David Raach

D1542660

WEST'S LAW SCHOOL
ADVISORY BOARD

CURTIS J. BERGER
Professor of Law, Columbia University

JESSE H. CHOPER
Professor of Law,
University of California, Berkeley

DAVID P. CURRIE
Professor of Law, University of Chicago

YALE KAMISAR
Professor of Law, University of Michigan

MARY KAY KANE
Dean and Professor of Law, University of California,
Hastings College of the Law

WAYNE R. LaFAVE
Professor of Law, University of Illinois

ARTHUR R. MILLER
Professor of Law, Harvard University

GRANT S. NELSON
Professor of Law,
University of California, Los Angeles

JAMES J. WHITE
Professor of Law, University of Michigan

CHARLES ALAN WRIGHT
Professor of Law, University of Texas

CALIFORNIA LEGAL ETHICS

Second Edition

By

Richard C. Wydick
Professor of Law
University of California, Davis

Rex R. Perschbacher
Professor of Law
University of California, Davis

This book is a California edition of Schwartz, Wydick & Perschbacher's
"Problems in Legal Ethics, Fourth Edition"

AMERICAN CASEBOOK SERIES®

WEST PUBLISHING CO.
ST. PAUL, MINN., 1997

This is a California edition of Schwartz, Wydick & Perschbacher's
"Problems in Legal Ethics, Fourth Edition", West Publishing Co., 1997

American Casebook Series, the key symbol appearing on the front
cover and the WP symbol are registered trademarks of West Publishing Co.
Registered in the U.S. Patent and Trademark Office.

COPYRIGHT © 1992 WEST PUBLISHING CO.
COPYRIGHT © 1997 By WEST GROUP
     610 Opperman Drive
     P.O. Box 64526
     St. Paul, MN 55164–0526
     1–800–328–9352

All rights reserved
Printed in the United States of America

Library of Congress Cataloging-in-Publication Data

Wydick, Richard C.
 California legal ethics / by Richard C. Wydick, Rex R.
Perschbacher. — 2nd ed.
  p. cm. — (American casebook series)
 Includes index.
 ISBN 0–314–21154–3 (hardcover)
 1. Legal ethics—California—Cases. 2. Practice of law—
California—Cases. I. Perschbacher, Rex R., 1946– . II. Title.
III. Series.
KFC76.5.A2W85 1997
174'.3'09794—dc21   97–8915
               CIP

ISBN 0–314–21154–3

*TEXT IS PRINTED ON 10% POST
CONSUMER RECYCLED PAPER*

Preface

This book is intended for use in California law school courses that teach the fundamentals of legal ethics. The book is to be used in conjunction with the current edition of West's *Professional Responsibility Standards, Rules & Statutes* (John Dzienkowski, ed.), which contains the California Rules of Professional Conduct, selected sections of the California Business and Professions Code, the ABA Model Rules of Professional Conduct, the ABA Model Code of Professional Responsibility, the ABA Code of Judicial Conduct, and other relevant material.

Chapter One of this book contains a set of readings on moral philosophy. The object is to help students see, at the outset, the connection between "legal ethics" and plain "ethics" or moral philosophy. The readings include parts of John Stuart Mill's essay on utilitarianism, a discussion of the golden rule, and parts of Immanuel Kant's discussion of the categorical imperative. We have been pleasantly surprised to find that law students generally welcome these readings as a refreshing change from the other material they read in law school. Teachers who prefer to dive directly into the substance of legal ethics can begin with Chapter Two, either omitting Chapter One or assigning it as background reading.

The Second Edition includes the following features:

• *The Problem Method:* Each chapter begins with a set of problems for discussion in the classroom. Some of the problems are drawn from decided cases, ethics opinions, and the writings of scholars in the field. Others are drawn from our own experience in teaching and law practice and from discussions we have had with judges and practicing lawyers. We have attempted to provide realistic problems—the kind that arise with disturbing frequency in the daily practice of law.

• *Background Readings:* For each major topic, we have included background reading material that illustrates the variety of sources to which a lawyer or judge can turn when seeking answers to ethics questions. The materials include ethics rules, judicial opinions, ethics committee opinions, and excerpts from articles and books written by judges, lawyers, and law teachers. Teachers who have used the first edition will note that in this second edition we have moved the ABA Model Code of Professional Responsibility to the Supplemental Readings section.

• *Supplemental Readings:* In each chapter, we have suggested supplemental readings from the ABA Model Code, from *The Law of Lawyering* by Geoffrey Hazard and William Hodes, from *Modern Legal Ethics* by Charles Wolfram, and from various drafts of the *Restatement (Third) of the Law Governing Lawyers*, which is nearing completion by the American Law Institute.

• *Descriptive Text:* Some chapters include text in which we attempt to pack a lot of information into a few pages. Examples are Chapter Two, which includes a description of the organized bar and its functions; Chapter Four, which includes a history of lawyer advertising and solicitation; and Chapter Six, which includes a brief summary of the law of legal malpractice.

• *Multiple Choice Questions:* At the end of each chapter (except the first), we have included some multiple choice questions. The Appendix at the back of the book gives our proposed answers and the reasoning behind them. Some of the questions review material that is covered elsewhere in the chapter, and others cover points that are not otherwise mentioned in the book.

We wish to thank our friend and colleague, Mortimer Schwartz, who retired from full-time law teaching in 1991. His contributions to the first and second editions of *Problems in Legal Ethics* endure in this book, and we are grateful for his continuing wise guidance and generous spirit.

We also wish to thank UCD law students Bridget Kayman and Kerry Branch for the excellent research and writing assistance they have given us in preparing this Second Edition.

RICHARD C. WYDICK
REX R. PERSCHBACHER

Davis, California
March 1997

Summary of Contents

CHAPTER 1. INTRODUCTION TO LEGAL ETHICS

I. How to Use This Book
II. Short Form Citations
III. Purposes of This Book
IV. "Ethics" and "Legal Ethics"
    A. The Relationship Between "Ethics" and "Legal Ethics"
    B. Utilitarianism
    C. The Golden Rule
    D. The Categorical Imperative

CHAPTER TWO. SOURCES AND APPLICATION OF LEGAL ETHICS RULES

I. The Organization of the Bar
    A. Admission to Practice in the Courts of a State
        1. Residency Requirements
        2. Character Requirements
        3. Admission to Practice in California
    B. Admission to Practice in Courts of Other States
    C. Admission to Practice in the Federal Courts
    D. Membership in Bar Associations
        1. State Bar Associations
        2. American Bar Association
        3. City, County, and Special Interest Bar Associations
II. Sources of Legal Ethics Rules
    A. State Codes of Conduct, Statutes, and Court Rules
    B. American Bar Association Model Code of Professional Responsibility
    C. American Bar Association Model Rules of Professional Conduct
        D. American Bar Association Code of Judicial Conduct
    E. Ethics Opinions and Ethics Hot Lines
III. Lawyer Disciplinary Proceedings
    A. Conduct Subject to Discipline
    B. How Discipline Is Imposed
    C. Types of Discipline
    D. Discipline by Federal Courts

CHAPTER 14. JUDICIAL CONDUCT

*

Table of Contents

CHAPTER 1. INTRODUCTION TO LEGAL ETHICS

  I. How to Use This Book
 II. Short Form Citations
III. Purposes of This Book
 IV. "Ethics" and "Legal Ethics"
      A. The Relationship Between "Ethics" and "Legal Ethics"
      B. Utilitarianism
      C. The Golden Rule
      D. The Categorical Imperative

      1. Responding to Your Adversary's Errors
      2. Conflicting Interests
      3. Confidentiality and Fraud

CHAPTER 2. SOURCES AND APPLICATION OF LEGAL ETHICS RULES

  I. The Organization of the Bar
      A. Admission to Practice in the Courts of a State
          1. Residency Requirements
          2. Character Requirements
          3. Admission to Practice in California
      B. Admission to Practice in Courts of Other States

CHAPTER 3. BEGINNING AND ENDING THE LAWYER–CLIENT RELATIONSHIP

CHAPTER 4. ADVERTISING AND SOLICITATION

CHAPTER 5. ATTORNEY FEES AND FIDUCIARY DUTIES

CHAPTER 6. COMPETENCE, DILIGENCE AND UNAUTHORIZED PRACTICE

CHAPTER 7. CONFIDENTIAL INFORMATION

CHAPTER 10. THE TRIAL LAWYER
AS TRUTH-SEEKER

CHAPTER 11. CONFLICTS OF INTEREST—LAWYERS, CLIENTS, AND THIRD PARTIES

CHAPTER 12. CONFLICTS OF INTEREST— CONFLICTS BETWEEN TWO CLIENTS

CHAPTER 13. LAWYERS IN LAW FIRMS AND SPECIALIZED PRACTICE AREAS

CHAPTER 14. JUDICIAL CONDUCT

Table of Cases

The principal cases are in bold type. Cases cited or discussed in the text
are roman type. References are to pages. Cases cited in principal
cases and within other quoted materials are not included.

Table of References to ABA Code

*

Table of References to ABA Model Rules

Table of References to California Rules of Professional Conduct

*

CALIFORNIA
LEGAL ETHICS

*

Chapter One

INTRODUCTION TO
LEGAL ETHICS

What This Chapter Covers

Reading Assignment

Wydick & Perschbacher, Chapter 1.

Discussion Problems

1. You represent client Claremont, who is the plaintiff in a civil action against five corporate defendants, each of which has its own lawyer. After extensive discovery, the case is almost ready for trial. Your secretary has just handed you a six page document that arrived on your fax machine a few minutes ago. The cover page states that the document was sent by one of the defense lawyers and that the intended recipients were the other four defense lawyers. Nothing on the cover page indicates that you were intended to receive the document; apparently the sender mistakenly speed-dialed your fax number along with those of the four defense lawyers. The "subject" line on the cover page states: "Confidential Memo to Defense Counsel re Settlement Negotiations in *Claremont*." The cover page is a standard law office form with the following boilerplate notice printed at the bottom: "This is a confidential communication protected by the attorney-client privilege, the work product doctrine, or both." You are aware that some law firms routinely use cover sheets with that boilerplate for all fax messages, whether or not they are confidential. Puzzled, you flip to the first page of the memo. The opening paragraph says: "I have discussed with my

client the idea of initiating settlement negotiations in the *Claremont* case. This memo states my client's position on settlement and outlines the negotiating tactics I think we should use with plaintiff's counsel." At that point you stop reading. What should you do now?

2. For many years you have served as legal counsel to the members of a family in a variety of matters. When the mother and father died, their son Samuel and daughter Dena each inherited about $750,000. Samuel is unmarried but has an 11 year-old child, Clara, who lives in his home under his care. You now represent Samuel in business, investment, and estate planning matters. From things Samuel has told you in confidence, and from things you have observed about him, you have concluded that he has developed a serious drug addiction problem that makes him unfit to take care of himself, his estate, and Clara. Now Dena has come to you and has asked you to petition the court to appoint a conservator for Samuel. You know from your prior dealings with Samuel that he will adamantly oppose this idea. What should you do?

3. Three years ago, lawyer Leon represented client Curtis in a worker's compensation matter. Pursuant to a settlement agreement, the compensation insurance company has since been sending Leon compensation checks once a month. In accordance with an agreement between Leon and Curtis, Leon deducts 10% from each check as his legal fee, and remits the remainder to Curtis. A week ago, during a routine review of the file, Leon discovered that the insurance company made a mistake in computing the amount of the monthly checks; it has been sending almost twice the amount that Curtis is entitled to receive under the settlement agreement. When Leon informed Curtis of this fact, Curtis said: "Well, I knew something must be wrong, but with inflation and all, I can barely make ends meet as it is. Don't rock the boat." What should Leon do?

HOW TO USE THIS BOOK

Each chapter of this book starts with a reading assignment. The reading assignments consist of some pages in this book, and (except for this first chapter) some portions of a paperback supplement called *Professional Responsibility Statutes, Rules, and Standards on the Legal Profession* (West). You will need a copy of the supplement to use in conjunction with this book.

The subsequent chapters also suggest some supplemental reading in other books that should be available in your local law library:

- G. Hazard & W. Hodes, *The Law of Lawyering* (2d ed. 1990);

- C. Wolfram, *Modern Legal Ethics* (1986); and

- Tentative Drafts of the *Restatement (Third) of the Law Governing Lawyers,* which is currently being prepared by the American Law Institute.

After you finish the assigned reading, work through the Discussion Problems posed at the beginning of the chapter. Make notes of your answers and your reasoning to use later in class, when you discuss the problems with your classmates and professor.

Finally, work the Multiple Choice questions at the end of each subsequent chapter. Some of these questions review material that is found elsewhere in the chapter. Other questions cover material that is not otherwise mentioned in the chapter, but you should be able to answer them from the assigned readings. In the Appendix at the end of this book, you will find proposed answers to the Multiple Choice questions.

SHORT FORM CITATIONS

The following table explains the short form citations used in this book:

ABA Code	American Bar Association Model Code of Professional Responsibility.
DR	Disciplinary Rule, a part of the ABA Code.
EC	Ethical Consideration, a part of the ABA Code.
ABA Model Rules	American Bar Association Model Rules of Professional Conduct.
CJC	American Bar Association Code of Judicial Conduct.
CRPC	California Rules of Professional Conduct.
Cal.Bus. & Prof.Code	California Business and Professions Code.
Hazard & Hodes	The Law of Lawyering (2d ed. 1990).
Wolfram	Modern Legal Ethics (1986).

PURPOSES OF THIS BOOK

This book will introduce you to the rules of ethics that apply to lawyers and judges in the United States. Every state has ethics rules that apply to lawyers, and a lawyer who does not follow them can be censured, or suspended from law practice, or disbarred. Likewise, every state has rules that govern the conduct of judges, and a judge who does not follow them can be censured, or suspended, or removed from the bench. Further, in most states, you cannot be admitted to practice law until you pass a bar examination that covers the ethics rules that apply to lawyers and judges.

Thus, this book has two purposes. First, we hope it will help you learn most of what you need to know about legal ethics to be admitted to law practice. Second, and far more important, we hope it will start you on a career-long process of studying, critically examining, and applying the legal ethics principles that you will study here.

"ETHICS" AND "LEGAL ETHICS"

The term "ethics," according to one dictionary, has several common meanings.[a] The *first* meaning is "the study of the general nature of morals and of the specific moral choices to be made by the individual in his relationship with others; the philosophy of morals. Also called 'moral philosophy.' " A *second* meaning is "the rules or standards governing the conduct of the members of a profession * * * [for example, the legal profession]."

Most of the reading you will do in this book concerns ethics in the second sense, that is, legal ethics. You will read the rules that lawyers and judges have devised to govern their own conduct in their professional relationships with others and among themselves. You will also read the thoughts of lawyers and judges on how those rules should be applied to specific situations. Some of these readings are in the form of judicial opinions; others are in the form of essays, and still others are in the form of ethics opinions written by members of the organized bar.

When you read this material, we suspect you will reach at least five conclusions:

(1) Some of the rules promulgated by the organized bar do not concern ethics issues. Some of them are intended to regulate more mundane aspects of lawyers' relations with clients, tribunals, and with other lawyers. Others are intended to regulate competition among lawyers and between lawyers and non-lawyers.

(2) Most of the rules that do concern ethics issues provide answers to questions that could not be answered by common sense or by consulting one's personal creed of moral behavior. In short, being an ethical person is no guarantee of being an ethical lawyer. For example, suppose lawyer A has made a settlement offer to lawyer B, who represents the adversary in a dispute. Lawyer A discovers that B has failed to convey the offer to her client and has thus breached her ethical obligation to keep her client informed. What should A do? One's common sense and personal moral creed might suggest that A should remedy B's ethics violation by telephoning B's client and conveying the offer directly. If A did that, however, he would violate a rule of legal ethics that prohibits a lawyer from communicating directly about a matter with a person who is represented in the matter by another lawyer. The purpose of the rule is to prevent a lawyer from overreaching a lay person, for example by inducing a damaging admission, or by effecting an unfavorable settlement of a dispute.

(3) The rules of legal ethics are silent on many ethics issues that commonly face members of the legal profession. What should guide you when there is "no rule on point"?

a. The quoted definitions are from the American Heritage Dictionary of the English Language (Houghton Mifflin 1978). Similar definitions are found in Webster's Third New International Dictionary (Merriam–Webster 1986) and The Random House Dictionary of the English Language (Random House 1968).

(4) Even when you can find a legal ethics rule on point, many of them are "open textured," or (to put it less gently) "highly ambiguous," either deliberately or as a result of "muddled thinking." [b] Professor Geoffrey Hazard offers this example:

[A] lawyer clearly has the power to file a suit that is well grounded in fact and warranted by current law. But given the indeterminancy of the governing legal rules, a lawyer also has the power, for practical purposes, to file a suit resting on no firmer ground than a client story that cannot be contradicted by indisputable evidence. The lawyer also is empowered to bring litigation that has no legal basis except a good faith argument for extrapolation of the law from its present state at any time. Since the boundaries of the impermissible are ill-defined, the lawyer's powers of office are correspondingly broad and legally unconstrained.[c]

(5) On occasion you may conclude that a rule of legal ethics permits, or even requires, conduct that offends your common sense and personal moral creed. What should guide you then?

This introductory chapter attempts to equip you with some tools that you can use later when you discover:

• that there is "no rule on point;" or

• that the rule on point is so "open textured" that you need more guidance; or

• that the rule on point permits or requires conduct that seems morally repugnant.

These tools are drawn from "ethics" in the first dictionary sense, that is, from writings on moral philosophy. We make no pretense of covering the field. Of the many important theories of ethics, we offer small fragments of only three: *utilitarianism,* as expressed by English philosopher and economist John Stuart Mill (1806–1873); the *golden rule* principle, as expressed in many of the world's religions; and the principle of the *categorical imperative,* as expressed by German philosopher Immanuel Kant (1724–1804). These three theories are partly rivals, but partly complementary. As you will see, they proceed from different premises. When applied to specific fact situations, they sometimes produce different conclusions, but other times they produce consistent conclusions. After you read about the three theories, we hope you will try them out on the Discussion Problems at the beginning of the chapter.

b. G. Hazard, *Ethical Opportunity in the Practice of Law,* 27 San Diego L.Rev. 127, 134 (1990).

c. *Id.*

UTILITARIANISM

John Stuart Mill [d]

There are few circumstances among those which make up the present condition of human knowledge, more unlike what might have been expected, or more significant of the backward state in which speculation on the most important subjects still lingers, than the little progress which has been made in the decision of the controversy respecting the criterion of right and wrong. From the dawn of philosophy, the question concerning the *summum bonum,* or, what is the same thing, concerning the foundation of morality, has been accounted the main problem in speculative thought, has occupied the most gifted intellects, and divided them into sects and schools, carrying on a vigorous warfare against one another. And after more than two thousand years the same discussions continue, philosophers are still ranged under the same contending banners, and neither thinkers nor mankind at large seem nearer to being unanimous on the subject, than when the youth Socrates listened to the old Protagoras, and asserted (if Plato's dialogue be grounded on a real conversation) the theory of utilitarianism against the popular morality of the so-called sophist.

* * *

The creed which accepts as the foundation of morals, Utility, or the Greatest Happiness Principle, holds that actions are right in proportion as they tend to promote happiness, wrong as they tend to produce the reverse of happiness. By happiness is intended pleasure, and the absence of pain; by unhappiness, pain, and the privation of pleasure. To give a clear view of the moral standard set up by the theory, much more requires to be said; in particular, what things it includes in the ideas of pain and pleasure; and to what extent this is left an open question. But these supplementary explanations do not affect the theory of life on which this theory of morality is grounded—namely, that pleasure, and freedom from pain, are the only things desirable as ends; and that all desirable things (which are as numerous in the utilitarian as in any other scheme) are desirable either for the pleasure inherent in themselves, or as means to the promotion of pleasure and the prevention of pain.

Now, such a theory of life excites in many minds, and among them in some of the most estimable in feeling and purpose, inveterate dislike. To suppose that life has (as they express it) no higher end than pleasure—no better and nobler object of desire and pursuit—they designate as utterly mean and grovelling; as a doctrine worthy only of swine, to whom the followers of Epicurus were, at a very early period, contemptuously likened; and modern holders of the doctrine are occasionally made the subject of equally polite comparisons by its German, French, and English assailants.

d. Reprinted from Great Books of the Western World. Copyright © 1952, 1990, Encyclopaedia Britannica, Inc.

When thus attacked, the Epicureans have always answered, that it is not they, but their accusers, who represent human nature in a degrading light; since the accusation supposes human beings to be capable of no pleasures except those of which swine are capable. If this supposition were true, the charge could not be gainsaid, but would then be no longer an imputation; for if the sources of pleasure were precisely the same to human beings and to swine, the rule of life which is good enough for the one would be good enough for the other. The comparison of the Epicurean life to that of beasts is felt as degrading, precisely because a beast's pleasures do not satisfy a human being's conceptions of happiness. Human beings have faculties more elevated than the animal appetites, and when once made conscious of them, do not regard anything as happiness which does not include their gratification.

* * *

According to the Greatest Happiness Principle, as above explained, the ultimate end, with reference to and for the sake of which all other things are desirable (whether we are considering our own good or that of other people), is an existence exempt as far as possible from pain, and as rich as possible in enjoyments, both in point of quantity and quality; the test of quality, and the rule for measuring it against quantity, being the preference felt by those who in their opportunities of experience, to which must be added their habits of self-consciousness and self-observation, are best furnished with the means of comparison. This, being, according to the utilitarian opinion, the end of human action, is necessarily also the standard of morality; which may accordingly be defined, the rules and precepts for human conduct, by the observance of which an existence such as has been described might be, to the greatest extent possible, secured to all mankind; and not to them only, but, so far as the nature of things admits, to the whole sentient creation.

* * *

[T]he assailants of utilitarianism seldom have the justice to acknowledge that the happiness which forms the utilitarian standard of what is right in conduct, is not the agent's own happiness, but that of all concerned. As between his own happiness and that of others, utilitarianism requires him to be as strictly impartial as a disinterested and benevolent spectator. In the golden rule of Jesus of Nazareth, we read the complete spirit of the ethics of utility: To do as you would be done by, and to love your neighbour as yourself, constitute the ideal perfection of utilitarian morality. As the means of making the nearest approach to this ideal, utility would enjoin, first, that laws and social arrangements should place the happiness, or (as speaking practically it may be called) the interest, of every individual, as nearly as possible in harmony with the interest of the whole; and secondly, that education and opinion, which have so vast a power over human character, should so use that power as to establish in the mind of every individual an indissoluble association between his own happiness and the good of the whole; especially between his own happiness and the practice of such modes of conduct, negative and positive, as regard for the universal happiness prescribes; so that not only he may be unable to conceive the possibility of happiness to himself, consistently with conduct opposed to the general good, but also that a direct impulse to promote the general good may be in every individual one of the habitual motives of action, and the sentiments connected therewith may fill a large and prominent place in every human being's sentient existence. * * *

* * *

The objectors to utilitarianism cannot always be charged with representing it in a discreditable light. On the contrary, those among them who entertain anything like a just idea of its disinterested character, sometimes find fault with its standard as being too high for humanity. They say it is exacting too much to require that people shall always act from the inducement of promoting the general interests of society. But this is to mistake the very meaning of a standard of morals, and confound the rule of action with the motive of it. It is the business of ethics to tell us what are our duties, or by what test we may know them; but no system of ethics requires that the sole motive of all we do shall be a feeling of duty; on the contrary, ninety-nine hundredths of all our actions are done from other motives, and rightly so done, if the rule of duty does not condemn them. It is the more unjust to utilitarianism that this particular misapprehension should be made a ground of objection to it, inasmuch as utilitarian moralists have gone beyond almost all others in affirming that the motive has nothing to do with the morality of the action, though much with the worth of the agent. He who saves a fellow creature from drowning does what is morally right, whether his motive be duty, or the hope of being paid for his trouble; he who betrays the friend that trusts him, is guilty of a crime, even if his object be to serve another friend to whom he is under greater obligations.

* * *

Utility is often summarily stigmatised as an immoral doctrine by giving it the name of Expediency, and taking advantage of the popular use of that term to contrast it with Principle. But the Expedient, in the sense in which it is opposed to the Right, generally means that which is expedient for the particular interest of the agent himself; as when a minister sacrifices the interests of his country to keep himself in place. When it means anything better than this, it means that which is expedient for some immediate object, some temporary purpose, but which violates a rule whose observance is expedient in a much higher degree. The Expedient, in this sense, instead of being the same thing with the useful, is a branch of the hurtful. Thus, it would often be expedient, for the purpose of getting over some momentary embarrassment, or attaining some object immediately useful to ourselves or others, to tell a lie. But inasmuch as the cultivation in ourselves of a sensitive feeling on the subject of veracity, is one of the most useful, and the enfeeblement of that feeling one of the most hurtful, things to which our conduct can be instrumental; and inasmuch as any, even unintentional, deviation from truth, does that much towards weakening the trustworthiness of human assertion, which is not only the principal support of all present social well-being, but the insufficiency of which does more than any one thing that can be named to keep back civilisation, virtue, everything on which human happiness on the largest scale depends; we feel that the violation, for a present advantage, of a rule of such transcendant expediency, is not expedient, and that he who, for the sake of a convenience to himself or to some other individual, does what depends on him to deprive mankind of the good, and inflict upon them the evil, involved in the greater or less reliance which they can place in each other's word, acts the part of one of their worst enemies. Yet that even this rule, sacred as it is, admits of possible exceptions, is acknowledged by all moralists; the chief of which is when the withholding of some fact (as of information from a malefactor, or of bad news from a person dangerously ill) would save an individual (especially an individual other than oneself) from great and unmerited evil, and when the withholding can only be effected by denial. But in order that the exception may not extend itself beyond the need, and may have the least possible effect in weakening reliance on veracity, it ought to be recognised, and, if possible, its limits defined; and if the principle of utility is good for anything, it must be good for weighing these conflicting utilities against one another, and marking out the region within which one or the other preponderates.

* * *

The corollaries from the principle of utility, like the precepts of every practical art, admit of indefinite improvement, and, in a progressive state of the human mind, their improvement is perpetually going on.

But to consider the rules of morality as improvable, is one thing; to pass over the intermediate generalisations entirely, and endeavour to test each individual action directly by the first principle, is another. It is a strange notion that the acknowledgment of a first principle is inconsistent with the admission of secondary ones. To inform a traveller respecting the place of his ultimate destination, is not to forbid the use of landmarks and direction-posts on the way. The proposition that happiness is the end and aim of morality, does not mean that no road ought to be laid down to that goal, or that persons going thither should not be advised to take one direction rather than another. * * * Whatever we adopt as the fundamental principle of morality, we require subordinate principles to apply it by; the impossibility of doing without them, being common to all systems, can afford no argument against any one in particular; but gravely to argue as if no such secondary principles could be had, and as if mankind had remained till now, and always must remain, without drawing any general conclusions from the experience of human life, is as high a pitch, I think, as absurdity has ever reached in philosophical controversy.

* * *

[Q]uestions of ultimate ends do not admit of proof, in the ordinary acceptation of the term. To be incapable of proof by reasoning is common to all first principles; to the first premises of our knowledge, as well as to those of our conduct. But the former, being matters of fact, may be the subject of a direct appeal to the faculties which judge of fact—namely, our senses, and our internal consciousness. Can an appeal be made to the same faculties on questions of practical ends? Or by what other faculty is cognisance taken of them?

Questions about ends are, in other words, questions what things are desirable. The utilitarian doctrine is, that happiness is desirable, and the only thing desirable, as an end; all other things being only desirable as means to that end. What ought to be required of this doctrine—what conditions is it requisite that the doctrine should fulfil—to make good its claim to be believed?

The only proof capable of being given that an object is visible, is that people actually see it. The only proof that a sound is audible, is that people hear it: and so of the other sources of our experience. In like manner, I apprehend, the sole evidence it is possible to produce that anything is desirable, is that people do actually desire it. If the end which the utilitarian doctrine proposes to itself were not, in theory and in practice, acknowledged to be an end, nothing could ever convince any person that it was so. No reason can be given why the general happiness is desirable, except that each person, so far as he believes it to be attainable, desires his own happiness. This, however, being a fact, we have not only all the proof which the case admits of, but all which it is possible to require, that happiness is a good: that each person's happiness is a good to that person, and the general happiness, therefore, a good to the aggregate of all persons. * * *

THE DEBATE OVER UTILITARIANISM

James Rachels [e]

The Resilience of the Theory

Classical Utilitarianism—the theory defended by [Jeremy] Bentham and [John Stuart] Mill—can be summarized in three propositions:

First, actions are to be judged right or wrong solely in virtue of their consequences. Nothing else matters. Right actions are, simply, those that have the best consequences.

Second, in assessing consequences, the only thing that matters is the amount of happiness or unhappiness that is caused. Everything else is irrelevant. Thus right actions are those that produce the greatest balance of happiness over unhappiness.

Third, in calculating the happiness over unhappiness that will be caused, no one's happiness is to be counted as more important than anyone else's. Each person's welfare is equally important. * * *

e. James Rachels, *The Elements of Moral Philosophy* 90–103 (1986), copyright 1986 by McGraw-Hill, Inc. Reproduced with permission. The reading consists of edited portions of Chapter 8, "The Debate over Utilitarianism."

The appeal of this theory to philosophers, economists, and others who theorize about human decision making has been enormous. The theory continues to be widely accepted, even though it has been challenged by a number of apparently devastating arguments. These antiutilitarian arguments are so numerous, and so persuasive, that many have concluded the theory must be abandoned. But the remarkable thing is that so many have *not* abandoned it. Despite the arguments, a great many thinkers refuse to let the theory go. According to these contemporary utilitarians, the antiutilitarian arguments show only that the classical theory needs to be *modified;* they say the basic idea is correct and should be preserved, but recast into a more satisfactory form.

In what follows, we will examine some of these arguments against Utilitarianism, and consider whether the classical version of the theory may be revised satisfactorily to meet them. * * *

Is Happiness the Only Thing That Matters?

The question *What things are good?* is different from the question *What actions are right?* and Utilitarianism answers the second question by referring back to the first one. Right actions, it says, are the ones that produce the most good. But what is good? The classical utilitarian reply is: one thing, and one thing only, namely happiness. * * *

The idea that happiness is the ultimate good * * * is known as *Hedonism.* Hedonism is a perennially popular theory that goes back at least as far as the ancient Greeks. It has always been an attractive theory because of its beautiful simplicity, and because it expresses the intuitively plausible notion that things are good or bad only on account of the way they make us *feel.* Yet a little reflection reveals serious flaws in the theory. The flaws stand out when we consider * * * [an example like this:]

A promising young pianist's hands are injured in an automobile accident so that she can no longer play. Why is this a bad thing for her? Hedonism would say it is bad because it causes her unhappiness. She will feel frustrated and upset whenever she thinks of what might have been, and *that* is her misfortune. But this way of explaining the misfortune seems to get things the wrong way around. It is not as though, by feeling unhappy, she has made an otherwise neutral situation into a bad one. On the contrary, her unhappiness is a rational response to a situation that *is* unfortunate. She could have had a career as a concert pianist, and now she cannot. *That* is the tragedy. We could not eliminate the tragedy just by getting her to cheer up.

* * *

We value all sorts of things, including artistic creativity and friendship, for their own sakes. It makes us happy to have them, but only because we *already* think them good. (We do not think them good *because* they make us happy—this is what I meant when I said that Hedonism "gets things the wrong way around.") Therefore we think it a misfortune to lose them, independently of whether or not the loss is accompanied by unhappiness. * * * [H]appiness is a response we have to the attainment of things that we recognize *as* goods, independently and in their own right. We think friendship is a good thing, and so having friends makes us happy. That is very different from first setting out after happiness, then deciding that having friends might make us happy, and then seeking friends as a means to this end.

* * *

Are Consequences All that Matter?

The claim that only consequences matter * * * [is] a necessary part of Utilitarianism. The most fundamental idea underlying the theory is that in order to determine whether an action would be right, we should look at *what will happen as a result of doing it.* If it were to turn out that some *other* matter is also important in determining rightness, then Utilitarianism would be undermined at its very foundation.

The most serious antiutilitarian arguments attack the theory at this point: they urge that various other considerations, in addition to utility, are important in determining whether actions are right. We will look at three such arguments.

1. *Justice.* Writing in the academic journal *Inquiry* in 1965, H.J. McCloskey asks us to consider the following case:

> Suppose a utilitarian were visiting an area in which there was racial strife, and that, during his visit, a Negro rapes a white woman, and that race riots occur as a result of the crime, white mobs, with the connivance of the police, bashing and killing Negroes, etc. Suppose too that our utilitarian is in the area of the crime when it is committed such that his testimony would bring about the conviction of a particular Negro. If he knows that a quick arrest will stop the riots and lynchings, surely, as a utilitarian, he must conclude that he has a duty to bear false witness in order to bring about the punishment of an innocent person.

This is a fictitious example, but that makes no difference. The argument is only that *if* someone were in this position, then on utilitarian grounds he should bear false witness against the innocent person. This might have some bad consequences—the innocent man might be executed—but there would be enough good consequences to outweigh them: the riots and lynchings would be stopped. The best consequences would be achieved by lying; therefore, according to Utilitarianism, lying is the thing to do. But, the argument continues, it would be wrong to bring about the execution of an innocent man. Therefore, Utilitarianism, which implies it would be right, must be incorrect.

2. *Rights.* Here is a case that is *not* fictitious; it is from the records of the U.S. Court of Appeals, Ninth Circuit * * * in the case of *York v. Story:*[f]

f. *York v. Story,* 324 F.2d 450 (9th Cir. 1963), *cert. denied,* 376 U.S. 939, 84 S.Ct. 794, 11 L.Ed.2d 659 (1964).

In October, 1958, appellant (Ms. York) went to the police department of Chino for the purpose of filing charges in connection with an assault upon her. Appellee Ron Story, an officer of that police department, then acting under color of his authority as such, advised appellant that it was necessary to take photographs of her. Story then took appellant to a room in the police station, locked the door, and directed her to undress, which she did. Story then directed appellant to assume various indecent positions, and photographed her in those positions. These photographs were not made for any lawful purpose.

* * *

Later that month, Story advised appellant that the pictures did not come out and that he had destroyed them. Instead, Story circulated these photographs among the personnel of the Chino police department. * * *

Ms. York brought suit against these officers and won. Her *legal* rights had clearly been violated. But what of the *morality* of the officers' behavior?

Utilitarianism says that actions are defensible if they produce a favorable balance of happiness over unhappiness. This suggests that we consider the amount of unhappiness caused to Ms. York and compare it with the amount of pleasure taken in the photographs by Officer Story and his cohorts. It is at least possible that more happiness than unhappiness was caused. In that case the utilitarian conclusion apparently would be that their actions were morally all right. But this seems to be a perverse way to approach the case. Why should the pleasure afforded Story and his cohorts matter at all? Why should it even count? They had no right to treat Ms. York in that way, and the fact that they enjoyed doing so hardly seems a relevant defense.

* * *

The moral to be drawn * * * is that Utilitarianism is at odds with the idea that people have *rights* that may not be trampled on merely because one anticipates good results. * * * Ms. York's right to privacy * * * [was] violated; * * * [and in other cases, other rights may be at issue]—the right to freedom of religion, to free speech, or even the right to life itself. It may happen that good purposes are served, from time to time, by ignoring these rights. But we do not think that our rights *should* be set aside so easily. The notion of a personal right is not a utilitarian notion. Quite the reverse: it is a notion that places limits on how an individual may be treated, regardless of the good purposes that might be accomplished.

3. *Backward–Looking Reasons.* Suppose you have promised someone that you will do something—say, you promised to meet him downtown this afternoon. But when the time comes to go, you don't want to do it—you need to do some work and would rather stay home. What should you do? Suppose you judge that the utility of getting your work

accomplished slightly outweighs the inconvenience your friend would be caused. Appealing to the utilitarian standard, you might then conclude that it is right to stay home. However, this does not seem correct. The fact that *you promised* imposes an obligation on you that you cannot escape so easily. * * *

[Utilitarianism is vulnerable to criticism because it looks only to *future* consequences.] However we normally think that considerations about the *past* also have some importance. The fact that you promised your friend to meet him is a fact about the past, not the future. * * * [Likewise] the fact that someone did not commit a crime is a good reason why he should not be punished. The fact that someone once did you a favor may be a good reason why you should now do him a favor. The fact that you did something to hurt someone may be a reason why you should now make it up to her. These are all facts about the past that are relevant to determining our obligations. But Utilitarianism makes the past irrelevant, and so it seems deficient for just that reason.

The Defense of Utilitarianism.

Taken together, the above arguments form an impressive indictment of Utilitarianism. The theory, which at first seemed so progressive and commonsensical, now seems indefensible; it is at odds with such fundamental moral notions as justice and individual rights, and seems unable to account for the place of backward-looking reasons in justifying conduct. The combined weight of these arguments has prompted many philosophers to abandon the theory altogether.

Many thinkers, however, continue to believe that Utilitarianism, in some form, is true. In reply to the arguments, three general defenses have been offered.

The First Line of Defense. The first line of defense is to point out that the examples used in the antiutilitarian arguments are unrealistic and do not describe situations that come up in the real world. * * *

The three antiutilitarian arguments share a common strategy. First, a case is described, and then it is noted that from a utilitarian point of view a certain action seems to be required * * *. It is then said that this action is not right. Therefore, it is concluded, the utilitarian conception of rightness cannot be correct.

This strategy succeeds only if we admit that the actions described *really would* have the best consequences. But the utilitarian need not admit this. He can object that, in the real world, bearing false witness does *not* have good consequences. Suppose, in the case described by McCloskey, the "utilitarian" tried to incriminate the innocent man in order to stop the riots. His effort might not succeed; his lie might be found out, and then the situation would be even worse than before. Even if the lie did succeed, the real culprit would remain at large, to commit additional crimes. Moreover, if the guilty party were caught later on, which is always a possibility, the liar would be in deep trouble, and confidence in the criminal justice system would be undermined.

The moral is that although one might *think* that one can bring about the best consequences by such behavior, one can by no means be certain of it. In fact, experience teaches the contrary: utility is not served by framing innocent people. Thus the utilitarian position is *not* at odds with common-sense notions of justice in such cases.

* * *

[F]ar from being incompatible with the idea that we should not violate people's rights, or lie or break our promises, Utilitarianism explains *why* we should not do those things. Moreover, apart from the utilitarian explanation, these duties would remain mysterious and unintelligible. What could be more mysterious than the notion that some actions are right "in themselves," severed from any notion of a good to be produced by them? Or what could be more unintelligible than the idea that people have "rights" unconnected with any benefits derived from acknowledgment of those rights? Utilitarianism is not incompatible with common sense; on the contrary, Utilitarianism *is* commonsensical.

The Second Line of Defense. The first line of defense contains more bluster than substance. While it can plausibly be maintained that *most* acts of false witness and the like have bad consequences in the real world, it cannot reasonably be asserted that *all* such acts have bad consequences. Surely, in at least some real-life cases, one can bring about good results by doing things that moral common sense condemns. * * * The first line of defense, then, is weak.

The second line of defense admits all this and proposes to save Utilitarianism by giving it a new formulation. * * * The troublesome aspect of the theory was this: the classical version of Utilitarianism implied that *each individual action* is to be evaluated by reference to its own particular consequences. If on a certain occasion you are tempted to lie, whether it would be wrong is determined by the consequences of *that particular lie.* This, the theory's defenders said, is the point that causes all the trouble; even though we know that *in general* lying has bad consequences, it is obvious that sometimes particular acts of lying can have good consequences.

Therefore, the new version of Utilitarianism modifies the theory so that individual actions will no longer be judged by the Principle of Utility. Instead, *rules* will be established by reference to the principle, and individual acts will then be judged right or wrong by reference to the rules. This new version of the theory is called *Rule–Utilitarianism,* to contrast it with the original theory, now commonly called *Act–Utilitarianism.*

Rule–Utilitarianism has no difficulty coping with the three antiutilitarian arguments. An act-utilitarian, faced with the situation described by McCloskey, would be tempted to bear false witness against the innocent man because the consequences of *that particular act* would be good. But the rule-utilitarian would not reason in that way. He would first ask, "What *general rules of conduct* tend to promote the greatest happiness?" Suppose we imagine two societies, one in which the rule "Don't bear false witness against the innocent" is faithfully adhered to, and one in which this rule is not followed. In which society are people likely to be better off? Clearly, from the point of view of utility, the first society is preferable. Therefore, the rule against incriminating the innocent should be accepted, and *by appealing to this rule,* the rule-utilitarian concludes that the person in McCloskey's example should not testify against the innocent man.

* * *

Rule–Utilitarianism cannot be convicted of violating our moral common sense, or of conflicting with ordinary ideas of justice, personal rights, and the rest. In shifting emphasis from the justification of acts to the justification of rules, the theory has been brought into line with our intuitive judgments to a remarkable degree.

The Third Line of Defense. Finally, a small group of contemporary utilitarians has had a very different response to the antiutilitarian arguments. Those arguments point out that the classical theory is at odds with ordinary notions of justice, individual rights, and so on; to this, their response is essentially, "So what?" * * * Our moral common sense is, after all, not necessarily reliable. It may incorporate various irrational elements, including prejudices absorbed from our parents, our religion, and the general culture. Why should we simply assume that our feelings are always correct? And why should we reject a plausible, rational theory of ethics such as Utilitarianism simply because it conflicts with those feelings? Perhaps it is the feelings, not the theory, that should be discarded.

* * *

What Is Correct and What Is Incorrect in Utilitarianism.

There is a sense in which no moral philosopher can completely reject Utilitarianism. The consequences of one's actions—whether they promote happiness, or cause misery—must be admitted by all to be extremely important. John Stuart Mill once remarked that, insofar as we are benevolent, we must accept the utilitarian standard; and he was surely right. Moreover, the utilitarian emphasis on impartiality must be a part of any defensible moral theory. The question is whether these are the *only* kinds of considerations an adequate theory must acknowledge. Aren't there *other* considerations that are also important?

If we consult what [Australian philosopher J.J.C.] Smart calls our "common moral consciousness," it seems that there are *many* other considerations that are morally important. * * * But I believe the radical act-utilitarians are right to warn us that "common sense" cannot be trusted. Many people once felt that there is an important difference between whites and blacks, so that the interests of whites are somehow more important. Trusting the "common sense" of their day, they might have insisted that an adequate moral theory should accommodate this "fact." Today, no one worth listening to would say such a thing. But who knows how many *other* irrational prejudices are still part of our moral common sense? * * * The strength of Utilitarianism is that it firmly resists "corruption" by possibly irrational elements. By sticking to the Principle of Utility as the *only* standard for judging right and wrong, it avoids all danger of incorporating into moral theory prejudices, feelings, and "intuitions" that have no rational basis.

The warning should be heeded. "Common sense" can, indeed, mislead us. At the same time, however, there might be at least some nonutilitarian considerations that an adequate theory *should* accept, because there *is* a rational basis for them. Consider, for example, the matter of what people deserve. A person who has worked hard in her job may deserve a promotion more than someone who has loafed, and it would be unjust for the loafer to be promoted first. * * * Now utilitarians might agree with this, and say that it can be explained by their theory—they might argue that it promotes the general welfare to encourage hard work by rewarding it. But this does not seem to be an adequate explanation of the importance of desert. The woman who worked harder has a superior claim to the promotion, *not* because it promotes the general welfare for her to get it, but *because she has earned it.* * * *

I believe [this way of thinking] has a rational basis, although it is not one that utilitarians could accept. We ought to recognize individual desert as a reason for treating people in certain ways—for example, as a reason for promoting the woman who has worked harder—because that is the principal way we have of treating individuals as autonomous, responsible beings. If in fact people have the power to choose their own actions, in such a way that they are *responsible* for those actions and what results from them, then acknowledging their deserts is just a way of acknowledging their standing as autonomous individuals. In treating them as they deserve to be treated, we are responding to the way they have freely chosen to behave. Thus in some instances we will not treat everyone alike, because people are not just members of an undifferentiated crowd. Instead, they are individuals who, by their own choices, show themselves to deserve different kinds of responses.

* * * [In short, Utilitarianism] emphasizes points that any adequate moral theory must acknowledge, * * * [but] Utilitarianism is not itself a fully adequate theory because there is at least one important matter—individual desert—that escapes its net.

ROOTS OF THE GOLDEN RULE

In his essay on utilitarianism, John Stuart Mill states: "In the golden rule of Jesus of Nazareth, we read the complete spirit of the ethics of utility: To do as you would be done by, and to love your neighbor as yourself, constitute the ideal perfection of utilitarian morality." Do you agree?

Mill's paraphrase of the golden rule draws on two passages from the New Testament. The first is toward the end of the Sermon on the Mount; Matthew reports Jesus as saying: "In everything, do to others what you would have them do to you, for this sums up the Law and the Prophets." [g] In the second passage, Matthew reports that an expert in the law tested Jesus with a question:

> Teacher, which is the greatest commandment in the Law? Jesus replied: " 'Love the Lord your God with all your heart and with all your soul and with all your mind.' This is the first and greatest commandment. And the second is like it: 'Love your neighbor as yourself.' All the law and the Prophets hang on these two commandments." [h]

The question put by the legal expert, and the reply Jesus gave, make plain that the golden rule is rooted in the law of the Jews. One prominent reference to it in the Torah comes in the 19th chapter of Leviticus:

> The Lord spoke to Moses, saying: "Speak to the whole Israelite community and say to them: You shall be holy, for I, the Lord your God, am holy. * * * Love your neighbor as yourself. I am the Lord." [i]

The principle expressed in the golden rule is also found in other cultures and religions of the world. H.T.D. Rost, a teacher of comparative religion and member of the Bahá'í faith, found expressions of the rule in some of the oral traditions of Africa and in many religions, including the following: [j]

● **Hinduism:** Do not to others what ye do not wish done to yourself; and wish for others too what ye desire and long for, for yourself. This is the whole of the Dharma, heed it well.[k]

● **Buddhism:** All shrink from suffering, and all love life; Remember that thou too are like to them; Make thine own self the measure of the others, and so abstain from causing hurt to them.[l]

● **Taoism:** To those who are good (to me), I am good; and to those who are not good (to me), I am also good; and thus (all) get to be good.[m]

● **Confucianism:** What you do not want done to yourself, do not

---

g. Matthew 7:12. The phrasing of the rule is similar in Luke's report of the Sermon on the Plain. Luke 6:31. These and other New Testament references in this section are to *The Bible* (New International Version, Zondervan 1978).

h. Matthew 22:35–40. See also Paul's letter to the church in Rome: "The commandments, 'Do not commit adultery,' 'Do not murder,' 'Do not steal,' 'Do not covet,' and whatever other commandments there may be, are summed up in this one rule:

'Love your neighbor as yourself.' " Romans 13:9.

i. Leviticus 19:1–2, 18, *The Torah: The Five Books of Moses* (Jewish Pub.Soc. of America 1962).

j. H.T.D. Rost, *The Golden Rule: A Universal Ethic* (George Ronald, Oxford 1986), copyright H.T.D. Rost, 1986.

k. *Id.* at 28.

l. *Id.* at 39.

m. *Id.* at 43.

do to others."[n]

● **Islam:** None of you (truly) believes until he wishes for his brother what he wishes for himself.[o]

Philosopher Marcus Singer observes that the golden rule is a moral principle, not a complete moral code.[p] That is to say, the golden rule does not tell us whether a particular act is right or wrong. Rather, the golden rule gives us a method or procedure for determining whether a particular act is right or wrong.

Singer distinguishes the golden rule from what he calls the "inversion" of the golden rule. The inversion states: "Do unto others as **they** would have you do unto them."[q] The inversion would lead to absurd consequences, Singer states. For example, if you would like to have all my property, then the inversion would require me to give it to you. Or, if you would like to have me as your slave for life, then I would have to become your slave for life. Because the inversion would require people to become totally selfless, it is unworkable as a moral principle.

In its best formulation, Singer says, the golden rule tells us to do unto others **as** we would have them do unto us.[r] In Singer's formulation, the word "**as**" is important; it signifies that we should treat others according to the same **standards** that we would wish to have applied to us. That does not mean that we should impose our own peculiar tastes on others. For example, suppose that I am especially fond of listening to heavy metal music in the middle of the night. The golden rule does not mean that I should play my heavy metal music at top volume in the middle of the night for the benefit of my neighbors. The golden rule teaches, instead, that I should conduct myself according to the same standards I would wish my neighbors to apply to me. I would not wish them to impose their musical tastes on me, and I should apply that same standard to my treatment of them.

THE CATEGORICAL IMPERATIVE

Immanuel Kant[s]

[The] moral worth of an action does not lie in the effect expected from it, nor in any principle of action which requires to borrow its motive from this expected effect. For all these effects—agreeableness of one's condition and even the promotion of the happiness of others—could have been also brought about by other causes, so that for this there would have been no need of the will of a rational being; whereas it is in this alone that the supreme and unconditional good can be found. The pre-eminent good which we call moral can therefore consist in

n. *Id.* at 49.

o. *Id.* at 103.

p. M. Singer, *The Golden Rule,* 38 Philosophy 293 (1963).

q. Id.

r. Id.

s. I. Kant, *Foundations of the Metaphysic of Morals,* translated by Thomas Kingsmill Abbott, reprinted from Great Books of the Western World. © 1952, 1990, Encyclopaedia Britannica, Inc.

nothing else than *the conception of law* in itself, *which certainly is only possible in a rational being,* in so far as this conception, and not the expected effect, determines the will. This is a good which is already present in the person who acts accordingly, and we have not to wait for it to appear first in the result.

But what sort of law can that be, the conception of which must determine the will, even without paying any regard to the effect expected from it, in order that this will may be called good absolutely and without qualification? As I have deprived the will of every impulse which could arise to it from obedience to any law, there remains nothing but the universal conformity of its actions to law in general, which alone is to serve the will as a principle, i.e., I am never to act otherwise than so *that I could also will that my maxim should become a universal law.* Here, now, it is the simple conformity to law in general, without assuming any particular law applicable to certain actions, that serves the will as its principle and must so serve it, if duty is not to be a vain delusion and a chimerical notion. The common reason of men in its practical judgments perfectly coincides with this and always has in view the principle here suggested.

Let the question be, for example: May I when in distress make a promise with the intention not to keep it? I readily distinguish here between the two significations which the question may have: Whether it is prudent, or whether it is right, to make a false promise? The former may undoubtedly often be the case. I see clearly indeed that it is not enough to extricate myself from a present difficulty by means of this subterfuge, but it must be well considered whether there may not hereafter spring from this lie much greater inconvenience than that from which I now free myself, and as, with all my supposed *cunning,* the consequences cannot be so easily foreseen but that credit once lost may be much more injurious to me than any mischief which I seek to avoid at present, it should be considered whether it would not be more *prudent* to act herein according to a universal maxim and to make it a habit to promise nothing except with the intention of keeping it. But it is soon clear to me that such a maxim will still only be based on the fear of consequences. Now it is a wholly different thing to be truthful from duty and to be so from apprehension of injurious consequences. In the first case, the very notion of the action already implies a law for me; in the second case, I must first look about elsewhere to see what results may be combined with it which would affect myself. For to deviate from the principle of duty is beyond all doubt wicked; but to be unfaithful to my maxim of prudence may often be very advantageous to me, although to abide by it is certainly safer. The shortest way, however, and an unerring one, to discover the answer to this question whether a lying promise is consistent with duty, is to ask myself, "Should I be content that my maxim (to extricate myself from difficulty by a false promise) should hold good as a universal law, for myself as well as for others?" and should I be able to say to myself, "Every one may make a deceitful promise when he finds himself in a difficulty from which he cannot otherwise extricate himself?" Then I presently become aware that while I can will the lie, I can by no means will that lying should be a universal law. For with such a law there would be no promises at all, since it would be in vain to allege my intention in regard to my future actions to those who would not believe this allegation, or if they over hastily did so would pay me back in my own coin. Hence my maxim, as soon as it should be made a universal law, would necessarily destroy itself.

I do not, therefore, need any far-reaching penetration to discern what I have to do in order that my will may be morally good. Inexperienced in the course of the world, incapable of being prepared for all its contingencies, I only ask myself: *Canst thou also will that thy maxim should be a universal law?* If not, then it must be rejected, and that not because of a disadvantage accruing from it to myself or even to others, but because it cannot enter as a principle into a possible universal legislation, and reason extorts from me immediate respect for such legislation. I do not indeed as yet *discern* on what this respect is based (this the philosopher may inquire), but at least I understand this, that it is an estimation of the worth which far outweighs all worth of what is recommended by inclination, and that the necessity of acting from *pure* respect for the practical law is what constitutes duty, to which every other motive must give place, because it is the condition of a will being good *in itself,* and the worth of such a will is above everything.

* * *

[Kant offers four examples, of which two are reproduced here.]

[(1) Suppose a man] finds himself forced by necessity to borrow money. He knows that he will not be able to repay it, but sees also that nothing will be lent to him unless he promises stoutly to repay it in a definite time. He desires to make this promise, but he has still so much conscience as to ask himself: "Is it not unlawful and inconsistent with duty to get out of a difficulty in this way?" Suppose however that he resolves to do so: then the maxim of his action would be expressed thus: "When I think myself in want of money, I will borrow money and promise to repay it, although I know that I never can do so." Now this principle of self-love or of one's own advantage may perhaps be consistent with my whole future welfare; but the question now is, "Is it right?" I change then the suggestion of self-love into a universal law, and state the question thus: "How would it be if my maxim were a universal law?" Then I see at once that it could never hold as a universal law of nature, but would necessarily contradict itself. For supposing it to be a universal law that everyone when he thinks himself in a difficulty should be able to promise whatever he pleases, with the purpose of not keeping his promise, the promise itself would become impossible, as well as the end that one might have in view in it, since no one would consider that anything was promised to him, but would ridicule all such statements as vain pretences.

* * *

[(2) Suppose a second man] who is in prosperity, while he sees that others have to contend with great wretchedness and that he could help them, thinks: "What concern is it of mine? Let everyone be as happy as Heaven pleases, or as he can make himself; I will take nothing from him nor even envy him, only I do not wish to contribute anything to his welfare or to his assistance in distress!" Now no doubt if such a mode of thinking were a universal law, the human race might very well subsist, and doubtless even better than in a state in which everyone talks of sympathy and good-will, or even takes care occasionally to put it into practice, but, on the other side, also cheats when he can, betrays the rights of men, or otherwise violates them. But although it is possible that a universal law of nature might exist in accordance with that maxim, it is impossible to *will* that such a principle should have the universal validity of a law of nature. For a will which resolved this would contradict itself, inasmuch as many cases might occur in which one would have need of the love and sympathy of others, and in which, by such a law of nature, sprung from his own will, he would deprive himself of all hope of the aid he desires.

* * *

If then there is a supreme practical principle or, in respect of the human will, a categorical imperative, it must be one which, being drawn from the conception of that which is necessarily an end for everyone because it is *an end in itself,* constitutes an *objective* principle of will, and can therefore serve as a universal practical law. The foundation of this principle is: *rational nature exists as an end in itself.* Man necessarily conceives his own existence as being so; so far then this is a *subjective* principle of human actions. But every other rational being regards its existence similarly, just on the same rational principle that holds for me so that it is at the same time an objective principle, from which as a supreme practical law all laws of the will must be capable of being deduced. Accordingly the practical imperative will be as follows: *So act as to treat humanity, whether in thine own person or in that of any other, in every case as an end withal, never as means only.* We will now inquire whether this can be practically carried out.

[To continue with the previous examples:]

[First,] as regards necessary duties, or those of strict obligation, towards others: He who is thinking of making a lying promise to others will see at once that he would be using another man *merely as a mean,* without the latter containing at the same time the end in himself. For he whom I propose by such a promise to use for my own purposes cannot possibly assent to my mode of acting towards him and, therefore cannot himself contain the end of this action. This violation of the principle of humanity in other men is more obvious if we take in examples of attacks on the freedom and property of others. For then it is clear that he who transgresses the rights of men intends to use the person of others merely as a means, without considering that as rational beings they ought always to be esteemed also as ends, that is, as beings who must be capable of containing in themselves the end of the very same action.

[Second,] as regards meritorious duties towards others: The natural end which all men have is their own happiness. Now humanity might indeed subsist, although no one should contribute anything to the happiness of others, provided he did not intentionally withdraw anything from it; but after all this would only harmonize negatively not positively with *humanity as an end in itself,* if every one does not also endeavour, as far as in him lies, to forward the ends of others. For the ends of any subject which is an end in himself ought as far as possible to be *my* ends also, if that conception is to have its *full* effect with me.

COMMENTARY ON KANT'S THEORY

Onora O'Neill [t]

A Simplified Account of Kant's Ethics

Kant's theory is frequently and misleadingly assimilated to theories of human rights. It is, in fact, a theory of human obligations; therefore it is wider in scope than a theory of human rights. (Not all obligations generate corresponding rights.) Kant does not, however, try to generate a set of precise rules defining human obligations in all possible circumstances; instead, he attempts to provide a set of *principles of obligation* that can be used as the starting points for moral reasoning in actual contexts of action. The primary focus of Kantian ethics is, then, on *action* rather than either *results,* as in utilitarian thinking, or *entitlements,* as in theories that make human rights their fundamental category. Morality requires action of certain sorts. But to know *what* sort of action is required (or forbidden) in which circumstances, we should not look just at the expected results of action or at others' supposed entitlements but, in the first instance, at the nature of the proposed actions themselves.

When we engage in moral reasoning, we often need go no further than to refer to some quite specific principle or tradition. We may say to one another, or to ourselves, things like "It would be hypocritical to pretend that our good fortune is achieved without harm to the Third World" or "Redistributive taxation shouldn't cross national boundaries." But when these specific claims are challenged, we may find ourselves pushed to justify or reject or modify them. Such moral debate, on Kant's account, rests on appeals to what he calls the *Supreme Principle of Morality,* which can (he thinks) be used to work out more specific principles of obligation. This principle, the famous Categorical Imperative, plays the same role in Kantian thinking that the Greatest Happiness Principle plays in utilitarian thought.

t. O. O'Neill, *The Moral Perplexities of Famine and World Hunger,* printed in *Matters of Life and Death: New Introductory Essays in Moral Philosophy* 319–24 (2d ed. 1986), edited by Tom Regan, copyright 1986 by McGraw–Hill, Inc. Reproduced with permission.

* * * Kant's moral thought often appears difficult [because] he offers a number of different versions of this principle, that he claims are equivalent, but which look very different. A straightforward way in which to simplify Kantian moral thought is to concentrate on just one of these formulations of the Categorical Imperative. For present purposes I shall choose the version to which he gives the sonorous name of *The Formula of the End in Itself.*

THE FORMULA OF THE END IN ITSELF

The "Formula of the End in Itself" runs as follows:

Act in such a way that you always treat humanity, whether in your own person or in the person of any other, never simply as a means but always at the same time as an end.

To understand this principle we need in the first place to understand what Kant means by the term *maxim.* The maxim of an act or policy or activity is the *underlying principle* of the act, policy or activity, by which other, more superficial aspects of action are guided.

* * *

When we want to work out whether a proposed act or policy is morally required we should not, on Kant's view, try to find out whether it would produce more happiness than other available acts. Rather we should see whether the act or policy is required by, or ruled out by, or merely compatible with maxims that avoid using others as mere means and maxims that treat others as ends in themselves.

* * *

USING OTHERS AS MERE MEANS

We use others as *mere means* if what we do reflects some maxim *to which they could not in principle consent.* Kant does not suggest that there is anything wrong about using someone as a means. Evidently every cooperative scheme of action does this. A government that agrees to provide free or subsidized food to famine-relief agencies both uses and is used by the agencies; a peasant who sells food in a local market both uses and is used by those who buy it. In such examples each party to the transaction can and does consent to take part in that transaction. Kant would say that the parties to such transactions use one another but do not use one another as *mere* means. Each party assumes that the other has its own maxims of action and is not just a thing or prop to be used or manipulated.

But there are other cases where one party to an arrangement or transaction not only uses the other but does so in ways that could only be done on the basis of a fundamental principle or maxim to which the other could not in principle consent. If a false promise is given, the party that accepts the promise is not just used but used as a mere means, because it is *impossible* for consent to be given to the fundamental principle or project of deception that must guide every false promise, whatever its surface character. Those who accept false promises *must* be kept ignorant of the underlying principle or maxim on which the "undertaking" is based. If this isn't kept concealed, the attempted promise will either be rejected or will not be a *false* promise at all. In false promising the deceived party becomes, as it were, a prop or tool—a *mere* means—in the false promisor's scheme. Action based on any such maxim of deception would be wrong in Kantian terms, whether it is a matter of a breach of treaty obligations, of contractual undertakings, or of accepted and relied upon modes of interaction. Maxims of deception *standardly* use others as mere means, and acts that could only be based on such maxims are unjust.

Another standard way of using others as mere means is by coercing them. Coercers, like deceivers, standardly don't give others the possibility of dissenting from what they propose to do. In deception, "consent" is spurious because it is given to a principle that couldn't be the underlying principle of *that* act at all; but the principle governing coercion may be brutally plain. Here any "consent" given is spurious because there was no option *but* to consent. If a rich or powerful landowner or nation threatens a poorer or more vulnerable person, group, or nation with some intolerable difficulty unless a concession is made, the more vulnerable party is denied a genuine choice between consent and dissent. While the boundary that divides coercion from mere bargaining and negotiation varies and is therefore often hard to discern, we have no doubt about the clearer cases. Maxims of coercion may threaten physical force, seizure of possessions, destruction of opportunities, or any other harm that the coerced party is thought to be unable to absorb without grave injury or danger. A moneylender in a Third World village who threatens not to make or renew an indispensable loan, without which survival until the next harvest would be impossible, uses the peasant as mere means. The peasant does not have the possibility of genuinely consenting to the "offer he can't refuse." The outward form of some coercive transactions may *look* like ordinary commercial dealings: but we know very well that some action that is superficially of this sort is based on maxims of coercion. To avoid coercion, action must be governed by maxims that the other party can choose to refuse and is not bound to accept. The more vulnerable the other party in any transaction or negotiation, the less their scope for refusal, and the more demanding it is likely to be to ensure that action is noncoercive.

In Kant's view, acts done on maxims that coerce or deceive others, so therefore cannot in principle have the consent of those others, are wrong. When individuals or institutions, or nation states act in ways that can only be based on such maxims they fail in their duty. They treat the parties who are either deceived or coerced unjustly. To avoid unjust action it is not enough to observe the outward forms of free agreement and cooperation; it is also essential to see that the weaker party to any arrangement has a genuine option to refuse the fundamental character of the proposal.

TREATING OTHERS AS ENDS IN THEMSELVES

For Kant, as for utilitarians, justice is only one part of duty. We may fail in our duty, even when we don't use anyone as mere means (by deception or coercion), if we fail to treat others as "ends in themselves." To treat others as "Ends in Themselves" we must not only avoid using them as mere means but also treat them as rational and autonomous beings with their own maxims. If human beings were *wholly* rational and autonomous then, on a Kantian view, duty would require only that they not use one another as mere means. But, as Kant repeatedly stressed, but later Kantians have often forgotten, human beings are *finite* rational beings. They are finite in several ways.

First, human beings are not ideal rational calculators. We *standardly* have neither a complete list of the actions possible in a given situation nor more than a partial view of their likely consequences. In addition, abilities to assess and to use available information are usually quite limited.

Second, these cognitive limitations are *standardly* complemented by limited autonomy. Human action is limited not only by various sorts of physical barrier and inability but by further sorts of (mutual or asymmetrical) dependence. To treat one another as ends in themselves such beings have to base their action on principles that do not undermine but rather sustain and extend one another's capacities for autonomous action. A central requirement for doing so is to share and support one another's ends and activities at least to some extent. Since finite rational beings cannot generally achieve their aims without some help and support from others, a general refusal of help and support amounts to failure to treat others as rational and autonomous beings, that is as ends in themselves. Hence Kantian principles require us not only to act justly, that is in accordance with maxims that don't coerce or deceive others, but also to avoid manipulation and to lend some support to others' plans and activities. * * *

Chapter Two

SOURCES AND APPLICATION OF LEGAL ETHICS RULES

What This Chapter Covers

Reading Assignment

Wydick & Perschbacher, Chapter 2

ABA Model Rules:

    Preamble, Scope and Terminology;

    Rules 5.5(a) and 8.1 through 8.5.

CRPC 1–100 through 1–300.

Cal.Bus. & Prof. Code §§ 6067–6068, 6076–6077, 6100–6117, 6125–6126.

Supplemental Reading

ABA Code:

Preamble and Preliminary Statement;

EC 1–1 through 1–6, and EC 8–6 through 8–7;

DR 1–101 through 1–103 and DR 3–101(B).

Hazard & Hodes:

Discussion of ABA Model Rules 5.5(a) and 8.1 through 8.5.

Wolfram:

Sections 1.1 through 1.6 (history and demographics of the legal profession);

Sections 2.1 through 2.7 (organization of the bar and sources of ethics guidance);

Sections 3.1 through 3.6 (professional discipline);

Sections 15.2 through 15.4 (admission to practice and character qualifications).

Cal.Bus. & Prof. Code §§ 6000–6228 (State Bar Act).

Cal.Family Code § 8800 (conflicts of interest in adoption proceedings).

––––––––

Discussion Problems

1.   Under the laws of the state of California, what requirements will you have to meet to be admitted to practice? [See Cal.Bus. & Prof.Code §§ 6060 & 6062.]

2.   In the *Kwasnik* case, *infra*:

a.   Trace the character investigation procedure that was followed. How were the facts determined? Who should bear the burden to show an applicant's good (or lack of good) character?

b.   Do you think that the decision in Kwasnik's case was correct given the circumstances?

c.   Should some conduct forever bar an applicant from becoming a lawyer? What about murder? child molestation? major securities or bank fraud? tax evasion? dozens of arrests at pro- or anti-abortion demonstrations? drunken driving convictions?

d.   If an applicant should be allowed to show rehabilitation, how long should the rehabilitation period be and who should decide? Can numerical standards be set?

3.   To practice in California, will you have to become a member of:

    a.   The state bar association?

    b.   The city or county bar association in the area where you open your office?

    c.   The American Bar Association?

4.   Suppose that you have recently been admitted to practice before the California Supreme Court.

    a.   Client Arnold asks you to represent him in a lawsuit pending in the United States District Court for the Northern District of California. Under what circumstances may you represent him?

    b.   Client Betty asks you to represent her in an appeal pending in the United States Court of Appeals for the Ninth Circuit. Under what circumstances may you represent her?

    c.   Client Carlos asks you to represent him in an appeal that is pending in the United States Supreme Court. Under what circumstances may you represent him?

    d.   Client Edgar asks you to defend him in an automobile negligence case pending in Arizona, right across the river from your office in California. Under what circumstances may you represent him?

    e.   Your law partner, attorney Thomas, suggests opening a branch office of the firm in Nevada. Thomas is admitted to practice in both California and Nevada; but you and the other lawyers in the firm are admitted only in California. Under what circumstances may the firm open the branch office? [*See* ABA Model Rule 7.5(b); ABA Code EC 3–9 and DR 2–102(D).]

5.   Lawyer Lawrence has come to you for legal advice. He has told you in confidence that he and a group of his friends formed a real estate investment venture. They entrusted him with a large sum of money to invest for them, but he diverted part of it for his own use. They have not yet discovered what he did, and he has asked you for legal guidance.

    a.   If Lawrence was acting in the real estate transaction in his personal capacity, not as a lawyer, is he subject to discipline by the state bar for what he did?

    b.   Do you have an ethical obligation to report him to the state bar?

6.   In the *Mountain* case and the *Drociak* case, *infra*:

    a.   How do you suppose the state bar first became aware of the misconduct?

    b.   Trace the procedure followed in each case. How were the facts determined? Who decided what discipline to impose?

    c.   Do you think the discipline imposed on lawyer Mountain was appropriate in the circumstances?

d. Do you think the discipline imposed on lawyer Drociak was appropriate in the circumstances?

THE ORGANIZATION OF THE BAR

In the United States, admission to the bar and lawyer discipline has traditionally been a matter of state concern. Lawyers are not admitted to practice in the United States, they are admitted to practice in a particular state or states. Separate rules govern admission to the various federal courts. Only recently has the states' near absolute control over their bars been challenged. However, the increased nationalization of commerce has broken down the model of local lawyer serving local client. Today, there are major law firms with offices in several cities and states throughout the United States and even the world. This increased practice across state lines and the increasing mobility of our population, including lawyers, has generated challenges to the states' residency requirements for membership in the bar. The consumer movement has also led to constitutional and antitrust challenges to the state bars' restrictions on lawyer advertising and fee regulation. These developments are discussed in this chapter and Chapter Four. Although this chapter focuses on admission to the bar, sources of ethics rules and lawyer discipline in general, in practice a lawyer will inquire into the admission, ethics, and discipline rules of the particular state(s) involved.

Admission to Practice in the Courts of a State

In most states, admission to practice law is gained by graduating from law school, passing the state's bar examination, and demonstrating that you possess good moral character.

1. Residency requirements

In the past, many states imposed residency requirements, but, since 1985, the Supreme Court has repeatedly struck down such requirements. In the first case, *Supreme Court of New Hampshire v. Piper,* 470 U.S. 274, 105 S.Ct. 1272, 84 L.Ed.2d 205 (1985), the Court held that the New Hampshire Supreme Court's refusal to swear in a Vermont resident who had passed the state's bar examination violated the Constitution's privileges and immunities clause. The Court established a narrow exception if a state can demonstrate "substantial" reasons for discriminating against non-residents and can show that the difference in treatment bears a close relation to those reasons. Using similar reasoning, in *Frazier v. Heebe,* 482 U.S. 641, 107 S.Ct. 2607, 96 L.Ed.2d 557 (1987), the Court invoked its supervisory power to invalidate a residency requirement imposed by the United States District Court for the Eastern District of Louisiana.

More recently, in *Supreme Court of Virginia v. Friedman,* 487 U.S. 59, 108 S.Ct. 2260, 101 L.Ed.2d 56 (1988), the Court struck down a Virginia rule that let permanent Virginia residents licensed out-of-state waive into the Virginia bar, but required non-Virginia residents to take the state bar examination. According to the Court, Virginia's rule violated the privileges and immunities clause because it burdened the right to practice law by discriminating among otherwise equally qualified applicants.

Finally, in *Barnard v. Thorstenn,* 489 U.S. 546, 109 S.Ct. 1294, 103 L.Ed.2d 559 (1989), the Court confronted perhaps its best chance to find "substantial" reasons to discriminate against nonresidents in bar admissions when it took up two New York and New Jersey lawyers' challenges to the Virgin Islands bar's one-year residency requirement. The Virgin Islands bar offered five justifications for its residency requirement: (1) the Virgin Islands' geographic isolation and communications difficulties would make it difficult for nonresidents to attend court proceedings on short notice; (2) delays in accommodating nonresident lawyers' schedules would increase the courts' caseloads; (3) delays in publication and lack of access to local statutory and case law would adversely affect nonresident lawyers' competence; (4) the bar does not have adequate resources to supervise a nationwide bar membership; and (5) nonresident bar members would be unable to take on a fair share of indigent criminal defense work.

The Supreme Court, in an opinion by Justice Kennedy, found none of the reasons substantial enough to justify excluding nonresidents from the Virgin Islands bar. Requiring nonresident lawyers to associate local counsel would satisfy the Virgin Islands' first two concerns, a solution the Court had also suggested in *Piper.* The Court rejected congested dockets and the difficulty in maintaining knowledge of local law as any justification for the exclusion of nonresidents from the bar. Dues paid by the nonresidents should supply the resources needed to meet the additional administrative burdens needed to supervise them. Only the fifth justification raised any serious concern. In *Piper,* the Court had recognized that nonresident lawyers could be required to share the burden of representing indigent criminal defendants as a condition of bar membership. In *Barnard,* the Court decided that requiring nonresident lawyers to meet this burden *personally* "is too heavy a burden on the privileges of nonresidents and bears no substantial relation to the [Virgin Islands'] objective." Justices Rehnquist, White and O'Connor dissented. They believed that "the unique circumstances of legal practice in the Virgin Islands * * * could justify upholding this simple residency requirement" under *Piper.*

The eventual impact of the residency-restriction cases may be ironic. In the past, some states allowed resident lawyers admitted in another state to "waive" into the bar without taking their own bar examination. Although this was often based on reciprocity (see below), it gave an advantage to lawyers who already resided in the state when they sought admission. Because the Supreme Court's decisions now require equality in treatment between in-state and out-of-state applicants to the bar, residence-based waivers are no longer allowed. These states must either allow any non-resident admission upon waiver on the same basis as residents, or abolish the waiver privilege. Illinois, for example, abolished the privilege rather than allowing waivers to non-residents (although the reciprocity privilege was later restored). The bottom line may be increased barriers to admission, rather than a relaxation of barriers for lawyers already in practice who wish to change or expand their geographical practices.

2. Character requirements

All states require that an applicant for admission to the bar possess "good moral character," although enforcement of this requirement is uneven and sporadic. Only two states—California and Florida—have paid staffs directly involved in screening bar applicants.[a] The elements of good moral character remain vague, but there is general agreement that they include honesty, respect for the law and respect for the rights of others. Applicants are most likely to get into difficulty for dishonesty on the bar application, recent criminal conduct, and fraud or other financial misdeeds. From time-to-time the bar has also sought to bar applicants on ideological, political, and moral grounds (especially persons whose sexual preferences or practices lack popular acceptance). In *Konigsberg v. State Bar,* 353 U.S. 252, 77 S.Ct. 722, 1 L.Ed.2d 810 (1957), the Supreme Court rejected mere membership in the Communist Party as proof that an applicant lacked good moral character. More difficult are cases involving past criminal conduct or misdeeds with an intervening passage of time or evidence of rehabilitation. Consider the following case.

KWASNIK v. STATE BAR OF CALIFORNIA

Supreme Court of California, 1990.
50 Cal.3d 1061, 269 Cal.Rptr. 749, 791 P.2d 319.

BY THE COURT:

Petitioner Richard E. Kwasnik seeks review of the refusal of the State Bar to certify him to this court for admission to the bar on the ground that he lacks the requisite good moral character. (Bus. & Prof.Code, § 6066; Cal.Rules of Court, rule 952(c); Rules Regulating Admission to Practice Law, rule I, § 11.) For the reasons set forth below, we conclude petitioner should be admitted to the bar.

FACTS

Petitioner graduated from Brooklyn Law School in June 1966. He was admitted to the practice of law in New York in 1967.

In November 1970 petitioner was involved in an automobile accident that resulted in the death of Steven Smilanich, a husband and father of three children. Although a grand jury investigated the accident, no criminal charges were filed. Petitioner pleaded guilty to "driving while impaired," a traffic infraction, and was fined $50.

a. Wolfram § 15.3.2, at 858.

The decedent's widow (hereafter Smilanich) and decedent's three minor children filed a wrongful death action against petitioner in a New York court, which resulted in a judgment against him in the amount of $232,234.16 in July 1974. Petitioner's automobile insurance carrier paid the policy limit of $10,000 to Smilanich. In 1975 Smilanich filed attachment proceedings against petitioner to enforce the judgment by garnishing his wages; he previously had made no payments on the judgment. Once he received a notice of levy, petitioner began making payments of approximately $42 every two weeks. Between 1975 and January 1980, petitioner paid $4,649. He has paid nothing since January 1980.

In November 1980, after Smilanich's attorney rejected a settlement offer of $15,000, petitioner filed a petition for bankruptcy in the United States Bankruptcy Court for the Southern District of Florida. * * * The only debt scheduled for discharge in the bankruptcy petition was the Smilanich judgment; petitioner listed none of his other then-existing debts. The Smilanich judgment was discharged by the bankruptcy court in March 1981.

A. Florida Bar Proceedings

[In 1980, the Florida State Bar found Kwasnik failed to meet their standards of conduct and fitness and refused to admit him. He sought reevaluation in 1986. The Florida bar again found he failed to meet their moral character requirements. However, the Florida Supreme Court rejected the bar's recommendation and held he had demonstrated sufficient rehabilitation to qualify for admission. In 1988 Kwasnik was admitted to practice in Florida.]

B. California Bar Proceedings

In July 1987 petitioner passed the Attorney's Examination of the California Bar Examination. His certification to practice was delayed, however, pending a moral character investigation. In June 1988 a formal hearing was held before a three-member hearing panel of the State Bar Court. Prior to the hearing petitioner entered a stipulation of facts with the State Bar. The hearing panel found that he had sustained his burden of proof that he is of good moral character and recommended that he be admitted to the California Bar.

Pursuant to a request for reconsideration, the hearing panel again recommended that he be admitted to the practice of law and issued a finding of facts that closely tracked the stipulation between the parties. First, it concluded that petitioner's description on his California Bar application of the disposition of the Smilanich suit as a "verdict for defendant" was not an intentional misstatement made to deceive. Second, it found that he accepted full responsibility for the three acts considered by the Florida Bar. Third, it concluded that the discharge of the Smilanich judgment in bankruptcy discharged both the legal and moral obligations of petitioner. Finally, it noted that except for the Smilanich matter petitioner's record is unblemished; that his conduct, as evidenced by the testimonial letters he submitted, established he is of a good moral character; and that he has an excellent reputation in the community for honesty, reliability, fairness and integrity. The hearing panel concluded that if he were admitted to the practice of law petitioner would be able to meet the professional and fiduciary duties of his practice.

The Review Department of the State Bar Court (hereafter the review department), however, made its own findings and disagreed with the hearing panel's conclusions. First, the review department detailed certain circumstances attendant on petitioner's bankruptcy: (1) between 1975 and 1979, when Kwasnik made payments only pursuant to garnishment proceedings, he earned an annual salary of between $15,000 and $32,000, totaling at least $100,000, while living rent-free at his mother's home and putting his wife through five years of college; and (2) petitioner misled Smilanich's attorney in 1980 by expressing an intention to take a one-year leave of absence when he had already accepted a new job in Florida.

Second, the review department cited a report issued by the Florida Bar after a formal rehabilitation hearing held in November 1986 on petitioner's application for reevaluation. The Florida Bar found that petitioner had taken no steps to fulfill his moral obligation to Smilanich since 1980. It noted that he had neither contacted the survivors nor made any further payment to them, despite the fact that he and his wife earned a combined income of $90,000 and owned $225,000 of equity in a home valued at $250,000. In addition, the review department noted that the Florida Bar found petitioner to be less than candid at the rehabilitation hearing, especially when asked why his New York home was in his wife's name.

Finally, the review department concluded that petitioner had demonstrated a lack of good moral character by failing to accept "any responsibility whatsoever for the Smilanich family which was victimized by his drunken driving." It found he ignored the rights of the Smilanich family under the wrongful death judgment until after garnishment proceedings were instituted, and then paid only the minimum in order to avoid the wage garnishment. Accordingly, in March 1989 the review department, by a vote of 11 to 4, found that petitioner did not possess the requisite good moral character and recommended that he not be admitted to the practice of law in California. The four members voting for petitioner's admission noted that the finding of lack of good moral character was based entirely on his failure to honor a moral obligation to pay a wrongful death judgment discharged in bankruptcy. They concluded petitioner should be admitted because he had successfully established his good moral character by his practice of law in sister jurisdictions and the attestations of judges and lawyers.

DISCUSSION

This court may admit to the practice of law any applicant whose qualifications have been certified to it by the Committee of Bar Examiners (hereafter the Committee). (Bus. & Prof.Code, § 6064.) To qualify, an applicant must, among other things, be of "good moral character." (Id., § 6060, subd. (b).)

"Good moral character" has traditionally been defined in California as the " 'absence of proven conduct or acts which have been historically considered as manifestations of "moral turpitude." ' " (*Hallinan v. Committee of Bar Examiners* (1966) 65 Cal.2d 447, 452, 55 Cal.Rptr. 228, 421 P.2d 76 (hereafter *Hallinan*).) Good moral character also is defined statutorily to include "qualities of honesty, fairness, candor, trustworthiness, observance of fiduciary responsibility, [observance] of the laws of the state and the nation and respect for the rights of others and for the judicial process." (Rule X, § 101(a)) * * *.

Because the commission of an act constituting "moral turpitude" is a statutory ground for disbarment (Bus. & Prof.Code, § 6106) and is perhaps the most frequent subject of inquiry in disciplinary proceedings, "insofar as the scope of inquiry is concerned, the distinction between admission and disciplinary proceedings is today more apparent than real." (*Hallinan,* supra, 65 Cal.2d at p. 452, 55 Cal.Rptr. 228, 421 P.2d 76.) The common issue is whether the applicant for admission or the attorney sought to be disciplined "is a fit and proper person to be permitted to practice law, and that usually turns upon whether he has committed or is likely to continue to commit acts of moral turpitude." (Id. at p. 453, 55 Cal.Rptr. 228, 421 P.2d 76.) * * *

The burden is on the applicant to prove good moral character. (*Hallinan,* supra, 65 Cal.2d at p. 451, 55 Cal.Rptr. 228, 421 P.2d 76.) If he is successful, the Committee must rebut that showing with evidence of bad character. Any applicant who is denied certification may seek review of the Committee's action in this court. (Bus. & Prof.Code, § 6066; Cal.Rules of Court, rule 952(c); Rules Regulating Admission to Practice Law, rule I, § 11.) In that review we give great weight to the Committee's findings, but they are not conclusive. We examine the evidence and make our own determination as to its sufficiency, resolving reasonable doubt in favor of the applicant. (*Hallinan,* supra, 65 Cal.2d at pp. 450–451, 55 Cal.Rptr. 228, 421 P.2d 76.)

Petitioner contends he has established his rehabilitation and good moral character. We agree. Petitioner introduced fifteen letters attesting to his character: seven from judges before whom he had appeared, seven from attorneys with whom he had practiced, and one from a pastor with whom he had worked on an interfaith council. The letters praise petitioner's personal and professional integrity and his reputation both as a competent trial attorney and as a member of the community.

Traditionally we have accorded significant weight to testimonials submitted by attorneys and judges regarding an applicant's moral fitness, on the assumption that such persons possess a keen sense of responsibility for the integrity of the legal profession. This is especially true when, as here, the references are aware of the circumstances that prompted the inquiry into the applicant's moral character.

In addition, the hearing panel and the review department both recognized that except for the events surrounding the wrongful death action, petitioner has an "unblemished record"; this is true not only of certain litigation in which petitioner was a party, in which his conduct did "not reflect badly on his moral character," but also of a 20–year period as a practicing member of the New York Bar, during which time he was never the subject of a disciplinary proceeding. Whether or not all petitioner's activities for which his superiors at the New York Legal Aid Society lauded him were simply part of his responsibilities, e.g., training and advising younger attorneys, there is extensive evidence that he acted diligently in that capacity. In addition, petitioner served competently in a fiduciary role as trustee of a $400,000 trust established by the City of New York for petitioner's parapalegic cousin; the Associate General Counsel of New York City who was in charge of that trust also submitted a letter on petitioner's behalf. Finally, as noted above, the Florida Supreme Court determined on the same evidence that petitioner was of good moral character and admitted him to the Florida Bar.

Business and Professions Code section 6106 states that an act of moral turpitude, dishonesty, or corruption constitutes a cause for disbarment or suspension of an attorney, regardless of whether the act is committed in his capacity as an attorney. Because the misconduct in this case is not in any way related to petitioner's practice of law, however, we should accord it less weight than we would professional misconduct in evaluating his moral fitness for admission to the bar. * * *

[Kwasnik and the State Bar disagreed over whether the State Bar refused to certify him *solely* because he obtained a bankruptcy discharge of the Smilanich judgment. The court reasoned that if the State Bar's denial was based on a claim that Kwasnik owed a moral obligation to the Smilanich family, it would violate the Bankruptcy Act § 525(a) [governmental unit may not deny a license to a person "solely because" he has not paid a debt that was discharged under the Bankruptcy Act] and the Constitution's supremacy clause by frustrating the purposes of Congress in enacting the Bankruptcy Act. The court found the evidence unrelated to the discharge was diminished by the passage of time and by the absence of similar, more recent misconduct, and thus did not reflect on his moral fitness to practice law. The court distinguished two other cases involving bankruptcy discharges in part because the debt Kwasnik discharged was unrelated to his practice of law, and was not a debt owed as a result of professional misconduct.]

DISPOSITION

* * * Accordingly, we order petitioner admitted to the California Bar. This holding is consistent with our charge to protect the public and its confidence in the legal profession rather than to impose punishment. (*Gary v. State Bar* (1988) 44 Cal.3d 820, 827, 244 Cal.Rptr. 482, 749 P.2d 1336.) The State Bar has presented no evidence that petition-

er is now a danger to the public in the practice of law or that he does not merit public confidence.

It is ordered that the Committee of Bar Examiners certify petitioner Richard E. Kwasnik to this court as a person qualified to be admitted to practice law.

[JUSTICE KENNARD'S and JUSTICE ARABIAN'S concurring opinions and CHIEF JUSTICE LUCAS' dissenting opinion are omitted.]

Note on Admission to Practice in California

The Committee of Bar Examiners, which is part of the State Bar of California, has the power to examine all applicants for admission to practice law in the State of California. [Rules Regulating Admission to Practice Law in California, Rule I § 2.] To be certified for admission, an applicant must be at least 18 years old, of good moral character, and a graduate of an accredited law school or a graduate of an unaccredited law school who passed the first year law students' examination. The applicant must also pass the General Bar Examination (or the Attorneys' Bar Examination if the applicant is admitted to practice in another state) and must pass the multi-state professional responsibility examination. [*Id.,* Rule II § 22, Rule IX § 92, Rule VI, Rule XI.] California also certifies people with additional skills in specialized areas of practice, including criminal law, family law, immigration and nationality law, taxation law, workers compensation law, and probate, estate planning and trust law. Certified specialists must demonstrate work experience, education and pass an examination in their area. [*See also* Chapter 4, *infra.*]

Once the applicant has fulfilled these requirements, the Examining Committee certifies the applicant to the Supreme Court for admission to the bar. If admitted, the applicant then takes an oath and becomes a member of the State Bar of California. [Cal.Bus. & Prof.Code §§ 6064, 6067.] An applicant who has been refused admission has the right to have his or her case reviewed by the California Supreme Court. [Cal.Bus. & Prof.Code § 6066.]

A member of the State Bar of California may be classified "active" or "inactive." [Cal.Bus. & Prof.Code § 6066.] A member is presumed an active member unless the member requests, or is involuntarily placed, on inactive status. [Cal.Bus. & Prof.Code § 6004.] Inactive members are not entitled to practice law. [Cal.Bus. & Prof.Code § 6006.] A member may be placed on involuntary inactive status for a number of reasons, including after a hearing where it was determined that the member is unable to practice law competently or without substantial threat of harm to his or her clients, or if there is a reasonable probability that the State Bar will prevail on the merits of an underlying disciplinary matter. [Cal.Bus. & Prof.Code § 6007.]

Since 1991, virtually all active California bar members have had to complete at least 36 hours of "minimum continuing legal education" (MCLE) every three years to retain their licenses to practice. At least four of the 36 hours must be devoted to legal ethics; one must relate to prevention and treatment of substance abuse and emotional distress; and another must relate to the elimination of bias in the legal profession.

ADMISSION TO PRACTICE IN OTHER STATES AND THE FEDERAL COURTS

An attorney who has been admitted in one state and who wants to represent a particular client in a court of another state may also petition that court to appear pro hac vice, i.e., "for this turn only." Each case requires a separate petition. In some jurisdictions, the attorney must enlist a local attorney as co-counsel. This requirement is to assure compliance with local procedure and provide accountability to the court, although some argue that it is really an economic device to protect the local bar.

A majority of the states have reciprocity arrangements that allow an attorney who has practiced in one state for a set number of years to gain full admission to practice in another state simply by filing a petition. But these arrangements are of no help to a lawyer from a state that does not reciprocate. Thus, if State A does not have an admission by petition procedure, but requires all attorneys from other states to take a bar examination, then even states that do permit admission by petition will require attorneys from State A to take a bar exam, though it may be a shorter one than is required of non-attorney applicants.

An attorney who wants to practice in a federal court must be separately admitted to the bar of that court, because each federal court maintains its own separate bar. Typically, admission is granted upon motion by an attorney who is already a member of that court's bar and who can affirm that the applicant is a person of good moral character. Admission to a federal district court typically requires that the applicant be admitted in the state in which the federal court sits. Admission to a federal court of appeal requires that the applicant be admitted in the courts of any state. Admission to the United States Supreme Court requires that the applicant have practiced before the courts of a state for at least three years.

LAWYER ASSOCIATIONS

Lawyers organize themselves into formal groups, not only because of tradition and natural inclination, but also because there is official encouragement to do so. ABA Code EC 9–6, itself a product of the organized bar, provides that every lawyer owes a solemn duty to cooperate with other lawyers in "supporting the organized bar through the devotion of * * * time, efforts, and financial support * * *." The Preamble to the ABA Model Rules suggests the goals sought by lawyer associations: to improve the law, legal education, the administration of justice, and the quality of services rendered by the legal profession; to promote law reform; to increase the availability of adequate legal assistance to those who cannot afford it; and to help preserve the independence of the legal profession by assuring that self-regulation is conducted in the public interest.

In the United States, lawyers have organized themselves into different kinds of groups according to geography (*e.g.*, the Ohio State Bar Association), age (*e.g.*, the Barristers Club of San Francisco, for lawyers under age 36), ancestry (*e.g.*, the Asian Bar Association), gender (*e.g.*, the National Association of Women Lawyers), and areas of legal interest (*e.g.*, the American Trial Lawyers Association).

1. *Nationwide Organizations*

There are dozens of nationwide organizations of lawyers. For example, the National Bar Association was organized in 1925 in response to discrimination against Black lawyers by other nationwide lawyer groups. Many of the present activities of the National Bar Association concern civil rights issues. The National Conference of Black Lawyers was formed in 1969 and is active in a variety of legal and political fields.

Another example is the National Lawyers Guild, formed in 1936 to work for social reform. In 1950, the House Un-American Activities Committee called it "the foremost legal bulwark of the Communist Party," [b] but that charge withered later in the decade.[c] Its present activities involve labor and immigration law, race relations, women's rights, disarmament, and prisoner rights.

A final example is the American Law Institute, formed in 1923. Its members are judges and lawyers from across the country, and its most well-known project is the Restatements of the Law.

2. *The American Bar Association*

The largest of the nationwide bar organizations is the American Bar Association. Described by one scholar as scarcely more than a minor social group when it was organized in 1878, it now has a membership of over 360,000—about half the lawyers in the country. The ABA holds itself out as the national voice of the legal profession.

The ABA functions through an elaborate structure consisting of its officers, the House of Delegates, the Board of Governors, and the Assembly. The House of Delegates is the designated source of control, policy formulation, and administration. Designed to be representative of the legal profession, it is made up of representatives or delegates from each state, from state and other bar associations, and from other organizations of the legal profession, such as the American Law Institute. The Board of Governors is empowered to perform, between meetings of the House of Delegates, the functions that the House itself might perform. The Assembly is composed of all members who register at the annual meeting. Members may present resolutions, and if

b. H.R.Rep. No. 3123, 81st Cong., 2d Sess. (1950). **c.** 1959 Atty.Gen.Ann.Rep. 259.

adopted by the Assembly, the resolutions are sent to the House of Delegates for approval, disapproval, or amendment.

Much of the ABA's work is accomplished through subgroups. The largest of these are called sections; they are devoted to distinct areas of practice or professional interest such as natural resources law, public utility law, anti-trust law, general practice, and tort and insurance practice. The sections have committees which focus on specific areas of interest. For example, the Section of International Law has more than 50 committees, including a committee on the law of the sea and a committee on international communications. Presently, there are more than 1,400 sectional committees.

One section of the ABA is the Law Student Division. Its goals include developing awareness of and participation in organized bar activities, further academic excellence, and promoting professional responsibility. The Law Student Division publishes its own journal, the Student Lawyer. Students who attend ABA-accredited law schools are eligible for membership, and presently some 28,000 law students belong to the Division.

In addition to the sections, there are approximately 70 smaller groups termed commissions, task forces, or committees. For example, the ABA Model Rules of Professional Conduct are the product of the Commission on Evaluation of Professional Standards.

ABA publications include the monthly American Bar Association Journal, which is distributed regularly to all members. Additionally, each section publishes a periodical which relates to its particular field of law and is sent automatically to each section member.

Another ABA function is to accredit law schools. Most states specify that only graduates of ABA-accredited law schools may take the bar examination, and ABA-accredited law schools accept transfer students only from other ABA-accredited schools. The ABA sets both quantitative and qualitative standards for accreditation. For example, it requires all students in accredited law schools to receive instruction in legal ethics, and that may well be why you are reading this book.

3. State Bar Associations

Each state has a statewide bar association, organized like the American Bar Association, although not so elaborately structured nor involved in so many activities. A significant distinction between the national organizations and many state bar associations is compulsory membership. Membership in all of the national organizations is voluntary. By contrast, many states require that all lawyers practicing in the state belong to the state bar association. The lawyer's license to practice law is membership in the state bar, which must be renewed annually by payment of dues. This form of compulsory membership is usually described as a *mandatory* or *integrated* bar.

Proponents of the mandatory bar claim that it can be more effective in fulfilling its professional responsibilities because it speaks and acts with one voice. Moreover, this effectiveness is enhanced by the predictable income from dues, which facilitates planning and budgeting. Opponents claim coerced membership is undemocratic, particularly when the organization acts or speaks out on some political, social or other matter outside the traditional scope of the legal profession. In a voluntary organization, the dissenter can always resign, but in an integrated bar exercising this option means leaving law practice. Critics also assert that mandatory bars beget their own ever-growing and increasingly expensive bureaucracies.

Critics of compulsory bar membership have had little success in making changes from within the bar associations. As a result, they have had to make their challenges in the courts, usually based on the Constitution. These challenges did not meet with much early success in state courts (which may have issued the very order unifying the bar that was being challenged). In 1961, in *Lathrop v. Donohue,* the Supreme Court rejected a constitutional challenge to the Wisconsin bar's membership requirement, and by the 1980's a majority of the states had unified bars.[d]

However, both practical and constitutional arguments against mandatory bar membership persisted, and in 1990 the Court returned to the question in *Keller v. State Bar of California,* 496 U.S. 1, 110 S.Ct. 2228, 110 L.Ed.2d 1 (1990). Members of the California state bar sued the bar claiming it was using their mandatory membership dues to advance ideological and political activities to which they were opposed in violation of their first amendment rights. The Court's decision focused on the free speech violations in found in the California bar's activities, and did not disturb *Lathrop*'s holding that involuntary membership in a state bar could be constitutionally compelled. Drawing upon cases giving union members the right to object to the use of a portion of their dues that supported political and ideological causes unrelated to collective-bargaining activities, the Court held the state bar could constitutionally fund activities "germane" to "regulating the legal profession and improving the quality of legal services" from the mandatory dues of all members. "It may not, however, in such manner fund activities of an ideological nature which fall outside of those areas of activity." The problem, the Court noted, is where to draw the line between permissible and prohibited activities:

> Precisely where the line falls between those State Bar activities in which the officials and members of the Bar are acting essentially as professional advisors to those ultimately charged with the regulation of the legal profession, on the one hand, and those activities having political or ideological coloration which are not reasonably related to the advancement of such goals, on the other, will not always be easy to discern. But the extreme ends of the spectrum

d. Wolfram § 2.3, at 37.

are clear: Compulsory dues may not be expended to endorse or advance a gun control or nuclear weapons freeze initiative; at the other end of the spectrum petitioners have no valid constitutional objection to their compulsory dues being spent for activities connected with disciplining members of the bar or proposing ethical codes for the profession.

496 U.S. at 15–16, 110 S.Ct. at 2237. The Court's opinion suggested there were several alternative means for the California bar to comply with its restrictions without abandoning either mandatory dues or compulsory bar membership. In the union dues context, *Chicago Teachers Union v. Hudson,* 475 U.S. 292, 106 S.Ct. 1066, 89 L.Ed.2d 232 (1986) upheld a procedure that required an adequate explanation of the basis for the fee, a reasonably prompt opportunity to challenge the amount of the fee before an impartial decisionmaker, and an escrow for the amounts reasonably in dispute while the challenges are pending. *Keller* may not have much of an impact on state bar finances. In California, the state bar spends almost 75% of its budget on lawyer discipline. Objecting members have been able to deduct from $1 to $4 annually from their $400 + in annual dues based on *Keller*'s restrictions. Lengthy annual hearings that determine the amount of deductible dues may lead to further challenges both to the hearings and to compulsory California bar membership.

As the *Keller* case notes, the State Bar of California is an integrated or mandatory bar association. Formed in 1927, the California bar has about 120,000 active members and continues to add over 5,000 members each year. It serves two basic functions. First, the State Bar acts as a regulatory agency overseeing the practice of law in the State of California; second, the State Bar is empowered to "aid in all matters pertaining to the advancement of the science of jurisprudence or to the improvement of the administration of justice." [Cal.Bus. & Prof.Code § 6031(a).] The latter function allows the State Bar to act as a trade association to lobby on behalf of the legal profession.

In its regulatory function, the State Bar presides over the admission to practice and discipline of attorneys. The State Bar also enforces laws regulating unauthorized practice and illegal solicitation [Cal.Bus. & Prof.Code §§ 6030, 6125–31, 6150–54], administers California's fee arbitration system, maintains a client security fund, and oversees the use of interest collected on client trust accounts for the representation of indigent people. [Cal.Bus. & Prof.Code §§ 6200–06, 6140.5, 6210–28.]

The State Bar also administers the California bar examination, accredits California law schools, provides continuing legal education for lawyers, publishes a monthly journal, and supports various sections and committees in specialized areas of the law.

4. *Local Bar Associations*

Bar associations organized on a local level, such as county or city, are voluntary in membership. Some are organized along subject or special interest lines such as trial practice. These organizations provide continuing professional education, act as a public voice on legal issues, serve as a medium for new lawyers to become acquainted with other practitioners, and function as social groups. Some local bar associations such as The Association of the Bar of the City of New York may be as powerful as statewide bar associations.

SOURCES OF GUIDANCE ON LEGAL ETHICS

1. State Rules, Statutes, and Rules of Court

Each state has a set of ethics rules that govern the lawyers in that state. In addition, some states have special statutes that govern the conduct of lawyers, and most courts have local rules that apply to all lawyers who appear before them. Thus, a lawyer who is beginning practice in a jurisdiction must consult several sources—the state ethics rules, the state statutes, and the local rules of court—to find out what is expected of him or her in that jurisdiction.

In 1989, the latest revisions to the Rules of Professional Conduct of the State Bar of California became effective. In addition to the Rules of Professional Conduct, the conduct of California attorneys is governed by article VI, section 9 of the California Constitution; the State Bar Act, found at Cal.Bus. & Prof.Code §§ 6000–6228; the California Code of Judicial Conduct; the California Rules of Court, Rules 901–22 pertaining to the censure, removal, retirement or private admonishment of judges; and state and county ethics opinions.

2. ABA Model Code of Professional Responsibility

In 1969, the American Bar Association promulgated the ABA Model Code of Professional Responsibility (the "ABA Code") as a model for the various states to follow in adopting their own sets of legal ethics rules. It was widely accepted, and within a few years almost all of the states had adopted ethics rules patterned closely on the ABA Code.

3. ABA Model Rules of Professional Conduct

In 1977, the ABA began work on the ABA Model Rules of Professional Conduct (the "ABA Model Rules"). The ABA Model Rules were designed to replace the ABA Code—that is, to become a new model for the states to follow. After extensive debate and a long process of compromise and amendment, a final version of the ABA Model Rules was adopted by the ABA House of Delegates in 1983.

The ABA Model Rules did not receive the quick, warm reception that the states had given the ABA Code fourteen years earlier. The debate over the ABA Model Rules served to focus attention on several key issues—particularly the confidentiality of client information—on which there was no clear consensus among the members of the legal profession. As of 1996, thirty-six states and the District of Columbia have adopted new legal ethics rules patterned on the ABA Model Rules, but most of those have made significant changes in important rules such as those concerning confidentiality of client information and solicitation of clients. A few other states have recently revised their legal ethics rules, drawing partly on the ABA Model Rules for guidance. The remaining states have thus far elected to retain their old rules patterned on the ABA Code.

The present lack of uniformity among the states has three consequences for you as a student of legal ethics. First, if you wish to be well-educated in legal ethics, you need to be familiar with both the ABA Code and the ABA Model Rules. Second, when you enter law practice in a state, you must promptly become familiar with that state's ethics rules. Third, as you work through the problems in this book, be critical. If the ABA Code and the ABA Model Rules provide different solutions to a problem, which solution is sounder? Would some different rule be better? Remember, the ethics rules you will study here are not graven in stone—they are subject to change, and they deserve the same critical analysis as any of the other rules you study in law school.

4. *ABA Code of Judicial Conduct*

In 1972, the American Bar Association promulgated the ABA Code of Judicial Conduct (the "CJC") as a model for the various states to follow in adopting their own sets of rules for judges. Most of the states adopted rules patterned closely on the CJC. In 1990 the ABA House of Delegates adopted a new Model Code of Judicial Conduct to replace the 1972 Code. Roughly half the states have now adopted the new model. California adopted the 1972 ABA Code with some modifications and California commentary. As a result of a voter initiative, California now has a new Code of Judicial Conduct, patterned on the 1990 ABA model. In addition, each state, including California, has statutes concerning judicial appointment, compensation, disqualification, and discipline.

5. *Advisory Opinions of Ethics Committees*

The ABA and many state and local bar associations have ethics committees—groups of lawyers who meet to consider, debate, and write opinions about questions of legal ethics. Some ethics committees publish their opinions, and these published opinions offer useful guidance on how the ethics rules apply to particular fact situations. They are not binding on any court or disciplinary body, but they are often cited as authority. The most convenient source of current ethics opinions is the ABA/BNA Lawyers' Manual on Professional Conduct, a looseleaf service published jointly by the American Bar Association and the Bureau of National Affairs, Inc. State and local bar associations in California publish ethics opinions for the guidance of their members. Particularly influential ethics opinions are those published by the Los Angeles and San Francisco County bar associations. Many of these opinions along with the statutes and rules can be found in the California Compendium on Professional Responsibility, published by The State Bar of California.

6. *Ethics Hot Lines*

Some state and local bar associations are willing to provide quick, rudimentary ethics advice by telephone. The Ethics Department of the ABA Center for Professional Responsibility operates ETHICSearch, an ethics research assistance service. The research assistance consists of referring the inquirer to ABA rules and standards, ABA ethics opinions, and other ABA materials relevant to the inquiry. The ABA ethics hotline can be reached by calling (312)988–5323 or by writing to 750 North Lake Shore Drive, Chicago, Illinois 60611, attention: Ethics Department. When using a telephone service, a careful lawyer should keep a record for the case file, including the question, the answer, and the identity of the person who responded to the question.

California attorneys may telephone the State Bar's Ethics Hotline at 1–800–2–ETHICS with inquiries. Hotline staff will discuss ethics questions with the caller and refer the caller to the appropriate authority, but the Hotline does not give advice.

7. *World-wide Web Sites*

Both the ABA and the California State Bar now maintain sites on the World-Wide Web. The ABA's is http://www.abanet.org; the California State Bar's is http://www.calbar.org.

DISCIPLINE

"Discipline" refers to the punishment or penalties imposed by a disciplining agency on an attorney who has breached a rule of professional ethics for which such action can be taken. A common disclaimer is that discipline is not intended as punishment but is for the protection of the public, the courts and the legal profession. To emphasize this, the word "sanctions" is frequently used in place of "penalty" or "punishment". Three types of discipline or sanctions are common: disbarment, suspension and reprimand (either public or private). All are available in California.

The mildest form of discipline is the reprimand, which is mild in the sense that such discipline does not limit the attorney's right to practice law. A private reprimand is an unpublished or private communication between the disciplining agency and the wrongdoing attorney and stating that certain conduct has been improper. A public reprimand is published, usually in a legal newspaper, a bar association newsletter or a bar journal and identifies the attorney as well as describes the improper conduct. A public reprimand thus ensures that at least some other members of the legal profession (and other readers of those publications) learn about the incident.

Suspension is a more stringent level of punishment because the attorney is prohibited from practicing law for the term of the suspension, which can range from several months to several years. Moreover, suspension may include the requirement that the attorney take and pass the legal ethics bar examination before being readmitted to active practice. Sometimes the suspension is stayed and the attorney is placed on conditional probation. For example, an attorney suffering from addiction to intoxicants or drugs may be permitted to continue practicing law but required to undergo psychiatric or other specialized supportive or rehabilitative help and to make progress reports on that help to the disciplining agency.

The most serious type of discipline is disbarment. Although disbarment typically means permanent removal from the practice of law, in some states a disbarred attorney may subsequently petition for readmission. Sometimes the petitioning attorney must retake the regular bar examination and the ethics examination to be readmitted. Until this year (1996), disbarred California lawyers could reapply for reinstatement after five years. A recent amendment to Rule of Procedure 662 of the State Bar Court gives that court discretion to set a reinstatement waiting period of either five or 10 years, or to disbar a California lawyer permanently.

Violation of the disciplinary rules and some statutes constitutes grounds for imposition of discipline. Moreover, an attorney can be disciplined for committing an illegal act that involves "moral turpitude." [ABA Model Rule 8.4(b); *see also* ABA Code DR 1–102(A)(3).] Moral turpitude is an imprecise term, but it certainly refers to the attorney's trustworthiness in the eyes of clients, the courts, other attorneys, and the public. The act which involves moral turpitude need not be committed in one's role as an attorney, but can be totally unrelated to the practice of law.

Discipline can also be imposed for specific statutory violations—for example statutes containing the attorney's oath, which provides that an attorney must support the Constitution and laws of the United States, maintain respect due to the courts, tell the truth, and not reject for any personal reason the cause of the defenseless or the oppressed.

The ABA Code and the ABA Model Rules do not prescribe specific disciplinary procedures and sanctions. These are contained in two separate documents, Model Rules for Lawyer Disciplinary Enforcement (1989)(procedure) and Standards for Imposing Lawyer Sanctions (1986)(sanctions), both produced by the American Bar Association and intended as models for the states to follow. The two documents essentially summarize the disciplinary process practiced by the states and the sanctions imposed, although variations do exist. In 1992, the ABA issued the ABA Recommendations for the Evaluation of Disciplinary Enforcement, suggesting various changes, including increased public access to disciplinary proceedings and records. [*See* ABA Recommendation 7.]

DISCIPLINE IN CALIFORNIA

In 1989, California restructured its disciplinary system and adopted a new set of Rules of Professional Conduct. The disciplinary system had been intensely criticized in the press and the state legislature for its leniency and the backlog of cases. Under this new structure, the Office of Intake/Legal Advice reviews and responds to all complaints, including written inquiries and complaints received through its toll-free hotline, plus reports from banks, courts, insurers and attorneys who received civil sanctions or criminal penalties, with the goal of resolving straightforward claims and eliminating meritless ones. If a quick resolution is not possible, the complaint is forwarded to Intake Investigators, who gather initial evidence regarding the complaint. The investigators are supervised by attorneys, and no complaint is dismissed without attorney approval. After talking with witnesses, the investigator contacts the attorney and presents the allegations.

If the claim cannot be resolved through this process, the file is forwarded to the Office of Investigation. Two types of claims are forwarded automatically—claims concerning monetary violations and claims concerning attorneys who are already under investigation.

Upon receiving a complaint, the Office of Investigation assigns the complaint to one of five investigative units. The investigator sends a letter to all involved parties to gather evidence, and then writes a Statement of the Case against the attorney, or closes the file if there are insufficient facts. If the investigator closes the file, the complainant may petition for review by the Complainant's Grievance Panel. The Administrative Compliance Unit will then review the case and make a recommendation to the Grievance Panel, which will determine whether the case should remain closed or should be reopened for further investigation.

If the case remains open, the file is forwarded to the Office of Trials, which prosecutes the matter before the State Bar Court and a Hearing Judge. The State Bar Court was created by 1988 legislation and was the first court of its kind in the United States. Funded exclusively by the members of the State Bar, the State Bar Court acts as an arm of the California Supreme Court in deciding all cases involving disciplinary proceedings brought against attorneys admitted to practice in California. There are nine full-time members of the court: six hearing judges and three review judges, one of whom is the presiding judge. Four of the six hearing judges are in Los Angeles; the other two are in San Francisco. At least one member of the State Bar Court must be a non-lawyer.

Subject to review by the California Supreme Court, the State Bar Court decides whether an attorney has violated any of the professional standards an attorney is required to maintain: the Business and Professions Code, the Rules of Professional Conduct and other California laws. If it finds that the standards have been violated, the State Bar Court then determines what sanctions or disciplinary action to impose based upon the facts and circumstances of the particular case. The Standards for Attorney Sanctions serve as guidelines for the extent of discipline to be imposed. The State Bar Court can issue private or public reprovals for offenses that are less serious. More serious acts of professional misconduct or conviction of serious crimes usually result in suspension from law practice or disbarment. [Cal.Bus & Prof. Code § 6078.]

An attorney who is disbarred is removed from membership in the State Bar of California and forbidden from practicing law in the State of California. Suspension allows an attorney to remain a member of the State Bar but prohibits the attorney from practicing law during the period of time that the suspension is in effect. An order suspending an attorney may be partially or totally stayed, and the attorney is then put on probation for up to five years. Attorneys may be placed on involuntary inactive status and precluded from practicing law even before all proceedings have been completed if the State Bar Court finds that the attorney presents a substantial threat of harm to clients or the public.

During the period of probation, or in addition to a reproval, the State Bar Court may impose various conditions such as restitution or refund to victims, passage of the Professional Responsibility Examination or payment of specified costs of the proceedings along with or instead of an actual suspension.

Before the enactment of the 1988 legislation, the State Bar could recommend disciplinary action, but the California Supreme Court had the ultimate power in deciding the actual discipline to be imposed. Now, the State Bar Court may suspend or permanently ban attorneys from practicing law, shifting much of the workload and responsibility from the Supreme Court to the State Bar Court, although an attorney may still appeal the imposition of discipline to the state's Supreme Court.

The California bar keeps careful records of all complaints about lawyers. A case history on a lawyer's professional life is thus established. Each incident—even those where no discipline or only mild discipline is imposed—may have increasing impact on subsequent charges by contributing to an overall pattern.

IN RE MOUNTAIN

Supreme Court of Kansas, 1986.
239 Kan. 412, 721 P.2d 264.

A formal complaint was filed against R. Keith Mountain, attorney respondent, by Arno Windscheffel, disciplinary administrator * * * alleging respondent violated the Lawyers Code of Professional Responsibility. Respondent answered denying he had violated his legal or ethical duty. A hearing before a disciplinary panel was held * * *. Respondent appeared in person and by his attorney * * *.

The panel made its final hearing report containing * * * findings of fact and conclusions of law * * *.

* * *

[A portion of the hearing panel's findings of facts can be paraphrased as follows. Mr. and Mrs. M, who wished to adopt a baby, contacted lawyer Mountain through a county health worker. The health worker told the M's about an expectant mother named A. S. who wanted to put her baby up for adoption. Mountain agreed to represent the M's for $500, of which $250 was paid in advance. Mountain then contacted A. S. and her grandmother.

[Mountain told the M's that A. S. and the grandmother needed $300 in financial help. The M's sent Mountain the money, and Mountain sent it on to A. S. Mountain then convinced A. S. and the grandmother that he was representing them, although they were on welfare and paid him no fee. The grandmother decided that the M's were not wealthy enough to adopt the child. Mountain then suggested other couples who would be willing to adopt the child and told the grandmother that she would receive $5,000 under a new arrangement with a different adopting couple.

[Shortly thereafter, Mountain sent the grandmother $500 in "prenatal expenses." The record did not disclose whether the $500 was advanced by Mountain or by someone else. Then Mountain called the M's, told them that the fetus indicated some abnormalities, that members of A. S.'s family were attempting to prevent the adoption, that the adoption would probably be "messy," and that the M's should abandon the adoption. Saddened, the M's agreed not to go on with the adoption. Meanwhile, Mountain had already made arrangements with another couple to adopt the baby, and the second couple paid Mountain a total of $17,000. Mountain did not disclose these facts to the M's. About two weeks later, the M's telephoned Mountain and asked questions about the adoption and medical tests. Mountain became adamant and told the M's that the adoption was off.

[The gynecologist who treated A. S. said that the medical tests on the fetus were normal, that Mountain had never called him to find out the results of the medical tests, and that he had never told Mountain about any abnormalities of the fetus.

[In due course, A. S. gave birth to a normal baby girl. Mountain arranged to have the baby adopted by the second couple. Mountain claimed that part of the $17,000 paid to him by the second couple was for a fee earned earlier in a different matter. Mountain paid about $750 for postbirth care of the baby and paid the grandmother $5,000; there was no showing about what happened to the rest of the $17,000.

[After the M's hired a new attorney, G, to look into the matter on their behalf, Mountain sent the M's $250 as a refund of the fee advance they had given him. He did not refund the $300 which the M's had advanced to him for financial support of A. S. When attorney G asked Mountain about the adoption, Mountain at first said that he had represented the M's but that A. S. had ultimately given the baby to a second couple and that Mountain had not handled the adoption by the second couple. Later, Mountain changed his story and claimed that he represented only A. S. and the grandmother throughout the entire matter.

[The hearing panel reached conclusions of law, a portion of which can be paraphrased as follows:

[1. Mountain represented the M's and at the same time represented the second couple in violation of the conflict of interest rules.

[2. Mountain made a false statement to the M's when he told them that the fetus was abnormal when in fact he had not conferred with the gynecologist.

[3. Mountain failed to carry out his agreement to represent the M's in the matter.

[4. Mountain made false statements to attorney G about Mountain's role in the matter.

[5. Mountain served as a procurer of a baby for adoption, which is morally repugnant and in violation of DR 1–102(A)(5) and (6).

[6. Mountain collected a clearly excessive fee from the second couple.]

Respondent took exceptions to the panel's final hearing report and took this appeal. Respondent neither filed a brief nor appeared for oral argument though personally notified.

We have examined the record and find substantial competent evidence to support the findings of fact of the hearing panel. The facts support the panel's conclusions of law * * *. We conclude the panel's recommendation that respondent be disbarred is appropriate.

IT IS THEREFORE ORDERED that R. Keith Mountain be and he is hereby disbarred from the practice of law in the State of Kansas and the Clerk of the Appellate Courts is directed to strike his name from the rolls of attorneys authorized to practice law in the State of Kansas. * * *

DROCIAK v. STATE BAR OF CALIFORNIA

Supreme Court of California, 1991.
52 Cal.3d 1085, 278 Cal.Rptr. 86, 804 P.2d 711.

THE COURT:

The Review Department of the State Bar Court recommends petitioner Joseph L. Drociak be suspended from the practice of law for one year, stayed, and that he be placed on probation for two years under certain conditions, including 30 days' actual suspension. Petitioner concedes he violated Business and Professions Code, section 6106 (commission of an act involving moral turpitude), section 6068, subdivision (d)(failing to employ "such means only as are consistent with truth"), and Rules of Professional Conduct, former rule 7–105(1)(same)(presently rule 5–200(B) under new Rules of Professional Conduct that became effective May 27, 1989)(all future section and rule references are to these respective sources unless otherwise indicated). The sole issue in the present proceeding is whether the recommended discipline is excessive. We adopt the recommendation of the review department.

I. Facts and procedure

The hearing panel found the following facts: Petitioner was admitted to practice law in 1964 and has no record of discipline. He has a solo practice of criminal and personal injury cases and employs support staff of six secretaries, paralegals and investigators.

In March 1985, petitioner was retained by Jane House to represent her in a personal injury action against Greyhound Bus Lines, Inc. (Greyhound). As was his custom with many of his clients, petitioner had House sign a number of undated, blank verification forms. In March 1986, petitioner filed a complaint on House's behalf. When Greyhound sought discovery through interrogatories and a request for documents, petitioner wrote to House, requesting she visit his office to prepare answers to the discovery requests. Between May and August 1986, he wrote four such letters to House but received no reply. He told counsel for Greyhound, Temple Harvey, that he had "temporarily lost contact" with House.

After receiving a number of extensions for discovery and still failing to contact House, petitioner consulted House's file and answered the interrogatories himself, attaching one of House's presigned verifications. Later he served responses to the request for documents, again attaching one of House's presigned verifications.

Trial in House v. Greyhound was set for November 1986. When petitioner failed to appear, the matter was dismissed.

[In late 1986 or early 1987, petitioner first learned that House had been dead since October 1985.]

* * *

The hearing panel concluded petitioner violated sections 6106 and 6068, subdivision (d), and former rule 7–105(1). Section 6106 provides, "The commission of any act involving moral turpitude, dishonesty or corruption * * * constitutes a cause for disbarment or suspension." Section 6068, subdivision (d), requires an attorney "To employ, for the purpose of maintaining the causes confided to him or her such means only as are consistent with truth, and never to seek to mislead the judge or any judicial officer by an artifice or false statement of fact or law." Former rule 7–105(1) tracks section 6068, subdivision (d), and likewise requires an attorney to "employ, for the purpose of maintaining the causes confided to him such means only as are consistent with truth * * *."

The panel found the following facts in aggravation: Petitioner's admission that he had other clients sign blank verifications demonstrated a "pattern of misconduct"; his acts disclosed dishonesty and concealment; his use of presigned verifications posed a threat to the administration of justice (in that unverified information in discovery responses might be inaccurate, and the opposing party might rely on that information in agreeing to an "undeserved" settlement); and petitioner "demonstrated no remorse for his actions."

The hearing panel found these facts in mitigation: In 25 years of practice, petitioner has no record of prior discipline; he believed his acts were in the best interests of his clients, many of whom move without leaving a forwarding address and are thus difficult to locate; there was no financial harm to House * * *; and petitioner was cooperative with the State Bar, and was "candid and open in his acknowledgment of his wrongful acts." (The last finding appears inconsistent with the final finding in aggravation.)

The hearing panel recommended the above-described discipline. The review department adopted the panel's findings and recommendation on a nine-to-four vote (three of the dissenters felt the discipline excessive; the fourth believed it too lenient and would have imposed ninety days' actual suspension).

II. *Challenge to various findings*

[Petitioner challenged certain ancillary "findings" made by the hearing panel and adopted by the review department as unsupported by the record. He claimed the findings cast him in a "false light" and led the review department to affirm the hearing panel's "excessive" recommendation of 30 days' actual suspension. The court agreed, adding, "we fail to understand why the review department adopted the findings in toto, without making appropriate modifications. For example, the hearing panel (a single referee who identified himself in the panel decision as 'an insurance defense attorney') twice characterized petitioner's law practice as a 'mill operation' and four times alluded to 'findings'— unsupported in the record, and certainly inflammatory—that petitioner allowed members of his staff to 'forge' clients' names to verifications."]
* * *

III. *Discipline*

It is well established that we exercise our independent judgment in determining whether the recommended discipline is appropriate, excessive, or inadequate. In exercising our authority we traditionally accord great weight to the review department's determination.

Petitioner insists this deference is inappropriate here in light of the unsupported "findings" described above (pt. II, *ante*) that may have improperly "colored" the review department's recommendation in this case. Even granting less than usual deference, however, we still conclude the review department's recommendation is appropriate.

* * *

The findings set out above are supported by the record and amply establish petitioner's misconduct.

* * *

The Standards for Attorney Sanctions for Professional Misconduct (Rules Proc. of State Bar; hereafter standards) make violation of section 6106 punishable by disbarment or actual suspension. (Std. 2.3.) The same provision applies to a violation of former rule 7–105(1). Likewise, standard 2.6(a) makes a violation of section 6068, subdivision (d), punishable by disbarment or suspension. We employ the standards as guidelines to determine the discipline necessary and appropriate to protect the public.

Petitioner insists that various factors in mitigation—his lengthy record without discipline, the asserted hardship on his office staff if he is compelled to cease practice even for a short period, his recent changes in office practices, the absence of harm to his client, and most important, his avowed intent to assist his client by his misconduct—make a 30–day actual suspension inappropriate.

We disagree. Discipline is imposed in order to protect the public by deterring future misconduct by attorneys. The impact of otherwise appropriate discipline on an attorney or his office staff is irrelevant to this purpose, and should not be considered by this court. Moreover, we have repeatedly rejected petitioner's assertion that his conduct is less culpable because he was motivated primarily by a desire to protect a client. (*Codiga v. State Bar* (1978) 20 Cal.3d 788, 793, 144 Cal.Rptr. 404, 575 P.2d 1186 ["deceit by an attorney is reprehensible misconduct whether or not harm results and without regard to any motive or personal gain"].) Petitioner's prior "clean" record is commendable, but it does not render the recommended 30–day actual suspension inappropriate.

Petitioner concedes there is no case involving the "particular misconduct" at issue here, but cites a number of cases in which attorneys received either less discipline than that recommended here for assertedly similar misrepresentations, or the same discipline in the face of more egregious violations. The State Bar also cites a number of assertedly similar cases, many with distinguishable aggravating facts, in which attorneys received the same (or greater) discipline recommended here. Exercising our independent judgment, on the facts of this case we are satisfied that the recommended discipline, including a 30–day actual suspension, is necessary and appropriate to protect the public and to deter future misconduct.

IV. *Disposition*

Petitioner is suspended from law practice for one year, which term will be stayed during two years of supervised probation. Conditions of this probationary period include: (i) 30 days' actual suspension and (ii) compliance with the terms set out in the review department's decision, including the requirements that he complete a course on law office management, and that he develop a law office management plan. In addition, petitioner shall take and pass the Professional Responsibility Examination within one year of the effective date of this order. This order is effective on finality of this decision in this court (see Cal.Rules of Court, rule 953(a)).

Note on Discipline in the Federal Courts

Discipline in the federal courts, like admission to practice, is handled separately by the particular district court, court of appeals or Supreme Court involved. Lawyers disciplined by a state court will not automatically receive federal court discipline. Likewise, lawyers disciplined by a federal court do not necessarily face discipline for the same conduct by the courts of their states of admission.

The federal courts exercise their power to discipline lawyers admitted to practice before the court based on their "inherent authority to suspend or disbar lawyers. This inherent power derives from the lawyer's role as an officer of the court which granted admission." [In re Snyder, 472 U.S. 634, 643, 105 S.Ct. 2874, 2880, 86 L.Ed.2d 504 (1985).] Rule 46(b) of the Federal Rules of Appellate Procedure provides a uniform rule for the courts of appeals. It subjects members of the federal court bar to suspension or disbarment by the court when a member "has been suspended or disbarred from practice in any other court of record, or has been guilty of conduct unbecoming a member of the bar of the court." The rule also provides the member an opportunity to show why he or she should not be disciplined. [See also Fed. R.App.P. 46(c).] The Supreme Court's Rule 8 is similar in substance. There is no uniform discipline rule in the federal district courts, and recent efforts to develop such a rule have stalled.

The *Snyder* case defined "conduct unbecoming a member of the bar" as "conduct contrary to professional standards that shows an unfitness to discharge continuing obligations to clients or the courts, or conduct inimical to the administration of justice. More specific guidance is provided by case law, applicable court rules, and the 'lore of the profession,' as embodied in codes of professional conduct." [472 U.S. at 645, 105 S.Ct. at 2881.] At the same time the Court rejected the idea that the federal court could simply apply the lawyer's licensing state's ethical code to evaluate the lawyer's conduct in federal court. "The state code of professional responsibility does not by its own terms apply to sanctions in the federal courts. Federal courts admit and suspend attorneys as an exercise of their inherent power; the standards imposed are a matter of federal law." [472 U.S. at 645 n. 6, 105 S.Ct. at 2881 n. 6.] But, the Court added: "The Court of Appeals was entitled, however, to charge petitioner with the knowledge of and the duty to conform to the state code of professional responsibility. The uniform first step for admission to any federal court is admission to a state court." [*Id.*] Many federal courts' local rules expressly incorporate the local state's rules of professional conduct as part of the federal court's standards. [*See, e.g.,* Local Rules for the United States District Court for the Northern District of California, Civil L.R. 11–3 (Standards of Professional Conduct)(1996).]

In *Snyder,* the Court reversed lawyer Robert Snyder's six-month suspension from practice in the Eighth Circuit. Snyder had written a "harsh" letter to the Chief Judge of the Eighth Circuit that was highly critical of fees for court appointments. The Supreme Court found Snyder's conduct did not rise to the level of "conduct unbecoming a member of the bar" warranting suspension from practice.

MULTIPLE CHOICE QUESTIONS

The multiple choice questions at the end of each of the following chapters of this book use some key words and phrases that are defined below. *Warning:* These definitions are similar, but not identical, to the ones used by the National Conference of Bar Examiners in the Multistate Professional Responsibility Examination.

- *Must* or *subject to discipline* asks whether the conduct described in the question subjects the attorney to discipline under the Disciplinary Rules of the ABA Code and the provisions of the ABA Model Rules.
- *Should* asks whether the conduct described in the question at least conforms to the level of conduct expected of the attorney pursuant to the ABA Code and the ABA Model Rules, regardless of whether the obligation arises under the Ethical Considerations, Comments, or Disciplinary Rules.
- *May* or *proper* asks whether the conduct described in the question is professionally appropriate in that it:
  — would not subject the attorney to discipline; and
  — is not inconsistent with the Ethical Considerations of the ABA Code and the Preamble and Comments to the ABA Model Rules; and
  — is not inconsistent with the ABA Code of Judicial Conduct.
- *Subject to liability for malpractice* asks whether the conduct described in the question subjects the attorney to liability for harm resulting from that conduct. Answer such questions according to generally accepted principles of law, bearing in mind the relationship between liability for malpractice and subjection to discipline.

1. Attorney Alford is admitted to practice before the highest court of State A, but not in State B. Client Clara lives in State A, but she runs a business in State B. She asks Alford to defend her in a lawsuit pending in a trial court of State B. The suit involves the proper interpretation of a State B business tax statute. Would it be *proper* for Alford to represent Clara?

    A. Yes, if the State B court admits him *pro hac vice,* that is, for the purpose of litigating this case.

    B. Yes, because State B cannot constitutionally discriminate against non-resident attorneys.

    C. No, because Clara's business is conducted in State B, and he is not admitted to practice in State B.

D.   No, because the suit involves the interpretation of a State B statute, and he is not admitted to practice in State B.

2.   Lawyer Linda is admitted to practice in State A, but not in State B. Her cousin asks her to write a letter recommending him for admission to practice law in State B. Linda knows that her cousin is educationally well-qualified to be a lawyer, but she regards him as thoroughly dishonest. *May* Linda write a letter stating that her cousin is fit to practice law?

A.   No, because Linda is not a member of the bar of State B.

B.   No, because Linda would be making a false statement of a material fact.

C.   Yes, because her belief about her cousin's lack of honesty is merely her own opinion.

D.   Yes, because the bar of State B will decide for itself whether her cousin is a person of good moral character.

3.   Law student Samuel has passed State C's bar examination. For which of the following reasons could State C constitutionally refuse to admit Samuel to practice?

I.   Samuel plans to live in neighboring State D and to commute to work at a law office in State C.

II.   For a brief period during his college years, Samuel was a member of the Communist Party.

III.   Samuel is not a citizen of the United States.

IV.   Two years ago, Samuel was convicted of federal tax fraud.

A.   None of the above.

B.   All of the above.

C.   II, III, and IV only.

D.   IV only.

4.   One of lawyer Leon's clients gave him a "Little Yellow Box," an electronic device that enables one to make long distance telephone calls from a pay phone without depositing any money. Leon used it occasionally to call his mother in Des Moines. Use of such a device is a misdemeanor under the applicable state law. Leon was arrested for using the device. At his trial, he denied ever having it in his possession. The judge did not believe him, found him guilty, and fined him $1,000. That same week, Leon's law partner, Leona, went backpacking in the mountains. She was arrested by a State Forest Ranger; unbeknownst to Leona, state law makes it a misdemeanor to build a campfire in a state forest without having a shovel and water bucket at hand. Leona pleaded guilty to the charge, and the judge fined her $1,000.

A.   Both Leon and Leona are *subject to discipline*.

B.   Neither Leon nor Leona is *subject to discipline*.

C.   Leon is *subject to discipline*, but Leona is not.

    D.   Leona is *subject to discipline*, but Leon is not.

    5.   When law student Sabrina was 17-years-old, a juvenile court in State A convicted her of shoplifting a $2,500 fur coat. She served eight months in a juvenile correction facility and thereafter was under the supervision of a parole officer for one year. After her parole, she completed high school, college, and law school, and she led a totally law-abiding life. When Sabrina applied for admission to practice law in State B, she was required to fill out a questionnaire. One question asked her to disclose "all convictions, including juvenile convictions." In answering that question she put "not applicable," on the theory that her juvenile offense in State A was irrelevant to her present moral character. The bar of State B did not learn about her State A conviction until six months after she had been admitted to practice in State B. Is Sabrina *subject to discipline*?

    A.   Yes, because she withheld a material fact when she answered the questionnaire.

    B.   Yes, because a person who has committed a crime involving dishonesty or false statement is disqualified from practicing law.

    C.   No, because her prior juvenile conviction was not relevant to her moral character at the time of her application to the bar.

    D.   No, because State B's questionnaire is an unconstitutional invasion of privacy.

    6.   Attorney Arner is a member of the bar of State C. While on vacation in State D, Arner was arrested and was ultimately convicted of a felony in State D—the sale of pornographic photographs of young children. Is Arner *subject to discipline* in State C?

    A.   No, because his conduct took place beyond the jurisdiction of State C.

    B.   Yes, because the sale of such photographs is an act involving moral turpitude.

    C.   No, because his conduct in State D was not connected with the practice of law.

    D.   Yes, because commission of any criminal act is grounds for professional discipline.

    7.   Client Cathcart hired lawyer Lindell to prepare an estate plan. In connection with that work, Cathcart told Lindell in strict confidence about a criminal fraud perpetrated by Cathcart's former lawyer, Foreman. Lindell urged Cathcart to report Foreman's conduct to the state bar. For unstated reasons, Cathcart refused to do so and refused to allow Lindell to do so. What is the *proper* course of conduct for Lindell in this situation:

    A.   To keep the information in confidence, as Cathcart has instructed.

B. To speak with Foreman in confidence, to inform him what Cathcart said, and to urge Foreman to rectify his fraud.

C. To report the information to the state bar, despite Cathcart's instruction not to do so.

D. To write an anonymous letter to the state bar, relating the facts disclosed by Cathcart.

Answers to the multiple choice questions will be found in the Appendix at the back of the book

Chapter Three

BEGINNING AND ENDING
THE LAWYER–CLIENT
RELATIONSHIP

What This Chapter Covers

Reading Assignment

Supplemental Reading

Hazard & Hodes:

Discussion of ABA Model Rules 1.16, 3.1, and 6.1 through 6.2.

Wolfram:

Sections 10.2.1 through 10.2.3 (accepting cases);

Sections 9.5 through 9.5.4 (ending the relationship);

Sections 16.7 through 16.9 (*pro bono* service);

Sections 11.2.3 through 11.2.5 (frivolous claims);

Restatement (Third) of the Law Governing Lawyers §§ 26, 28, 29, 30, 43–45, 49, 51–52, 56–58 (Proposed Final Draft No. 1, 1996).

Discussion Problems

1. When attorney Sheila was admitted to law practice a few years ago, she took the Attorney's Oath in which she promised "never to reject, for any consideration personal to [her]self, the cause of the defenseless or the oppressed." Sheila's grandparents narrowly escaped from Austria in 1939 to avoid the Holocaust. Although her law practice is primarily business-oriented, she has served in several cases as a vigorous and skillful advocate of individual civil liberties. The American Nazi Party has asked her to represent one of its members who was arrested for participating in an allegedly illegal street rally in her city. The Party has ample funds to pay a lawyer, but the other skilled trial lawyers in the city have refused to get involved in the case. Sheila believes that the city's refusal to issue a rally permit was a violation of the First Amendment, and she believes that she could present an effective defense. But she is repelled by the defendant and his political beliefs. Further, she knows that her reputation and her law practice will suffer because several of her business clients are among the prominent citizens who actively opposed the Nazi rally.

    a. Does Sheila have an ethical obligation to take the case?

    b. Suppose the defendant were indigent, that the Party could not fund his defense, and that the Public Defender could not represent him because of a conflict of interest. If the court appointed Sheila to defend him, may she refuse?

2. Suppose you have recently become a partner in a small law firm that has a broad, general practice. You are attending a partnership meeting where the item under discussion is a memorandum signed by all three of the newly-hired associates. They have asked the firm to establish a policy that permits and encourages every lawyer in the firm to devote the equivalent of 100 billable hours per year to representing indigent clients. (The lawyers in the firm average about 1,800 billable hours per year.) The state pays a modest fee to court-appointed counsel in criminal cases, but there is no compensation scheme for civil matters, and the state's legal services program has been sharply cut due to lack of

public funding. One of your partners has argued that to adopt the proposed policy, the firm will either have to cut its present overhead, or cut the present pay of the staff and the lawyers, or raise its fees to paying clients by about 5%. The discussion has come to a close. How will you vote on the proposal, and why?

3. From what you have learned thus far, give five illustrations in which a lawyer would be subject to discipline for accepting or continuing employment in a matter.

4. Judicial opinions sometimes state: "A client has a right to discharge a lawyer at any time, with or without cause, subject to liability for payment for the lawyer's services." Is there any situation in which the first part of that statement is not true?

5. Last August, California lawyer Simon agreed to represent plaintiff Noreen in a personal injury suit pending in California. Their fee agreement provided that Simon would receive 20% of the net recovered by settlement, or 30% of the net recovered after trial, or 40% of the net recovered after trial and appeal. The percentages were to be computed after deducting litigation expenses. The agreement further provided that in no event would Simon's fee be less than $5,000 nor more than $10,000. After Simon spent about 100 hours on the case, Noreen fired him for no apparent reason. She repaid $1,000 for litigation expenses he had advanced on her behalf, but she refused to pay him any fee. Later, she hired another lawyer who promptly settled the suit for $13,000, without incurring any additional litigation expenses. Assume that the reasonable value of Simon's 100 hours' work is $6,000. What are Simon's rights, if any, against Noreen?

6. Compare the *Holmes* case, *infra*, with the *Kriegsman* case, *infra*. Do you disagree with the result in either case? Why was the attorney allowed to withdraw in *Holmes*, but not in *Kriegsman*?

BEGINNING THE LAWYER–CLIENT RELATIONSHIP

A. DUTY TO TAKE SOME KINDS OF CASES

1. *General Rule: Lawyers Are Not Public Utilities*

In EC 2–26 the ABA Code states the general American rule: A lawyer is under no obligation to act as advisor or advocate for every person who may wish to become a client; but in furtherance of the objective of the bar to make legal services fully available, a lawyer should not lightly decline proffered legal employment. In other words, a lawyer is not a public utility obligated to take any client who walks into her office with money to pay her. Absent special circumstances, you are free to decide whom you will represent (assuming they want you) and whom you will not represent. You only have to answer to your conscience and your stomach.

2. *Exceptions to the General Rule*

THE ATTORNEY'S OATH

When you are admitted to law practice, you will take an oath, as required by state law. In some states, the oath is in brief form—a promise to uphold the constitution and laws of the state and the United States, and to perform the duties of an attorney to the best of your ability. But many states use this longer form:

It is the duty of an attorney:

a. To support the Constitution and laws of the United States and of this State;

b. To maintain the respect due to the courts of justice and judicial officers;

c. To counsel or maintain such actions, proceedings or defenses only as appear to him legal or just, except the defense of a person charged with a public offense;

d. To employ, for the purpose of maintaining the causes confided to him such means only as are consistent with truth, and never to seek to mislead the judge or any judicial officer by an artifice or false statement of fact or law;

e. To maintain inviolate the confidence, and at every peril to himself, to preserve the secrets of his client;

f. To abstain from all offensive personality, and to advance no fact prejudicial to the honor or reputation of a party or witness, unless required by the justice of the cause with which he is charged;

g. Not to encourage either the commencement or the continuance of an action or proceeding from any motive corrupt of passion or interest;

h. Never to reject, for any consideration personal to himself, the cause of the defenseless or the oppressed.

(California's even longer version of this oath can be found as Business and Professions Code § 6068.)

WHO SHOULD PAY WHEN THE CLIENT CANNOT?

Reread ABA Model Rules 6.1 and 6.2 and ABA Code EC 2–25. ABA Model Rule 6.1 is a watered-down version of an earlier draft that said:

A lawyer *shall* [emphasis added] render unpaid public interest legal service. A lawyer may discharge this responsibility by service in activities for improving the law, the legal system, or the legal profession, or by providing professional services to persons of limited means or to public service groups or organizations. A lawyer shall make an annual report concerning such service to appropriate regulatory authority.

When the draft was released, it generated considerable heat in the practicing bar. Here is a typical comment:

> True, many people can't afford a lawyer. But that is a problem of society as a whole. It ought to be solved by a general tax to support free legal services, not by a confiscatory levy on lawyers only. Should I have to bear more than my share of society's collective problem just because of the profession I am in?

What do you think of this line of argument? Do you support an ethics rule that requires all lawyers to perform a set amount of service *pro bono publico* each year?

In 1993, the ABA's House of Delegates voted narrowly to amend Rule 6.1 to emphasize the expectation that lawyers contribute a fixed number of hours per year to pro bono activities—with 50 hours as the default number—and that "a substantial majority of the (50) hours" be devoted to serving the poor either in person or through organizations. The Rule also calls upon lawyers to make voluntary financial contributions to organizations serving the poor. This amendment follows a 1988 vote of the House of Delegates supporting the 50 hour standard. In 1995, the ABA approved a resolution making the expansion of pro bono services a "critical priority."

Many state bar associations have made the same kind of aspirational pronouncement. The California bar's Board of Governors urges every lawyer in California to devote at least 50 hours of pro bono services annually to the indigent. Mandatory pro bono proposals are under consideration in some form in several states, but as of 1995, only Nevada has made pro bono service mandatory. Nevada lawyers have the choice of providing 20 hours of pro bono service a year or contributing $500 to a bar fund that then disperses the money to legal assistance groups. On a limited basis, some local bar associations and some counties operate mandatory pro bono programs.

If lawyers are merely urged to do pro bono work, will they do it? A 1985 ABA survey found that 75% of the lawyers surveyed think that lawyers ought to do pro bono work, but only 52% had actually done any during the prior year. A 1987 ABA study reported just 15.1 percent of the country's lawyers participate in formal pro bono programs. Only 10 percent of California lawyers donate any time to pro bono programs serving the poor, and among those, the average is under 30 hours contributed annually. ["Forgetting the Poor," California Lawyer, May 1990, pp. 17–18.] In the 1985 ABA survey, the most common excuse was "not enough time." The survey also found that over 50% of surveyed law firms and corporate law departments said they encourage their lawyers to do pro bono work. However, only 12% consider such work as a factor in evaluating lawyers for partnership, and only 10% count pro bono hours toward the quota of hours they expect lawyers to work. [*See* 71 A.B.A.J. 42 (Nov. 1985).] Until law firms and other employers begin to emphasize pro bono work, it is unlikely that attorneys will re-order their work to meet the 50 hour goal.

In criminal matters, public funds are generally available to provide modest compensation to private lawyers who represent indigent criminal defendants. But public funds are generally not available to compensate private lawyers who represent indigent persons in civil matters. May a court nevertheless order a private lawyer to provide free legal service to an indigent civil litigant?

What do you think of the answer provided by the court in Bothwell v. Republic Tobacco Co., below, and is the level of analysis needed to achieve the court's result worth the court's time and effort?

BOTHWELL v. REPUBLIC TOBACCO CO.

United States District Court, District of Nebraska, 1995.
912 F.Supp. 1221.

MEMORANDUM AND ORDER

PIESTER, UNITED STATES MAGISTRATE JUDGE.

Before me for consideration is a motion, submitted by plaintiff's appointed counsel, Paula Metcalf, seeking reconsideration and vacation of my order appointing her to represent plaintiff in this case. For the reasons set forth below, I shall grant the motion and vacate my order of appointment.

BACKGROUND

In March 1994 plaintiff Earl Bothwell, who at the time was incarcerated at the Hastings Correctional Center, submitted to this court a request to proceed in forma pauperis, a civil complaint, and a motion for appointment of counsel. I provisionally granted plaintiff's request to proceed in forma pauperis, pending receipt of trust account statements from his correctional institution. I then ordered that plaintiff's complaint be filed.

[Bothwell alleged he switched from smoking factory-manufactured cigarettes to his own rolled cigarettes when federal warning labels appeared on cigarette packages in 1969, mistakenly believing they were safer because loose tobacco came without warning labels. In 1986 Bothwell became aware that he suffered from emphysema, asthma, heart disease, and "bronchial and other respiratory diseases." He later learned that the loose tobacco products he had been using "were stronger that [sic] [factory-produced] cigarettes and were twice as harmful and deadly."

Eventually the magistrate judge required defendants to respond to Bothwell's strict liability and breach of implied warranty of fitness claims and granted his request for appointment of counsel.]

Following a series of motions to withdraw and appointments of substitute counsel, I appointed Paula Metcalf as plaintiff's counsel.

* * *

DISCUSSION

In her brief in support of her motion to reconsider and vacate [the order appointing her Bothwell's counsel], Metcalf contends that my order appointing her as counsel is "contrary to law and clearly erroneous" because "a federal court has no statutory or inherent authority to force an attorney to take an ordinary civil case for no compensation."

STATUTORY AUTHORITY

Insofar as concerns statutory authority, *Metcalf* is correct. Plaintiff in this case is proceeding in forma pauperis pursuant to 28 U.S.C. § 1915(d). In *Mallard v. United States District Court,* 490 U.S. 296, 109 S.Ct. 1814, 104 L.Ed.2d 318 (1989), the United States Supreme Court held, in a 5–4 decision, that section 1915(d) [3] does not authorize a federal court to require an unwilling attorney to represent an indigent litigant in a civil case. *Id.* at 300–08, 109 S.Ct. at 1817–22. In so holding, the Court focused on the language of section 1915(d), which provides that a court may "request" an attorney to accept a court appointment. *Id.* at 300–07, 109 S.Ct. at 1817–21. The Court examined other statutes and reasoned that, when Congress wanted to require compulsory service, it knew how to do so explicitly. The Court concluded that by using the term "request," Congress was demonstrating its desire not to require such service of attorneys who are appointed to represent indigent litigants. *Id.* However, the Court in *Mallard* left open the question of whether federal courts possess the inherent power to require an unwilling attorney to accept an appointment. *Id.* at 310, 109 S.Ct. at 1823.

INHERENT AUTHORITY

After conducting an extensive review of authority and commentary addressing this issue, I am convinced that a federal district court does possess the inherent power to compel an unwilling attorney to accept a civil appointment. The origin and scope of that power are discussed below.

[The court here reviewed three categories of inherent powers identified in the Third Circuit opinion, *Eash v. Riggins Trucking, Inc.,* 757 F.2d 557 (3d Cir.1985) (en banc).]

* * *

Specifically, then, this court's inherent power to compel representation of the indigent exists for two primary purposes: (1) to ensure a "fair and just" adjudicative process in individual cases; and (2) to maintain the integrity and viability of the judiciary and of the entire civil justice system. These two purposes mirror the dual functions that lawyers serve in the civil justice system. First, they act as advocates in individual cases working to peacefully resolve civil disputes between citizens. Second, by their ready availability to act in that capacity, they

---

3. Section 1915(d) provides as follows: The court may request an attorney to represent any [person claiming in forma pauperis status] unable to employ counsel and may dismiss the case if the allegation of poverty is untrue, or if satisfied that the action is frivolous or malicious. 28 U.S.C. § 1915(d).

preserve the credibility of the courts as a legitimate arm of the civil justice system. The following discussion explores the court's inherent authority to conscript unwilling counsel to achieve each of the foregoing purposes.

(1) "Fair and Just" Process in Individual Cases

As noted above, in seeking to bring about the fair and just resolution of a case, a court may exercise its inherent power to appoint individuals to act as "instruments" of the court. While it is established that a plaintiff has no constitutional right to counsel in a civil case, [cites] counsel nevertheless may be necessary in a particular civil proceeding to ensure fairness and justice in the proceeding and to bring about a fair and just outcome.

The American legal system is adversarial in nature. * * * Attorneys, because they are trained in the advocacy skills of cross examination and argument, are a necessary component in a properly functioning adversarial system. Thus, the notion that the adversarial system is an effective method for ferreting out the truth presumes that both sides have relatively equal access to adequate legal assistance from those trained in the art of advocacy.

Where one side is without adequate legal representation, the adversarial system may not be effective. * * *

If the lack of legal representation is the free choice of the unrepresented party or if it results from factors unrelated to the indigency of the plaintiff, our system is not offended. Where, however, one party is unable to obtain legal representation because of indigency, the resulting disparity of advocacy skills clearly offends the principle of "equality before the law" underlying our system. Further, a substantial disparity in access to legal representation caused by the indigency of one of the parties threatens the adversarial system's ability to produce a just and fair result.[9]

Access to legal representation in this country is gained primarily through the private market. For the most part, the market is an effective mechanism for providing legal services to those who need them. However, the market sometimes fails to provide counsel regardless of the merits of the claims at issue. Where the person whose claims have been rejected by the private market is indigent, he or she may seek representation through a legal aid organization. However, the ability of such organizations to meet the needs of the indigent has taken a serious hit over the past fifteen years in the form of reduced funding to the Legal Services Corporation ("LSC"), the federal entity responsible for funding state and local legal aid offices. In 1981 the LSC had almost reached its stated goal of providing two legal services lawyers for every 10,000 poor persons. In 1982, the LSC budget was slashed from $321 million to

---

9. Some might argue that this same reasoning applies in all cases where there is a disparity in the financial status of the parties because the party with greater wealth can hire a more qualified advocate. However, I do not subscribe to the view that a more expensive attorney is necessarily a better advocate.

$241 million. Those funding cuts resulted in a drastic reduction in the number of legal services attorneys, as well as the closing of many legal aid offices nationwide. The effect of those cuts is still felt today; to attain the 1981 ratio of lawyers to poor people, it is estimated that the current Legal Services Corporation budget would have to be nearly doubled. Rather than increasing that budget, however, the current Congress is considering further cuts in legal services funding. Also being considered are greater restrictions on the types of practice which legal aid organizations can provide to the indigent. Compounding the problem of legal access for the poor is the growing apathy of the private bar to the plight of many indigent litigants. The inevitable net result of these factors is that the poor, indeed most of the so-called "middle class," have less realistic access to advocacy services from lawyers.

The foregoing discussion establishes that: 1) courts possess the inherent power to bring to their assistance those "instruments" necessary to ensure a "fair and just" adjudicative process in individual cases; 2) in many, if not most, cases, due to the adversarial nature of our system, lawyers are a necessary component in ensuring such a "fair and just" process; 3) to a significant degree, neither the private marketplace nor public or charitable efforts provide indigent litigants with adequate access to legal assistance; and 4) to that extent, such failure threatens the reliability of the results of the adversarial process. On these bases, I conclude that, when indigency is the principal reason for disparate access to the civil justice system in an individual case, a federal court does possess the inherent authority to bring about a fair and just adjudicative process by conscripting an unwilling lawyer to represent the indigent party. A further basis for the existence of such authority is set forth below.

* * *

LAWYERS AS OFFICERS OF THE COURT

The extent to which attorneys are linked to the judiciary, as "officers of the court" or otherwise, has been the topic of much commentary over the past fifteen years.

One of the most oft-cited federal cases for the proposition that attorneys are "officers of the court" is United States v. *Dillon,* 346 F.2d 633, 636–37 (9th Cir.1965), cert. denied, 382 U.S. 978, 86 S.Ct. 550, 15 L.Ed.2d 469 (1966). In an appendix to its opinion in *Dillon,* the Court of Appeals for the Ninth Circuit traced the history of the officer-of-the-court doctrine to English common law. The court noted that English "*serjeants*-at-law" were required " 'from a very early period ... to plead for a poor man.' " *Id.* at 636 (quoting *Holdsworth's* History of English Law, vol. 2, p. 491 (3d ed., 1923)). The court further noted that, "in colonial America, there was, in addition to the common law, a more extensive statutory recognition of the obligation to represent indigents upon court order." *Id.* at 637. The court in *Dillon* concluded that "the obligation of the legal profession to serve indigents on court order is an ancient and established tradition, and that appointed counsel have generally been compensated, if at all, only by statutory fees ... usually payable only in limited types of cases." *Id.* at 635.

The accuracy of the historical justifications for the officer-of-the-court doctrine extolled by the Ninth Circuit in *Dillon* has been questioned recently by courts and commentators. These critics of the *Dillon* analysis contest the use of English tradition to support the doctrine. Under the ancient English legal system there were two classes of lawyers: attorneys or serjeants-at-law and barristers. Serjeants-at-law were considered an elite class of lawyers who enjoyed the privileges of the judiciary, including various immunities. Judicial appointments were made exclusively from their ranks. Serjeants-at-law took an oath to serve the King's people and uphold justice and were required to accept court appointments to represent the poor. Critics of *Dillon* concede that a serjeant-at-law truly was an officer of the court; they contend, however, that "[h]e has no counterpart in American practice." *Id.* Critics claim that modern American lawyers more closely resemble English barristers, who were not considered officers of the court.

The critics also challenge the *Dillon* court's reliance on colonial tradition, contending that there is no clear history in the American colonies of compelled representation in the civil context. These critics conclude that the officer-of-the-court doctrine may not properly be asserted as a justification for compelled representation of indigents.

The critics' challenges to the validity of the officer-of-the-court doctrine, while forceful, are flawed in several respects. First, the claim that there is no direct counterpart to the serjeants-at-law in the American legal system actually serves to underscore the void in needed representation of indigent litigants. Because there is no special class of attorneys in the American system whose primary task is to provide such representation in civil cases, and, as discussed above, the realistic opportunities available to the poor to participate in the civil justice system are, at best, extremely limited, there simply is, at present, no other source than the private bar capable of providing representation to indigents.

Second, even assuming that the historical foundation for the officer-of-the-court doctrine is not as solid as once thought, the fact remains that court-compelled appointments for indigents have been made for centuries. In fact, one legal historian has traced the requirement of indigent representation back to the ecclesiastical courts of the thirteenth century.

Third, quite apart from any role the officer-of-the-court doctrine may have played in England or the colonies, that doctrine has become and is part of the fabric of American jurisprudence.

Finally, critics of the officer-of-the-court doctrine have failed to recognize the role that the availability of lawyers has played and continues to play in maintaining the integrity of the civil justice system. Because the ready availability of lawyers is necessary to ensuring the perception, and indeed the reality, of fairness, their accessibility as officers of the court is necessary not only to the preservation of the justice system itself but to the ordered liberty of our society. For all of the foregoing reasons, I conclude that it is inappropriate to discard the officer-of-the-court doctrine as a justification for compelled representation of the indigent.

MONOPOLY OF LAWYERS

A further justification which has been advanced for the view that attorneys are obligated to comply with court-ordered appointments is the monopoly theory. Under that theory, attorneys must provide legal services to indigents without compensation by virtue of the exclusive privilege they have been granted to practice law. Regulation of attorney licensing limits the number of individuals who may practice law. As a result, those relatively few individuals who are licensed benefit financially, thereby compensating them for any financial losses incurred by representing indigents. Also, because meaningful access to the courts can be had only through these licensed attorneys, they are required to represent those who are unable to afford representation.

The monopoly theory has not escaped criticism. It has been challenged as an inaccurate portrayal of the American legal system. Specifically, critics have argued that no monopoly actually exists because every individual is free to represent themselves in court or, alternatively, to pursue a legal career. However, even if theoretically each potential litigant in the population at large had the intellectual capacity to become a lawyer, it is quite improbable that either their opponents or the courts in which they are embattled would stay the pursuit of claims while they did so. As discussed supra, meaningful access to the courts often requires representation by someone previously trained, if not experienced, in the practice of law. Thus, while the monopoly may not prevent a party from gaining access to the courts, it very well may prevent the administration of equal justice. Additionally, as one commentator has noted, "a litigant's freedom to pursue a legal career is 'sheer illusion' " due to the rigid training program and the prohibitive costs involved in obtaining a legal education.

It has been further argued by critics of the monopoly theory that, given the large number of attorneys in practice and competitive nature of the legal profession, no true monopoly exists. However, it is undeniable that licensed attorneys do benefit financially from the prohibition against the unauthorized practice of law.

Finally, critics claim that other groups enjoying monopolies as a result of state licensing, such as doctors, nurses, teachers, insurance agents, brokers, and pharmacists, do not bear an obligation to provide free services to the poor. While that is true, it misses the point. The practice of law—that is, the representation of others before the civil courts—is not simply a private enterprise. It is, in addition, a contribution to society's ability to manage its domestic affairs, a necessary condition of any civilized culture. Attorneys have a unique relationship to government not shared by other licensed groups. This relationship, which has been described as "symbiotic," places attorneys in "an intermediary position between the court and the public" where they are "inextricably linked to the public sector despite [their] dual position as a private businessperson."

By virtue of this special relationship between the bench and the bar, courts are dependent upon attorneys to aid in carrying out the administration of justice. While other professions also contribute to private gain and to the betterment of society's standards of living, no other group holds the exclusive key to meaningful participation in a branch of government and the protection of rights. This monumental difference between attorneys and other licensed groups justifies imposition of different conditions on the practice of the profession.

Ethical Obligation of Lawyers

An additional justification for the court's exercise of inherent power to compel representation is the ethical obligation of attorneys to provide representation to indigent litigants. This obligation arises from the law's ideals of professionalism and commitment to public service. In addition, the local rules of this court require availability for such service. NELR 83.4(f) provides:

> All members of the bar of this court are subject to be appointed to represent indigent litigants. This is an ethical obligation of attorneys in fulfillment of the underlying precepts of Canon 2 of the Code of Professional Responsibility.

NELR 83.4(f).

The "underlying precepts of Canon 2" require, inter alia, that a lawyer appointed to represent an indigent litigant "not seek to be excused" from that obligation "except for compelling reasons." Code of Professional Responsibility, EC 2–29. Rather, the attorney is to "find time to participate in serving the disadvantaged" and render "free legal services to those unable to pay reasonable fees." Id. at EC 2–25; see also Model Rule of Professional Conduct 6.1 ("a lawyer should aspire to render ... legal services without fee or expectation of fee to[ ] persons of limited means"). While these obligations are not expressed in mandatory terms, they clearly indicate that service to the indigent is an essential characteristic of any ethical attorney. Two aspects deserve further attention.

First, these moral and ethical obligations to provide legal services to the poor do not exist merely to prompt the practicing lawyer to be a "good" person, respected in the profession. Rather, they are a recognition of the critical role of the lawyer in ensuring the fair and just adjudication of disputes, and the need for such advocacy in ensuring the existence of the system.

Second, these obligations are not self-executing. Platitudes are nice, of course, but if these aspirational "goals" are to be achieved and to have any meaning in fact, there must be some mechanism for gaining compliance. It makes little sense to give only lip service to these ideals while the legitimacy of the court system is being challenged by other means of resolving private disputes. If our society is to have a legitimate civil justice system, the courts must be empowered to take necessary measures to create and maintain it. In a more genteel and public-spirited time, the mere suggestion by a court that a private attorney should provide free representation might be met with acceptance of the duty as a necessary means to ensure fairness and the justice system itself; perhaps that history contributes to the lack of mandatory requirements today. In any event, I view the attorney's ethical obligation to render services to the poor as the "flip side" of the court's inherent authority to provide "instruments" to ensure fairness and justice, and to maintain the relevance of the court system in resolving civil disputes. Both serve the same end: the preservation of a civil means to resolve private disputes.

A "New" Model?

As one commentator has recognized, the foregoing justifications can be combined into a cogent model justifying the exercise of inherent power to compel representation of the indigent. * * * Our governmental system is built partially upon the concept of citizens being able to redress their grievances and resolve their civil disputes in courts. A judiciary committed to observing notions of fairness, justice, and equality before the law is of paramount importance in maintaining public confidence in that system. Lawyers are essential in maintaining the system because the only realistic way the populace at large can obtain "equal justice" is through the advocacy of those trained in the law. If public confidence in the system wanes, in time, people will find, and indeed already have found, other, less civil, methods of resolving their differences. Thus, attorneys occupy a unique role in preserving the ordered liberty included in the concept of "domestic tranquility." They are therefore vital to preserving the viability of the third branch of government.

In accordance with the foregoing discussion, I conclude that, despite authority suggesting otherwise, * * * this court possesses the inherent power to compel representation of an indigent litigant. I further conclude that there are ample historical and theoretical justifications for the existence of that power.

However, the inquiry does not end there. A question remains as to whether that power should be exercised in this particular case.

Necessity of Exercising Authority

In deciding whether to exercise the authority to compel representation I first note that a court must exercise its inherent powers "with restraint and discretion." The common thread running through inherent powers jurisprudence is the concept of necessity. * * * Thus, while this court possesses the inherent power to compel representation of an indigent plaintiff, the power should be exercised only where reasonably necessary for the administration of justice. In other words, the appointment of counsel must be necessary to bring about a fair and just adjudicative process.

In * * * determining whether counsel should be appointed for an indigent plaintiff, the court should consider such factors as (1) the factual complexity of the case, (2) the ability of the plaintiff to investigate the facts, (3) the existence of conflicting testimony, (4) the plaintiff's ability to present his claims and (5) the complexity of the legal issues. An additional factor * * * is the plaintiff's ability to obtain counsel on his own. A plaintiff, before seeking appointment of counsel by the court, must diligently seek out private representation. Plaintiff alleges that he "tried several times ... to get an attorney [ ] in the Des Moines, Iowa area" to represent him. Notwithstanding plaintiff's apparent diligence, he has failed to obtain private counsel.

For reasons set forth more fully below, I conclude that plaintiff's failure to obtain private counsel was not the result of his indigency but rather a result of the "marketability," or lack thereof, of his claims. This "marketability" analysis, which I believe to be a proper additional consideration in determining whether to appoint counsel, involves an examination of the nature and circumstances of a particular case to determine whether the litigant's failure to obtain counsel is attributable to indigence, or instead to any of a number of other factors activated in the marketplace but unrelated to indigence. It requires some analysis of the market, the case, and the litigant, rather than a face-value acceptance of the market's exclusion of the litigant's claims as a true indicator of the claims' merit. Thus, the "marketability" analysis involves several steps.

The first step in the "marketability" analysis is to ask whether, realistically, there is a "market" of lawyers who practice in the legal area of the plaintiff's claims. Many indigent litigants, particularly prisoners, raise civil rights claims pursuant to 42 U.S.C. § 1983. There are relatively few private attorneys who practice in the area of civil rights. Also, there are few, if any, lawyers willing to assume cases on a contingent-fee basis where the indigent plaintiff primarily seeks forms of relief other than monetary damages, such as injunctive or declaratory relief. As a result, in many cases, there simply is no true "market" to look to when determining whether an indigent plaintiff should be appointed counsel. In such cases, there should be no further inquiry into the "marketability" of a plaintiff's claims. Rather, the appointment of counsel should rest on those other factors commonly used in determining whether to appoint counsel.

In cases where such a "market" of lawyers is found to exist, a second question must be addressed: Does the plaintiff have adequate access to that market? This inquiry is necessary for two major reasons. First, many indigent litigants are physically unable to access private counsel regardless of the merits of their claims. This is especially true where the litigant is incarcerated. The practical ability of prisoners and other institutionalized persons to communicate with private counsel is severely restricted. Second, there may be communication barriers of language or language skills; barriers of physical, emotional, or mental disabilities; or educational or cultural barriers that block understanding between attorney and client. The point is that the existence of lawyers "out there" in the private market does not establish their accessibility to a particular plaintiff. Where a "market" of attorneys exists but a party does not have adequate, realistic access to it, no further "marketability" inquiry is necessary because such inquiry could not yield a reliable conclusion regarding the involvement of indigence as a factor in the litigant's failure to obtain counsel.

If there is a market and the litigant had realistic access to it, the third step in the "marketability" analysis must be performed. That step requires an examination of the typical fee arrangements used in the particular area of the law implicated by the indigent plaintiff's complaint. Specifically, if contingent-fee or other low-cost financing arrangements are generally available in the area of law and would be feasible for the plaintiff, further examination is proper.

* * *

Once it is determined that an accessible market exists, that the plaintiff has the ability to access that market, and that feasible fee arrangements are available, the final and most important step in the analysis must be performed. The court must determine whether the market's rejection of the party's claims was the result of indigency, for, as noted above, indigency is the touchstone which authorizes the court to exercise the inherent power to correct unequal access to advocacy services. There are many factors to consider when a lawyer is approached about taking a person's claims into litigation. These factors might include, but would not be limited to, the merits of the claims; the existence of precedent to support the claims; the costs of investigating the claims, handling the discovery needed to prepare the case for trial, and trying the case; the relationship of those costs to the amount of a likely recovery, discounted by the probability of recovery; the lawyer's time available to pursue the claims and the impact upon his/her other practice obligations, as well as upon those of partners or associates; the likeability of the litigant; the popularity of the claims; and the potential settlement value of the claims. So long as the market's rejection of the claims was based on the interplay of these and other such factors, and not on the indigency of the plaintiff, the notions of equal justice discussed above are not offended and compelling an attorney to represent that plaintiff is not necessary to the achievement of a fair and just adjudicative process.

Applying the foregoing "marketability" analysis to this case, I first conclude that there was an adequate "market" of lawyers practicing in the general area of plaintiff's claims. Plaintiff raises product liability claims, as opposed to civil rights claims under 42 U.S.C. § 1983. As such, a greater number of private attorneys were available to represent him than would be for a typical indigent litigant.

* * *

I further conclude that plaintiff had ready access to that "market" of lawyers. Plaintiff is not incarcerated nor has he alleged any other substantial barriers which might have prevented him from communicating with private attorneys. He thus had the unfettered ability to communicate with private attorneys in his immediate locale and elsewhere. Additionally, many of the attorneys who work in products liability and personal injury claims do so on a contingent fee basis. Under a contingent fee arrangement, there typically is no requirement that the plaintiff advance costs, although the plaintiff would remain liable for them ultimately. Thus, despite plaintiff's indigency, there were feasible fee arrangements available to plaintiff.

The foregoing factors indicate that, unlike most cases initiated by indigent litigants, there was a "market" of private attorneys for plaintiff's claims and that, unlike most indigent litigants, plaintiff had open access to that market and has, in fact, accessed that market, albeit unsuccessfully. It thus is proper to determine whether that market's rejection of plaintiff's claims was the result of his indigency.

I conclude that it was not. The mere existence of indigency as a condition of the plaintiff did not prevent him from suggesting to lawyers that they consider his claims. Rather, he has had the same opportunity as middle- or upper-class plaintiffs to subject his claims to the scrutiny of tort attorneys. That this "market" of attorneys has thus far rejected his claims is the result of factors unrelated to his indigency. Primary among these factors is undoubtedly the enormous cost of litigating claims against tobacco companies.

* * *

Plaintiff asserts that most of the attorneys he contacted requested payment of a retainer which he was unable to afford. However, due to the enormous costs involved in this type of litigation and the unlikelihood of settlement, the amount of money required for an adequate retainer would likely be so great that even a middle-class or upper-middle-class citizen would be unable to afford it. As such, the rejection of plaintiff's claims was not based on his indigency, but rather on marketability factors such as the expenses involved and the unlikelihood of settlement.

Because it is the lack of marketability of his claims, as opposed to his indigency, which has prevented plaintiff from obtaining counsel, the notions of equal justice discussed above have not been offended. As such, it is not reasonably necessary to the administration of justice for this court to compel Metcalf to represent plaintiff. Accordingly, I shall not exercise this court's inherent authority to do so.[22]

---

22. Because I decline to exercise the court's inherent authority, I need not ad- dress Metcalf's contention that the exercise of that authority in this case would contra-

OUTLOOK FOR THE FUTURE

Because the court did not finally appoint Metcalf to represent Bothwell, Judge Piester declined to address Metcalf's objections to the appointment based on the Fifth and Thirteenth Amendments. Although claims of involuntary servitude may seem far-fetched, a California appellate court, in *Cunningham v. Superior Court of Ventura County,* 177 Cal.App.3d 336, 222 Cal.Rptr. 854 (2d Dist., 1986), concluded that an attorney ordered to represent an indigent defendant in a paternity action without compensation was denied equal protection of the law. *Cunningham* may be flawed as a constitutional equal protection case [for a contrary view, see *Madden v. Township of Delran,* 126 N.J. 591, 601 A.2d 211 (1992) (criminal representation)], but it does accurately represent the California courts' reluctance to find California lawyers are duty-bound to represent indigent clients without compensation. In 1985 in *Yarbrough v. Superior Court,* 39 Cal.3d 197, 216 Cal.Rptr. 425, 702 P.2d 583 (1985), the California Supreme Court confronted the question of whether an indigent prison inmate was entitled to appointed counsel to defend a wrongful death action. The court held that appointment of counsel may be appropriate as a last resort to protect an indigent inmate's access to court; but that the appointing court must consider several factors in addition to the prisoner's indigency: the possibility of a continuance, whether the inmate's interests are actually at stake, and whether counsel would be helpful under the circumstances. It reached no decision on Yarbrough's specific request. At the end of his opinion, Justice Kaus wrote:

> We are fully aware that we have not dealt with the issues which have triggered the flood of amicus briefs mentioned in footnote 1: the power of the trial court to appoint an unwilling attorney to represent an incarcerated civil defendant, as well as its power and duty to provide funds for counsel's services and costs and, of course, the source of such funds. The fact that we find that it would be premature to discuss these issues in this particular case should not be interpreted to mean that we find that courts are powerless in those regards. The problem is, however, primarily a legislative one. It is our hope that the Legislature, working closely with the State Bar and other interested groups, will use the respite afforded by our disposition on this case to enact a fair legislative solution to the vexing problems which, for the time being, have been placed on the judicial backburner.

[39 Cal.3d at 207, 216 Cal.Rptr. at 425, 702 P.2d at 589.] No legislative solution has yet been found, nor has the problem been removed from the "judicial backburner."

vene the Fifth and Thirteenth Amendments of the Constitution. However, the majority of courts which have addressed those issues have found no constitutional violations.

* * *

The California State Bar does have a program to fund legal services to indigent Californians using an IOLTA (Interest on Lawyers' Trust Accounts) system. Under the program all California lawyers must set up client trust accounts; those accounts not specifically earmarked for a particular client are pooled in accounts that earn interest that is then paid by the financial institutions to the State Bar's Legal Services Trust Fund Program. A 25–person commission administers the fund, determines which programs are eligible for funding, reviews recipients' budgets to insure compliance with the law, and evaluates the program and its providers. Money is distributed to "qualified legal services projects" (many of which also receive funds from the federal Legal Services Corporation), pro bono attorney projects, and "qualified support centers." Historically, the program, in operation since 1985, receives $1 million a month and distributes $12 million annually.

The Supreme Court has never directly considered the constitutionality of mandatory pro bono duties. The closest it came was in the 1989 case, *Mallard v. U.S. Dist. Court for Southern Dist. of Iowa*, 490 U.S. 296, 109 S.Ct. 1814, 104 L.Ed.2d 318 (1989) (cited in *Bothwell*), with inconclusive results. Mallard was an Iowa lawyer specializing in bankruptcy and securities law. The Iowa bar operates a Volunteer Lawyers Project (VLP), under which lawyers are randomly selected for assignment to parties appearing *in forma pauperis* in federal court under 28 U.S.C.A. § 1915(d). In June 1987, VLP asked Mallard to represent three prison inmates in a § 1983 civil rights action against prison officials. Mallard filed a motion to withdraw with the district court, claiming that he was not a litigator and that accepting the case would violate his ethical obligation to provide competent representation. He also asserted that the mandatory appointment exceeded the court's authority under § 1915(d) which provides, "The court may request an attorney to represent" an indigent litigant. The district court denied Mallard's motion, and the Supreme Court reversed in a 5–4 decision.

The Court held that § 1915(d) "does not authorize coercive appointments of counsel," but limited its decision to the specific language of § 1915(d). If Congress had intended assignments to be mandatory, it would have used "appoint" or "assign" or other mandatory language instead of "request." Accordingly, the Court left open the possibility that a court may have inherent power to require a lawyer to represent any indigent party without compensation. The majority cautioned:

> We do not mean to question, let alone denigrate, lawyers' ethical obligation to assist those who are too poor to afford counsel, or to suggest that requests made pursuant to § 1915(d) may be lightly declined because they give rise to no ethical claim. On the contrary, in a time when the need for legal services among the poor is growing and public funding for such services has not kept pace, lawyers' ethical obligations to volunteer their time and skills *pro bono publico* is manifest.

[490 U.S. at 310, 109 S.Ct. at 1822–23.] Justice Kennedy, concurring, added:

Our decision today speaks to the interpretation of a statute, to the requirements of the law, and not to the professional responsibility of the lawyer. Lawyers, like all those who practice a profession, have obligations to the State. Lawyers also have obligations by virtue of their special status as officers of the court. Accepting a court's request to represent the indigent is one of those traditional obligations.

[490 U.S. at 310–11, 109 S.Ct. at 1823.] The four dissenters criticized the majority's narrow and technical approach to the statute. In addition, they argued Mallard had joined the Iowa bar knowing of the implicit obligation to participate in the VLP. They concluded a more accurate interpretation of the word "request," would be "respectfully command."

RUSKIN v. RODGERS

Appellate Court of Illinois, 1979.
79 Ill.App.3d 941, 35 Ill.Dec. 557, 399 N.E.2d 623.

[Plaintiff sued defendant for specific performance of a written agreement for purchase of an apartment building and its conversion into condominiums. Plaintiff prevailed at trial. On appeal, defendant charged numerous errors, including the following.]

Defendant contends he was deprived of a fair trial because of denial by the trial court of defendant's motions for continuance and substitution of attorneys. * * * [D]efendant requested a continuance * * * two days before the previously set trial date.

In matters of this kind, the trial court possesses broad discretion in allowing or denying a motion for continuance. Denial of such a motion will not be disturbed on appeal unless there has been a manifest abuse of discretion or a palpable injustice. * * * Furthermore, because of the potential inconvenience to the parties, witnesses, and the court, especially grave reasons for granting a continuance must be given once a case has reached the trial stage.

In the case before us, the trial court denied a motion two days before trial. We cannot say the trial court manifestly abused its discretion or that its action resulted in a palpable injustice. The record does not reflect any lack of preparation by any of the able counsel in the trial court.

Defendant further contends the trial court erred in denying the motion for substitution of attorneys during the course of trial. Defendant contends that an individual has an absolute right to replace his attorney at any time with or without cause.

* * *

In the case before us, defendant attempted to discharge his attorney during the course of the trial. The attorney was at that time cross-examining the first witness. To allow defendant to substitute attorneys at this point would have been extremely disruptive to the trial and would have resulted in a significant and prejudicial delay. This is particularly true where, as here, the impetus behind the discharge of the attorney appeared to be predicated upon emotional whim rather than upon any apparent sound reason.

The [two] cases cited by defendant in support of the proposition that a client has an absolute right to discharge his attorney at all times are readily distinguishable. * * * Neither case goes to the issue of substitution of attorneys during the course of a trial. We find no error in this regard.

ROSENBERG v. LEVIN

Supreme Court of Florida, 1982.
409 So.2d 1016.

The issue to be decided concerns the proper basis for compensating an attorney discharged without cause by his client after he has performed substantial legal services under a valid contract of employment. * * *

We hold that a lawyer discharged without cause is entitled to the reasonable value of his services on the basis of quantum meruit, but recovery is limited to the maximum fee set in the contract entered into for those services. We have concluded that without this limitation, the client would be penalized for the discharge and the lawyer would receive more than he bargained for in his initial contract. * * *

The facts of this case reflect the following. Levin hired Rosenberg and Pomerantz to perform legal services pursuant to a letter agreement which provided for a $10,000 fixed fee, plus a contingent fee equal to fifty percent of all amounts recovered in excess of $600,000. Levin later discharged Rosenberg and Pomerantz without cause before the legal controversy was resolved and subsequently settled the matter for a net recovery of $500,000. Rosenberg and Pomerantz sued for fees based on a "quantum meruit" evaluation of their services. After lengthy testimony, the trial judge concluded that quantum meruit was indeed the appropriate basis for compensation and awarded Rosenberg and Pomerantz $55,000. The district court also agreed that quantum meruit was the appropriate basis for recovery but lowered the amount awarded to $10,000, stating that recovery could in no event exceed the amount which the attorneys would have received under their contract if not prematurely discharged.

The issue submitted to us for resolution is whether the terms of an attorney employment contract limit the attorney's quantum meruit recovery to the fee set out in the contract. This issue requires, however, that we answer the broader underlying question of whether in Florida quantum meruit is an appropriate basis for compensation of attorneys discharged by their clients without cause where there is a specific employment contract. The Florida cases which have previously addressed this issue have resulted in confusion and conflicting views.

* * *

There are two conflicting interests involved in the determination of the issue presented in this type of attorney-client dispute. The first is the need of the client to have confidence in the integrity and ability of his attorney and, therefore, the need for the client to have the ability to discharge his attorney when he loses that necessary confidence in the attorney. The second is the attorney's right to adequate compensation for work performed. To address these conflicting interests, we must consider three distinct rules.

CONTRACT RULE

The traditional contract rule adopted by a number of jurisdictions holds that an attorney discharged without cause may recover damages for breach of contract under traditional contract principles. The measure of damages is usually the full contract price, although some courts deduct a fair allowance for services and expenses not expended by the discharged attorney in performing the balance of the contract. Some jurisdictions following the contract rule also permit an alternative recovery based on quantum meruit so that an attorney can elect between recovery based on the contract or the reasonable value of the performed services.

Support for the traditional contract theory is based on: (1) the full contract price is arguably the most rational measure of damages since it reflects the value that the parties placed on the services; (2) charging the full fee prevents the client from profiting from his own breach of contract; and (3) the contract rule is said to avoid the difficult problem of setting a value on an attorney's partially completed legal work.

QUANTUM MERUIT RULE

To avoid restricting a client's freedom to discharge his attorney, a number of jurisdictions in recent years have held that an attorney discharged without cause can recover only the reasonable value of services rendered prior to discharge. This rule was first announced in *Martin v. Camp*, 219 N.Y. 170, 114 N.E. 46 (1916), where the New York Court of Appeals held that a discharged attorney could not sue his client for damages for breach of contract unless the attorney had completed performance of the contract. The New York court established quantum meruit recovery for the attorney on the theory that the client does not breach the contract by discharging the attorney. Rather, the court reasoned, there is an implied condition in every attorney-client contract that the client may discharge the attorney at any time with or without cause. With this right as part of the contract, traditional contract principles are applied to allow quantum meruit recovery on the basis of services performed to date. Under the New York rule, the attorney's cause of action accrues immediately upon his discharge by the client, under the reasoning that it is unfair to make the attorney's right to compensation dependent on the performance of a successor over whom he has no control.

The California Supreme Court, in *Fracasse v. Brent*, 6 Cal.3d 784, 494 P.2d 9, 100 Cal.Rptr. 385 (1972), also adopted a quantum meruit rule. That court carefully analyzed those factors which distinguish the attorney-client relationship from other employment situations and concluded that a discharged attorney should be limited to a quantum meruit recovery in order to strike a proper balance between the client's right to discharge his attorney without undue restriction and the attorney's right to fair compensation for work performed. The *Fracasse* court sought both to provide clients greater freedom in substituting counsel and to promote confidence in the legal profession while protecting society's interest in the attorney-client relationship.

Contrary to the New York rule, however, the California court also held that an attorney's cause of action for quantum meruit does not accrue until the happening of the contingency, that is, the client's recovery. If no recovery is forthcoming, the attorney is denied compensation. The California court offered two reasons in support of its position. First, the result obtained and the amount involved, two important factors in determining the reasonableness of a fee, cannot be ascertained until the occurrence of the contingency. Second, the client may be of limited means and it would be unduly burdensome to force him to pay a fee if there was no recovery. The court stated that: "[S]ince the attorney agreed initially to take his chances on recovering any fee whatever, we believe that the fact that the success of the litigation is no longer under his control is insufficient to justify imposing a new and more onerous burden on the client." *Id.* at 792, 494 P.2d at 14, 100 Cal.Rptr. at 390.

QUANTUM MERUIT RULE LIMITED BY THE CONTRACT PRICE

The third rule is an extension of the second that limits quantum meruit recovery to the maximum fee set in the contract. This limitation is believed necessary to provide client freedom to substitute attorneys without economic penalty. Without such a limitation, a client's right to discharge an attorney may be illusory and the client may in effect be penalized for exercising a right.

The Tennessee Court of Appeals, in *Chambliss, Bahner & Crawford v. Luther*, 531 S.W.2d 108 (Tenn.Ct.App.1975), expressed the need for limitation on quantum meruit recovery, stating: "It would seem to us that the better rule is that because a client has the unqualified right to discharge his attorney, fees in such cases should be limited to the value of the services rendered or the contract price, whichever is less." 531 S.W.2d at 113. In rejecting the argument that quantum meruit should be the basis for the recovery even though it exceeds the contract fee, that court said:

> To adopt the rule advanced by Plaintiff would, in our view, encourage attorneys less keenly aware of their professional responsibilities than Attorney Chambliss * * * to induce clients to lose

confidence in them in cases where the reasonable value of their services has exceeded the original fee and thereby, upon being discharged, reap a greater benefit than that for which they had bargained.

531 S.W.2d at 113. Other authorities also support this position.

CONCLUSION

We have carefully considered all the matters presented, both on the original argument on the merits and on rehearing. It is our opinion that it is in the best interest of clients and the legal profession as a whole that we adopt the modified quantum meruit rule which limits recovery to the maximum amount of the contract fee in all premature discharge cases involving both fixed and contingency employment contracts. The attorney-client relationship is one of special trust and confidence. The client must rely entirely on the good faith efforts of the attorney in representing his interests. This reliance requires that the client have complete confidence in the integrity and ability of the attorney and that absolute fairness and candor characterize all dealings between them. These considerations dictate that clients be given greater freedom to change legal representatives than might be tolerated in other employment relationships. We approve the philosophy that there is an overriding need to allow clients freedom to substitute attorneys without economic penalty as a means of accomplishing the broad objective of fostering public confidence in the legal profession. Failure to limit quantum meruit recovery defeats the policy against penalizing the client for exercising his right to discharge. However, attorneys should not be penalized either and should have the opportunity to recover for services performed.

Accordingly, we hold that an attorney employed under a valid contract who is discharged without cause before the contingency has occurred or before the client's matters have concluded can recover only the reasonable value of his services rendered prior to discharge, limited by the maximum contract fee. We reject both the traditional contract rule and the quantum meruit rule that allow recovery in excess of the maximum contract price because both have a chilling effect on the client's power to discharge an attorney. Under the contract rule in a contingent fee situation, both the discharged attorney and the second attorney may receive a substantial percentage of the client's final recovery. Under the unlimited quantum meruit rule, it is possible, as the instant case illustrates, for the attorney to receive a fee greater than he bargained for under the terms of his contract. Both these results are unacceptable to us.

We further follow the California view that in contingency fee cases, the cause of action for quantum meruit arises only upon the successful occurrence of the contingency. If the client fails in his recovery, the discharged attorney will similarly fail and recover nothing. We recognize that deferring the commencement of a cause of action until the occurrence of the contingency is a view not uniformly accepted. Deferral, however, supports our goal to preserve the client's freedom to discharge, and any resulting harm to the attorney is minimal because the attorney would not have benefited earlier until the contingency's occurrence. There should, of course, be a presumption of regularity and competence in the performance of the services by a successor attorney.

In computing the reasonable value of the discharged attorney's services, the trial court can consider the totality of the circumstances surrounding the professional relationship between the attorney and client. Factors such as time, the recovery sought, the skill demanded, the results obtained, and the attorney-client contract itself will necessarily be relevant considerations.

We conclude that this approach creates the best balance between the desirable right of the client to discharge his attorney and the right of an attorney to reasonable compensation for his services. * * *

HOLMES v. Y.J.A. REALTY CORP.

Supreme Court of New York, Appellate Division, 1987.
128 A.D.2d 482, 513 N.Y.S.2d 415.

[Attorney Donald J. Goldman appealed from the denial of his motion to be relieved as counsel for the defendants.] Plaintiff brought this action to recover damages for personal injuries allegedly sustained when she slipped and fell on a defective step at an apartment building owned by defendants. Since defendants maintained no liability insurance coverage, they independently retained Goldman to undertake their defense. Defendant Y.J.A. Realty Corp. ("Y.J.A.") is the landlord of the premises * * * [and] defendant Yori Abrahams is the sole shareholder, officer and director of the corporation.

It appears that a written retainer agreement was executed by Abrahams on behalf of himself and Y.J.A. when Goldman was hired by them. This retainer agreement provided that Goldman's legal fees would be billed periodically at the rate of $125 per hour for law office activity and $400 per day for each court appearance. The record contains Goldman's detailed itemized bill * * * for his legal services showing a balance due from these clients of $2,275.30 after crediting a payment on account of $3,500. Goldman averred that although a demand for payment of this bill had been made by him upon defendants for a period of over five months prior to his application to be relieved, defendants not only refused to make any payment (despite their financial ability to do so), but also that defendant Abrahams had verbally berated and abused him by accusations of disloyalty and conflict of interest. * * *

* * *

[O]nce representation of a client in litigation has commenced, counsel's right to withdraw is not absolute. Here, however, that is the beginning and not the end of the inquiry. DR 2–110(C)(1)(d) of the Code of Professional Responsibility states that an attorney's withdrawal from employment is permissible where a client "renders it unreasonably difficult for the lawyer to carry out his employment effectively." DR 2–110(C)(1)(f) provides for like relief where a client "deliberately disregards an agreement or obligation to the lawyer as to expenses and fees." Where a client repudiates a reasonable fee arrangement there is no obligation on the part of counsel to finance the litigation or render gratuitous services. * * * This application was supported by a detailed statement of legal services rendered which is an appropriate consideration on an application of this kind. * * * We note further that although the litigation has been pending for three years, no note of issue has yet been filed. Thus defendants will have ample time to retain new counsel if they be so advised. Nor will plaintiff be visibly prejudiced by any delay in trial attributable to this withdrawal. * * * [The motion to withdraw is granted.]

KRIEGSMAN v. KRIEGSMAN

Superior Court of New Jersey, Appellate Division, 1977.
150 N.J.Super. 474, 375 A.2d 1253.

Appellants Messrs. Rose, Poley, Bromley and Landers (hereinafter "the Rose firm") appeal from an order of the Chancery Division denying their application to be relieved as attorneys for plaintiff Mary-Ann Kriegsman in this matrimonial action.

On December 22, 1975, plaintiff, who had been previously represented by other counsel, retained the Rose firm to represent her in a divorce action against her husband, defendant Bernard Kriegsman. The Rose firm requested and received consent to substitution of attorneys from plaintiff's former attorney. Plaintiff then paid an initial retainer of $1,000, plus $60 in court costs, with the understanding that she would be responsible for additional fees and expenses as litigation progressed. In March 1976 plaintiff paid the Rose firm another $1,000, plus $44 which was to be applied against costs.

During the 3½ months that the Rose firm represented plaintiff prior to its motion the firm had made numerous court appearances and had engaged in extensive office work in plaintiff's behalf. The unusual amount of work required was necessitated in part by the fact that defendant appeared *pro se*, was completely uncooperative and had refused to comply with some of the orders entered by the court. As of April 5, 1976 the Rose firm alleged that it had spent 110 hours on plaintiff's case, billed at $7,354.50, and had incurred disbursements of approximately $242. Since, by then, plaintiff was on welfare and since she apparently did not have sufficient funds to pay the additional fees incurred, the Rose firm contended that they were entitled to be relieved from further representation. Plaintiff opposed the application before the court, pointing out

> First of all, this case, I think, has accumulated a file this thick. I think at this point, for another attorney to step in, it would be very difficult to acquaint himself with every motion that has been

brought up before this court. I feel that Mr. Koserowski [an associate in the Rose firm] has been with me, representing me, for four months, and when this case finally does go to trial, hopefully soon, he has all this knowledge at his fingertips. Whereas another attorney would have to, I don't know how they can, wade through all of this, and really become acquainted with it. That's the first thing. Secondly, when I first went to this law firm, I spoke to Mr. Rose, and he knew exactly my circumstances. He knew that there were very few assets in the marriage. He knew that I would have to borrow money from relatives to pay the thousand dollar retainer fee that they asked for. They knew that my husband was going to represent himself, which would be a difficult situation. They also knew that he had done certain bizarre things, such as sending letters to people, and doing strange things; so, therefore, we might expect a difficult case from him. Yet, they consented to take my case. Of course, I don't think any attorney can guess, when he consents to represent somebody, what might occur. I imagine some cases go to trial immediately things get resolved, and my case is probably the other extreme, where everything possible has happened. I think it's unfortunate, and I think they've done a very fine job of representing me. I feel they should continue.

Judge Cariddi in the Chancery Division agreed with plaintiff and denied the application of the Rose firm, but set the case down for trial within the month. The Rose firm appealed.

* * *

When a firm accepts a retainer to conduct a legal proceeding, it impliedly agrees to prosecute the matter to a conclusion. The firm is not at liberty to abandon the case without justifiable or reasonable cause, or the consent of its client. We are firmly convinced that the Rose firm did not have cause to abandon plaintiff's case, and that the trial judge properly exercised his discretion when he denied the firm's application and scheduled an early trial date. It was to plaintiff's and the firm's advantage that the matter be heard and disposed of as expeditiously as possible. With trial imminent, it would be extremely difficult for plaintiff to obtain other representation, and therefore she clearly would be prejudiced by the Rose firm's withdrawal.

* * *

Since the Rose firm undertook to represent plaintiff and demanded and was paid a retainer of $2,000, they should continue to represent plaintiff through the completion of trial. The firm should not be relieved at this stage of the litigation merely because plaintiff is unable to pay to them all of the fees they have demanded. *See Drinker, Legal Ethics*, 140, n. 4 (1953). We are not unmindful of the fact that the Rose firm has performed substantial legal services for plaintiff and clearly is entitled to reasonable compensation therefor. Nevertheless, an attorney has certain obligations and duties to a client once representation is undertaken. These obligations do not evaporate because the case becomes more complicated or the work more arduous or the retainer not as profitable as first contemplated or imagined. Attorneys must never lose sight of the fact that "the profession is a branch of the administration of justice and not a mere money-getting trade." Canons of Professional Ethics, No. 12. As Canon 44 of the Canons of Professional Ethics so appropriately states: "The lawyer should not throw up the unfinished task to the detriment of his client except for reasons of honor or self-respect." Adherence to these strictures in no way violates the constitutional rights of the members of the firm.

Affirmed.

FRIVOLOUS CLAIMS

ABA Model Rule 3.1 prohibits an attorney from taking a frivolous legal position—that is, a position that has no basis in existing law and that cannot be supported by a good faith argument for extending, modifying, or reversing the existing law. Under ABA Model Rule 1.16, an attorney must refuse employment (or must withdraw from employment) if the employment would require the attorney to violate a disciplinary rule or other law. ABA Code DR 2–109, DR 2–110(B), and DR 7–102(A)(1) and (2) are to the same general effect. California Business and Professions Code § 6068(c) and CRPC 3–200(A) and (B) similarly require California lawyers to "counsel or maintain such actions, proceedings, or defenses only as appear to him or her legal or just" and to withdraw from employment brought in bad faith or without a basis under the law.

Aside from professional discipline, what might happen to an attorney who pursues a frivolous claim on behalf of a client? One possibility is a suit against the attorney and client by the adversary for malicious prosecution. That tort requires the adversary to prove four elements: (1) the initiation or continuation of the underlying action; (2) lack of probable cause; (3) malice; and (4) favorable termination of the underlying action. [*See* Restatement (Second) of Torts, §§ 674–681B (1977).] In testing probable cause, courts that follow the modern view use an objective standard—would a reasonable attorney have pursued the claim? But some courts still use a subjective standard—did this attorney know that the claim was frivolous? The malice element can be established by proof of actual ill will or proof that the claim was commenced or pursued for an improper purpose; it can also be inferred from the lack of probable cause.

Another possibility is the imposition of sanctions in the underlying action against the offending attorney, or the client, or both. In recent years Rule 11 of the Federal Rules of Civil Procedure has become a popular device for imposing sanctions in civil actions in the federal courts. [*See generally,* Schwarzer, *Rule 11 Revisited,* 101 Harv.L.Rev. 1013 (1988).] Rule 11 requires every pleading and other court paper to be personally signed by an attorney (or by a litigant representing him- or herself). In "presenting" such a paper to the court (by signing, filing, submitting or advocating), the attorney or party certifies to the best of his or her "knowledge, information, and belief, formed after an inquiry reasonable under the circumstances,—": (1) the paper is not being presented for any improper purpose, such as harassment or to run up an opponent's expenses; (2) that the claims, defenses and other legal contentions are warranted by existing law or by a nonfrivolous argument for a change or reversal in existing law or the establishment of new law; (3) that the factual allegations have evidentiary support or are likely to have support after further investigation or discovery; and (4) that factual denials are likewise warranted by the evidence or identified as reasonably based on lack of information or belief. From 1983 through 1993 sanctions for a violation of Rule 11 were mandatory; since 1993 they are once again discretionary, must be no more than necessary for deterrence, and should not usually result in shifting attorney fee expenses between the parties. Additional safeguards against surprise sanction requests and a 21-day period to withdraw a paper challenged as violating the Rule, all contribute to a sense that the federal courts have pulled back from the acrimonious sanctioning battles of the past 10 years. But Rule 11 is not the only sanctioning authority available to the courts. For example, 28 U.S.C.A. § 1927 (1988) states that an attorney or other person who "so multiplies the proceedings in any case unreasonably and vexatiously" may be ordered personally to pay the "excess costs, expenses, and attorney fees" reasonably incurred by the victim. Frivolous federal court appeals can be sanctioned under Federal Rule of Appellate Procedure 38 and 28 U.S.C.A. § 1912 (1988). Even broader power to sanction lawyers for taking frivolous legal positions can be found in the "inherent power" doctrine. In *Chambers v. NASCO, Inc.,* 501 U.S. 32, 111 S.Ct. 2123, 115 L.Ed.2d 27 (1991), the Supreme Court ruled that federal courts have the inherent power to sanction bad faith conduct by lawyers and parties whether the conduct at issue is covered by one of the other sanctioning provisions or not. [*See generally,* Gregory P. Joseph, *Rule 11 is Only the Beginning,* A.B.A.J., May 1, 1988, at 62–65.]

Similar sanction provisions are available under state law rules or statutes. [*See, e.g.,* Cal.Code Civ.Proc. §§ 128.5 (court may order party or party's attorney to pay another party's reasonable expenses, including attorney's fees, incurred "as a result of bad-faith actions or tactics that are frivolous or solely intended to cause unnecessary delay") and 128.7 (the substantial equivalent of the amended Federal Rule 11).] California courts remain divided (and troubled) by section 128.5's apparent dual requirement: the action must be *both* totally without merit *and* brought in bad faith. *See, e.g., Llamas v. Diaz,* 218 Cal.App.3d 1043, 267 Cal.Rptr. 427 (1990) (plaintiffs' action for fraud found by both the trial and appellate courts to be "totally without [objective] merit"; but trial court found plaintiffs' counsel "sincerely believed there was a basis for recovery," negating subjective bad faith; sanctions under § 128.5 denied). *But see Weisman v. Bower,* 193 Cal.App.3d 1231, 238 Cal.Rptr. 756 (1987) ("section 128.5 permits the trial court to impose sanctions * * * only if the moving party meets its burden of proving that the opposing party's action or tactic was (1) totally and completely without merit, measured by the objective, 'reasonable attorney' standard, or (2) motivated solely by an intention to harass or cause unnecessary delay, measured by a subjective standard"). However, with the adoption of section 128.7 to apply to filings from 1995 through 1998, and possibly beyond, the California courts have moved in line with the Federal Rule 11 model.

MULTIPLE CHOICE QUESTIONS

Answer these questions under the ABA Code and
ABA Model Rules

1. For many years, lawyer Snyder has represented a professional football team, the Raptors, in business law matters. On the team's behalf, Snyder has filed a breach of contract case against the City Board of Commissioners concerning the stadium that the city leases to the Raptors. Snyder is counsel of record in the suit, and he has conducted all of the discovery for the Raptors. The trial date is fast approaching, and the Raptors' owners have retained a famous trial lawyer, Marvin Slick, to serve as Snyder's co-counsel and to do the actual trial work. Although Snyder envies Slick's win-loss record, he regards Slick as little more than a highly-educated con artist with whom he cannot possibly work. Which of the following *may* Snyder do?

    A. Immediately seek the court's permission to withdraw from the case.

    B. Promptly instruct the team owners to terminate their arrangement with Slick.

    C. Ask the team owners to consent to his withdrawal, if he believes that is in their best interests.

    D. Advise Slick to withdraw, if Snyder believes that is in the best interests of the team owners.

2. Attorney Arbuckle is admitted to practice in State A. The State A Rules of Court require court permission before an attorney can withdraw from a pending case. State A does not recognize attorney retaining liens on litigation files (that is, an attorney cannot keep the litigation files to secure payment of his or her fee). Arbuckle agreed to defend Clauzoff in a civil action for theft of the plaintiff's trade secrets. Clauzoff agreed to pay Arbuckle $60 per hour, and he gave Arbuckle a $1,200 advance on attorney fees. Three times, the plaintiff scheduled the taking of Clauzoff's deposition, and all three times Clauzoff failed to show up. Further, despite repeated promises, Clauzoff failed to send Arbuckle some documents that Arbuckle needed in order to draft responses to the plaintiff's interrogatories. After Arbuckle put in 50 hours on the case, he billed Clauzoff $1,800, but Clauzoff refused to pay the bill. Finally, Arbuckle decided to have nothing further to do with the

case; when plaintiff's counsel telephoned, Arbuckle told her that he was no longer the lawyer for Clauzoff. Clauzoff asked to have the litigation files and asked for a refund of the $1,200 advance, but Arbuckle refused both requests. Which of the following statements are correct?

I. Arbuckle is *subject to discipline* for stepping out of the case without the court's consent.

II. Arbuckle is *subject to discipline* for withdrawing from the case without adequate grounds.

III. Arbuckle is *subject to discipline* for refusing to give the litigation files to Clauzoff.

IV. Arbuckle is *subject to discipline* for refusing to refund the $1,200 fee advance to Clauzoff.

    A. All of the above.

    B. I and III only.

    C. II, III, and IV only.

    D. I, II, and III only.

3. Jason P. Worthington III is among the wealthiest men in New York society. When his son was arrested for selling illegal drugs to his prep school classmates, Worthington sought the legal services of the prestigious old firm of Bradbury & Crosswell. The Bradbury firm practices almost nothing but securities and banking law. For which of the following reasons *may* the Bradbury firm decline employment in the case?

I. That Worthington is not among the firm's regular clients.

II. That the firm is not experienced in criminal litigation.

III. That Worthington can obtain better service at lower fees from lawyers with more experience in criminal litigation.

IV. That the firm does not want to take time away from its regular work for a matter such as this one.

    A. All of the above.

    B. None of the above.

    C. III only.

    D. II only.

4. When attorney Hodges graduated from law school three years ago, she opened a solo practice in a small rural community close by the state's major prison. Her primary interests are family law and real estate law. Her practice is growing very slowly, despite her long work hours. She is barely able to make financial ends meet. The presiding judge of the local State District Court has asked her to serve as court-appointed counsel in a civil action that was originally filed *in propria persona* by an indigent inmate of the prison. From the roughly drawn complaint, the presiding judge believes there may be some merit in the inmate's allegations of brutality by some of the guards and gross neglect

on the part of the warden. State law allows attorney fees to be awarded to a plaintiff in a civil action of this type, but only if the plaintiff is victorious. Attorney Hodges realizes that she will not be paid for her work if she loses the case, and she is very concerned about the financial loss she may suffer if she takes time away from her regular practice. Further, she is worried about harming her reputation because the warden and many prison employees form the nucleus of her community. Which of the following statements are correct?

I. She *may* decline to serve on the ground that her practice is primarily in the fields of real estate and family law.

II. She *may* decline to serve if she believes in good faith that she cannot reasonably take the financial risk involved.

III. She *may* decline to serve if she believes in good faith that to serve would seriously injure her reputation in the community.

IV. She *may* decline to serve if she believes in good faith that some of her present clients will be offended if she takes the case.

    A.   All of the above.

    B.   None of the above.

    C.   II only.

    D.   I, II, and IV only.

    5. Lawyer Yeager has been retained by the officers of Amalgamated Finishers and Patternworkers Union, Local 453, to draft a new set of bylaws for the local. Yeager strongly disagrees with one of the provisions the officers want included in the new bylaws. The provision would deny members of the local the right to vote on some issues that involve the expenditure of union funds. Although Yeager believes that the provision is lawful and consistent with the national union charter, she believes it would be unwise and inconsistent with the best interests of the members of the local. If the union can obtain other counsel without serious loss, *may* Yeager withdraw from the matter?

    A.   Yes, but only if she obtains the consent of her client.

    B.   Yes, because her client is asking her to do something that is against her best judgment.

    C.   No, because she is obliged to carry out the lawful objectives of her client.

    D.   No, unless her client has breached the agreement under which she agreed to perform the work.

Answers to the multiple choice questions appear
in the Appendix at the back of the book

Chapter Four

ADVERTISING AND SOLICITATION

What This Chapter Covers

  I.   **Historical Summary**
 II. **The *Bates* case**
III. **Historical Summary, Continued**
IV. **The *Went For It* case**

Reading Assignment

Wydick & Perschbacher, Chapter 4

ABA Model Rules:

    Rules 7.1 through 7.5.

CRPC 1–320(B)–(C); 1–400; California Standards for Attorney Communications (printed after CRPC 1–400).

Skim Cal.Bus. & Prof.Code §§ 6150–54; 6157–6159.2.

Supplemental Reading

ABA Code:

    EC 2–1 through 2–15; EC 2–33; DR 2–101 through 2–105.

Hazard & Hodes:

    Discussion of ABA Model Rules 7.1 through 7.5.

Wolfram:

    Section 5.5 (specialization);

    Section 14.1 (client needs for legal services);

    Sections 14.2.1 through 14.2.4 (advertising);

    Section 14.2.5 (solicitation).

Discussion Problems

    1. Suppose you have just opened your law practice in a town where you do not know many people. In which of the following ways may you seek to build your clientele?

a. May you join a social club for the sole purpose of meeting new people and luring them as clients?

b. May you call on other lawyers at their offices and let them know that you are willing to take on work that they are too busy to handle?

c. May you volunteer to give a seminar on estate planning for the local chapter of Young Businesswomen of America, hoping to get legal business from some of those who attend?

d. May you list your name with the local court as a person who is willing to take court-appointed cases?

e. May you list your name with the lawyer referral service run by the local bar association? How does such a lawyer referral service operate?

f. May you place advertisements for your services? In what media? What restrictions are there on the content of your advertising?

g. May you publish a brochure that describes your law practice, states the kinds of matters you handle, and provides a schedule of the fees you charge for a variety of routine legal services? If so, how may you distribute the brochure? May you publish the same information on the World–Wide Web portion of the Internet?

2. Suppose that the Surgeon General has recently determined that prolonged exposure to a chemical known as DNXP causes a type of blood disease in humans. DNXP is used in the manufacture of certain types of plastics, and many plastics workers have contracted the disease. Lawyer Lovette practices personal injury and workers' compensation law in a town that has four plastics factories. She would like to represent afflicted plastics workers who wish to bring legal proceedings against their employers and the manufacturers of DNXP.

a. May she put an ad in the local newspaper, informing plastics workers of their legal rights respecting exposure to DNXP and inviting interested persons to contact her?

b. The town business directory provides a separate directory listing of all plastics workers, giving their names, postal addresses, e-mail addresses, and telephone numbers. May Lovette send an informative letter via the postal service to each plastics worker, inviting the worker to contact her for further information? Is your answer the same if Lovette uses e-mail rather than the postal service?

c. May Lovette hire a team of telephone callers who will use the business directory to phone each plastics worker, give a brief description of the DNXP problem, and invite the worker to contact Lovette for more information?

d. May Lovette stand on the public sidewalk outside the gates of one of the plastics factories at quitting time and pass out handbills that state her willingness to represent workers in DNXP cases? May she initiate conversations with workers on that subject?

3.   On your way down the courthouse hall after a hearing, you saw a tired-looking woman holding a crying infant. She was obviously confused and needed help. When you spoke to her, she handed you a paper and asked in halting English where she was supposed to go. The paper was a summons to appear that morning in an unlawful detainer action filed by her landlord. When you responded to her in her native language, her face broke into a wide smile. You briefly explained to her the nature of an unlawful detainer hearing, and you asked if she had a lawyer. When she said no, you offered to represent her at the hearing for a modest fee. Was your offer proper? Would it be proper if you had offered to represent her for free?[a]

If your prediction comes true, what role do you foresee for yourself 20 years from now?

HISTORICAL SUMMARY

A.   Advertising

Back in the 1800's, lawyers in the United States sometimes advertised their services in newspapers. But when the American Bar Association adopted its original Canons of Professional Ethics, in 1908, Canon 27 said:

> The most worthy and effective advertisement possible, even for a young lawyer, is the establishment of a well-merited reputation for professional capacity and fidelity to trust. This cannot be forced, but must be the outcome of character and conduct. * * * [S]olicitation of business by circulars or advertisements, or by personal communications, or interviews not warranted by personal relations, is unprofessional. * * * Indirect advertisement for business by furnishing or inspiring newspaper comments concerning causes in which the lawyer has been or is engaged * * * the importance of the lawyer's positions, and all other like self-laudation, defy the traditions and lower the tone of our high calling, and are intolerable.

In short, lawyers were to be passive receivers of legal business, not active seekers of it. A person who needed a lawyer could simply ask a friend or neighbor to recommend a good one, and in that fashion the trade of honest, competent lawyers would grow and prosper.

Over the years, Canon 27 was amended and re-amended to draw ever-finer distinctions about the precise ways in which lawyers could

------

a. Our thanks to Professor Monroe Freedman of the Hofstra University School of Law for inspiring this hypothetical question. He discusses the hypothetical in M. Freedman, *Lawyers' Ethics in an Adversary System* 118 (1975). *See also* Rhode, *Solicitation*, 36 J. Legal Educ. 317 (1986).

ethically hold themselves out to the public. A lawyer could have a "shingle," a small, dignified sign to mark the office door. A lawyer could be identified in a "reputable law list," a directory readily available to other lawyers (but not to ordinary citizens) that provided biographic information. A lawyer could make "customary use" of "simple professional cards," and could put limited kinds of information on a "letterhead," the formal stationery used in the office. Patent lawyers, trademark lawyers, and proctors in admiralty could so designate themselves in public communications, but ordinary lawyers could not tell the public what kinds of law they practiced.

As the complexity of the rules grew, so did the ingenuity of the lawyers who sought to evade them. The resulting tension created considerable work for those members of the profession who wrote ethics opinions and imposed discipline on the miscreants. When discipline was imposed, it was customarily coupled with a thorough denunciation. Thus, in censuring one Leon A. Berezniak, Esq., the Supreme Court of Illinois wrote:

> The advertisements of respondent are very obnoxious and disgusting, not only because they are gotten up after the manner of quack doctors and itinerant vendors of patent medicines and other cure-alls, but because of the fact that they contain statements that cast reflections upon the common honesty, proficiency, and decency of the profession generally of which he insists he is a distinguished member.[b]

Thus, in the period between 1910 and 1975, the bar and the courts created a remarkable body of law and lore, of which the following is but a small sample:

- A New York attorney was censured for (among other things) sending typewritten letters to businessmen with whom he had no prior relationship, inviting them to use him for their collection claims and other legal work.[c]

- A California attorney was censured for (among other things) putting signs on his house to advertise reduced fees for his services as lawyer, notary public, and tax consultant.[d]

- A Nebraska attorney was suspended for putting a classified advertisement in the local newspapers, offering to do divorces for "$15 and costs."[e]

- It was deemed unethical for an attorney-physician to state on his letterhead that he was both a lawyer and a doctor, and it was

b. *People ex rel. Chicago Bar Association v. Berezniak*, 292 Ill. 305, 127 N.E. 36 (1920).

c. *In re Gray*, 184 App.Div. 822, 172 N.Y.S. 648 (1918).

d. *Libarian v. State Bar*, 21 Cal.2d 862, 136 P.2d 321 (1943) (large signs); 25 Cal.2d 314, 153 P.2d 739 (1944) (small signs).

e. *State ex rel. Hunter v. Crocker*, 132 Neb. 214, 271 N.W. 444 (1937).

likewise unethical for him to send out formal announcements that he had opened an office for the practice of both professions.[f]

- It was deemed unethical for an attorney to have his name listed in boldface type in the telephone book.[g]

- An Arizona attorney was censured for (among other things) advertising by means of matchbooks printed with his name and profession.[h]

- It was deemed unethical for an attorney to send Christmas cards that mentioned his profession (except cards that merely pictured the scales of justice or a lawyer dressed as Santa Claus), and it was deemed unethical to send any sort of Christmas card to a present client, or to another lawyer, with whom the sender had no close personal or social relationship.[i]

- It was said that an attorney (hypothetically named Doe) could ethically erect a building and call it the "Doe Building," but not the "Doe Law Building" (nor even plain "Law Building," unless it were to be inhabited by numerous other lawyers).[j]

- It was said that an attorney could ethically allow his name to be put on a sign in the lobby of an office building, if the sign were used as a building directory, albeit a sign with a light.[k] However, a New York attorney was censured for using a neonlit sign in his office window.[l]

- A California attorney, who was called the "King of Torts," was suspended for allowing his name to be used in advertising an expensive Scotch whisky, where the court inferred that his intent was to promote his law practice as well as the whisky.[m]

B. Solicitation

Client-getting activity that involves personal contact (either face-to-face contact or live telephone contact) which is initiated by a lawyer (or the lawyer's agent) and a specific potential client is called "solicitation," to distinguish it from "advertising," which is general communication with the public at large. In the most blatant form of solicitation, "ambulance-chasing," the lawyer hires agents to urge injured people to employ the lawyer to represent them.[n]

Canon 28 of the 1908 ABA Canons of Professional Ethics was specifically directed at solicitation. It warned lawyers not to stir up litigation, nor to volunteer advice to a stranger to bring a lawsuit, nor to seek out injured persons or defects in land titles in the hope of gaining

f. ABA Formal Op. 183 (1938).

g. ABA Formal Op. 284 (1951).

h. *In re Maltby*, 68 Ariz. 153, 202 P.2d 902 (1949).

i. ABA Formal Op. 309 (1963).

j. ABA Informal Op. 441 (1961).

k. ABA Informal Op. 800 (1964).

l. *In re Duffy*, 19 A.D.2d 177, 242 N.Y.S.2d 665 (1963).

m. *Belli v. State Bar of California*, 10 Cal.3d 824, 112 Cal.Rptr. 527, 519 P.2d 575 (1974).

n. *See* Annot., *"Disbarment—Ambulance Chasing,"* 67 A.L.R.2d 859 (1959).

employment, nor to pay prison guards or hospital attendants for referring potential clients, nor to hire runners or agents to do any such dirty work.

Solicitation has traditionally been punished more harshly than advertising,[o] and for better reason. The bar and courts are concerned with the effect of solicitation on those solicited—especially unsophisticated lay people, when under stress and unable to exercise careful, informed judgment about the hiring of a lawyer.

C. The Forces of Change—Antitrust and the First Amendment

When the ABA Code was promulgated in 1969, it came complete with bans on advertising and solicitation. But simultaneously, it spoke of a lawyer's ethical obligation to help lay people recognize legal problems and to assure that legal service was available to all who needed it. Soon the bar began to feel the tension between these two positions.

In the early 1970s, distinguished members of the bar began to argue that lay people could not select a lawyer intelligently unless they were given more information than the ABA Code allowed. On another front, antitrust experts began to ponder the anti-competitive effects of the lawyer advertising ban. Ordinary commercial competitors could not lawfully agree to refrain from advertising.[p] Was the mantle of professionalism enough to protect lawyers from the Sherman Antitrust Act? The United States Justice Department thought not, and in 1976 it sued the American Bar Association as a conspiracy in restraint of trade.[q]

D. The *Bates* case

In the following pages, you will read *Bates v. State Bar of Arizona,* 433 U.S. 350, 97 S.Ct. 2691, 53 L.Ed.2d 810 (1977), which concerned two Arizona lawyers who violated Arizona's ban on lawyer advertising. The U.S. Supreme Court ruled that the advertising ban was immune from attack under the Sherman Antitrust Act because the ban had been promulgated by an arm of the state government, the Arizona Supreme Court. However, *Bates* holds that the First Amendment commercial speech doctrine protects attorney advertising that is truthful and not misleading. Ironically, the Court based its First Amendment conclusion on arguments that carry the strong flavor of antitrust: free competition among lawyers raises quality and reduces prices, and competition works best when consumers are well informed about their choices.

o. *Compare id. with* Annot., "Attorney Advertising—Discipline," 39 A.L.R.2d 1055 (1955).

p. *United States v. Gasoline Retailers Association,* Inc., 285 F.2d 688 (7th Cir. 1961) (agreement among gas stations not to post prices on curb signs held illegal per se).

q. *United States v. American Bar Association,* Civil No. 76–1182 (D.D.C. 1976). The suit was dismissed after the Supreme Court decision in *Bates v. State Bar of Arizona,* 433 U.S. 350, 97 S.Ct. 2691, 53 L.Ed.2d 810 (1977). *See* Trade Reg. Rptr., 1970–79 U.S. Antitrust Cases 53, 658 (1980).

BATES v. STATE BAR OF ARIZONA

Supreme Court of the United States, 1977.
433 U.S. 350, 97 S.Ct. 2691, 53 L.Ed.2d 810.

[In 1974, Arizona lawyers Bates and O'Steen opened a "legal clinic" to provide low cost service to people of moderate means. They did only "routine" legal work, and they made heavy use of paralegal assistants, standard legal forms, and modern office equipment. In 1976, they sought to increase their volume by running the newspaper ad that you see on the next page. When the State Bar of Arizona tried to discipline them, they appealed to the United States Supreme Court, claiming violations of the Sherman Act and the First Amendment free speech clause (as applied to the states through the Fourteenth Amendment). The Court rejected the Sherman Act argument because Arizona's advertising rules had been duly approved by the Arizona Supreme Court—the Sherman Act does not reach a restraint of trade that is conceived and supervised by a state government. But the Court held that lawyers' "commercial speech" is entitled to some protection under the First Amendment. As you will see from the following portions of the majority opinion, the Court's First Amendment analysis is, ironically, heavily seasoned with antitrust.]

The issue presently before us is a narrow one. First, we need not address the peculiar problems associated with advertising claims relating to the *quality* of legal services. Such claims probably are not susceptible of precise measurement or verification and, under some circumstances, might well be deceptive or misleading to the public, or even false. Appellee does not suggest, nor do we perceive, that appellants' advertisement contained claims, extravagant or otherwise, as to the quality of services. Accordingly, we leave that issue for another day. Second, we also need not resolve the problems associated with in-person solicitation of clients—at the hospital room or the accident site, or in any other situation that breeds undue influence—by attorneys or their agents or "runners." Activity of that kind might well pose dangers of over-reaching and misrepresentation not encountered in newspaper announcement advertising. Hence, this issue also is not before us. Third, we note that appellee's criticism of advertising by attorneys does not apply with much force to some of the basic factual content of advertising: information as to the attorney's name, address, and telephone number, office hours, and the like. The American Bar Association itself has a provision in its current Code of Professional Responsibility that would allow the disclosure of such information, and more in the classified section of the telephone directory. DR 2–102(A)(6) (1976). We recognize, however, that an advertising diet limited to such spartan fare would provide scant nourishment.

The heart of the dispute before us today is whether lawyers also may constitutionally advertise the *prices* at which certain routine services will be performed. Numerous justifications are proffered for the restriction of such price advertising. We consider each in turn:

1. *The Adverse Effect on Professionalism.* Appellee places particular emphasis on the adverse effects that it feels price advertising will have on the legal profession. The key to professionalism, it is argued, is

ADVERTISEMENT

DO YOU NEED A LAWYER?

LEGAL SERVICES
AT VERY REASONABLE FEES

* Divorce or legal separation--uncontested (both spouses sign papers)

$175 00 plus $20 00 court filing fee

* Preparation of all court papers and instructions on how to do your own simple uncontested divorce

$100 00

* Adoption--uncontested severance proceeding

$225 00 plus approximately $10 00 publication cost

* Bankruptcy--non-business, no contested proceedings

Individual
$250 00 plus $55 00 court filing fee

Wife and Husband
$300 00 plus $110 00 court filing fee

* Change of Name

$95 00 plus $20 00 court filing fee

Information regarding other types of cases furnished on request

Legal Clinic of Bates & O'Steen
617 North 3rd Street
Phoenix, Arizona 85004
Telephone (602) 252-8888

[E2922]

the sense of pride that involvement in the discipline generates. It is claimed that price advertising will bring about commercialization, which will undermine the attorney's sense of dignity and self-worth. The hustle of the marketplace will adversely affect the profession's service orientation, and irreparably damage the delicate balance between the lawyer's need to earn and his obligation selflessly to serve. Advertising is also said to erode the client's trust in his attorney: Once the client perceives that the lawyer is motivated by profit, his confidence that the attorney is acting out of a commitment to the client's welfare is jeopardized. And advertising is said to tarnish the dignified public image of the profession.

We recognize, of course, and commend the spirit of public service with which the profession of law is practiced and to which it is dedicated. The present Members of this Court, licensed attorneys all, could not feel otherwise. And we would have reason to pause if we felt that our decision today would undercut that spirit. But we find the postulated connection between advertising and the erosion of true professionalism to be severely strained. At its core, the argument presumes that attorneys must conceal from themselves and from their clients the real-life fact that lawyers earn their livelihood at the bar. We suspect that few attorneys engage in such self-deception. And rare is the client, moreover, even one of the [sic] modest means, who enlists the aid of an attorney with the expectation that his services will be rendered free of charge. *See* B. Christensen, Lawyers for People of Moderate Means 152–153 (1970). In fact, the American Bar Association advises that an attorney should reach "a clear agreement with his client as to the basis of the fee charges to be made," and that this is to be done "[a]s soon as feasible after a lawyer has been employed." Code of Professional Responsibility EC 2–19 (1976). If the commercial basis of the relationship is to be promptly disclosed on ethical grounds, once the client is in the office, it seems inconsistent to condemn the candid revelation of the same information before he arrives at that office.

Moreover, the assertion that advertising will diminish the attorney's reputation in the community is open to question. Bankers and engineers advertise, and yet these professions are not regarded as undignified. In fact, it has been suggested that the failure of lawyers to advertise creates public disillusionment with the profession. The absence of advertising may be seen to reflect the profession's failure to reach out and serve the community: Studies reveal that many persons do not obtain counsel even when they perceive a need because of the feared price of services or because of an inability to locate a competent attorney. Indeed, cynicism with regard to the profession may be created by the fact that it long has publicly eschewed advertising, while condoning the actions of the attorney who structures his social or civic associations so as to provide contacts with potential clients.

It appears that the ban on advertising originated as a rule of etiquette and not as a rule of ethics. Early lawyers in Great Britain viewed the law as a form of public service, rather than as a means of earning a living, and they looked down on "trade" as unseemly. *See* H. Drinker, Legal Ethics, 5, 210–211 (1953). Eventually, the attitude toward advertising fostered by this view evolved into an aspect of the ethics of the profession. *Id.*, at 211. But habit and tradition are not in themselves an adequate answer to a constitutional challenge. In this day, we do not belittle the person who earns his living by the strength of his arm or the force of his mind. Since the belief that lawyers are somehow "above" trade has become an anachronism, the historical foundation for the advertising restraint has crumbled.

2. *The Inherently Misleading Nature of Attorney Advertising.* It is argued that advertising of legal services inevitably will be misleading (a) because such services are so individualized with regard to content and quality as to prevent informed comparison on the basis of an advertisement, (b) because the consumer of legal services is unable to determine in advance just what services he needs, and (c) because advertising by attorneys will highlight irrelevant factors and fail to show the relevant factor of skill.

We are not persuaded that restrained professional advertising by lawyers inevitably will be misleading. Although many services performed by attorneys are indeed unique, it is doubtful that any attorney would or could advertise fixed prices for services of that type. The only services that lend themselves to advertising are the routine ones: the uncontested divorce, the simple adoption, the uncontested personal bankruptcy, the change of name, and the like—the very services advertised by appellants. Although the precise service demanded in each task may vary slightly, and although legal services are not fungible, these facts do not make advertising misleading so long as the attorney does the necessary work at the advertised price. The argument that legal services are so unique that fixed rates cannot meaningfully be established is refuted by the record in this case: The appellee, State Bar itself sponsors a Legal Services Program in which the participating attorneys agree to perform services like those advertised by the appellants at standardized rates. App. 459–478. Indeed, until the decision of this Court in *Goldfarb v. Virginia State Bar*, 421 U.S. 773, 95 S.Ct. 2004, 44 L.Ed.2d 572 (1975), the Maricopa County Bar Association apparently had a schedule of suggested minimum fees for standard legal tasks. We thus find of little force the assertion that advertising is misleading because of an inherent lack of standardization in legal services.

The second component of the argument—that advertising ignores the diagnostic role—fares little better. It is unlikely that many people go to an attorney merely to ascertain if they have a clean bill of legal health. Rather, attorneys are likely to be employed to perform specific tasks. Although the client may not know the detail involved in performing the task, he no doubt is able to identify the service he desires at the level of generality to which advertising lends itself.

The third component is not without merit: Advertising does not provide a complete foundation on which to select an attorney. But it seems peculiar to deny the consumer, on the ground that the information is incomplete, at least some of the relevant information needed to reach an informed decision. The alternative—the prohibition of advertising—serves only to restrict the information that flows to consumers. Moreover, the argument assumes that the public is not sophisticated enough to realize the limitations of advertising, and that the public is better kept in ignorance than trusted with correct but incomplete information. We suspect the argument rests on an underestimation of the public. In any event, we view as dubious any justification that is based on the benefits of public ignorance. *See Virginia Pharmacy Board v. Virginia Consumer Council*, 425 U.S., at 769–770, 96 S.Ct., at 1829–1830. Although, of course, the bar retains the power to correct omissions that have the effect of presenting an inaccurate picture, the preferred remedy is more disclosure, rather than less. If the naiveté of the public will cause advertising by attorneys to be misleading, then it is the bar's role to assure that the populace is sufficiently informed as to enable it to place advertising in its proper perspective.

3. *The Adverse Effect on the Administration of Justice.* Advertising is said to have the undesirable effect of stirring up litigation. The judicial machinery is designed to serve those who feel sufficiently aggrieved to bring forward their claims. Advertising, it is argued, serves to encourage the assertion of legal rights in the courts, thereby undesirably unsettling societal repose. There is even a suggestion of barratry. *See, e.g.,* Comment. A Critical Analysis of Rules Against Solicitation by Lawyers, 25 U.Chi.L.Rev. 674, 675–676 (1958).

But advertising by attorneys is not an unmitigated source of harm to the administration of justice. It may offer great benefits. Although advertising might increase the use of the judicial machinery, we cannot accept the notion that it is always better for a person to suffer a wrong silently than to redress it by legal action. As the bar acknowledges, "the middle 70% of our population is not being reached or served adequately by the legal profession." ABA, Revised Handbook on Prepaid Legal Services 2 (1972). Among the reasons for this underutilization is fear of the cost, and an inability to locate a suitable lawyer. Advertising can help to solve this acknowledged problem: Advertising is the traditional mechanism in a free-market economy for a supplier to inform a potential purchaser of the availability and terms of exchange. The disciplinary rule at issue likely has served to burden access to legal services, particularly for the not-quite-poor and the unknowledgeable. A rule allowing restrained advertising would be in accord with the bar's obligation to "facilitate the process of intelligent selection of lawyers, and to assist in making legal services fully available." ABA Code of Professional Responsibility EC 2–1 (1976).

4. *The Undesirable Economic Effects of Advertising.* It is claimed that advertising will increase the overhead costs of the profession, and that these costs then will be passed along to consumers in the form of increased fees. Moreover, it is claimed that the additional cost of practice will create a substantial entry barrier, deterring or preventing young attorneys from penetrating the market and entrenching the position of the bar's established members.

These two arguments seem dubious at best. Neither distinguishes lawyers from others, *see Virginia Pharmacy Board v. Virginia Consumer Council*, 425 U.S., at 768, 96 S.Ct., at 1828, and neither appears relevant to the First Amendment. The ban on advertising serves to increase the difficulty of discovering the lowest cost seller of acceptable ability. As a result, to this extent attorneys are isolated from competition, and the incentive to price competitively is reduced. Although it is true that the effect of advertising on the price of services has not been demonstrated, there is revealing evidence with regard to products; where consumers have the benefit of price advertising, retail prices often are dramatically lower than they would be without advertising. It is entirely possible that advertising will serve to reduce, not advance, the cost of legal services to the consumer.

The entry-barrier argument is equally unpersuasive. In the absence of advertising, an attorney must rely on his contacts with the community to generate a flow of business. In view of the time necessary to develop such contacts, the ban in fact serves to perpetuate the market position of established attorneys. Consideration of entry-barrier problems would urge that advertising be allowed so as to aid the new competitor in penetrating the market.

5. *The Adverse Effect of Advertising on the Quality of Service.* It is argued that the attorney may advertise a given "package" of service at a set price, and will be inclined to provide, by indiscriminate use, the standard package regardless of whether it fits the client's needs.

Restraints on advertising, however, are an ineffective way of deterring shoddy work. An attorney who is inclined to cut quality will do so regardless of the rule on advertising. And the advertisement of a standardized fee does not necessarily mean that the services offered are undesirably standardized. Indeed, the assertion that an attorney who advertises a standard fee will cut quality is substantially undermined by the fixed-fee schedule of appellee's own prepaid Legal Services Program. Even if advertising leads to the creation of "legal clinics" like that of appellants'—clinics that emphasize standardized procedures for routine problems—it is possible that such clinics will improve service by reducing the likelihood of error.

6. *The Difficulties of Enforcement.* Finally, it is argued that the wholesale restriction is justified by the problems of enforcement if any other course is taken. Because the public lacks sophistication in legal matters, it may be particularly susceptible to misleading or deceptive advertising by lawyers. After-the-fact action by the consumer lured by such advertising may not provide a realistic restraint because of the inability of the layman to assess whether the service he has received meets professional standards. Thus, the vigilance of a regulatory agency will be required. But because of the numerous purveyors of services, the overseeing of advertising will be burdensome.

It is at least somewhat incongruous for the opponents of advertising to extol the virtues and altruism of the legal profession at one point, and, at another, to assert that its members will seize the opportunity to mislead and distort. We suspect that, with advertising, most lawyers will behave as they always have: They will abide by their solemn oaths to uphold the integrity and honor of their profession and of the legal system. For every attorney who overreaches through advertising, there will be thousands of others who will be candid and honest and straightforward. And, of course, it will be in the latter's interest, as in other cases of misconduct at the bar, to assist in weeding out those few who abuse their trust.

In sum, we are not persuaded that any of the proffered justifications rise to the level of an acceptable reason for the suppression of all advertising by attorneys.

[The Court held that the First Amendment "overbreadth" doctrine did not apply in the context of lawyer advertising, but it ruled that the advertisement in question was not so obviously misleading as to be subject to regulation.]

In holding that advertising by attorneys may not be subjected to blanket suppression, and that the advertisement at issue is protected, we, of course, do not hold that advertising by attorneys may not be regulated in any way. We mention some of the clearly permissible limitations on advertising not foreclosed by our holding.

Advertising that is false, deceptive, or misleading of course is subject to restraint. *See Virginia Pharmacy Board v. Virginia Citizens Consumer Council*, 425 U.S., at 771–772, and n. 24, 96 S.Ct., at 1830–1831. Since the advertiser knows his product and has a commercial interest in its dissemination, we have little worry that regulation to assure truthfulness will discourage protected speech. And any concern that strict requirements for truthfulness will undesirably inhibit spontaneity seems inapplicable because commercial speech generally is calculated. Indeed, the public and private benefits from commercial speech derive from confidence in its accuracy and reliability. Thus, the leeway for untruthful or misleading expression that has been allowed in other contexts has little force in the commercial arena. Compare *Gertz v. Robert Welch, Inc.*, 418 U.S. 323, 339–341, 94 S.Ct. 2997, 3006–3007, 41 L.Ed.2d 789 (1974), and *Cantwell v. Connecticut*, 310 U.S., at 310, 60 S.Ct., at 906, with *NLRB v. Gissel Packing Co.*, 395 U.S., at 618, 89 S.Ct., at 1942. In fact, because the public lacks sophistication concerning legal services, misstatements that might be overlooked or deemed unimportant in other advertising may be found quite inappropriate in legal advertising. For example, advertising claims as to the quality of services—a matter we do not address today—are not susceptible of measurement or verification; accordingly, such claims may be so likely to be misleading as to warrant restriction. Similar objections might justify restraints on in-person solicitation. We do not foreclose the possibility that some limited supplementation, by way of warning or disclaimer or the like, might be required of even an advertisement of the kind ruled upon today so as to assure that the consumer is not misled. In sum, we recognize that many of the problems in defining the boundary between deceptive and nondeceptive advertising remain to be resolved, and we expect that the bar will have a special role to play in assuring that advertising by attorneys flows both freely and cleanly.

As with other varieties of speech, it follows as well that there may be reasonable restrictions on the time, place, and manner of advertising. *See Virginia Pharmacy Board v. Virginia Consumer Council*, 425 U.S., at 771, 96 S.Ct. at 1830. Advertising concerning transactions that are themselves illegal obviously may be suppressed. *See Pittsburgh Press Co. v. Human Relations Comm'n*, 413 U.S. 376, 388, 93 S.Ct. 2553, 37 L.Ed.2d 669 (1973). And the special problems of advertising on the electronic broadcast media will warrant special consideration.

The constitutional issue in this case is only whether the State may prevent the publication in a newspaper of appellants' truthful advertisement concerning the availability and terms of routine legal services. We rule simply that the flow of such information may not be restrained, and we therefore hold the present application of the disciplinary rule against appellants to be violative of the First Amendment.

The judgment of the Supreme Court of Arizona is therefore affirmed in part and reversed in part.

A. ABA Code Amendments after *Bates*

A few weeks after *Bates* was decided, the ABA amended the ABA Code to loosen the advertising ban a little, but not much. The amended ABA Code provisions purported to limit the types of information lawyers could advertise, and they retained many antique rules about law office signs, letterheads, professional cards and the like. Eventually, in the early 1980's, the ABA adopted the ABA Model Rules, which take a much more liberal approach to advertising and solicitation. The ABA Code provisions on advertising and solicitation are now of historical interest only (and, when you prepare for the Multistate Professional Responsibility Examination, you should disregard them.)

B. The *Ohralik* and *Primus* cases—Solicitation

The year after *Bates*, the Supreme Court decided a pair of cases that sketched the line between permissible and impermissible solicitation by lawyers.

In *Ohralik v. Ohio State Bar Association*, 436 U.S. 447, 98 S.Ct. 1912, 56 L.Ed.2d 444 (1978), the Court approved indefinite suspension from law practice for an old-fashioned ambulance chaser. Lawyer Ohralik learned about an auto accident in which two 18–year–old girls had been injured. He was casually acquainted with one of them and called her parents, who said she was in traction at the hospital. After visiting her parents at their home, he visited the girl in the hospital, offered to represent her, and asked her to sign a fee agreement. She said she would have to discuss it with her parents. With a tape recorder concealed under his raincoat, he returned to her parents' home where he volunteered some advice about how much they could recover under the uninsured motorist clause of their auto insurance policy. The parents told him that their daughter had telephoned and had agreed to let him represent her. He returned to the hospital two days later and had the girl sign a one-third contingent fee agreement.

Ohralik paid an uninvited visit to the second girl at her home, again carrying his concealed tape recorder. He told her about representing the first girl and about recovering money under the uninsured motorist clause. He asked if she wanted to file a claim, and she replied that she did not really understand what was going on. He then offered to represent her for a one-third contingent fee, to which she responded, "O.K." The next day, the second girl's mother told Ohralik that she and her daughter did not want to sue anyone or have him represent them, and that if they did decide to sue they would go to their own lawyer. Ohralik insisted that the girl had entered into a binding agreement; he refused to withdraw and ultimately tried to get the girl to pay him $2,466.66, representing one-third of his estimate of the worth of her claim.

The first girl also fired Ohralik and hired another lawyer to settle her claim. Ohralik sued her for breach of the contingent fee agreement, and he recovered $4,166.66, one-third of what she had received. After both girls complained to the state bar, Ohralik was suspended indefinitely from law practice.

The U.S. Supreme Court affirmed the disciplinary order, rejecting Ohralik's claim that the First Amendment protected his conduct. Unlike the advertisements approved in *Bates,* the Court said, in-person solicitation of fee-paying legal business poses significant dangers for the lay person who gets solicited. The lay person can be subjected to a high pressure sales pitch that demands immediate response and gives no time for comparison and reflection. Further, in-person solicitation gives no opportunity for counter-information by the organized bar, or others who might offer calmer advice.

Ohralik conceded that the state had a compelling interest in preventing fraud, undue influence, intimidation, overreaching, and other forms of vexatious conduct; however, he argued that the state could not discipline him without proving that his particular acts produced one of those evils. In short, Ohralik argued that the state must prove actual harm.

The Court rejected his argument, holding that a state may adopt prophylactic rules that forbid in-person solicitation of fee-generating legal business under circumstances that are likely to produce fraud, undue influence, or similar evils. Further, such a rule could be applied against Ohralik because he approached the girls when they were especially vulnerable, he urged his services upon them, he used a concealed tape recorder, he described his fee arrangement in a slick and tantalizing manner, and he refused to withdraw when asked to do so. All of this created a clear potential for overreaching, sufficient to justify the discipline imposed. [*Compare Ohralik with Edenfield v. Fane,* 507 U.S. 761, 113 S.Ct. 1792, 123 L.Ed.2d 543 (1993), which struck down a prophylactic rule against in-person solicitation by accountants. The Court said that accountants, unlike lawyers, are not trained in the arts of persuasion, and accountants' clients are less likely to be duped than lawyers' clients. Do you agree?]

The second of the two solicitation cases, *Ohralik v. Ohio State Bar Ass'n*, 436 U.S. 447, 98 S.Ct. 1912, 56 L.Ed.2d 444 (1978), offers a sharp contrast to the ambulance-chasing in *Ohralik*. Edna Smith Primus, a private practitioner in South Carolina, was a member and officer in the local chapter of the American Civil Liberties Union. At the request of another organization, she met with some women who allegedly had been sterilized, or threatened with sterilization, as a condition of receiving Medicaid benefits. She informed the women of their legal rights and suggested the possibility of a lawsuit. Later, the ACLU informed Primus that it would supply free legal counsel to the women who had been sterilized by one Dr. Clovis Pierce. Primus wrote a letter to one of the women to inform her of the ACLU offer. South Carolina publicly reprimanded Primus for solicitation.

In overturning the South Carolina reprimand, the U.S. Supreme Court distinguished Primus's conduct from Ohralik's conduct, saying that Primus had not been guilty of "in-person solicitation for pecuniary gain," but had simply conveyed an offer of free legal help by a recognized civil rights group. Further, the motive was partly political. Civil rights cases such as *NAACP v. Button*, 371 U.S. 415, 83 S.Ct. 328, 9 L.Ed.2d 405 (1963), establish that the First Amendment protects collective activity undertaken to gain meaningful access to courts and that the government can regulate such activity only with narrow specificity. The ACLU was seeking to use the sterilization litigation as a vehicle for political expression and association, as well as a means of communicating useful information to the public. That kind of speech is more precious than the commercial speech in *Ohralik*. Accordingly, the states may not regulate it without showing *actual* abuse; a showing of potential abuse is not enough. Since there was no evidence that Primus had overreached, or misrepresented, or invaded anyone's privacy, the discipline imposed on her was unconstitutional.

Could you draft a manageable disciplinary rule that embodies the Supreme Court's distinctions between Ohralik's conduct and Primus's conduct? How did the drafters of ABA Model Rule 7.3 deal with the problem? How did the drafters of CRPC 1–400 deal with the problem?

C. The Adoption of the ABA Model Rules

In 1983, the ABA House of Delegates adopted the ABA Model Rules, which included liberal provisions on advertising and solicitation that were drafted to comply with *In re R.M.J.*, 455 U.S. 191, 102 S.Ct. 929, 71 L.Ed.2d 64 (1982). In that case a unanimous Court ruled that under the commercial speech doctrine a state may flatly prohibit lawyer advertising that is false or misleading, and that a state may regulate advertising that is *not* misleading if the state can demonstrate that the regulation serves a substantial state interest, and that the regulation is no more extensive than is necessary to serve that interest.

In the years since 1983, the advertising and solicitation provisions of the ABA Model Rules have been amended several times, to keep up with the Supreme Court's decisions in the area.

D. The California Rules on Advertising and Solicitation

Like the ABA Model Rules, CRPC 1–400 was drafted to comply with the United States Supreme Court commercial speech decisions, and it has been amended several times to keep current with those decisions. One unique feature of California's approach is the California Standards for Attorney Communications (printed after CRPC 1–400). The standards create a set of rebuttable presumptions that certain kinds of advertising statements are misleading. The presumptions shift the burden of proof to the attorney in a disciplinary proceeding. Suppose, for example, that the state bar seeks to discipline an attorney for advertising that includes a guarantee or prediction about the outcome of a legal matter. The attorney would carry the burden of proving by a preponderance of the evidence that the guarantee or prediction was *not* misleading.

The California legislature has also gotten into the act by passing some attorney advertising statutes, Cal.Bus. & Prof.C. §§ 6157–6159.2. In some respects, the statutes are more restrictive than CRPC 1–400. After reading them, you can decide for yourself whether the statutes are a valuable addition to the law in this field.

E. The *Peel* case—Claims of Specialization

Unlike the medical profession, the organized bar has been slow to recognize specialization. As originally drafted, ABA Model Rule 7.4 allowed a lawyer to tell the public that she practices in a certain field, or that she restricts her practice to a certain field. However, the original rule prohibited a lawyer from stating or implying that she is a "specialist" in a field, subject to three exceptions:

- A lawyer admitted to practice in the U.S. Patent and Trademark Office could call herself a "patent attorney," or something similar;

- A lawyer engaged in admiralty practice could call herself a "proctor in admiralty," or something similar; and

- A lawyer could call herself a "certified specialist" in a field of law if she had been certified by the bar of her state.

Peel v. Attorney Reg. & Disciplinary Com'n, 496 U.S. 91, 110 S.Ct. 2281, 110 L.Ed.2d 83 (1990), involved a lawyer who had been certified as a specialist in trial advocacy, not by the bar of his state, but rather by the National Board of Trial Advocacy, a private organization that uses high, rigorously-enforced standards for certifying trial advocates. *Peel* establishes that a lawyer who is certified under those circumstances may call himself a certified specialist, provided that he identifies the organization that certified him and takes related steps to avoid misleading the public. ABA Model Rule 7.4 was subsequently amended to accord with the *Peel* decision. Similarly, California Standard for Attorney Communications 11 creates a presumption that it is misleading for an attorney to state or imply that she is a "certified specialist" unless she names the entity that certified her.

F. The *Zauderer, Shapero,* and *Went For It* cases—The Shadowland between Advertising and Solicitation

Zauderer v. Office of Disciplinary Counsel of the Supreme Court of Ohio, 471 U.S. 626, 105 S.Ct. 2265, 85 L.Ed.2d 652 (1985), involved a lawyer who placed a newspaper ad that was aimed at a narrow audience—users of the Dalkon Shield, an intrauterine contraceptive device that allegedly injured many women. A divided Court held that Zauderer could not be disciplined simply for placing an ad that concerned a specific legal problem and that was designed to lure a narrow group of potential clients. (He could, however, be disciplined for a misleading statement in the ad.) Justice O'Connor (joined by Burger, C.J. and Rehnquist, J.) dissented in part, arguing that the states should be free to prohibit lawyers from using ads that contain "free samples" of legal advice. Ordinary merchants can offer free samples of their wares, Justice O'Connor argued, but free samples of legal advice are too likely to mislead laypersons, who often lack the knowledge and experience to judge the sample before they buy.

If narrowly targeted newspaper ads are permissible, then what about solicitation letters mailed to potential clients whom the lawyer knows to be facing a specific, present legal problem? The Court answered that question in *Shapero v. Kentucky Bar Ass'n,* 486 U.S. 466, 108 S.Ct. 1916, 100 L.Ed.2d 475 (1988). Lawyer Shapero wanted to mail solicitation letters (which were assumed to be truthful and not misleading) to people he knew were facing foreclosure on their homes for failure to pay their debts. A slim majority of the Supreme Court held in Shapero's favor. The majority said the solicitation letters were more analogous to the targeted newspaper ads in *Zauderer* than they were to the in-person solicitation in *Ohralik.* In-person solicitation creates a grave risk that the lawyer will invade the client's privacy, overreach, or use undue influence. That risk is far less with a letter, which the recipient can set aside for later study, ignore entirely, or simply throw in the trash. Moreover, in-person solicitation cannot be policed because it happens in private and there is usually no certain proof of who said what, but solicitation letters can be policed by requiring copies to be sent to the regulatory agency. Thus, a state cannot ban solicitation letters outright, but it *can* impose *reasonable regulations* on their use.

In a vigorous dissent, Justice O'Connor (joined by Chief Justice Rehnquist and Justice Scalia) called for a reconsideration of the *Bates* case, which you read above. According to Justice O'Connor, *Bates* accepted a simplistic economics argument that attorney advertising would increase competition, raise quality, and lower price. That would be true in markets for ordinary goods, and it might even be true in the short run in the market for legal services. But in the long run, Justice O'Connor argued, allowing attorneys to hawk their wares will eventually destroy the professionalism that limits the "unique power" attorneys wield in our political system. If Justice O'Connor had it her way, states would have "considerable latitude" to ban advertising that is even "potentially" misleading and to ban even truthful advertising that undermines the substantial governmental interest in promoting high ethical standards in the legal profession.

As you will see below, Justice O'Connor did have it her way, at least partly, in *Florida Bar v. Went for It, Inc.*, 515 U.S. ___, 115 S.Ct. 2371, 132 L.Ed.2d 541 (1995). Writing for herself and four colleagues, she upheld a Florida rule that prohibits lawyers from mailing solicitation letters to victims and their families for 30 days following an accident.

FLORIDA BAR v. WENT FOR IT, INC.

Supreme Court of the United States, 1995.
515 U.S. ___, 115 S.Ct. 2371, 132 L.Ed.2d 541.

O'CONNOR, J. delivered the opinion of the Court, in which REHNQUIST, C.J., and SCALIA, THOMAS, and BREYER, JJ., joined.

Rules of the Florida Bar prohibit personal injury lawyers from sending targeted direct-mail solicitations to victims and their relatives for 30 days following an accident or disaster. This case asks us to consider whether such rules violate the First and Fourteenth Amendments of the Constitution. We hold that in the circumstances presented here, they do not.

* * *

[After a two year study of the effects of lawyer advertising on the public, the Florida Bar adopted rule 4–7.4(B)(1) which] provides that "[a] lawyer shall not send, or knowingly permit to be sent, ... a written communication to a prospective client for the purpose of obtaining professional employment if: (A) the written communication concerns an action for personal injury or wrongful death or otherwise relates to an accident or disaster involving the person to whom the communication is addressed or a relative of that person, unless the accident or disaster occurred more than 30 days prior to the mailing of the communication." * * *

* * *

[A Florida lawyer and his wholly-owned lawyer referral service challenged the rule. Relying on *Bates* and its progeny, the district court and the court of appeals held the rule unconstitutional. After reviewing the history of the commercial speech doctrine, Justice O'Connor wrote:]

Nearly two decades of cases have built upon the foundation laid by *Bates*. It is now well established that lawyer advertising is commercial speech and, as such, is accorded a measure of First Amendment protection. See, *e.g., Shapero v. Kentucky Bar Ass'n*, 486 U.S. 466, 472, 108 S.Ct. 1916, 1921, 100 L.Ed.2d 475 (1988); *Zauderer v. Office of Disciplinary Counsel of Supreme Court of Ohio*, 471 U.S. 626, 637, 105 S.Ct.

2265, 2274, 85 L.Ed.2d 652 (1985); *In re R.M.J.*, 455 U.S. 191, 199, 102 S.Ct. 929, 935, 71 L.Ed.2d 64 (1982). Such First Amendment protection, of course, is not absolute. We have always been careful to distinguish commercial speech from speech at the First Amendment's core. " '[C]ommercial speech [enjoys] a limited measure of protection, commensurate with its subordinate position in the scale of First Amendment values,' and is subject to 'modes of regulation that might be impermissible in the realm of noncommercial expression.' " *Board of Trustees of State University of N.Y. v. Fox,* 492 U.S. 469, 477, 109 S.Ct. 3028, 3033, 106 L.Ed.2d 388 (1989), quoting *Ohralik v. Ohio State Bar Assn.,* 436 U.S. 447, 456, 98 S.Ct. 1912, 56 L.Ed.2d 444 (1978). We have observed that " '[t]o require a parity of constitutional protection for commercial and noncommercial speech alike could invite dilution, simply by a leveling process, of the force of the Amendment's guarantee with respect to the latter kind of speech.' " 492 U.S., at 481, 109 S.Ct., at 3035, quoting *Ohralik, supra,* 436 U.S., at 456, 98 S.Ct., at 1918.

Mindful of these concerns, we engage in "intermediate" scrutiny of restrictions on commercial speech, analyzing them under the framework set forth in *Central Hudson Gas & Electric Corp. v. Public Service Comm'n of N.Y.,* 447 U.S. 557, 100 S.Ct. 2343, 65 L.Ed.2d 341 (1980). Under *Central Hudson,* the government may freely regulate commercial speech that concerns unlawful activity or is misleading. Commercial speech that falls into neither of those categories, like the advertising at issue here, may be regulated if the government satisfies a test consisting of three related prongs: first, the government must assert a substantial interest in support of its regulation; second, the government must demonstrate that the restriction on commercial speech directly and materially advances that interest; and third, the regulation must be " 'narrowly drawn.' " * * *

* * *

The Florida Bar asserts that it has a substantial interest in protecting the privacy and tranquility of personal injury victims and their loved ones against intrusive, unsolicited contact by lawyers. * * * This interest obviously factors into the Bar's paramount (and repeatedly professed) objective of curbing activities that "negatively affec[t] the administration of justice." * * *

The regulation, then, is an effort to protect the flagging reputations of Florida lawyers by preventing them from engaging in conduct that, the Bar maintains, " 'is universally regarded as deplorable and beneath common decency because of its intrusion upon the special vulnerability and private grief of victims or their families.' "

We have little trouble crediting the Bar's interest as substantial. On various occasions we have accepted the proposition that "States have a compelling interest in the practice of professions within their boundaries, and ... as part of their power to protect the public health, safety, and other valid interests they have broad power to establish standards for licensing practitioners and regulating the practice of professions."

Goldfarb v. Virginia State Bar, 421 U.S. 773, 792, 95 S.Ct. 2004, 2016, 44 L.Ed.2d 572 (1975); see also *Ohralik, supra,* 436 U.S., at 460, 98 S.Ct., at 1920–1921; *Cohen v. Hurley,* 366 U.S. 117, 124, 81 S.Ct. 954, 958–959, 6 L.Ed.2d 156 (1961). Our precedents also leave no room for doubt that "the protection of potential clients' privacy is a substantial state interest." See *Edenfield v. Fane,* 507 U.S. 761, 769, 113 S.Ct. 1792, 1799, 123 L.Ed.2d 543 (1993). In other contexts, we have consistently recognized that "[t]he State's interest in protecting the well-being, tranquility, and privacy of the home is certainly of the highest order in a free and civilized society." *Carey v. Brown,* 447 U.S. 455, 471, 100 S.Ct. 2286, 2295–2296, 65 L.Ed.2d 263 (1980). Indeed, we have noted that "a special benefit of the privacy all citizens enjoy within their own walls, which the State may legislate to protect, is an ability to avoid intrusions." *Frisby v. Schultz,* 487 U.S. 474, 484–485, 108 S.Ct. 2495, 2502–2503, 101 L.Ed.2d 420 (1988).

Under *Central Hudson's* second prong, the State must demonstrate that the challenged regulation "advances the Government's interest 'in a direct and material way.' " * * *

* * *

[The state cannot rely on speculation or conjecture; it must demonstrate that the harms it recites are real, and that the regulation will in fact alleviate them to a material degree.]

The Florida Bar submitted a 106–page summary of its 2–year study of lawyer advertising and solicitation to the District Court. That summary contains data—both statistical and anecdotal—supporting the Bar's contentions that the Florida public views direct-mail solicitations in the immediate wake of accidents as an intrusion on privacy that reflects poorly upon the profession. As of June 1989, lawyers mailed 700,000 direct solicitations in Florida annually, 40% of which were aimed at accident victims or their survivors. * * * A survey of Florida adults commissioned by the Bar indicated that Floridians "have negative feelings about those attorneys who use direct mail advertising." * * * Fifty–four percent of the general population surveyed said that contacting persons concerning accidents or similar events is a violation of privacy. * * * A random sampling of persons who received direct-mail advertising from lawyers in 1987 revealed that 45% believed that direct-mail solicitation is "designed to take advantage of gullible or unstable people"; 34% found such tactics "annoying or irritating"; 26% found it "an invasion of your privacy"; and 24% reported that it "made you angry." * * * Significantly, 27% of direct-mail recipients reported that their regard for the legal profession and for the judicial process as a whole was "lower" as a result of receiving the direct mail. * * *

The anecdotal record mustered by the Bar is noteworthy for its breadth and detail. With titles like "Scavenger Lawyers" (The Miami Herald, Sept. 29, 1987) and "Solicitors Out of Bounds" (St. Petersburg Times, Oct. 26, 1987), newspaper editorial pages in Florida have burgeoned with criticism of Florida lawyers who send targeted direct mail to victims shortly after accidents. The study summary also includes page upon page of excerpts from complaints of direct-mail recipients. For example, a Florida citizen described how he was " 'appalled and angered by the brazen attempt' " of a law firm to solicit him by letter shortly after he was injured and his fiancee was killed in an auto accident. * * * Another found it " 'despicable and inexcusable' " that a Pensacola lawyer wrote to his mother three days after his father's funeral. * * * Another described how she was " 'astounded' " and then " 'very angry' " when she received a solicitation following a minor accident. * * * Still another described as " 'beyond comprehension' " a letter his nephew's family received the day of the nephew's funeral. * * * One citizen wrote, " 'I consider the unsolicited contact from you after my child's accident to be of the rankest form of ambulance chasing and in incredibly poor taste.... I cannot begin to express with my limited vocabulary the utter contempt in which I hold you and your kind.' " * * * [W]e conclude that the Bar has satisfied the second prong of the *Central Hudson* test. * * *

[T]he Court of Appeals determined that this case was governed squarely by Shapero v. Kentucky Bar Assn., 486 U.S. 466, 108 S.Ct. 1916, 100 L.Ed.2d 475 (1988). Making no mention of the Bar's study, the court concluded that " 'a targeted letter [does not] invade the recipient's privacy any more than does a substantively identical letter mailed at large. The invasion, if any, occurs when the lawyer discovers the recipient's legal affairs, not when he confronts the recipient with the discovery.' " In many cases, the Court of Appeals explained, "this invasion of privacy will involve no more than reading the newspaper."

While some of *Shapero*'s language might be read to support the Court of Appeals' interpretation, *Shapero* differs in several fundamental respects from the case before us. First and foremost, *Shapero*'s treatment of privacy was casual. * * * [T]he State in *Shapero* did not seek to justify its regulation as a measure undertaken to prevent lawyers' invasions of privacy interests. * * * Rather, the State focused exclusively on the special dangers of overreaching inhering in targeted solicitations. * * * Second, in contrast to this case, *Shapero* dealt with a broad ban on all direct-mail solicitations, whatever the time frame and whoever the recipient. Finally, the State in *Shapero* assembled no evidence attempting to demonstrate any actual harm caused by targeted direct mail. The Court rejected the State's effort to justify a prophylactic ban on the basis of blanket, untested assertions of undue influence and overreaching. 486 U.S., at 475, 108 S.Ct., at 1922–1923. Because the State did not make a privacy-based argument at all, its empirical showing on that issue was similarly infirm.

* * *

[In the present case,] the harm targeted by the Florida Bar cannot be eliminated by a brief journey to the trash can. The purpose of the 30–day targeted direct-mail ban is to forestall the outrage and irritation with the state-licensed legal profession that the practice of direct solicitation only days after accidents has engendered. The Bar is concerned not with citizens' "offense" in the abstract, but with the demonstrable detrimental effects that such "offense" has on the profession it regulates. * * * Moreover, the harm posited by the Bar is as much a function of simple receipt of targeted solicitations within days of accidents as it is a function of the letters' contents. Throwing the letter away shortly after opening it may minimize the latter intrusion, but it does little to combat the former. * * *

Passing to *Central Hudson*'s third prong, we examine the relationship between the Florida Bar's interests and the means chosen to serve them. See *Board of Trustees of State University of N.Y. v. Fox,* 492 U.S., at 480, 109 S.Ct., at 3034–3035. With respect to this prong, the differences between commercial speech and noncommercial speech are manifest. In *Fox,* we made clear that the "least restrictive means" test has no role in the commercial speech context. "What our decisions require," instead, "is a 'fit' between the legislature's ends and the means chosen to accomplish those ends," a fit that is not necessarily perfect, but reasonable; that represents not necessarily the single best disposition but one whose scope is 'in proportion to the interest served,' that employs not necessarily the least restrictive means but ... a means narrowly tailored to achieve the desired objective." *Ibid.* (citations omitted). Of course, we do not equate this test with the less rigorous obstacles of rational basis review; in *Cincinnati v. Discovery Network, Inc.,* 507 U.S. ___, ___, n. 13, 113 S.Ct. 1505, 1510 n. 13, 123 L.Ed.2d 99 (1993), for example, we observed that the existence of "numerous and obvious less-burdensome alternatives to the restriction on commercial speech ... is certainly a relevant consideration in determining whether the 'fit' between ends and means is reasonable."

* * *

[Our view of this case might differ] if the Bar's rule were not limited to a brief period and if there were not many other ways for injured Floridians to learn about the availability of legal representation during that time. Our lawyer advertising cases have afforded lawyers a great deal of leeway to devise innovative ways to attract new business. Florida permits lawyers to advertise on prime-time television and radio as well as in newspapers and other media. They may rent space on billboards. They may send untargeted letters to the general population, or to discrete segments thereof. There are, of course, pages upon pages devoted to lawyers in the Yellow Pages of Florida telephone directories. * * * [T]he record contains considerable empirical survey information suggesting that Floridians have little difficulty finding lawyers when they need one. * * * Finding no basis to question the commonsense conclusion that the many alternative channels for communicating necessary information about attorneys are sufficient, we see no defect in Florida's regulation.

Speech by professionals obviously has many dimensions. There are circumstances in which we will accord speech by attorneys on public issues and matters of legal representation the strongest protection our Constitution has to offer. See, *e.g., Gentile v. State Bar of Nevada,* 501 U.S. 1030, 111 S.Ct. 2720, 115 L.Ed.2d 888 (1991); *In re Primus,* 436 U.S. 412, 98 S.Ct. 1893, 56 L.Ed.2d 417 (1978). This case, however, concerns pure commercial advertising, for which we have always reserved a lesser degree of protection under the First Amendment. Particularly because the standards and conduct of state-licensed lawyers have traditionally been subject to extensive regulation by the States, it is all the more appropriate that we limit our scrutiny of state regulations to a level commensurate with the " 'subordinate position' " of commercial speech in the scale of First Amendment values. *Fox,* 492 U.S., at 477, 109 S.Ct., at 3033, quoting *Ohralik,* 436 U.S., at 456, 98 S.Ct., at 1918–1919.

We believe that the Florida Bar's 30–day restriction on targeted direct-mail solicitation of accident victims and their relatives withstands scrutiny under the three-part *Central Hudson* test that we have devised for this context. The Bar has substantial interest both in protecting injured Floridians from invasive conduct by lawyers and in preventing the erosion of confidence in the profession that such repeated invasions have engendered. The Bar's proffered study, unrebutted by respondents below, provides evidence indicating that the harms it targets are far from illusory. The palliative devised by the Bar to address these harms is narrow both in scope and in duration. The Constitution, in our view, requires nothing more.

The judgment of the Court of Appeals, accordingly, is *reversed.*

[We have omitted the dissenting opinion of Justice Kennedy, joined by Justices Stevens, Souter, and Ginsburg.]

MULTIPLE CHOICE QUESTIONS

Follow the multiple choice instructions on page 55, above.

1. Mark Norris is a newscaster for the local television station. Every weeknight, following the evening news, he presents a ten-minute segment entitled "This Funny Town." It is patterned on an old-fashioned newspaper gossip column. Most of it concerns the private lives and peccadilloes of the prominent and would-be prominent citizens of the community. Judges and lawyers are among Mr. Norris's favorite subjects. He and attorney Philos have arrived at a tacit arrangement. Whenever Philos hears a piece of juicy gossip about a local judge or lawyer, he passes it along to Norris. In return, Norris frequently recommends Philos's legal services in his broadcasts. For example, Norris calls Philos "a fearless courtroom ace," or he states opinions such as: "if you want to win your case, hire Philos." Is Philos *subject to discipline?*

    A. Yes, because Philos is compensating Norris for recommending his services.

B. Yes, because a lawyer can be disciplined for demeaning other members of the legal profession.

C. No, unless he gives false or privileged information to Norris.

D. No, because Philos's conduct is a protected form of speech under the First and Fourteenth Amendments.

2. Three years ago, attorneys Hooten and Snod formed a law partnership called Hooten & Snod. A year later, Hooten died, and Snod continued practicing under the former firm name. Then Snod hired a salaried associate, attorney Tremble, and, the firm name was changed to Hooten, Snod & Tremble. The following year, Snod left law practice to become a commissioner on the Federal Trade Commission. Tremble took over the practice and continued to use the same name. Later, because he had more space in the office than he needed, he entered into a space-sharing agreement with attorney Gangler. The sign on the door now reads Tremble & Gangler, Attorneys at Law. Which of the following are correct?

I. After Hooten died, it was *proper* for Snod to continue using the firm name Hooten & Snod.

II. When Snod hired Tremble, it was *proper* to change the firm name to Hooten, Snod & Tremble.

III. After Snod joined the FTC, it was *proper* for Tremble to continue using Snod as part of the firm name.

IV. The present sign on the door is *proper*.

A. All of the above.

B. I, II, and III only.

C. I and II only.

D. I only.

3. Attorney Anton advertised on the local television station. His advertisement stated in relevant part: "The most I will charge you for any type of legal work is $100 per hour, and if your problem is not complicated, the hourly fee will be even lower." Which of the following propositions are correct?

I. If Anton does not retain a recording of the advertisement for at least two years, he will be *subject to discipline*.

II. If Anton charges $125 per hour for complicated legal work, he will be *subject to discipline* for using a misleading advertisement.

III. If Anton's advertisement fails to state that some other lawyers in the community charge substantially lower fees, he will be *subject to discipline*.

A. Only II is correct.

B. Only I and III are correct.

C. Only I and II are correct.

D. Only II and III are correct.

4. Lawyer Del Campos practices in a town in which 25% of the people are Mexican–American and another 20% have recently immigrated to the United States from Mexico. The bar of his state does not certify specialists in any field of law, but Del Campos has been certified as a specialist in immigration law by the American Association of Immigration Attorneys, a private organization with high, rigorously enforced standards. Del Campos wants to put an advertisement in the classified section of the local telephone book. Which of the following items of information *may* he include in his advertisement?

I. That he "serves clients who are members of the Continental Prepaid Legal Service Plan."

II. That he "speaks Spanish."

III. That he has been "certified as an immigration specialist by the American Association of Immigration Attorneys."

IV. That he can "arrange credit for fee payments."

     A. All of the above.

     B. None of the above.

     C. I, II, and IV only.

     D. I and III only.

5. Attorney Salmon published a brochure entitled, "What to Do When You Are Injured." It contains accurate, helpful information on obtaining medical treatment, recording details of the event, notifying insurance companies, not making harmful statements, and the like. The cover of the brochure identifies Salmon as a "Personal Injury Attorney" and gives his office address and telephone number. One afternoon, Salmon was standing in a crowd of people that saw a pregnant woman knocked down in a pedestrian crosswalk by a speeding car. A few days later, Salmon mailed the woman a copy of his brochure, together with a letter stating that he had witnessed the accident and was willing to represent her for a reasonable fee should she wish to sue the car driver. The bar in Salmon's state does not have a 30-day waiting period of the kind involved in *Went For It, Inc.*, above.

     A. Salmon is *subject to discipline,* both for sending the woman the brochure and for sending her the letter.

     B. Salmon is *subject to discipline* for sending the woman the letter, but not for sending her the brochure.

     C. Salmon is *subject to discipline* for offering his legal services, for a fee, to a person who was not a relative, client, or former client.

     D. Salmon's conduct was *proper.*

6. Attorney Gresler offered a free half-day seminar for nurses, hospital attendants, and emergency medical personnel on personal injury law as it relates to accident victims. During the seminar, he told the group about the importance of preserving items of physical evidence,

keeping accurate records of medical treatment, accurately recording statements made by the victim and others about the accident, and the like. At the close of the seminar, he passed out packets of his professional cards and invited the members of the group to give them to accident victims.

    A.   Gresler's conduct was *proper* in all respects.

    B.   Gresler is *subject to discipline* for passing out his professional cards and inviting the group to distribute them to accident victims.

    C.   Gresler is *subject to discipline* for holding the seminar and for asking the group to distribute his professional cards to accident victims.

    D.   Gresler is *subject to discipline* for giving legal advice to the members of the group, assuming that he had no prior professional relationship with them.

7.   After their graduation from law school, three young women formed a partnership to open a new law firm. They would like to call their firm the "Women's Law Collective." *May* they do so?

    A.   Yes, the use of a tradename is permitted in these circumstances.

    B.   No, because a law firm cannot use a tradename.

    C.   Yes, provided that they expand the tradename to include their own surnames.

    D.   No, because the use of a tradename for a law firm is deceptive.

8.   The firm of Wilkens & Crosse has existed for many years in Chicago. Now it wishes to open an office in Los Angeles. The Los Angeles office will be established as a separate partnership. Some of the proposed Los Angeles partners are admitted to practice only in California, and they will not become partners in the Chicago firm. Some of the Chicago partners are admitted to practice in both Illinois and California; they will retain their partnership in the Chicago firm, and they will also become partners in the Los Angeles firm. The letterheads of both firms will accurately identify which lawyers are admitted to practice in which jurisdictions. The two firms will regularly refer work back and forth, and each firm will be available to the other firm and its clients for consultation and advice. Further, on some occasions, partners and associates will be transferred from one firm to the other. Each firm will advertise itself as an "affiliate" of the other firm. Is the arrangement *proper*?

    A.   Yes, provided that the nature of the "affiliate relationship" is explained.

    B.   Yes, because "affiliate" is a broad term that can cover many kinds of relationships.

C.   No, because a partner of a firm in one state is not permitted to be a partner of a firm in a different state.

D.   No, because the arrangement contemplates the referral of work from one firm to the other in violation of the solicitation rule.

Answers to the multiple choice questions will be found in the Appendix at the back of the book

Chapter Five

ATTORNEY FEES AND FIDUCIARY DUTIES

What This Chapter Covers

I. **Attorney Fees**
    A.   Setting Fees
        1.   Excessive Fees
        2.   Factors in Fee Setting
        3.   Contingent Fees
    B.   Lending Money to Clients
    C.   Fee Forfeiture and Related Issues
    D.   Splitting Fees With Other Lawyers

II. **Fiduciary Duties**
    A.   Commingling
    B.   Safeguarding Property
    C.   Notifying Clients, Keeping Records, and Paying Promptly

Reading Assignment

Wydick & Perschbacher, Chapter 5

ABA Model Rules:

    Rules 1.5, 1.8(e), 1.15 and 3.8(f).

CRPC 2–200, 4–100, 4–200, and 4–210.

Cal.Bus. & Prof.Code §§ 6146–6149.5, 6210–6212.

Supplemental Reading

ABA Code:

    EC 2–16 through 2–23,

    EC 5–7 through 5–8, and EC 9–5;

    DR 2–106 through 2–107, DR 5–103, and DR 9–102.

Hazard & Hodes:

    Discussion of ABA Model Rules 1.5, 1.8(e), and 1.15.

Wolfram:

> Sections 9.2.1 through 9.2.4 (lawyer-client contracts, fees, and fee splitting);
>
> Sections 9.3.1 through 9.4.5 (various kinds of fee arrangements);
>
> Section 4.8 (safekeeping client funds and property).

Restatement (Third) of the Law Governing Lawyers §§ 46–58 (Proposed Final Draft No. 1, 1996).

Discussion Problems

1. After graduating from law school three years ago, Dolores became a solo practitioner in a medium-sized city. She has a general civil and criminal practice, and she puts in about 60 hours a week at the office. That yields her a weekly average of 40 billable hours. She takes a two-week vacation in the summer and another two weeks spread throughout the rest of the year. She and some other solo practitioners occupy a nicely furnished suite of offices under a lease-service arrangement. The leasing company provides them a good law library and also provides receptionist, secretary, delivery, and photocopy services. The lease-service fee plus Dolores's other overhead expenses total about $7,000 per month.

House painter Leonard wants Dolores to represent him in a dispute with an unhappy customer over a $6,000 unpaid painting bill. Dolores offers to handle the matter for an hourly fee, but Leonard wants a flat fee set in advance. Dolores has not handled precisely this kind of case before, and she knows that she will have to do about two hours worth of basic legal research that would be unnecessary for a more experienced lawyer. She estimates that, in addition to the two hours basic research, it will take her about 10 billable hours to complete the matter. Assume that the average lawyer in the community would charge Leonard about $1,000.

    a. What do you think would be a fair fee for Dolores to charge Leonard? How did you arrive at that figure?

    b. Suppose that Dolores quotes Leonard a flat fee of $1,500 and that they make an oral agreement to that effect. Is Dolores subject to discipline?

    c. Suppose Leonard wants a contingent fee rather than a flat fee. Dolores agrees to take the case for 35% of whatever amount she recovers for Leonard. Under what, if any, circumstances would that be proper?

    d. Suppose that Leonard paints portraits rather than houses, and that the amount in controversy is $60,000 rather than $6,000. How, if at all, would that change your estimate of a fair fee?

2. Attorney Kimberly represents client Marsha in a divorce proceeding in a noncommunity property jurisdiction. Marsha was married for 25 years to a successful business executive. Their two children have grown up and left home. Marsha has no independent wealth, nor has she any marketable job skills. Kimberly anticipates that the court will award Marsha a large sum of money when it grants the divorce.

    a. May Kimberly represent Marsha on a 25% contingent fee basis?

    b. May Kimberly advance the court costs, the investigation costs, the deposition reporter costs, and the like?

    c. Marsha has moved out of the family home, pending the divorce, and the court has been slow in acting on Kimberly's motion for a temporary living allowance. May Kimberly lend Marsha enough to make ends meet until the court acts?

3. Martin, a general business lawyer, has handled the affairs of Perello & Sons Plumbing Supply Co. for the past fifteen years. Old Mr. Perello and his two sons trust Martin implicitly, a sharp contrast to their attitude toward the rest of the legal profession. Martin believes that the Perellos have an excellent antitrust claim against a plumbing fixtures manufacturer who has refused to deal with them. Martin has a fair command of basic antitrust principles, but he knows he is no trial lawyer. He therefore takes the Perellos to see Cyrus, an antitrust litigator who customarily takes plaintiffs' cases on a contingent fee basis. To their considerable surprise, the Perellos discover that Cyrus is a decent human being, and they hire him on a contingent fee basis. But, just to make sure that Cyrus doesn't get out of hand, they want Martin to follow the case closely and to be prepared to advise them at any point along the way.

    a. How can Martin, Cyrus, and the Perellos arrange this in a way that is ethical and that protects each of their respective interests?

    b. Is there more than one way to do it?

4. Dringle bought a sailboat and a motorboat from Seaboard Marine Supply Company on credit, and he failed to make timely payments on either boat. Seaboard hired attorney Welch to collect the two debts. Welch sent a series of appropriate demand letters to Dringle. Finally, Dringle left a check, a message, and a set of keys at Welch's office. The message said: "Here is a check for the $7,500 I owe Seaboard on the sailboat. I have no way to pay for the motorboat, so here are the keys to it; you will find it tied to the dock at the City Marina." At the time, Welch was in trial and working 16 hours a day, so she put the message, the check, and the keys in an envelope, labeled it "Seaboard Marine," and put the envelope in her office safe. Her trial ended two weeks later, and that very day she deposited the check in her client trust account and notified Seaboard about the keys and the location of the motorboat. Did Welch handle the matter properly?

5. Suppose that you are a skilled criminal defense lawyer. A man named Smith, previously unknown to you, asks you to represent him in an impending federal criminal investigation. Smith tells you that he is the head of a church that solicits contributions by mail, telephone, and television and that the contributions are used to fund missionary activities in the United States and abroad. The federal prosecutor apparently contends that Smith's church is in fact an organized crime syndicate that uses a regular pattern of mail fraud and wire fraud to bilk millions of dollars from gullible people. Based on your initial conversation with Smith, you conclude that the case is loaded with difficult issues of criminal and constitutional law. Smith offers to pay you at your regular hourly rate, and from his briefcase he produces $15,000 in cash, to be used as an advance on attorney fees. What factors will you consider in deciding whether to represent Smith? If you decide to represent him, what will you do with respect to the $15,000 fee advance?

6. Attorney Arner agreed to represent client Corman in a suit against defendant Drews. Arner's written fee agreement with Corman provided that Arner would receive $75 per hour for his work, and that the fee "may be deducted from the proceeds of said litigation before payment thereof to" Corman. Corman won a judgment for $50,000, and Drews sent Arner a check in that amount, made payable to Corman. Arner consulted his time records and concluded that he had spent 153.3 hours on the case, for a total fee of $11,500. Arner endorsed the check with Corman's name and presented it at the bank where he maintained his client trust account. He had $38,500 deposited in the client trust account, and he took the other $11,500 in the form of a bank cashier's check, made payable to him personally. That same day, he wrote to Corman as follows:

> Drews' check came in today. I have expended 153.3 hours on the matter, for a total fee of $11,500. Accordingly, I am holding $38,500 for your account, and I will send you a check in that sum promptly upon receiving word from you that the fee computation is correct and in accordance with our agreement.

Did Arner handle the matter properly?

ROBERT L. WHEELER, INC. v. SCOTT

Supreme Court of Oklahoma, 1989.
777 P.2d 394.

KAUGER, JUSTICE.

The dispositive question is whether, after summary judgment was entered against Robert L. Scott (appellant/client) in a mortgage foreclosure proceeding, and after the trial court subsequently reduced the fee charged by Scott's attorney from $140,116.87 to $125,723.00, the fee was still excessive. After a careful examination of the standards enunciated in [prior cases,] we find that it was.

FACTS

* * * Robert L. Scott (client/appellant), a geologist and a geophysicist, hired Robert L. Wheeler (appellee/lawyer) to represent him after he was unable to pay a business loan. During the next ten months, Wheeler represented Scott in the collection and lien foreclosure action filed against Scott by the mortgagee, United Oklahoma Bank. In the first five months of Wheeler's representation, Scott was billed for legal services in the amount of $54,275.37 representing 524.5 hours and averaging 108.5 hours per month which he paid. During the next five months, Scott was billed $85,841.50 for legal services representing 753.4 hours, averaging 150.6 hours per month which he did not pay.

* * * [The bank then] moved for summary judgment. Two days before the hearing on the bank's motion, the lawyer told his client that if the attorney fees were not paid, he would withdraw from the case. Scott did not pay, and Wheeler did not withdraw. Instead, a first year associate was sent to oppose the bank's motion for summary judgment. The bank's motion was granted, and the attorney withdrew from the case * * *. Thereafter, Scott retained new counsel, and the case was settled.

* * * [Wheeler then] filed an action to collect unpaid attorney fees. Scott answered, asserting that the fees were excessive for the following reasons:

1) The case was never tried. Summary judgment was entered against him.

2) The client was billed a total of 1295.9 hours. However, a first year associate, who had failed to pass the bar at the first sitting, and who had been admitted to the bar for only five months before beginning work on the case, billed 853.5 hours at $110.00 an hour.

3) The firm representing the bank charged the bank $75,534.10 for 850 hours. These hours were for three attorneys with an average of ten to twenty years of experience, who normally bill at $150.00 an hour. However, because the lawyers are on retainer with the bank, they reduced their normal hourly rate in this case.

4) The bank's motion for summary judgment alleged that although a large amount of money and property was involved, the foreclosure was a simple case complicated by unfounded and legally unsound assertions by Scott's counsel. The bank's lawyer repeated these assertions at the hearing on attorney fees, and he also testified that his first year associates were billed at $85.00 an hour.

5) As prevailing party, the opposing attorney received $75,534.10 in attorney fees.

After hearing the evidence, the trial court reduced the hourly rate of the first year associate from $110.00 to $80.00, and the total attorney's fee from $140,116.87 to $125,723.00. Scott appealed. The Court of

Appeals affirmed * * *. We granted certiorari * * * to address the question of the reasonableness of the attorney fee.

* * *

A proper resolution of this case requires a thorough examination and balancing of the * * * [twelve factors we discuss below:] * * *

1. *Time and labor required*

The most visible and the most readily explainable portion of a bill for attorney fees is the time and labor expended by an attorney in performing services for a client. However, it is not the only relevant factor, and it must be considered in conjunction with the other enumerated criteria. Fees cannot be awarded on the basis of time alone—the use of time as the sole standard is of dubious value. Were fees to be calculated based only on the time spent on a case, worthy use of time would cease to be a virtue, a premium would be placed on inexperience, inefficiency, and inability, and expeditious disposition of litigation would go unrewarded.

Time spent in acquiring a basic law school education in the area of law concerned cannot be regarded as one of the determinative factors of a reasonable attorney fee. Attorneys are presumed to have acquired a working knowledge of fundamental legal principles as well as the ability to examine and apply the law. This does not mean that an attorney, within the limitations ordinarily necessary for a competent and skillful lawyer, should not be compensated for the time spent in necessary research. It does mean that if a lawyer takes on a case in an area in which he or she is totally unfamiliar or inexperienced, the client should not have to pay for every minute of the lawyer's preparation. Here, for example, a comparison of the time charged for preparation of the case by each of the law firms reflects that it is unlikely that billing 1295.9 billable hours, 853.5 of which were by a first year lawyer was proper when the prevailing law firm staffed by seasoned counsel charged for 850 hours. In short, a reasonable attorney's fee in a given case does not necessarily result from simple multiplication of the hours spent times a fixed hourly rate.

2. *Novelty or difficulty of issues*

The attorney for the prevailing party testified at the hearing, and he stated in his motion for summary judgment, that this was a simple case. He also noted that although a large sum of money was involved, the case had been unduly complicated by opposing counsel's unfounded and legally unsound assertions. One of the basic considerations in establishing the reasonable value of legal services is the type, extent, and difficulty of the services rendered. Substance must control over form. The intricacy and difficulty of the questions involved, and not necessarily the amount of manual legal work exhibited by the number of papers in the file of the case must control.

3. *The skill requisite to perform*

Another factor, which must be considered with the novelty or difficulty of the issues, is whether the services are routine, or whether exceptional skill or effort is required. Wheeler testified that he relied on his oil and gas expertise in designing his strategy. However, this expertise apparently did not come into play before summary judgment was entered because the attorney did not determine the value of the oil producing properties until after it was rendered. (The declining value of the properties was the reason given by the bank for settling the cause for less than the amount entered in its favor on summary judgment.)

4. *Loss of opportunity for other employment*

The fact that the employment for which compensation is sought deprived the attorney of the opportunity to secure other employment is another element of some significance in determining a reasonable fee. The court must consider not only the loss of other employment because of the time taken by the matter at hand, but also the fact that there may be involved in the matter certain elements which might cause the attorney to lose future business because of an association with the case. The attorney testified that this case neither required that he refuse to represent a potential client, nor did he introduce any evidence that his association with this case deprived him of future business.

5. *The customary fee*

Generally, courts consider the amounts customarily charged or allowed for similar services in the same locality. Only two witnesses were presented, and their testimony was conflicting. The expert called by Scott testified that the amount the prevailing party received, $75,-500.00, was reasonable compensation. The expert witness, who testified on behalf of Wheeler, stated that $140,000.00 was a reasonable fee.

6. *Whether the fee is fixed or contingent*

Although the court initially looks to the hourly rate for comparable representation where compensation is guaranteed, it must adjust the basic hourly rate where compensation is contingent by assessing the likelihood of success at the outset of the representation. Although contingent fee contracts are subject to restrictions, especially if the client is a minor, such agreements have generally been enforced unless the contract is unreasonable. The contingent fee system allows persons who could not otherwise afford to assert their claims to have their day in Court. In this case, a contingent fee is not involved. The parties agreed that the fee would be based on an hourly rate.

7. *Time limitations imposed by the client or circumstances*

This element is pertinent if an attorney must adjust the firm's other work load to accommodate the particular pressing needs of a client. Generally, additional fees have been allowed when the client failed timely to notify the attorney of such problems. There was no evidence implying any unusual time restrictions.

8. The amount involved and the results obtained

In establishing reasonable attorney fees, the court may properly consider the amount involved in litigation. This case involved over ten million dollars. However, this cannot be the sole component to be weighed. If the amount implicated, even though large in denomination, neither increases measurably the work nor enlarges the principles of law, it cannot be the deciding factor in setting a very high fee.

Closely related to the element of the amount or value of the property at issue, is the solution achieved by the attorney. While the court should consider all the guidelines, it must also contemplate the benefit to the client as a result of the services. The attorney testified that his client needed what he provided—time for opportunity to accomplish settlement—either to extend the client's loan or to make arrangements to fit his cash flow and current financial condition. (We note that after the attorney withdrew, the client and the bank settled.)

9. Experience, reputation, and ability of the attorney

The attorney's standing in the profession for learning, ability, skill, and integrity is recognized as a proper matter for consideration in assessing the value of the services provided and can be a basis for a higher award. The reverse is also true: inexperience, apparent lack of ability, or poor performance may reduce the award. Here, it appears from the time sheets and the appearances in court, that the primary attorney was the first year associate. The testimony by the expert witnesses indicated that the first year associate had not established a reputation in the legal community sufficient to command a higher fee.

10. The undesirability of the case

Apparently, this was an ordinary case to foreclose a lien which the client had little chance of winning, and that the client's best solution was the settlement obtained after the attorney withdrew from the case.

11. Casual or regular employment

The nature and length of the professional relationship between the client and the attorney is also subject to review. Clients who do not routinely employ the attorney should not expect the lower legal fees normally negotiated with clients who regularly hire or retain counsel. Scott was not a regular client.

12. Awards in similar cases

There was no evidence presented concerning awards in similar cases, other than the amount received by the prevailing party.

Conclusion

The proper determination of reasonable attorney fees requires a balancing and thorough consideration of the * * * [twelve factors we have discussed.] Apparently, the trial court gave too much weight to the time spent on the case and failed to consider adequately the other applicable standards. Setting attorney fees would be a simple matter if numbers could be inserted mechanically into a universally valid formula. Unfortunately, this is not the case. Here, it is obvious that much of the time expended was unnecessary by any reasonable standard. Under our detailed analysis of the guidelines—particularly the excessive time spent, the relative simplicity of the issues (except where they were needlessly multiplied and complicated by counsel), the very average lawyering skill required, the nonpreclusion of other employment, the entry of summary judgment, the customary fee, the absence of restrictive time limitations, and the inexperience of the lawyer who did the bulk of the work—we find that the fee allowed by the trial court is excessive.

* * *

[Reversed and remanded with directions.]

NOTE ON ATTORNEY FEES IN CALIFORNIA

"Unconscionable" vs. "Reasonable"

Note the differences between CRPC 4–200 and ABA Model Rule 1.5. The California rule is cast in the negative: an attorney's fee must not be "unconscionable." ABA Model Rule 1.5 is cast in the affirmative: an attorney's fee must be "reasonable." The term "unconscionable" was taken from old California cases that condemned fees so high as to "shock the conscience." The drafters of the California rule did not explain whether they intended the "unconscionable" standard to be different in substance from the ABA's "reasonable" standard. Note that the factors listed in CRPC 4–200(B) for determining "conscionability" are similar to those listed in ABA Model Rule 1.5(a) for determining "reasonableness," with these exceptions:

- The California list ignores the amount that other lawyers in the community would charge for similar work;

- The California list includes "the amount of the fee in proportion to the value of the services performed" (query whether that adds anything);

- The California list includes the "informed consent of the client" and the "relative sophistication of the client and lawyer."

Do you think that the *Wheeler* case would have been decided differently had it arisen in California?

Arbitration of Fee Disputes

Cal.Bus. & Prof.Code §§ 6200–6206 provide for arbitration of fee disputes between California lawyers and their California clients. Arbitration is voluntary for the client, but mandatory for the lawyer if the client desires it. Before suing a client to recover fees, a California lawyer must notify the client of the right to arbitrate. The client has 30 days following the notice to request arbitration. The parties may agree in writing to be bound by the arbitrators' decision; if they do not agree to be bound, either party is entitled to a court trial of the fee dispute after the arbitration. [*See* Rules of

Procedure for Fee Arbitrations and Enforcement of Awards by the State Bar of California, printed in California Rules of Court 1273–83 (West 1996).]

Contingent Fee Limitations

Note also that the California rules are silent on the propriety of contingent fees in criminal cases and marital relations cases. We have found no California cases that discuss whether a criminal defense lawyer may use a contingent fee. California law is murky on the use of contingent fees in marital relations cases. It has been said that a contingent fee is against public policy in a dissolution case if it encourages the break up of a marriage, but if the couple has already broken up and there is no hope of reconciliation, then a contingent fee is proper, especially if the client spouse could not otherwise afford counsel. [*Compare* Cal. Bar Op. 1983–72, *with Krieger v. Bulpitt,* 40 Cal.2d 97, 251 P.2d 673 (1953), *and* Coons v. Kary, 263 Cal. App.2d 650, 69 Cal.Rptr. 712 (1968).] A contingent fee to collect *past-due* spousal or child support payments is proper; those payments are like any other past-due debt. [Cal. Bar Op. 1983–72.] California law is unclear whether a contingent fee is proper to obtain *future* spousal or child support payments. [*Id.*] It can be argued that the lawyer is taking part of the money that is needed to support the spouse or child. [*See Kyne v. Kyne,* 60 Cal.App.2d 326, 140 P.2d 886 (1943).] But can't the same be said of a marital relations lawyer who is paid by the hour, or of a personal injury lawyer who takes a share of the plaintiff's disability award?

Written Fee Agreements

Note also that California law is stricter than the ABA Model Rules concerning written fee agreements. Cal.Bus. & Prof.Code § 6147 states the California requirements for contingent fee cases, and § 6148 states the requirements for other cases.

Loans to Clients

Concerning loans by a lawyer to a client, what differences do you see between ABA Model Rule 1.8(e) and CRPC 4–210? Do you favor California's more liberal rule? Early drafts of the Restatement of the Law Governing Lawyers § 48 would have allowed a lawyer to lend a client money to cover a client's expenses (food, shelter, medical care, basic business expenses and the like) during litigation, where financial hardship might otherwise force the client into an early settlement or dismissal. The lawyer could not offer or promise such a loan before being hired. The loan provision was initially approved by the membership of the American Law Institute in 1991, but it was later stricken by the ALI Council. In 1996 the ALI membership voted not to reinstate the loan provision. Do you see any policy reasons for prohibiting lawyers from lending their clients enough money to get along during litigation? Are there any opposing policy reasons?

Fee Splitting Between Lawyers

Read ABA Model Rule 1.5(e) and identify the three conditions that must be met when a lawyer splits her fee with another lawyer outside her own firm. Now read CRPC 2–200 and observe that it does not require any work or assumption of responsibility by the lawyer on the receiving end of the split. Thus, the California Rules permit one California lawyer to pay a "forwarding" or "referral" fee to another California lawyer who has done nothing except sign up the client and refer the matter to the paying lawyer. The policy reasons behind California's unusual position were summed up in *Moran v. Harris,* 131 Cal.App.3d 913, 182 Cal.Rptr. 519 (1982) as follows:

> If the ultimate goal is to assure the best possible representation for a client, a forwarding fee is an economic incentive to less capable lawyers to seek out experienced specialists to handle a case. Thus, with marketplace forces at work, the specialist develops a continuing source of business, the client is benefitted, and the conscientious, but less experienced lawyer is subsidized to completely handle the cases he retains and to assure his continued search for the referral of complex cases to the best lawyers in particular fields.

Do you find the argument convincing?

ABA FORMAL OPINION 93–379

American Bar Association Committee on Ethics
and Professional Responsibility, 1993 *

Consistent with the Model Rules of Professional Conduct, a lawyer must disclose to a client the basis on which the client is to be billed for both professional time and any other charges. Absent a contrary understanding, any invoice for professional services should fairly reflect the basis on which the client's charges have been determined. In matters where the client has agreed to have the fee determined with reference to the time expended by the lawyer, a lawyer may not bill more time than she actually spends on a matter, except to the extent that she rounds up to minimum time periods (such as one-quarter or one-tenth of an hour). A lawyer may not charge a client for overhead expenses generally associated with properly maintaining, staffing and equipping an office; however, the lawyer may recoup expenses reasonably incurred in connection with the client's matter for services performed in-house, such as photocopying, long distance telephone calls, computer research, special deliveries, secretarial overtime, and other similar services, so long as the charge reasonably reflects the lawyer's actual cost for the services rendered. A lawyer may not charge a client more than her disbursements for services provided by third parties like court reporters, travel agents or expert witnesses, except to the extent that the lawyer incurs costs additional to the direct cost of the third-party services.

The legal profession has dedicated a substantial amount of time and energy to developing elaborate sets of ethical guidelines for the benefit of

* Copyright © 1987 by the American Bar Association. All rights reserved. Reprinted by permission of the American Bar Association. Copies available from ABA Member Services, 750 North Lake Shore Drive, Chicago, IL 60611.

its clients. Similarly, the profession has spent extraordinary resources on interpreting, teaching and enforcing these ethics rules. Yet, ironically, lawyers are not generally regarded by the public as particularly ethical. One major contributing factor to the discouraging public opinion of the legal profession appears to be the billing practices of some of its members.

It is a common perception that pressure on lawyers to bill a minimum number of hours and on law firms to maintain or improve profits may have led some lawyers to engage in problematic billing practices. These include charges to more than one client for the same work or the same hours, surcharges on services contracted with outside vendors, and charges beyond reasonable costs for in-house services like photocopying and computer searches. Moreover, the bases on which these charges are to be assessed often are not disclosed in advance or are disguised in cryptic invoices so that the client does not fully understand exactly what costs are being charged to him.

The Model Rules of Professional Conduct provide important principles applicable to the billing of clients, principles which, if followed, would ameliorate many of the problems noted above. The Committee has decided to address several practices that are the subject of frequent inquiry, with the goal of helping the profession adhere to its ethical obligations to its clients despite economic pressures.

The first set of practices involves billing more than one client for the same hours spent. In one illustrative situation, a lawyer finds it possible to schedule court appearances for three clients on the same day. He spends a total of four hours at the courthouse, the amount of time he would have spent on behalf of each client had it not been for the fortuitous circumstance that all three cases were scheduled on the same day. May he bill each of the three clients, who otherwise understand that they will be billed on the basis of time spent, for the four hours he spent on them collectively? In another scenario, a lawyer is flying cross-country to attend a deposition on behalf of one client, expending travel time she would ordinarily bill to that client. If she decides not to watch the movie or read her novel, but to work instead on drafting a motion for another client, may she charge both clients, each of whom agreed to hourly billing, for the time during which she was traveling on behalf of one and drafting a document on behalf of the other? A third situation involves research on a particular topic for one client that later turns out to be relevant to an inquiry from a second client. May the firm bill the second client, who agreed to be charged on the basis of time spent on his case, the same amount for the recycled work product that it charged the first client?

The second set of practices involves billing for expenses and disbursements, and is exemplified by the situation in which a firm contracts for the expert witness services of an economist at an hourly rate of $200. May the firm bill the client for the expert's time at the rate of $250 per hour? Similarly, may the firm add a surcharge to the cost of computer-assisted research if the per-minute total charged by the computer company does not include the cost of purchasing the computers or staffing their operation?

The questions presented to the Committee require us to determine what constitute reasonable billing procedures; that is, what are the services and costs for which a lawyer may legitimately charge, both generally and with regard to the specific scenarios? This inquiry requires an elucidation of the Rule of Professional Conduct 1.5,[1] and the Model Code of Professional Responsibility DR 2–106.[2]

Disclosure of the Bases of the Amounts to Be Charged

At the outset of the representation the lawyer should make disclosure of the basis for the fee and any other charges to the client. This is a two-fold duty, including not only an explanation at the beginning of engagement of the basis on which fees and other charges will be billed, but also a sufficient explanation in the statement so that the client may reasonably be expected to understand what fees and other charges the client is actually being billed.

Authority for the obligation to make disclosure at the beginning of a representation is found in the interplay among a number of rules. Rule 1.5(b) provides that

When the lawyer has not regularly represented the client, the basis or rate of the fee shall be communicated to the client, preferably in writing, before or within a reasonable time after commencing the representation.

The Comment to Rule 1.5 gives guidance on how to execute the duty to communicate the basis of the fee:

In a new client-lawyer relationship ... an understanding as to the fee should be promptly established. It is not necessary to recite all the factors that underlie the basis of the fee, but only those that are directly involved in its computation. It is sufficient, for example, to

---

1. Rule 1.5 states in relevant part:

(a) A lawyer's fee shall be reasonable. The factors to be considered in determining the reasonableness of a fee include the following:

(1) the time and labor required, the novelty and difficulty of the questions involved, and the skill requisite to perform the legal service properly;

(2) the likelihood, if apparent to the client, that the acceptance of the particular employment will preclude other employment by the lawyer;

(3) the fee customarily charged in the locality for similar legal services;

(4) the amount involved and the results obtained;

(5) the time limitations imposed by the client or by the circumstances;

(6) the nature and length of the professional relationship with the client;

(7) the experience, reputation, and ability of the lawyer or lawyers performing the services; and

(8) whether the fee is fixed or contingent.

(b) When the lawyer has not regularly represented the client, the basis or rate of the fee shall be communicated to the client, preferably in writing, before or within a reasonable time after commencing the representation.

2. DR 2–106 contains substantially the same factors listed in Rule 1.5 to determine reasonableness, but does not require that the basis of the fee be communicated to the client "preferably in writing" as Rule 1.5 does.

state that the basic rate is an hourly charge or a fixed amount or an estimated amount, or to identify the factors that may be taken into account in finally fixing the fee. When developments occur during the representation that render an earlier estimate substantially inaccurate, a revised estimate should be provided to the client. A written statement concerning the fee reduces the possibility of misunderstanding. Furnishing the client with a simple memorandum or a copy of the lawyer's customary fee schedule is sufficient if the basis or rate of the fee is set forth.

This obligation is reinforced by reference to Model Rule 1.4(b) which provides that

A lawyer shall explain a matter to the extent reasonably necessary to permit the client to make informed decisions regarding the representation.

While the Comment to this Rule suggests its obvious applicability to negotiations or litigation with adverse parties, its important principle should be equally applicable to the lawyer's obligation to explain the basis on which the lawyer expects to be compensated, so the client can make one of the more important decisions "regarding the representation."

An obligation of disclosure is also supported by Model Rule 7.1, which addresses communications concerning a lawyer's services, including the basis on which fees would be charged. The rule provides:

A lawyer shall not make a false or misleading communication about the lawyer or the lawyer's services. A communication is false or misleading if it:

(a) contains a material misrepresentation of fact or law, or omits a fact necessary to make the statement considered as a whole not materially misleading.

It is clear under Model Rule 7.1 that in offering to perform services for prospective clients it is critical that lawyers avoid making any statements about fees that are not complete. If it is true that a lawyer when advertising for new clients must disclose, for example, that costs are the responsibility of the client, *Zauderer v. Office of Disciplinary Counsel*, 471 U.S. 626 (1985), it necessarily follows that in entering into an actual client relationship a lawyer must make fair disclosure of the basis on which fees will be assessed.

A corollary of the obligation to disclose the basis for future billing is a duty to render statements to the client that adequately apprise the client as to how that basis for billing has been applied. In an engagement in which the client has agreed to compensate the lawyer on the basis of time expended at regular hourly rates, a bill setting out no more than a total dollar figure for unidentified professional services will often be insufficient to tell the client what he or she needs to know in order to understand how the amount was determined. By the same token, billing other charges without breaking the charges down by type would not provide the client with the information the client needs to understand the basis for the charges.

Initial disclosure of the basis for the fee arrangement fosters communication that will promote the attorney-client relationship. The relationship will be similarly benefitted if the statement for services explicitly reflects the basis for the charges so that the client understands how the fee bill was determined.

PROFESSIONAL OBLIGATIONS REGARDING THE REASONABLENESS OF FEES

Implicit in the Model Rules and their antecedents is the notion that the attorney-client relationship is not necessarily one of equals, that it is built on trust, and that the client is encouraged to be dependent on the lawyer, who is dealing with matters of great moment to the client. The client should only be charged a reasonable fee for the legal services performed. Rule 1.5 explicitly addresses the reasonableness of legal fees. The rule deals not only with the determination of a reasonable hourly rate, but also with total cost to the client. The Comment to the rule states, for example, that "[a] lawyer should not exploit a fee arrangement based primarily on hourly charges by using wasteful procedures." The goal should be solely to compensate the lawyer fully for time reasonably expended, an approach that if followed will not take advantage of the client.

Ethical Consideration 2–17 of the Model Code of Professional Responsibility provides a framework for balancing the interests between the lawyer and client in determining the reasonableness of a fee arrangement:

> The determination of a proper fee requires consideration of the interests of both client and lawyer. A lawyer should not charge more than a reasonable fee, for excessive cost of legal service would deter laymen from utilizing the legal system in protection of their rights. Furthermore, an excessive charge abuses the professional relationship between lawyer and client. On the other hand, adequate compensation is necessary in order to enable the lawyer to serve his client effectively and to preserve the integrity and independence of the profession.

The lawyer's conduct should be such as to promote the client's trust of the lawyer and of the legal profession. This means acting as the advocate for the client to the extent necessary to complete a project thoroughly. Only through careful attention to detail is the lawyer able to manage a client's case properly. An unreasonable limitation on the hours a lawyer may spend on a client should be avoided as a threat to the lawyer's ability to fulfill her obligation under Model Rule 1.1 to "provide competent representation to a client." "Competent representation requires the legal knowledge, skill, thoroughness and preparation necessary for the representation." Model Rule 1.1. Certainly either a willingness on the part of the lawyer, or a demand by the client, to circumscribe the lawyer's efforts, to compromise the lawyer's ability to be as thorough and as prepared as necessary, is not in the best interests of the client and may lead to a violation of Model Rule 1.1 if it means the lawyer is unable to provide competent representation. The Comment to Model Rule 1.2, while observing that "the scope of services provided by a lawyer may be limited by agreement," also notes that an agreement "concerning the scope of representation must accord with the Rules.... Thus, the client may not be asked to agree to representation so limited in scope as to violate Rule 1.1...." [3]

On the other hand, the lawyer who has agreed to bill on the basis of hours expended does not fulfill her ethical duty if she bills the client for more time than she actually spent on the client's behalf.[4] In addressing the hypotheticals regarding (a) simultaneous appearance on behalf of three clients, (b) the airplane flight on behalf of one client while working on another client's matters and (c) recycled work product, it is helpful to consider these questions, not from the perspective of what a client could be forced to pay, but rather from the perspective of what the lawyer actually earned. A lawyer who spends four hours of time on behalf of three clients has not earned twelve billable hours. A lawyer who flies for six hours for one client, while working for five hours on behalf of another, has not earned eleven billable hours. A lawyer who is able to reuse old work product has not re-earned the hours previously billed and compensated when the work product was first generated. Rather than looking to profit from the fortuity of coincidental scheduling, the desire to get work done rather than watch a movie, or the luck of being asked the identical question twice, the lawyer who has agreed to bill solely on the basis of time spent is obliged to pass the benefits of these economies on to the client. The practice of billing several clients for the same time or work product, since it results in the earning of an unreasonable fee, therefore is contrary to the mandate of the Model Rules. Model Rule 1.5.

Moreover, continuous toil on or overstaffing a project for the purpose of churning out hours is also not properly considered "earning" one's fees. One job of a lawyer is to expedite the legal process. Model Rule 3.2. Just as a lawyer is expected to discharge a matter on summary judgment if possible rather than proceed to trial, so too is the lawyer expected to complete other projects for a client efficiently. A lawyer should take as much time as is reasonably required to complete a project, and should certainly never be motivated by anything other than the best interests of the client when determining how to staff or how much time to spend on any particular project.

---

3. Beyond the scope of this opinion is the question whether a lawyer, with full disclosure to a sophisticated client of the risks involved, can agree to undertake at the request of the client only ten hours of research, when the lawyer knows that the resulting work product does not fulfill the competent representation requirement of Model Rule 1.1.

4. Rule 1.5 clearly contemplates that there are bases for billing clients other than the time expended. This opinion, however, only addresses issues raised when it is understood that the client will be charged on the basis of time expended.

It goes without saying that a lawyer who has undertaken to bill on an hourly basis is never justified in charging a client for hours not actually expended. If a lawyer has agreed to charge the client on this basis and it turns out that the lawyer is particularly efficient in accomplishing a given result, it nonetheless will not be permissible to charge the client for more hours than were actually expended on the matter. When that basis for billing the client has been agreed to, the economies associated with the result must inure to the benefit of the client, not give rise to an opportunity to bill a client phantom hours. This is not to say that the lawyer who agreed to hourly compensation is not free, with full disclosure, to suggest additional compensation because of a particularly efficient or outstanding result, or because the lawyer was able to reuse prior work product on the client's behalf. The point here is that fee enhancement cannot be accomplished simply by presenting the client with a statement reflecting more billable hours than were actually expended. On the other hand, if a matter turns out to be more difficult to accomplish than first anticipated and more hours are required than were originally estimated, the lawyer is fully entitled (though not required) to bill those hours unless the client agreement turned the original estimate into a cap on the fees to be charged.

CHARGES OTHER THAN PROFESSIONAL FEES

In addition to charging clients fees for professional services, lawyers typically charge their clients for certain additional items which are often referred to variously as disbursements, out-of-pocket expenses or additional charges. Inquiries to the Committee demonstrate that the profession has encountered difficulties in conforming to the ethical standards in this area as well. The Rules provide no specific guidance on the issue of how much a lawyer may charge a client for costs incurred over and above her own fee. However, we believe that the reasonableness standard explicitly applicable to fees under Rule 1.5(a) should be applicable to these charges as well.

The Committee, in trying to sort out the issues related to these charges, has identified three different questions which must be addressed. First, which items are properly subject to additional charges? Second, to what extent, if at all, may clients be charged for more than actual out-of-pocket disbursements? Third, on what basis may clients be charged for the provision of in-house services? We shall address these one at a time.

A. General Overhead

When a client has engaged a lawyer to provide professional services for a fee (whether calculated on the basis of the number of hours expended, a flat fee, a contingent percentage of the amount recovered or otherwise) the client would be justifiably disturbed if the lawyer submitted a bill to the client which included, beyond the professional fee, additional charges for general office overhead. In the absence of disclosure to the client in advance of the engagement to the contrary, the client should reasonably expect that the lawyer's cost in maintaining a library, securing malpractice insurance, renting of office space, purchasing utilities and the like would be subsumed within the charges the lawyer is making for professional services.

B. Disbursements

At the beginning of the engagement lawyers typically tell their clients that they will be charged for disbursements. When that term is used clients justifiably should expect that the lawyer will be passing on to the client those actual payments of funds made by the lawyer on the client's behalf. Thus, if the lawyer hires a court stenographer to transcribe a deposition, the client can reasonably expect to be billed as a disbursement the amount the lawyer pays to the court reporting service. Similarly, if the lawyer flies to Los Angeles for the client, the client can reasonably expect to be billed as a disbursement the amount of the airfare, taxicabs, meals and hotel room.

It is the view of the Committee that, in the absence of disclosure to the contrary, it would be improper if the lawyer assessed a surcharge on these disbursements over and above the amount actually incurred unless the lawyer herself incurred additional expenses beyond the actual cost of the disbursement item. In the same regard, if a lawyer receives a discounted rate from a third-party provider, it would be improper if she did not pass along the benefit of the discount to her client rather than charge the client the full rate and reserve the profit to herself. Clients quite properly could view these practices as an attempt to create additional undisclosed profit centers when the client had been told he would be billed for disbursements.

C. In–House Provision of Services

Perhaps the most difficult issue is the handling of charges to clients for the provision of in-house services. In this connection the Committee has in view charges for photocopying, computer research, on-site meals, deliveries and other similar items. Like professional fees, it seems clear that lawyers may pass on reasonable charges for these services. Thus, in the view of the Committee, the lawyer and the client may agree in advance that, for example, photocopying will be charged at $.15 per page, or messenger services will be provided at $5.00 per mile. However, the question arises what may be charged to the client, in the absence of a specific agreement to the contrary, when the client has simply been told that costs for these items will be charged to the client. We conclude that under those circumstances the lawyer is obliged to charge the client no more than the direct cost associated with the service (*i.e.*, the actual cost of making a copy on the photocopy machine) plus a reasonable allocation of overhead expenses directly associated with the provision of the service (*e.g.*, the salary of a photocopy machine operator).

It is not appropriate for the Committee, in addressing ethical standards, to opine on the various accounting issues as to how one calculates direct cost and what may or may not be included in allocated overhead. These are questions which properly should be reserved for our colleagues in the accounting profession. Rather, it is the responsibility of the Committee to explain the principles it draws from the mandate of Model Rule 1.5's injunction that fees be reasonable. Any reasonable calculation of direct costs as well as any reasonable allocation of related overhead should pass ethical muster. On the other hand, in the absence of an agreement to the contrary, it is impermissible for a lawyer to create an additional source of profit for the law firm beyond that which is contained in the provision of professional services themselves. The lawyer's stock in trade is the sale of legal services, not photocopy paper, tuna fish sandwiches, computer time or messenger services.

CONCLUSION

As the foregoing demonstrates, the subject of fees for professional services and other charges is one that is fraught with tension between the lawyer and the client. Nonetheless, if the principles outlined in this opinion are followed, the ethical resolution of these issues can be achieved.

ABA FORMAL OPINION 94–389

American Bar Association Committee on Ethics
and Professional Responsibility, 1994 *

It is ethical to charge contingent fees as long as the fee is appropriate and reasonable and the client has been fully informed of the availability of alternative billing arrangements. The fact that a client can afford to compensate the lawyer on another basis does not render a contingent fee arrangement for such a client unethical. Nor is it unethical to charge a contingent fee when liability is clear and some recovery is anticipated. If the lawyer and client so contract, a lawyer is entitled to a full contingent fee on the total recovery by the client, including that portion of the recovery that was the subject of an early settlement offer that was rejected by the client. Finally, if the lawyer and client agree, it is ethical for the lawyer to charge a different contingent fee at different stages of a matter, and to increase the percentage taken as a fee as the amount of the recovery or savings to the client increases.

A. INTRODUCTION

The term contingent fees evokes an almost instantaneous visceral response among lawyers. Some view the contingent fee as the salvation of the impecunious,[1] a means to redress great wrongs, vindicate rights

---

* Copyright © 1987 by the American Bar Association. All rights reserved. Reprinted by permission of the American Bar Association. Copies available from ABA Member Services, 750 North Lake Shore Drive, Chicago, IL 60611.

1. As stated by the Pennsylvania Supreme Court:

If it were not for contingent fees, indigent victims of tortious accidents would be subject to the unbridled, self-willed partisanship of their tortfeasors. The person who has, without fault on his part, been injured and who, because of his injury, is unable to work, and has a large family to support, and has no money to engage a lawyer, would be at the mercy of the

and reform the law.[2] Others view it as an inducement to frivolous lawsuits which abuse tort laws,[3] and a means of exacting outrageously high fees for already overpaid lawyers.[4] This Committee does not propose in this opinion to take a role in this often intense public policy debate, which has been and will continue to be played out in Congress, state legislatures and other places in the political arena and within the profession.

Rather, the Committee confines its discussion here, in accordance with the specific question addressed to it, to the circumstances under which the charging of contingent fees could violate either the ABA Model Rules of Professional Conduct (1983, as amended) or the ABA Model Code of Professional Responsibility (1980). In particular, the Committee has been asked if it is an ethical violation for a lawyer to charge a contingent fee a) to a client who can otherwise afford to pay on a non-contingent basis or b) in a matter where liability is clear and some recovery is likely. The Committee has also been asked c) whether a personal injury lawyer operating under a contingent fee agreement is obliged to solicit an early settlement offer and d) whether the same lawyer can charge a contingent fee on the amount of recovery that was the subject of a rejected early settlement offer. Finally, the Committee has been asked if it is ethical to charge a contingent fee whose percentage increases e) as the litigation proceeds and f) as the recovery increases.

These are all appropriate questions of professional ethics, properly addressed to this Committee. Without taking sides on the inflammatory

---

person who disabled him because, being in a superior economic position, the injuring person could force on his victim, desperately in need of money to keep the candle of life burning in himself and his dependent ones, a wholly unconscionable meager sum in settlement or even refuse to pay him anything at all. Any society, and especially a democratic one, worthy of respect in the spectrum of civilization, should never tolerate such a victimization of the weak by the mighty.

Richette v. Solomon, 187 A.2d 910, 919 (Pa. 1963).

2. *See* Comment, *Judicial Regulation of Contingent Fee Contracts,* 48 J. Air L. & Comm. 151, 158 (1982); Pollack, *Book Review,* 90 Harv.L.Rev. 482, 484 (1976); Corboy, *Contingency Fees: The Individual's Key to the Courthouse,* 2 Litigation 27 (1976); R. Keeton, Venturing To Do Justice: Reforming Private Law (1969).

3. *See* Statements of Barry Keene, leader of the Association for California Tort Reform, that restrictions on contingent fees are necessary to "reduce financial incentives that encourage lawyers to file unnecessary, unwarranted and unmeritorious

suits." 9 ABA/BNA Lawyers' Manual on Professional Conduct No. 20 at 320 (1993).

4. *See* Brickman, *Contingent Fees Without Contingencies: Hamlet Without the Prince of Denmark,* 37 U.C.L.A.L.Rev. 29, 32–33 (1989); Grady, *Some Ethical Questions About Percentage Fees,* 2 Litigation 20 (1976). A study by the Rand Corporation, however, suggests that compensation received by attorneys on a contingent fee basis, if averaged over all cases, is similar to that received by attorneys compensated on an hourly basis. *See* P. Danzon, Rand Corporation Institute for Civil Justice, *Contingent Fees for Personal Injury Litigation,* Govt. Publication No. R–2458–HCFA at viii (June 1980). The study also suggests that prohibitions on contingency fees are likely to produce suboptimal compensation for plaintiffs and, hence, suboptimal deterrence of negligent actions because a substantial number of low and middle income plaintiffs would be deterred from filing suit. *Id. See also* Report of the Secretary's Commission on Medical Malpractice, U.S. Dep't. of Health Education and Welfare, *The Medical Malpractice Legal System at 87, 154* (Jan. 16, 1973).

and divisive policy issues these questions may evoke, the Committee can answer the questions in the hope of reminding the profession of important client safeguards that come into play in the contingent fee area. These safeguards, if followed, may go a long way toward reducing the larger controversy generated by contingent fees.

In the opinion of the Committee, the charging of a contingent fee, in personal injury and in all other permissible types of litigation, as well as in numerous non-litigation matters, does not violate ethical standards as long as the fee is appropriate in the circumstances and reasonable in amount, and as long as the client has been fully advised of the availability of alternative fee arrangements. The mere fact that liability may be clear does not, by itself, render a contingent fee inappropriate or unethical. Nor does the possibility that, as some have suggested, the profession's obligation to assure appropriateness and reasonableness is sometimes honored in its breach mean that contingent fees are inherently ethically questionable. Rather, any lapse from the applicable requirements by some members of the profession simply suggests that the profession should redouble its efforts to assure that the ethical obligations associated with entering into a contingent fee arrangement are fully understood and observed.

B. Contingent Fees Are Employed in Multiple Situations

It should be recognized at the outset that when we address contingent fees we are talking about a wide variety of situations. Contingent fees are no longer, if ever they were, limited to personal injury cases. Nor are contingent fees limited to suits involving tortious conduct. Contingent fees are now commonly offered to plaintiff-clients in collections, civil rights, securities and anti-trust class actions, real estate tax appeals and even patent litigation.

Nor is this compensation arrangement limited to plaintiffs. In this Committee's recent Formal Opinion 93–373, the Committee considered the ethical issues raised by the increasingly employed so-called "reverse contingent fees," in which defendants hire lawyers who will be compensated by an agreed upon percentage of the amount the client saves. The Committee concluded that as long as the fee arrangement reached between the lawyer and client realistically estimates the exposure of the defendant client, such a fee is consistent with the Model Rules.

Moreover, contingent fees are not limited to litigation practice. Fees in the mergers and acquisitions arena are often either partially or totally dependent on the consummation of a takeover or successful resistance of such a takeover. Additionally, fees on public offerings are often tied to whether the stocks or bonds come to market and to the amount generated in the offering. Banks are also hiring lawyers to handle loan transactions in which the fee for the bank's lawyers is dependent in whole or part on the consummation of the loan.

The use of contingent fees in these areas, for plaintiffs and defendants, impecunious and affluent alike, reflects the desire of clients to tie a lawyer's compensation to her performance and to give the lawyer incentives to improve returns to the client. The trend also may reflect a growing dissatisfaction with hourly rate billing.[5] Because of the growing importance and widespread use of contingent fees, the Committee will first address in detail the factors that should be considered before a lawyer and client enter into such a fee arrangement, and then address the specific questions occasioning this opinion.

C. The Decision by the Client to Enter Into a Contingent Fee Agreement Must Be an Informed One

Nothing in the Model Rules expressly prohibits a lawyer from entering into a contingent fee agreement with any client. Nevertheless, the lawyer must recognize that not all matters are appropriate for a contingent fee. For example, Model Rule 1.5(d) makes it clear that a contingent fee may never be agreed to, charged or collected in a criminal matter or divorce proceeding.[6] More to the point, in Informal Opinion 86–1521 this Committee concluded that, "when there is any doubt whether a contingent fee is consistent with the client's best interest," and the client is able to pay a reasonable fixed fee, the lawyer "must offer the client the *opportunity* to engage counsel on a reasonable fixed fee basis before entering into a contingent fee arrangement" (emphasis added). The Opinion pointed out that a client with a meritorious claim

> is entitled to representation and should not be required to relinquish a share of the claim to get representation if the client has the money to pay a reasonable fixed fee and is willing to assume the contingency risk. It may also be in some cases that a contingent fee arrangement is the only practical basis upon which a matter can be handled, but that decision should be made after consideration of the relevant facts and circumstances in consultation with the client....

In other words, regardless of whether the lawyer, the prospective client, or both, are initially inclined towards a contingent fee, the nature (and details) of the compensation arrangement should be fully discussed by the lawyer and client before any final agreement is reached.

---

5. For example, Zoe Baird, General Counsel of Aetna Casualty & Surety Co., at the 1992 ABA Annual Meeting asserted that billing based on hourly fees is a "deeply flawed economic system" which instead of focusing lawyers on resolving client problems, encourages "too much time spent on discovery, complicated and unproductive meetings, and long uncommunicative briefs". *See* ABA/BNA Lawyers' Manual on Professional Conduct, 8 Cur.Reps. 286–87 (9/9/92).

Shelby Rogers, General Counsel of Texas Commerce Bancshares, and Francis H. Musselman, Managing Partner of Milbank, Tweed, Hadley & McCoy, have similarly criticized the present system of hourly billing and advocated the use of contingent fees

and "success bonuses" as a means of ensuring a correlation between attorney work and value received by the client. *See* ABA/BNA Lawyers' Manual on Professional Conduct, 9 Cur.Reps. 254–55 (9/8/93); *see also* Salop & Litan, More Value for the Legal Dollar: a New Look at Attorney Client Fees and Relationships (Brookings Institute 1992).

This Committee has recently identified some ethical abuses that can accompany hourly billing in ABA Standing Committee on Ethics and Professional Responsibility. Formal Opinion No. 93–379 ("Billing for Professional Fees, Disbursements and Other Expenses").

6. The Model Code contains similar provisions in DR 2–106(C) and EC 2–20.

The extent of the discussion, of course, will depend on whether it is the lawyer or the client who initiated the idea of proceeding with the contingent fee arrangement, the lawyer's prior dealings with the client (including whether there has been any prior contingent fee arrangement), and the experience and sophistication of the client with respect to litigation and other legal matters.[7] Among the factors that should be considered and discussed are the following:

a. The likelihood of success;

b. The likely amount of recovery or savings, if the case is successful;

c. The possibility of an award of exemplary or multiple damages and how that will affect the fee;

d. The attitude and prior practices of the other side with respect to settlement;

e. The likelihood of, or any anticipated difficulties in, collecting any judgment;

f. The availability of alternative dispute resolution as a means of achieving an earlier conclusion to the matter;

g. The amount of time that is likely to be invested by the lawyer;

h. The likely amount of the fee if the matter is handled on a non-contingent basis;

i. The client's ability and willingness to pay a non-contingent fee;

j. The percentage of any recovery that the lawyer would receive as a contingent fee and whether that percentage will be fixed or on a sliding scale;

k. Whether the lawyer's fees would be recoverable by the client by reason of statute or common law rule;

l. Whether the jurisdiction in which the claim will be pursued has any rules or guidelines for contingent fees; and

m. How expenses of the litigation are to be handled.

Notwithstanding the foregoing, however, the inquiries prompting this opinion take the position that there are two particular circumstances where contingent fee arrangements are inappropriate. To these we now turn.

---

7. This procedure meets the lawyer's fiduciary obligations to the client without unnecessarily interfering with the lawyer's right to charge reasonable fees, Model Rule 1.5; ABA Standing Committee on Ethics and Professional Responsibility Formal Opinion 329; or the freedom of contract enjoyed by both lawyer and client. *See Venegas v. Mitchell,* 495 U.S. 82, 88 (1990) (parties are free to assign part of their recovery to an attorney if they believe that the contingency agreement will increase their likelihood of recovery); *Wells v. Sullivan,* 907 F.2d 367, 369–370 (2d Cir.1990) ("absent fraud or overreaching, courts must enforce such private contingency fee agreements, which are, after all, embodiments of the intentions and wishes of the parties.... [T]o deny [plaintiffs] the option of entering contingent fee arrangements would tend to defeat the general remedial purpose of the statute by unnecessarily restricting claimants' options in securing adequate counsel or counsel of their choice").

D. Contingent Fees May Be Appropriate when the Client Can Afford to Pay on Another Basis

Is a contingent fee appropriate when a client can afford to pay the lawyer on a non-contingent basis? Some commentators have suggested that because one of the fundamental reasons for allowing contingent fees is that they provide the poor equal access to the court system, such a fee may be inappropriate and unethical when the client is relatively well off or otherwise able to afford a lawyer.[8] However, as discussed above, there is nothing in the Model Rules to prevent a lawyer from entering into a contingent fee agreement with any client, regardless of the client's means, so long as the client's decision to enter into the arrangement is an informed one.

Moreover, to state that contingent fees are only appropriate for the indigent would ignore the reality of how expensive present day litigation can be. It is not uncommon for expenses and legal fees to total hundreds of thousands of dollars through trial.[9] Also, it is often difficult at the outset of a matter for the lawyer to estimate accurately how much time will be expended. Therefore, it may very well be in the client's best interests, whatever the client's apparent ability to pay the fee, to agree to pay a fixed percentage of any possible recovery, rather than assume liability for a possibly prohibitively expensive legal bill that will be owed even if the client recovers nothing.

The contingent fee system essentially shifts the risk of litigation or other legal endeavor from a risk averse client to the lawyer who may be more risk neutral because of his ability to recoup his losses through his handling of other legal matters on a contingent basis.

Even for those who can well afford to pay legal fees on a pay as you go basis, such as large corporations, the client's best interests may still be served by a contingent fee arrangement. In this way the corporation can use its financial resources, which would otherwise be spent in paying for legal services, for other business purposes until such time as the merger may be consummated or an identifiable fund is available from the proceeds of a public offering.

Furthermore, both the wealthy and the impecunious client may share the desire to give their lawyers the incentive to increase the actual proceeds to the client. At least some clients think contingent fee agreements are the best, if not the only way, to give such incentives. In their view the interests of the lawyer and the interests of the client are

---

8. *See* G. Hazard, W.W. Hodes, 2 Law of Lawyering § 1.5 at 118, 122–23 (1993 Supp.) (suggesting that lawyers should use a different fee system for clients who can afford to bear costs); J. O'Connell, The Injury Industry 48 (1971) ("[L]awyers will not normally take a personal injury case on other than a contingency fee no matter how wealthy the client … [this] suggests … that its use is so widespread today because it is profitable for lawyers"); Comment, *Are Contingent Fees Ethical Where Client is Able to Pay a Retainer?* 20 Ohio St.L.J. 329 (1959).

9. Fees and expenses can be especially high in certain hard fought and ground-breaking litigation. A prime example is the cigarette liability litigation which has cost law firms working on a contingent fee basis millions of dollars that has not been offset by any judgment or settlement. *See The Heat Is On*, ABA Journal, Sept. 1994, at 59.

only in true alignment when the lawyer's fee is totally contingent on a successful outcome for the client.

Thus, as discussed above, while the client's inability to pay legal fees on a non-contingent basis may be the determining factor in a conclusion that a contingent fee is appropriate, the fact that the client is able to pay such fees does not necessarily make a contingent fee inappropriate. Barring contingent fees for other than the impecunious would deny important benefits to which the well-to-do as well as the poor client are clearly entitled.

E.   In a Case in Which Liability Is Clear and Some Recovery Is Certain, a Fee Based on a Percentage of the Recovery Can Be Ethically Proper

The Committee has also been asked to consider whether it is ethical for a lawyer to accept a matter on a contingent fee basis when liability is clear and some recovery is certain. The argument put forward is that since the lawyer is sure that the matter will result in some recovery, there is no real contingency; thus, there is no justification for a contingent fee arrangement. A variation of this argument discussed more fully under caption G below, is found in a recent inquiry to this Committee which asks whether a lawyer to be compensated under a contingent fee arrangement is ethically obligated to solicit early settlement offers and whether a lawyer should be prohibited from charging a contingent fee on the amount of such offer, even if it is not accepted and the same amount is recovered after the case must go to trial.[10]

First, neither the Model Rules nor the Model Code mention any requirements regarding solicitation of early settlement offers and there is no valid basis for inferring such a requirement. *See* ABA Formal Opinion 329 (1972) (no reasonable method of fixing fees which takes into account the relevant factors set forth in the ethical rules is proscribed).

Second, the Committee is of the view that the argument may rest on a faulty notion as to the number of cases regarding which at the onset of the engagement the lawyer can say with certainty that the client will recover.[11] Defendants often vigorously defend and even win cases where liability seems certain.[12] Additionally, a previously undiscovered fact or

---

10. *See* Brickman, Horowitz & O'Connell, Rethinking Contingency Fees, at 28 (The Manhattan Institute 1994) (proposing that "[w]hen plaintiffs reject defendants' early offers, contingency fees may only be charged against net recoveries in excess of such offers").

11. A recent study indicates that the probability of recovery is presently *decreasing,* rather than increasing, in many types of lawsuits that are traditionally handled on a contingent fee basis. *See Stingier Jurors Doling Out Fewer Awards,* ABA Journal, Sept. 1994 at 20. This study shows that in medical malpractice cases the probability of

recovery at trial has decreased from 37% to 31%, and, in products liability cases from 51% to 43%. *Id.*

12. In a study of 8,231 closed medical malpractice cases in the State of New Jersey from 1977 to 1992, almost 10% of patients received no recovery at all in cases where the defendant doctors' conduct was rated indefensible. *See* M.I. Taragin, L.R. Willet, A. Pwilczek, R. Trout and J.L. Carson, *The Influence of Standard of Care and Severity of Injury on the Resolution of Medical Malpractice Claims,* 1992 Annals of Amer.Med. 780–784.

an unexpected change in the law can suddenly transform a case that seemed a sure winner at the outset of representation into a certain loser. *See, e.g., Central Bank of Denver v. First Interstate Bank of Denver*, 114 S.Ct. 1439 (1994) (where the Supreme Court held that a private plaintiff may not maintain an aiding and abetting suit under § 10(b) of the Securities Act of 1934, overruling every circuit court which for decades had allowed such suits).

Moreover, even in cases where there is no risk of non-recovery, and the lawyer and client are certain that liability is clear and will be conceded, a fee arrangement contingent on the amount recovered may nonetheless be reasonable.[13] As the increasing popularity of reverse contingent fees demonstrates, for almost all cases there is a range of possible recoveries. Since the amount of the recovery will be largely determined by the lawyer's knowledge, skill, experience and time expended, both the defendant and the plaintiff may best be served by a contingency fee arrangement that ties the lawyer's fee to the amount recovered.[14]

Also, an early settlement offer is often prompted by the defendant's recognition of the ability of the plaintiff's lawyer fairly and accurately to value the case and to proceed effectively through trial and appeals if necessary. There is no ethical reason why the lawyer is not entitled to an appropriate consideration for this value that his engagement has brought to the case, even though it results in an early resolution.

Given the foregoing, the Committee concludes that as a general proposition contingent fees are appropriate and ethical in situations where liability is certain and some recovery is likely.

That having been said, there may nonetheless be special situations in which a contingent fee may not be appropriate. For example, if in a particular instance a lawyer was reasonably confident that as soon as the case was filed the defendant would offer an amount that the client would accept, it might be that the only appropriate fee would be one based on the lawyer's time spent on the case since, from the information known to the lawyer, there was little risk of non-recovery and the lawyer's efforts would have brought little value to the client's recovery.[15] And even if, in

---

13. Evidence that, in such cases, free market forces may result in a substantially reduced contingent fee can be found in airline liability cases. In cases where airline insurers voluntarily sent out the "Alpert letter" which makes an early settlement offer *and concedes all legal liability,* average contingent fee rates dropped to 17% and were often only charged on a portion of the recovery. *See* L. Kriendler, *The Letter: It Shouldn't be Sent,* 12 The Brief 4, 38 (November 1982).

14. Similarly, in the case of reverse contingent fee arrangements, some savings from the amount the plaintiff demands is

almost always a certainty, yet as this Committee opined in Formal Opinion 93–373, there is nothing ethically improper about entering into a fee agreement that compensates the lawyer based on a percentage of the total saved.

15. Similar reasoning has led many courts to find that it is inappropriate to charge a contingent fee in cases involving first party insurance benefits where there is no risk of non-recovery and the lawyer merely submits the claim on behalf of the client. But courts have also found that contingent fees may be appropriate in these types of cases, if the lawyer performs addi-

such circumstances, after a full discussion, it were agreed between lawyer and client that a contingent fee was appropriate, the fee arrangement should recognize the likelihood of an early favorable result by providing for a significantly smaller percentage recovery if the anticipated offer is received and accepted than if the case must go forward through discovery, trial and appeal.[16]

F. FOLLOWING AN EARLY SETTLEMENT OFFER WHICH THE CLIENT REJECTS, IT IS ETHICAL FOR A LAWYER TO COLLECT A CONTINGENT FEE BASED ON THE ENTIRE RECOVERY, INCLUDING THAT PORTION WHICH WAS THE SUBJECT OF AN EARLY SETTLEMENT OFFER

The analysis in the preceding section regarding early settlement offers, however, does not mean, as an inquirer [17] has suggested, that in order to pass ethical muster a contingent fee agreement must limit the percentage recovery on the amount originally offered to the same small percentage suggested in Part E, if the client rejects the early offer, takes the case to trial and recovers no more than what was originally offered. In that example it would be ethical for the lawyer to provide for a significantly higher percentage contingent fee on the amount originally offered if the client chooses to go the full trial route. This higher fee would recognize the substantial time and effort that is required to take the matter to trial as well as the lawyer's assumption of the real risk that the plaintiffs will lose on the merits or that any judgment at trial may be less than the early offer.

The problem created by the inquirer's proposed limitation of the lawyers' contingent fee is that such a limitation penalizes both plaintiff and lawyer in cases where, even though liability is clear, there is an honest disagreement between the parties as to the amount owed in damages. Under those circumstances the plaintiff is entitled to reject the early offer and take his claim to a judge or jury represented by a fully compensated lawyer of his choosing. The circumstance that the fact finder eventually agrees with the defendant's evaluation of the case provides no ethical reason to interfere with a mutually agreed-upon contingent fee arrangement that was reasonable and appropriate at the onset of representation.[18] Such interference is particularly inappropriate given the fact that Model Rule 1.2 makes it clear that all decisions regarding the objectives of representation, including the acceptance and

---

tional services relating to the recovery by the client. *See In re Doyle,* 581 N.E.2d 669 (Ill.1991).

16. A recognition of the amount of additional work required to take a case through trial and appeals is reflected by several states which cap percentage fees in certain types of cases but allow the percentage charged to rise after certain milestones, i.e., 25% if settled before trial, 33½% if tried. *See* New Jersey Ct.R. 1.27(C)(f) (limiting fees in tort cases involving minors). States have also mandated differing percentages depending on the amount recovered. *See*

N.Y.Jud.L. § 474–A (McKinneys 1994 Supp); Conn.Gen.St.Ann. § 52–251(c)(1991).

17. *See* note 10, *supra.*

18. It should be noted that under one suggested proposal the plaintiff's lawyer is penalized even if the fact finder agrees with the plaintiff's valuation of the case, because the proposal would limit any fee on the portion of the judgment which equals the early settlement offer even if much more is awarded after trial. *See* Brickman et al., *supra* note 10.

rejection of settlement offers, are solely those of the client. It is the lawyer who is bound by the client's decision, not the other way around. The inquirer's proposal, however, results in the lawyer being penalized because she is required to pass on the client's rejection of the early offer and press forward with the litigation to a stage of the proceedings that the client chooses.

The argument for limiting contingent fees on the amount of an early offer finds no support in the ethical rules and seems to be based on the assumption that by making an early offer the defendant is conceding all liability up to that amount, thereby eradicating the possibility of non-recovery by the plaintiff. But early settlement offers are made for numerous reasons besides a concession of liability. And as any experienced trial lawyer knows, once an early settlement offer is rejected, the defendant and its lawyer will, in most cases, do their best to defend both against the fact of liability and the amount of damages owed. There is generally a real risk to the client and to the lawyer being paid on a contingent fee basis that such a defense will be successful. It is ethical for the lawyer to be compensated for both the time she expends to defeat any such defenses and the risk she assumes that the plaintiff will not prevail at trial or that a judgment awarded may never be collected.

The lawyer is also being compensated for the risk she assumes that the client will fire the lawyer, a right the client might exercise at any time. *See Hiscott & Robinson v. King,* 626 A.2d 1235 (Pa.Super.1993); *Covington v. Rhodes,* 247 S.E.2d 305 (N.C.App.1978); Comment on Model Rule 1.16(a)(3) ("a client has a right to discharge a lawyer at any time, with or without cause"); DR 2–110(B)(4), or that the client will insist on proceeding with the litigation through appeals or otherwise longer than the lawyer would proceed, if it were the lawyer's, rather than the client's decision.[19] *See* Model Rule 1.2. Additionally, the lawyer is being compensated for the often lengthy delay between the time work is performed and the time a fee is received.

G.   THERE IS NO ETHICAL REQUIREMENT FOR A PLAINTIFF'S LAWYER WHOSE COMPENSATION AGREEMENT IS CONTINGENT ON THE RECOVERY TO SOLICIT AN EARLY SETTLEMENT OFFER FROM THE DEFENDANT

An inquirer has asked whether, as an ethical matter, the plaintiff's lawyer must solicit an early offer of settlement. The Committee concludes that there is no such ethical requirement. First, neither the Model Rules nor the Model Code require any such solicitation. Second, the suggestion seems inequitable as no reciprocal requirement for the defendant to make an early settlement offer is imposed. Any require-

---

19. "The ordinary rule of construction of contingent fee contracts is that, absent an express provision otherwise, services rendered by the attorney in upholding a judgment on appeal are within the underlying contract." *Attorney Grievance Commission v. Korotki,* 569 A.2d 1224 (Md.1990). *See also* New York City Ethics Opinion 1986–6; Michigan State Bar Committee on Professional & Judicial Ethics Formal Opinion R–11 (1991). Conversely, if the client decides to voluntarily dismiss a case that the lawyer considers meritorious and likely to succeed, the lawyer cannot recover on a contingent fee contract.

ment to seek an early settlement offer would raise fundamental problems. Plaintiff's counsel, whether proceeding on a contingent fee basis or not, must be free (with appropriate consultation with the client) to select her own strategy. It may be that at the outset of the litigation, she doesn't have enough information about the defendant's conduct to make an intelligent evaluation of a settlement offer. For example, she may not know whether liability is clear or uncertain or whether exemplary damages may be available. Additionally, the plaintiff's damages at that juncture may still be a matter of significant uncertainty, with respect to either extent, permanence, or both. Finally, the plaintiff may have decided that he does not, under any circumstances, wish to settle or enter into settlement negotiations.

As an ethical matter, these are all matters to be decided between lawyer and client; there is no ground in the Model Rules for suggesting that the lawyer who is retained on a contingent basis and the plaintiff who retained her should be any less free than a lawyer who is compensated on some other basis to decide with her client whether and when to solicit or make a settlement offer. While the ethical rules require that any strategy pursued by the lawyer be directed to the client's best interests, it is not the role of the ethical rules to force lawyers to follow any specific litigation strategy or approach. Additionally, any proposed rule that seeks to dictate a particular strategy in all cases would be in conflict with Model Rule 2.1 which requires a lawyer to exercise her independent professional judgment on behalf of her client.

H. The Contingent Fee Arrangement Must Be Reasonable

In addition to the requirement that a fee be appropriate, Model Rule 1.5 requires that the fee, whether based on an hourly rate, a contingent percentage or some other basis, "shall be reasonable." Similarly, DR 2–106 prohibits a "clearly excessive fee," which is in turn defined as a "fee . . . in excess of a reasonable fee."[20]

In deciding whether a contingent fee arrangement is reasonable the lawyer must consider the following factors set forth in Model Rule 1.5(a):

(1) the time and labor required, the novelty and difficulty of the questions involved, and the skill requisite to perform the legal service properly;

(2) the likelihood, if apparent to the client, that the acceptance of the particular employment will preclude other employment by the lawyer;

(3) the fee customarily charged in the locality for similar legal services;

(4) the amount involved and the results obtained;

20. DR 2–106 provides that "[a] lawyer shall not enter into an agreement for, charge, or collect an illegal or clearly excessive fee." A fee is "clearly excessive" under DR 2–106 "when, after a review of the facts, a lawyer of ordinary prudence would be left with a definite and firm conviction that the fee is in excess of a reasonable fee."

(5) the time limitations imposed by the client or by the circumstances;

(6) the nature and length of the professional relationship with the client;

(7) the experience, reputation, and ability of the lawyer or lawyers performing the services.

Additionally, the lawyer must look again at, and discuss with the client, the factors that were considered in reviewing the appropriateness of the fee, discussed in Section C above.

We stress that the lawyer should take all these factors into account in evaluating every case. *See* ABA Formal Opinion 329 (1972). For this reason, a lawyer who always charges the same percentage of recovery regardless of the particulars of a case should consider whether he is charging a fee that is, in an ethical context, a *reasonable* one. One standard fee for all cases may have the effect, given the difference among cases, of both over- and under-compensating the lawyer. *Cf. In re Recorder's Court Bar Association v. Wayne Circuit Court,* 503 N.W.2d 885 (Mich.1993) (finding that a fixed fee system for compensating attorneys who represented indigent defendants that did not take into account the particulars of the case was unreasonable).

As with the question of appropriateness, the mere fact that liability may be clear and that some recovery is likely does not *per se* make any given contingent fee unreasonable. It is important to keep in mind that the reasonableness as well as the appropriateness of a fee arrangement necessarily must be judged at the time it is entered into. All contingent fee agreements carry certain risks: the risk that the case will require substantially more work than the lawyer anticipated; the risk that there will be no judgment, or only an unenforceable one; the risk of changes in the law; the risk that the client will dismiss the lawyer; and the risk that the client will require the lawyer to reject what the lawyer considers a good settlement or otherwise to continue the proceedings much further than in the lawyer's judgment they should be pursued. If a lawyer accepts a given risk—for example, the risk posed by the fact that the opposing party has a reputation for being intransigent in its approach to settlement—and offers a fee contract reflecting that risk, which is accepted by a fully informed client, the lawyer should not be required as a matter of ethics to give up the benefit of the agreement because the opposing party, to everyone's surprise, offers an early settlement that is acceptable to the client.[21] By the same token, a later development that increases the risk to the lawyer—for example, a statutorily imposed cap on liability, the loss of a summary judgment motion everyone expected to win, or the need to take three times the number of depositions originally

---

21. Brickman, *supra* note 4, at 87 ("It is not the actual effort expended by the attorney that is determinative of the legitimacy of the fee, but what a good faith, professionally informed estimate of anticipated effort and risk of non-recovery would have been prior to the *commencement of representation*"). (Emphasis added.)

anticipated—should not permit the lawyer to demand a new, more generous fee arrangement.[22]

I. The Percentage of a Contingent Fee May as an Ethical Matter Be Increased On the Basis of How Far the Lawyer Must Proceed in Prosecuting the Case

The Committee has also been asked whether it is ethical for a lawyer and client to enter into a fee agreement that provides for higher contingent fees after specific benchmarks, for example, 25% if the case settles within six months and 33% after trial. The higher contingent fee at advanced stages of the matter is meant to compensate the lawyer for the additional time and labor necessary in the case. As demonstrated in the factors set forth in Model Rule 1.5(a) set out above, the time and labor involved in a matter are among the reasonable bases for setting a fee. Therefore, it is the Committee's opinion that such a fee agreement is ethical as long as the overall fee is appropriate and reasonable. *See, e.g.,* Phila. Bar Assoc. Ethics Op. 93–11 (approving such a fee arrangement).

J. The Percentage of a Contingent Fee May Increase with the Amount of the Recovery

Finally, the Committee has been asked whether it is ethical for a lawyer to enter into a fee agreement that provides for a higher percentage fee as the amount of the recovery goes up or the amount of the savings increases: for example, 15% on the first $100,000 recovered or saved, 20% on the next hundred thousand, and 25% on everything thereafter. Such an arrangement on its face runs contrary to what several states have mandated in terms of reducing the percentage recovery as the amount recovered rises.[23] Nonetheless, as a matter of ethics, the Committee is of the view that a percentage that increases with the amount of the recovery can be permissible. Model Rule 1.5(a) refers, in connection with the reasonableness of a fee, to "results obtained," and the "ability of the lawyer or lawyers performing the services" as factors that may be considered. Since a higher recovery would, by definition, reflect the first of these factors and, in all likelihood, reflect the other as well, the Committee is of the view that such a fee agreement is ethical, so long as the matter for which the fee is charged is appropriate and the amount of the fee is reasonable. Indeed, many would say that this form of contingent fee agreement more closely

---

22. *See, e.g., Chase v. Gilbert,* 499 A.2d 1203 (D.C.1985) (A lawyer cannot modify a fee agreement even if he ends up performing significantly more services than were contemplated when agreement was entered into). Because reasonableness is judged at the time the contract is entered into, there is nothing necessarily unethical about charging a contingent fee on the portion of any recovery that is equal to an early settlement offer. *See* ABA Formal Opinion 329 ("[n]o reasonable method of fixing fees which takes into account the factors of DR 2–106(B) is proscribed by the Code of Professional Responsibility"). It should be noted, however, that extreme changes in circumstances occurring after negotiation of the fee agreement may lead a reviewing court to decide, ex post facto, that payment of the fee is unreasonable. *See, e.g., Mckenzie Construction Inc. v. Maynard,* 758 F.2d 97 (3d Cir.1985).

23. *See,* Calif.Bus. & Prof. Code § 6146 (West 1990); *see also* note 16, *supra.*

rewards the effort and ability the lawyer brings to the engagement than does a straight percentage fee arrangement, since everyone would agree that it is the last dollars, not the first dollars, of recovery that require the greatest effort and/or ability on the part of the lawyer. It may be that any lawyer would have been able to achieve a $100,000 verdict for a given plaintiff's injuries, but that only the most skilled would have been able to secure a $500,000 award plus an additional sum for exemplary damages.

K. Conclusion

A lawyer entering into a contingent fee arrangement complies with the ethical standards set forth in both the Model Rules of Professional Conduct and the Model Code of Professional Responsibility if the fee is both appropriate and reasonable and if the client has been fully informed of all appropriate alternative billing arrangements and their implications. Contingent fee arrangements are appropriate for both the affluent and those who cannot otherwise afford the lawyer's services. It is not necessarily unethical to charge a contingent fee when liability is clear and some recovery is anticipated. A lawyer compensated on a contingent basis has no obligation to solicit on behalf of the client an early settlement offer; further, she may collect a contingent fee on the total recovery, including any amount that was the subject of an early settlement offer. Finally, a lawyer may charge a different contingent fee at different stages of a matter, and may increase the percentage taken as a fee as the amount of the recovery or savings to the client increases.

FEE FORFEITURE AND RELATED ISSUES

The so-called War on Drugs, which commenced in the 1980s, produced a variety of statutes and prosecutorial practices that alter the professional relationship between criminal defendants and their defense counsel, not just in drug cases, but in all kinds of cases. Here are some well-known examples:

First, in the 1980s criminal prosecutors started subpoenaing criminal defense lawyers to testify before grand juries about their fees, the source of their fees, and their knowledge of unlawful activities by their clients. In response, some jurisdictions adopted legal ethics rules that restrict the practice. One example is ABA Model Rule 3.8(f), which forbids a prosecutor from subpoenaing a lawyer in a grand jury or other criminal proceeding to present evidence about a past or present client unless the prosecutor reasonably believes that the information sought (a) is not privileged; and (b) is essential to an ongoing investigation or prosecution; and (c) cannot be obtained in some other way. At one time the rule also required the prosecutor to get advance judicial approval (with a chance for an adversarial hearing) before issuing such a subpoena, but the ABA dropped that requirement in 1995 because it operated like a rule of criminal procedure rather than a legal ethics rule. [*Compare Baylson v. Disciplinary Board*, 975 F.2d 102 (3d Cir.1992), *cert.*

denied, 507 U.S. 9£ (1993), *with Whitehouse v. U.S. District Court,* 53 F.3d 1349 (1st Cir.1995).]

Second, Congress amended the tax law to require cash transactions of $10,000 or more to be reported to the Internal Revenue Service, along with the payor's name, address, and tax identification number. 26 U.S.C. § 6050I (1994). The IRS has refused to exempt lawyers from reporting legal fees paid in cash, even if the person who pays the fee wants to remain anonymous. Lawyers have challenged the reporting requirement on many grounds including the attorney-client privilege, the client's privilege against self-incrimination, and the client's right to effective assistance of counsel. Thus far these challenges have proven largely futile, and the IRS now fines lawyers who refuse to file complete reports. [*See United States v. Goldberger & Dubin,* 935 F.2d 501 (2d Cir.1991); *see also United States v. Blackman,* 72 F.3d 1418 (9th Cir.1995), *petition for cert. filed,* 64 U.S.L.W. 3865 (1996); *Ralls v. United States,* 52 F.3d 223 (9th Cir.1995); *United States v. Ritchie,* 15 F.3d 592 (6th Cir.1994), *cert. denied,* ___ U.S. ___, 115 S.Ct. 188, 130 L.Ed.2d 121 (1994); *United States v. Leventhal,* 961 F.2d 936 (11th Cir.1992); *but see United States v. Sindel,* 53 F.2d 874 (8th Cir.1995); *United States v. Gertner,* 873 F.Supp. 729 (D.Mass.1995), *questioned but affirmed on other grounds,* 65 F.3d 963 (1st Cir.1995).]

Third, 18 U.S.C. § 1957 (1994) makes it a felony to engage knowingly in a "monetary transaction in criminally derived property that is of a value greater than $10,000," and that is derived from certain kinds of unlawful activity. This statute provides for imprisonment for up to ten years and states that the prosecutor need not "prove that the defendant knew that the offense" from which the property was derived was "specified unlawful activity."

Fourth, the Comprehensive Forfeiture Act of 1984 amended the Continuing Criminal Enterprise statute (CCE), 21 U.S.C. §§ 848–53 (1994), and the Racketeer Influenced and Corrupt Organization Act (RICO), 18 U.S.C. §§ 1961–68 (1994), to provide that property and income derived from various illegal acts are subject to forfeiture to the government at the time the acts are committed. California has similar forfeiture statutes for drug cases, Cal. Health and Safety Code §§ 11469–95.

Neither RICO nor CCE nor the California drug statutes expressly include assets that are used to pay attorney fees, but prosecutors have used the statutes to go after fees paid by defendants to their defense lawyers. The object, the prosecutors say, is to separate criminals from the economic power base they need to continue their illegal activities. If forfeiture leaves a defendant without the funds to pay a lawyer, he is treated as an indigent; he has the right to appointed counsel, but he cannot use criminally-derived assets to pay the counsel of his choice.

Until 1989, the lower federal courts were split on whether to exempt attorney fees from federal forfeiture. The Supreme Court settled the issue in *United States v. Monsanto,* 491 U.S. 600, 109 S.Ct. 2657, 105

L.Ed.2d 512 (1989). Defendant Monsanto allegedly directed a heroin ring and was indicted under both RICO and CCE. The government obtained a restraining order freezing his house, apartment, and $35,000 in cash, pending trial. Monsanto sought to vacate the order so he could use the assets to pay his defense counsel. The Supreme Court held that the plain language of the forfeiture statute did not exempt attorney fees and that the restraining order was constitutional.

In another case decided the same day, *Caplin & Drysdale v. United States,* 491 U.S. 617, 109 S.Ct. 2646, 105 L.Ed.2d 528 (1989), the Court considered whether forfeiture of assets needed for attorney fees was consistent with the Fifth and Sixth Amendments. Defendant Reckmeyer, indicted under CCE, had paid the Caplin law firm $25,000 for legal services despite a court order that froze his assets. Caplin sought title to the $25,000 as well as $170,000 of other forfeited assets as compensation for its post-indictment defense of Reckmeyer. The Court held that the Sixth Amendment guarantees an indigent only the right to adequate representation, not the right to counsel of his choice. Further, the government gains title to all proceeds of illegal activity, and it has a compelling interest in abating the economic power of criminal enterprises. This interest overrides a criminal's interest in using the assets to pay for his defense. The Court found "no evidence that Congress intended to * * * [say] that 'crime does not pay, except for attorney's fees.' "

Both *Monsanto* and *Caplin & Drysdale* involved criminal defendants attempting to exempt attorney fees under *criminal* forfeiture statutes. The teachings of the two cases have, however, been extended to criminal defendants and *civil* forfeiture statutes. *See United States v. 501 Rimini Road,* 733 F.Supp. 1382, 1386 (S.D.Cal.1990); *United States v. 6250 Ledge Road,* 747 F.Supp. 505, 510 (E.D.Wis.1990), *aff'd,* 943 F.2d 721 (7th Cir.1991). They have likewise been extended to orders freezing the defendant's assets in some kinds of civil cases brought by the government. *See Securities and Exch. Comm'n v. Cherif,* 933 F.2d 403 (7th Cir.1991), *cert. denied,* 502 U.S. 1071 (1992) (civil securities fraud case); *United States v. Rogers,* 984 F.2d 314 (9th Cir.1993) (tax penalty case). *See also, United States v. Ursery,* 516 U.S. __, 116 S.Ct. 2135, 135 L.Ed.2d 549 (1996) (civil forfeiture is not penal; therefore, civil forfeiture followed by criminal punishment is not double jeopardy).

A few limits remain, however. In *United States v. Unimex, Inc.,* 991 F.2d 546 (9th Cir.1993), the corporate defendant was accused of money laundering and related offenses, and the government had seized all of its assets, including some assets that the corporation said were untainted. Being a corporation, the defendant was not entitled to appointed counsel, and no lay officer or shareholder could act as its counsel. The Ninth Circuit held that the government had deprived Unimex of its right to effective assistance of counsel by taking away all its assets, denying it a chance to show cause that some of the assets were nonforfeitable, and then forcing it to go to trial without counsel.

The Supreme Court has never decided whether the government must provide a defendant an adversarial hearing on the forfeitability of assets *before* placing them beyond a defendant's reach. In *United States v. Monsanto*, 924 F.2d 1186 (2nd Cir.1991) (en banc), the Second Circuit held that the government need not give an indicted defendant an adversarial hearing before taking initial control of assets that he needs to pay defense counsel; but, if the government seeks to *continue* the restraint during the pretrial phase of the case, the Fifth and Sixth Amendments require an adversarial hearing as to probable cause that the defendant committed the charged crimes and that the assets are properly forfeitable. A majority of the other federal circuits agree with the Second Circuit conclusion in *Monsanto*.

CLIENT TRUST ACCOUNTS

CRPC 4–100 and ABA Model Rule 1.15 require attorneys to keep clients' money and property separate from their own, to maintain adequate records, to notify clients promptly when money or property is received on their behalf, and to deliver promptly any money or property to which the client is entitled. [*Accord* ABA Code DR 9–102.]

A. What is a Client Trust Account?

Attorneys frequently receive money either from clients or on behalf of clients. For example, an attorney who does collection work may receive money from the client's debtor. Or, the plaintiff's attorney in a personal injury case may receive settlement money from the defendant or the defendant's insurance company. Or, the defense attorney in such a case may receive money from the defendant to be used in paying off a judgment. Or, an attorney in a business transaction may receive money from the client for use on the client's behalf later in the transaction. In each of these examples, the money belongs to the client, and the attorney must put it into a client trust account.

When a client turns over a relatively large sum to a lawyer to be held for a relatively long period, the lawyer should make a specific agreement with the client about how the sum is to be handled. Absent a specific agreement, the lawyer should put the sum into a separate, interest-bearing trust bank account. The interest, of course, belongs to the client, not to the lawyer. The lawyer should use a separate, interest-bearing trust account if the interest to be earned will exceed the cost of keeping a separate account. [*See Carroll v. State Bar*, 166 Cal.App.3d 1193, 213 Cal.Rptr. 305 (1985).]

Typically, however, a lawyer receives relatively small sums, to be held for relatively short periods, on behalf of numerous different clients. The lawyer traditionally lumps these sums together in a single trust account in a bank. Usually this account is a checking account, not a time deposit account, because a checking account makes transactions easier and provides a simple, clean record of what went where. Prior to the 1970's, banks did not pay interest on checking accounts; thus, in those days, the banks were blessed with free use of money that lawyers across the nation were holding for their clients. Further, even when banks began offering interest-bearing checking accounts, most lawyers did not take advantage of them because of the difficulty of prorating the interest among clients. In the 1980's, bar organizations discovered a way to end this gratuitous subsidy of the banking industry. At present, California and most other states require lawyers to use special interest-bearing accounts (called IOLTA, "Interest on Lawyers' Trust Accounts") for small sums that are to be held for relatively brief periods. The interest on these accounts is paid directly to the state bar which then uses it to fund legal service programs for the poor. [*See, e.g.*, Cal.Bus. & Prof.Code §§ 6210–6212.]

The bank in which a lawyer keeps her IOLTA account will typically deduct the routine bank service charges on the account from the interest the account earns; the bank will then send the remainder of the interest to the state bar. The lawyer may deposit a small amount of her own funds, or her office funds, into the client trust account to pay any additional bank service charges (such as check printing charges). [*See, e.g.*, CRPC 4–100(A)(1).] Aside from that small amount, the lawyer must not put her own funds or her office funds into the client trust account. Thus, a lawyer must not keep a "safety pad" of her own money in the client trust account to prevent overdrafts; to do that would constitute commingling. [*See* ABA Model Rule 1.15; CRPC 4–100(A).] When a client entrusts a lawyer with money to pay future expenses, the lawyer must put the money into the client trust account. The lawyer may then write checks on that account to pay the client's expenses as they arise. Needless to say, the lawyer must not write checks on the client trust account to pay the lawyer's personal expenses, or the law office expenses, or the expenses of some other client who has no funds in that account. Considering the statements made in this paragraph, we can draw the following conclusion about the balance in an IOLTA client trust account: the balance must always equal the total deposits of clients' money, plus a small sum of the lawyer's own funds for exceptional bank service charges, plus accrued interest that has not yet been paid by the bank to the state bar, minus the total amount properly disbursed on behalf of clients. If the balance is ever less than that amount, or more than that amount, the lawyer is in trouble.

B. What Goes Into the Client Trust Account?

Suppose that you have agreed to represent a client in some litigation. The two of you have signed a letter agreement in which you have agreed to do the work for a specified hourly fee. At the close of your initial two-hour interview with the client, she gives you $1,000. $100 is to pay your fee for the two-hour interview. $400 is an advance for costs and expenses that you will incur as the case proceeds—court filing fees, the sheriff's fee for serving the complaint, and the like. The remaining $500 is an advance to cover your fee for work that you will do on the case within the next few weeks. How much, if any, of the $1,000 must go into your client trust account?

Fee for Completed Work

Obviously the $100 payment for the initial two-hour interview does not go into your client trust account. That payment covers work you have already done—it belongs to you, and you would be guilty of commingling if you put it into your client trust account.

Advance for Costs and Expenses

What about the $400 that the client has advanced to you to cover costs and expenses? CRPC 4–100 and ABA Model Rule 1.15 require you to deposit advances for costs and expenses in the client trust account. [*But see* ABA Code DR 9–102(A) (advances for costs and expenses need not be put in client trust account).] The reason for putting the advance for costs and expenses in the client trust account is obvious; if you put it in your own account or your office account, you might spend it and have nothing left to pay the client's costs and expenses when they arise. Moreover, if you withdraw or get fired before the advance has been consumed, you must refund the remainder to the client. [*See* CRPC 3–700(D) and ABA Model Rule 1.16(d).]

Advance on Attorney Fees

What about the $500 advance on attorney fees? Neither CRPC 4–100, nor ABA Model Rule 1.15, nor ABA Code DR 9–102 offers specific guidance, and the law varies from state to state concerning the proper disposition of fee advances. [*See* Wolfram § 4.8 at 178–79; ABA/BNA Lawyers' Manual on Professional Conduct 45:109–111 (1993).] The confusion is compounded when an attorney's fee agreement with a client fails to spell out precisely what is intended. A frequent culprit in fee agreements is the term "retainer." Over the years, attorneys have used the term "retainer" in so many conflicting senses that it should be banished from the legal vocabulary.

Sometimes "retainer" means a fee that the client pays the attorney simply to be available should the client need legal assistance during a specified period or with respect to a specified matter. [*See* CRPC 3–700(D)(2) (defining "true retainer fee" as one "paid solely for the purpose of ensuring the availability of the attorney for the matter").] The attorney earns this kind of "retainer" by agreeing to be available, not by performing services. [Indeed, from the client's point of view, one benefit of such a "retainer" is to make a particular attorney *unavailable* to a potential adversary in the event of litigation.] This kind of "retainer" belongs to the lawyer when it is paid, and it should not be put into the client trust account. [*See* Wisconsin State Bar Formal Opinion E–86–9 (1986).] Like all attorney fees, this kind of "retainer" must be reasonable in amount; if it is excessive, the attorney is subject to discipline. When and if a "retainer" client actually needs legal services, the attorney will provide them for an additional hourly fee that is often lower than the attorney's ordinary rate.

Attorneys also use the term "retainer" to mean a lump sum paid by a client at the outset of a matter. Sometimes the fee agreement states that the "retainer" is to cover a specified amount of work, and that if more work is needed the client will pay for it at a specified rate. A retainer of that sort belongs to the attorney when it is paid, and it therefore does not go into the client trust account. [*See, e.g.,* Texas State Bar Op. 431 (1986).] Sometimes the fee agreement states that the "retainer" is "non-refundable." The New York Court of Appeal has held that "non-refundable retainer" fees are grounds for discipline because they inhibit the client's freedom to fire the lawyer and because a lawyer sometimes gets paid a large sum for little or no work. [*In re Cooperman,* 83 N.Y.2d 465, 611 N.Y.S.2d 465, 633 N.E.2d 1069 (1994).] Other states tolerate "non-refundable retainer" fee, but only when reasonable in amount; if a fee proves to be excessive, the lawyer must refund part of it.

Finally, attorneys sometimes use the term "retainer" to mean an advance payment of fees for work that the lawyer will perform in the future. If the attorney withdraws or is fired before completing the work, the attorney must refund the unearned portion of the advance. [*See* CRPC 3–700(D)(2); ABA Model Rule 1.16(d); *see also* ABA Code DR 2–110(A)(3).] Although the authorities are not uniform, the majority and more conservative view holds that the attorney should deposit this kind of advance payment in the client trust account. [For a thoughtful discussion of the issue, *see* L. Brickman, *The Advance Fee Payment Dilemma: Should Payments Be Deposited to the Client Trust Account or to the General Office Account?,* 10 Cardozo L.Rev. 647 (1989); *see also* Restatement of the Law Governing Lawyers § 56, comment f (Proposed Final Draft No. 1 (1996)).] At reasonable intervals, the attorney should provide the client an accounting of the number of hours expended and the amount that the attorney proposes to deduct from the advance. If the client does not dispute the amount, the attorney may then withdraw it from the client trust account and put it to his or her own use. [*See* ABA Model Rule 1.15(c).]

Perhaps the most important moral to draw from this discussion is: be clear when you draft your fee agreement with your client. If some primordial urge drives you to use the term "retainer," at least explain what you mean in terms that both you and the client will understand.

C. What Records Must the Attorney Keep?

CRPC 4–100(B)(3) and ABA Model Rule 1.15 require an attorney to keep "complete records" of all clients' money or property that comes into the attorney's possession, and to render appropriate accountings to the clients.

The State Bar of California has adopted some standards for the kinds of records lawyers should keep. [Trust Account Record Keeping Standards, operative January 1, 1993.] For clients' funds, the following records should be created and maintained for five years:

- A ledger sheet for each client. For each transaction, the ledger sheet should show the date, the amount, the purpose, the source or recipient, and the current balance for that client.

- A journal for each bank account. The journal should show the date, amount, and client affected by each transaction and should show the current account balance.

- All bank statements and cancelled checks.

- A monthly reconciliation (balancing) of the ledgers, journals, and bank documents.

For securities and other property the lawyer holds on behalf of the client, the lawyer should maintain a journal (again for five years) that shows:

- what the item is;

- for whom it is held;

- when it was received or distributed; and

- to whom it was distributed.

D.   What is a "Client Security Fund"?

The bar associations of California and some other states have established "client security funds," a source of money that can be used to reimburse the hapless clients of dishonest lawyers. [*See, e.g.,* Cal.Bus. & Prof.Code § 6140.5.]   Currently in California, $40 of a lawyer's annual State Bar membership fee goes to the client security fund.

Client security funds have two objectives. First, it is said that the legal profession owes defrauded clients a "debt of honor." Second, a client security fund may help improve the image of the profession and thus help preserve the lawyers' privilege of self-regulation. Client security funds are generally not large enough to provide full reimbursement to all claimants. Limits have been set on the amount a claimant can recover, and recovery may be denied if the loss is covered by the lawyer's or the claimant's insurance. [*See generally* Rules of Procedure, California Client Security Fund Matters, printed in California Rules of Court—State 1265–72 (West 1996).]

MULTIPLE CHOICE QUESTIONS

Answer these questions under the ABA Code and
ABA Model Rules

1.   Criminal defense lawyer Lenox agreed to represent defendant Denmon at Denmon's trial for arson. Lenox and Denmon orally agreed on the following attorney fee arrangement. If Denmon were acquitted, the fee would be $25,000. If Denmon were convicted of any lesser included offense, the fee would be $5,000. If Denmon were convicted of arson, the fee would be $500. Lenox further agreed to advance all litigation expenses, subject to Denmon's promise to repay Lenox whatever the outcome of the case. Which of the following statements are correct?

I.   Lenox *should* have put the fee agreement in writing.

II. It was *proper* for Lenox to agree to advance the litigation expenses.

III. Lenox is *subject to discipline* for charging a contingent fee in a criminal case.

IV. It was *proper* for Lenox to require Denmon to repay the advanced litigation expenses whatever the outcome of the case.

    A. Only I, II, and IV are correct.

    B. Only I and III are correct.

    C. Only II and IV are correct.

    D. All of the statements are correct.

2. Lawyer Leland is admitted to practice only in Kentucky. He regularly represents Holiday Hotels, Inc., a Kentucky corporation with its principal offices in Lexington. Holiday was sued for trademark infringement in Oregon, and Holiday asked Leland to oversee the case and to select appropriate Oregon counsel to do the trial work. With Holiday's approval, Leland selected Oregon attorney Alvarez, and Alvarez paid Leland $1,000 for the referral. Leland oversaw all of the work in the case, and he conducted all of the discovery that took place in Kentucky. Alvarez conducted all of the discovery that took place in Oregon, and he prepared the case for trial and served as trial counsel. At the conclusion of the case, Leland and Alvarez submitted separate bills to Holiday for their respective services.

    A. It was *proper* for Leland and Alvarez to bill Holiday separately, assuming that each bill was reasonable in amount.

    B. It was *proper* for Alvarez to pay Leland $1,000 for the referral, since the two lawyers shared the work and responsibility for the case.

    C. Leland and Alvarez *should* have submitted a single bill to Holiday, since the two lawyers shared the work and responsibility for the case.

    D. The arrangement was *proper,* unless the total fee Holiday paid was higher than it would have been absent the $1,000 referral fee.

3. After Carlson was injured in a car wreck, he was treated in the hospital for twelve days by physician Patino; she billed him $7,500 for her medical services. The wreck put Carlson out of work, and he had no way to pay Patino's bill. He hired attorney Aragon to sue the person who caused the wreck; in a written fee agreement, Aragon promised to do the work for a contingent fee. Aragon decided that Patino would make a good expert witness in the case. Aragon and Carlson agreed that Aragon would lend Carlson $7,500 to pay Patino's medical bill and that Aragon would advance the money needed to pay Patino at $100 per hour for the time she spent preparing to testify and testifying as an expert witness. Carlson agreed to pay back Aragon at the conclusion of the case.

A. Aragon is *subject to discipline* for taking the case on a contingent fee.

B. Aragon is *subject to discipline* for agreeing to lend Carlson the $7,500.

C. Aragon is *subject to discipline* for participating in an agreement to pay a witness for giving testimony.

D. Aragon is *subject to discipline* for agreeing to advance the money needed to pay Patino's expert witness fee.

4. Attorney Arnstein agreed to represent client Clemens in a products liability suit against Draxco, Inc. Clemens refused to discuss Arnstein's fee at the outset of the case; rather, Clemens insisted on a provision in the retainer agreement that Arnstein would do the work "for a reasonable fee, to be deducted from the proceeds" of the case. After a long period of discovery, Arnstein arranged a very favorable settlement between Clemens and Draxco. Draxco paid the $175,000 settlement by a check made payable to Arnstein. Arnstein immediately deposited the check in his client trust account and invited Clemens to come by the office to settle their affairs. When Clemens arrived, Arnstein gave him a bill for $25,000. He computed that amount by multiplying the number of hours he spent on the case (350) times his normal hourly rate ($65), and adding an extra $2,250 because of the generousness of the settlement he had achieved for Clemens. When Clemens looked at the bill, he turned scarlet and began to shout that the fee was outrageously high. Arnstein explained the basis of his charge, and he offered to arbitrate the matter through the local bar association, but Clemens refused. When Clemens demanded immediate payment of the entire $175,000, Arnstein gave him a check, drawn on his client trust account, in the amount of $150,000. Arnstein kept the other $25,000 in his client trust account, pending ultimate resolution of the fee dispute.

A. Arnstein's handling of the matter was *proper*.

B. Arnstein is *subject to discipline* for charging Clemens more than his normal hourly rate.

C. Arnstein is *subject to discipline* for depositing the entire proceeds of Draxco's check in his client trust account.

D. Arnstein is *subject to discipline* for keeping the $25,000 in his client trust account pending resolution of the fee dispute.

5. Client Fujitomi entrusted lawyer Lee with $10,000, to be used six weeks later to close a business transaction. Lee immediately deposited it in her client trust account; at the time, it was the only money in that account. Later that same day, the local bar association called Lee and asked her to rush out to the Municipal Court to take over the defense of an indigent drunkard, Watkins, who was being tried for violating an obscure municipal statute. Because of chaos in the Public Defender's Office, Watkins was being tried without benefit of counsel. By the time Lee arrived, the judge had already found Watkins guilty and sentenced him to pay a fine of $350 or spend 30 days in jail. Under a

peculiar local rule of court, the only way to keep Watkins from going to jail was to pay the fine immediately and to request a trial *de novo* in the Superior Court. Therefore, Lee paid the fine with a check drawn on her client trust account, and Watkins promised to repay her within one week.

A. Lee's handling of the Watkins matter was *proper*.

B. Lee *should* have allowed Watkins to go to jail.

C. Had Lee paid Watkins' fine out of her personal bank account, that would have been *proper*.

D. Lee would be *subject to discipline* for handling the matter in any manner other than she did.

6. Attorney Ayers represents client Canfield as plaintiff in a suit to compel specific performance of a contract. Canfield contracted to purchase Thunderbolt, a thoroughbred race horse, from defendant Dennis in exchange for $1,500,000 worth of corporate bonds owned by Canfield. Canfield transferred the bonds to Dennis, but Dennis refused to deliver Thunderbolt. Two months before the scheduled trial date, Canfield gave Ayers the following instructions: "I am leaving tomorrow on a six-week sailing trip through the South Pacific, and you will not be able to reach me by mail or phone. If Dennis makes any reasonable settlement offer before I return, please accept it, but try to get the horse if you can." A week later, Dennis's lawyer called Ayers and said: "Dennis wants to capitulate. He will either return the bonds, or he will turn over Thunderbolt. He insists on an immediate response, so call me back this afternoon." Ayers believes in good faith that Thunderbolt is a tired nag, worth far less than $1,500,000. Further, Ayers discovers that it will cost nearly $1,000 to keep Thunderbolt in a safe, bonded stable until Canfield's return. What *should* Ayers do?

A. Get the bonds and put them in a safe deposit box until Canfield returns.

B. Tell Dennis's lawyer that he cannot respond until Canfield returns.

C. Get Thunderbolt and house him in the safe, bonded stable at Canfield's expense until Canfield returns.

D. Get Thunderbolt and turn him out to pasture on Ayers' farm until Canfield returns.

*Answers to the multiple choice questions will be found
in the Appendix at the end of the book*

Chapter Six

COMPETENCE, DILIGENCE, AND UNAUTHORIZED PRACTICE

What This Chapter Covers

Reading Assignment

Wydick & Perschbacher, Chapter 6

ABA Model Rules:

> Scope, note 6 [printed at the beginning of the ABA Model Rules];
>
> Rules 1.1 through 1.4, 1.8(h), and 5.3 through 5.5.

CRPC 1–200, 1–300 through 1–320, 3–110, 3–400, 3–500 and 3–510

Cal.Bus. & Prof.Code §§ 6105, 6125–6126.

Supplemental Reading

ABA Code:

> EC 3–1 through 3–9, EC 6–1 through 6–6, EC 7–4 through 7–9;
>
> DR 3–101 through 3–103;

DR 6–101 through 6–102.

Hazard & Hodes:

Discussion of ABA Model Rules 1.1, 1.3 through 1.4, 1.8(h), and 5.3 through 5.5(b).

Wolfram:

Section 5.1 (definition and regulation of competence);

Sections 5.2 through 5.5 (education, bar exams, continuing education requirements, and specialization);

Sections 5.6.1 through 5.6.6 (law of legal malpractice);

Section 5.6.7 (limiting malpractice liability);

Section 5.6.8 (malpractice insurance);

Sections 15.1.1 through 15.1.4 (unauthorized practice).

Restatement (Third) of the Law Governing Lawyers §§ 30–34 (Proposed Final Draft No. 1, 1996).

———

Discussion Problems

1. Lawyer Layton graduated at the top of her class from a famous law school that provides a "national" legal education, and she now practices probate law in California, the only jurisdiction in which she is licensed to practice. Purely for her own enjoyment, Layton regularly uses her home computer to communicate about legal topics with strangers on the Internet. A few months ago, Layton responded to a request for legal advice made by one Cushing, a woman from Rhode Island. Cushing's request was directed to any lawyer willing to answer, not specifically to Layton. Cushing's request described a blatant act of malpractice committed by the Rhode Island lawyer who represented her in her Rhode Island divorce case. The malpractice had occurred 35 months earlier; Cushing realized at the time that the divorce lawyer had made a grave mistake, but she had never done anything about it. Cushing's Internet message asked whether she had a valid claim against the divorce lawyer for malpractice. Layton, relying on her national education at the famous law school, and without doing a scrap of legal research, sent an e-mail message to Cushing, expressing her opinion that the divorce lawyer's conduct was indeed actionable malpractice, and advising Cushing that it was not too late to sue because the statute of limitations for legal malpractice is four years. If Layton had spent a few minutes in the law library or on WESTLAW, she would have discovered that the Rhode Island statute of limitation is three years, not four. Cushing, lulled into inaction by Layton's advice, did not get around to suing the divorce lawyer until two months later, at which point she discovered that the three year statute of limitations had run.

a. Is Layton guilty of practicing law in Rhode Island without a license?

b. Is Layton subject to discipline for incompetence?

c. Is Layton liable to Cushing for legal malpractice?

2. Client Cameron hired the firm of Alarcon & Brown to represent her as plaintiff in a products liability action. Cameron gave the firm a $5,000 advance on attorney fees. The firm's management committee assigned the case to associate attorney Anson. Before doing any significant amount of work on the case, Anson left the firm for personal reasons. The management committee then reassigned the case to associate Benson. Due to his heavy work load, Benson did not get around to filing the complaint for 10 months. Eventually the case came to trial before Judge Jergins as trier of fact. Judge Jergins took the case under submission for 18 months, despite a state statute that requires judges to decide cases within 90 days. During that 18 months, Benson did nothing to speed Judge Jergins along, believing that to do so might annoy him to Cameron's detriment. Ultimately Judge Jergins entered judgment in Cameron's favor, but Cameron was angry that justice had been so long delayed. Does Cameron have a valid claim for legal malpractice? Is this an appropriate case for professional discipline? If so, who should be disciplined?

3. While attempting to board a commercial airliner, Chandler was personally injured and publicly humiliated by an employee of the airline company. She hired attorney Adams to sue the company. Adams neglected the matter, and Chandler eventually complained to the state bar. When Adams received a letter of inquiry from the state bar, he checked Chandler's file and discovered that he had let the statute of limitations on Chandler's claim run. Adams met with Chandler, told her honestly what happened, and offered to pay her $6,500 out of his own pocket. That amount was $2,000 more than the medical costs she had incurred as a result of the personal injury. Chandler accepted this offer and signed a form prepared by Adams that released him "from all further responsibility and liability in the aforementioned matter." Adams gave Chandler his personal check for $6,500; the back of the check stated: "Endorsement acknowledges full payment and release of all claims." Adams duly reported the settlement to the state bar. Did Adams handle the matter properly?

4. Crampton lost the use of his right leg when a nurse gave him improper medication at the hospital. Crampton consulted attorney Arlene; she told Crampton that she had never handled a medical malpractice claim before, but that she would do her best on Crampton's behalf. Ultimately Crampton's case went to trial and was lost. Then Crampton sued Arlene for legal malpractice, claiming these defects in Arlene's performance:

a. Arlene had a choice of venue in the case. She chose to litigate in a rural community, rather than in a large metropolitan area where the jury might well have been more sympathetic to a medical malpractice claim.

    b.   Arlene failed to consult with any expert on hospital operations; an expert could have testified that the number of nurses at the hospital was insufficient to give proper care to all the patients.

    c.   Arlene used only one expert medical witness at the trial, and the jury might have been more impressed had several experts testified.

    d.   Arlene failed to find out whether there were any eyewitnesses around (aides or other nurses) when Crampton received the improper medication.

    e.   Arlene failed to discover a State Department of Health regulation setting the proper staff/patient ratio in hospitals.

Is Arlene guilty of malpractice for taking on the case in the first place? Do any of the five defects constitute good grounds for a legal malpractice claim?

    5.   Lawyer Levitt got a phone call this afternoon from lawyer Huffington, house counsel for Infoscope, Inc., a large software company that Levitt had previously represented in several matters. Huffington told Levitt that a consumer had sued Infoscope in Levitt's jurisdiction for violating the Nelson–Sturgis Act, a federal consumer protection law. Huffington explained that Infoscope had been sued in a half dozen similar cases in other jurisdictions, and that Infoscope had won every case on summary judgment. Huffington said: "Our lawyers in the prior cases have already researched every possible legal question, and I will send you a complete set of the legal memos they prepared for us. Further, we have already been through extensive discovery, and I will send you all the documents, deposition transcripts, and other materials collected in the earlier cases." Then Huffington made Levitt a proposal, as follows: "Our Board of Directors is tired of high legal bills, and the Board has allocated $125,000 to dispose of this case. That's to cover legal fees, litigation expenses, and settlement or judgment—everything. I'm offering you the case on that basis. It should be a good money-maker for you. You'll start by sending the plaintiff a set of interrogatories, and I can supply you with the set we used successfully in the two most recent cases. You will also need to take the plaintiff's deposition, but I can give you a complete outline of all the points to cover. Finally, you'll need to move for summary judgment, but I'll supply you with the motion papers and briefs from the prior cases. Whatever part of the $125,000 is left over will be your legal fee." May Levitt represent Infoscope on the terms Huffington has proposed?

    6.   Attorneys Ames, Bell, and Chen are the three shareholders in a law firm that is organized as a professional corporation. The hardest working person in the firm is Daley, a non-lawyer. Her title is "Office Manager," and her duties include keeping the financial and billing records, supervising the office staff, and managing the client file system.

When she has time, she also helps the lawyers with research and prepares drafts of routine legal documents.

a. Daley's brother and sister want to buy a small piece of real estate as an investment, and they want to keep the legal costs as low as possible. Over the years, Daley has picked up enough knowledge of real estate law to know exactly what to do. Would it be proper for Daley to do the basic legal work, provided that Chen looks over the work to make sure that it is accurate and complete?

b. One of Daley's friends selected Ames, Bell, & Chen to represent him in a major matter, thanks largely to his friendship with Daley. May the firm pay Daley a bonus equal to 10% of the fees earned in this matter?

c. The firm proposes to set up a retirement program that will be funded in part by fees earned by the lawyers. Would it be proper to include Daley as a participant in the retirement program?

d. The state's professional corporation statute requires corporate officers to be shareholders. Bell is officially named as the corporate treasurer, but in fact Daley does all the financial work. May the attorneys sell Daley a token number of shares and name her as the corporate treasurer?

LEGAL MALPRACTICE

A. The Relationship between Legal Malpractice and Discipline by the Bar

As used here, the term "legal malpractice" refers to the attorney's civil liability to a client or other injured person for professional misconduct or negligence. Malpractice actions differ from disciplinary actions. First, the forum for a malpractice action is a civil court, not a disciplinary hearing. Second, in a malpractice action the attorney's adversary is an injured person, not a disciplinary authority. Third, the purpose of a malpractice action is to obtain compensation for the injured person, not necessarily to punish the attorney nor to protect the public. [*See generally* Manuel R. Ramos, *Legal Malpractice*: *The Profession's Dirty Little Secret*, 47 Vand.L.Rev. 1657 (1994).]

Suppose that an attorney violates one of the rules of legal ethics. Does that automatically mean that the attorney has also committed legal malpractice? What answer is provided by paragraph 6 of the Scope section at the beginning of the ABA Model Rules? Is an ethics violation admissible as evidence of negligence? [*See Fishman v. Brooks*, 396 Mass. 643, 487 N.E.2d 1377 (1986) (ethics violation is "not itself an actionable breach of duty to a client," but if the client can show that the ethics rule was "intended to protect one in his position, a violation of that rule may be some evidence of the attorney's negligence"); *see also*

Geoffrey Hazard, *Foreward* to the Restatement of Law Governing Lawyers (Proposed Final Draft No. 1, 1996).]

B. Theories of Legal Malpractice Liability

A number of legal theories are available to the plaintiff in a legal malpractice case, and the choice of theory may be important because of differences in the measure of damages and the applicable statutes of limitations.

One possible theory is intentional tort. For instance, an attorney can be sued for misuse of funds, or abuse of process, or misrepresentation.

A second possible theory is breach of general fiduciary duties. When acting as a fiduciary, an attorney undertakes the ordinary duties of a fiduciary, including loyalty, confidentiality, and honest dealing.

A third possible theory is breach of contract. One source of contractual duties is the written or oral agreement by which the client hires the attorney to perform legal services. Even if there is no express contract, a court may be willing to imply a promise by the attorney to use ordinary skill and care to protect the client's interests.

The fourth and most common theory is unintentional tort—ordinary negligence. Here the plaintiff must prove the familiar elements of a negligence case: a duty of care, a breach of that duty, actual cause, proximate cause, and damages. These elements are discussed in the following paragraphs.

1) The Duty of Care

In a legal malpractice action there can be two points of dispute about the element of duty. First, to whom does an attorney owe a duty of care? Second, what is the appropriate standard of care?

Obviously, an attorney owes a duty of care to a client. Sometimes it is not clear whether a person has become a client. A person can become a client without formal fanfare and without paying a fee to the attorney. A court is especially likely to imply an attorney-client relationship when a person asks the attorney for help, reasonably believes that the attorney has agreed to provide help, and ultimately discovers that the attorney has not done so. [*See, e.g., De Vaux v. American Home Assur. Co.*, 387 Mass. 814, 444 N.E.2d 355 (1983).]

Does an attorney owe a duty of care to anyone other than a client? The modern trend of authority holds that an attorney owes a duty of care to third parties whom the client intended to benefit from the attorney's rendition of legal services. For example, suppose client C hires attorney A to draft a will leaving C's estate to T. If A drafts the will negligently and the estate passes to C's heirs instead of T, then T has a valid malpractice claim against A. [*See, e.g., Lucas v. Hamm*, 56 Cal.2d 583, 15 Cal.Rptr. 821, 364 P.2d 685 (1961), cert. denied, 368 U.S. 987, 82 S.Ct. 603, 7 L.Ed.2d 525 (1962).] But courts have not expanded an attorney's liability for negligence (as distinct from intentional wrong) to third parties that were not intended to benefit from the attorney's services. For instance, an attorney is not liable for negligence to his client's adversary in litigation.

What is the appropriate standard of care? If the attorney defendant is a general practitioner, then the standard of care is the skill and knowledge ordinarily possessed by attorneys under similar circumstances. R. Mallen & J. Smith, *Legal Malpractice* § 15.2 (3d ed. 1989). If the attorney purports to be an expert or specialist in a field of law, then the standard of care is the skill and knowledge ordinarily possessed by experts or specialists in that field. [*Id.* § 15.4.] The relevant geographic area for measuring the standard of care is the jurisdiction in which the defendant attorney is admitted to practice. Thus, rural lawyers should be held to the same standard as their cousins in the big city. [*See Russo v. Griffin*, 147 Vt. 20, 510 A.2d 436 (1986); *see also* Note, *The Locality Rule*, 64 N.D.L.R. 661 (1988).]

2) Breach of the Duty of Care

The standard wisdom teaches that lawyers are not liable for "mere errors in judgment." Thus, in *Hodges v. Carter*, 239 N.C. 517, 80 S.E.2d 144 (1954), it was said:

> An attorney who acts in good faith and in an honest belief that his advice and acts are well-founded and in the best interest of his client is not answerable for a mere error of judgment or for a mistake in a point of law which has not been settled by the court of last resort in his state and on which reasonable doubt may be entertained by well-informed lawyers.

But note carefully the last three words of that quotation. The judgment must be a *well-informed* judgment, not one made in ignorance. A lawyer is expected to know the settled principles of law; if she does not know them, she is expected to look them up using the standard research techniques used by ordinarily prudent attorneys. If the answers are there to be found, and if she does not find them, she has breached the duty of care. [*See Smith v. Lewis*, 13 Cal.3d 349, 118 Cal.Rptr. 621, 530 P.2d 589 (1975).] If a principle of law is unsettled and open to debate, the attorney is expected to do reasonable research and to "make an informed decision as to a course of conduct based upon an intelligent assessment of the problem." [*Id.*]

In the trial of a case, an attorney is often called upon to make tactical decisions, such as what questions to ask a witness on cross-examination. The attorney will not be second-guessed in a later malpractice case, so long as the tactical decision was based on a well-informed judgment. An attorney can, however, be held liable for failing to conduct a reasonable fact investigation, or failing to find and interview key witnesses, or failing to consult with appropriate experts, or failing to discover pertinent statutes, regulations, and the like. [*See Woodruff v. Tomlin*, 616 F.2d 924 (6th Cir. 1980).]

3) Actual Cause

As in ordinary negligence litigation, a malpractice plaintiff must prove actual cause—that the injury would not have happened *but for* the defendant's negligent act. For instance, suppose that attorney A represents client C in a contract suit. The trial court enters a large judgment against C, and C instructs A to petition the appellate court for review. Attorney A negligently fails to file the petition, and C sues A for malpractice. To win the malpractice action, C must prove that the appellate court probably would have granted the petition and probably would have reached a result more favorable to C. [*See Daugert v. Pappas*, 104 Wash.2d 254, 704 P.2d 600 (1985).]

4) Proximate Cause

Again as in ordinary negligence litigation, a malpractice plaintiff must prove, not just actual cause, but proximate cause—that it is fair to hold defendant liable for unexpected injuries or for expected injuries that happen in unexpected ways.

For example, suppose that H (age 75) marries W (age 25). Each has children from a prior marriage. H wants his estate to pass to W's children, not to his own who are already well provided for. Attorney A negligently drafts H's will in a way that will accomplish that result only if W outlives H. Then W is killed in a car crash, and H dies a few months later without having changed his will. W's children sue attorney A for malpractice, and A argues lack of proximate cause. Since a reasonably prudent attorney should have foreseen that H might outlive W, and might not change his will after W's death, a court would probably conclude that proximate cause has been established.

5) Damages

A malpractice plaintiff must prove damages—for example, the value of a lost cause of action, or the value of property lost through a defect in title. The plaintiff can recover for loss that flows directly from the attorney's wrong, and also for loss that flows indirectly, but foreseeably, from the attorney's wrong. [*See Mallen & Smith, supra*, §§ 16.1–16.14.]

For instance, suppose that client C hires attorney A to defend him in a suit for alleged theft of trade secrets belonging to C's former employer. Due to A's negligence, C lost the case and had to pay a large judgment to the former employer. Further, the loss so injured C's professional reputation that no one would hire him. If the injury to C's reputation was foreseeable, A will be liable to C, not only for the amount of the judgment, but also for C's loss of earnings. [*Id.* §§ 16.12–16.14.]

C. Vicarious Liability

Under ordinary principles of *respondeat superior*, an attorney is liable for injuries caused by employees acting within the scope of their employment. Thus, an attorney is responsible for her secretary's negligence in failing to transmit an important message or for the negligence of an attorney employed by her to assist in the trial of a case.

Likewise, under general principles of partnership law, each partner in a law partnership is liable for the negligence of the other partners in the ordinary course of the partnership business. The laws of many states allow law firms to incorporate. In the past, incorporation produced significant tax advantages, but many of those advantages have since been eliminated by tax reform. [*See* Finley & King, *Should Your Practice be Incorporated?*, 3 Juris 8 (July, 1987).] In some states, incorporation does nothing to shield an attorney from vicarious liability for the malpractice of others in the firm. In other states, only the corporation and the actual tortfeasors are liable for malpractice, but in some such states the limited liability applies only if the corporate shareholders have provided adequate protection (through insurance or otherwise) for the victims of their malpractice. [*See* Mallen & Smith, *supra*, § 5.4.]

D. Malpractice Insurance

Neither the CRPC, nor the ABA Code nor the ABA Model Rules requires lawyers to carry malpractice insurance,[a] but the majority of contemporary American lawyers regard malpractice insurance as an essential, albeit expensive, part of law practice. Americans tend to be quick in looking to courts to resolve conflicts. Further, a client who has been injured by a lawyer's ineptitude often prefers to sue for malpractice, rather than start disciplinary proceedings, which are typically slow and which provide no monetary solace to the injured client. Money may seem better than blood, and unhappy clients can be tempted by malpractice verdicts that occasionally reach the multimillion dollar mark.

In comparison shopping for malpractice insurance, be aware that policies differ dramatically in their features. [*See generally* H. Robert Fiebach, *Shopping for Malpractice Insurance*, A.B.A.J., March 1993 at 98; R. Minto & M. Morton, *The Anatomy of Legal Malpractice Insurance: A Comparative View*, 64 N.D.L.Rev. 547 (1988); F. Goldfein, *Legal Malpractice Insurance*, 61 Temple L.Rev. 1285 (1988).] For example:

• In former years, some insurers offered "occurrence" policies, which covered the lawyer for acts or omissions made during the policy term, regardless of when the claim was asserted. At present, a lawyer can obtain only a "claims made" policy, which covers the lawyer for unforeseen claims made during the policy period, no matter when the act or omission occurred. If the lawyer has changed jobs or changed insurance companies, she may need supplemental "prior acts" coverage, to prevent gaps in her insurance coverage.

• Liability policies generally require the insured to defend the lawyer against covered claims. Most policies give the insurer the right to select defense counsel, but others allow the insured lawyer to partici-

---

a. A California lawyer who takes business from a State Bar approved lawyer referral service must either carry malpractice insurance or else provide proof of financial responsibility. The limits of the insurance policy must be at least $100,000 for each occurrence and at least $300,000 aggregate per year. [Minimum Standards for a Lawyer Referral Service in California § 6.3 (1989), printed in California Rules of Court 1151–54 (West 1991).]

pate in the selection. Further, policies differ respecting the decision to settle a case. Most require the consent of the insured lawyer, but some policies provide that if the lawyer refuses to settle, the insured's liability is limited to the amount for which the claim could have been settled. Other policies provide that if the insurer and the insured disagree on whether to settle, a peer review panel will make the final decision.

• The limits of liability can make an important difference in the cost of insurance. The higher the policy limits, the higher the premium. A policy with limits of $500,000/$1 million usually means that the insurer will pay no more than $500,000 for all claims arising out of a single act (regardless of the number of claimants), and will pay no more than $1 million for all claims during the policy term. Policies differ in how they treat the expenses of defending claims. Typically, defense costs are included in the policy limits, which means that the lawyer should buy policy limits high enough to cover both potential liability and defense costs.

• The type of deductible provision can also make an important difference in the cost of a policy. A lawyer who self-insures for the first $100,000 of liability will obviously pay a lower premium than one whose policy has a deductible of only $10,000. Further, most policies provide for a per claim deductible, but a few specify an aggregate deductible during the policy term.

• Policies differ as respects the persons who are covered. The cost of a policy depends partly on whether it covers only the present lawyers and non-lawyers in the firm, or whether it also covers predecessor firms, persons formerly with the firm, and lawyers who are "of counsel" to the firm. Further, some policies do not cover employees of the firm unless an additional premium is paid.

• Policies vary in the kinds of acts and omissions they cover. All of them cover the conduct of the insured when rendering professional legal services to others, but some also cover conduct as a fiduciary (for example, as a trustee or executor), some cover judicially imposed sanctions (under F.R.Civ.P. 11, for example), and some cover practice-related personal injury such as false arrest, libel, and malicious prosecution.

• All policies contain exclusions, and the number and breadth of exclusions will affect the cost of the insurance. Typical exclusions are for claims of dishonest, fraudulent, or criminal conduct, claims arising from incidental legal service provided to a business owned by the insured, claims arising out of the insured's conduct as an officer or director of a business, claims of sexual harassment or illegal discrimination, and claims that the insured knew or should have known about the time he or she bought the policy.

When shopping for insurance, remember that (as with other products and services) you generally get about what you pay for. A bargain premium is no bargain if you get less coverage than you expect and need. Information in insurance company brochures and statements by sales representatives are helpful, but in the end there is no substitute for carefully studying the insurance policy itself.

THE ETHICS OF SECOND–RATE LEGAL SERVICE

Is it ethical for a lawyer to supply second-rate legal service to a client who does not want to pay for first-rate service? At what point do client-imposed limits on the budget, the means, and the scope of a representation prevent the lawyer from doing a competent, diligent job?

The ethics committee of the Association of the Bar of the City of New York explored those two issues in a report entitled *The Evolving Lawyer–Client Relationship and its Effect on the Lawyer's Professional Obligations* [51 The Record 441 (1996).] The committee began by observing that the nature of law practice has changed dramatically over the past two decades. In prior years, clients tended to defer to their lawyers, usually letting the lawyers select the means for resolving a matter, and usually letting the lawyers decide how much time and money the matter required. [*See id.* at 441–45.] All that has changed, the committee said. Competition has increased in the legal profession. Clients, both the rich and the poor, have become sensitive to the cost of legal services. Advances in technology have removed communications barriers between client and attorney, thus allowing the client to keep close track of what the lawyer is doing. Institutional clients are demanding more control over details that were traditionally left to the lawyer's judgment, such as which lawyers in a firm will work on a case, when and how much discovery should be conducted, and what tactics the lawyers should pursue at what stages of the case. [*Id.*] As a consequence,

> [r]ather than retain an attorney to handle a matter as he or she deems appropriate, many clients today demand involvement not only in defining the objectives of a representation but also in selecting the means to achieve the objectives. The relationship increasingly is being defined by lawyer and client alike as a joint venture. [*Id.* at 441.]

Do the ethics rules prohibit a lawyer from acceding to a client's budget limit that is too low to let the lawyer handle a matter in the way the lawyer thinks best? Is there a point at which a lawyer must stop a client from dictating the details of how a matter is handled? Consider the following guidance from the ABA Code, the ABA Model Rules, and the Restatement of the Law Governing Lawyers.

A. The ABA Code and ABA Model Rules

The ABA Code requires a lawyer to represent a client "competently" [ABA Code DR 6–101 and EC 6–1] and "zealously within the bounds of the law." [*Id.* DR 7–101(A) and EC 7–1.] Similarly, the ABA Model Rules require a lawyer to represent a client "competently" [ABA Model Rule 1.1; *accord* CRPC 3–110], but in place of "zealous" representation, the Model rules call for the lawyer to act "with reasonable diligence and promptness in representing a client." [*Id.* Rule 1.3.] Comment 1 to Rule 1.3 explains that a

> lawyer should act with commitment and dedication to the interests of the client and with zeal in advocacy upon the client's behalf. However, a lawyer is not bound to press for every advantage that might be realized for a client. A lawyer has professional discretion in determining the means by which a matter should be pursued. [ABA Model Rule 1.3, Comment 1.]

The ABA Code's mention of "zeal within the bounds of the law" is significant. If the client wants the lawyer to pursue an unlawful objective, the lawyer must refuse. Similarly, if the client wants the lawyer to pursue a lawful objective but by unlawful means, the lawyer must refuse. The "bounds of the law" include not only rules of law, but also the rules of legal ethics. Thus, if the client wants the lawyer to do something that would subject the lawyer to professional discipline, the lawyer must refuse. [*See* The Record, *supra,* at 450–51.] Therefore, when the client seeks the lawyer's service, but the client insists on a budget too low to let the lawyer provide the service competently and diligently, the lawyer must decline the representation. [*Id.;* ABA Model Rule 1.16(a)(1); *accord* CRPC 3–700(B)(2).]

It is up to the client to decide the *objectives* of the representation (so long as they are within the bounds of the law). [*See* ABA Model Rule 1.2(a) and (c)–(e).] With the client's consent, however, the lawyer may set a *limit* on those objectives. (For example, "I will set up a licensing program for you, but first you need to get a patent lawyer's advice about the validity of your patent.") [*See* ABA Model Rule 1.2(c).]

The ABA Code posits a distinction between the *objectives* of the representation and the *means* by which those objectives are achieved. [*See* The Record, *supra,* at 452.] ABA Code DR 7–101(A) says that the lawyer must "seek the lawful objectives of the client through reasonably available means permitted by law and the Disciplinary Rules." To oversimplify: the client decides where we are going, and the lawyer decides how to get us there. Ethical Consideration 7–7 states:

> In certain areas of legal representation not affecting the merits of the cause or substantially prejudicing the rights of a client, a lawyer is entitled to make decisions on his own. But otherwise the authority to make decisions is exclusively that of the client, and if made within the framework of the law, such decisions are binding on the lawyer.

Thus, it is the client who gets to decide whether to issue the stock, or whether to get the divorce, or whether to settle the litigation, or whether to plead not guilty, or whether to take the appeal. [ABA Code EC 7–7.]

The ABA Model Rules recognize that the distinction between objectives and means is not as clear as the ABA Code might make it seem. Comment 1 to ABA Model Rule 1.2 explains:

Both lawyer and client have authority and responsibility in the objectives and means of representation. The client has ultimate authority to determine the purposes to be served by legal representation, within the limits imposed by law and the lawyer's professional obligations. Within those limits, a client also has a right to consult with the lawyer about the means to be used in pursuing those objectives. At the same time, a lawyer is not required to pursue objectives or employ means simply because a client may wish that the lawyer do so. A clear distinction between objectives and means sometimes cannot be drawn, and in many cases the client-lawyer relationship partakes of a joint undertaking. In questions of means, the lawyer should assume responsibility for technical and legal tactical issues, but should defer to the client regarding such questions as the expense to be incurred and concern for third persons who might be adversely affected. Law defining the lawyer's scope of authority in litigation varies among jurisdictions.

B. The Restatement of the Law Governing Lawyers

The Restatement of the Law Governing Lawyers provides additional guidance about the division of authority between the client and the lawyer.

Section 30 states that (subject to limits stated elsewhere in the Restatement) a client and lawyer may agree to limit a duty that a lawyer would otherwise owe to a client if the limitation is *reasonable,* and if the client is *adequately informed* and gives *consent.* [Restatement of the Law Governing Lawyers § 30 (Proposed Final Draft No. 1, 1996).] One of the illustrations in § 30 concerns a corporation that wants to impose a tight budget on the lawyer who will defend it in a law suit. The lawyer explains to the corporation's house counsel that the budget will not allow for much discovery, which will reduce the chances of winning. If the corporation consents after being properly informed about the consequences, and if the limitation on the lawyer's duty is reasonable in the circumstances, the corporation will have effectively waived its right to more thorough representation. One consequence of that waiver is that the corporation cannot later claim that the lawyer committed malpractice by failing to do more discovery. The commentary to § 30 suggests that a *reasonable* agreement to limit the lawyer's duty would *not* violate the general rule that prohibits a lawyer from trying to escape malpractice liability by prospective contract with the client. [*Compare* Restatement § 30, Comment a (Proposed Final Draft No. 1, 1996), *with* Restatement § 76 (Tent. Draft No. 7, 1994) and ABA Model Rule 1.8(h).]

In a similar vein, § 32 of the Restatement allows lawyers and their clients to allocate between themselves the authority to make most decisions about the representation. The law, however, makes some decisions nondelegable, for example, a criminal defendant's decision to waive a jury trial. [*See* Restatement § 33(2) (Proposed Final Draft No. 1, 1996).]

Comment b to § 32 explains that the lawyer and client start in a default position in which the lawyer has

> broad authority to make choices advancing the client's interests. But the client may limit the lawyer's authority by agreement or instructions. The lawyer or the client may insist at the outset of the representation on an agreement defining the lawyer's authority. The lawyer is also protected if the client ratifies the lawyer's unauthorized act. Ideally, clients and lawyers will discuss decision-making authority, making allocations that both understand and approve. A lawyer who acts beyond authority is subject to disciplinary sanctions and to suit by the client.... [Restatement § 32, comment b (Proposed Final Draft No. 1, 1996).]

The commentary goes on to explain that the best allocation of authority in a particular case will depend on the client's sophistication and desire to be involved, the extent to which the lawyer and client understand each other and work well together, the significance and complexity of the decisions to be made, the need for speedy action, and similar considerations. [*See id.,* comment c.]

Let us suppose that the lawyer and client begin their relationship by allocating to the lawyer all decisions about, say, negotiation tactics. As the matter progresses, suppose that the client issues an express instruction about something that is clearly within the lawyer's zone of decision. If the instruction calls for the lawyer to act unethically or illegally, the lawyer should explain the situation and the risks to the client and seek to be relieved of the instruction. If the client will not relent, the lawyer *must* withdraw (after obtaining the court's permission if that is required). [*See id.,* comment d; see also *id.* § 44(2)(a); ABA Model Rule 1.16(a)(1).]

Suppose that the client instructs the lawyer to do something that is neither unlawful nor unethical, but that the lawyer believes is foolhardy or obnoxious. Once again, the lawyer should explain the situation and the risks to the client and seek to be relieved of the instruction. [*See* Restatement, *supra,* § 32, comment d (Proposed Final Draft No. 1, 1996); ABA Model Rule 1.16(b)(3).] If the client will not relent, the lawyer *may* withdraw (after obtaining the court's permission if that is required). In this situation, "a lawyer may not continue a representation while refusing to follow a client's continuing instruction." [Restatement, *supra* § 32, comment d.]

Suppose that the client instructs the lawyer to do something that is not unlawful, nor unethical, nor foolhardy, nor obnoxious, but that the lawyer thinks is plain bad judgment and is likely to backfire on the client. Suppose that the lawyer carefully explains the situation and the risks to the client and seeks to be relieved of the instruction, but that the client will not relent. The lawyer then does as the client has instructed. Just as the lawyer feared, the action turns out to harm the client. Can the client now recover from the lawyer for malpractice? No, answers the Restatement, not if the lawyer adequately explained the risks to the client. [*Id.*]

MULTIPLE CHOICE QUESTIONS

Answer these questions under the ABA Code and
ABA Model Rules

1. On June 1st, client Catlin hired attorney Acevedo to sue defendant Degan for securities fraud. Catlin and Acevedo realized that the complaint would have to be filed by September 15th to be within the statute of limitations. Acevedo was very busy with other matters. Starting in mid-August, Catlin telephoned Acevedo every few days to see what progress Acevedo was making. Acevedo repeatedly assured Catlin that he was assembling the facts and preparing preliminary drafts of the complaint, but in truth Acevedo was doing nothing on the case. On September 10th, Catlin learned from Acevedo's secretary that Acevedo had still not started to work on the case. At that point, Catlin fired Acevedo and hired a different lawyer who was able to get the complaint on file by September 15th. Although Acevedo did not charge Catlin any fee, Catlin reported the matter to the state bar. Which of the following is most nearly correct?

   A. If Acevedo would have been able to complete the necessary work by September 15th, his conduct was *proper*.

   B. Since Catlin suffered no damage due to Acevedo's delay, Acevedo's conduct was *proper*.

   C. Even though Catlin suffered no damage due to Acevedo's delay, Acevedo is *liable for malpractice*.

   D. Acevedo is *subject to discipline* for neglecting Catlin's case and for lying to Catlin about the status of the matter.

2. Lawyer Lloyd was an associate attorney employed by the law partnership of Ames & Baker. Client Cress hired Ames to sue one of his competitors for false advertising. Ames assigned Lloyd to do the necessary research and draft the complaint. Lloyd confined her research to state law. Any reasonably competent general practitioner would have discovered a more favorable body of parallel federal law under Section 43(a) of the Lanham Act. Ames eventually brought the case to trial on state law theories only, and Cress lost. Had the case been tried under the Lanham Act, Cress would have won a large judgment. Which of the following propositions are correct?

   I. Lloyd is *liable for malpractice*.

   II. If Lloyd is *liable for malpractice*, then so is Ames.

   III. If Lloyd and Ames are *liable for malpractice*, then so is Baker.

   IV. None of the three lawyers is *liable for malpractice*.

   A. Only IV is correct.

   B. Only I is correct.

C. Only I, II, and III are correct.

D. Only I and II are correct.

3. The Community Association for the Homeless (CAH) is a non-profit charitable corporation that provides food and temporary shelter for homeless persons. CAH subsists on charitable donations and volunteer labor provided by members of the community. CAH owns a large old home in the downtown area, but it has virtually no other assets. Seeking to assist CAH in a time of financial need, Corliss Cheng decided to lend CAH $500,000, interest-free, for two years. Lawyer Landsman offered his services without a fee to represent CAH in the transaction and to prepare the necessary loan papers. Cheng was not represented by a lawyer in the transaction. Landsman prepared a suitable promissory note. The officers of CAH duly executed the note and presented it to Cheng in return for the $500,000. A year later, CAH was overcome by financial disaster; the corporation was dissolved, and its creditors took over its few remaining assets. Cheng received only $2,000. Any reasonably competent general practitioner would have advised Cheng to secure the interest-free loan by obtaining a deed of trust on CAH's large old home. Cheng sued Landsman for legal malpractice. Which of the following is most nearly correct?

A. Landsman is *liable for malpractice* in the suit brought by Cheng.

B. Landsman is not *liable for malpractice* because he did the legal work as a volunteer, not for a fee.

C. Landsman is not *liable for malpractice* because he did not purport to represent Cheng in the transaction.

D. Landsman is not *liable for malpractice* because the injury to Cheng was not foreseeable.

4. Attorney Applegate represented client Cortez as plaintiff in an employment discrimination action against Delta Corporation. After considerable pretrial discovery, Applegate and Cortez concluded that Delta had indeed unlawfully discriminated against Cortez but that they probably would be unable to convince a jury of that fact. They decided not to pour any more money into pretrial discovery and to trust to good luck when the case came to trial. Before the case was set for trial, Delta moved for summary judgment. Delta's motion was granted, and the case was dismissed. Then Delta sued Applegate for legal malpractice, alleging that he was negligent in advising Cortez to maintain the suit against Delta and that Delta had been injured to the extent of its litigation costs and attorney fees. In Delta's action against Applegate, which of the following is most nearly correct?

A. Applegate is not *liable for malpractice*, even if he lacked a good faith belief that Cortez would win at trial.

B. Applegate is *liable for malpractice* if he lacked a good faith belief that Cortez would win at trial.

C. Applegate is not *liable for malpractice* because his conduct was not the actual cause of Delta's injury.

D. Applegate is *liable for malpractice* if he was negligent in advising Cortez to oppose Delta's motion for summary judgment.

5. For many years attorney Abrams has done all of the routine business law work for Carmondy Corporation. Now Carmondy has asked him to represent it in negotiating a contract to supply electronic components to the U.S. Navy. Abrams knows nothing about government contract law except that it is a highly specialized field governed by a mass of technical regulations. Which of the following would be *proper* for Abrams to do?

I. To decline to represent Carmondy, and to charge Carmondy a nominal fee for finding Carmondy a lawyer who specializes in government contract law.

II. To agree to represent Carmondy, provided that Carmondy will consent to the association of a lawyer who specializes in government contract law.

III. To agree to represent Carmondy, and then to subcontract the substantive legal work to a lawyer who specializes in government contract law.

IV. To agree to represent Carmondy, intending to master the field of government contract law with reasonable speed and efficiency.

     A. All of the above.

     B. None of the above.

     C. II or III only.

     D. I, II, or IV only.

6. Attorney Aoki and client Cramer entered into a written agreement in which Aoki agreed to represent Cramer in a real estate venture in return for a specified hourly fee. The agreement provided that any malpractice or fee dispute would be arbitrated by a neutral arbitrator selected by mutual agreement. Eventually Aoki and Cramer did get into a dispute. Cramer refused to pay Aoki's quarterly bill, and Aoki refused to do any more work until Cramer paid. Cramer also threatened to sue Aoki for malpractice, claiming that he had lost money because of her negligent advice. Which of the following propositions are correct?

I. Aoki is *subject to discipline* for trying to avoid a law suit for malpractice by including the arbitration provision in her contract with Cramer.

II. Aoki is *subject to discipline* for refusing to do further work until Cramer paid her bill.

III. It would be *proper* for Aoki to insist that Cramer abide by the arbitration provision in their contract.

IV. If Aoki wants to settle her dispute with Cramer, she *should* advise Cramer to obtain independent representation for that purpose.

    A.   I, II, and IV only.

    B.   III and IV only.

    C.   II and III only.

    D.   I and IV only.

    7.   Solo practitioner Pearce hired non-lawyer Nelson to serve as her secretary and all-purpose assistant. Pearce put Nelson in charge of her client trust account and her office account and instructed her about how the accounts were to be handled. Several months later, Pearce learned that Nelson had a criminal record, including two prior convictions for embezzlement from a former employer. Since Nelson appeared to be handling the accounts properly, Pearce decided to leave well enough alone. After several more months, Pearce noticed that $1,500 was missing from the office account. Nelson explained that she had borrowed the money to pay her mother's funeral expenses and that she would repay it out of her next paycheck. Nelson did repay the money, and Pearce decided to let Nelson continue to manage the accounts. Then, a year later, Nelson disappeared along with $30,000 from Pearce's client trust account. The clients whose money was taken sued Pearce for negligence and breach of fiduciary duties. Which of the following propositions are correct?

    I.   Pearce is *subject to discipline* for allowing a non-lawyer to handle her client trust account.

    II.   If Pearce did not adequately supervise Nelson's handling of the client trust account, then Pearce is *subject to discipline*.

    III.   Pearce is *liable for malpractice* to the injured clients if she was negligent in allowing Nelson to handle the client trust account.

    IV.   If Pearce had a subjective, good faith belief that Nelson was trustworthy, then Pearce is not *liable for malpractice* to the injured clients.

    A.   II and III only.

    B.   I, II, and III only.

    C.   IV only.

    D.   II and IV only.

    8.   Supervising lawyer Liggett assigned paralegal Prentice to search through the massive business files of Liggett's client to find documents responsive to a federal court order for production of documents. After several months' work, Prentice ended up with 170 large cartons full of documents that were responsive to the court order. Most of the documents were harmless, but a few were quite damaging to the legal position taken by Liggett's client. Instead of arranging the documents in the same logical order in which she found them in the client's files, Prentice intentionally jumbled the order of the documents. Her purpose was to make it exceedingly difficult, if not impossible, for the adversary to find the damaging documents and to understand their significance.

Before the documents were produced for the adversary, Prentice told Liggett what she had done. Liggett responded: "Good—that ought to slow the bastards down. In the future, however, don't do anything like that without checking with me first; we might get in trouble otherwise." Which of the following statements are correct?

I. Since document production requires the skill and judgment of a lawyer, Liggett is *subject to discipline* for delegating the task to Prentice, even if he had adequately supervised her work.

II. Liggett's conduct was *proper* since he admonished Prentice and instructed her not to engage in similar conduct in the future.

III. Assuming that all responsive documents were produced, Liggett's conduct was *proper,* since the adversary has no right to insist that the documents be arranged in any particular order.

IV. Even if all responsive documents were produced, Liggett is *subject to discipline* because he failed to take steps to mitigate the consequences of Prentice's misconduct.

    A.   II only.

    B.   I and IV only.

    C.   IV only.

    D.   II and III only.

*Answers to the multiple choice questions will be found
in the Appendix at the back of the book*

Chapter Seven

CONFIDENTIAL INFORMATION

What This Chapter Covers

Reading Assignment

Wydick & Perschbacher, Chapter 7

ABA Model Rules:

Rules 1.2(d), 1.6, 1.8(b), 1.9(b), 3.3, 3.4(a), and 4.1.

CRPC 3–310(D).

Cal.Bus. & Prof.Code § 6068(e).

Cal.Evid.Code §§ 950–962.

Supplemental Reading

ABA Code:

EC 4–1 through 4–6 and EC 7–1;

DR 4–101 and DR 7–101 through 7–102.

Hazard & Hodes:

Discussion of ABA Model Rules 1.6, 1.8(b), 1.9(b), 3.3, 3.4(a), and 4.1.

Wolfram:

Sections 6.1.1 through 6.1.4 (confidentiality principle);

Sections 6.2.1 through 6.2.4 (confidentiality and the Constitution);

Sections 6.3.1 through 6.3.8 (attorney-client privilege);

Sections 6.4.1 through 6.4.10 (waivers, exceptions, and extensions);

Sections 6.5.1 through 6.5.6 (corporate client);

Sections 6.6.1 through 6.6.3 (work product rule);

Sections 6.7.1 through 6.7.8 (lawyer's duties).

Restatement (Third) of the Law Governing Lawyers §§ 111–117A (Proposed Final Draft No. 1, 1996).

––––––

Discussion Problems

1. In your law school course in evidence law, you studied (or will study) the attorney-client privilege. Briefly stated, the attorney-client privilege gives the client a legal right to prevent a witness from revealing confidential communications between the client and his or her attorney, or the agents of either of them. The privilege applies whenever a governmental body can use the twin powers of subpoena and contempt to compel the giving of information. How does the attorney-client privilege differ from the attorney's ethical duty to preserve the client's confidential information? Consider the following situations:

a. While standing around at a P.T.A. potluck supper, lawyer L gossips with a friend about the reasons that L's client V wants to divorce her husband. Does the attorney-client privilege apply at P.T.A. potluck suppers? Does the ethical duty?

b. Lawyer L is defending client X in a drunk driving case. Through her own investigation, L learns from a loquacious bartender that X stops in for several double martinis every night after work. Does the attorney-client privilege protect that information? If not, is L free to reveal it to whomever she wishes?

c. Client Y tells lawyer L in confidence that he wants to purchase Blackacre to build a new shopping center. Acting as an undisclosed principal, lawyer L instructs her agent to buy Blackacre, hoping to turn a quick profit on resale to Y. Has L violated the attorney-client privilege? Has she violated the ethical duty?

d. Suppose instead that lawyer L buys Greenacre, the adjoining parcel, knowing that it will triple in value when Y builds the shopping center on Blackacre. Has L violated the ethical duty?

e. Client Z told lawyer L in confidence: "Yesterday I burned down my barn on purpose; it is now a heap of ashes. I want you to represent me in collecting the money on my fire insurance policy." L declined to represent Z, who then hired lawyer M to pursue the insurance claim. (Having learned his lesson, Z did not tell M about burning the barn.) The insurance company refused to pay, asserting that Z burned the barn on purpose. At the trial of Z's insurance claim, the insurance company lawyer called L to the witness stand and asked: "What did Z tell you about burning the barn?"

(1) Should the court sustain Z's claim of attorney-client privilege?

(2) When Z left L's office, should L have warned the insurance company that Z was planning to file a fraudulent claim?

2. Dorman is in jail, awaiting trial for the first-degree murder of a young girl. Attorney Anthony is appointed by the court to defend Dorman. Dorman tells Anthony in confidence that he killed not only that girl, but also two other young girls. Dorman tells Anthony where he hid the other two bodies. Anthony goes to the hiding place and discovers that Anthony has told him the truth. Nobody else knows that the other two girls are dead; their parents and the police are searching for them as runaway children. What should Anthony do?

3. On the afternoon of August 11th last year, a woman walked into your law office, stated her name, and said in confidence: "I'm the driver the police are looking for in that fatal hit and run accident last week." You agreed to represent her, and you advised her about the wisdom of surrendering to the police, but she rejected your advice. The police have never discovered the identity of the hit and run driver. Just prior to the expiration of the statute of limitations, the parents of the hit and run victim filed a wrongful death action against a Jane Doe defendant. Acting on a hunch, the parents' lawyer has subpoenaed you as a deposition witness and has asked you for the names of all persons who consulted you on the afternoon of August 11th. What should you do?

4. Your law practice includes some criminal defense work. A few minutes ago, one of your steady clients stormed into your office, waiving a pistol and announcing that he just killed his probation officer. You have urged him to allow you to surrender him to the authorities, but he has refused, stating that they will catch him sooner or later and that he wants to enjoy his last bit of freedom. He has laid the pistol on your desk, and he is about to walk out. What should you do about the pistol?

5. Your client, Enos Furman, is in the business of leasing expensive equipment to farmers. First, he arranges long term equipment leases with the farmers. Then he borrows money from banks to purchase the equipment; he uses the long term leases as security for the bank loans. You have acted as Furman's lawyer in ten of these lease-loan transactions over the past two years. Today he revealed to you, in strict confidence, that some of the leases he used in those transactions were fake—he forged them and thus tricked the banks into lending him money which he has long since spent. He has solemnly promised you that he will never do that again, and he has asked you to serve as his lawyer in a series of new lease-loan transactions. What are your ethical obligations in this situation?

---

* * *

WASHINGTON v. OLWELL

Supreme Court of the State of Washington, 1964.
64 Wash.2d 828, 394 P.2d 681.

May an attorney refuse to produce, at a coroner's inquest, material evidence of a crime by asserting the attorney-client privilege or by claiming the privilege against self-incrimination on behalf of his client? These are the issues raised in this appeal.

September 18, 1962, a coroner's inquest was held for the purpose of investigating the circumstances surrounding the death of John W. Warren. Several days prior to the date of the inquest, appellant was served with a subpoena duces tecum, which said, in part:

> "* * * bring with you all knives in your possession and under your control relating to Henry LeRoy Gray, Gloria Pugh or John W. Warren."

Thereafter, at the coroner's inquest the following exchange took place between a deputy prosecutor and appellant:

> "* * *
>
> "Q. Now, Mr. Olwell, did you comply with that? [Subpoena]
>
> "A. I do not have any knives in my possession that belong to Gloria Pugh, or to John W. Warren, and I did not comply with it as to the question of whether or not I have a knife belonging to Henry LeRoy Gray.
>
> "Q. Now, I would ask you, do you have a knife in your possession or under your control relating to or belonging to Henry LeRoy Gray?
>
> "A. I decline to answer that because of the confidential relationship of attorney and client; and to answer the question would be a violation of my oath as an attorney.
>
> "* * *
>
> "Q. And for the record, Mr. Olwell, in the event you do have in your possession a knife or knives that would be called for under the subpoena duces tecum, I take it your answer would be that you received these at the time you were acting as the attorney for Mr. Gray, is that correct?
>
> "A. That is correct."

Further, on examination by the coroner, the following occurred:

> "Mr. Sowers: * * * As the Coroner of King County I order you to do so [answer] under the provisions of the law set forth in the legislature under R.C.W. 36.24.050.
>
> "Mr. Olwell: I decline to surrender any of my client's possessions, if any, because of the confidential relationship of attorney and

client because under the law I cannot give evidence which under the law cannot be compelled from my client himself."

The events preceding the issuance of the subpoena and the coroner's inquest (as shown by the record as supplemented by some undisputed statements in the parties' briefs) are substantially as follows: Henry LeRoy Gray and John W. Warren engaged in a fight on September 7, 1962, which resulted in Warren's being mortally injured by knife wounds. On or about September 8, 1962, Gray was taken into custody by the Seattle Police Department and placed in jail. During his incarceration, Gray admitted the stabbing of Warren and was willing to cooperate and to aid in the investigation of the homicide. According to a detective of the police department, Gray was not sure what became of the knife he had used in the fight with Warren.

September 10, 1962, David H. Olwell, appellant, was retained as attorney for Gray, who was still confined in jail. Mr. Olwell conferred with his client and then, between the time of that conference and the issuance of the subpoena duces tecum, he came into possession of certain evidence (a knife). It is not clear whether appellant came into possession of this knife through his own investigation while acting as attorney for Gray or whether possession of it was obtained as the result of some communication made by Gray to Olwell during the existence of their attorney and client relationship. This factor is important in determining whether the evidence could be considered as a privileged communication (which is discussed below.)

Therefore, at the time of the inquest, appellant was in possession of a knife that, at that time, was considered as a possible murder weapon.[1] Thereafter the coroner issued the subpoena duces tecum previously quoted.

Appellant appeared at the coroner's inquest and the exchange between appellant, the deputy prosecutor, and the coroner took place as described above. At that time, appellant refused to comply with the subpoena duces tecum and raised the issues presented in this appeal. Thereafter, appellant was cited to appear in the Superior Court of King County, where he was found to be in contempt because of his actions at the coroner's inquest on September 18, 1962. Appellant was given 10 days within which to purge himself of contempt, and, upon his failure to do so, an order was entered adjudging him to be in contempt and directing that he serve two days in the county jail. From that order finding him in contempt, Mr. Olwell appeals.

* * *

To be protected as a privileged communication, information or objects acquired by an attorney must have been communicated or

---

1. It is stated in respondent's brief that, on April 25, 1963, Henry LeRoy Gray was tried and convicted of murder and is now serving a life sentence for the crime. Furthermore, a knife other than the one involved in this proceeding was subsequently discovered to be the weapon used by Gray in the fight.

delivered to him by the client, and not merely obtained by the attorney while acting in that capacity for the client. Dupree v. Better Way, Inc., 86 So.2d 425 (Fla.1956). See, also, 97 C.J.S. Witnesses § 283. This means that the securing of the knife in this case must have been the direct result of information given to Mr. Olwell by his client at the time they conferred in order to come within the attorney-client privilege. Although there is no evidence relating thereto, we think it reasonable to infer from the record that appellant did, in fact, obtain the evidence as the result of information received from his client during their conference. Therefore, for the purposes of this opinion and the questions to be answered, we assume that the evidence in appellant's possession was obtained through a confidential communication from his client. If the knife were obtained from a third person with whom there was no attorney-client relationship, the communication would not be privileged, and the third person could be questioned concerning the transaction.[3]

Further, communications concerning an alleged crime or fraud, which are made by a client to the attorney after the crime or the fraudulent transaction has been completed, are within the attorney-client privilege, as long as the relationship of attorney and client has been established. Therefore, we find nothing significant in the fact that the communication was made after and concerned the events of a homicide.

In the present case we do not have a situation that readily lends itself to the application of one of the general rules applicable to the attorney-client privilege. Here, we enter a balancing process which requires us to weigh that privilege (which is based on statute and common law), and, as discussed later herein, the privilege against self-incrimination (which is constitutional), against the public's interest in the criminal investigation process. Generally speaking, the public interest at times must yield to protect the individual. Also, we must not lose sight of the policy behind the attorney-client privilege, which is to afford the client freedom from fear of compulsory disclosure after consulting his legal adviser.

* * *

On the basis of the attorney-client privilege, the subpoena duces tecum issued by the coroner is defective on its face because it requires the attorney to give testimony concerning information received by him from his client in the course of their conferences. The subpoena names the client and requires his attorney to produce, in an open hearing, physical evidence allegedly received from the client. This is tantamount to requiring the attorney to testify against the client without the latter's consent. RCW 36.24.080 makes testifying in a coroner's inquest similar to testifying in a superior court, and, therefore, the attorney-client privilege should be equally applicable to witnesses at a coroner's inquest.

---

3. The state suggests that the knife was obtained from Gray's ex-wife, but it failed to offer any proof of this alleged fact to show that a privileged communication did not, in fact, exist.

We, therefore, hold that appellant's refusal to testify at the inquest for the first reason stated by him was not contemptuous.

We do not, however, by so holding, mean to imply that evidence can be permanently withheld by the attorney under the claim of the attorney-client privilege. Here, we must consider the balancing process between the attorney-client privilege and the public interest in criminal investigation. We are in agreement that the attorney-client privilege is applicable to the knife held by appellant, but do not agree that the privilege warrants the attorney, as an officer of the court, from withholding it after being properly requested to produce the same. The attorney should not be a depository for criminal evidence (such as a knife, other weapons, stolen property, etc.), which in itself has little, if any, material value for the purposes of aiding counsel in the preparation of the defense of his client's case. Such evidence given the attorney during legal consultation for information purposes and used by the attorney in preparing the defense of his client's case, whether or not the case ever goes to trial, could clearly be withheld for a reasonable period of time. It follows that the attorney, after a reasonable period, should, as an officer of the court, on his own motion turn the same over to the prosecution.

We think the attorney-client privilege should and can be preserved even though the attorney surrenders the evidence he has in his possession. The prosecution, upon receipt of such evidence from an attorney, where charge against the attorney's client is contemplated (presently or in the future), should be well aware of the existence of the attorney-client privilege. Therefore, the state, when attempting to introduce such evidence at the trial, should take extreme precautions to make certain that the source of the evidence is not disclosed in the presence of the jury and prejudicial error is not committed. By thus allowing the prosecution to recover such evidence, the public interest is served, and by refusing the prosecution an opportunity to disclose the source of the evidence, the client's privilege is preserved and a balance is reached between these conflicting interests. The burden of introducing such evidence at a trial would continue to be upon the prosecution. [The court then explains that the client's Fifth Amendment privilege against self-incrimination could not serve as a shield for the attorney.]

As was previously stated, the attorney should not be a depository for the suppression of such criminal evidence. If the attorney is given such evidence by his client, he should not be able to assert the privilege against self-incrimination which is personal to the client and must be claimed by the client alone. The attorney can aid in its preservation by informing the client of his right to claim the privilege against self-incrimination.

Because the subpoena duces tecum in this case is invalid, since it required the attorney to testify without the client's consent regarding matters arising out of the attorney-client relationship, the order of the trial court finding appellant to be in contempt and punishing him therefor is hereby reversed with directions to dismiss this proceeding.

PEOPLE v. MEREDITH

Supreme Court of California, 1981.
29 Cal.3d 682, 175 Cal.Rptr. 612, 631 P.2d 46.

Defendants Frank Earl Scott and Michael Meredith appeal from convictions for the first degree murder and first degree robbery of David Wade. Meredith's conviction rests on eyewitness testimony that he shot and killed Wade. Scott's conviction, however, depends on the theory that Scott conspired with Meredith and a third defendant, Jacqueline Otis, to bring about the killing and robbery. To support the theory of conspiracy the prosecution sought to show the place where the victim's wallet was found, and, in the course of the case this piece of evidence became crucial. The admissibility of that evidence comprises the principal issue on this appeal.

At trial the prosecution called Steven Frick, who testified that he observed the victim's partially burnt wallet in a trash can behind Scott's residence. Scott's trial counsel then adduced that Frick served as a defense investigator. Scott himself had told his former counsel that he had taken the victim's wallet, divided the money with Meredith, attempted to burn the wallet, and finally put it in the trash can. At counsel's request, Frick then retrieved the wallet from the trash can. Counsel examined the wallet and then turned it over to the police.

The defense acknowledges that the wallet itself was properly admitted into evidence. The prosecution in turn acknowledges that the attorney-client privilege protected the conversations between Scott, his former counsel, and counsel's investigator. Indeed the prosecution did not attempt to introduce those conversations at trial. The issue before us, consequently, focuses upon a narrow point: whether under the circumstances of this case Frick's observation of the *location* of the wallet, the product of a privileged communication, finds protection under the attorney-client privilege.

This issue, one of first impression in California, presents the court with competing policy considerations. On the one hand, to deny protection to observations arising from confidential communications might chill free and open communication between attorney and client and might also inhibit counsel's investigation of his client's case. On the other hand, we cannot extend the attorney-client privilege so far that it renders evidence immune from discovery and admission merely because the defense seizes it first.

Balancing these considerations, we conclude that an observation by defense counsel or his investigator, which is the product of a privileged communication, may not be admitted unless the defense by altering or removing physical evidence has precluded the prosecution from making that same observation. In the present case the defense investigator, by removing the wallet, frustrated any possibility that the police might later discover it in the trash can. The conduct of the defense thus precluded the prosecution from ascertaining the crucial fact of the location of the wallet. Under these circumstances, the prosecution was entitled to present evidence to show the location of the wallet in the trash can; the trial court did not err in admitting the investigator's testimony.

* * *

We first summarize the evidence other than that relating to the discovery and location of the victim's wallet. * * *

On the night of April 3, 1976, Wade (the victim) and Jacqueline Otis, a friend of the defendants, entered a club known as Rich Jimmy's. Defendant Scott remained outside by a shoeshine stand. A few minutes later codefendant Meredith arrived outside the club. He told Scott he planned to rob Wade, and asked Scott to go into the club, find Jacqueline Otis, and ask her to get Wade to go out to Wade's car parked outside the club.

In the meantime, Wade and Otis had left the club and walked to a liquor store to get some beer. Returning from the store, they left the beer in a bag by Wade's car and reentered the club. Scott then entered the club also and, according to the testimony of Laurie Ann Sam (a friend of Scott's who was already in the club), Scott asked Otis to get Wade to go back out to his car so Meredith could "knock him in the head."

When Wade and Otis did go out to the car, Meredith attacked Wade from behind. After a brief struggle, two shots were fired; Wade fell, and Meredith, witnessed by Scott and Sam, ran from the scene.

Scott went over to the body and, assuming Wade was dead, picked up the bag containing the beer and hid it behind a fence. Scott later returned, retrieved the bag, and took it home where Otis and Meredith joined him.[2]

We now recount the evidence relating to Wade's wallet, basing our account primarily on the testimony of James Schenk, Scott's first appointed attorney. Schenk visited Scott in jail more than a month after the crime occurred and solicited information about the murder, stressing that he had to be fully acquainted with the facts to avoid being "sandbagged" by the prosecution during the trial. In response, Scott gave Schenk the same information that he had related earlier to the police. In addition, however, Scott told Schenk something Scott had not revealed to the police: that he has seen a wallet, as well as the paper bag, on the ground near Wade. Scott said that he picked up the wallet, put it in the paper bag, and placed both behind a parking lot fence. He also said that he later retrieved the bag, took it home, found $100 in the wallet and divided it with Meredith, and then tried to burn the wallet in his kitchen sink. He took the partially burned wallet, Scott told Schenk, placed it in a plastic bag, and threw it in a burn barrel behind his house.

---

2. Meredith offered an alibi defense. He testified that he spent the evening at the Kit-Kat Club and another club across the street, and was never in the vicinity of Rich Jimmy's. Two witnesses partially corroborated his alibi.

Schenk, without further consulting Scott, retained Investigator Stephen Frick and sent Frick to find the wallet. Frick found it in the location described by Scott and brought it to Schenk. After examining the wallet and determining that it contained credit cards with Wade's name, Schenk turned the wallet and its contents over to Detective Payne, investigating officer in the case. Schenk told Payne only that, to the best of his knowledge, the wallet had belonged to Wade.

The prosecution subpoenaed Attorney Schenk and Investigator Frick to testify at the preliminary hearing. When questioned at that hearing, Schenk said that he received the wallet from Frick but refused to answer further questions on the ground that he learned about the wallet through a privileged communication. Eventually, however, the magistrate threatened Schenk with contempt if he did not respond "yes" or "no" when asked whether his contact with his client led to disclosure of the wallet's location. Schenk then replied "yes," and revealed on further questioning that this contact was the sole source of his information as to the wallet's location.

At the preliminary hearing Frick, the investigator who found the wallet, was then questioned by the district attorney. Over objections by counsel, Frick testified that he found the wallet in a garbage can behind Scott's residence.

Prior to trial, a third attorney, Hamilton Hintz, was appointed for Scott. Hintz unsuccessfully sought an *in limine* ruling that the wallet of the murder victim was inadmissible and that the attorney-client privilege precluded the admission of testimony concerning the wallet by Schenk or Frick.

At trial Frick, called by the prosecution, identified the wallet and testified that he found it in a garbage can behind Scott's residence. On cross-examination by Hintz, Scott's counsel, Frick further testified that he was an investigator hired by Scott's first attorney, Schenk, and that he had searched the garbage can at Schenk's request. Hintz later called Schenk as a witness: Schenk testified that he told Frick to search for the wallet immediately after Schenk finished talking to Scott. Schenk also stated that Frick brought him the wallet on the following day; after examining its contents Schenk delivered the wallet to the police. Scott then took the stand and testified to the information about the wallet that he had disclosed to Schenk.

The jury found both Scott and Meredith guilty of first degree murder and first degree robbery. It further found that Meredith, but not Scott, was armed with a deadly weapon. Both defendants appeal from their convictions.

Defendant Scott concedes, and we agree, that the wallet itself was admissible in evidence. Scott maintains, however, that Evidence Code section 954 bars the testimony of the investigator concerning the location of the wallet. We consider, first, whether the California attorney-client privilege codified in that section extends to observations which are the product of privileged communications. We then discuss whether that privileged status is lost when defense conduct may have frustrated prosecution discovery.

Section 954 provides, "[T]he client * * * has a privilege to refuse to disclose, and to prevent another from disclosing, a confidential communication between client and lawyer * * *." Under that section one who seeks to assert the privilege must establish that a confidential communication occurred during the course of the attorney-client relationship.

Scott's statements to Schenk regarding the location of the wallet clearly fulfilled the statutory requirements. Moreover, the privilege did not dissolve when Schenk disclosed the substance of that communication to his investigator, Frick. Under Evidence Code section 912, subdivision (d), a disclosure which is "reasonably necessary" to accomplish the purpose for which the attorney has been consulted does not constitute a waiver of the privilege. If Frick was to perform the investigative services for which Schenk had retained him, it was "reasonably necessary," that Schenk transmit to Frick the information regarding the wallet.[3] Thus, Schenk's disclosure to Frick did not waive the statutory privilege.

The statutes codifying the attorney-client privilege do not, however, indicate whether that privilege protects facts viewed and observed as a direct result of confidential communication. To resolve that issue, we turn first to the policies which underlie the attorney-client privilege, and then to the cases which apply those policies to observations arising from a protected communication.

The fundamental purpose of the attorney-client privilege is, of course, to encourage full and open communication between client and attorney. "Adequate legal representation in the ascertainment and enforcement of rights or the prosecution or defense of litigation compels a full disclosure of the facts by the client to his attorney * * *. Given the privilege, a client may make such a disclosure without fear that his attorney may be forced to reveal the information confided to him." (*City & County of S.F. v. Superior Court, supra,* 37 Cal.2d at p. 235, 231 P.2d 26. *See also People v. Canfield* (1974) 12 Cal.3d 699, 705, 117 Cal.Rptr. 81, 527 P.2d 633; *People v. Atkinson* (1870) 40 Cal. 284, 285.)

In the criminal context, as we have recently observed, these policies assume particular significance: " 'As a practical matter, if the client

---

3. Although prior cases do not consider whether section 912, subdivision (d) applies to an attorney's investigator, the language of that subdivision covers the circumstances of the instant case. An investigator is as "reasonably necessary" as a physician or psychiatrist (*People v. Lines* (1975) 13 Cal.3d 500, 119 Cal.Rptr. 225, 531 P.2d 793), or a legal secretary, paralegal or receptionist. (*See Anderson v. State* (Fla.App. 1974) 297 So.2d 871; *City & County of S.F. v. Superior Court* (1951) 37 Cal.2d 227, 231 P.2d 26). Because the investigator, then, is a person encompassed by the privilege, he stands in the same position as the attorney for purposes of the analysis and operation of the privilege; the investigator cannot then disclose that which the attorney could not have disclosed. (*City & County of S.F. v. Superior Court, supra,* 37 Cal.2d at p. 236, 231 P.2d 26, *see also* Evid.Code, § 952 and Law Revision Com. comment thereto.) Thus, the discussion in this opinion of the conduct of defense counsel, and of counsel's right to invoke the attorney-client privilege to avoid testifying, applies also to a defense investigator.

knows that damaging information could more readily be obtained from the attorney following disclosure than from himself in the absence of disclosure, the client would be reluctant to confide in his lawyer and it would be difficult to obtain fully informed legal advice.' * * * Thus, if an accused is to derive the full benefits of his right to counsel, he must have the assurance of confidentiality and privacy of communication with his attorney." (*Barber v. Municipal Court* (1979) 24 Cal.3d 742, 751, 157 Cal.Rptr. 658, 598 P.2d 878, citing *Fisher v. United States* (1976) 425 U.S. 391, 403, 96 S.Ct. 1569, 1577, 48 L.Ed.2d 39.)

Judicial decisions have recognized that the implementation of these important policies may require that the privilege extend not only to the initial communication between client and attorney but also to any information which the attorney or his investigator may subsequently acquire as a direct result of that communication. In a venerable decision involving facts analogous to those in the instant case, the Supreme Court of West Virginia held that the trial court erred in admitting an attorney's testimony as to the location of a pistol which he had discovered as the result of a privileged communication from his client. That the attorney had observed the pistol, the court pointed out, did not nullify the privilege: "All that the said attorney knew about this pistol, or where it was to be found, he knew only from the communications which had been made to him by his client confidentially and professionally, as counsel in this case. And it ought therefore, to have been entirely excluded from the jury. It may be, that in this particular case this evidence tended to the promotion of right and justice, but as was well said in *Pearce v. Pearce*, 11 Jar. 52, in page 55, and 2 De Gex & Smale 25–27: 'Truth like all other good things may be loved unwisely, may be pursued too keenly, may cost too much.' " (*State of West Virginia v. Douglass* (1882) 20 W.Va. 770, 783.)

This unbearable cost, the *Douglass* court concluded, could not be entirely avoided by attempting to admit testimony regarding observations or discoveries made as the result of a privileged communication, while excluding the communication itself. Such a procedure, *Douglass* held, "was practically as mischievous in all its tendencies and consequences, as if it has required [the attorney] to state everything, which his client had confidentially told him about this pistol. It would be a slight safeguard indeed, to confidential communications made to counsel, if he was thus compelled substantially, to give them to a jury, although he was required not to state them in the words of his client." (*Id.*, at p. 783.)

More recent decisions reach similar conclusions. In *State v. Olwell* (1964) 64 Wash.2d 828, 394 P.2d 681, the court reviewed contempt charges against an attorney who refused to produce a knife he obtained from his client. The court first observed that "[t]o be protected as a privileged communication * * * the securing of the knife * * * must have been *the direct result of information* given to Mr. Olwell by his client." The court concluded that defense counsel, after examining the physical evidence, should deliver it to the prosecution, but should not reveal the source of the evidence; "[b]y thus allowing the prosecution to recover such evidence, the public interest is served, and by refusing the prosecution an opportunity to disclose the source of the evidence, the client's privilege is preserved and a balance reached between these conflicting interests." (P. 685.)[4] (See also *Anderson v. State* (D.C.App. Fla.1974) 297 So.2d 871.)

Finally, we note the decisions of the New York courts in *People v. Belge* (Sup.Ct.1975) 83 Misc.2d 186, 372 N.Y.S.2d 798, affirmed in *People v. Belge* (App.Div.1975) 50 A.D.2d 1088, 376 N.Y.S.2d 771. Defendant, charged with one murder, revealed to counsel that he had committed three others. Counsel, following defendant's directions, located one of the bodies. Counsel did not reveal the location of the body until trial, 10 months later, when he exposed the other murders to support an insanity defense.

Counsel was then indicted for violating two sections of the New York Public Health Law for failing to report the existence of the body to proper authorities in order that they could give it a decent burial. The trial court dismissed the indictment; the appellate division affirmed, holding that the attorney-client privilege shielded counsel from prosecution for actions which would otherwise violate the Public Health Law.[5]

The foregoing decisions demonstrate that the attorney-client privilege is not strictly limited to communications, but extends to protect observations made as a consequence of protected communications. We turn therefore to the question whether that privilege encompasses a case in which the defense, by removing or altering evidence, interferes with the prosecution's opportunity to discover that evidence.[7]

---

4. The parties discuss an earlier Washington case. *State v. Sullivan* (1962) 60 Wash.2d 214, 373 P.2d 474. Defendant in that case revealed the location of the victim's body to his counsel, who informed the sheriff. At trial the prosecution called defense counsel to testify to the location. The appellate court reversed the conviction, apparently on the ground that it was unnecessarily prejudicial to call defense counsel as a prosecution witness when sheriff's deputies and other witnesses who had seen the body were available.

The *Sullivan* court stated a general rule which supports the result we reach here— that attorney-client communications remain privileged "regardless of the manner in which it is sought to put the communications in evidence, whether by direct examination, cross-examination, or *indirectly as by bringing of facts brought to knowledge solely by reason of a confidential communication.*" (P. 476, quoting 58 Am. Jur., Witnesses, § 466.) (Emphasis by the *Sullivan* court.) The decision expressly left open, however, whether defense counsel could be

called to prove the location of the body if other witnesses were unavailable.

5. In each of the cases discussed in text, a crucial element in the court's analysis is that the attorney's observations were the direct product of information communicated to him by his client. Two decisions, *People v. Lee* (1970) 3 Cal.App.3d 514, 83 Cal.Rptr. 715 and *Morrell v. State* (Alaska 1978) 575 P.2d 1200, held that an attorney must not only turn over evidence given him by *third parties*, but also testify as to the source of that evidence. Both decisions emphasized that the attorney-client privilege was inapplicable because the third party was not acting as an agent of the attorney or the client.

7. We agree with the parties' suggestion that an attorney in Schenk's position often may best fulfill conflicting obligations to preserve the confidentiality of client confidences, investigate his case, and act as an officer of the court if he does not remove evidence located as the result of a privileged communication. We must recognize, however, that in some cases an examination of

In some of the cases extending the privilege to observations arising from protected communications the defense counsel had obtained the evidence from his client or in some other fashion removed it from its original location (*State v. Olwell, supra*, 394 P.2d 681; *Anderson v. State, supra*, 297 So.2d 871); in others the attorney did not remove or alter the evidence (*People v. Belge, supra*, 372 N.Y.S.2d 798; *State v. Sullivan, supra*, 373 P.2d 474). None of the decisions, however, confronts directly the question whether such removal or alteration should affect the defendant's right to assert the attorney-client privilege as a bar to testimony concerning the original location or condition of the evidence.

When defense counsel alters or removes physical evidence, he necessarily deprives the prosecution of the opportunity to observe that evidence in its original condition or location. As the Amicus Appellate Committee of the California District Attorneys Association points out, to bar admission of testimony concerning the original condition and location of the evidence in such a case permits the defense in effect to "destroy" critical information; it is as if, he explains, the wallet in this case bore a tag bearing the words "located in the trash can by Scott's residence," and the defense, by taking the wallet, destroyed this tag. To extend the attorney-client privilege to a case in which the defense removed evidence might encourage defense counsel to race the police to seize critical evidence. (See *In re Ryder* (E.D.Va.1967) 263 F.Supp. 360, 369; Comment, *The Right of a Criminal Defense Attorney to Withhold Physical Evidence Received From His Client* (1970) 38 U.Chi.L.Rev. 211, 227–228.)

We therefore conclude that courts must craft an exception to the protection extended by the attorney-client privilege in cases in which counsel has removed or altered evidence. Indeed, at oral argument defense counsel acknowledged that such an exception might be necessary in a case in which the police would have inevitably discovered the evidence in its original location if counsel had not removed it. Counsel argued, however, that the attorney-client privilege should protect observations of evidence, despite subsequent defense removal, unless the prosecution could prove that the police probably would have eventually discovered the evidence in the original site.

We have seriously considered counsel's proposal, but have concluded that a test based upon the probability of eventual discovery is unworkably speculative. Evidence turns up not only because the police deliberately search for it, but also because it comes to the attention of policemen or bystanders engaged in other business. In the present case, for example, the wallet might have been found by the trash collector.

evidence may reveal information critical to the defense of a client accused of crime. If the usefulness of the evidence cannot be gauged without taking possession of it, as, for example, when a ballistics or fingerprint test is required, the attorney may properly take it for a reasonable time before turning it over to the prosecution. (*Olwell, supra*, 394 P.2d pp. 684–685.) Similarly, in the present case the defense counsel could not be certain the burnt wallet belonged in fact to the victim: in taking the wallet to examine it for identification, he violated no ethical duty to his client or to the prosecution. (*See generally Legal Ethics and the Destruction of Evidence* (1979) 88 Yale L.J. 1665.)

Moreover, once physical evidence (the wallet) is turned over to the police, they will obviously stop looking for it; to ask where, how long, and how carefully they would have looked is obviously to compel speculation as to theoretical future conduct of the police.

We therefore conclude that whenever defense counsel removes or alters evidence, the statutory privilege does not bar revelation of the original location or condition of the evidence in question.[8] We thus view the defense decision to remove evidence as a tactical choice. If defense counsel leaves the evidence where he discovers it, his observations derived from privileged communications are insulated from revelation. If, however, counsel chooses to remove evidence to examine or test it, the original location and condition of that evidence loses the protection of the privilege. Applying this analysis to the present case, we hold that the trial court did not err in admitting the investigator's testimony concerning the location of the wallet.

EXCEPTIONS TO THE ETHICAL DUTY OF CONFIDENTIALITY

A. Self–Defense

Re-read ABA Model Rule 1.6(b). Note that it permits a lawyer to reveal a client's confidential information in "self-defense," for example: to defend against a claim of legal malpractice or ineffective assistance of counsel; to defend against a civil or criminal charge that the lawyer was involved in the client's wrongdoing; and to obtain relief against a client who has breached a fee agreement or the like. [*Accord* ABA Code DR 4–101(C)(4); Restatement of the Law Governing Lawyers §§ 116–17 (Proposed Final Draft No. 1, 1996).]

B. Future Crimes

Now examine the part of ABA Model Rule 1.6(b) that concerns future crimes. Suppose that a client goes to his lawyer and, in confidence, asks for some legal advice in conjunction with his plan to commit two future crimes: (1) a fraud that will bilk innocent people of their life savings, and (2) a brutal murder, to cover up the fraud. If the lawyer is brought into court, sworn as a witness, and asked what the client said, the lawyer will have to answer truthfully. In court, the applicable law is

---

8. In offering the evidence, the prosecution should present the information in a manner which avoids revealing the content of attorney-client communications or the original source of the information. In the present case, for example, the prosecutor simply asked Frick where he found the wallet; he did not identify Frick as a defense investigator or trace the discovery of the wallet to an attorney-client communication.

In other circumstances, when it is not possible to elicit such testimony without identifying the witness as the defendant's attorney or investigator, the defendant may be willing to enter a stipulation which will simply inform the jury as to the relevant location or condition of the evidence in question. When such a stipulation is proffered, the prosecution should not be permitted to reject the stipulation in the hope that by requiring defense counsel personally to testify to such facts, the jury might infer that counsel learned those facts from defendant. (Cf. *People v. Hall* (1980) 28 Cal.3d 143, 152, 167 Cal.Rptr. 844, 616 P.2d 826.)

the attorney-client privilege, and the privilege does not protect communications in which the client seeks the lawyer's services to aid in the planning or commission of an ongoing or future crime or fraud. [*See* Christopher Mueller & Laird Kirkpatrick, Evidence § 5.22 (1995).]

Suppose that after the client states his evil plan, the lawyer tries to talk him out of it. The client flies into a rage, vows to carry out the plan, and storms out of the lawyer's office. The lawyer is convinced that the client will really do it. May the lawyer warn the appropriate authorities and the intended victims in an effort to foil the client's plan? This situation is governed, not by the attorney-client privilege, but by the lawyer's ethical duty of confidentiality. The ABA Code, which used to apply in almost every state, allowed the lawyer to voluntarily reveal the client's confidentially stated intent to commit **any kind** of crime, together with information needed to prevent the crime from being committed. [*See* ABA Code DR 4–101(C)(3).]

The ABA Model Rules drafting committee proposed a rule that would allow the lawyer to reveal the client's confidential information: (1) to stop the client from committing a crime that would cause imminent death or substantial bodily injury; (2) to stop the client from committing a crime or fraud that would cause substantial financial injury; and (3) to rectify the consequences of a client's crime or fraud in furtherance of which the lawyer's services had been used. When the committee's draft came before the ABA House of Delegates, the delegates threw out the second and third categories, leaving only the first; that is why ABA Model Rule 1.6(b) covers only future crimes that will cause imminent death or substantial bodily injury.

The House of Delegates' radical surgery on the draft rule started lawyers across the country thinking seriously about confidentiality and its limits. The end result was a many-sided division of authority. Only ten states accepted the ABA Model Rules position, which allows the lawyer to reveal only those future crimes that will cause imminent death or substantial bodily injury. [*See* Steven Gillers & Roy D. Simon, Regulation of Lawyers: Statutes and Standards 74–78 (1996); *see also* Restatement of the Law Governing Lawyers § 117A, Reporter's Note (Proposed Final Draft No. 1, 1996).] Close to twenty states allow the lawyer to reveal future crimes that will cause imminent death, substantial bodily injury, or substantial financial injury. [*Id.*] Several states created their own variations. For example, some *permit* revelation of crimes that will cause financial injury, but *require* revelation of crimes that will cause imminent death or substantial bodily injury. [*Id.*] A few states *require* the revelation of *both* kinds of crimes. [*Id.*]

C. Noisy Withdrawal

ABA Model Rule 1.2(d) prohibits a lawyer from assisting a client to commit a crime or fraud, and ABA Model Rule 4.1(b) requires the lawyer to disclose material facts to a third person "when disclosure is necessary to avoid assisting a criminal or fraudulent act by a client, unless disclosure is prohibited by Rule 1.6." [ABA Model Rule 4.1(b).] As originally proposed by the drafting committee, the disclosure provision did not contain the "unless" clause—the lawyer's duty to disclose would have covered even confidential information. Again the House of Delegates rebelled; it added the "unless" clause, which means that the lawyer must not disclose information that is protected by the duty of confidentiality.

In a way, the proponents of the original draft got the last laugh. They persuaded the House of Delegates to add the following Comments to ABA Model Rule 1.6, to explain what a lawyer is supposed to do when she discovers that her client is using, or is planning to use, her services to carry out a crime or fraud:

- If the lawyer's services will be used by the client in materially furthering a course of criminal or fraudulent conduct, the lawyer must withdraw, as stated in Rule 1.16(a)(1).

- After withdrawal the lawyer is required to refrain from making disclosure of the clients' confidences, except as otherwise provided in Rule 1.6. Neither this rule nor Rule 1.8(b) nor Rule 1.16(d) prevents the lawyer from *giving notice of the fact of withdrawal, and the lawyer may also withdraw or disaffirm any opinion, document, affirmation, or the like.* [ABA Model Rule 16, Comments 14 and 15 (emphasis added).]

What do the italicized words contemplate? May the lawyer give notice of withdrawal to anyone other than the client? To whom? May the lawyer give notice to anyone other than the client that she is disavowing a prior opinion, document, affirmation, or the like? To whom? What will the recipient of the notice be likely to think? [*See* Ronald Rotunda, *The Notice of Withdrawal and the New Model Rules of Professional Conduct: Blowing the Whistle and Waiving the Red Flag,* 63 Or.L.Rev. 455 (1984).] The ABA ethics committee explained the so-called "noisy withdrawal" provision in ABA Formal Op. 92–366, which you will read below.

D. The Restatement Position

The American Law Institute revisited the topic of confidentiality in preparing the Restatement of the Law Governing Lawyers. As presently drafted, the Restatement permits a lawyer to reveal a client's confidential information: (a) if doing so will advance the client's interests, or (b) if the client consents, or (c) if required by law, or (d) if needed in the lawyer's self-defense, or (e) if needed in a compensation dispute, or (f) if needed to prevent death or serious bodily injury, whether caused by a crime or something else, and whether caused by the client or someone else, and (g) if needed to prevent future substantial financial loss as a result of the client's crime or fraud in the commission of which the lawyer's services were or are being employed. [*See* Restatement of the Law Governing Lawyers §§ 113–117A (Proposed Final Draft No. 1, as amended by the ALI membership in May, 1996), reported in 64 U.S.L.W. 2739 (1996).]

E. The California Position

California's position on exceptions to the lawyer's duty of confidentiality is muddled. [*See* Roger C. Cramton, *Proposed Legislation Concerning a Lawyer's Duty of Confidentiality*, 22 Pepperdine L.Rev. 1467 (1995); Fred C. Zacharias, *Privilege and Confidentiality in California* 28 U.C.Davis L.Rev. 367 (1995).] California is the only state in the nation whose legal ethics rules do not contain a rule about confidentiality. Instead of having a comprehensive confidentiality rule, California limps along with one sentence of the Attorney's Oath: "It is the duty of an attorney . . . [t]o maintain inviolate the confidence, and at every peril to himself or herself to preserve the secrets, of his or her client." [Cal.Bus. & Prof.Code §§ 6067 and 6068(e).] The sex free pronouns are a modern addition, but otherwise the sentence is a ceremonial relic of the 19th century, cribbed from David Dudley Field's civil procedure code, which in turn had taken it from an old oath used in Switzerland. [*See* Charles W. Wolfram, *The U.S. Law of Client Confidentiality: Framework for an International Perspective,* 15 Fordham Int'l L.J. 529, 534 (1991–2).]

Taken at face value, § 6068(e) has no exceptions whatsoever: the attorney must stay mum, even if doing so will violate a court order, or will cause the death of an innocent child, or will end civilization as we know it. Various California ethics committees have disagreed with one another about whether some common sense exceptions should be read into § 6068(e) [*See* Zacharias, *supra,* at 371 n. 14.] Further, some California judicial decisions have recognized exceptions to the duty of confidentiality. For example, in an attorney's suit to collect a fee from a client, the attorney may offer evidence about relevant confidential communications between himself and the client. [*See, e.g., Carlson, Collins, Gordon & Bold v. Banducci,* 257 Cal.App.2d 212, 227–28, 64 Cal.Rptr. 915, 923 (1967).] In that situation, the client cannot assert the attorney-client privilege because of the exception for claimed breaches of the duties running between attorney and client. [Cal.Evid.Code § 958.] By necessary implication, there must be a corresponding exception to the ethical duty of confidentiality because the attorney is voluntarily initiating the offer of evidence. [*See* Wolfram, *supra* at 535 n. 17.]

In 1987, and again in 1991, the State Bar of California tried to clean up the confidentiality muddle by proposing rule changes to the California Supreme Court. The Supreme Court sent the 1987 proposal back with a comment which revealed that the Justices did not understand the difference between the attorney-client privilege and the ethical duty of confidentiality. The Supreme Court sent the 1991 proposal back with no comment at all. [The history is sketched in the Report to the Board of Trustees of the Los Angeles County Bar Association from the association's Committees on Evaluation of Professional Standards and the State Bar (March 8, 1996).]

In 1993, the California legislature deepened the muddle by amending the California Evidence Code to make the attorney-client privilege inapplicable if "the lawyer reasonably believes that disclosure of any confidential communication relating to representation of a client is necessary to prevent the client from committing a criminal act that the lawyer believes is likely to result in death or substantial bodily harm." [Cal.Evid.Code § 956.5.] The amendment might have been an attempt to repair a supposed flaw in California's version of the attorney-client privilege, or it might have been a fumbling effort to codify a future crime exception to the ethical duty of confidentiality. [*See* Zacharias, *supra* at 374–96.] Neither the text of the amendment nor its legislative history reveals clearly what the legislature thought it was doing. [*Id.*]

At the time of this writing, the State Bar of California is trying once again to get the California Supreme Court to approve an ethics rule that will shrink (but not eliminate) the muddle. The new proposal will amend the CRPC by adding a Rule 3–100, which will create an exception to the ethical duty of confidentiality that is expressed in Cal.Bus. & Prof.Code § 6068(e). The exception will allow a lawyer to reveal a client's confidence if the lawyer "reasonably believes the disclosure is necessary to prevent the client from committing a criminal act that the member believes is likely to result in death or substantial bodily harm." The proposal does not touch on *other* possible exceptions to the ethical duty that have been created, or implied, or hinted at in California case law and ethics committee opinions. The proposal does, however, include a disclaimer of any intent to diminish or preclude reliance on "other exceptions ... recognized under California law."

ABA FORMAL OPINION 92–366

American Bar Association Committee on Ethics
and Professional Responsibility, 1992 *

A lawyer who knows or with reason believes that her services or work product are being used or are intended to be used by a client to perpetrate a fraud must withdraw from further representation of the client, and may disaffirm documents prepared in the course of the representation that are being, or will be, used in furtherance of the fraud, even though such a "noisy" withdrawal may have the collateral effect of inferentially revealing client confidences.

When a lawyer's services have been used in the past by a client to perpetrate a fraud, but the fraud has ceased, the lawyer may but is not required to withdraw from further representation of the client; in these circumstances, a "noisy" withdrawal is not permitted.

The Committee has been asked its views on what the ABA Model Rules of Professional Conduct (1983, amended 1992) require, and what the Rules permit, a lawyer to do when she learns that her client has used her work product to perpetrate a fraud, is continuing so to use it, or plans so to use it in the future. The answers to these questions require

* Copyright © 1987 by the American Bar Association. All rights reserved. Reprinted by permission of the American Bar Association. Copies available from ABA Member Services, 750 North Lake Shore Drive, Chicago, IL 60611.

a somewhat difficult reconciliation of the text and commentary of three Rules: Rule 1.6, imposing a broad requirement of confidentiality;[1] 1.2(d), prohibiting a lawyer from assisting client crime or fraud;[2] and Rule 1.16(a)(1), requiring withdrawal from a representation where continued representation would result in a violation of the Rules.[3]

As more fully explained below, the Committee's conclusions are these:

First, the lawyer *must* withdraw from any representation of the client that, directly or indirectly, would have the effect of assisting the client's continuing or intended future fraud.

1. Rule 1.6 Confidentiality of Information

(a) A lawyer shall not reveal information relating to representation of a client unless the client consents after consultation, except for disclosures that are impliedly authorized in order to carry out the representation, and except as stated in paragraph (b).

(b) A lawyer may reveal such information to the extent the lawyer reasonably believes necessary;

(1) to prevent the client from committing a criminal act that the lawyer believes is likely to result in imminent death or substantial bodily harm; or

(2) to establish a claim or defense on behalf of the lawyer and the client, to establish a defense to a criminal charge or civil claim conduct in which the client was involved, or to respond to allegations in any proceeding concerning the lawyer's representation of the client.

2. Rule 1.2 Scope of Representation

* * *

(d) A lawyer shall not counsel a client to engage, or assist a client, in conduct that the lawyer knows is criminal or fraudulent, but a lawyer may discuss the legal consequences of any proposed course of conduct with a client and may counsel or assist a client to make a good faith effort to determine the validity, scope, meaning or application of the law.

3. Rule 1.16 Declining or Terminating Representation

(a) Except as stated in paragraph (c), a lawyer shall not represent a client or, where representation has commenced, shall withdraw from the representation of a client if:

(1) the representation will result in violation of the rules of professional conduct or other law;

(2) the lawyer's physical or mental conduction materially impairs the lawyer's ability to represent the client; or

(3) the lawyer is discharged.

(b) except as stated in paragraph (c), a lawyer may withdraw from representing a client if withdrawal can be accomplished without material adverse effect on the interests of the client, or if:

(1) the client persists in a course of action involving the lawyer's services that the lawyer reasonably believes is criminal or fraudulent;

(2) the client has used the lawyer's services to perpetrate a crime or fraud;

(3) a client insists upon pursuing an objective that the lawyer considers repugnant or imprudent;

(4) the client fails substantially to fulfill an obligation to the lawyer regarding the lawyer's services and has been given reasonable warning that the lawyer will withdraw unless the obligation is fulfilled;

(5) the representation will result in an unreasonable financial burden on the lawyer or has been rendered unreasonably difficult by the client; or

(6) other good cause for withdrawal exists.

(c) When ordered to do so by a tribunal, a lawyer shall continue representation notwithstanding good cause for terminating the representation.

(d) Upon termination of representation, a lawyer shall take steps to the extent reasonably practicable to protect a client's interests, such as giving reasonable notice to the client, allowing time for employment of other counsel, surrendering papers and property to which the client is entitled and refunding any advance payment of fee that has not been earned. The lawyer may retain papers relating to the client to the extent permitted by other law.

Second, the lawyer *may* withdraw from all representation of the client, and *must* withdraw from all representation if the fact of such representation is likely to be known to and relied upon by third persons to whom the continuing fraud is directed, and the representation is therefore likely to assist in the fraud.

Third, the lawyer may disavow any of her work product to prevent its use in the client's continuing or intended future fraud, even though this may have the collateral effect of disclosing inferentially client confidences obtained during the representation. In some circumstances, such a disavowal of work product (commonly referred to as a "noisy" withdrawal) may be necessary in order to effectuate the lawyer's withdrawal from representation of the client.

Fourth and finally, if the fraud is completed, and the lawyer does not know or reasonably believe that the client intends to continue the fraud or commit a future fraud by use of the lawyer's services or work product, the lawyer may withdraw from representation of the client but may not disavow any work product.

The facts we have been asked to assume by the instant inquiry are as follows: The client is a small, non-public company specializing in the business of providing lighting fixtures in new office buildings and other new commercial structures. Its principal assets are receivables and work in progress. For the past three years, the lawyer has been the principal outside counsel to the client, handling a variety of general corporate matters. A year ago, the lawyer acted as counsel for the client in negotiating and drafting loan documents pursuant to which the client obtained from a bank a $5 million unsecured loan for office expansion and working capital. The loan was for a three-year term during which only interest was payable, on a monthly basis, the principal being payable at the end of the three years. At the loan closing, the lawyer as counsel for the client issued a formal opinion to the bank in the customary form to the effect that (i) the client had been duly organized and was in good standing as a foreign corporation in every state where the nature of its business required such qualification; (ii) the loan transaction had been duly authorized by all necessary corporate action and the loan documents had been properly executed on behalf of the client by its duly authorized officers; (iii) all obligations cited in the loan documents were enforceable against the client in accordance with their terms (subject only to the application and effect of bankruptcy and insolvency laws and the like); and (iv) all installation contracts were enforceable obligations under applicable law against the client's customers.

The bank at closing relied not only on the lawyer's opinion but in addition on the client's audited financial statements which were accompanied by an unqualified opinion in the usual form from the client's independent auditors. The audited financial statements showed the client as a sound enterprise financially, with a net worth in excess of $15 million, and with no outstanding indebtedness other than to trade creditors. The treasurer of the client executed and submitted to the bank a certificate accompanying the audited financial statements warranting that, at the date of the loan closing, there had been no material adverse change in the financial condition of the client, and that the audited financial statements accurately reflected its financial condition at the date of the loan closing. The bank thereupon closed the loan and advanced the full $5 million loan proceeds to the client.

Unknown to the lawyer, and also to the accounting firm, the chief executive officer and the treasurer of the client have for the past three years been engaged in a fraud, manufacturing millions of dollars worth of false lighting installation contracts. In many cases, the fraud was facilitated because the client actually did some work in the building in question. The fraud essentially consisted of altering the original contracts, or forging change orders, so as to inflate the contract amount. As a result, the client's audited financial statements for the past three years (including the statements on which the bank relied in closing the loan) were materially misleading. In fact, the company's net worth is less than the $5 million borrowed from the bank.

The CEO and the treasurer have now confessed the fraud to the lawyer but not to the independent auditors or anybody else. They have represented to the lawyer that they have ceased creating bogus contracts. However, they are unwilling to issue corrected financial statements, which of course would disclose the prior fraud. In addition, they have told the lawyer that they are planning to retain a new law firm as outside counsel and do not intend to disclose the prior fraud to that firm, so that the new firm will be available to use for certain future assignments involving the false financial statements that they believe the lawyer would be ethically precluded from handling by virtue of what she has learned about the client's true financial situation. These assignments may include new loan transactions, but they may also simply consist of ongoing dealings with the bank from which the first loan was fraudulently obtained, e.g., maintaining a line of credit. Further reliance by the bank on the fraudulent financial statements would of course necessarily entail reliance as well on the lawyer's opinion vouching for the principal asset reflected therein. Implicit in the proposed substitution of counsel is recognition by the CEO and the treasurer that a lawyer who knew of their intention to continue a fraudulent course of conduct against the bank and represented the company in dealing with the bank would be knowingly assisting the fraud, in violation of her ethical responsibilities.

The CEO and the treasurer have said they will do everything within their power to strengthen the company financially during the two years remaining before the $5 million debt to the bank matures. The lawyer believes that they are sincere. She also believes their assertions that, although there is a serious threat of insolvency, the client company ultimately will survive because it is slowly developing a good volume of honest business. All agree, however, that even if the client survives, it is unrealistic to expect that the full $5 million indebtedness to the bank can be repaid at maturity. The CEO and the treasurer have asked the lawyer to remain publicly and officially as counsel to the company, so that she may assist the company's survival efforts in ways that would not directly implicate the opinion in which she expressed confidence in the fabricated installation contracts on which the company's false financial statements are based.

As permitted by Rule 1.13, the lawyer has informed the third member of the client's board of directors, who was not involved in the fraud, of all these facts. After discussing the matter with the CEO and treasurer, the third board member advised the lawyer that he believes the company will survive, and that for the time being he intends to take no action with respect to the fraud other than to assist the CEO and treasurer in avoiding the company's insolvency.

Thus it is that the lawyer knows that so much of her opinion as certifies to the enforceability of the installation contracts is false and its use by the client has been fraudulent. The lawyer also knows, by virtue of the client's representations to her, that the client intends further use of her opinion to defraud the bank and/or other third parties. The lawyer recognizes that in these circumstances, even if the client had not proposed to replace her as counsel, she would be required by Rule 1.16(a)(1)[4] to withdraw from further representation of the client in matters directly involving her opinion, the fraudulent contracts to which her opinion referred, or the false financial statements that rest upon the fraudulent contracts. She believes that she would also be required to withdraw from representation of the client in any matters involving a continuing relationship with the bank from which the $5 million loan was fraudulently obtained, since her very presence as a representative of the client could lull the bank into a continuing reliance on its erroneous view of the company's financial condition, as reflected in her false opinion that the installment contracts were enforceable obligations. In either case she believes she would be put in the position of assisting the client's continuing fraudulent course of conduct in violation of Rule 1.2(d).[5] Her "assistance" would stem in material part from an invited, and assumed, reliance by the bank on her prior representations about the enforceability of the client's installation contracts, and, by extension, about the client's financial situation generally. Her remaining in the role of counsel to the client in matters involving the bank would discourage inquiry into the soundness of the loan and perhaps even encourage the bank to make further extensions of credit. Indeed, the lawyer is persuaded that her remaining as counsel to the company in *any* capacity, knowing what she does about the company's true financial situation and its intention to continue to deal with third parties as if the fraudulent statements were genuine, is likely to bring her into conflict with Model Rule 1.2(d).

---

4. *See* note 3, *supra.*   **5.** *See* note 2, *supra.*

The Committee agrees that Rule 1.16(a)(1) compels the lawyer to "withdraw from the representation" of the company in any matters involving her opinion, the fraudulent contracts, the erroneous financial statements or the bank, since continued representation would constitute assisting the client in a course of conduct known to be fraudulent in violation of Rule 1.2(d).

It is not clear from the facts presented to the Committee whether severance of the *entire* relationship is ethically compelled in this case, as the lawyer apparently believes, or whether she is ethically required to withdraw from representation of the client only in matters relating to the fraud. We do not believe that knowledge of a client's ongoing fraud necessarily requires the lawyer's withdrawal from representation wholly unrelated to the fraud, even if the fraud involves the lawyer's past services or work product. On the other hand, complete severance may be the preferred course in these circumstances, in order to avoid any possibility of the lawyer's continued association with the client's fraud. We would simply point out, however, that withdrawal from matters totally unrelated to the fraud is more likely to be permissive, and governed by Rule 1.16(b), than mandatory under Rule 1.16(a)(1).

The question then arises, what if anything may or must the lawyer do, beyond the simple silent act of ceasing further activity on behalf of the client, if she is obliged to withdraw under Rules 1.16(a)(1) and 1.2(d)? [6]

Specifically, may she withdraw or disaffirm opinions or other documents that she has issued in the course of her representation?

The lawyer is subject to the general prohibition of Rule 1.6 [7] against disclosing information relating to her representation of the company, and the text of this Rule itself contains no exception that would permit her to reveal the fraud to the bank, to the client's stockholders, to the new law firm the company has retained, or to anyone else. Nor is disclosure explicitly authorized by any other ethical rule.[8] Therefore, the lawyer may not, as a general matter, reveal the client's fraud even in order to save innocent third parties from being victimized or herself from potential civil or even criminal liability. The question we address

---

6. Withdrawal by counsel, without more, may put the bank on notice that something is wrong, and engender additional inquiries that would discourage further reliance on the fraudulent opinion letter. If withdrawal alone does have this effect, then the lawyer may not do anything further. However, since a silent unexplained withdrawal is far less likely to prevent a violation of Rule 1.2(d) than a "noisy" one, see note 9 *infra,* in most instances a lawyer who wishes to avoid a Rule 1.2(d) violation will have to consider more than a silent withdrawal.

7. *See* note 1, *supra.*

8. The provisions of Rules 1.13 (Organization as Client) and 4.1(b) (Truthfulness in Statements to Others) are expressly limited by reference in their text to the prohibitions of Rule 1.6. Rule 3.3 (Candor Towards the Tribunal), whose text contains an explicit exception to the confidentiality requirement of Rule 1.6, is inapplicable in this situation, since the fraud is not implicated in any matter presently before a tribunal. Any argument that Rule 4.1(a) (a lawyer may not "knowingly" make a false statement of material fact) applies in this situation fails in the face of the fact that the lawyer did not know at the time she vouched for the installation contracts that they were false.

is whether the lawyer may nonetheless in the circumstances here in question accompany her withdrawal from the representation with disaffirmance of the formal opinion on which the bank relied in making the loan, and which she now knows to be based upon false information provided her by the client, in order to avoid providing assistance in violation of Rule 1.2(d). Such a "noisy" withdrawal is, of course, likely to have the collateral consequence of disclosing, inferentially, information relating to the representation that is otherwise protected as a client confidence under Rule 1.6.[9]

For reasons discussed below, we believe that Rule 1.6 should not necessarily and in every case "trump" other ethical rules with which it collides, at least to the extent that a lawyer should be allowed (if indeed she should not be required) to withdraw assistance that has unknowingly been provided to a continuing or future fraudulent project in order to comply fully with her obligation to "withdraw" so as to avoid "assisting" client fraud under Rules 1.16(a)(1) and 1.2(d).

Such a "noisy" withdrawal, with its potential for indirectly signaling the client's past wrongdoing, notwithstanding the strict obligation of confidentiality otherwise imposed by the black letter text of Rule 1.6, is clearly contemplated in the following Comment to that Rule:

WITHDRAWAL

If the lawyer's services will be used by the client in materially furthering a course of criminal or fraudulent conduct, the lawyer must withdraw, as stated in Rule 1.16(a)(1).

After withdrawal the lawyer is required to refrain from making disclosure of the client's confidence, except as otherwise provided in Rule 1.6. Neither this rule nor Rule 1.8(b) nor Rule 1.16(d) prevents the lawyer from giving notice of the fact of withdrawal, and *the lawyer may also withdraw or disaffirm any opinion, document, affirmation, or the like.*

Where the client is an organization, the lawyer may be in doubt whether contemplated conduct will actually be carried out by the organization. Where necessary to guide conduct in connection with this Rule, the lawyer may make inquiry within the organization as indicated in Rule 1.13(b). (Emphasis added)

---

9. Unlike a silent, unexplained withdrawal, *see* note 6 *supra*, a lawyer's explicit disaffirmance of work product prepared by the lawyer in the course of the representation, may well be understood as amounting to a representation by the lawyer that the client information on which the disaffirmed document relied is untrustworthy, thereby necessitating the withdrawal. That follows from the fact that it is only in those very circumstances that the lawyer may disaffirm the documents prepared in the course of the representation. Indeed, the whole point of a "noisy" withdrawal is to ensure that those to whom it is communicated understand that the lawyer will no longer take responsibility for the contents of the documents which were prepared in reliance on client representations. Every lawyer and every individual or entity involved in the transaction which has had occasion to rely upon those documents is likely to so interpret their unilateral disaffirmance by the lawyer who prepared them. It must be recognized, therefore, that a "noisy" withdrawal may result in a disclosure of "information relating to representation" that is generally prohibited by Rule 1.6.

The questions presented by the Comment are, first, in just what circumstances it contemplates a "noisy" withdrawal; and second, whether the Comment correctly interprets the confidentiality requirements of Rule 1.6 in stating that a "noisy" withdrawal is permissible in any circumstances.

As to the first question, we think it clear that the Comment would allow disaffirmance only in circumstances where the lawyer's withdrawal is ethically *required* because of the client's intention of using the lawyer's services (absent effective withdrawal) in a continuing or future fraud. The first of the three paragraphs of the Comment addresses the situation in which "the lawyer's services will be used by the client in materially furthering a course of criminal or fraudulent conduct," a situation in which the lawyer "must withdraw, as stated in Rule 1.16(a)(1)." The third paragraph concerns the lawyer's doubt as to the client's intention to carry out "contemplated conduct," plainly a reference to the "criminal or fraudulent conduct" referred to in the first paragraph. It would strain common rules of construction to conclude that the middle of three related paragraphs of text, containing the disaffirmance provision, was intended to address broader circumstances than those to which the first and third paragraph are limited: *viz.*, the situation in which withdrawal is mandatory. Disaffirmance is, thus, not contemplated by the Comment where the lawyer's withdrawal from representation is only optional, under Rule 1.16(b).[10] It follows that disaffirmance is not allowed where the fraud is completed, and the client does not, so far as the lawyer knows or reasonably believes, intend to make further fraudulent use of the lawyer's services.

A more difficult question is whether the "Withdrawal" Comment to Rule 1.6, asserting in effect that the confidentiality requirement of the Rule is subject to an exception for "noisy" withdrawals, correctly inter-

---

10. To the extent that the annotations to Model Rule 1.6 may be read to suggest that a "noisy" withdrawal is authorized in circumstances governed by Rule 1.16(b), where withdrawal from representation is not mandatory but merely permissible, we disagree. *See* ANNOTATED MODEL RULES OF PROFESSIONAL CONDUCT at 100 (1992). That said, however, we note that Rule 1.16(b) permits (but does not require) withdrawal if (1) "the client persists in a course of action involving the lawyer's services that the lawyer reasonably believes is criminal or fraudulent," or (2) "the client has used the lawyer's services to perpetrate a crime or fraud." The difference between the situation described in 1.16(b)(1) and that contemplated by 1.16(a)(1), where failure to withdraw would violate the prohibition in Rule 1.2(d) against assisting client fraud, appears to lie in the extent to which the lawyer is persuaded that her client's intended course of conduct is in fact wrongful. (Note that the degree of certitude here at issue relates to the wrongfulness of the client's intended conduct, and *not* the likelihood that the conduct will actually occur— as to which the lawyer need only have a "reasonable belief" to trigger the mandatory withdrawal obligation of Rule 1.16(a)(1).) Once she *knows* that what her client intends to do is fraudulent, as opposed to merely "reasonably believing" that it is, as contemplated under 1.16(b)(1), her duty to resign the representation under Rule 1.16(a)(1) becomes clear, as does her obligation to disaffirm if necessary. Disavowal of work product is not permissible in cases where withdrawal is voluntary under Rule 1.16(b)(1) rather than mandatory under Rule 1.16(a)(1) precisely because voluntary withdrawal occurs by definition in circumstances where the lawyer does not know that the client's intended course of conduct is fraudulent, and hence does not have the same need to make her withdrawal effective so as to avoid assisting that fraud.

prets the text of that Rule in its interplay with the other pertinent Rules. We are cognizant, in this connection, of the observation in the "Scope" section of the Rules that Comments "are intended as guides to interpretation, but the text of each Rule is authoritative." See *Annotated Model Rules of Professional Conduct* at 10 (1992). We are also mindful of the fact that the House of Delegates, which adopted this Comment (along with the entire body of Commentary to the Rules) at its Annual Meeting in 1983, had six months earlier rejected a proposal of the Commission on Evaluation of Professional Standards (known as the "Kutak Commission") that would have included in Rule 1.6 a provision giving a lawyer the discretion to reveal information relating to the representation of a client to the extent the lawyer reasonably believed necessary "to rectify the consequences of a client's criminal or fraudulent act in the furtherance of which the lawyer's services had been used" (proposed Model Rule 1.6(b)(2), Final Draft of the Proposed Model Rules of Professional Conduct, May 30, 1981).[11] The effect of the two actions of the House of Delegates, taken together, was to reject an explicit exception to the obligation of confidentiality with respect to client fraud in the text of Rule 1.6, but to adopt a statement in the Comment to the effect that an exception relating to that general subject—albeit a substantially narrower one—was to be implied.

The question before us is, at heart, whether the "Withdrawal" Comment is appropriately to be given meaning—i.e., viewed as legitimate interpretation of the Rules—or instead simply ignored. We think the former: that the Comment correctly reflects the need to interpret Rule 1.6's requirement of confidentiality in light of what Rules 1.2(d) and 1.16(a)(1) require of a lawyer in a situation where continued representation of the client will entail the lawyer's assisting in the client's continuing or future fraud and withdrawal is therefore mandatory.

We note that neither Rule 1.16(a)(1) nor Rule 1.2(d) is qualified, as are other possibly relevant provisions of the Rules, *see* note 8, *supra,* by a caveat that compliance is subject to the obligation to protect client confidences contained in Rule 1.6. While it is also true that neither Rule contains language explicitly overriding the confidentiality requirement of Rule 1.6 (as do Rule 3.3 and, of course, Rule 1.6 itself), the absence from their text of a preemption clause does not seem to us necessarily determinative of the proper course of conduct in a situation where compliance with Rules 1.16(a)(1) and 1.2(d) appears to require conduct that may have the collateral consequence of disclosing client confidences.

---

11. In 1991 this Committee proposed an amendment to Rule 1.6 that would have incorporated the "rectification" provision defeated in 1983 into the text of Rule 1.6. The proposal was again defeated after sharp debate in the House of Delegates. *See* 60 U.S.L.W. 2122 (August 20, 1991). A number of states adopting the Model Rules have amended their rules to allow or require disclosure of client fraud. *See* G.C. HAZARD & W.W. HODES, THE LAW OF LAWYERING, App. 4, 1259–66 (2d ed. 1990). *See also* RESTATEMENT (THIRD) OF THE LAW GOVERNING LAWYERS §§ 117(A), 117(B) (Tentative Draft No. 3, 1990) (duty of confidentiality permits disclosure of crime or fraud threatening substantial financial loss; one proposed alternative would permit disclosure only where the lawyer's services have been used, the other would not).

In the absence of a clear textual indication of how such a conflict should be resolved,[12] the Committee believes that the confidentiality requirement of Rule 1.6 should not be interpreted so rigidly as to prevent the lawyer from undertaking to the limited extent necessary that which is required to avoid a violation of Rules 1.2(d) and 1.16(a)(1).

We also note that the exception from the requirement of confidentiality that we recognize in this case is different from the exceptions spelled out in the text of Rules 1.6 and 3.3, which explicitly authorize revelation of client confidences.[13] The exception here (if "exception" is an appropriate term to describe the inevitable consequences of one rule's operation upon another) simply results from a recognition that fulfillment of the lawyer's obligations under Rules 1.16(a)(1) and 1.2(d) may have the collateral effect of inferentially revealing a confidence. Under these circumstances, we are comfortable concluding that the lawyer should not be prevented from fulfilling those two obligations by a construction of Rule 1.6 as necessarily imposing a categorical bar.[14]

12. The commentary to these Rules sends somewhat confusing and even contradictory messages about how they should be interpreted in relationship to one another. For example, a Comment to Rule 1.2(d) ("Criminal, Fraudulent and Prohibited Transactions") suggests that the obligation to protect client confidences should take precedence over the obligation not to assist a client's fraud: "The lawyer is not permitted to reveal the client's wrongdoing, except where permitted by Rule 1.6." On the other hand, a Comment to Rule 1.6 ("Disclosure Adverse to Client") somewhat cryptically appears to negate this suggestion: in discussing the general duty not to disclose, the Comment "distinguishes" several situations, the first of which is a lawyer's counseling or assisting a client in conduct that is criminal or fraudulent in violation of Rule 1.2(d), the necessary implication being that this is a situation in which disclosure adverse to the client may be permissible. This Comment notes that a lawyer's "innocent involvement" in "past conduct" by the client that was criminal or fraudulent does not violate Rule 1.2(d). Again, the implication is that a lawyer's "involvement" in ongoing conduct that she "knows" is fraudulent may permit or require disclosure. This same Comment to Rule 1.6 also identifies the lawyer's duty not to use false evidence in violation of Rule 3.3(a)(4) as a "special instance" of the Rule 1.2(d) duty not to assist. The question then arises whether the provision specifically overriding the confidentiality requirement of Rule 1.6 in Rule 3.3, *see* note 8, *supra*, should also be read into Rule 1.2(d). We need not, for purposes of this opinion, resolve all of these ambiguities and uncertainties.

13. Professor Hazard has suggested that the "noisy" withdrawal provision in the Comment to Rule 1.6 could also be interpreted as a "modest but significant" attempt to "enlarge" the "self defense" exception to Rule 1.6(b)(2). *See* HAZARD, *Rectification of Client Fraud: Death and Revival of a Professional Norm*, 33 EMORY L.J. 271, 290 (1984). Paragraph (b)(2) allows disclosure of confidences "to the extent the lawyer believes necessary . . . to establish a defense to a criminal charge or civil claim against the lawyer based upon conduct in which the client was involved, or to respond to allegation in any proceeding concerning the lawyer's representation of the client." The Committee does not share, or for purposes of this opinion rely on, the view that the permissibility of a "noisy" withdrawal rests upon Rule 1.6(b)(2).

14. The two other Rules referred to in the second paragraph of the "Withdrawal" Comment overlap Rule 1.6 in suggesting a duty of confidentiality in more narrowly defined situations: Rule 1.8(b) (Conflict of Interest: Prohibited Transactions) provides that a lawyer shall not use information relating to representation of a client to the disadvantage of a client without consent of the client, "except as permitted or required by Rule 1.6 or Rule 3.3 [Candor Toward the Tribunal];" Rule 1.16(d) provides that after termination of representation a lawyer shall take steps reasonably necessary to protect a client's interests, such as giving reasonable notice and surrendering papers or property to which the client is entitled. Our conclusion respecting the need to interpret the confidentiality requirement of Rule 1.6 in light of the requirements imposed by Rule 1.2(d) and 1.16(a)(1) applies as well to any

This reading of Rule 1.6 finds ample support in the text of Rules 1.16(a)(1) and 1.2(d). Under the mandate of Rule 1.16(a)(1) that a lawyer shall withdraw if the "representation will result in a violation," the term "representation" must be read to include a lawyer's permitting the client's continued use of the lawyer's pre-existing work product. Similarly, under the injunction in Rule 1.2(d) that a lawyer shall not "assist a client in conduct the lawyer knows is criminal or fraudulent," the term "assist" must be reasonably construed to cover a failure to repudiate or otherwise disassociate herself from prior work product the lawyer knows or has reason to believe is furthering the client's continuing or future criminal or fraudulent conduct. It would follow from such a construction of these key terms in Rules 1.16(a)(1) and 1.2(d) that a lawyer's disavowal of work product would be an essential accompaniment to the lawyer's withdrawal from representation. Indeed, it would also follow that such a disaffirmance might be necessary in order to make the withdrawal effective; that is, the lawyer may be required to do more than simply decline to perform further services in order to fully effectuate a "withdrawal" from representation under Rule 1.16(a)(1) and to avoid "assistance" under Rule 1.2(d). In this view, where the client avowedly intends to continue to use the lawyer's work product, this amounts to a *de facto* continuation of the representation even if the lawyer has ceased to perform any additional work. The representation is not completed, any more than the fraud itself is completed.[15] In order to fully effectuate the withdrawal mandated by Rule 1.16(a)(1), and to avoid assisting client fraud as mandated by Rule 1.2(d), the lawyer may have to repudiate her preexisting work product in addition to refusing to perform any further work for the client.

Such a construction of these key terms in Rules 1.16(a)(1) and 1.2(d) reinforces this conclusion that a lawyer's disavowal of work product may be an appropriate accompaniment to the lawyer's withdrawal from representation; indeed, it may be necessary, in order to make the withdrawal effective.

Two consequences flow from this interpretation of these key terms in Rules 1.16(a)(1) and 1.2(d). First, it provides a rationale for limiting a "noisy" withdrawal to circumstances where the withdrawal is mandatory. Absent imperatives imposed by these other two Rules, that a lawyer disassociate herself from a client's ongoing wrongdoing in order to avoid assisting it, it is neither necessary nor appropriate to permit

implied obligation of confidentiality deriving from these two other Rules.

15. We do not mean to suggest that disaffirmance would be similarly appropriate long after the lawyer has ceased her association with the client. The possibility of disaffirmance of work product arises in the first place precisely because the work product is perceived as a continuation of the representation, and its repudiation is therefore part and parcel of the mandatory withdrawal. We express no view on a lawyer's obligations when she discovers long after she has ceased to represent a client that the client intends to make use of her work product to the detriment of third parties. In any event, as a practical matter, we doubt that such a situation is likely to arise.

disavowal of work product and possible consequent revelation of client confidences.

The second conclusion logically to be drawn from this construction of the Rules is that the lawyer's ability to disaffirm work product, and thus attempt to disassociate herself from further client fraud based upon that work product, cannot depend upon whether the client or the lawyer is the first to act in discontinuing the representation. The possibility of a noisy withdrawal cannot be preempted by a swift dismissal of the lawyer by the client. Whenever circumstances exist that would otherwise require a lawyer to withdraw, disaffirmance may be in order even if the client fires her before she has a chance to do so.

Applying Rule 1.6, so construed, we conclude that the instant inquiry presents a situation in which a "noisy" withdrawal would be proper since the client has declared itself determined to engage in further fraudulent conduct that will implicate the lawyer's past services, and the lawyer knows it. Withdrawal from further representation of the client is therefore mandated by Rule 1.16(a)(1). And, if the lawyer reasonably believes that her withdrawal in silence will be ineffective to prevent the client from using the lawyer's work product to accomplish its unlawful purpose, in order to avoid violating Rule 1.2(d), she may take the additional step of disaffirming her work product, with the hope and expectation that this will prevent reliance on that work product by future victims of the client's continuing fraud. Indeed, disavowal of her opinion may be the only way of making her withdrawal effective.

But disaffirmance should be a last resort, and should in any event go no further than necessary to accomplish its purpose of avoiding the lawyer's assisting the client's fraud. Before taking this drastic step, the lawyer should determine whether the circumstances are such that disaffirmance is necessary to disassociate herself from the client's fraud, or whether measures short of disaffirmance will suffice. We can envision situations in which the lawyer's simple silent withdrawal from representation would be sufficient to accomplish this end.[16] We can also envision situations in which the lawyer's intention to disaffirm, announced to the client, would accomplish the same result as actual disaffirmance. And even where disaffirmance is necessary, it may be enough to take measures short of notifying the bank. For example, it may be sufficient for the lawyer to notify the client's new lawyers that she can no longer stand behind the opinion she gave at the loan closing about the enforceability of the installation contracts. Finally, if the bank must be notified, in disaffirming her work product the lawyer should take only such steps as are reasonably necessary to accomplish the intended purpose of preventing use of her work product in the client's fraud. The lawyer may and indeed must decline to discuss or otherwise reveal anything about the disaffirmed work product beyond the simple fact that she no longer stands behind it.

---

16. *See* note 6, *supra.*

It bears emphasis that the conclusion of this opinion has not been easily reached. It has required clarification and reconciliation of contradictory text and conflicting directives from different parts of the Rules and their commentary, a by-product of the ambivalence with which the legal profession has historically approached the problem of a client determined to engage in illegal conduct.[17] We are keenly aware of, and support, the high importance placed by the profession on the duty to keep client confidences. And in finding an implied exception to this duty, we are mindful of the fact that limited exceptions to it are spelled out explicitly in the text of Rule 1.6 itself and in the text of Rule 3.3. *See* note 8, *supra*. Moreover, it has not escaped us that on two occasions, one as recent as a year ago, the ABA's House of Delegates flatly rejected a proposal to make explicit in the text of Rule 1.6 an exception that would permit disclosure in circumstances involving client fraud.

It should be pointed out, however, that the proposal to amend Rule 1.6 that was twice rejected by the House of Delegates would have carved out a much larger exception to Rule 1.6's obligation of confidentiality than is presented by the foregoing interpretation of the Rules: the Kutak Commission's "rectification" provision would have permitted a lawyer to disclose explicitly and directly, and not merely inferentially, a client's fraud, in order to rectify its consequences and not merely to prevent its continuation, regardless of whether it was ongoing or entirely a thing of the past.[18] Our present opinion reads the Rules as permitting limited disclosure *only* where the client is determined to continue the fraudulent conduct which the lawyer has unwittingly facilitated, or to make use of the lawyer's services or work product in a future fraud, and there is no other way for the lawyer to avoid giving assistance to such continuing or future fraud in violation of Rule 1.2(d). In these limited circumstances, where silence would result in a violation of the lawyer's duty under Model Rule 1.2(d) not to assist a client's ongoing or intended future fraud, we are persuaded that her duty to keep client confidences must give way to the extent necessary to avoid this result.

[Three members of the eight member committee dissented. The dissenting opinion is not included here.]

MULTIPLE CHOICE QUESTIONS

Answer these questions under the ABA Code and
ABA Model Rules

1. In which of the following situations would the information received by the attorney be covered by *both* the attorney-client privilege and the ethical duty to preserve the client's confidential information?

---

17. *See* note 12, *supra*. It may also be noted that the two sentences of the second paragraph of the "Withdrawal" Comment appear flatly inconsistent since a "noisy" withdrawal will almost certainly be viewed as a signal by the lawyer that third parties should no longer trust the client information upon which the disaffirmed document relied. *See* note 9, *supra,* and accompanying text.

18. *See* text accompanying note 11, *supra.*

I. Lawyer L is defending client C in a tax fraud case. With C's consent, L hires a tax accountant to examine C's records, to talk with C, and to prepare some worksheets for L to use in defending the case. The accountant turns the worksheets over to L.

II. L is representing C in a boundary line dispute with C's neighbor. When combing through the county land records, L discovers that C's grantor apparently had no legal title to the land he purported to grant to C.

III. L is defending C in a first degree murder case. In the course of her investigation, L talks to a taxi driver who tells L that he remembers that on the night in question C rode in his taxi to an address near the scene of the murder.

IV. L represents C in an action for breach of an oral contract. When preparing the case for trial, L stumbles across an old newspaper clipping, reporting C's conviction of a felony in a distant state 15 years ago.

    A. All of the above.

    B. I, III, and IV only.

    C. I only.

    D. III only.

2. Client Christenson asked attorney Alder to prepare some legal papers in connection with Christenson's proposed public sale of investment shares in a real estate venture. Alder advised Christenson that it would be a felony under state law to sell the shares without first registering them with the State Commissioner of Real Estate. Assume that a reasonable lay person would not realize, without a lawyer's advice, that this conduct would be criminal. When Christenson heard Alder's advice, he told Alder simply to abandon the project. Later Alder learned that Christenson went ahead and sold the shares to the public without registering them. Which of the following items are correct?

I. Since Christenson sought Alder's aid in committing a future crime, the attorney-client privilege does not cover the communications between them.

II. Alder *must* contact the State Commissioner of Real Estate and reveal what he told Christenson.

III. Alder *may* contact Christenson and urge him to take appropriate steps to rectify his wrong.

IV. It would be *proper* for Alder not to tell any outsider about his communications with Christenson.

    A. I, II, and III only.

    B. III and IV only.

    C. II and III only.

    D. IV only.

3. Lawyer Lorenz represents client Cramer in a complex business case. The defendant has demanded production of a mass of Cramer's records that contain vital, confidential business information. The defendant has agreed to a protective order that prohibits it from misusing the information, and it has agreed to accept xerographic copies in lieu of the original records. Lorenz's office does not have a copying machine big enough to do the job efficiently. In these circumstances:

A. Lorenz *must* do the copying job herself on her small, slow office machine.

B. Lorenz *must* tell Cramer to make the copies himself, using his own facilities.

C. Lorenz *may* select a trustworthy copying firm to do the work, provided that she makes sure the firm's employees preserve the confidentiality of the records.

D. Lorenz *may* select a trustworthy copying firm to do the work, provided that she is personally present to supervise the work.

4. Attorney Aquino defended Dempsey in a criminal assault case. Before trial, Dempsey told Aquino in confidence that he beat up the victim without provocation. Due to Aquino's hard work, coupled with a stroke of luck, the jury found Dempsey not guilty. Then Dempsey refused to pay Aquino's fee. Aquino wrote to Dempsey as follows: "The jury found you not guilty, but your victim can still sue you for civil damages. If you do not pay my fee, and if I have to sue you to collect it, I will have to reveal the whole truth in open court, to explain why the amount of my fee is reasonable. Think this over carefully. I hope to receive your check by return mail." Which of the following is most nearly correct?

A. Even though heavy-handed, Aquino's letter was *proper* because he was simply explaining to Dempsey the consequences of refusing to pay the fee.

B. If Aquino sues Dempsey to collect the fee, Aquino will be *subject to discipline* because a lawyer is prohibited from using a civil suit to collect a fee.

C. Aquino's letter was *proper* because a lawyer is required to settle fee disputes amicably if possible.

D. If Aquino sues Dempsey to collect the fee, Aquino *may* reveal Dempsey's confidential communications, but only to the extent necessary to establish his claim against Dempsey.

5. Client Colbert has retained lawyer Lamb to represent her in divorce proceedings instituted by Colbert's husband. Colbert has moved out of the family home and is living in a distant town; she no longer sees her husband or their children. Colbert tells Lamb in confidence that, before the separation, she had been physically abusing the children. A state statute requires physicians and psychotherapists to report to the

police all suspected cases of child abuse. The statute makes no mention of attorneys. Which of the following is most nearly correct?

A. If Lamb reports the child abuse to the police, he will be *subject to discipline*.

B. Lamb *may* report the child abuse to the police if he believes that the interests of justice will be served by doing so.

C. Lamb *must* report the child abuse to the police, because the state policy favors the protection of children.

D. Lamb *must* report the child abuse to the police, because child abuse is a crime that may result in death or serious bodily injury.

6. Eight years ago, attorney Arnott represented client Coleman in connection with a murder investigation. Coleman repeatedly assured Arnott that he was innocent. The investigation proved futile, and Coleman was never formally charged with any crime. At present Arnott is representing client Curtis in a child custody dispute between Curtis and her ex-husband. In that connection, Curtis tells Arnott in confidence about a murder committed eight years earlier by one Coleman, a friend of her ex-husband. The details revealed by Curtis make it clear that Arnott's former client, Coleman, did commit the murder. Curtis insists that Arnott not tell anyone about the murder for fear that Coleman or some of her ex-husband's other friends may retaliate against her or her children. Which of the following is most nearly correct?

A. Assuming that there is no statute of limitations on the crime of murder, Arnott *may* reveal the information to the prosecutor without Curtis's consent.

B. Arnott *must* reveal the information to the prosecutor because Coleman's evasion of the law is a continuing crime.

C. Arnott *must* keep the information in confidence unless Curtis changes her mind and consents to have it revealed.

D. Arnott *may* reveal the information to the prosecutor without the consent of either Curtis or Coleman, provided that he asks the prosecutor not to disclose the source of the information.

7. Lawyer Ling represented clients Clark and Craddock who were the sole partners in a business joint venture. In that connection, Clark and Craddock met frequently with Ling to discuss confidential matters relating to the business. One day Clark alone came to Ling's office. Before Ling could stop him, Clark disclosed that he had usurped a business opportunity that properly belonged to the joint venture. Ling informed Clark that she could not advise him on that topic. Further, Ling promptly withdrew as counsel to Clark and Craddock. Ultimately Craddock sued Clark for the usurpation. Craddock's lawyer subpoenaed Ling to testify at a deposition about the statements Clark made to Ling. At the deposition, Clark's lawyer asserted the attorney-client privilege on

Clark's behalf. Ultimately the court ordered Ling to disclose what Clark said. Which of the following is most nearly correct?

A. It was *proper* for Ling to withdraw as counsel to Clark and Craddock. Further, Ling *must* disclose what Clark said.

B. It was *proper* for Ling to withdraw as counsel to Clark and Craddock. However, Ling will be *subject to discipline* if she discloses that Clark said.

C. Ling is *subject to discipline* for withdrawing as counsel to Clark and Craddock. Further, Ling will be *subject to discipline* if she discloses what Clark said.

D. Even if Ling believes that the court order is correct, she *must* refuse to disclose what Clark said.

Answers to the multiple choice questions will be found
in the Appendix at the end of the book

Chapter Eight

CANDOR IN LITIGATION

What This Chapter Covers

I. The Attorney's Duty of Candor in Litigation
   A. Candor About the Law
   B. Candor About the Facts
   C. False Evidence
   D. The Client Perjury Problem

Reading Assignment

Wydick & Perschbacher, Chapter Eight

ABA Model Rules:

Rules 1.6, 3.3, and 4.1.

CRPC 3–700(B) and (C); 5–200.

Cal.Bus. & Prof.Code §§ 6068(d) and (e).

Supplemental Reading

ABA Code:

EC 7–23 through 7–27;

DR 4–101, DR 7–101 through DR 7–102, and DR 7–106(B).

Hazard & Hodes:

Discussion of ABA Model Rules 1.6, 3.3, and 4.1.

Wolfram:

Sections 12.3.1 through 12.3.5 (advocates and evidence);

Sections 12.4.1 through 12.4.6 (advocates and witnesses);

Sections 12.5.1 through 12.5.4 (advocates and perjury);

Sections 12.6.1 through 12.6.6 (client wrongdoing outside of litigation);

Sections 12.7 through 12.10 (other disclosure duties).

Discussion Problems

1. Suppose you represent the defendant in a diversity of citizenship case that is in trial in the United States District Court for the Southern District of New York. The applicable law is that of the State of New York. One disputed legal issue is vital—in a malpractice action, what is the appropriate standard of care for a doctor of veterinary medicine who holds herself out as a specialist in ruminant epidemiology? The plaintiff's lawyer has failed to cite a very recent appellate decision that would support the plaintiff's position. So far as you know, the trial judge is unaware of the decision, but you know about it because it was reported in the current issue of U.S. Law Week. In which of the following situations would you have an ethical duty to call the decision to the trial judge's attention?

    a. Suppose it were a New York Court of Appeals decision in a veterinary malpractice case?

    b. Suppose it were an Arizona Supreme Court decision in a veterinary malpractice case?

    c. Suppose it were a New York Court of Appeals decision in a legal malpractice case involving a lawyer who held himself out as an expert in Robinson-Patman price discrimination litigation?

Are there any tactical reasons to go beyond what the ethics rules require?

2. Suppose you represent the defendant at the trial of a negligence case. The plaintiff has engaged in extensive discovery, but she has not found out about eyewitness X, an impartial third party who saw the accident clearly. X's testimony would establish that your client was at fault. At the trial, plaintiff's case in chief is insufficient to get the case to the jury, but the defect could be cured by X's testimony. Plaintiff is about to close her case in chief. When she does, it will be time for you to move for a directed verdict. You know that X lives nearby and is available as a witness. What will you do?

3. Suppose that you are the in-house counsel for a drug company that has been sued in a state court products liability case. You have hired outside attorney Adney to defend the company. Technically speaking, you have the ultimate responsibility for all litigation matters, but you try never to second-guess the judgments of outside counsel. In the case at hand, the plaintiff alleges that he got bleeding stomach ulcers from taking Luxair, a drug made and sold by the company as a remedy for male pattern baldness. The active ingredient in Luxair is a chemical known as phlogestin. Plaintiff alleges that the company knew all along that Luxair creates a grave risk of stomach ulcers in males past age 40. Plaintiff demanded production of a host of documents, including "all documents relating to Luxair and the risk of stomach ulcers." When attorney Adney's paralegals searched the company files, they found no documents that mention both Luxair and stomach ulcers. However, in the company files pertaining to a different drug product that also

contains phlogestin, the paralegals found a "smoking gun," namely a packet of research reports. The reports show that when defendant put Luxair on the market, it knew beyond doubt that phlogestin significantly increases the risk of stomach ulcers in males past age 40. Adney plans not to produce the research reports because they were not in the files pertaining to Luxair and they do not mention Luxair. Do you agree with Adney's plan?

4. Suppose that you are the defense lawyer for Decker who is charged with first degree murder. He has told you that he is innocent and that he was miles away from the scene of the crime, playing cards with three friends. You have interviewed the three friends, and they confirm his story. You plan to use Decker and the three friends as defense witnesses at Decker's jury trial.

    a. Suppose that ten weeks before the trial, your investigator hands you information that clearly shows, beyond any fleeting whiff of doubt, that Decker and his friends are lying and that Decker did commit the murder. When you confront Decker, he says: "You are my lawyer, not my jury. I want to testify and to have my friends testify for me. Let the jury decide whether I am guilty." What should you do?

    b. Suppose the same facts, except that you get the information and confront Decker ten minutes before you are to begin presenting the defense case-in-chief. What should you do?

    c. Suppose that you do not get the information until ten minutes after you have presented the testimony of Decker and his friends. When you confront Decker, he says: "Your information is correct; I murdered that guy. But I think the jury believed me and my friends. Leave well enough alone." What should you do?

    d. Suppose that you do not get the information until ten weeks after the jury has acquitted Decker. When you confront Decker, he says: "Your information is correct; I murdered that guy. But obviously the jury believed me and my friends. Leave well enough alone." What should you do?

    e. Suppose that the information you receive from your investigator leaves some small room for doubt. When you confront Decker, he reaffirms his story about the card game. Does that change your answers to questions a through d?

    f. Compare your answers to questions a through e with your answer to Discussion Problem 5 in Chapter 7. Are they consistent? If not, what accounts for the differences?

THE TRILEMMA: TRUST, CONFIDENTIALITY, AND CANDOR

If a dilemma is a beast with two horns, then perhaps a trilemma has three. [*See* Monroe Freedman, *Perjury: The Lawyer's Trilemma*, 1 Litigation 26 (# 1, Winter 1975).] We lawyers may occasionally face such a beast in a criminal defense matter:

Horn One: We are told to seek the client's trust and to find out everything the client knows about the case.

Horn Two: We are told to preserve our client's confidential information (except in very limited situations).

Horn Three: We are told to act with candor, to refrain from presenting evidence we know is false, and (in some situations) to reveal our client's frauds.

At the outset, consider ABA Code DR 7–102(B)(1), which says:

A lawyer who receives information clearly establishing that * * * [h]is client has, in the course of the representation, perpetrated a fraud upon a person or tribunal shall promptly call upon his client to rectify the same, and if his client refuses or is unable to do so, he shall reveal the fraud to the affected person or tribunal, except when the information is protected as a privileged communication.

The "except" clause at the end was added by the ABA House of Delegates in a 1974 amendment to the ABA Code. Shortly thereafter, ABA Formal Opinion 341 (1975) interpreted the term "privileged communication" to include not only material that is protected by the attorney-client privilege, but also all other material that is protected by the ethical duty of confidentiality. That interpretation makes the "except" clause virtually swallow the rule. Do you see why? Eighteen states added the 1974 amendment to their own versions of the ABA Code, but the remainder did not.

Next, consider the advice formerly offered to criminal defense lawyers in Standard 4–7.7 of the ABA Standards for the Defense Function. When the ABA House of Delegates approved the other Standards for the Defense Function in 1979, it reserved judgment on 4–7.7, thus leaving the matter open for resolution by the drafters of the ABA Model Rules. [Standard 4–7.7 was eventually disapproved by the ABA Ethics Committee in 1987. *See* ABA Formal Op. 87–353, *infra*.] Standard 4–7.7 reads as follows:

Standard 4–7.7 Testimony by the Defendant

(a) If the defendant has admitted to defense counsel facts which establish guilt and counsel's independent investigation established that the admissions are true but the defendant insists on the right to trial, counsel must strongly discourage the defendant against taking the witness stand to testify perjuriously.

(b) If, in advance of trial, the defendant insists that he or she will take the stand to testify perjuriously, the lawyer may withdraw from the case, if that is feasible, seeking leave to the court if necessary, but the court should not be advised of the lawyer's reason for seeking to do so.

(c) If withdrawal from the case is not feasible or is not permitted by the court, or if the situation arises immediately preceding trial or during the trial and the defendant insists upon testifying perjuriously in his or her own behalf, it is unprofessional conduct for the lawyer to lend aid to the perjury or use the perjured testimony. Before the defendant takes the stand in these circumstances, the lawyer should make a record of the fact that the defendant is taking the stand against the advice of counsel in some appropriate manner without revealing the fact to the court. The lawyer may identify the witness as the defendant and may ask appropriate questions of the defendant when it is believed that the defendant's answers will not be perjurious. As to matters for which it is believed the defendant will offer perjurious testimony, the lawyer should seek to avoid direct examination of the defendant in the conventional manner; instead, the lawyer should ask the defendant if he or she wishes to make any additional statement concerning the case to the trier or triers of the facts. A lawyer may not later argue the defendant's known false version of facts to the jury as worthy of belief, and may not recite or rely upon the false testimony in his or her closing argument.

Next, consider the views expressed by Professor Monroe Freedman in his book, *Lawyers' Ethics in an Adversary System* 27–47 (Bobbs-Merrill 1975). Professor Freedman poses the question thus:

> Is it ever proper for a criminal defense lawyer to present perjured testimony? One's instinctive response is in the negative. On analysis, however, it becomes apparent that the question is an exceedingly perplexing one. [*Id.* at 27.]

He goes on to explain as follows:

> A frequent objection to the position that the attorney must go along with the client's decision to commit perjury is that the lawyer would be guilty of subornation of perjury. Subornation, however, consists of willfully procuring perjury, which is not the case when the attorney indicates to the client that the client's proposed course of conduct would be unlawful, but then accepts the client's decision. Beyond that, there is a point of view, which has been expressed to me by a number of experienced attorneys, that the criminal defendant has a "right to tell his story." What that suggests is that it is simply too much to expect of a human being, caught up in the criminal process and facing the loss of liberty and the horrors of imprisonment, not to attempt to lie to avoid that penalty. For that reason, criminal defendants in most European countries do not testify under oath, but simply "tell their stories." It is also note-

worthy that subsequent perjury prosecutions against criminal defendants in this country are extremely rare. However, the judge may well take into account at sentencing the fact that the defendant had apparently committed perjury in the course of the defense. That is certainly a factor that the attorney is obligated to advise the client about whenever there is any indication that the client is contemplating perjury. [*Id.* at 31–32.]

One possibility, says Professor Freedman, is simply for the criminal defense lawyer to withdraw from the case. But that is no answer, he says, because the client will simply get a new lawyer. The client will now know that the law profession's pledge to preserve confidential information is not all it is cracked up to be. So the client will not tell the new lawyer the truth. The identical perjured testimony will ultimately be presented in court. Further, the new lawyer (being ignorant of the truth) will have no chance to discourage the client from lying.

The problem is compounded when the criminal defendant is indigent, argues Professor Freedman. In many jurisdictions, a public defender or appointed counsel can withdraw only for extraordinary reasons. To get the court's permission to withdraw, the lawyer must either tip off the judge to the client's guilt, or mislead the judge by giving some contorted reason for withdrawal. The judge is not likely to allow withdrawal in the middle of trial, or close to trial, unless the judge is convinced that the reason for withdrawal is compelling. Further, in many jurisdictions, the judge who presides at trial will also impose the sentence on the defendant.

Professor Freedman argues that the solution proposed in ABA Defense Function Standard 4–7.7 is no solution at all. It has two flaws:

> The first is purely practical: The prosecutor might well object to testimony from the defendant in narrative form rather than in the conventional manner, because it would give the prosecutor no opportunity to object to inadmissible evidence prior to the jury's hearing it. The Standards provide no guidance as to what the defense attorney should do if the objection is sustained. More importantly, experienced trial attorneys have often noted that jurors assume that the defendant's lawyer knows the truth about the case, and that the jury will frequently judge the defendant by drawing inferences from the attorney's conduct in the case. There is, of course, only one inference that can be drawn if the defendant's own attorney turns his or her back on the defendant at the most critical point in the trial, and then, in closing argument, sums up the case with no reference to the fact that the defendant has given exculpatory testimony. [*Id.* at 37.]

Professor Freedman further argues that ABA Defense Function Standard 4–7.7 does not reflect universal agreement among lawyers about the proper course of conduct. Many respectable lawyers, he suggests, believe that the proper course is for the criminal defense counsel to call the defendant as a witness and to question him in the ordinary manner. Professor Freedman concludes as follows:

> I continue to stand with those lawyers who hold that "the lawyer's obligation of confidentiality does not permit him to disclose the facts he has learned from his client which form the basis for his conclusion that the client intends to perjure himself." What that means— necessarily, it seems to me—is that the criminal defense attorney, however unwillingly in terms of personal morality, has a professional responsibility as an advocate in an adversary system to examine the perjurious client in the ordinary way and to argue to the jury, as evidence in the case, the testimony presented by the defendant. [*Id.* at 40–41.]

The committee that drafted the ABA Model Rules rejected both Professor Freedman's advice and the advice given in Standard 4–7.7, and in 1983 the ABA House of Delegates adopted present Model Rule 3.3. Read that rule carefully, especially the Comment paragraphs labeled 4 through 14. What does Rule 3.3 require a criminal defense lawyer to do when she learns that her client is about to tell, or has already told, a false story under oath?

In *Nix v. Whiteside,* 475 U.S. 157, 106 S.Ct. 988, 89 L.Ed.2d 123 (1986), Chief Justice Burger (writing for himself and four others) traveled well out of his way to put a judicial stamp of approval on the procedure envisioned in ABA Model Rule 3.3. Defendant Whiteside was charged with murdering a marijuana dealer. Attorney Robinson was appointed to represent him. At first, Whiteside told Robinson that he stabbed the victim just as the victim was "pulling a pistol from underneath the pillow on the bed." [*Id.* at 160.] Whiteside said he had not actually seen a gun, but he was convinced that the victim had one. No gun was found at the scene. Robinson advised Whiteside that the existence of an actual gun was not critical to a claim of self-defense, and that a *reasonable belief* that there was a gun would suffice.

About a week before trial, Whiteside told Robinson for the first time that he had seen something "metallic" in the victim's hand. [*Id.* at 161.] When Robinson inquired further, Whiteside said: "In Howard Cook's case there was a gun. If I don't say I saw a gun, I'm dead." Robinson again explained that a reasonable belief would suffice, but Whiteside insisted on testifying that he had seen "something metallic." [*Id.*] At that point, Robinson told Whiteside that if Whiteside testified to that story, it would be Robinson's duty "to advise the Court of what he was doing," and Robinson said he would also "probably be allowed to impeach that particular testimony." [*Id.*] Robinson also indicated that he would try to withdraw if Whiteside insisted on testifying falsely.

Thus warned, Whiteside did not testify about having seen something metallic. Instead, he testified that he "knew" the victim had a gun, and he believed that the victim was reaching for it. On cross-examination, he admitted that he did not actually see a gun in the victim's hand. He was found guilty of second degree murder and sentenced to 40 years in prison. After exhausting his appeals, he claimed on federal habeas corpus that Robinson's refusal to let him testify as he wished was a denial of the effective assistance of counsel guaranteed by the Sixth Amendment.

The narrow issue presented to the Supreme Court was whether Whiteside was deprived of his right to effective counsel when his counsel told him that if he testified to a story the counsel believed was false, the counsel would try to withdraw and (failing that) would tell the judge that the story was false. The Court held that Whiteside was not deprived of the effective assistance of counsel—Robinson's conduct fell within the wide range of acceptable responses to proposed client perjury.

The Chief Justice explained that an ineffective assistance claim requires (a) serious error by the lawyer, and (b) prejudice to the defendant. Robinson did not make a serious error. A criminal defense attorney must be loyal to the client, but only within the bounds of lawful conduct. The attorney must not assist the client in presenting false evidence. True, a criminal defendant does have a constitutional right to testify in his own defense. [*See Rock v. Arkansas,* 483 U.S. 44, 49–53, 107 S.Ct. 2704, 2707–2710, 97 L.Ed.2d 37 (1987).] But, Burger said, if he testifies falsely, he must bear the consequences. Part of the consequences may be withdrawal of counsel or revelation of the perjury by the counsel. Moreover, Whiteside was not prejudiced. He ended up testifying truthfully at the trial. Perhaps he was deprived of counsel's help in presenting perjury, but the Constitution does not guarantee the right to have counsel's help in presenting perjury.

In a terse concurring opinion, Justice Brennan pointed out that much of the Chief Justice's opinion was unnecessary to the decision in the case:

> [L]et there be no mistake: the Court's essay regarding what constitutes the correct response to a criminal client's suggestion that he will perjure himself is pure discourse without the force of law. * * * Lawyers, judges, bar associations, students, and others should understand that the problem has not now been "decided." [*Id.* at 177.]

Shortly after *Nix v. Whiteside,* the ABA ethics committee promulgated ABA Formal Opinion 87–353, *infra,* expressing the committee's view about the trilemma issue. [For a dissection and analysis of *Nix* and Opinion 87–353, see Monroe Freedman, Understanding Lawyer's Ethics 129–41 (1990).]

ABA FORMAL OPINION 87–353

American Bar Association Committee on Ethics
and Professional Responsibility, 1987 *

If, prior to the conclusion of the proceedings, a lawyer learns that the client has given testimony the lawyer knows is false, and the

* Copyright © 1987 by the American Bar Association. All rights reserved. Reprinted by permission of the American Bar Association. Copies available from ABA Mem-

lawyer cannot persuade the client to rectify the perjury, the lawyer must disclose the client's perjury to the tribunal, notwithstanding the fact that the information to be disclosed is information relating to the representation.

If the lawyer learns that the client intends to testify falsely before a tribunal, the lawyer must advise the client against such course of action, informing the client of the consequences of giving false testimony, including the lawyer's duty of disclosure to the tribunal. Ordinarily, the lawyer can reasonably believe that such advice will dissuade the client from giving false testimony and, therefore, may examine the client in the normal manner. However, if the lawyer knows, from the client's clearly stated intention, that the client will testify falsely, and the lawyer cannot effectively withdraw from the representation, the lawyer must either limit the examination of the client to subjects on which the lawyer believes the client will testify truthfully; or, if there are none, not permit the client to testify; or, if this is not feasible, disclose the client's intention to testify falsely to the tribunal.

The professional obligations of a lawyer relating to client perjury as now defined by the Model Rules of Professional Conduct (1983), particularly in Model Rule 3.3(a) and (b), require a reconsideration of Formal Opinion 287 (1953), which was based upon an interpretation of the earlier Canons of Professional Ethics (1908), and Informal Opinion 1314 (1975), which interpreted the predecessor Model Code of Professional Responsibility (1969, revised 1980).[1] Formal Opinion 287 discussed in part the lawyer's responsibility with regard to false statements the lawyer knows that the client has made to the tribunal. Informal Opinion 1314 dealt with the lawyer's duty when the lawyer knows of the client's intention to commit perjury.

FORMAL OPINION 287

Formal Opinion 287 addressed two situations: one, a civil divorce case; the other, the sentencing procedure in a criminal case. In the civil matter, the client informs his lawyer three months after the court has entered a decree for divorce in his favor that he had testified falsely about the date of his wife's desertion. A truthful statement of the date would not have established under local law any ground for divorce and would have resulted in the dismissal of the action as prematurely brought. Formal Opinion 287 states that under these circumstances, the lawyer must advise the client to inform the court of his false

---

ber Services, 750 North Lake Shore Drive, Chicago, IL 60611.

1. The Committee notes that other prior opinions of this Committee relating to client perjury are not consistent with Model Rule 3.3. These include Formal Opinions 341 (1975) and 216 (1941) and Informal

Opinions 1318 (1975) and 869 (1965). Lawyers are cautioned to investigate the applicable local ethical rules and opinions governing a lawyer's responsibility with relation to client perjury, since local standards may differ from Rule 3.3 as adopted by the ABA House of Delegates in August, 1983.

testimony, and that if the client refuses to do so, the lawyer must cease representing the client.[2] However, Formal Opinion 287 concluded that Canon 37 of the Canons of Professional Ethics (dealing with the lawyer's duty to not reveal the client's confidences) prohibits the lawyer from disclosing the client's perjury to the court.

In this factual situation, Model Rule 3.3 also does not permit the lawyer to disclose the client's perjury to the court, but for a significantly different reason. Contrary to Formal Opinion 287, Rule 3.3(a) and (b) require a lawyer to disclose the client's perjury to the court if other remedial measures are ineffective, even if the information is otherwise protected under Rule 1.6, which prohibits a lawyer from revealing information relating to representation of a client. However, under Rule 3.3(b), the duty to disclose continues only "to the conclusion of the proceeding...." From the Comment to Rule 3.3, it would appear that the Rule's disclosure requirement was meant to apply only to those situations where the lawyer's knowledge of the client's fraud or perjury occurs prior to final judgment and disclosure is necessary to prevent the judgment from being corrupted by the client's unlawful conduct.[3] Therefore, on the facts considered by Formal Opinion 287, where the lawyer learns of the perjury after the conclusion of the proceedings— three months after the entry of the divorce decree[4]—the mandatory disclosure requirement of Rule 3.3 does not apply and Rule 1.6, therefore, precludes disclosure.

In the criminal fact setting, Formal Opinion 287 is directly contrary to the Model Rules with regard to one part of its guidance to lawyers. Briefly, the criminal defense lawyer is presented with the following three situations prior to the sentencing of the lawyer's client: (1) the judge is told by the custodian of criminal records that the defendant has no criminal record and the lawyer knows this information is incorrect based on his own investigation or from his client's disclosure to him; (2) the judge asks the defendant whether he has a criminal record and he falsely answers that he has none; (3) the judge asks the defendant's lawyer whether his client has a criminal record.

Formal Opinion 287 concluded that in none of the above situations is the lawyer permitted to disclose to the court the information he has concerning the client's actual criminal record. The opinion stated that such a disclosure would be prohibited by Canon 37, which imposed a paramount duty on the lawyer to preserve the client's confidences. In

---

2. This requirement of withdrawal from the representation stated in Formal Opinion 287 is inconsistent with Model Rule 1.16, which, under the facts posited in the Opinion, provides only for discretionary withdrawal.

3. This explanation, at least, is consistent with the distinction between information relating to continuing crime, which is not protected by the attorney-client privilege, and information relating to past crime, which is protected. *See, e.g.,* In re Grand Jury Proceedings, 680 F.2d 1026 (5th Cir. 1982) (discussing crime/fraud exception to attorney-client privilege).

4. The Committee assumes that there were no further proceedings and that this was a final decree. This is not to say, however, that the judgment could not be set aside by the court if the court subsequently learns of the fraudulent representations of the client.

situations (1) and (3) Opinion 287 is still valid under the Model Rules, since there has been no client fraud or perjury, and, therefore, the lawyer is prohibited, under Rule 1.6, from disclosing information relating to the representation.[5] However, in situation (2), where the client has lied to the court about the client's criminal record, the conclusion of Opinion 287 that the lawyer is prohibited from disclosing the client's false statement to the court is contrary to the requirement of Model Rule 3.3.[6] This rule imposes a duty on the lawyer, when the lawyer cannot persuade the client to rectify the perjury, to disclose the client's false statement to the tribunal for the reasons stated in the discussion of Rule 3.3 below.[7]

Change in Policy in Model Rule 3.3

Model Rule 3.3(a) and (b) represent a major policy change with regard to the lawyer's duty as stated in Formal Opinions 287 and 341 when the client testifies falsely. It is now mandatory, under these Model Rule provisions, for a lawyer, who knows the client has committed perjury, to disclose this knowledge to the tribunal if the lawyer cannot persuade the client to rectify the perjury.

The relevant provisions of Rule 3.3(a) are:

(a) A lawyer shall not knowingly:

. . .

(2) fail to disclose a material fact to a tribunal when disclosure is necessary to avoid assisting a criminal or fraudulent act by the client;

. . .

(4) offer evidence that the lawyer knows to be false. If a lawyer has offered material evidence and comes to know of its falsity, the lawyer shall take reasonable remedial measures.

Rule 3.3(a)(2) and (4) complement each other. While (a)(4), itself, does not expressly require disclosure by the lawyer to the tribunal of the client's false testimony after the lawyer has offered it and learns of its falsity, such disclosure will be the only "reasonable remedial [measure]"

---

5. Although in situation (3), where the court puts a direct question to the lawyer, the lawyer may not reveal the client's confidences, the lawyer, also, must not make any false statements of fact to the court. Formal Opinion 287 advised lawyers facing this dilemma to ask the court to excuse the lawyer from answering the question. The Committee can offer no better guidance under the Model Rules, despite the fact that such a request by the lawyer most likely will put the court on further inquiry, as Opinion 287 recognized.

6. The validity of Formal Opinion 287 in this regard was initially put in question in 1969 when the ABA adopted DR 7–102(B)(1). This provision required a lawyer to reveal to an affected person or tribunal any fraud perpetrated by the client in the course of the representation discovered by the lawyer. Because of its apparent inconsistency with DR 4–101, prohibiting a lawyer from revealing a confidence or secret of the client, DR 7–102(B)(1) was amended in 1974 to provide an exception to the duty to reveal the client's fraud when the information is protected as a privileged communication. Formal Opinion 341 (1975) interpreted the words "privileged communication" to encompass confidences and secrets under DR 4–101, thereby making the amendment consistent with Formal Opinion 287.

7. The Comment to Rule 3.3 suggests that the lawyer may be able to avoid disclosure to the court if the lawyer can effectively withdraw. But the Committee concludes that withdrawal can rarely serve as a remedy for the client's perjury.

the lawyer will be able to take if the client is unwilling to rectify the perjury. The Comment to Rule 3.3 states that disclosure of the client's perjury to the tribunal would be required of the lawyer by (a)(4) in this situation.

Although Rule 3.3(a)(2), unlike 3.3(a)(4), does not specifically refer to perjury or false evidence, it would require an irrational reading of the language: "a criminal or fraudulent act by the client," to exclude false testimony by the client. While broadly written to cover all crimes or frauds a client may commit during the course of the proceeding, Rule 3.3(a)(2), in the context of the whole of Rule 3.3, certainly includes perjury.

Since 3.3(a)(2) requires disclosure to the tribunal only when it is necessary to "avoid assisting" client perjury, the important question is what conduct of the lawyer would constitute such assistance. Certainly, the conduct proscribed in Rule 3.3(a)(4)—offering evidence the lawyer knows to be false—is included. Also, a lawyer's failure to take remedial measures, including disclosure to the court, when the lawyer knows the client has given false testimony, is included. It is apparent to the Committee that as used in Rule 3.3(a)(2), the language "assisting a criminal or fraudulent act by the client" is not limited to the criminal law concepts of aiding and abetting or subornation. Rather, it seems clear that this language is intended to guide the conduct of the lawyer as an officer of the court as a prophylactic measure to protect against client perjury contaminating the judicial process. Thus, when the lawyer knows the client has committed perjury, disclosure to the tribunal is necessary under Rule 3.3(a)(2) to avoid assisting the client's criminal act.

Furthermore, as previously indicated, contrary to Formal Opinions 287 and 341 and the exception provided in DR 7–102(B)(1) of the Model Code, the disclosure requirement of Model Rule 3.3(a)(2) and (4) is not excused because of client confidences. Rule 3.3(b) provides in pertinent part: "The duties stated in paragraph (a) . . . apply even if compliance requires disclosure of information otherwise protected by Rule 1.6." Thus, the lawyer's responsibility to disclose client perjury to the tribunal under Rule 3.3(a)(2) and (4) supersedes the lawyer's responsibility to the client under Rule 1.6.

APPLICATION TO CRIMINAL CASES—EFFECT OF *NIX V. WHITESIDE*

The Comment to Rule 3.3 makes it clear that this disclosure requirement applies in both civil and criminal cases. However, the Comment states that if such disclosure by a lawyer would constitute a violation of a criminal defendant's constitutional rights to due process and effective assistance of counsel, "[t]he obligation of the advocate under these Rules is subordinate to such a constitutional requirement." Subsequent to the publishing of this Comment, however, the Supreme Court of the United States held in *Nix v. Whiteside,* 475 U.S. 157, 106 S.Ct. 988, 994–97, 89 L.Ed.2d 123, 134–37 (1986) that a criminal defendant is not entitled to the assistance of counsel in giving false testimony and that a lawyer who refuses such assistance, and who even threatens the client with disclosure of the perjury to the court if the client does testify falsely, has not deprived the client of effective assistance of counsel. Some states, nevertheless, may rely on their own applicable constitutional provisions and may interpret them to prohibit such a disclosure to the tribunal by defense counsel. In a jurisdiction where this kind of ruling is made, the lawyer is obligated, of course, to comply with the constitutional requirement rather than the ethical one.

As stated earlier, the obligation of a lawyer to disclose to the tribunal client perjury committed during the proceeding, which the lawyer learns about prior to the conclusion of the proceeding, represents a reversal of prior opinions of this Committee given under earlier rules of professional conduct. However, the Committee has done nothing more in this opinion than apply the ethical rule approved by the American Bar Association when it adopted Rule 3.3(a) and (b) of the Model Rules of Professional Conduct. Even so, a question may be raised whether this application is incompatible with the adversary system and the development of effective attorney-client relationships.[8]

The Committee believes it is not. Without doubt, the vitality of the adversary system, certainly in criminal cases, depends upon the ability of the lawyer to give loyal and zealous service to the client. And this, in turn, requires that the lawyer have the complete confidence of the client and be able to assure the client that the confidence will be protected and honored. However, the ethical rules of the bar which have supported these basic requirements of the adversary system have emphasized from the time they were first reduced to written form that the lawyer's duties to the client in this regard must be performed within the bounds of law.

For example, these ethical rules clearly recognize that a lawyer representing a client who admits guilt in fact, but wants to plead not guilty and put the state to its proof, may assist the client in entering such a plea and vigorously challenge the state's case at trial through cross-examination, legal motions and argument to the jury. However, neither the adversary system nor the ethical rules permit the lawyer to participate in the corruption of the judicial process by assisting the client in the introduction of evidence the lawyer knows is false. A defendant does not have the right, as part of the right to a fair trial and zealous representation by counsel, to commit perjury. And the lawyer owes no duty to the client, in providing the representation to which the client is entitled, to assist the client's perjury.

On the contrary, the lawyer, as an officer of the court, has a duty to prevent the perjury, and if the perjury has already been committed, to prevent its playing any part in the judgment of the court. This duty the lawyer owes the court is not inconsistent with any duty owed to the client. More particularly, it is not inconsistent with the lawyer's duty to preserve the client's confidences. For that duty is based on the lawyer's need for information from the client to obtain for the client all that the

---

8. *See* Freedman, *Professional Responsibility of the Criminal Defense Lawyer: The* *Three Hardest Questions,* 64 Mich.L.Rev. 1469 (1966).

law and lawful process provide. Implicit in the promise of confidentiality is its nonapplicability where the client seeks the unlawful end of corrupting the judicial process by false evidence.

It must be emphasized that this opinion does not change the professional relationship the lawyer has with the client and require the lawyer now to judge, rather than represent, the client. The lawyer's obligation to disclose client perjury to the tribunal, discussed in this opinion, is strictly limited by Rule 3.3 to the situation where the lawyer *knows* that the client has committed perjury, ordinarily based on admissions the client has made to the lawyer.[9] The lawyer's suspicions are not enough. *United States ex rel. Wilcox v. Johnson,* 555 F.2d 115, 122 (3d Cir.1977).

INFORMAL OPINION 1314

So far, this opinion has discussed the duty of the lawyer when the lawyer learns that the client has committed perjury. The lawyer is presented with a different dilemma when, prior to trial, the client states an intention to commit perjury at trial. This was the situation addressed in Informal Opinion 1314 (1975). The Committee, in that opinion, stated that the lawyer in that situation must advise the client that the lawyer must take one of two courses of action: withdraw prior to the submission of the false testimony, or, if the client insists on testifying falsely, report to the tribunal the falsity of the testimony.

The Committee distinguished, in Informal Opinion 1314, the situation where the lawyer does not know in advance that the client intends to commit perjury. In that case, the Committee stated that when the client does commit perjury, and the lawyer later learns of it, the lawyer may not disclose the perjury to the tribunal because of the lawyer's primary duty to protect the client's confidential communications. As stated earlier in this opinion, the Committee believes that Model Rule 3.3 calls for a different course of action by the lawyer.

The duty imposed on the lawyer by Informal Opinion 1314—when the lawyer knows in advance that the client intends to commit perjury, to advise the client that if the client insists on testifying falsely, the lawyer must disclose the client's intended perjury to the tribunal—was based on the Committee's reading of DR 7–102(A)(4), (6) and (7). These provisions prohibit a lawyer from: (1) knowingly using perjured testimony or false evidence; (2) participating in the creation or preservation of evidence the lawyer knows to be false; and (3) counseling or assisting the client in conduct the lawyer knows to be illegal or fraudulent. However, none of these prohibitions *requires* disclosure to the tribunal of any information otherwise protected by DR 4–101. Although DR 4–101(C)(3) permits a lawyer to reveal a client's stated intention to commit

---

9. The Committee notes that some trial lawyers report that they have avoided the ethical dilemma posed by Rule 3.3 because they follow a practice of not questioning the client about the facts in the case and, therefore, never "know" that a client has given false testimony. Lawyers who engage in such practice may be violating their duties under Rule 3.3 and their obligation to provide competent representation under Rule 1.1. ABA Defense Function Standards 4–3.2(a) and (b) (1979) are also applicable.

perjury, this exception to the lawyer's duty to preserve the client's confidences and secrets is only discretionary on the part of the lawyer.

Informal Opinion 1314 in this regard is more consistent with Model Rule 3.3(a)(2) than with any provision of the Model Code, upon which the opinion was based. However, the Committee does not believe that the mandatory disclosure requirement of this Model Rule provision is necessarily triggered when a client states an intention to testify falsely, but has not yet done so. Ordinarily, after warning the client of the consequences of the client's perjury, including the lawyer's duty to disclose it to the court, the lawyer can reasonably believe that the client will be persuaded not to testify falsely at trial. That is exactly what happened in *Nix v. Whiteside*. Under these circumstances, the lawyer may permit the client to testify and may examine the client in the normal manner. If the client does in fact testify falsely, the lawyer's obligation to make disclosure to the court is covered by Rule 3.3(a)(2) and (4).

In the unusual case where the lawyer does know, on the basis of the client's clearly stated intention, that the client will testify falsely at trial, and the lawyer is unable to effectively withdraw from the representation, the lawyer cannot examine the client in the usual manner. Under these circumstances, when the client has not yet committed perjury, the Committee believes that the lawyer's conduct should be guided in a way that is consistent, as much as possible, with the confidentiality protections provided in Rule 1.6, and yet not violative of Rule 3.3. This may be accomplished by the lawyer's refraining from calling the client as a witness when the lawyer knows that the only testimony the client would offer is false; or, where there is some testimony, other than the false testimony, the client can offer in the client's defense, by the lawyer's examining the client on only those matters and not on the subject matter which would produce the false testimony. Such conduct on the part of the lawyer would serve as a way for the lawyer to avoid assisting the fraudulent or criminal act of the client without having to disclose the client's confidences to the court. However, if the lawyer does not offer the client's testimony, and, on inquiry by the court into whether the client has been fully advised as to the client's right to testify, the client states a desire to testify, but is being prevented by the lawyer from testifying, the lawyer may have no other choice than to disclose to the court the client's intention to testify falsely.

This approach must be distinguished from the solution offered in the initially ABA–approved Defense Function Standard 7.7 (1971). This proposal, no longer applicable,[10] permitted a lawyer, who could not dissuade the client from committing perjury and who could not withdraw, to call the client solely to give the client's own statement, without being questioned by the lawyer and without the lawyer's arguing to the

---

10. This particular Standard was not approved by the ABA House of Delegates during the February, 1979 meeting when the Standards were reconsidered and otherwise approved.

jury any false testimony presented by the client. This "narrative" solution was offered as a model by the ABA and supported by a number of courts [11] on the assumption that a defense lawyer constitutionally could not prevent the client from testifying falsely on the client's own behalf and, therefore, would not be assisting the perjury if the lawyer did not directly elicit the false testimony and did not use it in argument to the jury.

The Committee believes that under Model Rule 3.3(a)(2) and the recent Supreme Court decision of *Nix v. Whiteside,* 475 U.S. 157, 106 S.Ct. 988, 89 L.Ed.2d 123 (1986), the lawyer can no longer rely on the narrative approach to insulate the lawyer from a charge of assisting the client's perjury. Despite differences on other issues in *Nix v. Whiteside,* the Justices were unanimous in concluding that a criminal defendant does not have the constitutional right to testify falsely. More recently, this ruling was made the basis of the holding by the Seventh Circuit in *United States v. Henkel,* 799 F.2d 369 (7th Cir.1986) that the defendant "had no right to lie" and, therefore, was not deprived of the right to counsel when the defense lawyer refused to present the defendant's testimony which he knew was false.

OTHER VIEWS ABOUT THE TRILEMMA

Most jurisdictions have accepted the ABA's approach to the trilemma issue, but it has been rejected in some jurisdictions that do a big part of the nation's legal business. New York, for instance, has kept its version of ABA Code DR 7–102(B)(1), which obliges a lawyer to reveal a client's fraud on a tribunal *except* when the lawyer learns about it through a confidence or secret.

Lawyers in California get no guidance at all, aside from an unqualified promise in the Attorney's Oath to protect the client's secrets and confidences at all costs, coupled with a smattering of case law that condones a narrative approach similar to ABA Standard for the Defense Function 4–7.7. [*Compare* Calif.Bus. & Prof.Code §§ 6067 and 6068(d)– (e) *with People v. Gadson,* 19 Cal.App.4th 1700, 24 Cal.Rptr.2d 219 (1993); *see also People v. Guzman,* 45 Cal.3d 915, 248 Cal.Rptr. 467, 755 P.2d 917 (1988), *cert. denied,* 488 U.S. 1050 (1989).]

The District of Columbia has written a variation on the narrative approach into its ethics rules, as follows:

> When the witness who intends to give evidence that the lawyer knows to be false is the lawyer's client and is the accused in a criminal case, the lawyer shall first make a good faith effort to dissuade the client from presenting the false evidence; if the lawyer is unable to dissuade the client, the lawyer shall seek leave of the tribunal to withdraw. if the lawyer is unable to dissuade the client or to withdraw without seriously harming the client, the lawyer may

---

11. *See, e.g.,* United States v. Campbell, 616 F.2d 1151, 1152 (9th Cir.), *cert. denied,* 447 U.S. 910, 100 S.Ct. 2998, 64 L.Ed.2d 861 (1980); State v. Lowery, 111 Ariz. 26, 28–29, 523 P.2d 54, 56–57 (1974).

put the client on the stand to testify in a narrative fashion, but the lawyer shall not examine the client in such manner as to elicit testimony which the lawyer knows to be false, and shall not argue the probative value of the client's testimony in closing argument. [District of Columbia Rule 3.3(b).]

The National Association of Criminal Defense Lawyers has rejected both the ABA's approach and the narrative approach. Formal Opinion 92–2 of the association's ethics committee argues that the ABA approach undermines both the criminal defendant's privilege against self-incrimination and his right to the effective assistance of counsel. [NACDL Formal Op. 92–2, The Champion, March 1993 at 23.] The narrative approach is unworkable because it signals the judge and jury what is going on. Further, the opinion argues, the lawyer must not intentionally remain ignorant of the facts; remaining ignorant hobbles the lawyer's ability to defend the client on legitimate grounds and removes the lawyer's chance to talk the client out of committing perjury. The ethics committee says that the lawyer can usually convince the client not to commit perjury. If the lawyer cannot do that, the lawyer may withdraw if doing so will not prejudice the client. It is better, however, not to withdraw; instead, the lawyer should stay in the case and continue trying to talk the client out of committing perjury. If the lawyer *knows beyond a reasonable doubt* that the client's story will be false, and if the lawyer cannot dissuade the client, the lawyer should nevertheless allow the client to testify and should examine the client in the ordinary manner. Finally, the committee says, the lawyer "should argue the client's testimony to the jury in summation to the extent that sound tactics justify doing so." [*Id.* at 28.]

You have now been exposed to several ways to approach the trilemma: the ABA approach described in ABA Model Rule 3.3 and elaborated in ABA Formal Opinion 87–353; the narrative testimony approach described in ABA Standards for the Defense Function 4–7.7 and partly altered in District of Columbia Rule 3.3; and the approach described by Professor Freedman and partly altered in NACDL Formal Op. 92–2. Can you think of any better approach? Is there any approach that does not compromise an important value?

The trilemma arises in the context of criminal defense. The candor issues faced by lawyers in civil litigation are related but different. What differences do you see? The following ABA ethics opinion discusses lack of candor in civil discovery proceedings.

ABA FORMAL OPINION 93–376

American Bar Association Committee on Ethics
and Professional Responsibility, 1993 *

A lawyer in a civil case who discovers that her client has lied in responding to discovery requests must take all reasonable steps to

* Copyright © 1987 by the American Bar Association. All rights reserved. Reprint- ed by permission of the American Bar Association. Copies available from ABA Mem-

rectify the fraud, which may include disclosure to the court. In this context, the normal duty of confidentiality in Rule 1.6 is explicitly superseded by the obligation of candor toward the tribunal in Rule 3.3. The lawyer must first attempt to persuade the client to rectify the situation or, if that proves impossible, must herself take whatever steps are necessary to ensure that a fraud is not perpetrated on the tribunal. In some cases this may be accomplished by a withdrawal from the representation; in others it may be enough to disaffirm the work product; still others may require disclosure to opposing counsel; finally, if all else fails, direct disclosure to the court may prove to be the only effective remedial measure for client fraud most likely to be encountered in pretrial proceedings.

The Committee has been asked to address the ethical obligations of a lawyer in a civil case who is informed by her client after the fact that the client lied in responding to interrogatories and deposition questions, and supplied a falsified document in response to a request for production of documents.

The Committee most recently reviewed the professional obligations of a lawyer with regard to client fraud in the context of an adjudicative proceeding in ABA Formal Opinion No. 87–353 (1987). In that opinion, dealing with client perjury, the Committee reconsidered several earlier opinions in light of the Model Rules of Professional Conduct (1983, amended 1993), particularly Rule 3.3 ("Candor Toward the Tribunal").[1] The Committee adopted a complementary interpretation of Rules 3.3(a)(2) and (4) and concluded that the lawyer's responsibility to disclose client perjury to the tribunal under Rule 3.3 superseded the lawyer's responsibility to keep client confidences under Rule 1.6.[2] "It is

ber Services, 750 North Lake Shore Drive, Chicago, IL 60611.

1. Rule 3.3 Candor Toward the Tribunal

(a) A lawyer shall not knowingly:

(1) make a false statement of material fact or law to a tribunal;

(2) fail to disclose a material fact to a tribunal when disclosure is necessary to avoid assisting a criminal or fraudulent act by a client;

(3) fail to disclose to the tribunal legal authority in the controlling jurisdiction known to the lawyer to be directly adverse to the position of the client and not disclosed by opposing counsel; or

(4) offer evidence that the lawyer knows to be false. If a lawyer has offered material evidence and comes to know of its falsity, the lawyer shall take reasonable remedial measures.

(b) The duties stated in paragraph (a) continue to the conclusion of the proceed-

ing, and apply even if compliance requires disclosure of information otherwise protected by Rule 1.6.

(c) A lawyer may refuse to offer evidence that the lawyer reasonably believes is false.

(d) In an ex parte proceeding, a lawyer shall inform the tribunal of all material facts known to the lawyer which will enable the tribunal to make an informed decision, whether or not the facts are adverse.

2. Rule 1.6 Confidentiality of Information

(a) A lawyer shall not reveal information relating to representation of a client unless the client consents after consultation, except for disclosures that are impliedly authorized in order to carry out the representation, and except as stated in paragraph (b).

(b) A lawyer may reveal such information to the extent the lawyer reasonably believes necessary:

now mandatory, under these Model Rule provisions, for a lawyer, who knows the client has committed perjury, to disclose this knowledge to the tribunal if the lawyer cannot persuade the client to rectify the perjury.'' The opinion goes on to state that

> It is apparent to the Committee that, as used in Rule 3.3(a)(2), the language "assisting a criminal or fraudulent act by the client" is not limited to the criminal law concepts of aiding and abetting or subornation. Rather, it seems clear that this language is intended to guide the conduct of the lawyer as an officer of the court as a prophylactic measure to protect against client perjury contaminating the judicial process.

It is with this overall purpose in mind that the Committee now addresses the application of the Model Rules in the pretrial situation presented by the current inquiry.

A lawyer represents the agent for an insurance company in a contract action filed by an insured against both the company and the agent. The lawsuit was filed on a policy requiring proof of claim within 60 days of loss. The insured alleged that he had put such proof in the regular mail addressed to the agent on the 59th day, thereby providing timely notice under law and complying with the terms of the policy. Unfortunately, the insured did not obtain a mailing receipt or other evidence of posting. Subsequently, the insurance company refused to pay the claim on the ground that the required notice was never received.

Because the defendant agent would not be amenable to a trial subpoena, he was one of the first to be deposed after suit was filed. At the deposition, the plaintiff/insured hoped to prove timely mailing and receipt by the agent, while the defendants hoped to establish a basis for summary judgment in view of the lack of such timely mailing or receipt, as indicated by evidence offered by the agent in pretrial discovery. When asked at the deposition if he had received proof of claim by the 60th day, the agent replied that he had not, and produced a copy of his office mail log confirming this, which was marked as an exhibit in the deposition.

The deposition was transcribed according to local custom and the agent later stopped by the lawyer's office to review and sign it. The next day the lawyer sent a letter to plaintiff's counsel, pointing out plaintiff's serious problem of lack of proof of compliance with the policy requirement of timely notice, and enclosing a draft copy of a motion for summary judgment. She intended to file the motion as soon as she received notice from the court reporter that the deposition had been duly signed, sealed and filed with the court. Failing a favorable ruling on

(1) to prevent the client from committing a criminal act that the lawyer believes is likely to result in imminent death or substantial bodily harm; or

(2) to establish a claim or defense on behalf of the lawyer in a controversy between the lawyer and the client, to establish a defense to a criminal charge or civil claim against the lawyer to allegations in any proceeding concerning the lawyer's representation of the client.

said motion (or reasonable settlement proposal by plaintiff), the lawyer planned to use the deposition at trial pursuant to Federal Rule of Evidence 804(b)(1).

Several days later, on a business trip, the lawyer ran into her client the agent, at the airport. In the course of discussing the status of the case and the upcoming trial, the agent advised the lawyer that he had lied about not receiving insured's notice. In fact, it had arrived in his office on the 60th day and his secretary had entered its receipt in the office mail log with other incoming correspondence before placing the mail on his desk. The agent, however, had shredded the letter and altered the mail log to conceal the fact of receipt.

In circumstances where a lawyer has offered perjured testimony or falsified evidence in an adjudicative proceeding, the Model Rules, like the predecessor Model Code of Professional Responsibility (1969, amended 1980), adopt the view that remedial measures must be taken. *See* Rule 3.3, Comment. Although Rule 1.6 generally affords protection to client confidences, its confidentiality requirement is qualified by its own provisions, and by the effect of other Rules. Most notably in this context, the duty of confidentiality mandated by Rule 1.6 is explicitly superseded by the duty of disclosure in Rule 3.3. *See* Rule 3.3(b).[3] Thus, as was made clear in Formal Opinion No. 87–353, disclosure of a client's perjury is required by Rule 3.3 where a lawyer has offered material evidence to a tribunal and comes to know of its falsity, or when disclosure of a material fact is necessary to avoid assisting a criminal or fraudulent act by the client.

In the case at hand, there is no issue as to knowledge on the lawyer's part of the client's fraud; the client has made a direct admission to the lawyer after the fact. Similarly, there is no doubt that the perjury and other fraudulent acts of the client relate to a material fact, in that a necessary element of plaintiff's case is at issue. However, because the client's misrepresentations took place during pretrial discovery and none occurred in open court, the question arises whether the applicable rule of conduct is Rule 3.3 or Rule 4.1 ("Truthfulness in Statement to Others").[4] The issue is whether perjury or fraud in pretrial discovery should be regarded as a lack of candor toward the tribunal, governed by Rule 3.3, or untruthfulness toward the opposing party and counsel, as to which Rule 4.1 is the applicable provision. Unlike the duty of candor toward a "tribunal" in Rule 3.3, the duty of truthfulness toward "others" in Rule 4.1 does not expressly trump the duty to keep client confidences in Rule 1.6. If it is Rule 4.1 rather than

---

3. *See* Note 1 *supra.*

4. Rule 4.1 Truthfulness in Statements to Others

In the course of representing a client a lawyer shall not knowingly:

(a) make a false statement of material fact or law to a third person; or

(b) fail to disclose a material fact to a third person when disclosure is necessary to avoid assisting a criminal or fraudulent act by a client, unless disclosure is prohibited by Rule 1.6.

Rule 3.3(a) that applies in this context, the prohibition on disclosure of client confidences in Rule 1.6 must be given full effect.

It is clear that once the deposition is signed and filed and the motion for summary judgment submitted to the court, a fraud has been committed upon the tribunal which would trigger application of Rule 3.3(a). Indeed, we think that even before these documents are filed there is potential ongoing reliance upon their content which would be outcome-determinative, resulting in an inevitable deception of the other side and a subversion of the truth-finding process which the adversary system is designed to implement. Support for this view is found in case law holding that the duty of a lawyer under Rule 3.3(a)(2) to disclose material facts to the tribunal implies a duty to make such disclosure to opposing counsel in pretrial settlement negotiations. *See, e.g., Kath v. Western Media, Inc.*, 684 P.2d 98, 101 (Wyo.1984) (letter contradicting testimony of a key witness should have been disclosed to opposing counsel in connection with settlement negotiations, under Rule 3.3 and DR 7–102(A)); *Virzi v. Grand Trunk Warehouse and Cold Storage Co.*, 571 F.Supp. 507, 509 (E.D.Mich.1983) (fact that client had died should have been disclosed to opposing counsel in pretrial settlement negotiations.)

Further supporting the applicability of Rules 3.3(a)(2) and (4) to pretrial discovery situations is the fact that while paragraphs (a)(1) and (3) presuppose false or incomplete statements made *to* the *tribunal,* neither paragraph (a)(2) nor (a)(4) expresses any such condition precedent that the *tribunal* must have been aware of the crime, fraud, or false evidence.

The Committee is therefore of the view that, in the pretrial situation described above, the lawyer's duty of candor toward the tribunal under Rule 3.3 qualifies her duty to keep client confidences under Rule 1.6. Continued participation by the lawyer in the matter without rectification or disclosure would assist the client in committing a crime or fraud in violation of Rule 3.3(a)(2).[5] Although the perjured deposition testimony and the altered mail log may not become evidence until they are offered in support of the motion for summary judgment or actually introduced at trial, their potential as evidence and their impact on the judicial process trigger the lawyer's duty to take reasonable remedial measures under Rule 3.3(a)(4), including disclosure if necessary, according to the complementary interpretation of paragraphs (a)(2) and (a)(4) in ABA Formal Opinion No. 87–353.

It is important to note, however, that the Committee does not assert, nor should it be inferred from its analysis of Rule 3.3(a) in Opinion No. 87–353, that disclosure to the tribunal is the first and only appropriate remedial measure to be taken in situations arising under Rule 3.3(a)(4). As the Comment to Rule 3.3 makes clear, the duties of

---

5. The more general prohibition against assisting client fraud contained in Rule 1.2(d) would also be violated were the lawyer to continue to represent the client in the matter without taking steps to rectify the fraud, up to and including giving notice of withdrawal and disaffirmance of her work product. See ABA Formal Opinion No. 92–366 (August 8, 1992).

loyalty and confidentiality owed to her client require a lawyer to explore options short of outright disclosure in order to rectify the situation. Thus, the lawyer's first step should be to remonstrate with the client confidentially and urge him to rectify the situation. It may develop that, after consultation with the client, the lawyer will be in a position to accomplish rectification without divulging the client's wrongdoing or breaching the client's confidences, depending upon the rules of the jurisdiction and the nature of the false evidence. For example, incomplete or incorrect answers to deposition questions may be capable of being supplemented or amended in such a way as to correct the record, rectify the perjury, and ensure a fair result without outright disclosure to the tribunal. Although this approach would not appear to be feasible in the case at hand, it is nevertheless the type of reasonable remedial measure that should be explored initially by a lawyer when confronted by a situation in which she realizes that evidence she has offered or elicited in good faith is false.

In this case, if efforts to persuade the client to rectify fail, the lawyer must herself act to see that a fraud is not perpetrated on the tribunal. At a minimum she must withdraw from the representation, so as to avoid assisting the client's fraud in violation of Rules 3.3 and 1.2(d). *See* Rule 1.16(a)(1) (withdrawal mandatory where continued representation would result in a violation of rules of professional conduct). However, the Committee observed in Opinion No. 87–353, "withdrawal can rarely serve as a remedy for the client's perjury." While withdrawal may enable the lawyer to avoid knowing participation in the commission of perjury, Rule 3.3(a)(4) specifically requires the lawyer to do more than simply distance herself from the client's fraud when she has offered evidence that she learns was false; she must take "reasonable remedial measures" to alert the court to it. Moreover, under paragraph (b) of Rule 3.3, the lawyer's duties in this regard "continue to the conclusion of the proceeding," presumably even if the lawyer has withdrawn from the representation before this time.

It is possible that so-called "noisy withdrawal" procedures could be effective in the instant case, albeit in a way that is tantamount to disclosure. *See* ABA Formal Opinion No. 92–366 (August 8, 1992). Utilization of the withdrawal/disaffirmance approach suggested by Opinion No. 92–366 is appealing as a remedial measure because it is less intrusive on the confidential relationship between lawyer and client than outright disclosure to the tribunal under Rule 3.3(a). It may also have the advantage of directly and expeditiously rectifying the fraud in a way that does not compromise the tribunal and prevent the case from proceeding. On the other hand, "noisy withdrawal" may not be an entirely effective means of dealing with the type of client fraud likely to occur in the pretrial stages of a case. For instance, withdrawal would not be sufficient to correct the fraud's impact on the case if the plaintiff decided to drop his or her lawsuit because of a perceived lack of proof prior to or notwithstanding the "noisy withdrawal." Also, a "noisy withdrawal" does not necessarily put either successor counsel or the opposing party on notice as to *why* the documents are being disaffirmed. Thus, notwithstanding withdrawal and disaffirmance, the fraud could continue to adversely affect the proceedings and ultimate disposition of the case. Direct disclosure under Rule 3.3, to the opposing party or if need be to the court, may prove to be the only reasonable remedial measure in the client fraud situations most likely to be encountered in pretrial proceedings.

MULTIPLE CHOICE QUESTIONS

Answer these questions under the ABA Code and ABA Model Rules

1. State X and State Y each have state trademark registration statutes that are substantially similar in purpose and wording to the Lanham Act (the federal trademark registration statute). For many years, Daisy Dairy has used the mark "Daisy" on dairy products it sells in State X, and it has registered the mark under the State X statute. Recently Noxatox Chemical began using the "Daisy" mark on cockroach poison it sells in State X. Daisy Dairy sued Noxatox under State X law in a State X court for intentional infringement of the "Daisy" mark. The complaint asks for an injunction, for an award of the profits made by Noxatox, and for money damages. Noxatox moved for summary judgment on the grounds that dairy products and cockroach poison do not compete with each other, that no sensible consumer could be deceived by the use of the same mark on such widely different goods, and that Daisy Dairy could not possibly have suffered monetary injury. The trial judge who will hear the motion is not well versed in trademark law, and the lawyer for Daisy Dairy failed to discover several pertinent court decisions. Which of the following decisions *must* the lawyer for Noxatox call to the judge's attention?

I. A United States Supreme Court decision which holds that the Lanham Act authorizes an injunction to stop intentional infringement, even where the defendant's goods do not compete with the plaintiff's goods.

II. A decision of the United States Court of Appeals for the federal circuit that includes State X and State Y, holding that an injunction can be issued under the Lanham Act where the nature of the defendant's goods could cast a distasteful or odious image on the plaintiff's goods.

III. A decision of the Supreme Court of State Y which holds that the State Y registration statute authorizes an accounting of the defendant's profits in a case of intentional infringement, even where the plaintiff cannot prove monetary injury.

IV. A decision of the Supreme Court of State X which holds that in actions for intentional trespass to real property, State X trial judges have the power of courts of equity to fashion equitable remedies, even where the plaintiff cannot prove monetary injury.

A. All of the above.

    B.   None of the above.

    C.   I, II, and IV only.

    D.   I and IV only.

    2.   Lawyer Penny represents client Paul in a family law matter. When Paul and Donna were divorced, the court gave Paul custody of their infant son and gave Donna "reasonable" visiting rights. Paul is a busy accountant and often stays late at his office. While Paul is working, the baby stays at a baby sitter's house. Donna has started making unannounced visits to the baby sitter's house on the evenings when Paul works late. Paul believes Donna may try to kidnap the baby and disappear. Paul asks Penny to apply immediately for a temporary restraining order that forbids Donna from going near the sitter's house. In this jurisdiction, a temporary restraining order can be granted in an *ex parte* proceeding, without giving the adversary any notice or chance to be heard. An affidavit from the sitter states that when Donna makes her surprise visits, the baby cries and refuses to eat or sleep for hours thereafter. Just as Penny is leaving her office to go to the judge's chambers, her investigator arrives with three additional pieces of information. First, when Paul works late, the sitter sometimes leaves a ten-year-old neighbor girl in charge of the baby while the sitter grocery shops and runs errands. Second, Donna's unannounced visits are motivated by her concern for the baby's safety. Third, when Paul works late, Donna could conveniently keep the baby at her house until Paul is through at the office.

    What *should* Penny do?

    A.   She *should* present the judge with only those facts that favor Paul's position.

    B.   She *should* present the judge with the facts that favor Paul's position, but she *should* respond candidly if the judge specifically asks for information that is adverse to Paul's position.

    C.   She *should* present the judge with all the relevant facts, even those that are adverse to Paul's position.

    D.   She *should* call Paul and tell him that she is withdrawing the application for a temporary restraining order.

    3.   The law of State X requires child adoptions to be approved by the court. Further, it prohibits cohabiting couples from adopting a child unless they are validly married. Attorney Anderson represented clients Clara and Carl in an adoption proceeding. They assured her that they were validly married. Among the papers she presented to the court in connection with the adoption proceeding was copy of Carla's and Carl's Certificate of Marriage, duly certified by the custodian of public records. In due course, the court approved the adoption. A year later, Carla and Carl returned to Anderson's office. Carla explained to her as follows: "When we came to you about the adoption, there's something we didn't tell you, because we didn't want to get into lots of complications. Carl was married once before. His wife moved out, and he hasn't heard from

her since. When he and I began dating, we fell in love so fast that there wasn't time for him to go through a divorce before we got married. We don't want to do anything that might risk losing our child, but this has been bothering us, and we thought we should come to you for advice." What *should* Anderson do in this situation?

A. Advise Carla and Carl about the legal effect of the prior marriage on their current status and on the adoption.

B. Decline to advise Carla and Carl, thus avoiding the assistance of a continuing fraud.

C. Advise Carla and Carl to reveal their fraud to the court that approved the adoption, and warn them that she will do so if they do not.

D. Bring the matter to the attention of the court that approved the adoption, and let the court decide what remedial action is appropriate in the circumstances.

4. Client Curtis hired lawyer Lomax to defend him in a civil antitrust action brought by Pucci, a former retail distributor of products that Curtis sold to Pucci. Pucci alleges that Curtis terminated him as a distributor because Pucci sold the products below a minimum retail price set by Curtis. Pucci further alleges that the termination resulted from a secret agreement between Curtis and other distributors that Curtis would terminate any distributor who sold below the minimum retail price. Assume that such an agreement, even if coerced, would violate the antitrust law. When Lomax was preparing Curtis for his deposition, Lomax asked Curtis why he terminated Pucci. Curtis answered: "Because Pucci was a price cutter. My other distributors pressured me to do it." At that point, Lomax said: "If you say that at your deposition, you will lose this case. Before you say more, let me tell you about the law that applies here. If you, using your own business judgment, terminated Pucci because he was not doing a good job, or because he was not displaying or advertising your products effectively, then the termination would be lawful. If, on the other hand, you let your other distributors talk you into terminating him because his prices were too low, the termination would probably be unlawful. Now go back to your office, refresh your memory of this event, and we will talk again tomorrow morning about your reasons for terminating Pucci." Was Lomax's conduct *proper*?

A. Yes, because a lawyer has a duty to represent a client with zeal, using all lawful means to achieve the client's objectives.

B. No, because it is improper for a lawyer to discuss the substance of a client's testimony with the client before the client testifies.

C. Yes, because a lawyer has a duty to advise a client fully about the law that applies to a matter.

D. No, because it is improper for a lawyer to invite a client to give false testimony.

5. Attorney Arossio was defending Doyle in a drunk driving case. The state's drunk driving statute specifies a fine up to $1,000 for a first offense. For a second offense, it specifies a fine up to $10,000, plus a mandatory jail sentence of 60 days up to one year. Doyle told Arossio in confidence that he had one prior conviction for drunk driving. Arossio consulted the public records and found that Doyle's prior conviction had never been properly recorded. Doyle decided to plead guilty. The hearing transcript shows the following colloquy:

> The Court: Your guilty plea will be accepted, Mr. Doyle. Ms. Prosecutor, are there priors in this case?
>
> Prosecutor: No, your Honor. The People ask the maximum fine of $1,000.
>
> The Court: Very well. Mr. Arossio, since your client is a first-timer, I'm inclined toward a fine of $750. Is that acceptable?

For which of the following responses would Arossio be *subject to discipline*?

I. Yes, thank you, your Honor.

II. My client will accept the court's judgment, your Honor.

III. Since my client's blood-alcohol level wasn't much above the mark, and since his record is clean, I would ask your Honor for a fine of not more than $500.

IV. There's been a mistake, your Honor. My client has a prior conviction that does not appear on the record.

     A. None of the above.

     B. III and IV only.

     C. I, II, and III only.

     D. IV only.

6. Over the past several months, you and lawyer Lauder have been representing your respective clients in a complicated contract negotiation. The proposed contract has been drafted, redrafted, and revised dozens of times during the negotiation. Finally, your respective clients have struck a bargain; their bargain includes a key provision that your client long resisted and ultimately accepted with great reluctance. The final version of the contract has been typed by Lauder's secretary and has been signed by Lauder's client. Lauder has sent it to you for signature by your client. You have read it carefully, and you have discovered that the secretary left out the provision mentioned above. Which of the following *may* you do?

     A. Without consulting your client, call Lauder and direct her attention to the missing provision.

     B. Call your client, explain the situation, and do whatever your client directs.

C. Call your client, explain the situation, and advise him to sign the contract.

D. Call Lauder's client and ask whether he ultimately decided not to insist on the provision.

Answers to the multiple choice questions will be found
in the Appendix at the end of the book

Chapter Nine

FAIRNESS IN LITIGATION

What This Chapter Covers

Reading Assignment

Wydick & Perschbacher, Chapter 9

ABA Model Rules:

    Rules 3.1 through 3.9.

CJC:

    3(B)(7) and (9); and 4(D)(5).

CRPC 2–100, 3–210, 5–100, 5–200, 5–220, 5–300, 5–310 and 5–320.

Cal.Bus & Prof.Code §§ 6068(b), (c), (d), (f) and (g); 6103; 6128(a).

Supplemental Reading

ABA Code:

    EC 7–1 through 7–39;

DR 7–101 through 7–110.

Hazard & Hodes:

Discussion of ABA Model Rules 3.1 through 3.9.

Wolfram:

Sections 11.3.1 through 11.3.3 (advocates and judges);

Sections 11.4.1 through 11.4.4 (advocates and jurors);

Sections 11.5 (advocates and adversary lawyers);

Sections 12.1.1 through 12.1.3 (courtroom forensics);

Sections 12.2.1 through 12.2.3 (public comment);

Sections 12.4.1 through 12.4.6 (advocates and witnesses).

ABA, A Lawyer's Creed of Professionalism (1988) (in West's Selected Statutes, Rules and Standards on the Legal Profession).

Discussion Problems

1. You represent twelve plaintiffs in an action against Monolith Consolidated Industries, Inc., for race discrimination in employment. The case will be tried before a jury. As is customary in your community, the names and addresses of the 150 citizens on the jury panel have been published in the local newspaper.

    a. May you hire a private investigator to find out whatever he can about the attitudes of individual jury panel members toward race discrimination?

    b. May you have your paralegal assistant search the public records in the County Records Office to find out which jury panel members own real property? To find out the political party affiliation of those jury panel members who are registered to vote?

    c. In the jurisdiction where you plan to practice, do trial lawyers usually obtain information about jury panel members in advance of *voir dire*? How do they obtain it?

2. During the trial of the above case, you and one of the jurors find yourselves riding the elevator together on the way up to the courtroom one morning.

    a. Suppose the juror turns to you and says: "Well, good morning, counselor! Do you have some red-hot testimony to keep us all awake today?" How should you respond?

    b. Suppose the juror turns to you and says: "Well, good morning, counselor! What did you think of that lousy ball game on TV last night?" How should you respond?

3. During the noon recess in the above case, you are having lunch at a cafe near the courthouse. You observe a female juror sitting at a

secluded table in the back, talking in hushed tones with a young man, a law student who works part-time as a paralegal for the firm that represents your adversary, Monolith Consolidated. What, if anything, should you do about that?

4. In the above case, the jury returned a verdict against your clients; judgment was entered accordingly, and the jury was dismissed.

a. On your way out of the courthouse, may you stop to chat with one of the jurors, to ask for her comments on the way you presented the evidence and on your closing argument?

b. The day after the trial ended, you learned that during jury deliberations the foreman asked the bailiff for a deposition transcript that had been used at the trial. Part of the transcript had been received in evidence, but the rest had not. Apparently, the bailiff delivered the entire transcript to the jury room. May you interview some of the jurors to find out whether this is true?

5. At the pretrial conference in the above case, you and counsel for Monolith Consolidated exchanged lists of prospective trial witnesses. Monolith Consolidated's list included Erna Tuttle, an investigator employed by the State Fair Employment Practices Commission. Without consulting counsel for Monolith Consolidated, you interviewed Ms. Tuttle before trial. You learned that she had investigated Monolith Consolidated for the Commission and had come away with a very favorable impression of Monolith Consolidated's hiring practices. Was it proper for you to interview her?

6. Prior to trial, and without consulting counsel for Monolith Consolidated, you contacted several former and current Monolith Consolidated employees to see if they had information that would support plaintiffs' claims. Was this proper?

7. One of your trial witnesses in the above case was Edgar Taylor, a former assembly line employee of Monolith Consolidated. At the trial, he testified about a conversation he had overheard between a union official and the head of Monolith Consolidated's personnel department. Shortly after he overheard that conversation, Monolith Consolidated laid him off. He had to move out of state to find a new job. When you asked him to be a witness at the trial, he refused, stating that he did not want to take the time away from his new job. To convince him to come, you promised him that your clients would pay:

a. His travel, hotel, meal, and incidental expenses;

b. His lost wages, due to time away from his job; and

c. One hundred dollars per day, as compensation for his time and trouble in coming to testify.

Was that proper?

8. In preparing the above case for trial, you requested production of a large volume of Monolith Consolidated's employment records. After the usual preliminary skirmishing, adversary counsel finally agreed to

produce them. As is common in such cases, you and adversary counsel orally agreed that Monolith Consolidated would copy the records (at your clients' expense), deliver the copies to you, and keep the originals available should you wish to examine them. The copies Monolith Consolidated delivered to you (nine large boxes full) were legible, but so light as to be extremely tedious to read. Later, after you had paid the copying bill, you learned (quite by accident) that adversary counsel had instructed the copying machine operator to "make the copies hard to read." What should you do in this situation?

9. At the final pretrial conference in the above case, the trial judge heard oral argument on the admissibility of several key items of evidence. The trial judge decided not to rule on the point until her law clerk could complete his own search of the authorities. Two days later, while reading the newest advance sheets, you found an evidence decision that directly supports the argument you were making. What is the proper way for you to call the new decision to the court's attention?

10. The trial of the above case has attracted considerable attention from the local news media. The trial judge has forbidden cameras and recorders inside the courtroom, but during every recess reporters swarm around the trial participants, asking questions. Late one afternoon, the trial judge calls the evening recess just after Monolith Consolidated has completed the direct examination of one of its key witnesses. You gravely doubt the credibility of this witness, and tomorrow morning you will have your chance to cross-examine. As you walk down the courthouse steps, news reporters surround you, asking for your comment on the witness's testimony and on your plans for tomorrow's cross-examination. Considering both ethics and tactics, how will you respond?

11. What marks the line between the conduct of a colorful, vigorous advocate and the conduct of a shyster? Before you answer, consider *In re Vincenti, infra.*

IN RE WARLICK

Supreme Court of South Carolina, 1985.
287 S.C. 380, 339 S.E.2d 110 (as modified on rehearing).

Respondent was temporarily suspended from the practice of law on November 9, 1983, following his conviction in federal court for contempt. The Executive Committee, by a divided vote, recommended respondent be disbarred. * * *

In preparation for a personal injury trial in federal court, respondent hired a private investigator to conduct a jury investigation. The investigator's activities included personal contacts with jurors and their family members. Respondent was aware of the personal contact, and was questioned about the propriety of his actions by the investigator, who referred respondent to this Court's decision in *Matter of Two Anonymous Members of South Carolina Bar*, 278 S.C. 477, 298 S.E.2d 450 (1982). Respondent advised the investigator to continue personal contacts He thereafter selected a jury which contained at least three jurors who had been personally contacted. The lawsuit was settled prior to trial.

Respondent was convicted of contempt of court following a bench trial. * * *

Respondent * * * asserts error in the panel's failure to allow him to present evidence concerning the facts which led to the conviction. During the hearing, respondent attempted to offer testimony to show that his involvement in contacting jurors was nonculpable. That issue was decided adversely to respondent in the criminal proceeding. He is prohibited from offering evidence inconsistent with essential elements of the crime for which he was convicted. * * * Respondent was not prohibited from offering mitigating evidence, which he is clearly entitled to do.

Respondent's law partner received a public reprimand for his peripheral involvement in this case. * * * However disbarment is appropriate where, as here, an attorney's improper juror contact is informed or intentional. * * *

[On petition for rehearing, the discipline was reduced from permanent disbarment to indefinite suspension of the right to practice.]

LIND v. MEDEVAC, INC.

California Court of Appeal, First District, 1990.
219 Cal.App.3d 516, 268 Cal.Rptr. 359.

PETERSON, ASSOCIATE JUSTICE.

[Attorney B. Mark Fong, Jr. and his law firm appeal from the trial court's award of sanctions against them for contacting jury members after trial of a personal injury action.]

I. FACTUAL AND PROCEDURAL BACKGROUND

In July 1984, Edward P. Lind, by and through his conservator Wendell J. Lind, (plaintiff) filed a complaint for personal injuries. Named as defendants were Medevac, Inc.; its employees, Dana Young and Carol Ferguson; and others. Plaintiff was represented by attorney Marc C. Barulich of the firm of Barulich and Barulich. Defendants were represented by appellants B. Mark Fong, Jr. and his law firm, Robert A. Harlem, Inc. & Associates.

In January 1988, the matter was tried before a jury which rendered a judgment in favor of defendants. Plaintiff then moved for a new trial or in the alternative for judgment notwithstanding the verdict (JNOV). The motions were based, inter alia, upon allegations of jury misconduct. Defendants opposed the motion, noting that plaintiff had not submitted juror affidavits in support of the motion for new trial as required by Code of Civil Procedure section 658. In reply, plaintiff claimed that he had been prevented from obtaining juror affidavits by a letter defense counsel had sent to the jurors. The text of that letter is as follows:

"Dear [Juror]: [¶] This is to thank you again for your service as a juror. I know that my clients, Carol Ferguson and Dana Young[,] are glad at last to put the events of four years ago behind them. [¶] On occasion, following a jury trial, the losing side will hire an investigator to contact the trial jurors. The purpose of these investigators is to impeach the jury's verdict. The [investigator] will ask you about your deliberations in the jury room and will prepare a statement for your signature. This statement will then be presented to the judge to convince him to set aside the jury's verdict as improper. [¶] You are under no obligation to speak with these investigators and need not sign anything. You worked with your fellow jurors to reach a fair result. I would not want to see that result set aside because of sharp investigative tactics. [¶] Please contact me should anyone attempt to speak with you about your jury service. I would like to be present should you choose to speak with an investigator. [¶] Should you have any questions or wish to discuss the case, please do not hesitate to contact me. Again, thank you for your time and service. [¶] Very truly yours, [/S/] B. Mark Fong"

The court denied the motion for JNOV concluding the verdict was supported by substantial evidence. The motion for new trial was denied because it was not supported by any juror affidavits. However, the trial judge expressed disapproval of the letter appellants had sent to the jurors, and set a hearing for Fong and his law firm to show cause why they should not be sanctioned for "deliberately interfering" with plaintiff's right to obtain juror affidavits to support a motion for new trial.

* * * After hearing the arguments of counsel, the court imposed sanctions of $20,000 against appellants, holding the letter they sent violated the rules of professional conduct in that it was likely to adversely influence the jurors in their present and future jury service. This timely appeal followed.

II. DISCUSSION

Appellants challenge the court's imposition of sanctions on both substantive and procedural grounds. Substantively, they argue that the letter they sent was proper and did not violate the rules of professional conduct. Procedurally, appellants claim that the trial court lacked the authority to impose sanctions in the manner in which it did.

A. The Letter

At the time these proceedings were held, former rule 7–106 of the Rules of Professional Conduct (now rule 5–320) provided in part, "(D) After discharge of the jury from further consideration of a case with which the member of the State Bar was connected, the member of the State Bar shall not ask questions of or make comments to a member of that jury that are intended to harass or embarrass the juror or to influence the juror's actions in future jury service. [¶] (E) A member of the State Bar shall not conduct directly or indirectly an out of court investigation of either a venireman or a juror of a type likely to influence the state of mind of such venireman or juror in present or future jury service."

* * *

* * * The trial court properly rejected the argument that a juror's "present" jury service could not be affected *solely* because counsel's contact with the juror came after the jury was discharged. We affirm the trial court's implicit finding that the Rules of Professional Conduct concerning counsel's contact with jurors remain fully applicable in the period from jury discharge to expiration of the time for filing new trial motions in the case in which those jurors served.

The trial court did not commit error in finding the letter which appellants sent to the jurors in the present case violated rule 7–106. That finding was supported by substantial evidence. The letter asserts that a fellow member of the bar might employ "sharp investigative tactics" to "impeach" the jury's verdict and have it set aside as "improper." The lower court found this letter could easily adversely influence a juror in his "present" or "future" jury service. Taken as a whole, the letter advising a juror, inter alia, that the verdict of his jury could be "impeach[ed]" and set aside as "improper" certainly implies such juror may be falsely importuned to say or do something which might lead to that result, i.e., to the false conclusion the jury or some of its members undertook some wrongful or unlawful act in arriving at a verdict. This implication is clearly brought into focus by the letter's assertion that "sharp investigative tactics" may be used to accomplish this objective, thereby suggesting a subversive and false result is likely to be sought by losing counsel through his own actions or those of his post-trial investigator. It is common knowledge that it is increasingly difficult to obtain willing citizens to serve as members of a jury. Letters such as the one sent by appellants in the present case unprofessionally denigrate anticipated and unproven conduct of opponents, and will only exacerbate the reluctance of some persons to undertake jury service for fear their decisions will be falsely attacked and overturned by reason of unprofessional and improper conduct of counsel designed to achieve that result. They are likely, incidentally, to be perceived by jurors as converting the performance of their civic responsibility to serve as jurors into the center of a distasteful and acrimonious post-trial dispute between lawyers whose motives, they are told, are suspect and misleading.

The trial judge was justified in determining that the true purpose of the letter was to achieve the chilling result of preventing attempts by the losing side to communicate with jurors after their discharge, in a legitimate effort to determine if juror misconduct existed as grounds for a new trial, and to obtain permitted affidavits concerning any such misconduct.

Appellants urge it has been a "common experience" among trial lawyers that, after a trial has been completed, investigators acting on behalf of the losing party will privately approach jurors and use various plausible stories in order to "trick[ ]" the jurors into making statements which do not fairly reflect the nature of the jurors' deliberations. Thus, they claim they should not be sanctioned for warning jurors about potential abuses by investigators. We find this argument unpersuasive. Were we to adopt this rationale, we would do little more than approve unprofessional conduct of counsel on the ground like conduct of the other side was anticipated. We decline to sanction preemptive strikes of this nature. Attorneys who individually or through investigators employ such tactics may well be subject to discipline by the court, as well as appropriate authorities of the State Bar.

An attorney wishing to protect a verdict against such tactics can do so within the ethical mandates of the rules of professional conduct. For example, an attorney who wins a trial by jury should not be barred from writing jurors post verdict, thereby requesting that he be notified of any post-trial contact with the jurors by the adverse side; and that he be further allowed either to be present for any interviews granted the adverse side, or to discuss with the juror any telephonic or written communications received from the adverse side.

* * *

[The appellate court reversed and remanded the sanction award. The trial court had based its sanction on its inherent power to control proceedings under California Code of Civil Procedure § 128. However, under California case law, attorney fees could only be awarded under § 128.5, not § 128. Therefore, the case was remanded to the trial court to consider whether Fong and his firm had acted in bad faith or engaged in frivolous tactics to justify sanctions under § 128.5 (see Chapter 3, supra). The opinion added, "We also leave to the sound discretion of the trial court whether appellants' conduct was sufficiently serious to warrant review by the disciplinary authorities of the California State Bar."]

PUBLIC COMMENTS ABOUT PENDING LITIGATION

A. Background

Although the idea of public and media access to trials is firmly rooted in American jurisprudence—indeed, the right to a public trial is part of the Sixth Amendment protection for the criminally accused—excessive publicity may also interfere with the equally important right to a fair trial. As a result, the interests of the media and the courts are sometimes at odds. Added to this mix is the danger that lawyers for the state, the accused, and the parties in civil actions may seek to argue their cases outside of court, using the media for the benefit of their clients or themselves. Historically, the First Amendment has required a showing of "actual prejudice or a substantial and imminent threat to fair trial" [*Nebraska Press Ass'n v. Stuart,* 427 U.S. 539, 96 S.Ct. 2791, 49 L.Ed.2d 683 (1976)] in order to restrict press coverage during a criminal trial, but has allowed trial courts to restrain lawyers' speech before and during trial on a significantly lower showing. [*See Sheppard v. Maxwell,* 384 U.S. 333, 362–63, 86 S.Ct. 1507, 1522, 16 L.Ed.2d 600 (1966).] Lawyers may also have ethical limitations on what they may say in advance of and during trial, although this must be balanced against their obligation to represent their clients zealously and effectively within the bounds of the law.

B. The ABA enters the fray

The ABA's Canons of Professional Ethics (1908) "[g]enerally ... condemned" newspaper publications by lawyers regarding pending or anticipated litigation because of the danger they would "interfere with a fair trial" and "otherwise prejudice the due administration of justice." When the ABA Code was promulgated in 1969, it relied upon recommendations of the Advisory Committee on Fair Trial and Free Press, created in 1964 on the recommendation of the Warren Commission's report on the assassination of President Kennedy. The Advisory Committee developed the ABA Standards Relating to Fair Trial and Free Press which covered the disclosure of information regarding criminal proceedings. The ABA used those standards in developing ABA Model Rule of Professional Responsibility 3.6. Meanwhile, the Supreme Court had identified the need for such a rule in *Sheppard v. Maxwell,* and, in 1966, the Judicial Conference of the United States authorized a special subcommittee to study whether further guidelines needed to be laid down to implement *Sheppard.* The result of that report was the "reasonable likelihood of prejudicing a fair trial" test used in the ABA 1969 Model Code. DR 7–107 of the Model Code used the laundry list of acceptable and prohibited statements similar to the Model Code's approach to advertising. [*See* Chapter 4, *supra.*] Ten years later, when the ABA amended its guidelines, the ABA changed the test from "reasonable likelihood" to "clear and present danger." ABA Standard for Criminal Justice 8–1.1 (as amended in 1978) (2d ed. 1980, Supp.1986).

The Model Rules of Professional Conduct, drafted in the early 1980's, did not grant as much protection to lawyers who made extrajudicial statements when fair trial rights were involved. The MRPC adopted yet another test, the "substantial likelihood of material prejudice" test. By 1991, 32 states had adopted either wholly or with minor variations ABA Model Rule 3.6. Eleven states had adopted DR 7–107's milder "reasonable likelihood of prejudice" test. Only Virginia had explicitly adopted the "clear and present danger" standard, and four other states had adopted arguably similar standards.

C. The *Gentile* case

In *Gentile v. State Bar of Nevada,* 501 U.S. 1030, 111 S.Ct. 2720, 115 L.Ed.2d 888 (1991), the Supreme Court directly addressed whether state-imposed limitations on extrajudicial statements in criminal cases violated the right of free speech. Gentile, a Nevada lawyer, represented Sanders in a criminal trial. Sanders was charged with stealing drugs and money used in an undercover operation conducted by the Las Vegas police. The trial attracted a great deal of publicity. During pre-trial press conference, Gentile made several inflammatory statements, accusing a detective of actually stealing the drugs and travelers' checks and framing Sanders. Six months later, a jury acquitted Sanders on all counts.

The State Bar of Nevada filed a complaint against Gentile for violating Nevada Supreme Court Rule 177 (almost identical to the then-current ABA Model Rule of Professional Conduct 3.6). The rule prohibited attorneys from making any "extrajudicial statement" that a reasonable person would expect to be spread among the public and materially prejudice the proceedings. The disciplinary board found Gentile guilty of violating the bar rule. In a 5 to 4 decision, the Supreme Court reversed.

In an opinion by Justice Rehnquist, the Court stated that "[t]he regulation of attorneys' speech is limited." Advocating a "less demanding standard" for attorney's speech regarding their pending cases, the Court upheld the "substantial likelihood of materially prejudicing that proceeding" test. However, the Court struck down parts of the Nevada rule which specified that an attorney could make "general" statements about the defense without "elaboration." This standard would prove confusing to any attorney, since the language made it very unclear when one's statements were protected by the safe harbor provision of "general." Additionally, the Court pointed out that the general versus elaboration directions failed to even consider that a general statement could materially prejudice a case just as much as any elaboration on the defense. Consequently, the Court upheld the general test but struck down the more explicit language of the rule.

D. Current Rules

In 1994, the ABA House of Delegates amended Model Rules 3.6 and 3.8 to reflect the *Gentile* decision. The amended Rule 3.6 moved to the comments section the portion of the rule which delineated what kind of statements would be held to be prejudicial. The ABA also added a section to the rule allowing a lawyer to attempt to mitigate negative publicity not of the attorney's or client's creation notwithstanding paragraph (a)'s bar on extrajudicial statements. Notably, the ABA deleted a comment acknowledging that no rules could satisfy all the interests of a fair trial and those of free speech. The addition of subsection (g) to Rule 3.8 imposed an additional responsibility on criminal prosecutors to "refrain from making extrajudicial comments that have a substantial likelihood of heightening public condemnation of the accused."

E. California

At the time of the *Gentile* decision, California had no rule regulating lawyers' out-of-court statements. As a direct result of the criminal prosecution of the athlete O.J. Simpson and the massive pretrial publicity used by both the prosecution and defense in that case, in 1994 the California legislature passed a statute directing the State Bar to submit "a rule of professional conduct governing pretrial publicity and extrajudicial statements made by attorneys concerning adjudicative proceedings." [Cal.Bus. & Prof.Code § 6103.7.] The statute also suggested using ADA Model Rule 3.6 as a basis for the California rule. After considerable debate, the State Bar submitted "without recommendation" a proposed rule applicable only to jury trials and that restricted only those statements that posed a "clear and present danger" to the proceedings. Following a further exchange between the State Bar and the California Supreme Court during which the State Bar President stated his opposition to the proposed rule, the court adopted a rule substantially similar to Model Rule 3.6 giving more limited protection to lawyers who make out-of-court statements. [See CRPC § 5–120.]

MATTER OF VINCENTI

Supreme Court of New Jersey, 1983.
92 N.J. 591, 458 A.2d 1268.

Under some circumstances it might be difficult to determine precisely the point at which forceful, aggressive trial advocacy crosses the line into the forbidden territory of an ethical violation. But no matter where in the spectrum of courtroom behavior we would draw that line, no matter how indulgent our view of acceptable professional conduct might be, it is inconceivable that the instances of respondent's demeanor that we are called upon to review in these proceedings could ever be countenanced. The record lays bare a shameful display of atrocious deportment calling for substantial discipline.

I.

A panel of the local ethics committee (Committee) prepared a carefully documented report of 60 pages, unanimously adopted by the Committee as its presentment charging respondent with unethical conduct. With equally meticulous care the Disciplinary Review Board (DRB) embodied its determination, with which we are in accord, in a Decision and Recommendation. Our independent review of the entire record leads us to the same conclusion as was reached by the DRB, whose full opinion we here set forth and adopt as our own.

* * *

The respondent represented D.K., the defendant in a child abuse/neglect case involving the defendant's four children. * * * During this proceeding, respondent's in-court conduct, his out of court conduct towards lawyers, witnesses and bystanders in the courthouse, and his written communiques and applications relative to the D.K. proceeding reached a level of impropriety that mandated the filing of a 22 count ethics complaint.

* * *

It is sufficient to note examples of respondent's numerous improprieties here. He was frequently sarcastic, disrespectful and irrational, and accused the Court on numerous occasions of, *inter alia*, collusion with the prosecution, cronyism, racism, permitting the proceedings to have a "carnival nature", conducting a kangaroo court, prejudging the case, conducting a "cockamamie charade of witnesses" and barring defense counsel from effectively participating in the proceedings, conducting a sham hearing, acting outside the law, being caught up in his "own little dream world", and ex-parte communications with the prosecutor together with other equally outrageous, disrespectful and unsupported charges. These and other comments were made frequently throughout the proceedings and continued at length.

* * *

[In one instance] the respondent reviewed a witness's files while she was testifying and failed to return them thereafter. The Deputy Attorney General located the files on the counsel table and returned them to the witness, at the witness's request. The respondent, in open court, then accused the Deputy Attorney General of stealing the files, and accused her of being a "bald-faced liar", and "a thief, a liar and a cheat". He also filed an ethics complaint against the Deputy Attorney General for her actions. * * *

[The] respondent further alleged that the trial judge had participated in extortion as well as cronyism, bias, prejudice, racism and religious bigotry during the trial, again without any basis in fact.

The respondent's improprieties continued. The respondent directed the following letter * * * to the trial judge, the text of which is set forth below:

> I wish to extend my sincerest good wishes for your speedy recovery from the obvious breakdown you suffered in chambers yesterday, Tuesday, December 11 * * *.

> Hopefully, with some rest and relaxation from your most taxing schedule, you will be in a position to resume your judicial duties more appropriately than exhibited on the eleventh.

> If, however, you feel somehow justified in pressing your demand for written recommendations, I must supply them, if for no other purpose than to demonstrate my client's continuing bona fides herein.

> I must admit, with no small degree of trepidation, that we have no confidence in your rationality vis-a-vis this case. Your activities on the eleventh and throughout the trial clearly demonstrate an irrational predisposition to chastise Mr. D.K. and defense counsel. The cronyism I wrote of in our motion for new trial continues unabated.

> You have simply closed your mind to our position and have retreated into a dream world not unlike the somnambulist in the early German classic story at the turn of the century.

> How do we make any kind of recommendations to you while you sleep-walk through your judicial duties. How does one get through to you.

* * *

The statements made by respondent in that letter speak for them-selves.

* * *

In addition to respondent's outrageous in-court conduct and equally outrageous written applications and communications, respondent, on numerous occasions, also engaged in reprehensible behavior towards witnesses, potential witnesses, opposing counsel, and other attorneys outside the courtroom but inside the Courthouse. A sampling of the improprieties follows:

1. On September 26 * * * outside the courtroom, respondent and Assistant Public Defender Eisert were discussing the issues of visitation. Argument ensued, during which, among other obscenities, respondent told Eisert to "go screw himself" * * *, and referred to Eisert as * * * "schmuckface", all in the presence of a number of individuals, some of whom were involved in the case.

2. On October 31 * * * Deputy Attorney General Rem and Eisert agreed to meet with respondent, at his request, for a settlement confer-ence. The Lawyer's Lounge was selected. In addition to addressing insults at Rem, respondent referred to a female attorney, also in the lounge, as "Miss Wrinkles" [and] "Miss Bags" * * *.

3. Respondent on several occasions either unnecessarily subpoe-naed individuals to testify or threatened those under subpoena by opposing counsel.

4. On December 6, 1979, in the Courthouse corridor, after attempt-ing to intimidate a witness by directing her to answer everything he asked, while his secretary wrote down her responses, respondent advised an attorney named Pearson who was standing with the witness but not involved in the proceeding to "just keep your god damn nose out of my business".

* * *

Respondent's performance did not conclude there. While Eisert, Pearson and Rem were conversing in the Courthouse, respondent ap-proached, stating loudly that Rem should not be believed since "* * * she's a bald-faced liar". He then called Rem "fuckface", and while walking away again made the suggestion "* * * shove it up your ass". Within the next several minutes, respondent twice approached the group, each time pushing into Rem, causing her to lurch against a desk in the hallway.

* * *

We would hope, through this opinion, to serve some more salutary purpose than just the distasteful meting out of well-deserved public discipline to Mr. Vincenti. As pointed out earlier, * * * this ethics proceeding unveils conduct so bizarre, so outrageous, as not to bring us close to what in some other case might be the difficult problem of distinguishing between permissibly vigorous advocacy and an ethical transgression. Although we need not here attempt with exquisite precision to delineate the difference, it may nevertheless be useful to restate, in general terms, the obligation of New Jersey lawyers, that they may readily avoid entanglements of the sort that brings respondent before us.

Models abound. We adopt one formulated by Justice Frankfurter:

> Certainly since the time of Edward I, through all the vicissitudes of seven centuries of Anglo-American history, the legal profession has played a role all its own. The bar has not enjoyed prerogatives; it has been entrusted with anxious responsibilities. One does not have to inhale the self-adulatory bombast of after-dinner speeches to affirm that all the interests of man that are comprised under the constitutional guarantees given to "life, liberty and property" are in the professional keeping of lawyers. It is a fair characterization of the lawyer's responsibility in our society that he stands "as a shield," to quote Devlin, J., in defense of right and to ward off wrong. From a profession charged with such responsibilities there must be exacted those qualities of truth-speaking, of a high sense of honor, of granite discretion, of the strictest observance of fiduciary responsibility, that have, through the centuries, been compendiously described as "moral character." [*Schware v. Board of Examiners*, 353 U.S. 232, 247, 77 S.Ct. 752, 760–761, 1 L.Ed.2d 796, 806 (1957) (Frankfurter, J., concurring).]

* * *

Respondent is suspended from the practice of law for one year and until the further order of the Court.

MULTIPLE CHOICE QUESTIONS

Answer these questions under the ABA Code and
ABA Model Rules

1. At the trial of a routine civil case in a United States District Court, defense lawyer Westerman presented the testimony of an insurance company investigator. On cross examination, plaintiff's lawyer established that on the day before the trial began, the investigator spent three hours in Westerman's office going over his testimony. On that occasion, Westerman showed the investigator some handwritten notes from the insurance company files, in an effort to refresh the investigator's recollection of some important dates. Plaintiff's counsel asked to have the notes brought to court the next morning; after hearing oral argument on the point, the judge ordered Westerman to bring them the next morning. Westerman responded: "I'll bring them, judge, on the next cold day in Hell." The judge looked startled but chose to overlook the remark. Westerman intentionally failed to bring the notes to court the following day. Which of the following are correct?

I. Westerman is *subject to discipline* for discussing the investigator's testimony with him before the trial.

II. Westerman is *subject to discipline* for using the notes to refresh the investigator's memory of dates.

III. Westerman is *subject to discipline* for his rude remark to the judge.

IV. Westerman is *subject to discipline* for intentionally violating the Federal Rules of Evidence.

V. Westerman is *subject to discipline* for intentionally violating the judge's order.

    A. All of the above.

    B. II and V only.

    C. I, II, III, and IV only.

    D. III, IV, and V only.

2. Lawyer Lexington represents the plaintiffs in a civil action. His clients are three members of the congregation of All Souls' Divine Missionary Church, suing on behalf of themselves and others similarly situated. The defendants are All Souls' Divine Missionary Church, Inc., (a corporation) and Pastor Dorset, the spiritual leader of the church and president of the church corporation. Pastor Dorset and the church corporation are represented by separate defense lawyers. The complaint alleges that Pastor Dorset misappropriated large amounts of church money, and that the Board of Elders, acting as corporate directors, knew about it and failed to stop him. In the early discovery phase of the case, lawyer Lexington conducted a lengthy, private interview with the church bookkeeper, an employee of the church corporation; she brought the church books with her to the interview, and she and Lexington went over them in great detail. Lexington did this without the knowledge or consent of either defense lawyer. Which of the following is most nearly correct?

    A. Lexington's conduct was *proper*, since the bookkeeper was not a party to the lawsuit.

    B. Lexington's conduct was *proper*, since the bookkeeper was neither an officer nor a high-ranking employee of the church corporation.

    C. Lexington is *subject to discipline*; he should have obtained the consent of both defense lawyers.

    D. Lexington is *subject to discipline*; he should have obtained the consent of the church corporation's defense lawyer.

3. Client Terpin hired attorney Altmont to study her past and present tax records and to give her legal advice in connection with the filing of her federal income tax return for the current year. Altmont did the necessary work, rendered the legal advice, and then she sent Terpin a bill for services. When Terpin received the bill, she stormed into Altmont's office to protest the amount. The more that Altmont tried to explain how she had computed the bill, the angrier Terpin grew. Final-

ly, Terpin stood up, leaned across the desk, and punched Altmont in the nose, hard. When Altmont regained her composure, she said in a quiet voice: "My dear lady, sit down. Listen carefully to what I am about to tell you. I have examined your tax records for the past five years, and you know as well as I do what they reveal. The statute of limitations on federal tax fraud is six years. Further, you have injured my nose. In this state, you can get up to one year in jail for criminal assault and battery. Now let us hear no more nonsense about my bill. Do you understand me?"

A. Altmont is *subject to discipline* for using this method to collect her bill.

B. Altmont's conduct was *proper*, because a lawyer may use reasonable means, short of a civil suit, to resolve a fee dispute.

C. Altmont's conduct was *proper*, provided that her statements about the statute of limitations and the jail term were accurate.

D. Altmont is *subject to discipline* for giving unsolicited legal advice to her client.

4. Attorney Paxton represents plaintiff Parker on a contingent fee basis in an action against Dougal Corp. for breach of an alleged employment contract between Dougal Corp. and Parker. Attorney Daniels represents Dougal Corp. in the matter. Dougal Corp. instructs Daniels to offer the plaintiff $35,000 to settle the case, and Daniels duly telephones Paxton and makes the offer of settlement. Paxton says he will take it up with Parker and get back to Daniels in due course. When Daniels hears nothing for two weeks, he calls Paxton back, but Paxton refuses to take Daniels' telephone call. Then Daniels writes Paxton a formal letter, re-making the settlement offer, requesting that Paxton consult Parker about it, and requesting a prompt response. Again, Daniels hears nothing from Paxton. Finally Daniels develops a strong suspicion that Paxton has not communicated the settlement offer to Parker. *May* Daniels send Parker a carbon copy of his letter to Paxton?

A. No, because Daniels is not allowed to communicate directly with Parker.

B. Yes, if Daniels reasonably believes that Paxton has failed to communicate the settlement offer to Parker.

C. No, since Daniels cannot be sure that Paxton failed to communicate the settlement offer to Parker.

D. Yes, because the carbon copy would simply advise Parker of Daniels' prior communication with Paxton.

5. Crebs had an automobile accident in his sportscar, injuring his girl friend, Victoria, who was riding in the front seat without her seatbelt fastened. Crebs consulted lawyer Limpett about his possible legal liability to Victoria. After making sure that Victoria had not already retained counsel, Limpett went to visit her, to find out how badly she was injured and to obtain her description of what happened the

night of the accident. Victoria asked Limpett whether he thought she should make a claim against Crebs. Limpett gave her his honest opinion: litigation can be costly and time-consuming, and Crebs' liability was debatable. Further, he told her, since her medical expenses were fully covered by her own health insurance, she had little to gain by suing Crebs.

A.   Limpett's conduct was *proper*, since Victoria was not represented by counsel when Limpett spoke with her.

B.   Limpett's conduct was *proper*, because he gave Victoria his honest opinion about the matter.

C.   Limpett's conduct was *proper*, provided that his visit with Victoria was an overture to a good faith settlement of the matter.

D.   Limpett is *subject to discipline*, even if his ultimate objective was to reach a fair settlement of the matter.

Answers to the multiple choice questions will be found
in the Appendix at the end of the book

Chapter Ten

THE TRIAL LAWYER AS TRUTH–SEEKER

What This Chapter Covers

I. The Trial Lawyer as Truth-Seeker
 A. Courtroom Tactics
 B. The Duties of the Criminal Prosecutor
  1. The Prosecutor's Primary Goal
  2. Decision to Prosecute
  3. Duty to Disclose Evidence
 C. The Duties of the Criminal Defense Lawyer
  1. The Defense Counsel's Goal
  2. Zeal Within the Bounds of the Law

Reading Assignment

Wydick & Perschbacher, Chapter 10

Review ABA Model Rules:

 Rules 3.1 through 3.9.

Review CRPC 3–200, 5–110, 5–200 and 5–220.

Review Cal.Bus & Prof.Code §§ 6068(b), (c), (d), (f) and (g); 6103; 6128(a).

Supplemental Reading

Review ABA Code:

 EC 7–1 through 7–10 and EC 7–13;

 DR 7–101 through 7–110.

Hazard & Hodes:

 Discussion of ABA Model Rules 3.1 through 3.9.

Wolfram:

 Sections 10.1 through 10.2.3 (adversary system and professional detachment);

 Sections 10.3.1 through 10.3.2 (zealous partisanship);

Sections 10.5.1 through 10.5.4 (justice v. merits in criminal defense);

Sections 12.1.1 through 12.1.3 (courtroom forensics);

Sections 13.10.1 through 13.10.6 (prosecutor's duties).

ABA Standards Relating to the Administration of Criminal Justice (The Prosecution Function; The Defense Function) (1979, 1982).

Discussion Problem

For this class consider the following transcript of events that occur just before and during a preliminary hearing in a criminal case, *People v. Link.* Defendant Link is charged with two felonies, robbery and attempted rape. The first scene takes place in the hallway of the courthouse. The victim, Polly Tate, is talking to Clyde Rollins, the prosecuting attorney. Al Wirtz, counsel for the defendant, overhears a part of this conversation. Later the scene shifts to the courtroom where the preliminary hearing is in progress.

PEOPLE v. LINK

SCENE: *Prosecutor is talking to a victim of a robbery and attempted rape in a hallway outside of the courtroom.*

Rollins: I understand, Miss Tate.

Miss Tate: I'm just telling you that I can't be sure, that's all.

Rollins: All crime victims feel that way, Miss Tate. But look at it this way, there's a man in there who is guilty of robbery and attempted rape, and we won't be able to do a thing about it if you don't help us this afternoon in this preliminary hearing. We're never gonna be able to turn this problem of crime around if people like that continue to get off.

(Wirtz appears, undetected by Rollins and Tate. He overhears the following:)

Miss Tate: I don't know. It was so dark and I was scared, really scared. It all happened so fast, you know, it makes me wonder. You know, I saw something just like this on TV last night, and the girl picks this guy out of the line-up and then it turns out that she was wrong. That's what I wonder about. And besides, I had a couple of drinks before I left the bar. I mean, what if I made a mistake?

Rollins: Let me put your mind to rest about that. The man you identified is definitely the right person. We have a statement from his co-defendant that incriminates him. They got it right after he was arrested. We know he has a prior record for armed robbery.

(Wirtz withdraws, still undetected)

Miss Tate: Oh, well * * *

Rollins: Can we go in now? Can we?

Miss Tate: I still * * *

Rollins: Can we?

Miss Tate: Will I be first?

Rollins: Yes, but just relax. All you have to do is tell the truth and you'll be fine. Now when the, ah, defense attorney gets a chance to ask you questions, just answer what he asks. Don't volunteer anything that they might be able to use to get this guy off the hook. Oh, and you don't have to mention anything about these last-minute self-doubts that you have. You don't want to see a guy like this, with this kind of record, get off, do you?

Miss Tate: (*Shakes her head no*). I'm ready.

Scene: *The courtroom. The preliminary hearing is in progress.*

Judge: You may proceed, Mr. Rollins.

Rollins: State your name and address, please.

Miss Tate: My name is Polly Tate. I live in the Royal Apartments in Arlington.

Rollins: And what is your occupation?

Miss Tate: I'm a student part-time, and I also work nights as a waitress, at Frank's Place. It's a bar.

Rollins: Directing your attention to the evening of July 10th at or about 12:30 a.m. Did anything unusual happen that evening?

Miss Tate: Yes, that was the night I was attacked.

Rollins: Would you please tell the court what happened in your own words?

Miss Tate: I got off work a little late as usual. My car was in the parking lot next door where I usually keep it and so I was walking, and you know, I've walked through that lot a hundred times, but there was something different about it that night. I thought I heard something but I wasn't sure. * * * I never thought it could be so dark out there. Anyway I started to hurry, and by the time I got to the car my hands were shaking, and I had trouble with the keys and that's when this guy came at me out of the dark. I guess he was hiding behind one of the cars. He, um, grabbed at me, and, um, he pulled on my purse, and I pulled back. * * * I don't know why. * * * I guess I should have given it to him, maybe then he would have left me alone, but I didn't, and um, he had hold of me and the purse, and I could tell that he was angry. You know what I mean? And then he dropped the purse and that's when I broke and ran away * * *. I was scared. I was really scared. I tried to run, you know, but the, uh, the ground was real uneven and I started to stumble and that's when he caught up with me * * *. I didn't see that he had a knife then, but he shov * * * shoved me to the ground, and I thought this is really it. I can still see it. The blade seemed to give off flashes of light. The he said * * * "Shut up and hold still or I'll cut your face." And then he was on top of me and he was tearing at my clothes and then, uh, I felt this smashing pain and my whole head was spinning * * *. I guess that I decided that I was never going to get out of it alive. And then this other guy, he came up and he started, uh, shaking the guy who was on top of me and he said something like, um, "Hey, this wasn't in the plan," and, uh, he said, uh, something like "Let's split, we've already got the pocketbook," and, uh, they must have run off then, but I didn't actually see them go. I must have passed out because the next thing I knew the policemen were there.

Rollins: Miss Tate, Miss Tate. Ah, I'd like to go back over your testimony to clarify some points. Did you say that you were shoved to the ground?

Miss Tate: Yes.

Rollins: And you were pushed into a sexual position?

Miss Tate: Yes.

Rollins: And the man that got on top of you, he said something else, didn't he?

Wirtz: Objection, your honor! This is leading, repetitious and aimed at prejudicing the court.

Judge: Overruled. You may answer the question.

Miss Tate: I guess I forgot to include this earlier. He said, uh, "Now you're gonna get what you want."

Rollins: Did you get a good look at the man who robbed and assaulted you that night?

Miss Tate: Yes.

Rollins: Do you see that person in this courtroom?

Miss Tate: I do. That's him.

Rollins: Let the record indicate that the witness has identified the defendant, John Link. Are you certain that this is the same man?

Miss Tate: Yes. I'm positive.

Rollins: When the defendant struggled with you, were you injured?

Wirtz: I object!

Rollins: I'm only trying to show the extent of the assault, your honor.

Judge: Overruled.

Rollins: What were your injuries?

Miss Tate: He broke my nose when he hit me.

Rollins: Were you taken to a hospital?

Wirtz: Objection, your honor!

Rollins: Tell us about the treatment, Miss Tate.

Miss Tate: I had to have surgery, twice.

Rollins: Were you hospitalized for some time after the assault?

Miss Tate: Yes.

Wirtz: I object to this entire line of questioning, your honor.

Judge: Cross-examine, Mr. Wirtz?

Wirtz: Thank you, your honor * * *. Have you discussed your testimony in this case with the prosecutor, Miss Tate?

Miss Tate: Yes, I have.

Wirtz: Did the prosecutor ever say anything to you about any of the other evidence in this case?

Miss Tate: No, not that I recall.

Rollins: Objection. I object to counsel's insinuation.

Wirtz: Are you prepared to take the stand and say that you haven't raised these issues with this witness?

Rollins: Your honor, I'm not the witness in this case.

Judge: Proceed, counsel. Let's get on with this.

Wirtz: All right, your honor. It is your testimony, then, that it was very dark when you were attacked and that you were very frightened? Is that correct?

Miss Tate: Yes, that's what I said.

Wirtz: And nevertheless you say that you're positive that you could identify John Link, that there's no question in your mind about that?

Miss Tate: No, none at all.

Wirtz: This man whose features you remember so clearly, had you ever seen him before the events you described?

Miss Tate: No.

Wirtz: The place you work, this Frank's Place. Can you describe the typical clientele, Miss Tate?

Miss Tate: Sure. They're almost always men, older guys, working types. They start coming in about cocktail hour, and it's pretty busy from then until closing time.

Wirtz: Did you ever leave the bar at closing time with one of the customers?

Miss Tate: Not very often.

Wirtz: Isn't it a fact, Miss Tate, that you regularly left the bar with customers?

Miss Tate: It was safer that way. That was the only reason. I wouldn't say it was regular, either.

Wirtz: Isn't it a fact that it was you who picked these men up? That you agreed to have sexual relations with them?

Rollins: Objection, your honor. Counsel is making wild allegations that he has no intention of substantiating. He is simply harassing the witness.

Wirtz: I can prove my allegations, your honor.

Judge: Are you prepared to produce witnesses in this matter, counsel?

Wirtz: I am, your honor. I'm calling two "customers" and I'm simply laying the foundation for that now. I will also establish that Miss Tate had been drinking immediately before she was allegedly assaulted.

Rollins: Whether counsel has witnesses or not, I don't see the relevance of this part of the cross-examination. The prior sexual conduct and drinking habits of this witness have no bearing on her veracity.

Wirtz: I'm showing that this witness made a regular practice of picking up men from the bar, just as she did on the night of July 10th, and that's highly relevant, your honor.

Judge: I'll overrule the objection.

Wirtz: Thank you, your honor.

Associate Counsel (whispering to Wirtz): Al, the judge is wrong on that. Prior bad conduct is not admissible to show credibility. There's a new case directly against us, and we don't have anything on her conduct for the night in question.

Wirtz (whispering): Let's not make the other side's arguments for them, okay? I've got enough problems already.

Wirtz: Miss Tate, I'm going to rephrase that last question. Is it your testimony that you did not leave Frank's Place with one of the customers that night?

Miss Tate: No, I didn't.

Wirtz: And you deny that you had a fight with one of them and then called the police with this story?

––––––––

In preparing for the class discussion, read the *Tyler* case and the passages in this chapter by Judge Jerome Frank, Professor Monroe Freedman, Professor Geoffrey Hazard and practicing lawyer Barry Winston. Then consider these questions:

1. In what, if any, respects should a criminal prosecutor be held to an ethical standard different from other lawyers?

2. How far may a lawyer go in shaping the testimony of a witness?

3. In advising a client, or in working with a witness, may a lawyer explain the legal and practical consequences of a given set of facts before asking the client or witness to state the facts?

4. Is it proper for a lawyer to try to impeach the credibility of a witness whom the lawyer knows to be telling the truth?

5. Why are trial lawyers forbidden to express their personal opinions when presenting a case to the trier of fact?

6.   What are the ethical duties of a criminal defense lawyer when representing a client whom he or she knows to be guilty?

COURTS ON TRIAL

Jerome Frank, 82–85 (1949).

What is the role of the lawyers in bringing the evidence before the trial court? As you may learn by reading any one of a dozen or more handbooks on how to try a law-suit, an experienced lawyer uses all sorts of stratagems to minimize the effect on the judge or jury of testimony disadvantageous to his client, even when the lawyer has no doubt of the accuracy and honesty of that testimony. The lawyer considers it his duty to create a false impression, if he can, of any witness who gives such testimony. If such a witness happens to be timid, frightened by the unfamiliarity of court-room ways, the lawyer, in his cross-examination, plays on that weakness, in order to confuse the witness and make it appear that he is concealing significant facts. Longenecker, in his book *Hints On The Trial of a Law Suit* (a book endorsed by the great Wigmore), in writing of the "truthful, honest, over-cautious" witness, tells how "a skilful advocate by a rapid cross-examination may ruin the testimony of such a witness." The author does not even hint any disapproval of that accomplishment. Longenecker's and other similar books recommend that a lawyer try to prod an irritable but honest "adverse" witness into displaying his undesirable characteristics in their most unpleasant form, in order to discredit him with the judge or jury. "You may," writes Harris, "sometimes destroy the effect of an adverse witness by making him appear more hostile than he really is. You may make him exaggerate or unsay something and say it again." Taft says that a clever cross-examiner, dealing with an honest but egotistic witness, will "deftly tempt the witness to indulge in his propensity for exaggeration, so as to make him 'hang himself.' And thus," adds Taft, "it may happen that not only is the value of his testimony lost, but the side which produces him suffers for seeking aid from such a source"— although, I would add, that may be the only source of evidence of a fact on which the decision will turn.

"An intimidating manner in putting questions," writes Wigmore, "may so coerce or disconcert the witness that his answers do not represent his actual knowledge on the subject. So also, questions which in form or subject cause embarrassment, shame or anger in the witness may unfairly lead him to such demeanor or utterances that the impression produced by his statements does not do justice to its real testimonial value." Anthony Trollope, in one of his novels, indignantly reacted to these methods. "One would naturally imagine," he said, "that an undisturbed thread of clear evidence would be best obtained from a man whose position was made easy and whose mind was not harassed; but this is not the fact; to turn a witness to good account, he must be badgered this way and that till he is nearly mad; he must be made a laughing-stock for the court; his very truths must be turned into falsehoods, so that he may be falsely shamed; he must be accused of all manner of villainy, threatened with all manner of punishment; he must be made to feel that he has no friend near him, that the world is all against him; he must be confounded till he forget his right hand from his left, till his mind be turned into chaos, and his heart into water; and then let him give his evidence. What will fall from his lips when in this wretched collapse must be of special value, for the best talents of practiced forensic heroes are daily used to bring it about; and no member of the Humane Society interferes to protect the wretch. Some sorts of torture are as it were tacitly allowed even among humane people. Eels are skinned alive, and witnesses are sacrificed, and no one's blood curdles at the sight, no soft heart is sickened at the cruelty." This may be a somewhat overdrawn picture. Yet, referring to this manner of handling witnesses, Sir Frederic Eggleston recently said that it prevents lawyers from inducing persons who know important facts from disclosing them to lawyers for litigants. He notes, too, that "the terrors of cross-examination are such that a party can often force a settlement by letting it be known that a certain * * * counsel has been retained."

The lawyer not only seeks to discredit adverse witnesses but also to hide the defects of witnesses who testify favorably to his client. If, when interviewing such a witness before trial, the lawyer notes that the witness has mannerisms, demeanor-traits, which might discredit him, the lawyer teaches him how to cover up those traits when testifying: He educates the irritable witness to conceal his irritability, the cocksure witness to subdue his cocksureness. In that way, the trial court is denied the benefit of observing the witness's actual normal demeanor, and thus prevented from sizing up the witness accurately.

Lawyers freely boast of their success with these tactics. They boast also of such devices as these: If an "adverse," honest witness, on cross-examination, makes seemingly inconsistent statements, the cross-examiner tries to keep the witness from explaining away the apparent inconsistencies. "When," writes Tracy, counseling trial lawyers, in a much-praised book, "by your cross-examination, you have caught the witness in an inconsistency, the next question that will immediately come to your lips is, 'Now, let's hear you explain.' Don't ask it, for he may explain and, if he does, your point will have been lost. If you have conducted your cross-examination properly (which includes interestingly), the jury will have seen the inconsistency and it will have made the proper impression on their minds. If, on redirect examination the witness does explain, the explanation will have come later in the case and at the request of the counsel who originally called the witness and the jury will be much more likely to look askance at the explanation than if it were made during your cross-examination." Tracy adds, "Be careful in your questions on cross-examination not to open a door that you have every reason to wish kept closed." That is, don't let in any reliable evidence, hurtful to your side, which would help the trial court to arrive at the truth.

"In cross-examination," writes Eggleston, "the main preoccupation of counsel is to avoid introducing evidence, or giving an opening to it, which will harm his case. The most painful thing for an experienced practitioner * * * is to hear a junior counsel laboriously bring out in cross-examination of a witness all the truth which the counsel who called him could not" bring out "and which it was the junior's duty as an advocate to conceal." A lawyer, if possible, will not ask a witness to testify who, on cross-examination, might testify to true facts helpful to his opponent.

Nor, usually, will a lawyer concede the existence of any facts if they are inimical to his client and he thinks they cannot be proved by his adversary. If, to the lawyer's knowledge, a witness has testified inaccurately but favorably to the lawyer's client, the lawyer will attempt to hinder cross-examination that would expose the inaccuracy. He puts in testimony which surprises his adversary who, caught unawares, has not time to seek out, interview, and summon witnesses who would rebut the surprise testimony. "Of course," said a trial lawyer in a bar association lecture in 1946, "surprise elements should be hoarded. Your opponent should not be educated as to matters concerning which you believe he is still in the dark. Obviously, the traps should not be uncovered. Indeed, you may cast a few more leaves over them so that your adversary will step more boldly on the low ground believing it is solid."

These, and other like techniques, you will find unashamedly described in the many manuals on trial tactics written by and for eminently reputable trial lawyers. The purpose of these tactics—often effective—is to prevent the trial judge or jury from correctly evaluating the trustworthiness of witnesses and to shut out evidence the trial court ought to receive in order to approximate the truth.

In short, the lawyer aims at victory, at winning in the fight, not at aiding the court to discover the facts. He does not want the trial court to reach a sound educated guess, if it is likely to be contrary to his client's interests. Our present trial method is thus the equivalent of throwing pepper in the eyes of a surgeon when he is performing an operation.

ETHICS IN THE PRACTICE OF LAW

Geoffrey C. Hazard, Jr., 127–35.
Yale University Press (1978)[a]

No question of legal ethics is more difficult than the question whether an advocate can help suppress the truth in order to protect his

---

a. Professor Hazard teaches at Yale Law School, and he was the Reporter for the commission that drafted the ABA Model Rules. In *Ethics in the Practice of Law,* he reports and comments on discussions held at Seven Springs, New York, by a group of lawyers, judges, and law teachers about contemporary problems in legal ethics.

client. In so far as litigation is concerned, the effect is to immobilize the law's enforcement. A lawyer can, within the limits of the law, obstruct its enforcement by advising his client to refuse to testify. At the borderland of the law, and without much risk to himself, he can go a considerable way in helping his client build a coverup. For example, he can advise the client about the consequences of preserving records or indicate to him the legal consequences of a certain line of testimony that the client might give. To the extent that such advice is given and acted upon, the effect is much the same as putting a client on the stand when it is known that his testimony will be false: The truth of the matter, which might have been discovered if the lawyer had not been involved, will less likely be discovered because he is involved. The problem is whether the benefits are worth that cost.

Paradoxically, the primary benefit of the system is often said to be the promotion of truth. For every instance in which truth is suppressed or distorted by the adversary system, it is thought there are more instances in which the system uncovers truth that otherwise would not have been uncovered. There is no practicable way to test this claim. It is worth considering, however, whether the situation would really be much better if we gave up the adversary system in favor of the interrogative system. But even if the claim were false we might want to keep the rule as it is. Under the present system, using ostensibly open competition for discovery of the truth, the law has troubles with suppression and distortion; what sort of troubles would it have if we depended on *ex officio* procedures for getting the evidence? If the truth suffers from our use of the adversary system, we ought to consider how it might suffer if we used some other system. In our political culture, the interrogative system of trial could well turn out to resemble Congressional hearings.

The real value of the adversary system thus may not be its contribution to truth but its contribution to the ideal of individual autonomy. This is the rationale underlying many rules that obscure the truth, such as the privilege against self-incrimination and the rule that private premises may not be searched without a warrant. The proposition, as applied to the adversary system, is that there is good in being able to say what one wants to say, even if it involves the commission of perjury. Stated baldly, the proposition is shocking. The norms of our society condemn lying, although it is perhaps worth noting that the biblical rule is the much narrower proposition that one should not bear false witness against a neighbor. At any rate, conventional morality does not openly recognize the value of being able to lie. Still, our commitment to truthfulness may actually go no further than homily; when it comes to serious business such as negotiation and diplomacy, most people accept the utility, the inevitability, and perhaps even the desirability of dissimulation in various forms.

Why should dissimulation not be acceptable in court? There are many cultures in which it is assumed that parties to legal conflict lie on their own behalf; no pretense is made that they should be expected to do otherwise. The common law formerly exhibited the same attitude, for it did not allow testimony from a criminal defendant or any "party in interest" in civil litigation. The present ethical dilemma in the adversary system may therefore be ultimately traceable to the abolition of the common law rules of witness disqualification.

The reform of the common law rules occurred in the nineteenth century. It was based on the proposition that few injustices would result if interested persons were allowed to testify. It was believed that with cross-examination and the good sense of the jury, the truth will out most of the time. Perhaps it is time that this premise was reexamined, for it seems evident that if the stakes involved in a lawsuit are substantial, if the outcome depends on the truth, and if the parties are authorized to give evidence as to what the truth is, the parties will distort their submissions to the maximum extent possible. The artistry and self-consciousness of the distortion will of course vary. In many cases it may be supposed that at least one party will tell the unvarnished truth, hoping if not trusting that it will be seen as such. But to require a party to choose between imprisonment or financial self-destruction on the one hand, and complete truthfulness on the other, is to impose a moral burden that may simply be too heavy. And, directly to the point of the present discussion, it imposes nearly as difficult a burden on the advocate who must advise the party in making the choice.

There is much ambivalence concerning the advocate's responsibility in this respect. The rules clearly say that, even in the defense of criminal cases, the advocate may not assist his client in committing perjury or in otherwise fabricating or suppressing evidence. In practice, lawyers often wind up violating these rules, some of them quite frequently. But they seek escapes from moral responsibility for having done so.

There are several escapes. It is said that no client is guilty until found so by a court; therefore, one cannot know what the truth is until then; therefore, one cannot conclude that a client's testimony will constitute perjury. This is pure casuistry. Of course there are doubtful situations, but there are also ones that are not doubtful. A thing is not made true or not by a court's pronouncing on it, and a lawyer can reach conclusions about an issue without having a judge tell him what to think.

Another escape is for the advocate to indicate to the client how inconvenient it would be if the evidence were such and so, and leave it to the client to do the dirty work—well illustrated in "the lecture" in *Anatomy of a Murder*.[b] Another is for the advocate to pretend that the rules governing his responsibility are different from what they are—to

b. Professor Hazard's reference is to a story written by a lawyer, John D. Voelker, under the pen name Robert Traver, *Anatomy of a Murder* (1958). In the story, an accused murderer tells his defense counsel what happened on the night in question. Defense counsel then explains that if the facts are as stated, the defendant will probably be executed. "But, on the other hand, if you acted in a blind rage, there is a possibility of saving your life. Think it over, and we will talk about it tomorrow." Is there something wrong with doing that? *See* Monroe Freedman, 64 Mich.L.Rev. 1469, 1478–82 (1966); see also Monroe Freedman, Understanding Lawyers' Ethics 143–60 (1991).

pretend that duty to client requires aiding him in whatever the client feels he must do to vindicate himself in court. The advocate is then absolved because he is merely an instrument.

As the situation stands, the advocate is supposed to be both the champion of his client and a gatekeeper having a duty to prevent his client from contaminating the courtroom. In principle, these responsibilities are compatible. The duty to the court simply limits the ways in which a lawyer can champion his client's cause. In practice, however, the duties have come to be in perhaps uncontrollable conflict.

The sources of this conflict are located in the depths of our system of advocacy. An important factor in the advocate's ability to control the conflict is the set of rules that describe his relationship to the client and the cause. In other legal systems, these relationships are quite different from what they are in this country. In the English system, for example, the barrister is insulated from the case in several important ways. An English barrister has no continuing relation with any client; his fee is fixed before trial in negotiations to which he is not a party and on a basis unrelated to eventual victory or defeat; the case is placed with a barrister through a solicitor as intermediary; and barristers as a group are small in number, aristocratic, clannish, and closely tied to the judiciary. The barrister thus is strongly identified as an officer of the court and as a gatekeeper concerning what kind of evidence will be offered. In the continental system, the advocate is insulated from the client by somewhat similar conventions; equally important, he has a much more limited responsibility in the trial because the judge and not the advocate is primarily responsible for eliciting the facts.

In the American system, however, the advocate's relationship to his client's cause is much more dependent and intimate. In litigation involving "repeat business" clients, the advocate or his firm usually is also counsel under retainer to the client. In litigation involving "one shot" clients, such as plaintiff's injury claims, the lawyer's fee is usually contingent on the outcome. In any event, the advocate is expected and permitted to investigate the facts and interrogate witnesses before trial, thus becoming a party to the evidence before its presentation in court. A much wider range of harassing tactics is indulged in American litigation. Hence, the advocate's situation in our version of the adversary system is fairly defined by Shaw's description of marriage: it "combines the maximum of temptation with the maximum of opportunity." It is not difficult to see why the lawyer may be relatively ineffective as a source of restraint on his client.

The advocate who represents large corporations rarely confronts the problems of client perjury or fabrication or destruction of evidence. But he faces problems that are similar if more subtle. What does a lawyer do with the client who wants to fight the case to the bitter end, even though the advocate thinks that the other side's case is substantially just and that the matter should be settled? What does he do in a case where he is convinced that the other side is wrong on the merits but also convinced that the judge or jury or administrative hearing officer will be prejudiced against his corporate client? Does this justify the use of harassing tactics? If the case has a political aspect, may he delay its progress in the hope that there will be a change in administration? If so, within what limits? Legitimate and illegitimate techniques shade into each other—vigorous maneuver into harassment, careful preparation of witnesses into subornation of perjury, nondisclosure into destruction of evidence. At some point in deterioration of rules of form, an expert in rough and tumble becomes simply a thug.

This brings in view another serious problem of the adversary system. The trial lawyer can become completely immersed in his lawsuits, to the point where they become his identity and their outcome the sole criterion of his professional stature. Indeed, it is often only with difficulty that a modern trial specialist can maintain distance between himself and his craft. The whole tendency of his work leads him to hold, with Vince Lombardi, that winning is not the most important thing but the only thing. And the result can be that he becomes incapacitated to give his client detached advice about the prospects of ultimate victory and the advisability of settling through compromise. The problem can be especially severe in "big" cases for and against big corporations, because one such case can for several years be the vocation of a good part of a firm or agency's litigation staff. But it is inherent in the system. An English barrister is reported to have remonstrated, upon the prospect of compromising a bitter suit between heirs to a large fortune, "What? And allow that magnificent estate to be frittered away among the beneficiaries?"

If it is possible that the adversary system can work satisfactorily, and necessary that it must do so because no other system of adjudication is likely to be any better, it remains true that the system in its present form is pretty sick. The problem can be posed in terms of the attitude with which the advocate should approach a case. One approach, whether in reality or in idealized form we cannot be entirely sure, is that of the English barrister. In this approach, the advocate undertakes a dispassionate analysis of the facts and a magisterial consideration of the law with the aim of establishing common ground with his opposite number and thereupon settling the case on the basis of truth and legal justice, or at worst, isolating for trial the issues of fact or law that prove intractable. A lot of litigation in this country is actually determined this way, when the advocates trust each other's competence, integrity, and judgment. But a lot of litigation is conducted otherwise. In the other approach the advocate is a streetfighter—aggressive, guileful, exploitive. Some clients seem to want it that way, at least until they find out that two can play the game. At any rate many clients suppose that is the way litigation inevitably must be conducted and approach their counsel with a corresponding set of expectations. The advocate in turn can confirm and exploit these expectations, providing fulfillment of the prophecy if he wishes. As the institution of adversary adjudication now stands, the advocate has very strong inducements to oblige.

If the adversary system is to be changed, it will not be a simple undertaking. The system as it exists expresses a number of strongly held beliefs and ideals. One is that justice should be free. It is this proposition that supports the rule that the loser in litigation does not have to pay the winner's expenses. From this in turn follows the contingent fee system and the lack of inhibitions on running up an opposing party's costs, with the corresponding impairment of the advocate's gatekeeper function. Another belief is that entry into the legal profession should be relatively democratic. From this proposition it follows that admission is relatively easy, levels of training uneven, and professional esprit de corps weak. From this it follows that the images of professional lawyers are fuzzy and the potential for self-policing correspondingly low. Another is that litigation should secure not only justice under law but natural and popular justice. From this it follows that litigation often has inherently political, redistributive, and sometimes subversive characteristics, which infuse not only the merits of the controversies but the way they are prosecuted or defended. The "Chicago Seven" trial is an illustration. Still another belief is the notion that militant advocacy is an especially genuine and efficacious expression of social conscience. Exemplars of this style are the relentless prosecutor, the fearless vindicator of the oppressed, the wiley strategist for the establishment. It would be better if there were a larger constituency that understood, with Judge Learned Hand, that being in litigation, whatever its outcome, can justly be compared with sickness and death.

Perhaps the problem is this: We can have a system that does not charge user fees, lets everyone play, seeks both law and common justice, and is subject to few inhibitions in style. We can also have a system in which a trial is a serious search for the truth or at least a ceremony whose essential virtue is solemnity. But we probably cannot have both. So long as the advocate in the American system is supposed to be at once a champion in forensic roughhouse and a guardian of the temple of justice, he can fulfill his responsibilities only if he combines extraordinary technical skill with an unusually disciplined sense of probity. That seems to be asking too much of any profession.

Note on Witness Coaching

As these excerpts from Professor and Hazard and Judge Frank indicate, a persistent problem in the adversary system is lawyers' pretrial preparation of witnesses. This technique and its ethical and practical problems are explored in a recent article by Professor Richard Wydick, *The Ethics of Witness Coaching,* 17 Cardozo L.Rev. 1 (1995). Wydick begins with the "standard wisdom" about witness coaching:

> First, a lawyer may discuss the case with the witnesses before they testify. A lawyer in our common law adversary system has an ethical and legal duty to investigate the facts of the case, and the investigation typically requires the lawyer to talk with the witnesses—the people who know what happened on the occasion in question. Moreover, the adversary system benefits by allowing

lawyers to prepare witnesses so that they can deliver their testimony efficiently, persuasively, comfortably, and in conformity with the rules of evidence.

Second, when a lawyer discusses the case with a witness, the lawyer must not try to bend the witness's story or put words in the witness's mouth. As an old New York disciplinary case puts it: "[The lawyer's] duty is to extract the facts from the witness, not to pour them into him; to learn what the witness does know, not to teach him what he ought to know."

Third, a lawyer can be disciplined by the bar for counseling or assisting a witness to testify falsely or for knowingly offering testimony that the lawyer knows is false. [*Id.* at 1–2.]

According to Wydick, when a lawyer interviews and prepares a witness, the lawyer typically does these things:

- discusses the witness's perception, recollection, and possible testimony about the events in question;

- reviews documents and other tangible items to refresh the witness's memory or to point out conflicts and inconsistencies with the witness's story;

- reveals other tangible or testimonial evidence to the witness to find out how it affects the witness's story;

- explains how the law applies to the events in question;

- reviews the factual context into which the witness's testimony will fit;

- discusses the role of the witness and effective courtroom demeanor;

- discusses probable lines of cross-examination that the witness should be prepared to meet;

- rehearses the witness's testimony, by role playing or other means. [*Id.* at 4–5.]

From this, he elaborates 23 different "legitimate reasons for a lawyer's statement of question to a witness":

- to investigate the facts, that is, to find out about the events in question;

- to find out what the witness perceived and can testify to from personal knowledge;

- to determine how accurately the witness perceived the events and what conditions may have hindered or assisted his perception;

- to test the witness's memory about what he perceived;

- to discover how certain the witness is about what he remembers;

- to determine adverse or favorable conditions that may have affected the witness's memory;

- to refresh the witness's memory of things he once remembered but has since forgotten;

- to find out whether exposure to relevant documents, other items of tangible or testimonial evidence, or some non-evidentiary stimulus will help refresh the witness's memory;

- to test the witness's ability to communicate his recollections accurately;

- to find out what the witness means by words or expressions he used in his story;

- to test the witness's truthfulness;

- to warn the witness that his credibility may be attacked and that some kinds of acts in his past may be exposed in open court;

- to ascertain whether the witness has a good or bad character as respects truthfulness;

- to find out whether the witness has previously been convicted of a crime that could be used to impeach his credibility;

- to uncover instances of non-criminal conduct that could be used to impeach the witness's credibility;

- to discover whether the witness's story has been influenced by bias or prejudice;

- to find out whether the witness's story has been influenced, properly or improperly, by the statements or conduct of some other person;

- to find out whether the witness has previously made statements that are either consistent or inconsistent with his present story;

- to test the witness's demeanor in response to various stimuli he may encounter when he testifies (for example, the witness's likely response to harsh questioning by a cross-examiner);

- to explain the role of a witness, the obligations imposed by the oath, and the formality of court proceedings;

- to inform the witness about the physical surroundings in which he will testify, the persons who will be present, and the logistical details of being a witness;

- to explain to the witness why he should listen to questions carefully, not guess, not volunteer information that has not been asked for, be alert to objections, and the like;

- to advise the witness about appropriate attire and physical appearance in court, distracting mannerisms, inappropriate language and demeanor, and the effective delivery of testimony. [*Id.* at 16–18.]

These are all acceptable practices. Nevertheless, when a lawyer is left alone with a witness, the fallibility of human memory also allows lawyers to alter the witness' story and the witness' memory itself. Wydick divides "witness coaching" into three "grades":

Grade One witness coaching is where the lawyer knowingly and overtly induces a witness to testify to something the lawyer knows is false. "Overtly" is used to mean that the lawyer's conduct is "openly" or "on its face" an inducement to testify falsely. Grade One witness coaching obviously interferes with the court's truth-seeking function and corrodes the morals of both the witness and the lawyer. Sometimes it goes undetected by adversaries, judges, and disciplinary authorities, but when it is detected, it can and should be punished under the present lawyer disciplinary rules and perjury statutes.

Grade Two witness coaching is the same as Grade One, except that the lawyer acts *covertly*. Thus, Grade Two is where the lawyer knowingly but covertly induces a witness to testify to something the lawyer knows is false. "Covertly" is used to mean that the lawyer's inducement is masked. It is transmitted by implication. Grade Two witness coaching is no less harmful to the court's truth-seeking function than Grade One, nor less morally corrosive, nor less in breach of the lawyer disciplinary rules and perjury statutes, but it is less likely to be detected and successfully punished. Grade Two witness coaching falls within a range of conduct that cannot be effectively controlled by disciplinary rules or criminal laws and that it must therefore be controlled by a lawyer's own informed conscience. To have an *informed* conscience about witness coaching, a lawyer needs to understand how messages get transmitted covertly between a speaker and a hearer. To that end, the article describes philosopher Paul Grice's "theory of conversational implicature" and suggests a method of analysis that incorporates Grice's theory.

Grade Three witness coaching is where the lawyer does not knowingly induce the witness to testify to something the lawyer knows is false, but the lawyer's conversation with the witness nevertheless alters the witness's story. Given the malleable nature of human memory, Grade Three witness coaching is very hard to avoid. It lacks the element of corruption that Grades One and Two have, but it does alter a witness's story and can thus interfere with the court's truth-seeking function. Therefore, when a lawyer's conversation with a witness serves a proper purpose, such as refreshing the witness's memory, the lawyer should nonetheless conduct the conversation in the manner that is least likely to produce inaccurate testimony. [*Id.* at 3–4.]

Finally, Wydick suggests methods for conducting a non-suggestive witness interview to minimize the dangers of improper witness suggestion, which include (1) using recall first, and then recognition; (2) using neutral questions; and (3) ordering questions based on the pattern the witness is likely to have used when originally storing the information. [*Id.* at 41–52.]

THE PROSECUTOR'S SPECIAL DUTIES

Prosecutors have the unique power to bring criminal prosecutions on behalf of the government. This power also entails a special duty to exercise the power in a responsible fashion. Ethical Consideration 7–13 of the ABA Code states this special role this way: "The responsibility of a public prosecutor differs from that of the usual advocate; his duty is to seek justice, not merely to convict." [*See also* Comment to ABA Model Rule 3.8.] But the prosecutor is also an advocate in the adversary system of criminal litigation. Thus the prosecutor is asked to assume a dual role as a partisan advocate and a quasi-judicial officer—a role difficult to achieve in practice.

The special ethical responsibilities of the prosecutor include restraint in prosecuting charges without probable cause; protecting the accused's right to counsel and other important pretrial rights; disclosing evidence that negates guilt or mitigates the offense or sentence; and exercising restraint in litigation tactics and out-of-court statements. [*See* ABA Model Rule 3.8; ABA Code DR 7–103.]

An important feature of the prosecutor's special duty is the obligation to disclose evidence that may assist the defense. The ethical duty of disclosure goes beyond the bare due process requirements of the fifth and fourteenth amendments. [*See* Hazard & Hodes § 3.8:501, at 697–98.]

The Supreme Court set out the constitutional minimum in *Brady v. Maryland*, 373 U.S. 83, 83 S.Ct. 1194, 10 L.Ed.2d 215 (1963), and explained it more fully in *United States v. Bagley*, 473 U.S. 667, 105 S.Ct. 3375, 87 L.Ed.2d 481 (1985). As explained in *Bagley*, the due process clause requires a prosecutor to disclose evidence that favors the defendant with respect to guilt on the merits, or impeachment of prosecution witnesses, or punishment for the offense. Five Justices agreed that the duty to disclose applies when a failure to disclose "undermines confidence in the outcome of the trial," and thus "deprives the defendant of a fair trial." This standard is met if there is a "reasonable probability" that, had the evidence been disclosed, "the result of the proceeding would have been different." The five Justices also agreed that this same standard applies, irrespective of whether the defense lawyer has made a specific request for the material, or a general request, or no request at all. [*See* Justice White's concurring opinion, 473 U.S. at 685, 105 S.Ct. at 3385.]

Now examine ABA Model Rule 3.8 and ABA Code DR 7–103(B). In what respects do these provisions appear to impose a standard that is higher than the constitutional minimum?

The wisdom of having an ethical standard that is higher than the constitutional minimum is illustrated by *Read v. Virginia State Bar*, 233 Va. 560, 357 S.E.2d 544 (1987). Virginia's version of ABA Code DR 7–103(B) requires prosecutors to disclose exculpatory material only when "required by law." [Virginia Code of Professional Responsibility DR 8–102(A)(4).] In the *Read* case, an eye-witness had identified the defendant from photographs and at a pretrial line-up. But, after observing the defendant during the first day of trial, the eye-witness changed his story and told the prosecutor's office that he was *certain* that the defendant was *not* the person he saw at the scene of the crime. The defense lawyers knew that the eye-witness was a proposed witness for the prosecution. Prosecutor Read did not call the eye-witness during the prosecution case-in-chief. When the eye-witness learned that he would not be called as a prosecution witness, he voluntarily informed the defense lawyers about his changed story. The defense arranged to have him available as a defense witness. Prosecutor Read closed the prosecution case-in-chief without mentioning the eye-witness. Only when it became apparent that the defense would call the eye-witness did Read attempt a hasty disclosure of the change of story.

The Virginia State Bar Disciplinary Board recommended that Read be disbarred because he was apparently willing to see the defendant convicted of arson and murder without permitting the jury to consider the eye-witness's changed story. The Virginia Supreme Court refused to follow the Board's recommendation, holding that the *Brady* due process standard was satisfied because defense counsel eventually got the exculpatory information in time to use it at trial. True enough—but doesn't that miss the point?

THE DUTIES OF THE CRIMINAL
DEFENSE LAWYER

A lawyer who represents a client accused of a criminal offense also has duties that diverge from the general rules for litigating lawyers. Professor Wolfram comments that "[t]he effective limits on a defense lawyer's loyalty and zeal are quite unclear and can probably be captured only by a vague phrase such as 'advocacy in good faith.'" [Wolfram, at 589.] Model Rule 3.1 contains a special exemption from the prohibition against making frivolous claims: "A lawyer for the defendant in a criminal proceeding, * * * may nevertheless so defend the proceeding as to require that every element of the case be established." California's list of attorney duties requires lawyers "[t]o counsel or maintain such actions, proceedings or defenses only as appear ... legal or just, *except the defense of a person charged with a public offense.*" (emphasis added) Thus the criminal defense lawyer may require the prosecution to put on its proof even if there is no non-frivolous defense. Exceptions such as these are necessary to preserve the presumption that a criminal defendant is innocent until proven guilty. In fact, the American Bar Association in 1979 adopted a distinct set of standards for both criminal prosecutors and defense counsel. [*See* American Bar Association, *Standards Relating to the Administration of Criminal Justice,* "Prosecution and Defense Function" (1979).] One of the enduring questions for defense counsel is what means she can use to defend her client, particularly if she is convinced of the client's guilt. This problem and related issues are explored in this chapter and in Chapters 7, 8, and 9.

PEOPLE v. TYLER

California Court of Appeal, First District, 1991.
233 Cal.App.3d 1456, 285 Cal.Rptr. 371.

DOSSEE, ASSOCIATE JUSTICE.

[Defendant was convicted in a jury trial of second degree robbery. On appeal, he claims the trial court made improper comments to the jury.]

I. Trial Court's Comments

At closing argument, the trial court twice interrupted defense counsel and remarked that defense counsel was not allowed to express his belief in his client's innocence. At the outset, the court interjected as follows:

"MR. PINKNEY [Defense Counsel]: Good morning, Ladies and Gentlemen. [¶] We're going to start off first with a question. The question to you is: [¶] In our system, what can an innocent man without an alibi do? [¶] I'm going to repeat that because that's a very important question in this case.

"THE COURT: All right. Ladies and Gentlemen of the Jury, *I don't want you to assume by that statement by defense counsel that he's taking the position or expressing a position that his client is innocent because his client is presumed to be innocent.* [¶] All right? [¶] Go ahead.

"MR. PINKNEY: It's important to point out that the word 'I' was not used in a statement. Again, the question to you is: In our system, what can an innocent man without an alibi do? [¶] He can do no more than to enter a plea of not guilty." (Emphasis added.)

Later, after defense counsel had discussed the presumption of innocence, defense counsel stated: "Now in this case, Mr. Tyler has the jury defense. That is, he turns to the jury system. He turns to the jury and asks the jury to perform its role in the system. Because of the presumption of innocence and because Mr. Tyler, the accused, has no burden of proof, as you sit there right now, as you sit there and think about my comments and the comments of the district attorney, you are under an obligation to perceive him as no different than an innocent man without an alibi."

The court then interrupted again:

"THE COURT: Wait a minute. Wait a minute * * *. *You can't say that* * * *. [¶] Now, Ladies and Gentlemen of the Jury, *it's* *improper for defense counsel to express an opinion that his client is innocent.* It's improper. He is presumed to be innocent. I don't want you to take that statement by defense counsel as an expression of his opinion that his client is innocent of these charges. If that's the conclusion you've come to, disregard it because his client is presumed to be innocent. *For him to take the position that his client is innocent no matter how he frames it is improper.* [¶] All right? [¶] So bear that in mind. [¶] All right. Go ahead, Mr. Pinkney.

"MR. PINKNEY: I've tried, and this is the first time I believe the word 'I' has come. I'll try to be careful about how I articulate that position, and I'll continue to try to be careful. If you hear me use the word 'I' to suggest something about my personal feelings, you are to disregard it, as the Court just instructed you. And the same is true of the district attorney. So watch that. Sometimes we're human. We use the word and we don't mean to.

"Now, let's go back to the significance in our legal system of the presumption of innocence and the fact that Mr. Tyler does not have the burden of proof, has no burden. [¶] What does that mean? What does it mean to say that you have to presume that the accused is innocent? [¶] I submit to you that it means nothing different than what I said a few minutes ago. [¶] Now, Mr. Tyler can do no more than through his plea tell you that he is not guilty, that he denies all the allegations." (Emphasis added.)

Defendant argues that the trial court's comments were improper and prejudicial in that they conveyed the message that defense counsel could not and did not believe defendant was innocent. * * *

* * *

Defendant also asserts that the trial court erred in applying to defense counsel a rule that is applicable only to prosecutors. We cannot agree. It is well established that a prosecutor may not express a personal opinion as to the defendant's guilt because of the danger that jurors will interpret the opinion as being based on facts at the prosecutor's command which were not adduced at trial. Although we have been cited to no case applying that rule to prohibit defense counsel from expressing a personal opinion as to the defendant's innocence, we find no reason why defense counsel are not equally barred from expressing their personal beliefs. Jurors are just as likely to interpret defense counsel's remarks as being based on outside knowledge. As the Attorney General correctly notes, rule 5–200(E) of the Rules of Professional Conduct prohibits all attorneys from asserting personal knowledge of the facts at issue.[1]

In the present case, however, we agree that defense counsel's remarks were not objectionable. They were in the nature of argument,

---

1. Rule 5–200(E) of the Rules of Professional Conduct decrees that in presenting a matter at court, an attorney "[s]hall not assert personal knowledge of the facts at issue, except when testifying as a witness."

urging the jury to find defendant innocent, rather than expressions of a personal belief. Nevertheless, we perceive no harm resulting from the trial court's comments. The trial court explained that an expression of opinion is improper because the defendant is presumed innocent. Defense counsel, too, emphasized the presumption of innocence.

* * *

The judgment is affirmed.

"PROFESSIONAL RESPONSIBILITY OF THE CRIMINAL DEFENSE LAWYER: THE THREE HARDEST QUESTIONS"

Monroe Freedman, 64 Mich.L.Rev. 1469 (1966).

In almost any area of legal counseling and advocacy, the lawyer may be faced with the dilemma of either betraying the confidential communications of his client or participating to some extent in the purposeful deception of the court. This problem is nowhere more acute than in the practice of criminal law, particularly in the representation of the indigent accused. The purpose of this article is to analyze and attempt to resolve three of the most difficult issues in this general area:

1. Is it proper to cross-examine for the purpose of discrediting the reliability or credibility of an adverse witness whom you know to be telling the truth?

2. Is it proper to put a witness on the stand when you know he will commit perjury?

3. Is it proper to give your client legal advice when you have reason to believe that the knowledge you give him will tempt him to commit perjury?

These questions present serious difficulties with respect to a lawyer's ethical responsibilities. Moreover, if one admits the possibility of an affirmative answer, it is difficult even to discuss them without appearing to some to be unethical. It is not surprising, therefore, that reasonable, rational discussion of these issues has been uncommon and that the problems have for so long remained unresolved. In this regard it should be recognized that the Canons of Ethics, which were promulgated in 1908 "as a general guide," are both inadequate and self-contradictory.

* * *

The first[c] of the difficult problems posed above will now be considered: Is it proper to cross-examine for the purpose of discrediting the reliability or the credibility of a witness whom you know to be telling the

---

c. This passage presents Professor Freedman's thoughts on the first problem only. For his thoughts on the other two, see 64 Mich.L.Rev. 1469 (1966); see also, Monroe Freedman, Understanding Lawyers' Ethics 161–71 (1990) where Professor Freedman expands on and partly modifies his views on this issue.

truth? Assume the following situation. Your client has been falsely accused of a robbery committed at 16th and P Streets at 11:00 p.m. He tells you at first that at no time on the evening of the crime was he within six blocks of that location. However, you are able to persuade him that he must tell you the truth and that doing so will in no way prejudice him. He then reveals to you that he was at 15th and P Streets at 10:55 that evening, but that he was walking east, away from the scene of the crime, and that, by 11:00 p.m., he was six blocks away. At the trial, there are two prosecution witnesses. The first mistakenly, but with some degree of persuasion, identifies your client as the criminal. At that point, the prosecution's case depends on this single witness, who might or might not be believed. Since your client has a prior record, you do not want to put him on the stand, but you feel that there is at least a chance for acquittal. The second prosecution witness is an elderly woman who is somewhat nervous and who wears glasses. She testifies truthfully and accurately that she saw your client at 15th and P Streets at 10:55 p.m. She has corroborated the erroneous testimony of the first witness and made conviction virtually certain. However, if you destroy her reliability through cross-examination designed to show that she is easily confused and has poor eyesight, you may not only eliminate the corroboration, but also cast doubt in the jury's mind on the prosecution's entire case. On the other hand, if you should refuse to cross-examine her because she is telling the truth, your client may well feel betrayed, since you knew of the witness's veracity only because your client confided in you, under your assurance that his truthfulness would not prejudice him.

The client would be right. Viewed strictly, the attorney's failure to cross-examine would not be violative of the client's confidence because it would not constitute a disclosure. However, the same policy that supports the obligation of confidentiality precludes the attorney from prejudicing his client's interest in any other way because of knowledge gained in his professional capacity. When a lawyer fails to cross-examine only because his client, placing confidence in the lawyer, has been candid with him, the basis for such confidence and candor collapses. Our legal system cannot tolerate such a result.

> The purposes and necessities of the relation between a client and his attorney require, in many cases, on the part of the client, the fullest and freest disclosures to the attorney of the client's objects, motives and acts * * *. To permit the attorney to reveal to others what is so disclosed, would be not only a gross violation of a sacred trust upon his part, but it would utterly destroy and prevent the usefulness and benefits to be derived from professional assistance.

The client's confidences must "upon all occasions be inviolable," to avoid the "greater mischiefs" that would probably result if a client could not feel free "to repose [confidence] in the attorney to whom he resorts for legal advice and assistance." Destroy that confidence, and "a man would not venture to consult any skillful person, or would only dare to tell his counsellor half his case."

Therefore, one must conclude that the attorney is obligated to attack, if he can, the reliability or credibility of an opposing witness whom he knows to be truthful. The contrary result would inevitably impair the "perfect freedom of consultation by client with attorney," which is "essential to the administration of justice."

WHY I DEFEND GUILTY CLIENTS

Barry T. Winston [d]

Let me tell you a story. A true story. The court records are all there if anyone wants to check. It's three years ago. I'm sitting in my office, staring out the window, when I get a call from a lawyer I hardly know. Tax lawyer. Some kid is in trouble and would I be interested in helping him out? He's charged with manslaughter, a felony, and driving under the influence. I tell him sure, have the kid call me.

So the kid calls and makes an appointment to see me. He's a nice kid, fresh out of college, and he's come down here to spend some time with his older sister, who's in med school. One day she tells him they're invited to a cookout with some friends of hers. She's going directly from class and he's going to take her car and meet her there. It's way out in the country, but he gets there before she does, introduces himself around, and pops a beer. She shows up after a while and he pops another beer. Then he eats a hamburger and drinks a third beer. At some point his sister says, "Well, it's about time to go," and they head for the car.

And the kid tells me, sitting there in my office, the next thing he remembers, he's waking up in a hospital room, hurting like hell, bandages and casts all over him, and somebody is telling him he's charged with manslaughter and DUI because he wrecked his sister's car, killed her in the process, and blew fourteen on the Breathalyzer. I ask him what the hell he means by "the next thing he remembers," and he looks me straight in the eye and says he can't remember anything from the time they leave the cookout until he wakes up in the hospital. He tells me the doctors say he has postretrograde amnesia. I say of course I believe him, but I'm worried about finding a judge who'll believe him.

I agree to represent him and send somebody for a copy of the wreck report. It says there are four witnesses: a couple in a car going the other way who passed the kid and his sister just before their car ran off the road, the guy whose front yard they landed in, and the trooper who investigated. I call the guy whose yard they ended up in. He isn't home. I leave word. Then I call the couple. The wife agrees to come in

d. © 1986, *Harper's Magazine.* Mr. Winston's article first appeared under the title, "Stranger Than True: Why I Defend Guilty Clients," at page 70 of the December, 1986, issue of *Harper's.* It is reprinted here with special permission. Mr. Winston is a 1961 graduate of the University of North Carolina School of Law. He is engaged in general civil and criminal trial practice in Chapel Hill, North Carolina.

the next day with her husband. While I'm talking to her, the first guy calls. I call him back, introduce myself, tell him I'm representing the kid and need to talk to him about the accident. He hems and haws and I figure he's one of those people who think it's against the law to talk to defense lawyers. I say the D.A. will tell him it's O.K. to talk to me, but he doesn't have to. I give him the name and number of the D.A. and he says he'll call me back.

Then I go out and hunt up the trooper. He tells me the whole story. The kid and his sister are coming into town on Smith Level Road, after it turns from fifty-five to forty-five. The Thornes—the couple—are heading out of town. They say this sports car passes them, going the other way, right after that bad turn just south of the new subdivision. They say it's going like a striped-ass ape, at least sixty-five or seventy. Mrs. Thorne turns around to look and Mr. Thorne watches in the rearview mirror. They both see the same thing: halfway into the curve, the car runs off the road on the right, whips back onto the road, spins, runs off on the left, and disappears. They turn around in the first driveway they come to and start back, both terrified of what they're going to find. By this time, Trooper Johnson says, the guy whose front yard the car has ended up in has pulled the kid and his sister out of the wreck and started CPR on the girl. Turns out he's an emergency medical technician. Holloway, that's his name. Johnson tells me that Holloway says he's sitting in his front room, watching television, when he hears a hell of a crash in his yard. He runs outside and finds the car flipped over, and so he pulls the kid out from the driver's side, the girl from the other side. She dies in his arms.

And that, says Trooper Johnson, is that. The kid's blood/alcohol content was fourteen, he was going way too fast, and the girl is dead. He had to charge him. It's a shame, he seems a nice kid, it was his own sister and all, but what the hell can he do, right?

The next day the Thornes come in, and they confirm everything Johnson said. By now things are looking not so hot for my client, and I'm thinking it's about time to have a little chat with the D.A. But Holloway still hasn't called me back, so I call him. Not home. Leave word. No call. I wait a couple of days and call again. Finally I get him on the phone. He's very agitated, and won't talk to me except to say that he doesn't have to talk to me.

I know I better look for a deal, so I go to the D.A. He's very sympathetic. But. There's only so far you can get on sympathy. A young woman is dead, promising career cut short, all because somebody has too much to drink and drives. The kid has to pay. Not, the D.A. says, with jail time. But he's got to plead guilty to two misdemeanors: death by vehicle and driving under the influence. That means probation, a big fine. Several thousand dollars. Still, it's hard for me to criticize the D.A. After all, he's probably going to have the MADD mothers all over him because of reducing the felony to a misdemeanor.

On the day of the trial, I get to court a few minutes early. There are the Thornes and Trooper Johnson, and someone I assume is Holloway. Sure enough, when this guy sees me, he comes over and introduces himself and starts right in: "I just want you to know how serious all this drinking and driving really is," he says. "If those young people hadn't been drinking and driving that night, that poor young girl would be alive today." Now, I'm trying to hold my temper when I spot the D.A. I bolt across the room, grab him by the arm, and say, "We gotta talk. Why the hell have you got all those people here? That jerk Holloway. Surely to God you're not going to call him as a witness. This is a guilty plea! My client's parents are sitting out there. You don't need to put them through a dog-and-pony show."

The D.A. looks at me and says, "Man, I'm sorry, but in a case like this, I gotta put on witnesses. Weird Wally is on the bench. If I try to go without witnesses, he might throw me out."

The D.A. calls his first witness. Trooper Johnson identifies himself, tells about being called to the scene of the accident, and describes what he found when he got there and what everybody told him. After he finishes, the judge looks at me. "No questions," I say. Then the D.A. calls Holloway. He describes the noise, running out of the house, the upside down car in his yard, pulling my client out of the window on the left side of the car and then going around to the other side for the girl. When he gets to this part, he really hits his stride. He describes, in minute detail, the injuries he saw and what he did to try and save her life. And then he tells, breath by breath, how she died in his arms.

The D.A. says, "No further questions, your Honor." The judge looks at me. I shake my head, and he says to Holloway, "You may step down."

One of those awful silences hangs there, and nothing happens for a minute. Holloway doesn't move. Then he looks at me, and at the D.A., and then at the judge. He says, "Can I say something else, your Honor?"

All my bells are ringing at once, and my gut is screaming at me, Object! Object! I'm trying to decide in three-quarters of a second whether it'll be worse to listen to a lecture on the evils of drink from this jerk Holloway or piss off the judge by objecting. But all I say is, "No objections, your Honor." The judge smiles at me, then at Holloway, and says, "Very well, Mr. Holloway. What did you wish to say?"

It all comes out in a rush. "Well, you see, your Honor," Holloway says, "it was just like I told Trooper Johnson. It all happened so fast. I heard the noise, and I came running out, and it was night, and I was excited, and the next morning, when I had a chance to think about it, I figured out what had happened, but by then I'd already told Trooper Johnson and I didn't know what to do, but you see, the car, it was upside down, and I did pull that boy out of the lefthand window, but don't you see, the car was upside down, and if you turned it over on its wheels like it's suppose to be, the left-hand side is really on the right hand side, and your Honor, that boy wasn't driving that car at all. It was the girl that was driving, and when I had a chance to think about it the next morning, I realized that I'd told Trooper Johnson wrong, and I was scared and I didn't know what to do, and that's why"—and now he's looking right at me—"why I wouldn't talk to you."

Naturally, the defendant is allowed to withdraw his guilty plea. The charges are dismissed and the kid and his parents and I go into one of the back rooms in the courthouse and sit there looking at one another for a while. Finally we recover enough to mumble some Oh my Gods and Thank yous and You're welcomes. And that's why I can stand to represent somebody when I know he's guilty.

MULTIPLE CHOICE QUESTIONS

Answer these questions under the ABA Code and ABA
Model Rules

1. The court has appointed you to defend Charles Carter at his trial for kidnapping. Carter is an indigent person, and he suffers a mild form of mental handicap. (After appropriate investigation, you have concluded that his handicap is not so severe as to require the appointment of a guardian to act for him.) One of the key elements of kidnapping is "asportation," that is, moving the victim from one place to another. In doing legal research for Carter's case, you have found an old decision of the highest court of the state which clearly holds that the kind of conduct with which Carter is charged *cannot* constitute asportation. The precise point has not been considered in any later decision in this state. You believe that the old decision is unsound; it makes no common sense, and it is against the trend of more modern decisions in other jurisdictions. You are pondering what use, if any, to make of the decision in defending Carter. You have talked over the problem with Carter, but he was unable to grasp the subtlety of it, and he ended up telling you to do whatever you thought was best. Which of the following *should* you do in this situation?

A. Cite the old decision to the court and inform the court *ex parte* of your doubts about its continued validity.

B. Ignore the old decision and base Carter's defense on whatever other grounds are available.

C. Use the old decision in whatever way you think will be of most value to Carter's defense, even though you believe that the old decision is unsound.

D. Take the problem up with Carter a second time, explaining it to him as best you can, and letting him make the ultimate decision about what to do.

2. District Attorney Smith is faced with making a decision about whether or not to bring criminal charges against one Elmo Owens. Which of the following factors *may* Smith consider in making her decision?

I.   That the punishment for this crime is, in Smith's opinion, much more harsh than Owens' particular case would warrant.

II.   That Smith herself has a reasonable doubt about Owen's guilt.

III.   That the alleged victim of the crime is reluctant to testify about it.

IV.   That the person who made the complaint about Owens may have been motivated by a desire to "get even" with Owens over a different matter.

V.   That Owens is willing and able to cooperate in the apprehension and conviction of another person who seems clearly guilty of a related course of criminal conduct.

    A.   All of the above.

    B.   None of the above.

    C.   II only.

    D.   II, III, and IV only.

3.   Deputy District Attorney Sanford has been assigned to prosecute defendant Rossi for arson.   Shortly after the fire was extinguished, a three-person team of arson experts was sent by the City fire department to determine the cause of the fire.   The team concluded that the fire was set by a professional arsonist, and the team's report so states.   Shortly before trial, Sanford learned that Beaumont, the youngest and least experienced member of the team, had originally concluded that the fire resulted from an explosion in the furnace.   Beaumont had tried to convince the other two team members that his conclusion was correct, but they ultimately prevailed, and Beaumont signed the report without dissent.   Sanford does not plan to offer the report in evidence at trial, and he does not plan to call any of the three team members as witnesses.   Rather, he plans to use the testimony of two independent experts to establish that arson caused the fire.   Which of the following *should* Sanford do concerning the information about Beaumont?

    A.   Disclose it to Rossi's counsel, since it may be useful in Rossi's defense.

    B.   Recommend to his superior that the charges against Rossi be dismissed, since the information creates a reasonable doubt about Rossi's guilt.

    C.   Wait to see whether Rossi's counsel asks for the information in the regular course of criminal discovery.

    D.   Do nothing about it since he does not plan to offer the report or the testimony of the team members at the trial.

4.   Lawyer Loach represents the Alliance for Nature as plaintiff in a suit against the State Highway Commission to block construction of an eight lane freeway across tidal wetlands that serve as a breeding and feeding ground for ducks, geese, and other migratory waterfowl.   The judge heard eight days of live testimony at a hearing on plaintiff's

motion for a preliminary injunction. Loach's closing argument to the judge includes the following passages; which of them are *proper*?

I. Your Honor has heard the testimony of the so-called "experts" on behalf of the Commission. Your Honor has heard that every one of these "impartial scientists" is on the regular staff payroll of the Commission. These people earn their daily bread by going around testifying in favor of State highway projects! Can Your Honor possibly believe that they are impartial in what they say?

II. I've heard tell that Your Honor's father was the best duck hunter in this county—one of the best in the whole state. And I've heard tell that you, too, are a mighty fine shot, Your Honor, and that your first love is getting out in the wilds on a foggy morning with your two fine Golden Labrador retrievers, in search of ducks. How will Your Honor feel when the foggy quiet is replaced by the roar of trucks and the stink of the exhaust fumes? And what would your father have thought about it, God rest his soul?

III. At this hearing, there simply wasn't time to present to the Court all the reasons why this freeway would be a disaster. But for twenty years or so, I've been an avid member of the Audubon Society, and I've spent many hours out in those wetlands watching birds. I'd say there are at least fifteen species of waterfowl that breed there every spring. That's their last small sanctuary in this part of the State. Without it, they will disappear. And the State Highway Commissioners want to take it away.

IV. Your Honor heard the testimony of Chief Commissioner Smeltzer. Your Honor examined a copy of the judgment convicting him of federal tax evasion—a felony, Your Honor. Your Honor heard citizens of this county testify under oath that Chief Commissioner Smeltzer's reputation for truthfulness is deplorable. Your Honor will have to decide for himself whether to believe a single word Commissioner Smeltzer uttered on this witness stand.

    A. I, III, and IV only.

    B. II only.

    C. II, III, and IV only.

    D. I and IV only.

5. In a complicated commercial law case brought by Parker Finance Company against Dumont National Bank, Parker's lawyer dawdled through three years of pretrial discovery. In exasperation, the judge finally set the case for trial in 30 days. A week before the trial date, Parker's lawyer filed a last minute notice to take the depositions of seven non-party witnesses. One of them was Katzenmeier, a retired executive who was once Dumont's president. Katzenmeier left Dumont with ill-feelings, but he remained on friendly terms with Dennert, Dumont's lawyer in the *Parker* case. On Saturday afternoon, Katzenmeier telephoned Dennert and said:

A little bird just told me that Parker's lawyer wants to take my deposition Tuesday afternoon. I haven't been served with a subpoena yet, but I guess one is coming, and I want to know what to do. If I'm asked the right questions, I'm going to have to say some things that will hurt Dumont and will hurt me too. My wife and I have plans to leave Tuesday morning for a year-long tour of South America. We've been planning this trip ever since I retired, and we've had the plane tickets and itinerary set for over nine months. If I have to stay around for this deposition, it's going to wreck our entire schedule and cost us a bundle for new plane tickets. What do you think I ought to do?

How *should* Dennert respond?

A. "Katz, you know I'd be happy to advise you on this if I could, but I can't. I think you should call your own lawyer right away, because you do need some legal advice in this situation."

B. "Katz, there's no reason for you and your wife to ruin your travel plans just to be nice to Parker. The judge is already mad because they've stalled so long. Just make sure no process server finds you between now and Tuesday."

C. "Katz, don't worry about a thing. If a process server happens to tag you between now and Tuesday, just toss the subpoena in the trash. I'll make sure the judge understands the situation."

D. "Katz, you are in a tough position here. If I were you, I'd call up Parker's lawyer and try to work out something reasonable."

6. Lawyer Lester represented the wife in a dissolution of marriage proceeding in State X. The court entered a final order of dissolution, awarded custody of the children to the wife, enjoined the husband from having any contact with the children until further order of the court, and ordered the husband to pay child support and alimony to the wife. A State X statute permits court orders in domestic relations cases to be enforced by criminal contempt proceedings. The statute also authorizes courts to appoint private attorneys as special prosecutors in such criminal contempt proceedings. The husband in the above case repeatedly contacted his children in violation of the court order; further, he repeatedly failed to make the required alimony and child support payments. Lester sought and obtained a court order appointing him as special prosecutor in proceedings to punish the husband for criminal contempt. At the contempt hearing, when cross-examining the husband and when making his closing argument, Lester repeatedly referred to the husband as "Sammy Scofflaw," "Sam the wife-beater," and "the child molester." There was no evidence in either the dissolution proceeding or the contempt proceeding to suggest that the husband had molested children or beat his wife.

I. Lester is *subject to discipline* for his comments about wife beating and child molesting.

II. It was *proper* for Lester to seek and accept appointment as special prosecutor in the criminal contempt proceeding.

III.   Lester's comments about wife beating and child molesting were *proper* expressions of personal opinion.

IV.   Lester *should* have declined to serve as special prosecutor in the criminal contempt proceeding.

> A.   II and III only.
>
> B.   I and II only.
>
> C.   I and IV only.
>
> D.   III and IV only.

Chapter Eleven

CONFLICTS OF INTEREST— LAWYERS, CLIENTS, AND THIRD PARTIES

What This Chapter Covers

Reading Assignment

Wydick & Perschbacher, Chapter 11

ABA Model Rules:

    Rules 1.2, 1.7, 1.8, 1.10, 1.13, 1.14, 2.1, 3.7, and 5.4(c).

CRPC 1–600, 3–120, 3–300, 3–310, 3–320, 3–600, 4–210, 4–300, 4–400 and 5–210.

Cal.Bus. & Prof.Code § 6106.8.

Supplemental Reading

ABA Code:

    EC 5–1 through 5–13; EC 5–21 through 5–24; EC 7–7 through 7–12;

DR 2–103(D)(4), DR 5–101 through 5–104, DR 5–107(A) and (B), and DR 7–101.

Hazard & Hodes:

Discussion of ABA Model Rules 1.2, 1.7, 1.8, 1.10, 1.13, 1.14, 2.1, 3.7, and 5.4(c).

Wolfram:

Sections 4.2 through 4.7 (respective authority of attorney and client);

Sections 7.1.1 through 7.1.7 (general principles of conflicts of interest);

Sections 7.2.1 through 7.2.4 (effect of client consent to conflict);

Sections 7.5.1 through 7.5.2 (trial lawyer as witness);

Sections 7.6.1 through 7.6.6 (imputed disqualification);

Sections 8.3.1 through 8.3.5 (corporations and other entities as clients);

Sections 8.4.1 through 8.4.3 (indemnity insurance conflicts);

Sections 8.8.1 through 8.8.4 (conflicts due to third party control);

Sections 8.11.1 through 8.11.5 (business dealings with client);

Sections 8.12.1 through 8.12.4 (gifts and favors from client).

Restatement (Third) of the Law Governing Lawyers §§ 27–28, 31–34, 38–39, 48, 55, 201–204, 206–208, 212, 215–216 (Proposed Final Draft No. 1, 1996).

Discussion Problems

1. Attorney Wharton's law practice consists primarily of insurance defense work. Hamilton Casualty Co. has hired her to defend Silas Combs in a negligence case. The plaintiff in the case alleges that Combs' rice field was plowed negligently, so as to cause a large quantity of water to escape into plaintiff's adjoining tomato field. The water caused plaintiff's tomatoes to rot before harvest. Plaintiff's complaint demands $125,000 in damages. Combs' insurance policy with Hamilton Casualty has a top liability limit of $100,000. After extensive discovery, the case was set for trial. Six weeks before the trial date, plaintiff's lawyer called Wharton and offered to settle the case for $90,000. What are Wharton's ethical obligations in this situation?

2. Consider the following transcript. It depicts a meeting between Glenn Sparks (the president of a large electric appliance manufacturing corporation) and Helen Wilson (the in-house general counsel for the corporation). Ms. Wilson and Mr. Sparks discuss three legal problems that face the corporation.

The first problem concerns a new stock issue. Ms. Wilson has discovered a potentially embarrassing contingent liability that should be disclosed in the SEC registration statement. Mr. Sparks foresees practical problems if it is disclosed, and he attempts to resolve the issue by relieving Ms. Wilson of her duties in connection with the stock issue.

The second problem concerns a products liability suit in which it appears that the corporation's interests might be served by delay and by putting the plaintiff through expensive discovery proceedings.

The third problem is related to the second. The plaintiff's own discovery in the products liability suit may uncover some highly questionable conduct by the corporation involving secret payments to labor union inspectors. Ms. Wilson has repeatedly advised against this conduct, but to no avail.

As you read the transcript, consider these questions:

● Who is Ms. Wilson's client here?

● Has Mr. Sparks asked Ms. Wilson to do anything that you regard as clearly illegal or clearly unethical?

● If so, has Ms. Wilson sufficiently insulated herself from the illegal or unethical conduct?

● Has she effectively served her client?

IN RE ELECTRO CORPORATION*

SCENE: *The president of a large corporation calls the general counsel to his office to discuss some business matters.*

Secretary: Office of the General Counsel.

Sparks: This is Glenn Sparks. Ask Mrs. Wilson to come in right away.

Secretary: Yes sir.

Receptionist: He's waiting for you.

Sparks: Where the hell did you dig this up?

Wilson: We found it by accident. It surprised me too.

Sparks: Why didn't you find it six months ago before I took over?

Wilson: It was a fluke. Normally no one would be looking for something like this, Glenn. When we started to prepare the SEC registration statement on that new stock issue, we just hired a new attorney. I asked him to track down all possible contingent liabilities, just to give him some practice. Of course, he reviewed the abstract of title. That's when it turned up.

Sparks: So you're telling me that the corner of our main plant sits on Katchitorian's property, huh?

Wilson: I'm afraid so.

---

* Reprinted with permission of the American Bar Association.

Sparks: That S.O.B. He's fought this company for years.

Wilson: The defect qualifies as a contingent liability. It'll have to be disclosed in the registration statement.

Sparks: Damn it. Katchitorian will be all over us the minute the word gets out * * * No one else knows about this but you and me. Is that right?

Wilson: Um, the lawyer who found it, but no one else, and I doubt anyone will be looking for it. The irony is that in another six months it would solve itself. We'd be able to acquire clear title by adverse possession.

Sparks: Six months! We can't delay the stock offering that long.

Wilson: Well, that would solve the disclosure problem.

Sparks: Yes, but what would happen to stockholder confidence? All of a sudden, for no apparent reason, the industry's leading corporation delays an offering that everyone's already expecting. Do you realize what that could mean to the company?

Wilson: It's a messy situation, Glenn. I think you should take it back to the board.

Sparks: The board? I can't do that. I've got the board's approval. The details are my responsibility. You know my policy, we can handle this at staff level. I'll be damned if I'm going to go back and tell them our factory is sitting on someone else's property.

Wilson: Well, I can't approve the registration statement, not unless everything's there.

Sparks: There's a way out of this. You won't have to approve, Helen. I'll retain outside counsel to handle this. That was our original plan, anyway.

Wilson: But what about accounting? They still might want to talk, and if they ask me directly, I'll have to tell the truth.

Sparks: I'll tell them to talk to the outside firm. They won't know anything about it. If they insist on seeing you, well let's hope that they don't ask you the direct question. Then it won't have to come out, will it?

Wilson: I'll do whatever you want me to, Glenn, but I want you to know the liabilities at issue here, and I also want to make it clear to you that I will have to respond if I'm asked. Frankly, I'm most worried about the board, about not telling them.

Sparks: I understand, Helen * * * I'm taking you off the registration altogether and we'll let our accountants and the outside attorneys hammer it out. That'll get you off the hook, won't it? Does it sound okay to you?

Wilson: Alright. If they don't come looking for me, I won't go looking for them.

Sparks: Okay, that takes care of that problem. Now I've got another one for you.

Wilson: The registration statement?

Sparks: No, it's about that other matter you've been pestering me about. That lawsuit. You know, the toaster that started the fire, where the fellow got burned?

Wilson: Oh yes. I was going to ask you about that.

Sparks: I ordered an engineering review to see if the filament could actually reach a temperature hot enough to start the fire.

Wilson: What did they find out?

Sparks: Well, there may be a problem. It's not that clear, but the tests seem to indicate about ten percent of the toasters coming off the line are below our safety levels. The engineers need to run more tests, but that'll take time. We're going to have to stall.

Wilson: Um, the plaintiff's attorney will start discovery any day, Glenn. We can't delay indefinitely.

Sparks: I know, I know.

Wilson: Well, we just can't risk it. If it gets out that non-union truckers delivered the shipments, you know what that means.

Sparks: That'll lead to the under the table payments.

Wilson: From a highly irregular corporate slush fund.

Sparks: I'm trying to stop that, Helen. We don't need payoffs to stay on top.

Wilson: It's got to stop. That's for sure. We could have some problems with criminal liability here. I've been saying that for years.

Sparks: I really inherited a mess here. It's been going on for so long, it's hard to change.

Wilson: It could hurt the company if it gets out, Glenn. Even if you put a stop to it before then, the accountants might want to look at this as well.

Sparks: I know, I know. This is all top priority with me—you know that—but I can't perform miracles. We've got to stall for time.

Wilson: Then why not settle this one? You're going to buy a bunch of lawsuits if this goes to court.

Sparks: Oh, I doubt it. Most people won't have the kind of injuries this guy did. And we're going to settle this one, just as soon as he decides he can't hold us up.

Wilson: Well, I'm sure he'd be willing to adjust the damages. I think it's a mistake for his lawyers to start taking depositions.

Sparks: I talked this over with Ned Franks, our insurance lawyer. I'd like the two of you to work together and delay it for a while. Raise every technicality and objection you can to the discovery request and make it expensive. I doubt the plaintiff is ready for a real fight when he sees that it's going to be an expensive, long, drawn-out litigation. I'm betting that he'll settle for something more reasonable.

Wilson: I told Franks to tell plaintiff's attorney that his time will be well compensated in the event of a settlement.

Sparks: Did he think that would work?

Wilson: Yes. And he's a good judge of things like that. I told him I'd do whatever I could to help out.

Sparks: You can help me too, Helen. Stay on top of this mess, will you? Keep me informed. I'd really appreciate that.

Wilson: Will do.

Sparks: Thanks, Helen.

3.   After attorney Sarah graduated from law school, she opened her own law office in a small seaside village. She longs for a cottage on the beach, but she has been unable to find one at the right price. Client Willis has retained her to help him find a way out of his financial distress. Among his few solid assets is a lovely cottage on a secluded end of the beach. Willis has been unable to pay the taxes on the cottage, and Sarah has advised him to put it up for public auction.

   a.   At the auction, may Sarah have her brother bid for her as undisclosed principal?

   b.   Suppose, instead, that Sarah simply agrees to buy the cottage directly from Willis, subject to the tax debt. Under what, if any, circumstances would that be proper?

   c.   Suppose, instead, that Sarah agrees to lend Willis enough money to pay off the back taxes on his cottage. Under what, if any, circumstances would that be proper?

4.   Jefferson and Herchberger are involved in a boundary line suit concerning twelve acres of land that lies in a valley between their two farms. Lawyer Lennihan represents Herchberger in the suit.

   a.   May Lennihan purchase from Jefferson a 30% interest in that twelve acres?

   b.   May Lennihan purchase from Herchberger a 30% interest in that twelve acres?

   c.   May Lennihan agree with Herchberger to do the legal work in exchange for a 30% interest in that twelve acres if Herchberger wins the suit?

5.   Client Curt hired attorney Annette to advise him during some difficult business negotiations with Danforth Corporation. The negotiations extended over many months; during that time, Annette developed

a good working relationship with Curt and a thorough understanding of the factual and legal problems at hand. Only four people were present at the negotiating sessions: Curt, Annette, Danforth's vice-president, and Danforth's house counsel. Ultimately the negotiations failed, and Danforth sued Curt. A key contested issue at trial will be whether Curt made a certain statement during one of the negotiating sessions. Curt wants Annette to represent him at trial, but Danforth has moved to disqualify her on the ground that she may have to testify about Curt's making the alleged statement.

    a. Should the court grant the motion to disqualify?

    b. May Annette's law partner, Elmwood, serve as Curt's trial lawyer?

    c. Does your answer to either question depend on whether Annette's testimony would be for Curt or against Curt?

6. For many years, attorney Alice has looked after the legal and financial affairs of her client Chadbourne, an aged widower. Chadbourne has asked Alice to prepare a new will for him, but he does not know whom to name as executor. He does not want an institutional executor, and he has no suitable friends or relatives.

    a. May Alice suggest herself as executrix?

    b. May Alice accept as thanks for all her kindness to Chadbourne over the years a modest picture frame she has admired when visiting Chadbourne's townhome?

    c. May Alice accept Chadbourne's valuable townhome if given to her as a gift? What if it is left to her in Chadbourne's will?

7. The law firm of Shubert, DeWitt, & Howe specializes in family law matters. The firm has three partners and four associate lawyers.

    a. Partner Rhonda Howe is representing client Curt Clinton in a pending dissolution of marriage proceeding. Howe's own marriage was recently dissolved, so she is especially sympathetic to Clinton's situation. On several occasions, she and Clinton have discussed Clinton's legal problems over long dinners. Howe now finds herself quite attracted to Clinton as a person, and she believes the attraction is mutual. What advice would you give Howe in this situation?

    b. Partner Shubert has been asked to represent client Cummings in a child custody dispute with Cummings' ex-husband. The ex-husband is represented by attorney Arnott, a partner in a different law firm. Arnott and Shubert are engaged to be married in the near future. Shubert believes that Cummings' matter could be handled adequately by the senior associate in Shubert's firm. What advice would you give Shubert in this situation?

ALLOCATING DECISION–MAKING BETWEEN LAWYER AND CLIENT

Under the traditional understanding of the lawyer-client relationship, the respective roles of lawyer and client are easy to state, but difficult to apply. The primary relationship is that of agent and principal, but the lawyer-agent's professional obligations require adjustment of the conventional agency relationship. Here is a statement of the more-or-less standard view from the California Supreme Court:

> The allocation of decision-making authority between client and attorney is a difficult problem. It involves practical, ethical and philosophical considerations. (See Burt, Conflict and Trust Between Attorney and Client (1981) *69 Georgetown L.J. 1015;* Note, Balancing Competing Discovery Interests in the Context of the Attorney–Client Relationship: A Trilemma (1983) *56 So.Cal.L.Rev. 1115;* Martyn, Informed Consent in the Practice of Law (1980) *48 Geo. Wash.L.Rev. 307;* Spiegel, Lawyering and Client Decisionmaking: Informed Consent and the Legal Profession (1979) *128 U.Pa.L.Rev. 41;* Spiegel, The New Model Rules of Professional Conduct: Lawyer–Client Decision Making and the Role of Rules in Structuring the Lawyer–Client Dialogue, 1980 Am.Bar Found. Research J. 1003; Lehman, The Pursuit of a Client's Interest (1979) *77 Mich.L.Rev. 1078.*) Clear guidance on the scope of an attorney's implied and apparent authority and the legal consequences of the allocation of that authority would benefit both attorneys and clients. Unfortunately, the majority fail to give any guidance.

> A reading of the cases and authorities reveals that when courts refer to "substantial rights," they mean important or "essential" rights, rights " 'affecting the merits of the cause' " or "serious steps" in the litigation. For example, the decision to settle or dismiss a cause of action affects a "substantial right," and an attorney must obtain the client's consent before taking either action. Similarly, because a "substantial right" is affected, an attorney has no independent authority to waive the right to appeal, to eliminate an essential defense, to dispose of a client's property, or to stipulate to a finding of negligence irrespective of the record.

> When no substantial right is implicated, an attorney must be free to act independently. It is essential to the efficient conduct of the client's case and the accomplishment of the client's ultimate goals that an attorney have the authority to make independent decisions in the day-to-day management of civil litigation. This authority "[allows] the lawyer-professional to apply his technical expertise[.]" (Spiegel, The New Model Rules of Professional Conduct: Lawyer–Client Decision Making and the Role of Rules in Structuring the Lawyer–Client Dialogue, supra, Am.Bar Found. Research J. at p. 1004.) It also protects the lawyer's professional reputation and preserves the lawyer's role as an officer of the court.

The effective management of litigation requires independent decisions by the attorney regarding not only procedural matters but also certain substantive matters—for example, it may include the legal theories or arguments to be advanced. Routine and technical matters, including those ordinary matters which arise in the course of litigation, may be handled independently by the attorney as a necessary aspect of the professional management of the case. On the other hand, decisions which affect "substantial rights," whether they be denominated "procedural" or "substantive," must involve the client.

Rather than define the standard as "substantial rights" versus "procedural matters," the inquiry should seek to differentiate between decisions affecting important, substantial rights and decisions on routine matters. This approach would provide the practitioner with more useful guidance.

Blanton v. Womancare, Inc., 38 Cal.3d 396, 409–10, 696 P.2d 645, 653–55, 212 Cal.Rptr. 151, 159–60 (1985) (Bird, C.J., concurring). [*See also* ABA Model Rule 1.2.]

Applying these rules becomes even more complicated when the identity of the client is elusive or when more than one representative claims to speak for the client. In this chapter we first take up the problem of conflicts between directions from the client and others who may purport to speak for the client or represent the "true" interests of the client. We next take up the issue of determining just who is the client. Finally, the chapter deals with conflicts between the interests of the client and those of the client's own lawyer.

EMPLOYERS INSURANCE OF WAUSAU v. ALBERT D. SEENO CONSTRUCTION CO.

United States District Court, N.D.California, 1988.
692 F.Supp. 1150.

[Plaintiff, Employers Insurance of Wausau ("Wausau"), issued various insurance policies to defendant, Albert D. Seeno Construction Company ("Seeno"), a real estate developer, in connection with Seeno's construction of a large number of homes. Buyers of several hundred Seeno homes brought claims against Seeno for construction defects. After Seeno submitted the claims to Wausau, Wausau and Seeno disagreed over whether the claims were covered by Wausau's policies. Wausau reserved its rights to deny coverage, and Seeno exercised its rights to obtain independent *Cumis* counsel paid for by Wausau.[1] After further disagreements arose, Wausau brought this action, seeking a declaration it is not liable for the third-party claims. Wausau moved to disqualify

---

1. *See, e.g., San Diego Navy Federal Credit Union v. Cumis Ins. Society, Inc.,* 162 Cal.App.3d 358, 208 Cal.Rptr. 494 (1984) (clearly establishing insured's right to select independent counsel paid for by insurer where an actual or potential conflict has arisen between insured and insurer); * * *.

Seeno's counsel, Archer; and Seeno cross-moved to disqualify Wausau's primary counsel, Robins.]

* * *

I. CROSS-MOTIONS TO DISQUALIFY UNDER CUMIS

Both parties bring motions to disqualify based on alleged breaches of the duties of counsel in the *Cumis* context, i.e., where the insured has exercised its right to select independent counsel paid for by the insurer because a conflict or potential conflict has arisen between the insurer and the insured. In brief, the insurer Wausau argues that the insured Seeno's choice of *Cumis* counsel, the Archer firm, has failed properly to represent Wausau's interests. Seeno, on the other hand, argues that the counsel chosen by Wausau, the Robins firm, has failed properly to represent Seeno's interests.

A. *Wausau's Motion to Disqualify the Archer Firm*

Plaintiff's first argument for disqualification of Seeno's counsel Archer is based on that firm's conceded double role as 1) *Cumis* counsel opposing liability in the underlying home buyers' claims, and 2) counsel asserting coverage by Wausau.[3] Plaintiff argues that in its *Cumis* counsel role Archer is representing Wausau as well as Seeno, and that it is therefore an improper concurrent representation of adverse interests for Archer to represent Seeno in a coverage dispute such as the instant case, where Seeno's interests are directly adverse to Wausau.[4]

Plaintiff relies chiefly on cases stating that counsel retained by an insurer to defend an insured have both the insured and the insurer as clients. *E.g., Bogard v. Employers Casualty Co.,* 164 Cal.App.3d 602, 609, 210 Cal.Rptr. 578 (1985) ("The attorney hired by the insurance company to defend in an action against the insured owes fiduciary duties to two clients: the insurer and the insured." (citations omitted)). Wausau argues that the *Cumis* line of decisions has not changed the dual duties of liability defense counsel; it simply allows the insured rather

---

3. For clarity, the Court shall use the term "liability" to refer to the potential liability of the insured or the insurer to a third party, and the term "coverage" to refer to the potential liability of the insurer to the insured, unless otherwise indicated.

4. The following are the most pertinent California Rules in this regard:

Rule 4–101. Accepting Employment Adverse to a Client

A member of the State Bar shall not accept employment adverse to a client or former client, without the informed and written consent of the client or former client, relating to a matter in reference to which he has obtained confidential information by reason of or in the course of his employment by such client or former client.

Rule 5–102. Avoiding the Representation of Adverse Interests

(A) A member of the State Bar shall not accept professional employment without first disclosing his relation, if any, with the adverse party, and his interest, if any, in the subject matter of the employment. A member of the State Bar who accepts employment under this rule shall first obtain the client's written consent to such employment.

(B) A member of the State Bar shall not represent conflicting interests, except with the written consent of all parties concerned.

[For current California versions, *see* CRPC 3–310—eds.]

than the insurer to select such counsel. *Cumis* counsel thus always represents both the insured and the insurer.

Wausau views *Cumis* counsel as properly concerned only with minimizing liability to third parties, and as necessarily completely *neutral* with respect to any coverage dispute between its two clients, the insured and the insurer. Accordingly, Wausau asserts that *Cumis* counsel is "independent" not of the insurer but rather in the sense that such counsel seeks to minimize liability in a neutral fashion, independent of any regard for the coverage position of either client. According to this argument, as *Cumis* counsel chosen by Seeno, Archer represents Wausau as well as the insured, and it is therefore a patent conflict for Archer also to represent Seeno's interests against Wausau in this coverage action.

* * *

In *Cumis,* the California Court of Appeal recognized that:

> In the usual tripartite relationship existing between insurer, insured and counsel, there is a single, common interest shared among them. Dual representation by counsel is beneficial since the shared goal of minimizing or eliminating liability to a third party is the same. A different situation is presented, however, when some or all of the allegations in the [third-party] complaint do not fall within the scope of coverage under the policy. In such a case, the standard practice of an insurer is to defend under a reservation of rights where the insurer promises to defend but states it may not indemnify the insured if liability is found.

Id. at 364, 208 Cal.Rptr. 494.

In such situations, the court found, a conflict arises between the insurer and the insured, because it is in the insurer's interest for the third-party action to establish that any liability is outside the coverage of the policy, while it is in the insured's interest to show the opposite. After reviewing the ethical dilemma posed for counsel in this conflict situation, the *Cumis* court held that:

> [T]he [Model Code] Canons of Ethics impose upon lawyers hired by the insurer an obligation to explain to the insured and the insurer the full implications of joint representation in situations where the insurer has reserved its rights to deny coverage. If the insured does not give an informed consent to continued representation, counsel must cease to represent both. Moreover, * * * the insurer must pay the reasonable cost for hiring independent counsel by the insured. The insurer may not compel the insured to surrender control of the litigation.

162 Cal.App.3d at 375, 208 Cal.Rptr. 494 (citations omitted).

* * *

Plaintiff Wausau does not challenge *Cumis* itself and indeed concedes the right and has paid the considerable cost of defendant Seeno to be provided with *Cumis* counsel to defend many of the home buyers' claims. However, Wausau asserts that because the Archer firm is *Cumis* liability counsel, it is impermissible conflict for Archer to serve also as Seeno's coverage counsel. This argument thus requires that the Court determine whether *Cumis* counsel represent or owe duties to the insurer such that *Cumis* counsel cannot represent the insured in coverage disputes with the insurer.

The starting point for determining to whom *Cumis* counsel owe what duties is the seminal California case *Executive Aviation, Inc. v. National Ins. Underwriters,* 16 Cal.App.3d 799, 94 Cal.Rptr. 347 (1971). In finding that an insurer was obligated to pay for the fees of independent counsel selected by the insured, the court followed the "reasonable solution" proposed in *Prashker v. United States Guarantee Co.,* 1 N.Y.2d 584, 154 N.Y.S.2d 910, 136 N.E.2d 871 (1956), stating that:

> [W]here a conflict of interest has arisen between an insurer and its insured, the attorney to defend the insured in the tort suit should be selected by the insured and the reasonable value of the professional services rendered assumed by the insurer. If the insured and the insurer are represented by two different attorneys, each of whom is pledged to promote and protect the prime interests of his client, adequate representation is guaranteed and the deleterious effect of the conflict of interest imposed on an attorney who attempts the difficult task of representing both parties is averted.

Executive Aviation, 16 Cal.App.3d at 809, 94 Cal.Rptr. 347. Like the New York Court of Appeals in *Prashker,* the *Executive Aviation* court thus appears to have assumed that *Cumis* counsel would represent only the insured, and that the insurer would be entitled to counsel that would represent only the insurer.

Similarly, the *Cumis* court itself contemplated that being "the insureds' *independent* counsel" meant representing the insureds, and being independent of the insurer. *Cumis,* 162 Cal.App.3d at 375, 208 Cal.Rptr. 494 (emphasis added). Thus, the court quoted with approval statements such as:

> "Where a question exists as to whether an occurrence is within coverage, independent counsel *representing the insured's interests* is required. The insurer is contractually obligated to pay for *insured's independent counsel.*"

Id. at 374, 208 Cal.Rptr. 494 (quoting Dondanville, *Defense Counsel Beware: The Perils of Conflicts of Interest,* 26 Trial Law.Guide 408, 415 (1982)) (emphasis added). Nor does the *Cumis* court appear to have believed that it is ethically possible to continue joint representation without consent once conflict has arisen. To take another example quoted by the court: " 'once the insurer decides to assert a coverage defense, the same attorney may not represent both the insured and the insurer.' " *Id.* (quoting Committee on Professional Responsibility of the State Bar of Louisiana Opinion No. 342, 22 La.B.J. O–132 [within insert following page 46] (1974)). Indeed, it was precisely because "dual agency" representation is ethically impossible that the *Cumis* court required the insurer to pay for independent counsel for the insureds. *Id.* at 364–65 & n. 4, 374–75, 208 Cal.Rptr. 494. Since the attorney initially chosen by the insurer cannot ethically serve in both such capacities, the same logic requires the conclusion that the *Cumis* attorney for the insured may not either.

Other cases support the same conclusion.[9] For example, in *Bogard,* the court of appeal clearly recognized that *Cumis* counsel is hired to fulfill the insurer's duty to provide "independent counsel to represent the *insured's* interests" in order to avoid "the impossible ethical dilemma with which the attorney representing both insured and insurer in such a [conflict] situation is faced." *Bogard,* 164 Cal.App.3d at 613, 210 Cal.Rptr. 578 (emphasis added); *see also id.* at 614, 210 Cal.Rptr. 578. Likewise in *United Pacific Ins. Co. v. Hall,* 199 Cal.App.3d 551, 245 Cal.Rptr. 99 (1988), the court had no doubt that "[t]he obligation of an insurer to provide independent *Cumis* counsel for an insured is premised on the ethical inability of an attorney to represent conflicting interests." *Id.* at 556, 245 Cal.Rptr. 99 (citation omitted). Nor has the Court discovered any case holding that *Cumis* counsel are somehow exempted from the ethical rules that make it impossible to represent conflicting interests without consent.

Case law thus leaves little doubt that *Cumis* counsel represent solely the insured, and accordingly that there is no ethical requirement that prevents *Cumis* counsel from representing the insured in coverage actions adverse to the insurer as well as in liability matters.[10]

* * *

9. Wausau's attempt to rely on *MGIC Indemnity Corp. v. Weisman,* 803 F.2d 500 (9th Cir.1986), is not compelling, although that case does contain the following broad language:

> When [counsel] took the defense of the suits against the [insureds], the [insureds] were their clients. But it is an untenable simplification to say that they had no duty to the [insurer] they knew would pay the legal fees of the [insureds]. A lawyer may have more than a single client in a lawsuit. A "client" is the person or entity on whose behalf a lawyer acts. [Counsel] were acting for the insurer as well as for the insured[s] * * *.
>
> * * * Anyone paying legal bills would want to know, and would be entitled to know, that the lawyers being paid were the very lawyers who started the suits they were now being compensated to defend. The alleged failure to disclose their activity would have been a breach of the fiduciary duty [counsel] owed [the insurer].

Id. at 504. * * *

* * *

[I]t would certainly be "an untenable simplification," *MGIC,* 803 F.2d at 504, to read *MGIC* as holding that one who pays a lawyer's fee always becomes a client or that the lawyer automatically owes such a person duties of loyalty and candor. *See, e.g., Cumis,* 162 Cal.App.3d 358, 208 Cal.Rptr. 494; Model Code Ethical Canons ("EC") 5–1, 5–21 to 5–23; Model Code Disciplinary Rule ("DR") 5–107(A)–(B); Los Angeles Bar Association Ethics Committee Opinion No. 439 (February 24, 1986) [hereinafter Bar Opinion No. 439] at 5–6.

* * *

10. The Court also notes that an opinion of the Los Angeles Bar Association Ethics Committee on facts quite similar to those in this case has reached the same result, stating that:

> The clear implication of [*Cumis*] is that there is no attorney-client relationship between the insured's counsel and the insurer despite the fact that the insurer is paying for the independent counsel * * *.

At least one other factor indicates that Wausau's view of the role of *Cumis* counsel is unlikely to be accepted in California. The *Cumis* line of cases evolved out of express concern that counsel representing the insurer as well as the insured might prejudice the insured's coverage and liability positions by favoring the insurer's coverage position. *See, e.g., Cumis,* 162 Cal.App.3d at 364, 208 Cal.Rptr. 494 (" 'The [insurance] Carrier is required to hire independent counsel because an attorney in actual trial would be tempted to develop the facts to help his real client, the Carrier Company, as opposed to the Insured, for whom he will never likely work again. * * * A lawyer who does not look out for the Carrier's best interest might soon find himself out of work.' " (quoting trial court opinion)). Given the nature of this problem and the courts' determination to alleviate it, it seems highly unlikely that the *Cumis* line of decisions or the legislature's codification of it meant to allow the essential nature of the joint representation to remain the same, and merely to allow the insured rather than the insurer to make the initial selection of the counsel that would represent both of them. Rather, the Court believes that the *Cumis* decisions intended to eliminate the ethical dilemmas and temptations that arise along with conflict in joint representations, and that they accomplished this through mandating the insured's right to *Cumis* counsel that represent only the insured.

This is not to say, however, that *Cumis* counsel necessarily owe *no* duties to the insurer. The Court simply holds that any such duties do not as a matter of law create an attorney-client relationship between *Cumis* counsel and the insurer or otherwise make *Cumis* counsel vulnerable to disqualification at the instance of the insurer. The Court accordingly concludes that *Cumis* counsel do not as a matter of law have a relationship with the insurer that precludes such counsel from representing the insured in coverage disputes adverse to the insurer. Plaintiff has not shown that in law or fact the Archer firm has represented Wausau's interests, and it therefore cannot be concluded that Archer has breached the ethical strictures against representation of adverse interests. Plaintiff's first argument to disqualify the Archer firm is unavailing.

[The court also denied Seeno's motion to disqualify Wausau's counsel, finding Wausau's primary counsel did not represent Seeno either as a matter of law or as a matter of fact. Finally, the court denied Wausau's motion to disqualify Seeno's counsel based on the ground that a lawyer who had previously represented Wausau was now a partner in the Archer firm that represented Seeno. The court found grounds for

* * * Moreover *Cumis* holds that such an attorney[-]client relationship is impossible. Bar Opinion No. 439 at 5–6. The committee therefore found it entirely proper for *Cumis* counsel representing the insured in a third-party action to represent the insured in the coverage case against the insurer as well. *See id.* at 6.

However, it should be obvious that this conclusion in no way suggests that the insurer is answerable for the cost of the insured's counsel's work in coverage actions; that expense of course must ordinarily be borne by the insured.

the disqualification, but denied the motion because Wausau's counsel delayed in bringing it.]

ETHICS IN THE PRACTICE OF LAW

Geoffrey C. Hazard, Jr., pp. 43–44, 46, 48–52.

The lawyer's professional responsibilities may not end with concern for his client, but clearly they start there. Confidential information is a secret if it relates to a client, valuable evidence if it relates to someone else. Conflict with the client must be avoided, conflict with everyone else is what a lawyer is retained to handle. How far a lawyer is prepared to go in partisan aggressiveness is the measure of what he will do, at the same time, for a client and to other people. Identifying the client is thus critical in the lawyer's orientation to "relevant others" and in their orientation to him.

In the traditional lore of the legal profession, identifying the client is not a problem. The client is the troubled fellow who walks into the office, papers in hand, wanting someone to help him in a legal matter. If all real world lawyer-client relationships began this way and involved nothing else, the question of client identity would always be answered before the relationship begins.

For the lawyer retained by an organization such as a corporation or government agency, identifying the client is much more complicated. Client identity is ambiguous, continuously problematic, and requires resolution by conscious choice. * * *

It is a problem that the Code of Responsibility simply evades. The Code says:

> A lawyer employed or retained by a corporation or similar entity owes his allegiance to the entity and not to a stockholder, director, officer, employee, representative, or other person connected with the entity.

The counterpart rule for government lawyers says it is the government that is the client. When the legal matter in question is between the organization and an outsider, these propositions are truisms—of course the client is the organization. When the legal matter poses a question within the corporation or the government, however, the "entity" referent provides no help. The unanswered question for the lawyer is: What individual should I treat as representing the organization so I can know whom to represent? Or, conversely: Whom should I decide to represent so I can know what individual to treat as the organization?

* * *

Corporate financial or legal crises * * * are directly the result of action or inaction by the corporation's officers and other employees working under their direction. Legal liability for the consequences begins with them, for the officers sometimes can be held personally liable to the corporation for getting it into trouble and may also be liable to outsiders, such as the government or creditors. If the derelictions are ones that the board of directors knew about, or should have known about if they had fulfilled their supervisory responsibility, the directors may be personally liable to the stockholders and to outsiders. The corporation itself is liable to third persons injured by the misconduct, such as victims of antitrust violations, but the existence and extent of its liability can depend on whether the conduct in question was "unauthorized," that is, violative of company policy. All these forms of potential liability increase if the conduct is persisted in and may take on an additional intentional quality if persisted in after counsel has appraised them to be wrongful. Furthermore, they may occasion not only damages liability but also criminal penalties and such sanctions as loss of license (for licensed industries) and delistment as an eligible contractor (for companies doing business with government agencies).

When a legal problem of this sort comes to the attention of the lawyer for the corporation, he has two issues to contend with. The first is how he should conduct himself apart from the question of client identity. * * *

Beyond this, the lawyer has to deal with the problem of identifying his client. The problem is difficult both morally and legally. The question has a moral aspect because the lawyer is faced with subordinating and perhaps seriously injuring the interest of a person who has trusted him in the past. * * * In the corporate setting, the individual can have been a business friend of long standing. When the heretofore client begins unburdening himself, he is only doing what the lawyer has encouraged him to do in the past. If the lawyer refuses to listen, he must appear to be violating a trusting relationship and to be abandoning a friendship. On the other hand, if the lawyer does listen, he can hear things that implicate not only the heretofore client but the organization that both of them are being paid to serve. And if the lawyer listens, he knows that the person before him supposes that the disclosure is confidential. If the lawyer is not certain that he can keep the disclosure confidential, his listening to it is the first step of what can turn out to be a betrayal of a confidence, and therefore a grave moral wrong.

In terms of the lawyer's legal obligations, the situation is equally complex. When the corporate officer begins talking, the lawyer must be mindful that a lawyer-client relationship is in the making. At this point, if the lawyer treats the corporate officer as the client, and if he learns things that may subject the officer to criminal or civil liability, the lawyer is bound by the rule of confidentiality not to disclose the matters to others, for example to the board of directors. But the lawyer's general retainer, if we may call it that, is to the corporation. The board will consider that it "is" the corporate client, and expect the lawyer eventually to advise the board what to do, including advice about the possibility of proceeding against the executive. The lawyer may find himself unable to do that without violating his professional duty to the executive. The board will then feel at least disappointed and very likely betrayed.

On the other hand, if the lawyer treats the executive as a nonclient, he must consider giving him some sort of "Miranda warning," that is, tell him that any disclosures he makes may have to be revealed to the board and perhaps to others. Giving a "Miranda warning" represents a decision by the lawyer that his client is the board of directors and not the officer. If such a warning is given, the lawyer will leave the executive in the lurch, perhaps requiring him to go elsewhere for legal advice and therewith drawing some kind of line between himself and the company he has been bound to serve.

* * *

The next stage remove is the board of directors. Until it has received the bad news, the board most likely will have been highly supportive of—or perhaps dominated by—the officers whose conduct is immediately in question. The board may well be unreceptive to the lawyer's message unless it is solidly documented, but documentation may be lacking. If the lawyer does not disclose to the board what he knows, and the board "is" the corporation, then he is holding out on his client. If he does disclose, he may have betrayed what the executive thought was a confidence. Furthermore, when he takes the matter to the board he implicates the board members in the problem, because their responsibility and potential legal liability is affected by the extent of their knowledge. If they then take appropriate remedial action, their very action can alert potential adversaries of something afoot that may be the basis of legal action against the corporation. If they do not act, they may be regarded as having violated their duties to the stockholders and perhaps have become accomplices so far as concerns liability to outsiders. And so the lawyer may have to consider the stockholders as the "client."

PHILLIPS v. CARSON

Supreme Court of Kansas, 1987.
240 Kan. 462, 731 P.2d 820.

[Plaintiff Thelma Phillips sued attorney David Carson and his law firm for legal malpractice in connection with personal loans Carson obtained from Phillips. The lower court granted summary judgment against Carson. It also granted summary judgment in favor of Carson's law firm on the theory that Carson was not acting within the ordinary course of the firm's partnership business in connection with the personal loans he obtained from Phillips. The Supreme Court of Kansas affirmed the summary judgment against Carson and reversed the summary judgment in favor of the law firm.]

Mrs. Phillips and her husband, Robert L. Phillips, and Mr. and Mrs. Carson had been friends for several years prior to Mr. Phillips' death in 1978. Mrs. Phillips retained Carson and his law firm to handle the estate of her deceased husband. * * *

While the estate was pending, Mrs. Phillips paid fees totaling $80,000 to the firm. Carson told her that this fee was to take care of all of her legal business until the estate was closed. * * *

* * *

In August 1980, Carson told Mrs. Phillips that he was having financial problems, and Mrs. Phillips loaned him $200,000. Carson told her that she would be fully secured, and he gave her a note and a second mortgage on some Arizona property. These documents were properly executed and the mortgage was filed of record. In 1981, Phillips loaned Carson an additional $70,000. Because of his representations, she believed that this loan would get him over his current financial difficulties. She was concerned that he might harm himself, and she thought this loan would increase the chances that her first loan would be repaid. Later, Carson asked Mrs. Phillips to release her mortgage on the Arizona property so that he could refinance and sell that or another property. He offered her a mortgage on 90 acres he owned in Wyandotte County, and told Mrs. Phillips that this would put her in a better position. She relied upon Carson's statement that she would be better secured and she trusted his advice as her attorney. On March 29, 1982, Mrs. Phillips released her mortgage on the Arizona property, and Carson gave her a new promissory note for $274,933.70, which included past due interest as principal. Carson also prepared and executed a mortgage on the Wyandotte County property to Mrs. Phillips, but he failed to file that mortgage with the Register of Deeds.

Carson at no time advised Mrs. Phillips to seek independent counsel regarding the loan transactions, and she did not discuss them with other partners of the Carson firm or with other counsel. In May 1982, Mrs. Phillips called Carson's office and learned that her mortgage had not been filed of record. She sought independent counsel, who secured the mortgage and filed it for record on July 23, 1982. Mrs. Phillips then demanded payment in full from Carson; it was not forthcoming. On September 10, 1982, Carson filed a Chapter 11 petition in the United States Bankruptcy Court. * * *

* * *

By her petition filed in this action, plaintiff claims that Carson, while acting as attorney for her and within the scope and course of the law partnership business and authority, and while acting in a fiduciary relationship towards her, negligently performed or failed to perform those legal duties entrusted to him to be performed on behalf of the plaintiff, listing some six allegedly negligent acts or omissions. These include negligently advising or failing to advise her of the legal nature, extent, and effect of the mortgage she was to receive, of the effect of her releasing the mortgage on the Arizona property, and of the extent of the superior liens on the Wyandotte County land; failing to timely draft the note and mortgage; failing to record the mortgage and perfect plaintiff's security interest; failing to fully advise her of the effect upon her of his financial consolidation; and filing his Chapter 11 petition which, under the circumstances, left her totally unsecured. She contends that a fiduciary relationship existed between Carson, the individual members of the firm, the partnership, and the plaintiff. She seeks actual damages of $274,933.70 plus accruing interest and costs.

* * *

[The Supreme Court rejected Carson's arguments that the summary judgment against him was improper. Though rarely granted in negligence cases, summary judgment is proper if there are no disputed issues of fact, and the Supreme Court agreed that there were none here.]

The Code of Professional Responsibility, by which attorneys in this state are governed, states:

"DR 5–104 *Limiting Business Relations with a Client.*

(A) A lawyer shall not enter into a business transaction with a client if they have differing interests therein and if the client expects the lawyer to exercise his professional judgment therein for the protection of the client, unless the client has consented after full disclosure." 235 Kan. cxlvi.

A comment on this section of the Kansas Code of Professional Responsibility, pertinent here, is as follows:

"It is not uncommon for attorneys to engage in business transactions with clients and other nonlawyers. Despite intentions to the contrary, members of the bar quite often use their legal knowledge or give advice on behalf of such joint efforts. In these situations courts are prone to find the existence of an attorney-client relationship upon the complaint of the lay party. The existence of retainer or fee charge is usually immaterial.

* * *

"An attorney who is confronted with the possibility of a joint business venture with a client is cautioned to consider the increased malpractice and ethical risks along with the financial considerations. In all such situations there should be a complete disclosure, and the client should be strongly urged to seek independent legal and other professional advice."

* * *

The trial court * * * found that Carson breached his professional duty to plaintiff by failing to advise her to secure outside independent legal and financial advice. * * * [That conclusion is] supported by the undisputed facts.

In *Ford v. Guarantee Abstract & Title Co.*, 220 Kan. 244, 553 P.2d 254 (1976), we summarized the duty of attorney to client * * *:

"The relationship of an attorney to his client is fiduciary in character, binding the attorney to the highest degree of fidelity and good faith to his client on account of the trust and confidence imposed.''

"A fiduciary relation does not depend upon some technical relation created by, or defined in, law. It may exist under a variety of circumstances, and does exist in cases where there has been a special confidence reposed in one who, in equity and good conscience, is bound to act in good faith and with due regard to the interests of the one reposing the confidence.''

Under the extensive factual record before us, we agree with the trial court that there existed an attorney and client relationship between Carson and Mrs. Phillips during the time that Carson secured loans from Mrs. Phillips, advised her or failed to advise her about them, and agreed to take care of preparing and filing all necessary documents in connection therewith. That relationship gave rise to the duty upon the attorney to properly, competently, and adequately counsel, advise, and represent the client. That duty was breached, not only in failing to file the final mortgage of record, but also in failing to advise Mrs. Phillips of the legal ramifications of the transaction, in failing to advise her of the legal consequences of the changes in security, in failing to recommend that she secure independent counsel, and in other ways pointed out by the trial court * * *. Finally, we agree with the trial court that Carson's extensive breaches of the Code of Professional Responsibility proximately caused injury to his client, and that she sustained substantial actual damages.

* * *

[The Supreme Court next considered the summary judgment granted in favor of Carson's law firm. The trial court ruled that Carson had clearly acted outside the scope of the partnership business in connection with the loans.]

The evidence here is clear that Carson and the partnership were representing Mrs. Phillips and were her attorneys for the primary purpose of probating the estate of her deceased husband. Additionally, the firm charged her a fee which was to cover not only the probate matter, but all other legal services she might require individually during the term of the probate. Additional legal services were provided for her * * * without additional charge.

Advising a client on the propriety of making loans, the legality and sufficiency of proposed security, the method of ascertaining the value of the security, the method of recording security documents and the like are all matters well within the scope of the general practice of law. Had Mrs. Phillips been considering a loan to a third person and had a member of the partnership advised her as Carson did (or as he failed to advise her), there would be little question of the firm's responsibility in the event that she sustained damages as a result of that action or omission. Similarly, the preparation of notes and mortgages, and the filing of mortgages for record, are matters well within the scope of the general practice of law handled daily by lawyers throughout this state.

* * *

Mrs. Phillips asserts that there is a factual question * * * regarding whether the transactions were apparently authorized by the partnership. She claims that it is the reasonable belief of the third party concerning the existence of apparent authority that is determinative. Certainly when a lawyer is consulting with a client on legal matters in the lawyer's office, the appearances to the client and the reasonable belief of the client are persuasive upon the issue. As the firm points out, however, the indication of authority must come from the principal. * * *

While in this case no partner in the firm told Phillips that Carson's actions were within his authority as a partner, no one told her that his actions were not within his authority as a member of the law firm. Two of the firm's employees, Doreen Benton and Judy Tranckino, did personal work for Mr. Carson, including preparation of the notes and mortgages herein. While Mrs. Phillips knew Mrs. Benton did personal work for Carson, no one told her that Benton's work on this project was not as a firm employee. The fact that Benton and Tranckino did personal work for Carson was known and not objected to by the other members of the law firm. Letters from Carson to Mrs. Phillips regarding this loan were on firm stationery and mailed in firm envelopes. Using firm supplies and personnel for personal business was apparently an acceptable practice within the firm. There was no firm policy prohibiting a partner from transacting business with a client, the only restriction regarding acceptance of a client being that a partner could not represent a client if doing so would cause a conflict with other clients of the firm. Whether Carson was apparently carrying on the usual business of the partnership, or whether his wrongful acts or omissions were in the usual course of business or with the authority of his partners * * * [are unresolved issues of material fact.]

The summary judgment entered by the trial court in favor of Thelma L. Phillips and against David W. Carson is affirmed. The summary judgment entered in behalf of the partnership * * * is reversed.

AAA PLUMBING POTTERY CORP. v. ST. PAUL INSURANCE CO. OF ILLINOIS

United States District Court, N.D. Illinois, 1995.
1995 WL 608548.

MEMORANDUM OPINION AND ORDER

PLUNKETT, DISTRICT JUDGE.

This matter is before us on defendant St. Paul Insurance Company of Illinois' ("St. Paul") motion for a protective order and to disqualify attorney Barry B. Gross ("Gross") from representing the plaintiffs, AAA

Plumbing Pottery Corporation ("AAA") and its parent, Kokomo Sanitary Pottery Corporation ("Kokomo"), in this case. The plaintiffs have sued St. Paul for bad faith failure to settle a fraud action brought by Jerry D. Britton, which went to trial and resulted in a verdict against AAA in excess of $3,000,000. The current motion is based upon Gross' involvement in AAA's post-trial conduct and in settling the case following the verdict, all of which, St. Paul contends, make him a necessary witness whose testimony may be prejudicial to AAA. For the reasons set forth below, we grant the motion to disqualify Gross. In addition, St. Paul's request for a protective order is granted in part and denied in part.

BACKGROUND

I. The Workers Compensation Claims

[In two prior workers compensation actions brought by Britton, an AAA employee, AAA's insurance company, St. Paul, defended the actions on behalf of AAA. Around June 6, 1991, Britton's attorney proposed settling all of Britton's claims he might have against AAA for $200,000.] St. Paul rejected the demand, but, according to AAA, it never communicated the settlement offer to AAA.

St. Paul and AAA settled the workers compensation cases in November 1992 for $75,000.

II. The Britton Fraud Case

On June 7, 1991, Britton brought a civil action for fraud * * * against AAA * * *. Britton alleged that AAA * * * had fraudulently induced him to return to work prematurely in June 1989 by misrepresenting that his doctor had approved his return to a specific job assignment, and that this conduct had led to his second back injury and permanent disability. Britton was again represented by Bohanan. [While St. Paul was named a defendant in this action, AAA, according to St. Paul, never filed an employer's liability claim under their insurance policy. AAA asserts that St. Paul rejected its demand for defense and coverage regarding the lawsuit.] In any event, AAA hired its own attorneys, the Alabama law firm of Henslee, Bradley & Robertson, P.C., to defend it in the Britton case.

* * * On October 7, 1993, when the [Britton] trial was nearly over, AAA contacted William Gifford, a partner at Shefsky Froelich & Devine, Ltd. [a Chicago law firm] ("SF & D") asking for his advice regarding settlement of the case. After obtaining certain information regarding the lawsuit from AAA, Gifford consulted with Gross, a senior partner at SF & D, before advising AAA. Gross recommended that Gifford inquire about insurance coverage for the suit and that he advise AAA to follow the advice of its Alabama counsel with regard to settlement, as they were the most knowledgeable about the case. Gifford did so. Nonetheless, AAA refused to offer $100,000 to $125,000 to Britton, ignoring the advice of both SF & D and its Alabama attorneys, as well as the recommendation of the Alabama judge presiding over the trial. AAA instead offered

only $50,000, which Britton rejected. The case went to the jury, which awarded Britton compensatory damages of $1,314,000 and punitive damages of $2,000,000.

III.   After the Verdict

AAA filed a motion for judgment notwithstanding the verdict, or, alternatively, for a new trial or remittitur, which SF & D prepared, wholly or in part. [To support its claim that the punitive damage award was excessive, AAA claimed that the judgment was uninsured and paying it would put AAA out of business.]

After the verdict, SF & D also advised AAA to convey security interests, or mortgages, * * * in virtually all of its fixed assets in favor of affiliated corporations, to protect those assets from attachment. AAA did so.   Gifford's notes indicate that, apparently after the mortgages were recorded, two SF & D partners who worked on the security documents advised him that they could be considered fraudulent conveyances, but that Gross instructed him to go forward with them anyway. [The move left Britton unable to collect his judgment.]

[Britton's attorney] smelled a rat and promptly moved to set aside the mortgages as fraudulent conveyances.   In addition, he pointed to the mortgages in his post-trial papers as one reason why the punitive damage award was proper.   He also threatened to file another action against AAA on Britton's behalf, on the grounds that the mortgages were fraudulent conveyances and that AAA had allegedly failed to tender the Britton case to its insurers, leaving Britton unable to collect his judgment.

Although SF & D prepared the JNOV papers in the Britton case, it never obtained the Alabama court's permission to appear pro hac vice. Gifford explained at his deposition that AAA did not want the court and Britton to see that it was being represented by (and paying the fees of) a Chicago law firm at the same time it was claiming indigency regarding payment of the judgment, and his contemporaneous notes indicate that he was not to sit at counsel table or be introduced. * * *

IV.   The Britton Settlement

Before the post-trial motions were decided, AAA settled with Britton for $950,000, allegedly without St. Paul's knowledge. * * * In return, Britton assigned his rights to the judgment, along with any claim he might have against St. Paul, to Kokomo [AAA's parent corporation]. * * *

[A provision in the settlement agreement specifically releasing two additional claims, including one based upon AAA's failure to tender the Britton case to St. Paul, was eventually deleted.] St. Paul suggests, based upon Gifford's deposition testimony, that Gross made the deletion. Its effect is that all of Britton's claims against AAA were lumped together under the terms of the settlement agreement, and there is no allocation among the claims, according to St. Paul.   Moreover, AAA seeks in this action to hold St. Paul responsible for the full amount of the settlement agreement, despite the fact that these two claims clearly fall outside the provisions of the Policy.

As part of the settlement document, AAA and Kokomo executed a promissory note in favor of Britton, under which they agreed to pay him fifty percent of any recovery they obtain in this case, after payment of attorneys' fees.

V. This Lawsuit

In this case, AAA has sued St. Paul for bad faith in failing to communicate the June 6, 1991, settlement offer, alleging that it was denied any opportunity to independently settle Britton's claims against it (Count I). It also asserts a claim of negligence on the same facts (Count II). It further alleges that St. Paul breached the terms of the Policy because Britton's claim in the fraud case arose from his work-related injury in June 1989 (Count III). Kokomo asserts a claim on behalf of Britton for the $2,364,000 of the judgment which was not paid under the settlement agreement (Count IV).

St. Paul has filed a counterclaim, seeking a declaration that it did not engage in bad faith and has no obligation to indemnify AAA. It has also asserted as one of its affirmative defenses that the settlement of the Britton case was made in bad faith, is collusive and fraudulent, unjustly enriched AAA and Kokomo, and violates public policy.

AAA and Kokomo are represented by SF & D. Gross is apparently the senior attorney responsible for this case, and he signed the complaint. Gifford is not participating in this action.

St. Paul has notified AAA and Kokomo of its intent to call Gross and Gifford as witnesses. Gifford has already been deposed, and at least some of SF & D's files relating to the Britton case have been produced. In bringing this motion, St. Paul originally sought to disqualify Gifford also, but, upon SF & D's representation that he is not participating in this case, it has withdrawn that request.

DISCUSSION

St. Paul contends that Gross' involvement in the Britton case makes him a necessary witness in this action. They argue that under Rule 3.7 of the Rules of Professional Conduct for the Northern District of Illinois, Gross must be disqualified from representing AAA in this case.

Rule 3.7 states, in pertinent part:

(b) If a lawyer knows or reasonably should know that the lawyer may be called as a witness other than on behalf of the client, the lawyer may act as an advocate in a trial or evidentiary proceeding unless the lawyer knows or reasonably should know that the lawyer's testimony is or may be prejudicial to the client.

The court has the discretion to determine whether an attorney acting as an advocate may appear as a witness without withdrawing from the case. United States v. Morris, 714 F.2d 669, 671 (7th Cir. 1983). In addition, the court may decide whether to permit an attorney to be called as a witness, and may forbid it "where evidence is easily available from other sources and absent 'extraordinary circumstances' or 'compelling reasons.'" United States v. Dack, 747 F.2d 1172, 1176 n. 5 (1984) (quoting United States v. Johnston, 690 F.2d 638, 644 (7th Cir.1982)).

St. Paul raises fifteen different factual issues on which it would ostensibly require Gross' testimony. We find most to be without merit or not to be "facts" at all. However, there are two related issues which give us pause. It is undisputed that Gross had a hand in drafting the settlement agreement, although there is substantial dispute between the parties as to how large his role was. Gross' timesheets for the early part of 1994 indicate that he made a number of entries for reviewing and revising the settlement document. The frequency of these entries indicate that his involvement was not merely that of a senior partner who does a quick review before a document is finalized. While others may have negotiated basic terms, such as the amount of money, it appears that Gross had a hand in structuring of the agreement. St. Paul has called the legitimacy of that settlement into question through its affirmative defenses. In the same vein, through discovery, St. Paul has obtained a draft of the settlement agreement in which Britton's release of his fraudulent conveyance and failure to tender claims against AAA was specifically mentioned. That provision was crossed out by hand on the draft, and the word "general" was written in the margin. The handwriting may be that of Gross. The claims based upon the fraudulent conveyances and the failure to tender are clearly beyond the scope of the Policy, yet AAA has sued St. Paul for the entire amount of the settlement. The fact that the release in the settlement agreement was intended to include those claims, the deletion of the specific mention of them, and the overall structure of the settlement agreement are issues upon which Gross' testimony is important. While others participated in negotiating and drafting that agreement, it is unlikely that they can testify as to Gross' precise role; he is the best source of that information. Moreover, they certainly could not testify as to Gross' reasoning and judgments; he is the only source of that information.[8]

Our inquiry does not stop there, for we must also determine whether Gross' testimony may be prejudicial to AAA. St. Paul obviously intends to use Gross' testimony to prove its affirmative defense that the settlement agreement was entered into in bad faith. Since the opposing party intends to use Gross' testimony to help prove its affirmative defense, Gross' testimony may well be prejudicial to AAA. There is sufficient likelihood of this that his disqualification is appropriate.

St. Paul has also made a brief argument that SF & D should be disqualified. It argues that under Rule 1.7(b), SF & D's representation of AAA and Kokomo would be materially limited by the firm's own

---

8. Our analysis regarding Gross' role in the settlement agreement does not mean that St. Paul must limit its examination of him to that issue. It means simply that St. Paul has sufficiently demonstrated that his testimony is necessary on this issue to sustain its burden of showing that disqualification is appropriate.

interests. All of its arguments, however, go to Gross' conduct, or AAA's request in its complaint for the attorneys' fees it incurred in defending and settling the Britton case. SF & D can be disqualified only under Rule 1.10, which addresses imputed disqualifications. Under Rule 1.10(a), a firm may be disqualified only where one of its attorneys has an actual conflict of interest under Rules 1.7, 1.8(c), or 1.9. St. Paul has not established that Gross has a conflict of interest and cannot represent AAA under Rule 17.(b); it has only established that Gross is a necessary witness and cannot appear as an advocate at the trial or in an evidentiary hearing in this case under Rule 3.7. However, we note that this situation may change if the plaintiffs attempt to rebut St. Paul's affirmative defense that the settlement agreement was made in bad faith by using an advice of counsel defense. If that should occur, a conflict of interest may exist, and we would reexamine the issue. At this time, however, SF & D is not disqualified from representing the plaintiffs in this suit.

Finally, St. Paul has asked for a protective order barring Gross from participating in the depositions in this case. Its arguments are unpersuasive, except to the extent that a videotape of a deposition may be replayed at trial in place of the witness' trial testimony. Under that circumstance, Gross may not participate in the deposition or appear on the videotape. Otherwise, he is free to participate in any depositions taken in this action.

Conclusion

For the forgoing reasons, we grant defendant St. Paul Insurance Company of Illinois' motion to disqualify Barry B. Gross from representing the plaintiffs in this case. St. Paul's request for a protective order is granted in part and denied in part as set forth above.

CALIFORNIA EXTENDS SEXUAL HARASSMENT PROTECTION TO CLIENTS

California has emphasized protection for clients from their lawyers in personal matters, first in CRPC 3–120 prohibiting most sexual relations between lawyers and their clients, and, more recently, in extending protection from sexual harassment to professional relationships, including the lawyer-client relationship. Consider the following legislation, based on a legislative declaration that "sexual harassment occurs not only in the workplace, but in relationships between providers of professional services and their clients."

CALIFORNIA CIVIL CODE:

§ 51.9. Sexual harassment; business, service and professional relationships

(a) A person is liable in a cause of action for sexual harassment when the plaintiff proves all of the following elements:

(1) There is a business, service, or professional relationship between the plaintiff and defendant. Such a relationship includes any of the following:

(A) Physician, psychotherapist, or dentist-patient.

(B) Attorney, marriage, family or child counselor, licensed clinical social worker, master of social work, real estate agent, real estate appraiser, accountant banker, trust officer, financial planner, loan officer, collection service, contractor, or escrow loan officer-client.

(C) Executor, trustee, or administrator beneficiary.

(D) Landlord or property manager-tenant.

(E) Teacher-student.

(F) A relationship that is substantially similar to any of the above.

(2) The defendant has made sexual advances, solicitations, sexual requests, or demands for sexual compliance by the plaintiff that were unwelcome and persistent or severe, continuing after a request by the plaintiff to stop.

(3) There is an inability by the plaintiff to easily terminate the relationship without tangible hardship.

(4) The plaintiff has suffered or will suffer economic loss or disadvantage or personal injury as a result of the conduct described in paragraph (2).

* * *

MULTIPLE CHOICE QUESTIONS

Answer these questions under the ABA Code and
ABA Model Rules

1. Lawyer Lenschell, born and raised in a peaceful rural community, has recently opened his law office in a rough district in the big city. As yet, Lenschell lacks sophistication in big city ways. Timothy came to Lenschell's office and introduced himself as the "boyfriend" of Tina, a young woman who was just arrested on a prostitution charge. Timothy retained Lenschell to represent Tina and paid him an appropriate fee in advance. Timothy explained to Lenschell that in prostitution cases in this district, a guilty plea usually results in a $500 fine, but no jail sentence. But if the defendant pleads not guilty, goes to trial, and is found guilty, the judge usually imposes a jail sentence. Timothy further explained that Tina did not want to go to jail, that he would pay her fine for her, and that Lenschell should therefore advise her to plead guilty. Lenschell met Tina for the first time at the courthouse, shortly before her case was to be called on the criminal calendar for entry of her plea. In their hurried conference, Tina told Lenschell that in big city parlance, "boyfriend" means pimp. Further, she said that she wanted to escape

from Timothy and from her life as a prostitute, and that she wanted to plead not guilty, thus risking a jail sentence, rather than become further indebted to Timothy. What is the *proper* course of conduct for Lenschell to follow in this situation?

    A. To adhere to the instructions given by Timothy, and to advise Tina to plead guilty.

    B. To give Tina whatever legal assistance she needs in entering her plea of not guilty.

    C. To withdraw from the matter promptly, without advising Tina one way or the other on what plea to enter.

    D. To telephone Timothy and ask for further instructions in light of Tina's unwillingness to plead guilty.

    2. Lawyer Lattimer is on the in-house legal staff of Centennial Corporation, a major manufacturer of steel shipping containers. She regularly provides legal advice to Vice-President Markler, the executive in charge of sales and marketing. In the course of a routine preventive law project, Lattimer discovered that Markler had participated in a series of telephone conferences with his counterparts at the company's two main competitors. Further, she discovered that each such conference was promptly followed by an increase in the prices charged by the three companies. When Lattimer took this up with Markler, she first reminded him that she was not his personal lawyer, but rather the corporation's lawyer. Then she said: "If you have been discussing prices with our competitors, we may be in deep trouble. Your telephone conferences may violate the Sherman Antitrust Act, and that could mean civil and criminal liability, both for you and for the corporation. And, as you know, the corporation has a rule against rescuing executives who get in antitrust trouble." Markler responded as follows: "Ms. Lattimer, I know you're a good lawyer, but you don't know much about the real world. You can't run a business these days if you try to trample on your competition. Now don't worry yourself about my telephone conferences, because I'm sure you have better things to do with your time." If Markler remains uncooperative, which of the following expresses the *proper* course for Lattimer to take?

    A. Draft a careful, complete memorandum about the matter for her own files, and maintain her conversation with Markler in strict confidence.

    B. Describe the relevant facts in a carefully drafted letter to the Antitrust Division of the United States Department of Justice, and request an advisory opinion on the legality of the described conduct.

    C. Describe the entire matter to Markler's immediate corporate superior, the Executive Vice President, and advise him to put a stop to Markler's activity.

    D. Describe the relevant facts in a memorandum to the corporate Board of Directors, and advise the Board that she will resign unless something is done to stop Markler.

    3. Attorney Tillis is a partner in the 138 person firm of Dahlberg & Sneed. The firm is located in a state that has adopted the ABA Model Rules of Professional Conduct. The Citizens Alliance for Coastal Preservation has asked Tillis to represent the Alliance in a public interest law suit against Vista del Oro, Inc., a real estate developer. Vista del Oro owns several thousand acres of beautiful coastline, about an hour's drive from the largest city in the state. It is building homes to sell to the public. When the project is complete, the entire area will be fenced off to prevent access by non-owners. The Alliance seeks to force Vista del Oro to provide access paths across the property, so that members of the public can get from the state highway to the public beaches. Attorney Prentice is also a partner in Dahlberg & Sneed. He is a member of the Board of Directors of Vista del Oro, and he owns seven of the vacation home sites as a personal investment. No Dahlberg & Sneed lawyer has ever represented Vista del Oro, and none will do so in the present case. After careful consideration, Tillis has concluded that his representation of the Alliance would not be adversely affected by Prentice's interest. Under the ABA Model Rules, which of the following conditions *must* be met if Tillis is to represent the Alliance?

    I. The Alliance consents after full disclosure.

    II. Vista del Oro consents after full disclosure.

    III. Prentice resigns as a director of Vista del Oro.

    IV. Prentice sells his seven home sites.

        A. All of the above.

        B. III only.

        C. I and II only.

        D. I only.

    4. In a private treble damage case arising under the federal price discrimination law (the Robinson–Patman Act), the defendant wants to prove that it had a good faith belief that its pricing system was lawful. As evidence of its good faith, the defendant wants to prove that, five years ago, the Federal Trade Commission carefully reviewed the defendant's pricing system and decided not to institute proceedings against the defendant. The proof of this is a letter from the FTC to defendant's lawyer, Smithers. At the treble damage trial, the defendant will need Smithers' testimony to authenticate the letter—Smithers will simply testify that he received the letter from the FTC. The defendant wants Smithers and his law partner, Hillner, to serve as its trial counsel in the treble damage case. Which of the following is correct?

    A. Neither Smithers nor Hillner *may* serve.

    B. Both Smithers and Hillner *may* serve.

C. Only Hillner *may* serve.

D. Smithers and Hillner *may* serve, but only if the plaintiff consents.

5. Client Parsons has asked lawyer Ekimoto to represent her, and nine other representatives of a plaintiff class, in an employment discrimination class action against Consolidated Telephone and Telegraph Corporation. The size of the plaintiff class and the size of the potential recovery are hard to estimate, but the case would conceivably produce a total recovery of nearly 15 million dollars. Lawyer Ekimoto and her two brothers are the beneficiaries of a trust fund established by their late parents. Among the trust assets are 1,000 shares of Consolidated common stock. Consolidated has 30 million shares of common stock outstanding. If Ekimoto reasonably believes that her interest in Consolidated will not affect her representation of the plaintiffs, *may* she serve as plaintiffs' counsel?

A. Yes, since the interest of a trust beneficiary is not regarded as disqualifying.

B. Yes, if she obtains the consent of the class representatives after full disclosure of her interest.

C. No, since even a small adverse financial interest creates an appearance of impropriety.

D. No, since there are other counsel available who could serve the plaintiff class without any potential conflict.

6. Biochemist Belloni invented a "gene-splicing" process for making snake antitoxins. The invention was a major breakthrough because Belloni's antitoxins were far cheaper and more reliable than the natural variety produced from the venom of live snakes. She obtained a U.S. Patent on her process. Shortly thereafter, she was sued in a declaratory judgment action brought by United Laboratories, Inc. United sought a declaration that her U.S. Patent was invalid. Belloni asked lawyer Lothrup to represent her in the case. Lothrup agreed to do so on the following terms: (1) Belloni would pay Lothrup for the necessary legal work at Lothrup's regular hourly rate; (2) Lothrup would advance the litigation expenses, subject to repayment by Belloni no matter what the outcome of the case; and (3) at the outset, Belloni would assign to Lothrup a 10% ownership interest in the U.S. Patent.

A. The arrangement is *proper,* assuming that the total Lothrup earns from it is reasonable.

B. Lothrup is *subject to discipline* because the arrangement requires Belloni to pay back the advanced litigation expenses even if she loses the declaratory judgment case.

C. Lothrup is *subject to discipline* because the arrangement provides for an advance of litigation expenses by the lawyer in a civil case.

D. Lothrup is *subject to discipline* because the arrangement gives her a personal financial interest in the U.S. Patent which is the subject of the declaratory judgment case.

7. A statute of State X requires prison inmates to be provided "sanitary living conditions, suitable education and recreation facilities, and competent medical treatment." The statute authorizes inmates who are deprived of these benefits to sue the State Commissioner of Prisons for equitable relief. The statute also permits (but does not require) the courts to order the state to pay the attorney fees of successful inmate plaintiffs. At the request of the local bar association, private attorney Andrate agreed to represent a group of indigent inmates who were allegedly being deprived of proper medical attention at a State X prison. After extensive discovery proceedings, the State Commissioner of Prisons offered to settle the case by entering into a consent decree that would give the inmates all the equitable relief they could ever hope to receive, provided that Andrate would not request an award of attorney fees. What *should* Andrate do with respect to the settlement offer?

A. Explain it to his clients and let them decide whether to accept it or reject it.

B. Reject it on behalf of his clients because it does not provide for an award of attorney fees.

C. Accept it on behalf of his clients, even though it does not provide for an award of attorney fees.

D. Reject it on behalf of his clients because to do otherwise would discourage private attorneys from representing indigent inmates in future cases.

*Answers to the multiple choice questions will be found
in the Appendix at the end of the book*

Chapter Twelve

CONFLICTS OF INTEREST—
CONFLICTS BETWEEN
TWO CLIENTS

What This Chapter Covers

Reading Assignment

Wydick & Perschbacher, Chapter 12

ABA Model Rules:

    Rules 1.7, 1.8(b), (g), and (i), 1.9 through 1.12, and 6.3.

CRPC 1–120 and 3–310

Cal.Bus. & Prof.Code § 6068(e).

Supplemental Reading

ABA Code:

    EC 5–14 through 5–20 and EC 9–3;

    DR 5–105 through 5–107 and DR 9–101.

Hazard & Hodes:

    Discussion of ABA Model Rules 1.7, 1.8(b), (g), and (i), 1.9 through 1.12, and 6.3.

Wolfram:

    Sections 7.3.1 through 7.3.4 (simultaneous representations);

    Sections 7.4.1 through 7.4.3 (former-client conflicts);

    Sections 7.6.1 through 7.6.6 (imputed disqualification);

Sections 8.4.1 through 8.4.3 (indemnity insurance conflicts);

Section 8.5 (buyer-seller conflicts);

Section 8.6 (conflicts in divorce cases);

Sections 8.9.1 through 8.10.3 (present and former government lawyers);

Section 8.15 (settling related cases).

Restatement (Third) of the Law Governing Lawyers §§ 201–204, 209–211, 213–214 (Proposed Final Draft No. 1, 1996).

_____

Discussion Problems

1. The County Association of Real Estate Dealers (CARED) is a trade association composed of all the licensed real estate brokers and dealers in the county. Over the years, CARED has provided its members with standard forms of legal documents for use in routine real estate transactions. Last year, the state passed a new statute that requires all legal documents affecting consumers to be expressed in "clear, simple English." Any document that does not comply is void. CARED hired attorney Adler to draft a new standard form apartment lease to comply with the new state statute. Adler did so, and CARED distributed the new form to its members. Dearbourne Realty & Investment Company (a CARED member) used the new form to lease one of its own apartment units to one Leon Beckner. Now Beckner seeks to have attorney Adler represent him in a law suit against Dearbourne to have the lease declared void. One of Beckner's several arguments is that two key paragraphs of the lease are totally incomprehensible to the average person. Adler has re-examined the two paragraphs and is inclined to agree that Beckner is very likely correct. May Adler represent Beckner in the law suit?

2. Aaron, Bropovski, and Carter were riding in a car driven by Duffy. The car was hit, head-on, by a truck driven by Emerson. Aaron, Bropovski, Carter, and Duffy have asked you to represent them in a suit against Emerson and his employer, United Fat and Tallow, Inc. Under what circumstances may you represent the four plaintiffs in this case?

3. You are one of only five lawyers in the little town of Sand Springs. You represent Sand Springs Hardware Company in a civil suit against Virgil McQuillan to collect $338 on an overdue charge account. Last week, McQuillan and one of his friends got drunk and were arrested trying to climb into the back window of a saloon after closing hours. They were charged with burglary, a felony. Neither man has funds to pay a lawyer.

   a. McQuillan's friend is being represented by the County Public Defender, but she has declined to represent McQuillan too, on the ground that to do so would pose a conflict of interest. Is her position sound?

   b.   The court has asked you to defend McQuillan in the felony case. How should you respond to the court's request?

4.   Two years ago, you represented Mr. W in setting up a close corporation for his business and for certain personal investments. That work has long since been completed, and you have not represented Mr. W since then. Now Mrs. W has asked you to represent her in divorce proceedings against Mr. W. The two of them are in sharp disagreement over the division of property, child support obligations, and alimony. Assume that this jurisdiction does not have community property. Under what, if any, circumstances may you represent Mrs. W?

5.   Review the *Employers Insurance of Wausau v. Albert D. Seeno Construction Co.* case from Chapter 11, *supra.* The third part of that opinion (omitted from the text) deals with Wausau's motion to disqualify Seeno's counsel, the Archer firm, because an attorney in the Archer firm, Lageson, had previously been a partner in a firm (the B firm) representing Wausau. Lageson's previous association with the B firm and his defense of Wausau and its insureds in numerous cases is undisputed. Less than two years earlier, Lageson left the B firm for the Archer firm, where he also handles liability cases as *Cumis* counsel for Wausau's insureds. Lageson's particular role in both firms and his access to confidential information in connection with the representations is sharply disputed. The Archer firm is counsel of record in direct opposition to Wausau in the *Seeno* case.

   a.   Should Lageson personally be disqualified from representing Seeno in *Wausau v. Seeno*?

   b.   If Lageson is personally disqualified, should the entire Archer firm also be disqualified?

   c.   Are there any steps the Archer firm could have taken to avoid its imputed disqualification? Examine as best you can the solutions under the ABA Code, the ABA Model Rules, the approach of the Restatement and the California rules.

   d.   If you believe sufficient screening procedures can protect a private firm from disqualification, can you see why the former client who is the firm's adversary still might feel uneasy?

   e.   As a soon-to-be member of the bar, what effect will the courts' decisions to allow or reject screening as a partial solution to imputed disqualification have on you and your employment decisions?

6.   Until ten months ago, attorney Barneo was an Administrative Law Judge for the State Consumer Protection Commission. The Commission's Enforcement Division brought proceedings against Mandel Toy Company to stop Mandel from selling some allegedly dangerous toy rifles. The Commission attorney moved for a preliminary cease and desist order. Barneo was assigned to hear the motion. She declined to

issue the order, stating on the record that "the evidence of dangerousness looks exceedingly thin at this time." Several months later, Barneo resigned her position and entered the private practice of law. Ultimately, after a full hearing before a different Administrative Law Judge, Mandel was ordered to take the toy rifles off the market. That order is now before the Appellate Division of the Commission, and Mandel has asked Barneo to argue the appeal on its behalf. May she do so?

7. For three years after his graduation from law school, attorney Toulmin worked on the legal staff of the State Revenue Bureau. Among many other things, he drafted a set of regulations to define what constitutes a valid deduction for travel expense in connection with a business or profession. His draft was adopted by the Bureau without significant change. Later, he resigned from public service and became an associate in the private firm of Leonard & Levy. Senior partner Leonard has been asked to defend a dentist, Karis Borloff, in a civil suit brought by the State Revenue Bureau to collect back taxes. One of the legal issues in Borloff's case will be the proper interpretation and application of the travel expense regulations drafted by Toulmin. Under what, if any, circumstances may senior partner Leonard represent Borloff?

STATE FARM MUTUAL AUTOMOBILE INSURANCE COMPANY v. K.A.W.

Supreme Court of Florida, 1991.
575 So.2d 630.

GRIMES, JUSTICE

* * *

David Wilkerson was driving a rental car in which his wife and infant daughter were passengers when it was struck by another car. The Wilkersons retained the law firm of Sheldon J. Schlesinger, P.A. (Schlesinger firm) and filed suit against the driver and owner of the other vehicle and others for injuries suffered by the three of them in the accident. The action included a count against petitioner State Farm Mutual Automobile Insurance Company (State Farm), the Wilkersons' insurer, for uninsured motorist coverage. The Wilkersons also filed a separate malpractice action against various health care providers for alleged negligent treatment of their daughter after the accident. The Schlesinger firm represented the Wilkersons in the malpractice action.

After the personal injury action had proceeded for approximately one year, the Wilkersons added new defendants, including petitioners Interstate Fire and Casualty Company and Continental Casualty Company, which had issued uninsured motorist insurance to Wilkerson's employer. The following year, the Wilkersons' attorneys determined that David Wilkerson's negligence may have contributed to the automobile accident. Thereupon, Mr. Wilkerson discharged the Schlesinger firm as his counsel in the personal injury action and retained a former member of the Schlesinger firm as new counsel. Shortly thereafter, Mrs. Wilkerson and her daughter filed a second amended complaint in that action, adding David Wilkerson as a defendant. The Schlesinger firm continued to represent Mrs. Wilkerson and the daughter in that action, and Mr. Wilkerson consented to be sued up to the limits of his insurance coverage. The firm also continued to represent all three Wilkersons in the medical malpractice action.

Asserting their exposure as liability insurers of Mr. Wilkerson, each of the petitioners filed motions seeking the disqualification of the Schlesinger firm in the personal injury action. Petitioners objected to the potential for the Schlesinger firm to use confidential information gained during the course of the prior representation of Mr. Wilkerson in this action against him. In opposition to the motion, David Wilkerson filed an affidavit stating that he did not consider anything he discussed with Sheldon Schlesinger privileged because he had disclosed everything in his deposition and he did not feel that Mr. Schlesinger's representation of his wife and daughter disadvantaged him in any way. Mrs. Wilkerson also submitted an affidavit in which she stated that she and her daughter would be prejudiced if the Schlesinger firm were required to withdraw.

The trial court refused to disqualify the Schlesinger firm, finding that the petitioners lacked standing to request disqualification in the face of Mr. Wilkerson's consent to the firm's representation of his wife and child. In addition, the court found that the petitioners failed to show clearly and convincingly that they would be prejudiced or that the continued representation would interfere with the fair and impartial administration of justice. The Fourth District Court of Appeal denied the insurers' petitions for writ of certiorari, finding no proof of substantial prejudice or circumstances calling into question the fair and efficient administration of justice.

While not addressed by the majority opinion below, we shall first discuss the question of the petitioners' standing. The Wilkersons contend that an attorney may not be disqualified where the former client has consented to the representation.

* * * The rule urged by the Wilkersons is based on the premise that rules governing attorney conduct are intended for the protection of the client, who may either explicitly or implicitly waive that protection. On the other hand, the petitioners argue that they have standing because as insurance companies they will be liable for the payment of any judgment against David Wilkerson in this action.

* * *

The ethical principle at issue is an attorney's duty to maintain the confidences of his client. That principle is embodied in two rules of professional conduct. Rule Regulating The Florida Bar 4–1.6(a) provides that "[a] lawyer shall not reveal information relating to representation of a client * * * unless the client consents after disclosure to the client."

The duty of confidentiality continues after termination of the attorney-client relationship. *See* Comment to rule 4–1.6.

Rule Regulating The Florida Bar 4–1.9 provides:

A lawyer who has formerly represented a client in a matter shall not thereafter:

(a) Represent another person in the same or a substantially related matter in which that person's interests are materially adverse to the interests of the former client unless the former client consents after consultation; or

(b) Use information relating to the representation to the disadvantage of the former client except as rule 4–1.6 would permit with respect to a client or when the information has become generally known.[1]

The purpose of the requirement that an attorney maintain client confidences is two-fold. It advances the interests of the client by encouraging a free flow of information and the development of trust essential to an attorney-client relationship. *Developments in the Law: Conflicts of Interest in the Legal Profession,* 94 Harv.L.Rev. 1244, 1316 (1981). However, it also serves a second purpose fundamental to a fair adversary system. Our legal system cannot function fairly or effectively if an attorney has an informational advantage in the form of confidences gained during a former representation of his client's current opponent. *Id.* at 1315–16; * * *.

The question then is whether the insurers may "stand in the shoes" of their insured for purposes of seeking disqualification of the Schlesinger firm on grounds of conflict of interest. Comments to the Rules of Professional Conduct indicate that under certain circumstances someone other than the client may request disqualification. Thus, where a conflict "is such as clearly to call in question the fair or efficient administration of justice, opposing counsel may properly raise the question." Comment to Rule Regulating The Florida Bar 4–1.7. * * *

We find that the facts of this case call into question the fair administration of justice. Mr. Wilkerson is not exposed to any personal liability because he may be sued only up to the amount of any available insurance coverage. * * * This is, in reality, not an action between Mr.

---

1. Rule Regulating The Florida Bar 4–1.7 is also pertinent here. That rule provides:

(a) A lawyer shall not represent a client if the representation of that client will be directly adverse to the interests of another client, unless:

(1) The lawyer reasonably believes the representation will not adversely affect the lawyer's responsibilities to and relationship with the other client; and

(2) Each client consents after consultation.

Mr. Wilkerson is, in effect, both a former client of the Schlesinger firm for purposes of rule 4–1.9 (in the personal injury action) and a current client for purposes of rule 4–1.7 (in the medical malpractice action). The duty of confidentiality is present regardless of whether Mr. Wilkerson is viewed as the firm's former or current client.

[The Florida Rules are identical to ABA Model Rules 1.6, 1.7 and 1.9 as they existed before amendment in 1989—eds.]

Wilkerson and his child, but an action by the mother and child against the parent's insurance carriers. Mr. Wilkerson is in a position adverse to his daughter in theory only. He reasonably hopes to enhance his daughter's chance of recovery. The petitioners, on the other hand, will be acting in Mr. Wilkerson's defense, attempting to persuade the fact finder that he was not negligent in the automobile accident in order that they may avoid liability. Because of this situation, Wilkerson's consent to the firm's representation of his wife and daughter does not end the inquiry. Information disclosed by Mr. Wilkerson to his attorneys during the course of the attorney-client relationship could be used to prove that Mr. Wilkerson was negligent. This is adverse to the petitioners who are obligated to act in his defense. The unfairness of the situation results from the fact that Mrs. Wilkerson and her daughter have a potential informational advantage over those who must defend Mr. Wilkerson which was gained as a result of her law firm's former representation of Mr. Wilkerson in this action. It defies logic to suggest that the petitioners do not have a legitimate interest in seeking to prevent the opposing parties from using confidential information obtained from their insured through a prior attorney-client relationship. We conclude that the petitioners have standing to request the law firm's disqualification.

We next address the issue of the appropriate standard to apply to determine whether the Schlesinger firm should be disqualified. In conflict-of-interest cases such as this arising under the former Code of Professional Responsibility, one seeking to disqualify opposing counsel was required to show that (1) an attorney-client relationship existed, thereby giving rise to an irrefutable presumption that confidences were disclosed during the relationship, and (2) the matter in which the law firm subsequently represented the interest adverse to the former client was the same or substantially related to the matter in which it represented the former client. This standard was based on the Code of Professional Responsibility, Canon 4, which provided that an attorney should preserve the confidences and secrets of a client.

* * * The Rules of Professional Conduct requiring confidentiality serve the same purposes as the confidentiality requirements of the Code of Professional Responsibility. Similarly, the need for the irrefutable presumption continues to exist, just as under the former code. The presumption acknowledges the difficulty of proving that confidential information useful to the attorney's current client was given to the attorney. It also protects the client by not requiring disclosure of confidences previously given to the attorney. *See Government of India v. Cook Indus., Inc.,* 422 F.Supp. 1057, 1060 (S.D.N.Y.1976) (if two actions are substantially related, court will not require proof that attorney had access to confidential information, nor give weight to attorney's assertion that he had no access to and did not possess confidential information), *aff'd,* 569 F.2d 737 (2d Cir.1978).

Accordingly, we disagree with the court below that actual proof of prejudice is a prerequisite to disqualification under these circumstances. The Schlesinger firm represented Mr. Wilkerson in the personal injury action for more than two years, and the existence of this relationship raised the irrefutable presumption that confidences were disclosed. Moreover, the firm continues to represent Mr. Wilkerson in the medical malpractice action. Under Florida law, Mr. Wilkerson could be found liable in the instant case not only for those injuries which were sustained by his daughter in the automobile accident but also for any injuries she received as a result of any subsequent medical malpractice. Thus, even now Mr. Wilkerson may be disclosing confidences to the Schlesinger firm as his counsel in the medical malpractice action which could be used against him by the Schlesinger firm in the instant case.

In reaching our decision, we do not imply any misconduct on the part of the Schlesinger firm. In this respect, we find the statement in *Rotante v. Lawrence Hospital,* 46 A.D.2d 199, 200, 361 N.Y.S.2d 372, 373 (1974), apropos:

> While these facts neither indicate nor imply any departure from professional conduct or breach of any ethical canon, we cannot escape the conclusion that this is a situation rife with the possibility of discredit to the bar and the administration of justice. Obviously Mr. Turkewitz cannot erase from his mind the confidences he received from his former client or the plan of defense he envisaged. Though we do not dispute his good faith or the good faith of the firm representing plaintiff, both the possibility of conflict of interest and the appearance of it are too strong to ignore.

We quash the decision below and direct that the Schlesinger firm be disqualified from further representation of Mrs. Wilkerson and her minor child in this action.

It is so ordered.

* * *

ROSENFELD CONSTRUCTION COMPANY, INC. v. SUPERIOR COURT

California Court of Appeal, Fifth District, 1991.
235 Cal.App.3d 566, 286 Cal.Rptr. 609.

OPINION

VARTABEDIAN, ASSOCIATE JUSTICE.

This is a petition for writ of mandate following respondent court's denial of the motion of petitioner, Rosenfeld Construction Company, Inc., to disqualify the law firm of Wild, Carter, Tipton & Oliver (hereafter Wild) in its representation of real parties in interest, Paul Sivas and Jeanet Sivas. * * *

PROCEDURAL AND FACTUAL BACKGROUND

Petitioner brought a motion for disqualification of opposing counsel, the Wild firm, on the basis it had formerly represented petitioner in a related matter.

The memorandum in support of the motion recited that in 1982, John Rosenfeld, petitioner's president, consulted Wild for advice and representation in a dispute with Mr. and Mrs. George Lawson regarding the Lawsons' failure to pay petitioner for constructing a home; * * *.

* * *

Wild acknowledged it represented petitioner for nearly four years in "relatively few matters," including the Lawson controversy.

The Lawsons had contended that the construction of their home was defective in the following respects: cabinetry, flooring, doors, water penetration into rooms and foundation, roof penetrations, moldings, painting, tile work and the grading of the property on which the house was constructed.

On November 18, 1988, real parties initiated a lawsuit against petitioner, alleging that it breached its contract with them by failing to construct their residence in conformity with the construction contract and industry standards, in particular in the following areas: cabinetry, flooring, doors, water penetration, painting, and grading of the lot on which the house was constructed.

At the time the lawsuit was commenced, real parties were represented by the law firm of Dowling, Magarian, Phillips & Aaron (hereafter Dowling). On January 8 or 9, 1991, as a consequence of attorney Steven E. Paganetti's change of employment from the Dowling firm to Wild, the Wild firm was substituted as counsel for real parties.

Petitioner's attorney, D. Tyler Tharpe, received the notice of substitution of attorneys on January 14, 1991. Tharpe had been present at the deposition of John Rosenfeld nearly a year earlier, at which time Rosenfeld had mentioned that petitioner was once represented by Wild. On February 1, 1991, Tharpe reviewed the deposition testimony, which reminded him of petitioner's prior representation by Wild.

On February 4, 1991, the next business day, Tharpe called the matter to John Rosenfeld's attention; on that same day, Rosenfeld instructed Tharpe to contact Wild, demanding that it immediately withdraw as counsel for real parties. Tharpe did so. Wild declined.

Before respondent court, petitioner argued that the appropriate test to apply to determine if disqualification was necessary was the substantial relationship standard. Claiming that the subject matters of the two lawsuits were substantially related, petitioner asked the court to disqualify Wild from the representation of real parties in the instant matter.

Rosenfeld's declaration in support of the motion to disqualify contained his statement that he spent "dozens of hours" with Robert H. Oliver, Trevor C. Clegg, William H. Leifer, and Victor D. Ryerson of the Wild firm concerning the Lawson dispute. Rosenfeld declared:

"[O]ver the course of those many years (1) I surrendered to WCT & O [Wild] all of the business' work files relating to the Lawson project, (2) I explained in detail to each of the above-mentioned attorneys at WCT & O my company's manner of operation, methods of construction and provision of warranty work, and (3) I disclosed to the same attorneys my strategies as they relate to handling customer complaints and the attorneys shared their strategies with me."

In his supplemental declaration, Rosenfeld further declared:

"3. * * * Every attorney who assisted in representing ROSENFELD in the Lawson controversy met with me at one time or another, some more than others, and I shared confidential information with them about the nature of the complaints and the manner of ROSENFELD's construction as it related to the complaints. During the course of the prior representation, I shared my strategies with the WCT & O attorneys and they shared their strategies with me related to proving ROSENFELD's case against the Lawsons and defeating the Lawsons' claims against ROSENFELD.

"4. There is no question in my mind that the attorneys at WCT & O, owing to their extended representation of ROSENFELD, each had access to and actually accessed information which is confidential in nature and which is substantially related to the present action."

Four attorneys from Wild submitted declarations in opposition to the motion.

Robert Oliver declared that his firm represented Rosenfeld personally or the petitioner corporation "in relatively few matters through approximately 1985." He acknowledged that Wild represented petitioner in the controversy with the Lawsons and that the case ultimately involved litigation and arbitration, * * *.

Oliver further declared that Paganetti had not discussed the "substance of the Rosenfeld Construction Company, Inc./Lawson case" with him. Oliver went on:

"The file containing the *Rosenfeld Construction vs. Lawson* case has been closed for several years and stored in a location removed from our law offices. Only upon receiving correspondence alleging conflicts of interest was the file brought to this office so that declarations could be prepared by various partners in this firm."

William H. Leifer submitted a declaration in which he admitted he had reviewed the office file entitled Rosenfeld Construction Company, Inc. v. Lawson et al. Leifer noted:

"Even after reviewing the file and reviewing the documents that I could find in the file, I still have no recollection of ever having talked to John Rosenfeld in person. * * * I have not in any fashion discussed with Mr. Paganetti any of the issues having to do with the Lawson matter and could not because I have no actual knowledge of the underlying facts giving rise to that case and I was not involved in any of the merits of the case except on a very limited basis as to the fact that it concerned a residence."

Trevor Clegg acknowledged that in 1983 he prepared and filed a complaint seeking foreclosure of petitioner's mechanic's lien on the Lawsons' residence and damages for breach of contract Clegg went on to note:

"4. * * * In the course of preparing the complaint, I did conduct discussions with Mr. John Rosenfeld, * * * To the best of my recollection, those discussions were neither lengthy nor detailed. They did touch on the Lawsons' complaints, but with the exception noted below, I do not recall any extended or detailed discussion of those complaints. * * *

"5. The one complaint that Mr. Rosenfeld and I discussed in some detail involved land subsidence or slippage around and under the Lawson residence. Mr. Rosenfeld maintained that the entire problem was the Lawsons' fault. * * *

"6. The only materials in our file that we received from Rosenfeld Construction consisted of rather unenlightening communications to and from the Lawsons and the Contractors License Board; a few scribbled notes by Mr. Rosenfeld; and a chronology of events prepared by Mr. Rosenfeld."

Paganetti declared that he never had any conversations with any of his fellow attorneys at Wild concerning the Lawson matter, nor had he seen any written documents relating to the Lawson matter. * * *

The minute order of the court's ruling reads in its entirety, "Motion to disqualify is denied. No present counsel at 'Wild, Carter, Tipton & Oliver' have sufficient knowledge of prior 'Rosenfeld' representation to disqualify the firm from representing the Sivas. The court finds no actual or potential present conflict."

* * *

DISCUSSION

* * *

Rule 3–310 of the State Bar Rules of Professional Conduct provides for the avoidance of representation of adverse interests.[2] It has long been recognized that knowledge obtained by one member of a firm of lawyers is imputed to all the other members. "The imputed knowledge theory holds that knowledge by any member of a law firm is knowledge

---

2. Rule 3–310 of the State Bar of Professional Conduct (23 West's Ann.Cal. Codes, Civil and Crim.Rules, 1991 supp. pamph., p. 551) provides in pertinent part:

"(A) If a member has or had a relationship with another party interested in the representation, or has an interest in its subject matter, the member shall not accept or continue such representation without all affected clients' informed written consent.

"_____

"(D) A member shall not accept employment adverse to a client or former client where, by reason of the representation of the client or former client, the member has obtained confidential information material to the employment except with the informed written consent of the client or former client."

by all of the attorneys in the firm, partners as well as associates." (*Chadwick v. Superior Court* [1980] 106 Cal.App.3d 108, 116, 164 Cal. Rptr. 864.)

In 1953, the United States District Court for the Southern District of New York decided *T.C. Theatre Corp. v. Warner Bros. Pictures* (S.D.N.Y.1953) 113 F.Supp. 265, in which the court held "[a] lawyer's duty of absolute loyalty to his client's interest does not end with his retainer. He is enjoined for all time, except as he may be released by law, from disclosing matters revealed to him by reason of the confidential relationship. Related to this principle is the rule that where any substantial relationship can be shown between the subject matter of a former representation and that of a subsequent adverse representation, the latter will be prohibited." (*Id.* at p. 268.) Further, "the former client need show no more than that the matter embraced within the pending suit wherein his former attorney appears on behalf of his adversary are substantially related to the matters or cause of action wherein the attorney previously represented him, the former client. The court will assume that during the course of the former representation confidences were disclosed to the attorney bearing on the subject matter of the representation. It will not inquire into their nature and extent. Only in this manner can the lawyer's duty of absolute fidelity be enforced and the spirit of the rule relating to privileged communications be maintained." (*Id.* at pp. 268–269.)

The court went on to note that to require a client to show the nature of the confidential information "would tear aside the protective cloak drawn about the lawyer-client relationship. For the court to probe further and sift the confidences in fact revealed would require the disclosure of the matters intended to be protected by the rule * * *. No client should ever be concerned with the possible use against him in future litigation of what he may have revealed to his attorney." (*T.C. Theatre Corp. v. Warner Bros. Pictures, supra,* 113 F.Supp. at p. 269.)

In 1983, a California court first used the substantial relationship standard in *Global Van Lines, Inc. v. Superior Court* (1983) 144 Cal. App.3d 483, 192 Cal.Rptr. 609. That court held:

> "When a substantial relationship has been shown to exist between the former representation and the current representation, and when it appears by virtue of the nature of the former representation or the relationship of the attorney to his former client confidential information material to the current dispute would normally have been imparted to the attorney or to subordinates for whose legal work he was responsible, the attorney's knowledge of confidential information is presumed. [Citation.]
>
> "This is the rule by necessity, for it is not within the power of the former client to prove what is in the mind of the attorney. Nor should the attorney have to 'engage in a subtle evaluation of the extent to which he acquired relevant information in the first representation and of the actual use of that knowledge and information in

the subsequent representation.' [Citations.]" (*Global Van Lines, supra,* 144 Cal.App.3d at p. 489, 192 Cal.Rptr. 609.)

* * *

Subsequently, our court decided *River West, Inc. v. Nickel* (1987) 188 Cal.App.3d 1297, 234 Cal.Rptr. 33, in which we reversed the trial court's order disqualifying counsel for a conflict of interest. In *River West,* the prior representation occurred more than 27 years earlier and the moving party had notice of the conflict over 3 years before he made the motion to disqualify. We determined that due to the long wait in bringing the motion to disqualify, an exception to the substantial relationship test could be found.

* * *

While an exception was found on the particular facts, our court in *River West* left no doubt that the substantial relationship test is the proper standard. "Therefore, in the usual case when the substantial relationship of the matters is established, the inquiry ends and the disqualification should be ordered. If it were otherwise, a weighing process would be inevitable. The rights of the former client would be lined up against those of the new client, perhaps to the detriment of both. The purpose of the substantial relationship test is to avoid such an inquiry." (*River West, Inc. v. Nickel, supra,* 188 Cal.App.3d at p. 1304, 234 Cal.Rptr. 33.)

"Disqualification of an attorney from representing a former client does not require proof of actual possession of confidential information."

While the substantial relationship test is central to the determination of attorney disqualification, the standard itself has not received much critical scrutiny. Yet both parts of the test, "substantial" and "relationship," are susceptible to a variety of meanings and interpretations.

The recent case of *H.F. Ahmanson & Co. v. Salomon Brothers, Inc.* (1991) 229 Cal.App.3d 1445, 280 Cal.Rptr. 614 recognized the need for greater specificity in dealing with the standard. "The word 'substantial,' like other nonquantifiable denominators of measurement, is subject to a variety of interpretations. Use of the word 'relationship' implies a connection, but offers no guidance as to *what* is being connected: subject matters, facts, or issues." (*Id.* at p. 1453, 280 Cal.Rptr. 614.) The *Ahmanson* court looked to *Silver Chrysler Plymouth, Inc. v. Chrysler Mot. Corp.* (2d Cir.1975) 518 F.2d 751, 757, for an analysis of the substantial relationship test found in Judge Adams's concurring opinion. Judge Adams suggested that a court should "focus on the similarities between the two factual situations, the legal questions posed, and the nature and extent of the attorney's involvement with the cases. As part of its review, the court should examine the time spent by the attorney on the earlier cases, the type of work performed, and the attorney's possible exposure to formulation of policy or strategy." (*Id.* at p. 760, conc. opn. of Adams, J.)

The *Ahmanson* court thus analyzed the question of whether a substantial relationship existed by applying three factors: factual similarity, legal similarity, and nature and extent of the attorney's involvement with the cases.

Here, the record does not reflect that the court applied the substantial relationship standard nor that significant inquiry was made concerning the three factors stated in *Ahmanson*. The respondent court, without benefit of the specific analysis contained in *Ahmanson* (which was not filed until May 7, 1991), merely determined that no present counsel at the law firm in question had "sufficient knowledge of prior 'Rosenfeld' representation" to disqualify the firm. The court then found no actual or potential present conflict existed.

We find no authority that supports the notion that, standing alone, the present recollection of the members of the firm is an adequate criterion.

The respondent court failed to apply the appropriate standard. * * * We therefore return the matter to respondent court to allow the court to evaluate the motion in light of the appropriate standard.

In supplemental briefing, real parties suggest that if we determine the motion for disqualification was improperly denied, respondent court should be instructed to institute or impose a screening procedure such as we approved in *Higdon v. Superior Court* (1991) 227 Cal.App.3d 1667, 278 Cal.Rptr. 588 to avoid disqualification.

Higdon presented a very different situation—we were confronted with a case of first impression, involving the novel circumstance of a former judicial officer joining a law firm. In *Higdon,* we determined whether a former court commissioner, and the law firm he had joined, would be disqualified from representing the husbands in two separate dissolution actions. The former court commissioner had not represented any of the parties but had heard contested matters in the same actions. *Higdon* did not involve any allegation of conflict of interests or passage of confidential information, far less a presumption. Nor did it present a question of a firm's split loyalty in representing a present client whose interests may be in conflict with those of a prior client of the firm. By contrast, here, if the respondent court determines a "substantial relationship" exists, there is a conclusive presumption that confidential information has passed to the prior attorney.

In *Higdon*, while the former court commissioner was personally disqualified from handling a matter which he had previously heard as a judge, the remainder of the firm could avoid disqualification so long as it was proven that he had been and would continue to be screened from any participation in the case. We recognized there that existing California law resulted from very different circumstances concerning practicing attorneys changing employment and "California precedent has not rushed to accept the concept of disqualifying the attorney but not the firm, nor has it enthusiastically embarked upon erecting Chinese walls.' " (*Higdon v. Superior Court, supra,* 227 Cal.App.3d 1667, 1679,

278 Cal.Rptr. 588, quoting *Klein v. Superior Court* (1988) 198 Cal.App.3d 894, 912, 244 Cal.Rptr. 226.)

Here, real parties' request would result in the *firm* being disqualified and the member *attorney* being allowed to continue representing the client. Screening under these circumstances would be even more drastic than the converse relationship criticized in *Klein*. Should the respondent court find the current representation is substantially related to the former, creating the conclusive presumption that the Wild firm possesses confidential information of its former client, petitioner, a screening procedure cannot suffice to safeguard against the conflicting representations.

Real parties argue further that they will be prejudiced if they must obtain new representation at this point. However, this argument fails to recognize that real parties had been represented by the *firm* employing Paganetti, not the individual attorney alone. The instant problem arose when real parties obtained new representation. Real parties were represented for some years by Dowling until they chose to substitute Wild. The determination of whether a client follows an attorney to a new firm should include some scrutiny of the conflicts of interest that might result. While attorneys should be able to move freely from membership in one firm to another and clients should be allowed their choice of an individual attorney, the importance of maintaining public respect for and belief in the integrity of the legal profession should not take a back seat to other considerations.

The right to counsel of one's choice must be balanced with "the paramount objective of maintaining public confidence in the impartiality of the courts and the integrity of its professional bar."

We remand this matter to respondent court with instructions to apply the appropriate standard to determine if there exists a substantial relationship between the prior representation and the current representation based on the facts, the legal issues, and the nature and extent of involvement of the attorneys.

DISPOSITION

The petition for writ of mandate is granted; respondent court is ordered to set aside its order denying the motion for disqualification. Respondent court shall hold another hearing wherein it will consider relevant material bearing on the issue of whether or not there exists a substantial relationship between the present representation and the prior representation. If it finds such a substantial relationship, the court shall grant the motion for disqualification. The parties shall bear their own costs of the instant proceeding.

* * *

CHO v. SUPERIOR COURT

California Court of Appeal, Second District, 1995.
39 Cal.App.4th 113, 45 Cal.Rptr.2d 863.

EPSTEIN, ASSOCIATE JUSTICE.

The issue in this case is whether a law firm must be disqualified as counsel in a lawsuit after employing the retired judge who had presided over the action and had received ex parte confidences from the opposing party in the course of settlement conferences. We conclude that screening procedures are not sufficient to preserve public trust in the justice system in these circumstances and therefore the firm must be disqualified.

FACTUAL AND PROCEDURAL SUMMARY

[Cho is the plaintiff in Jennifer Donghee Cho v. Cho Hung Bank and Jang W. Lee (No. BC080299) pending in the Los Angeles County Superior Court. Cho moved to disqualify the law firm of Graham & James, counsel for Cho Hung Bank, after Eric E. Younger, the judge who had presided over the action, retired and joined Graham & James in an "of counsel" capacity.

Judge Younger held three settlement conferences at various stages of the proceedings. According to Cho, her "posture in the settlement conferences accordingly changed at such stages, not the least of which was disclosure of Cho's bottom line settlement." Cho's lawyer also stated that Judge Younger had been privy to confidences relating to the merits of Cho's case because: "In separate conference, Judge Younger asked plaintiff's counsel to speak candidly about the strengths and weaknesses of plaintiff's case, to which counsel responded openly and divulged information to His Honor in confidence. No such information would have been divulged but for the fact that it was in a confidential setting."

Judge Younger retired in late December 1994, with the Cho action still pending. Graham & James substituted into the lawsuit as counsel for Cho Hung Bank on February 17, 1995. Within the next few days, a partner at Graham & James, Stephen Owens, reviewed the court docket sheet and discovered for the first time that Judge Younger had presided over the case until his retirement. Mr. Owens had heard that Judge Younger was joining the firm, and he told the managing partner, Henry David, of Judge Younger's role in the action. After researching the issues, Graham & James decided to impose a " 'cone of silence' " around Judge Younger before he began his formal relationship with the firm. A memorandum was circulated throughout Graham & James directing all personnel that Judge Younger was not to be involved in the action in any way; that it was not to be discussed in his presence; that Judge Younger was not to discuss his role or any information he had obtained; and that he was not to have access to any files or written materials about the action.

Judge Younger began his work with Graham & James on March 1, 1995. Cho's attorney first learned of this at a deposition on March 22, 1995. On the same day Graham & James delivered a letter to the court and counsel in the action formally informing them of Judge Younger's relationship with that firm, and of the steps taken to screen him from any involvement in the action.]

DISCUSSION

This case presents an issue of first impression in California— whether a law firm must be disqualified when it employs a former judge who in his official capacity received ex parte confidences, bearing on the merits of a lawsuit over which he was presiding, from an adverse party in the identical litigation in which the motion to disqualify is brought. We conclude that the firm must be disqualified.

* * *

The parties acknowledge that Judge Younger is disqualified from participating in the action by virtue of his role as judge. There is no California rule of professional conduct which governs the issue of disqualification of Graham & James. Petitioner urges us to adopt the "substantial relationship" test applied in *Rosenfeld* [*supra,* p. 327.]. * * * Cho Hung Bank argues that we should apply the analysis employed by the court in *Higdon v. Superior Court*, 227 Cal.App.3d 1667, 278 Cal.Rptr. 588 (1991). As we shall explain, neither analysis resolves the issues presented here.

The reported decision closest to ours is *Higdon v. Superior Court*, *supra,* 227 Cal.App.3d 1667, 278 Cal.Rptr. 588. In that case, a court commissioner resigned and joined a law firm representing a party to a marital dissolution action on which he had heard contested matters. There was no indication that the commissioner had been party to confidences divulged by either side in the case.

The *Higdon* court ruled that * * * absent consent by the opposing party, the former commissioner was disqualified from participating in the case as an attorney under the rationale of rule 1.12(a) of the American Bar Association Model Rules of Professional Conduct. That rule provides: "[A] lawyer shall not represent anyone in connection with a matter in which the lawyer participated personally and substantially as a judge or other adjudicative officer, arbitrator or law clerk to such a person, unless all parties to the proceeding consent after consultation."

Turning to the question whether the former commissioner's firm must be disqualified, the court concluded: "... no conflict of interest is even alleged here; rather the appearance of impropriety is asserted as the sole basis supporting recusal of Thomas's firm. *Except for authorized ex parte matters* and instances of unethical behavior, a judge's role in a court proceeding does not present the opportunity for confidentiality with a party. (See Cal.Code of Jud.Conduct, canon 3.) Nonetheless, the parties' and the public's perception of impropriety needs to be alleviated by a process which assures that neither the former judge nor his law firm has or will receive an unfair advantage. Screening serves this purpose. A trial court hearing a recusal motion thus must look beyond the mere allegation of appearance of impropriety to determine whether appropriate screening has occurred and whether screening can effectively continue to protect against the former judge's participation." (227 Cal.App.3d at p. 1680, 278 Cal.Rptr. 588, italics added.) The court concluded that the law firm should be given an opportunity to establish that the former commissioner, now attorney, had been effectively screened from the case. If that requirement was satisfied, the *Higdon* court directed the trial court to deny the motion for recusal of the firm. (*Id.* at pp. 1680–1681, 278 Cal.Rptr. 588.)

In reaching this conclusion, the *Higdon* court considered another provision of rule 1.12 of the ABA Model Rules of Professional Conduct, which addresses recusal of a law firm employing a former judicial officer: " '(c) If a lawyer is disqualified by paragraph (a), no lawyer in a firm with which that lawyer is associated may knowingly undertake or continue representation in the matter unless: [¶] (1) the disqualified lawyer is screened from any participation in the matter and is apportioned no part of the fee therefrom; and [¶] (2) written notice is promptly given to the appropriate tribunal to enable it to ascertain compliance with the provisions of this rule.' " (227 Cal.App.3d at p. 1676, 278 Cal.Rptr. 588.)

The protection of the confidences of litigants has been a primary focus of rules of professional conduct in California and as drafted by the American Bar Association. (See Rules Prof.Conduct, rule 3–310(E); *Flatt v. Superior Court*, 9 Cal.4th 275, 283, 36 Cal.Rptr.2d 537, 885 P.2d 950 [discussing fiduciary duty of confidentiality in context of Rules of Professional Conduct]; ABA Model Rules Prof.Conduct, rules 1.6; 1.9; and 1.10.) Public attorneys moving to the private sector are treated separately under the American Bar Association's Model Rules of Professional Conduct, rule 1.11 (Model Rules). Subdivision (b) of that rule provides: "[A] lawyer having information that the lawyer knows is confidential government information about a person acquired when the lawyer was a public officer or employee, may not represent a private client whose interests are adverse to that person in a matter in which the information could be used to the material disadvantage of that person. A firm with which that lawyer is associated may undertake or continue representation in the matter only if the disqualified lawyer is screened from any participation in the matter and is apportioned no part of the fee therefrom." Similarly, under the Model Rules, a former judge may not represent anyone in connection with a matter in which he or she "participated personally and substantially as a judge...." (Model Rules, rule 1.12(a).) The rule on vicarious disqualification of the law firm employing a former judicial officer parallels the rule for former public attorneys: the disqualified attorney must be screened from participation, receive no share of the fee, and notice must be given to the appropriate tribunal. (Model Rules, rule 1.12(c).)

The integrity of the judicial process demands that litigants have confidence that a judicial officer who has been privy to revelations regarding the case in the course of settlement conferences will not later become aligned with the opposition. Unlike the disqualification of a former private sector attorney who has governmental information, here the former judge became privy to the confidences of private parties to the litigation.

We are presented with a situation in which the judge's role did include receiving confidences from petitioner's counsel ex parte during repeated settlement conferences. The case is analogous to that of a mediator who was disqualified from representing a litigant in a subsequent matter related to an earlier case in which the mediator had received confidences from the parties. (*Poly Software International, Inc. v. Su* (D.Utah 1995) 880 F.Supp. 1487.)

[In *Poly Software* the district court required disqualification of a former mediator and his firm from representing parties involved in the mediation against other parties to the mediation.]

* * *

We agree with the analysis in *Poly Software* that disqualification of both the individual attorney and his or her firm is required where the attorney has been privy to confidences of a litigant while acting as a neutral mediator. * * *

All manner of issues are discussed in confidence at a settlement conference, including the strengths and weaknesses of each party's case, and the amount the party is willing to pay or receive in settlement. "[A] settlement conference judge does not decide anything—he merely uses his judicial status to help the parties reach a settlement if reasonably possible. To this end it has been said that the judge should actively participate in the negotiating process to 'break the ice' between litigants who may be reluctant to settle. The judge should also use any expertise he may have in the subject area of the litigation to express his opinions of the settlement value of the various causes of action against the different defendants or of the range in which negotiations may realistically proceed. He should listen to and carefully evaluate the parties' personal contentions so they will feel they have had their 'day in court' if the case is settled. [Citations.]" (*Horton v. Superior Court* (1987) 194 Cal.App.3d 727, 733, 238 Cal.Rptr. 467.)

No amount of assurances or screening procedures, no "cone of silence," could ever convince the opposing party that the confidences would not be used to its disadvantage. When a litigant has bared its soul in confidential settlement conferences with a judicial officer, that litigant could not help but be horrified to find that the judicial officer has resigned to join the opposing law firm—which is now pressing or defending the lawsuit against that litigant. No one could have confidence in the integrity of a legal process in which this is permitted to occur without the parties' consent.

Petitioner has urged us to adopt the "substantial relationship" test applied in *Rosenfeld Construction Co. v. Superior Court* (1991) 235 Cal.App.3d 566, 286 Cal.Rptr. 609.

We have no quarrel with * * * the *Rosenfeld* court's policy analysis, but we find that it does not apply to this case. Here, Judge Younger had no previous attorney-client relationship with petitioner. Moreover, the motion to disqualify was brought in the identical action in which Judge Younger served as settlement judge. Under these circumstances, the "substantial relationship" test does not apply. The common theme between the disqualification opinions discussed in *Rosenfeld* and our case is the vital importance of maintaining confidences disclosed in the course of litigation to ensure public trust in the judicial system.

* * *

DISPOSITION

[The Court of Appeal directed the Superior Court to vacate its order denying petitioner's motion to disqualify Graham & James and to enter a new order granting the motion.]

A. M. WOOD, P.J., and HASTINGS, J., concur.

IMPUTED DISQUALIFICATION AND SCREENING

Legal ethics rules and case law begin with the assumption that lawyers working together in a single firm share each other's, and their clients', secrets and confidences. [See ABA Model Rule 1.6, comment.] This assumption is based on the realities of practice as well—both office routine and financial rewards are shared within a firm. Generally, the assumption works well; no one seriously suggests that two partners within a single firm could represent adversaries in litigation. One consequence of this assumption is that lawyers within a firm must also share each other's disqualifications for conflicts of interest; one lawyer's conflicts are imputed to all other lawyers in the firm. [See generally ABA Model Rule 1.10(a) and comment 6.] In a time of increased lawyer mobility, imputed disqualification rules can quickly spread taints when lawyers move among firms, and the result can spin out of control.

Under the ABA Code, imputed disqualification became a near absolute rule. DR 5–105(D) provided that if any one lawyer in a firm was disqualified, all lawyers in the firm were. There was no exception for client consent or waiver. [Wolfram § 7.6.2, at 394.] The ABA Model Rules have adopted a much more flexible approach that does not apply to all disqualifying associations. For example, spousal and other family conflicts [Rule 1.8(i)] and the lawyer witness rule [Rule 3.7] do not come within the automatic disqualifications. There is no automatic disqualification for all lawyers with whom a departing lawyer had been associated [Rule 1.10(b).] Most imputed disqualifications can be cured by informed client consents. [Rule 1.10(c).]

Nevertheless, imputed disqualification rules regularly create problems for law firms when a lawyer moves from one firm to another. If a client or former client of the former firm is involved as an adversary with a client of the newly associated firm, both firms could end up disqualified, and, in sharply contested matters, removing the disqualification by client consent is unlikely. The proposed favored solution from the bar is to protect the new firm by screening off the tainted lawyer. Such devices are sometimes referred to as "Chinese walls" or "ethical walls." Their approval in the courts has been decidedly mixed and largely limited to former government lawyers moving to private practices. [See Model Rule 1.11 approving such screening and the discussion in *Rosenfeld* and *Cho, supra.*] The Model Rules do not formally accept the device in private firm to private firm moves. However, after intense debate, the ALI, in section 204 of its Proposed Final Draft No. 1 of the Restatement of the Law Governing Lawyers recently approved using screening to remove imputed disqualification in the purely private setting. Section 204(2) applies only when "(a) any confidential client information communicated to the personally prohibited lawyer is unlikely to be significant in the subsequent matter"; (b) when adequate screening measures are in place; and (c) when "timely and adequate notice of the screening has been provided to all affected clients." According to comment d(ii):

> Screening must assure that confidential client information, if any, that the personally-prohibited lawyer possesses will not pass from that lawyer to any other lawyer in the firm. The screened lawyer should be prohibited from talking to any other person in the firm about the matter as to which the lawyer is prohibited, sharing documents about the matter, and the like. Further, the screened lawyer should receive no direct financial benefit, based upon the outcome of the matter, such as a financial bonus or a larger share of firm income directly attributable to the matter. However, it is not impermissible that the lawyer receives compensation and benefits under standing arrangements established prior to the representation. An adequate showing of screening ordinarily requires affidavits by the personally-prohibited lawyer and by a lawyer responsible for the screening measures. A tribunal can require that other appropriate steps be taken.

Despite the movement toward accepting screening, prominent commentators such as Professor Wolfram remain skeptical that the "screening lawyer foxes * * * will carefully guard the screened-lawyer chickens." [Wolfram § 7.6.4 at 402.] The courts have found screening adequate only in limited factual contexts, often involving dilatory disqualification of counsel motions in litigation.

The California State Bar decided not to adopt an imputed disqualification rule as part of its Rules of Professional Conduct. The drafters feared (1) the proposed rule (3–300) would establish *de facto* standards for trial courts' rulings on disqualification motions; (2) a bright-line rule could not adequately cover the myriad situations caused by the movement of lawyers and non-lawyer employees between firms; and (3) Business and Professions Code section 6068(e) [client confidences] and Rule 1–120 [aiding and abetting rules violations] taken together address the central issues of the protection of client confidences for purposes of imposing discipline. Thus imputed disqualifications will continue to be decided on a case-by-case basis in California, as the *Rosenfeld* and *Cho* cases, *supra,* indicate.

MULTIPLE CHOICE QUESTIONS

Answer these questions under the ABA Code and
ABA Model Rules

1. After they graduated from law school, Cheryl and Dennis were married and went to work for separate law firms in a large city. Cheryl's practice is primarily trademark litigation, and Dennis's practice is primarily general business counseling; only rarely does he become involved in trial work. One of Dennis's regular business clients sued a major corporation for trademark infringement. Dennis and his law firm appear on the pleadings as counsel for plaintiff, but, in fact, all of the trial work is being done by another firm that specializes in trademarks. The defendant's lead counsel died suddenly, and his firm withdrew from the case. Now the defendant has asked Cheryl and her firm to take over the defense. Which of the following is most nearly correct?

A. If Cheryl and her firm agree to represent the defendant, then Dennis and his firm *must* seek their client's permission to withdraw.

B. Cheryl and her firm *must* decline to represent the defendant, since to do so would create an appearance of impropriety.

C. If the respective clients consent after full disclosure of the situation, then Cheryl and Dennis *may* participate on opposite sides of the case.

D. Cheryl and Dennis *may* participate on opposite sides of the case, since the mere fact that they are married creates neither an actual nor an apparent conflict of interest.

2. Law partners Norman and Enid are too busy to spend much time discussing their legal work with each other. For many years, Enid's major client has been Eratec Corporation, a diversified electronics firm with worldwide operations. Most of Norman's time is devoted to his work as outside general counsel for North American Industries, Inc. It is a diversified manufacturing company with operations in Canada, the United States, and Mexico. Enid filed a law suit in the United States on behalf of a French subsidiary of Eratec. The defendant was a Canadian joint venture. When Enid received the answer to the complaint, he was shocked to discover that North American was one of the three joint venturers, and that Norman was listed on the caption of the answer as "Of Counsel" to the joint venture. Immediately after Enid called this to Norman's attention, Norman explained the situation to North American

and to the lead counsel for the joint venture. Both readily consented to the removal of his name from the pleading. Enid then continued in the case as counsel for the plaintiff, Eratec's French subsidiary. Which of the following is most nearly correct?

A. Enid and Norman handled the matter in a *proper* manner, since Norman had his name removed from the pleading promptly after the conflict of interest was discovered.

B. Enid is *subject to discipline*, even though Norman's name was promptly removed from the pleading.

C. Neither Enid nor Norman is *subject to discipline*, since the conflict of interest was unintentional and was remedied as soon as it was discovered.

D. Enid handled the matter in a *proper* manner, but Norman is subject to discipline for failing to discover the conflict of interest at the outset.

3. R, S, T, and U are four sellers of high-speed photoimage reproductor disks. U falsely advertises its disks, and U's false statements injure R, S, and T by causing some of their customers to buy instead from U. But R, S, and T are not sure of the precise amount of business each lost. The three of them hire Attorney A to represent them in a suit against U for an injunction and damages, and A agrees to take the case for a 30% contingent fee. After extensive discovery, U's attorney calls A with a settlement offer: U will consent to a court order enjoining U from using the allegedly false statements in future advertising, and U will pay a total of $100,000, in return for a full release of all claims by R, S, and T. In A's opinion, the consent order would adequately protect R, S, and T from future harm, but A believes in good faith that $100,000 is ridiculously low and would not compensate R, S, and T for their past losses. Which of the following is most nearly correct?

A. A *must* reject U's settlement offer, since he does not believe in good faith that $100,000 would sufficiently compensate R, S, and T for their past losses.

B. A *must* let R, S, and T decide what to do about U's settlement offer, even though he represents them on a contingent fee basis, and even though he believes that $100,000 is not enough to compensate them for their past losses.

C. A *may* accept U's settlement offer, provided that he distributes the $100,000 equitably among R, S, and T, and provided that he does not take any portion of it as his fee.

D. A *may* reject U's settlement offer, since he does not believe in good faith that $100,000 would sufficiently compensate R, S, and T for their past losses.

4. Wife Wendy and husband Harry ask attorney Anna to represent both of them in a dissolution of marriage proceeding in a state that allows "no-fault" dissolution. The couple has no children. Wendy is a

successful young pediatrician, and Harry is an unemployed computer programmer. They want Anna to represent both of them because separate lawyers may cost more and may stir up antagonism, and because they hope Anna can help them reach a property and support agreement that is mutually acceptable. Which of the following is most nearly correct?

A. If Anna represents both, she will be *subject to discipline* for counseling both sides in an adversary proceeding.

B. Anna *may* represent both, provided that she obtains from them separate covenants not to sue her later for legal malpractice.

C. If Anna represents both, she will be *subject to discipline* because Wendy's and Harry's interests are in present, actual conflict.

D. Anna *may* represent both, provided that she reasonably believes that she can serve both effectively and that both consent after full disclosure of the disadvantages of joint representation.

5. Tillingham, Wadsworth & DePew is a sprawling corporation law firm with 100 partners, 200 associates, and branch offices in eight major cities. Reynard DePew is the senior partner in charge of the firm's Washington, D.C., branch office. A year ago, he was retained by Transpac Oil Company to prepare some Transpac executives to testify before a Senate committee in opposition to proposed antitrust legislation that would require all integrated oil companies to divest themselves of their retail service stations. In connection with this work, DePew received truckloads of confidential documents from Transpac concerning competitive conditions in the retail end of the oil industry. DePew did not share this confidential information with anyone in the firm's Denver branch office, nor did he ever discuss the matter with anyone in the Denver office; indeed, no one in the Denver office even knew that DePew was working on the matter. Eight months after the matter was concluded, the Independent Service Station Dealers of America asked the firm's Denver office to represent it as plaintiff in an antitrust action against nine major integrated oil companies, including Transpac. *May* the Denver office accept the case without Transpac's consent?

A. No, because the case is substantially related to the work DePew did for Transpac.

B. Yes, provided that the Dealers Association consents after full disclosure.

C. Yes, provided that the firm concludes that it can effectively represent the Dealers Association and that DePew is screened off from the case and does not share any fees earned in the case.

D. Yes, because the Denver office never received any of Transpac's confidential information from DePew.

6. Lawyer Leggett is a partner in a private law firm that represents numerous landlords who rent apartments to low-income families.

Leggett is also a member of the Board of Directors of the County Legal Aid Society. Some of the other directors are non-lawyers. The society offers free legal services to low-income clients in a variety of civil matters. The legal services are actually provided by paid lawyers on the society staff or by volunteer lawyers from the community. Up to now, the society has not had enough funding to offer services in landlord-tenant disputes. Recently it acquired a new source of funds, and now the Board of Directors needs to decide whether to add landlord-tenant disputes to the society's list of services. Leggett knows that an affirmative answer will adversely affect his firm's landlord clients. Which of the following is most nearly correct?

A. Leggett is *subject to discipline* for being a director of a legal services organization in which some directors are non-lawyers.

B. Leggett's participation in the decision will make him *subject to discipline*, no matter which way he votes.

C. Leggett *may* participate in the decision, but if he votes "no," he will be *subject to discipline*.

D. Leggett *may* participate in the decision, but if he votes "yes," he will be *subject to discipline*.

7. When attorney Aldrich was in private practice, she defended client Costa in two criminal assault and battery cases. The cases were three years apart, and both times the victim was Vincent, Costa's brother-in-law. Costa was convicted in both cases. Thereafter, Aldrich was elected County Prosecutor. As County Prosecutor, Aldrich hires and fires deputy prosecutors and generally supervises their work. As time permits, she also personally prepares and tries some cases. Her former client Costa is in trouble again, this time for the apparent first-degree murder of Vincent. A state statute requires all first-degree murder prosecutions to be conducted under the "direct, immediate, and personal supervision" of the County Prosecutor. The statute further provides that the State Attorney General's Office shall take over any criminal prosecution in which the local County Prosecutor cannot act due to conflict of interest. Which of the following is most nearly correct?

A. Aldrich *should* ask the State Attorney General's Office to take over the prosecution because she and her deputies have a conflict of interest.

B. Aldrich *may* personally prepare and prosecute the case because it arises out of a transaction separate and distinct from those in which she represented Costa.

C. Aldrich *may* assign one of her deputies to prepare and prosecute the case, so long as she undertakes "direct, immediate, and personal supervision" of the work.

D. Aldrich *should* assign one of her deputies to prepare and prosecute the case and then carefully screen herself off from any personal participation in the case.

*Answers to the multiple choice questions appear
in the Appendix at the end of the book*

Chapter Thirteen

LAWYERS IN LAW FIRMS AND SPECIALIZED PRACTICE AREAS

What This Chapter Covers

Reading Assignment

Wydick & Perschbacher, Chapter 13

ABA Model Rules:

> Rules 1.10 (Comment: Definition of "Firm"), 1.17, 2.2, 2.3, 5.1 through 5.7.

CRPC 1–100(B), 1–300, 1–310, 1–320, 1–500 and 2–400.

Cal.Bus. & Prof.Code §§ 6125–6127.

Supplemental Reading

ABA Code:

> EC 4–6, EC 5–20, EC 5–24.

> DR 2–108, DR 3–101 through DR 3–103, DR 4–101(D), DR 5–105(D), DR 5–107.

Hazard & Hodes:

> Discussion of ABA Model Rules 1.10, 1.17, 2.2, 2.3, and 5.1 through 5.7.

Wolfram:

> Sections 8.7.1 through 8.7.4 (lawyer as mediator);
>
> Section 8.8.4 (lawyer control by other lawyer);
>
> Sections 13.4.1 through 13.4.4 (lawyer as evaluator);
>
> Section 13.6 (mediation);
>
> Section 13.7.3 (house counsel);
>
> Section 16.2.1 through 16.2.5 (forms of law practice; respective duties of supervising and subordinate lawyers);
>
> Section 16.3.1 through 16.3.2 (nonlawyer employees of lawyers);
>
> Section 16.4 (dual practice);
>
> Section 16.5.1 through 16.5.5 (group legal services);
>
> Section 16.7.4 (legal services lawyering and lawyer-client relationships).

Restatement (Third) of the Law Governing Lawyers §§ 202, 211 (Proposed Final Draft No. 1, 1996).

ABA Standards of Practice for Lawyer Mediators in Family Disputes.

Discussion Problems

1. Lasar is a senior partner in the 20–lawyer firm of Fimrite, Steele & Lasar. Fimrite Steele's style of new lawyer training can best be described as "sink or swim." Newly-hired associates are given tasks by the firm's partners and are expected to carry them out on their own, asking for help from the partners when needed. The firm is proud of the substantial responsibility given to its associates "right off the bat." New associate Allen was thrilled when within one month after joining Fimrite Steele, she was given responsibility for preparing a new will and trust arrangement for Clint, one of the firm's longtime estate planning clients. Lasar, as the supervising partner for Clint's matters, gave Allen an example of the firm's "standard estate package" to use as a model for her assignment. Allen was concerned about several provisions in the model such as designating managing partner Fimrite as executor and designating a major banking client of the firm as trustee of the trust. However, Allen thought it best to stick with the model and not ask Lasar any questions that might make her look bad or be tagged as a troublemaker.

    a. Has Allen acted properly in this matter?

    b.   What are Lasar's ethical obligations in the matter?

    c.   Should the Fimrite Steele firm be held accountable in any way?

    d.   What if Allen, instead of just carrying out the assignment, expressed her concerns about the firm's practices to the state agency that oversees fiduciary practices. As a result, the agency then launched an investigation of Fimrite Steele's practices. When the firm's partners learned of Allen's role in informing the agency, she was immediately fired. Does Allen have any recourse against Fimrite Steele for her firing?

    2.   For the past eight years, your law firm has represented client Anton in a variety of venture capital projects. Now Anton has a new project. He, Benson, and Chung want to form a business entity to manufacture and sell a revolutionary new sonar surgical device. Chung has received an apparently valid United States Patent on the device, and she has the know-how that is needed to manufacture it efficiently. Benson is an expert in marketing surgical equipment. Anton has neither technical nor marketing skills, but he has the capital that the new venture will need. Anton, Benson, and Chung have asked you to represent all three of them in organizing the new venture.

    a.   Under what, if any, conditions may you represent all three of them?

    b.   What, if anything, will you tell them respecting the confidential information they will disclose to you?

    c.   What will be your role if the three of them come to a parting of the ways?

    3.   For the past four years, the law firm of Ayers & Alfred has been defending client Clayton Industries in a series of related products liability cases in which the plaintiffs seek hundreds of millions of dollars for injuries caused by an allegedly defective Clayton product. The damage claims exceed Clayton's assets ten-fold. International Bank & Trust Company is now deciding whether to renew Clayton's multi-million dollar line of credit. Clayton has asked Ayers & Alfred to prepare a candid evaluation of the products liability cases and to furnish it to International's loan department. What are the ethical obligations of Ayers & Alfred in this situation?

    4.   Describe the practice of law as you foresee it 20 years from now. In framing your prediction, consider what you have read here and elsewhere about:

- The Supreme Court's likely approach to lawyer advertising and solicitation in future cases;

- The alleged over-supply of lawyers in the United States;

- The alleged unmet needs of middle and low income people for affordable legal services;

- The alleged transformation of law practice from a selfless profession into a selfish business;

- The increasing recognition of legal specialties, that is, lawyers who claim expertise in narrow fields of law; and

- The growing role of high technology in law practice.

If your prediction comes true, what role to you foresee for yourself 20 years from now?

LEGAL EDUCATION AND PROFESSIONAL DEVELOPMENT—AN EDUCATIONAL CONTINUUM

Report of The Task Force on Law Schools and the Profession:
Narrowing the Gap, pp. 29–34, 75, 77–78, 80, 88, 95.
(American Bar Association, Section of Legal Education
and Admission to the Bar, 1992).

THE DIVERSE PRACTICE SETTINGS

Historically the lawyer in America was an independent professional who was neither employed by another nor dependent on others to help the lawyer provide legal services. The lawyer was also a generalist, personally ready to render whatever legal service a private client might require. The vast majority of lawyers were sole practitioners, either as a full-time or a part-time occupation. Many supplemented their income and filled out their time in other activities—real estate, banking or political office—but employment of lawyers by public agencies and private organizations was virtually non-existent until the late 19th century.

Nor were law firms the usual practice setting. In urban centers some lawyers shared office space or entered into loose partnership arrangements, but this was not common. A study found that as late as 1872, only 14 law firms in the entire country had even four lawyers; three had as many as five lawyers; and only one had six.[1] The gradual emergence of the law firm as a common mode of private practice began only in the last quarter of the 19th century to provide the legal services which were required by those leading the great expansion of industry, commerce and finance.[2]

Since 1970 there has been a steady movement of law firms of all sizes from smaller practice units into larger. Private practice has become a spectrum of different practice units, differentiated not only by size but by clients, by the kind of legal work performed, by the amount

1. See W.K. Hobson, *Symbol of the New Profession: Emergence of the Large Law Firm 1870–1915* reprinted in THE NEW HIGH PRIESTS: LAWYERS IN POST-CIVIL WAR AMERICA, at 5–7 (Gawalt ed., 1984); J.W. HURST, THE GROWTH OF AMERICAN LAW: THE LAW MAKERS, Chapter 13: "The Uses of the Bar" (1950).

2. By 1898, 67 firms had five lawyers or more and by 1915 there were 240, with the firms predominately in New York City, Chi-

cago and Boston. The pattern of law firm growth continued and by 1924 there were 101 firms of seven lawyers or more in the five largest American cities, with a total lawyer complement of 1,303 (id.) out of approximately 137,500 lawyers in the United States at the time. See R.L. ABEL, American Lawyers, Table 32, at 290 (1989).

of specialization, by the extent of employment of salaried associates and other support staff, and by the degree of bureaucratization of the practice.

The accompanying table tracks the movement in firm size from smaller practice units to larger, reflects the drop in the percentage of lawyers who are sole practitioners and the growth during the 1980s in the size of large law firms, with the greatest growth in the percentage of lawyers in law firms of 51 lawyers or more.[13]

The table reflects the steady movement toward larger and larger law firms in which a greater percentage of lawyers' time is devoted to business law and less to the representation of individuals.

At the same time, new forms of organization have been developed for providing legal services to individuals of modest means and new methods for financing such services. A sector of "new providers" of legal services for individual clients and client groups has emerged. Increasing numbers of sole and small-firm practitioners are participating in these new delivery systems which together are estimated today to provide potential access to legal services for more than 70 million middle-income Americans.[14]

In addition, substantial new provision has been made of services for the poor. Although some legal services have always been provided by various members of the bar to those unable to pay for them, during the past 25 years organized legal services to the poor have been greatly expanded by increased numbers of legal aid attorneys, now funded both publicly and privately, and by public defenders employed by government. Such services have been supplemented by a great many new programs of organized pro bono services furnished by lawyers in private practice.

There are two other major segments of law practice today in which legal services are provided outside the traditional setting of private practice. One is comprised of those providing in-house legal services to corporations and other private organizations, and the second is made up of the lawyers employed by government in all of its functions. The private bar historically has provided legal services both to corporate clients and to governments, but since the late 19th century there has been a steady trend toward bringing law work "in-house," both for corporations and for governmental departments and agencies, and toward employing salaried lawyers instead of retaining individual lawyers and law firms on a fee basis, to handle at least part of the client's legal matters.[15]

13. Sources: B.A. Curran. *The Legal Profession in the 1980s: A Profession in Transition,* 20 Law & Society Rev. 19 (1986); American Bar Foundation 1988 Supplement to the Lawyer Statistical Report.

14. *See* National Resource Center for Consumers of Legal Services, *Legal Plan Letter* (Special Census Issue, August 30, 1991).

15. *See* Eve Spangler, Lawyers for Hire Salaried Professionals at Work (1986).

	1960		1970		1980		1985		1988	
	Private Practitioners N = 206,000	All Lawyers N = 285,933	Private Practitioners N = 240,000	All Lawyers N = 355,242	Private Practitioners N = 370,111	All Lawyers N = 542,205	Private Practitioners N = 460,206	All Lawyers N = 655,191	Private Practitioners N = 519,941	All Lawyers N = 723,189
Sole Practitioners	64%*	46%**	52%	35%	48%	33.2%	47%	33%	46.2%	33.2%
2 to 10 Lawyer firms	N/A	N/A	N/A	N/A	32%	21.5%	28.3%	19.9%	25.1%	18.0%
11 to 50 lawyer firms	N/A	N/A	N/A	N/A	12.6%	8.7%	13.6%	9.6%	14.1%	10.2%
51 or more lawyer firms	N/A	N/A	N/A	N/A	7.3%	5%	11.2%	7.9%	14.6%	10.5%
	Percentage of all lawyers in private practice: 72%		Percentage of all lawyers in private practice: 67.6%		Percentage of all lawyers in private practice: 68.3%		Percentage of all lawyers in private practice: 70.2%		Percentage of all lawyers in private practice: 71.9%	

N/A—not available from existing data base.
*percent of private practitioners.
**percent of all lawyers.

THE "LARGE FIRM" PHENOMENON

The more than 75,000 lawyers in the 600 largest law firms are the most prominent sector of the profession today. They trace their origins to Wall Street, not to Main Street. It is clear that the emergence of what came to be referred to as the "Wall Street law firms" has profoundly affected both the structure and the operations of many law firms of both large and of lesser size. In addition, it has had a significant effect upon the profession generally, as well as upon recruitment and placement policies at many law schools, if not upon curricula.[149] One recent study concludes that the elite large firms have been the "critical catalysts" of recent changes in the legal profession.[150]

[Since the 1960s,] it has been said that the large law firm became "the most conspicuous feature in the American legal landscape." [159]

This "transformation" of large law firms in the 1970s and 1980s has been systematically analyzed, first, by Robert Nelson in his *Partners With Power* and later by Galanter & Palay in their *Tournament of Lawyers* who view the transformation against what they describe as "a dramatic expansion of the scale and scope of the whole world of legal institutions." [160]

The elements of that transformation are the subject of extensive comment.[161] The most obvious feature of the transformation was the exponential growth in the size of firms, to which the structure and mode of operation of the larger firms was highly conducive. The rate of growth in the very largest firms was truly phenomenal. The average size of the 20 largest firms grew more than fourfold from 1968 (128 lawyers) to 1987 (527 lawyers). While the median number of lawyers in the 200 largest firms between 1975 and 1987 grew from 68 lawyers to 205, the number of firms with more than 100 lawyers grew from 45 in 1975 to 247 in 1987.[162]

Galanter & Palay present a compelling demonstration of the inevitability of such exponential growth when law firms are structured around a system that maintains a leveraged ratio of associates-to-partners

---

149. *See* R.L. NELSON, PARTNERS WITH POWER: SOCIAL TRANSFORMATION OF THE LARGE LAW FIRM, (1988), at 1.

150. R.H. Sanders & E.D. Williams, *Why Are There So Many Lawyers? Perspectives on a Turbulent Market,* 14 Law & Soc. Inquiry 478 (1989).

159. R.L. Abel, *supra* note 2, at 182.

160. GALANTER & PALAY, Tournament of Lawyers 37 (1991).

161. In addition to NELSON and GALANTER & PALAY, *supra* notes 149 and 50, see, for example, S. Brill, *The Law Business in the Year 2000,* American Lawyer (Management Report, June 1989); *Symposium: The Growth of Large Law Firms and Its Effect on the Legal Profession and Legal Education,* 64 IND. L.J. 423 (1989) which includes the following contributions: E. Freidson, "Theory and the Professions," (at 423); B.G. Garth, "Legal Education and Large Law Firms: Delivering Legality or

Solving Problems," (at 433); B.C. Danner, "Looking at Large Law Firms—Any Role Left for the Law Schools?," (at 447); J.F. Fitzpatrick, "Legal Future Shock: The Role of Large Law Firms by the End of the Century," (at 461); J.A. Stanley, "Should Lawyers Stick to Their Last?," (at 473); R.E. Rosen, "The Inside Counsel Movement, Professional Judgment and Organizational Representation," (at 479); L.M. Friedman, Robert W. Gordon, Sophie Pirie and Edwin Whatley, "Law, Lawyers and Legal Practice in Silicon Valley: A Preliminary Report," (at 555); J. Flood, "Megalaw in the U.K.: Professionalism or Corporatism? A Preliminary Report," (at 569); D.A. MacDonald, "Speculations by a Customer About the Future of Large Law Firms," (at 593). *See also,* M. STEVENS, POWER OF ATTORNEY: THE RISE OF THE GIANT LAW FIRMS (1986).

162. See R.L. ABEL, *supra* note 2, at 182–184.

combined with a fixed policy of "up-or-out/promotion-to-partner." [163] Strict adherence to such a system compels an increasing number of associates to be made partners and hiring still more associates to replace the new partners.[164] This in turn compels a continuing search for more legal business to utilize fully the firm's legal resources.

In due course, to help maintain the leveraging ratio of associates to partners, many firms lowered their rate of promotion-to-partner, while others introduced multi-tiered staffs of senior lawyers, specialists, a second tier of associates, as well as an increased number of non-lawyer professionals.[172]

IN-HOUSE COUNSEL

[F]rom the late 19th century a few large corporations found law so pervasive to their operations that they hired lawyers to work full time in the management of the business and called them "general counsel." As demands grew, additional lawyers were added to corporate payrolls and corporate law departments gradually grew in size and number. In addition, in larger corporations, matters of corporate governance in the course of time came to be centered in the office of the corporate secretary and it became common to have lawyers serve in that position and on the secretary's staff when the function was not a part of the law department's responsibilities.

Serving as inside or staff counsel to a business or eleemosynary institution is today an established practice-setting for as many as 10 percent of the legal profession. Such employment places the individual lawyer in the dual position of being responsible to and sharing the culture both of the profession of which he or she is a member and of the institution by which he or she is employed. It is important that new lawyers entering this organizational setting of dual cultures be acquainted with how in-house counsel can properly accommodate in a principled manner to the two cultures and conduct themselves faithfully to the profession's ethical rules. It suggests the desirability that instruction in professional ethics address issues commonly faced by in-house counsel and their appropriate resolution.

LAWYERS EMPLOYED BY GOVERNMENT

[The survey notes that an estimated 40,000 private attorneys are retained to provide legal services to the approximately 39,000 local government units in the United States; another 20–22,000 lawyers serve as district attorneys and assistant district attorneys for local government; and others work as defense counsel, in probation offices; and still

---

163. GALANTER & PALAY, *supra* note 50, at 77–110; See A.W. Thorner, *Legal Education in the Recruitment Marketplace: Decades of Change,* 1987 Duke L.Rev. 276, 278.

164. The authors postulate that the progressive growth rate of many law firms reached a point in the early 1970s of "expo-

nential" growth which would continue until operation policies were modified either by choice or the compulsion of circumstance.

172. T.C. FISCHER, LEGAL EDUCATION, LAW PRACTICE AND THE ECONOMY: A NEW ENGLAND STUDY 283 (1990).

other lawyers are employed by local government to provide a variety of civil legal services. Thus, an estimated 50,000 lawyers are employed in local government. State attorneys general offices employ some 8,278 full-time and 236 part-time attorneys, and unknown tens of thousands other lawyers are employed doing civil work for attorneys general offices, with other lawyers working for state agencies and the legislature. Probably as many as 40,000 lawyers work for the federal government with 7,280 lawyers employed by the Department of Justice alone.]

NEW FORMS OF LEGAL PRACTICE

Although traditionally lawyers practiced either as sole practitioners or in partnerships, both the ABA Code and the ABA Model Rules allow lawyers to form professional corporations as long as all the shareholders, officers, and directors are lawyers. [Model Rule 5.4(d).] These rules and state law allow lawyers to practice in the form of the professional corporation (P.C.) to gain the tax advantages of other corporations. However, the corporate form of business has generally not provided lawyer-shareholders a shield against malpractice liability as a result of the acts of other lawyer-shareholders in the professional corporation. Lawyers are also able to practice as members of group legal service plans, although this form of practice initially encountered strong opposition within the ABA, probably motivated by fear of competition from such plans. The official concern was a danger that the lawyer's professional independence could be compromised by nonlawyer owner or management. Restrictive provisions in the Model Code have since been superseded by the more benign controls of Model Rule 5.4.

More recently, the older forms of professional incorporation lost the tax advantages that originally led to this form of practice, and newer forms have emerged. In a limited liability company (LLC), individual lawyer members are liable for their own misconduct, but may limit their personal liability while still gaining the tax treatment accorded to general partners. This form of practice remains controversial; only a few states explicitly allow professionals to organize as LLC's, and the liability limitations have not been fully tested in the courts. [See Susan S. Fortney, Am I My Partner's Keeper? Peer Review in Law Firms, 66 Colo.L.Rev. 329, 330–333 (1995).] A second emerging form of practice is the limited liability partnership (LLP), which also limits a nonparticipating partners' liability for the negligent acts of other partners. California law permits lawyers to practice in the form of limited liability partnerships, and the State Bar has issued rules requiring lawyers to register with the Bar. For a fuller discussion of these new practice forms and their implications, see Robert R. Keatinge & George W. Coleman, *Practice of Law by Limited Liability Partnerships and Limited Liability Companies,* Symposium Issue of the Professional Lawyer 5 (1995).

LAW FIRM BREAKUPS

The last two decades have seen disturbing new phenomena become a regular part of law practice—law firm mergers, downsizing (reducing and deferring the hiring of new associates, staff layoffs, forced separation of associates and partners), break-ups, and sometimes bankruptcy of small and large law firms. These major transformations of firms raise ethical issues for the lawyers involved among themselves and in relation to their clients. What notice do firms owe their lawyers in advance of a merger or break-up? What notice should lawyers give their firms and their clients if they are leaving the firm? Can firms limit the practice opportunities of departing partners as other businesses do, or is this an improper limitation on the lawyer's right to practice law? An entire new area of legal practice has arisen consisting of advising and counseling firms and their lawyers over these issues. [See Barbara B. Buchholz, *Graceful Exits,* 81 ABA Journal 76 (Aug. 1995); Pamela A. Bresnahan, *Breaking Up Is Hard to Do,* 81 ABA Journal 94 (Nov. 1995).] Although they have tried, firms cannot prohibit their lawyers from leaving and letting clients know of their impending move, so they have tried other economic disincentives to at least limit the grabbing off of their best clients when lawyers move. Model Code DR 2–108 and Model Rule 5.6 appear to limit, if not prohibit, the use of noncompetition clauses in partnership agreements, and restrict the use of payments to the departing partners as a means of limiting competition. However, their use has produced a major split between the courts of New York and California over payments for unbilled work and work in progress when the partners depart. In *Cohen v. Lord, Day & Lord,* 75 N.Y.2d 95, 551 N.Y.S.2d 157, 550 N.E.2d 410 (1989), New York's Court of Appeals held that clauses that allow firms to withhold fees on grounds a departing partner forfeited them by practicing at a competing firm are unethical noncompetition agreements that limit clients' choice of lawyers. In *Howard v. Babcock,* 6 Cal.4th 409, 863 P.2d 150, 25 Cal.Rptr.2d 80 (1993), the California Supreme Court upheld the inclusion of a similar clause on the ground that law firms should not be treated any differently than other businesses as long as the restriction is reasonable. For a full treatment of these issues see ROBERT W. HILLMAN, HILLMAN ON LAWYER MOBILITY: THE LAW AND ETHICS OF PARTNER WITHDRAWALS AND LAW FIRM BREAKUPS (1994).

ANCILLARY BUSINESS ACTIVITIES

Probably for as long as there have been lawyers, lawyers have occasionally offered other non-legal services to their clients. In fact, ABA Model Rule 2.1 encourages lawyers when giving advice to clients to "refer not only to law but to other considerations such as moral, economic, social and political factors, that may be relevant to the client's situation." Clients often expect business advice, real estate advice, and even marital advice from their lawyers. A flat refusal to respond to such requests may well cost the lawyer the client. Less nobly, lawyers have occasionally, perhaps often, operated non-law businesses either as a part of their firm or as a related entity. For example, a lawyer practicing real estate may well operate a title business as well. A well-connected Washington, D.C. megafirm may offer its clients lobbying services in addition to legal work. According to the comment to ABA Model Rule 5.7, ancillary law-related services include, "title insurance, financial planning, accounting, trust services, real estate counseling, legislative lobbying, economic analysis, social work, psychological counseling, tax return preparations, and patent, medical or environmental counseling."

Such "ancillary" operations pose several dangers. Clients may be confused over whether they are a client of the firm or of the ancillary business; non-lawyers may influence the law practice in ways inconsistent with the lawyers' professional obligations; the non-law business and law practice may raise serious conflict of interest problems. Perhaps operating an ancillary business makes it painfully clear that the law practice is a business as well. Whatever the reasons, until recently the bar's ethical rules either ignored the issue of ancillary businesses or flatly prohibited their operation in connection with a law practice. Beginning in the late 1980's, competing interests within the ABA began to develop conflicting rule proposals on ancillary businesses. One group offered a highly restrictive proposal that would confine ancillary business activities within the law firm to activities incidental to the provision of legal services and limit such services to clients of the law firm. Another group favored a rule that (a) generally permitted ancillary business activities both within the law firm and offered through related entities if the law firm disclosed the relationship to its clients; (b) generally treated a client-customer as a client of the law firm unless the client-customer was fully informed to the contrary; and (c) provided safeguards that client-customers would be treated in accordance with the lawyers' professional obligations. In August 1991, the ABA adopted the restrictive alternative as Model Rule 5.7. In less than a year, it was repealed. No state had adopted the Rule. After a two year hiatus, the ABA, in 1994, adopted the current Rule 5.7. The current rule does little more than remind lawyers that they are subject to the rules of professional responsibility when providing "law-related services" unless the client understands that these services are not legal services and do not enjoy the protection of the lawyer-client relationship. [*See also* ABA Formal Opinion 94–388 (1994).] Can you find a better way through these competing interests?

LAW FIRM DISCIPLINE

Discipline has traditionally been a matter between the bar and its individual members. The entire range of sanctions seems appropriate only to punish an individual lawyer. Nevertheless, it is apparent that law firm culture has a significant effect on the individual members of the firm, particularly those newly admitted to practice who are developing habits of practice, often by modeling their behavior on those lawyers they observe practicing on a day-to-day basis—the partners and more senior associates of the firm that has hired them. Entire law firms have been found liable *as firms* for malpractice, and for violations of regulatory regimes by administrative agencies vigorously exercising their supervisory function. Some disciplinary rules are already applicable to law firms—conflict of interest rules usually require disqualification of the entire firm, as do rules on mandatory withdrawal. Article 5 of the ABA Model Rules deals with law firm issues. Finally, other sanction rules, particularly the current version of Federal Rule of Civil Procedure 11, allow sanctioning a law firm. [See Fed.R.Civ.P. 11(c).] Recently a few commentators, notably Professor Schneyer in his article, *Professional Discipline for Law Firms?* 77 Cornell L.Rev. 1 (1991), and bar organizations in California and New York have suggested or studied discipline of entire law firms for ethical misconduct attributable to them. In its study, of *Discipline for Law Firms,* The Association of the Bar of the City of New York [48 Rec.A.B. City N.Y. 628 (1993)] identified these reasons for extending discipline to law firms: (1) to improve the practice environment for lawyers within the firm that will discourage ethical violations by its members; (2) to enhance self-policing of conduct by firms; (3) to bring the rules into line with the group character of modern practice and its supervisory structure; (4) to enhance the ethical supervision of non-lawyer employees of firms; (5) to overcome the difficulty of assessing blame on individual lawyers; (6) to provide counter incentives to a climate that encourages cutting corners; and (7) to address organizational problems that may be the cause of ethical violations, such as conflicts checking, billing procedures, and oversight of client funds.

Difficulties remain with any proposal for law firm discipline. Firms cannot be disbarred, and even a total firm suspension seems inappropriate. Thus far, law firm discipline remains under consideration; no state bar has adopted a rule that disciplines firms.

GENERAL DYNAMICS CORP. v. SUPERIOR COURT

Supreme Court of California, 1994.
7 Cal.4th 1164, 32 Cal.Rptr.2d 1, 876 P.2d 487.

ARABIAN, JUSTICE.

We granted review to consider an attorney's status as "in-house" counsel as it affects the right to pursue claims for damages following an allegedly wrongful termination of employment. Specifically, we are asked to decide whether an attorney's status as an employee bars the pursuit of implied-in-fact contract and retaliatory discharge tort causes of action against the employer that are commonly the subject of suits by *non*-attorney employees who assert the same claims.

We conclude that, because so-called "just cause" contractual claims are unlikely to implicate values central to the attorney-client relationship, there is no valid reason why an in-house attorney should not be permitted to pursue such a contract claim in the same way as the nonattorney employee. Our conclusion with respect to the tort cause of action is qualified; our holding seeks to accommodate two conflicting values, both of which arise from the nature of an attorney's professional role: the fiducial nature of the relationship with the client, on the one hand, and the duty to adhere to a handful of defining ethical norms, on the other. As will appear, we conclude that there is no reason inherent in the nature of an attorney's role as in-house counsel to a corporation that in itself precludes the maintenance of a retaliatory discharge claim, *provided* it can be established without breaching the attorney-client privilege or unduly endangering the values lying at the heart of the professional relationship.

Although the effect of the attorney-client relationship is to produce a remedy more limited than that available to the nonattorney employee, the similarities between the position of in-house attorneys and their non-attorney colleagues nevertheless justify an analogous cause of action. The complete economic dependence of in-house attorneys on their employers is indistinguishable from that of nonattorney employees who *are* entitled to pursue a retaliatory discharge remedy. Moreover, as we explain, the position of in-house counsel is especially sensitive to those fundamental ethical imperatives derived from an attorney's professional duties, as well as organizational pressures to ignore or subvert them. On balance, these considerations favor allowing a tort claim for discharges for reasons that contravene an attorney's mandatory ethical obligations or for which a non-attorney employee could maintain such a claim and a statute or ethical code provision permits the attorney to depart from the usual rule that client matters remain confidential.

The trial courts have at their disposal several measures to minimize or eliminate the potential untoward effects on both the attorney-client privilege and the interests of the client-employer resulting from the litigation of such wrongful termination claims by in-house counsel. Thus, we also hold that, in those instances where the attorney-employee's retaliatory discharge claim is incapable of complete resolution without breaching the attorney-client privilege, the suit may not proceed. That result, however, is rarely, if ever, appropriate where, as in this case, the litigation is still at the pleadings stage.

I

Andrew Rose, an attorney, began working for General Dynamics Corporation (hereafter General Dynamics) as a 27–year–old contract administrator at its Pomona plant in 1978. He progressed steadily within the organization, earning repeated commendations and, after 14 years with the company, was in line to become a division vice-president and general counsel. On June 24, 1991, he was fired, abruptly and wrongfully.

So Rose alleged in the complaint for damages that began this litigation. The complaint also alleged that although the stated reason for his discharge was a loss of the company's confidence in Rose's ability to represent vigorously its interests, the "real" reasons motivating his firing had more to do with an attempt by company officials to cover up widespread drug use among the General Dynamics work force, a refusal to investigate the mysterious "bugging" of the office of the company's chief of security, and the displeasure of company officials over certain legal advice Rose had given them, rather than any loss of confidence in his legal ability or commitment to the company's interests.

The complaint relied on two main theories of relief. First, it alleged that General Dynamics had, by its conduct and other assurances, impliedly represented to Rose over the years that he was subject to discharge only for "good cause," a condition that the complaint alleged was not present in the circumstances under which he was fired. Second, the complaint alleged that Rose was actually fired for cumulative reasons, all of which violated fundamental public policies: in part because he spearheaded an investigation into employee drug use at the Pomona plant (an investigation, the complaint alleged, that led to the termination of more than 60 General Dynamics employees), in part because he protested the company's failure to investigate the bugging of the office of the chief of security (allegedly a criminal offense and, since it involved a major defense contractor, a serious breach of national security), and in part as a result of advising General Dynamics officials that the company's salary policy with respect to the compensation paid a certain class of employees might be in violation of the federal Fair Labor Standards Act, possibly exposing the firm to several hundred million dollars in backpay claims.

General Dynamics filed a general demurrer to the complaint, asserting that Rose had failed to state a claim for relief. Because he had been employed as an in-house *attorney,* the company contended, Rose was subject to discharge at any time, "for any reason or for no reason." The trial court overruled the demurrer and the Court of Appeal [upheld the trial court.] * * *

II

The last two decades have seen a marked rise in the number and professional stature of so-called in-house or corporate counsel. Increasingly, large corporations have turned inward for the acquisition of legal services, for a host of reasons ranging from cost incentives, to the increasing complexity of the regulatory environment, to the programmatic style characteristic of such organizations. According to a study conducted in the early 1980's, 50,000 lawyers were on corporate payrolls, a figure double that of 15 years earlier; a more recent survey indicates that more than 10 percent of all lawyers in the United States are employed in-house by corporations.[2]

2. (See, e.g., Wolfram, Modern Legal Ethics (1986 ed.) § 13.7.3, at pp. 736–738 & fns. 89–99 [hereafter Wolfram]; Giesel, The Ethics or Employment Dilemma of In–House Counsel (1990) 5 Geo.J.Legal Ethics 535, 540–545 & accompanying fns. [hereafter Giesel]). For an account of the rise of the corporate legal department and its implications for the traditional "outside" law firm, see the series of articles in volume 37 of the Stanford Law Review. (Chayes & Chayes, Corporate Counsel and the Elite Law Firm (1984) 37 Stan.L.Rev. 277; Comment 301; Comment (1984) 37 Stan.L.Rev. 305.)

The growth in the number and role of in-house counsel has brought with it a widening recognition of the descriptive inadequacy of the nineteenth century model of the lawyer's place and role in society—one based predominantly on the small- to middle-sized firm of like-minded attorneys whose economic fortunes were not tethered to the good will of a single client—and of the social and legal consequences that have accompanied that transformation. Unlike the law firm partner, who typically possesses a significant measure of economic independence and professional distance derived from a multiple client base, the economic fate of in-house attorneys is tied directly to a single employer, at whose sufferance they serve. Thus, from an economic standpoint, the dependence of in-house counsel is indistinguishable from that of other corporate managers or senior executives who also owe their livelihoods, career goals and satisfaction to a single organizational employer.

Moreover, the professional relationship between the in-house attorney and the client is not the "one shot" undertaking—drafting a will, say, or handling a piece of litigation—characteristic of the outside law firm. Instead, the corporate attorney-employee, operating in a heavily regulated medium, often takes on a larger advisory and compliance role, anticipating potential legal problems, advising on possible solutions, and generally assisting the corporation in achieving its business aims while minimizing entanglement in the increasingly complex legal web that regulates organizational conduct in our society. This expansion in the scope and stature of in-house counsel's work, together with an inevitably close professional identification with the fortunes and objectives of the corporate employer, can easily subject the in-house attorney to unusual pressures to conform to organizational goals, pressures that are qualitatively different from those imposed on the outside lawyer. Even the most dedicated professionals, their economic and professional fate allied with that of the business organizations they serve, may be irresistibly tempted to cut corners by bending the ethical norms that regulate an attorney's professional conduct.

Indeed, the analogy of in-house counsel's position to that of his or her lay colleagues in the executive suite is inexact only because, as a licensed professional, an attorney labors under unique ethical imperatives that exceed those of the corporate executive who seeks, say, a tort remedy after being terminated for refusing to join a conspiracy to violate the antitrust laws. We turn, then, to a consideration of the effects of in-house counsel's professional role and ethical duties on access to judicial remedies for alleged wrongful termination that are available to the nonattorney colleague.

III

A

If there is a unifying theme in this conflict, it is the claim of General Dynamics that our opinion in *Fracasse v. Brent* (1972) 6 Cal.3d 784, 100 Cal.Rptr. 385, 494 P.2d 9 (*Fracasse*) is dispositive of all issues tendered against it by Rose in his complaint. Because *Fracasse* cloaks the client in an unfettered, absolute right to discharge an attorney at any time and for any reason, General Dynamics argues, the complaint cannot state a claim against the company that is judicially cognizable; the trial court should thus have sustained General Dynamics's demurrer without leave to amend.

In *Fracasse, supra,* 6 Cal.3d 784, 100 Cal.Rptr. 385, 494 P.2d 9, an attorney entered into a contingent fee contract with a client to represent her as a plaintiff in a personal injury lawsuit. Not long afterward—and before any recovery had been made on her behalf—the client decided to end the relationship. She discharged the attorney, and retained other counsel to pursue her claim. The former attorney then filed a declaratory relief action against her, alleging that he had been discharged without cause and in breach of the contingency fee agreement, and seeking a judgment that he was entitled to his one-third contingency fee as a percentage of any sum ultimately recovered by his former client. The trial court sustained the client's demurrer, ruling that the complaint failed to state a claim for relief.

Although the core proposition established by our opinion in *Fracasse, supra,* 6 Cal.3d at page 790, 100 Cal.Rptr. 385, 494 P.2d 9, affirming the trial court, undoubtedly remains valid—we concluded that "a client should have both the right and the power at any time to discharge his attorney with or without cause"—our holding in that case does not support the sweeping scope urged for it by General Dynamics. It should be evident to anyone reading our opinion in *Fracasse* that we confronted there one of the most common of the traditional forms of the lawyer-client relationship: the potential claimant who seeks redress by hiring an independent professional to prosecute her claim for personal injuries.

* * *

Entwined with our concern for the specific risks facing the contingent-fee plaintiff who has lost faith in her attorney was an underlying perception that, whatever the circumstances, *no* client should be forced to suffer representation by an attorney in whom that confidence and trust lying at the heart of a fiduciary relationship has been lost. It is not surprising, given this chain of reasoning, that our opinion in *Fracasse, supra,* 6 Cal.3d 784, 100 Cal.Rptr. 385, 494 P.2d 9, should establish as bedrock law what remains probably the central value of the lawyer-client relationship—the primary of fiducial values and its corollary: the unilateral right of the client to sever the professional relationship at any time and for any reason.

That rule, which we reaffirm today, some 22 years after our decision in *Fracasse, supra,* 6 Cal.3d 784, 100 Cal.Rptr. 385, 494 P.2d 9, does not mean, however, that the "absolute" right of the personal injury client to discharge unilaterally his attorney permits *all* clients to terminate the attorney-client relationship under all circumstances without consequence. The sources of contract and tort claims in wrongful termination cases are analytically distinct from the circumstances confronting the contingent-fee plaintiff that propelled our analysis in *Fracasse*. Given these disparate origins, it is unlikely that the client's undoubted power to discharge the attorney at will is one that can be invoked under all circumstances *without consequence*. Even in *Fracasse*, we recognized the requirement that the dissatisfied personal injury contingent fee client compensate discharged counsel, limiting that obligation, in light of the peculiar risks associated with contingent fee undertakings, to the reasonable value of any services provided in the event of a recovery.

Additionally, General Dynamics' claim of an unqualified immunity from any liability for terminating in-house counsel is inconsistent with the law in other areas, notably claims grounded in alleged violations of antidiscrimination laws and statutory rights to public collective bargaining.

* * *

B

How does the fundamental rule of the client's unilateral power of discharge announced in *Fracasse, supra*, 6 Cal.3d 784, 100 Cal.Rptr. 385, 494 P.2d 9, apply in the circumstances of this case? First, Rose's complaint does not contest the right of General Dynamics to terminate a member of its corporate legal department at any time or for any reason, nor could it. It simply asserts that there is a cost to be paid for such an action under the circumstances alleged in the complaint—either in lost wages and related damages in the case of the implied-in-fact contract claim, or as tort damages in the case of the public policy tort claim. In neither case, however, is the client's power to rid itself of an attorney in whom it has lost confidence thwarted. To the extent that General Dynamics's claim that its "unfettered" right to discharge a member of its corporate legal department means that it may do so without liability of any kind under all circumstances, that is not, and never has been, the law of this state.

As a threshold matter, then, we do not feel constrained by our opinion in *Fracasse, supra*, 6 Cal.3d 784, 100 Cal.Rptr. 385, 494 P.2d 9, from considering the proposition that, under circumscribed conditions, an in-house attorney may pursue a wrongful discharge claim for damages against his corporate employer *even though* a judgment ordering his reinstatement is *not* an available remedy. We turn to a consideration of the merits of plaintiff's claims that his termination breached an implied-in-fact agreement with General Dynamics and violated fundamental public policies, as well as the possible limitations on the vitality of such claims when brought by in-house counsel.

IV

* * *

Perhaps the overriding distinction between *Fracasse, supra*, 6 Cal.3d 784, 100 Cal.Rptr. 385, 494 P.2d 9, and this case lies in the allegations of the complaint that the plaintiff was hired as a "career oriented" employee with an expectation of permanent employment, provided his performance was satisfactory; that he was promised job security and substantial retirement benefits; that he regularly received outstanding performance reviews, promotions, salary increases, and commendations throughout his 14–year tenure; and that the company abruptly terminated him without adhering to its published discharge procedures.

These pleadings, we conclude, adequately allege that a "course of conduct, including various oral representations, created a reasonable expectation" that the plaintiff would not be terminated without good cause. The factual allegations of the complaint being sufficient to withstand a general demurrer, we see no reason in policy, at least at the outset, why the plaintiff's status as an in-house attorney should operate to defeat his contract claim. It is true, as we have just affirmed, that General Dynamics has a right to discharge any member of its general counsel's staff in whom it has lost confidence. That right does not mean, however, that it may do so without honoring antecedent contractual obligations to discharge an attorney-employee only on the occurrence of specified conditions.

In short, implied-in-fact limitations being a species of contract, no reason appears why an employer that elects to limit its at-will freedom to terminate the employment relationship with in-house counsel should not be held to the terms of its bargain.

* * *

We agree that, as creatures of contract, implied-in-fact limitations on a client-employer's right to discharge in-house counsel are not likely to present issues implicating the distinctive values subserved by the attorney-client relationship. Such suits can thus for the most part be treated as implied-in-fact claims brought by the nonattorney employee.

* * *

V

A

We turn next to an evaluation of Rose's claim that he was discharged for multiple reasons, each of which violated a "fundamental polic[y] that [is] delineated in constitutional or statutory provisions" of the law of this state. (*Gantt v. Sentry Insurance* (1992) 1 Cal.4th 1083, 1095, 4 Cal.Rptr.2d 874, 824 P.2d 680.) Unlike implied-in-fact contract claims, which, as discussed above, arise out of the conduct and expectations of the parties to the employment relationship, so-called public policy wrongful discharge claims are pure creatures of law.

* * *

According to a recent count, 43 jurisdictions have adopted the so-called "retaliatory discharge" cause of action as a restraint on the employer's historical at-will power of termination. In California, refinements in the doctrine of wrongful discharge in violation of public policy have engrafted two prominent restraints on the vitality of such claims. The first is the requirement, explicated in our decision in *Gantt v. Sentry Insurance, supra,* 1 Cal.4th at page 1095, 4 Cal.Rptr.2d 874, 824 P.2d 680, that the public policy at issue must be one that is not only "fundamental" but is clearly established in the Constitution and positive law of the state. The second restriction is the requirement that, even though established by positive law, the policy subserved by the employee's conduct must be a truly public one, that is, "affect[ing] a duty which inures to the benefit of the *public at large* rather than to a particular employer or employee." (Foley v. Interactive Data Corp., 47 Cal.3d 654, 699, 765 P.2d 373, 254 Cal.Rptr. 211 (1988.))

There is a third characteristic of such claims that warrants our attention, one that may, in the case of in-house counsel, be of surpassing significance. That characteristic is well stated in *Foley, supra,* 47 Cal.3d 654, 254 Cal.Rptr. 211, 765 P.2d 373, where we explained that "decisions recognizing a tort action for discharge in violation of public policy *seek to protect the public, by protecting the employee* who refuses to commit a crime [citations] . . ., who reports criminal activity to proper authorities [citations], or who discloses other illegal, unethical, or unsafe practices [citation]" (id. at p. 670, 254 Cal.Rptr. 211, 765 P.2d 373, italics added).

* * *

B

This foundational *public* rationale is especially important in the case of the attorney-employee. Perhaps the defining feature of professionals as a class is the extent to which they embody a dual allegiance. On the one hand, an attorney's highest duty is to the welfare and interests of the client. This obligation is channeled, however, by a limiting and specifically *professional* qualification: attorneys are required to conduct themselves *as such,* meaning that they are bound at all events not to transgress a handful of professional ethical norms that distinguish their work from that of the nonattorney.

Some (but not all) of these professional norms incorporate important *public* values. Lawyers are given wide professional license in part because of ethical restraints on their discretion designed to further (or at least not endanger) the public weal. The minimal ethical standards that distinctively define the lawyer as a professional are, of course, those embodied in the codes of ethics, and, in California, in the Rules of Professional Conduct. These standards are in turn linked by their nature and goals to important values affecting the public interest at large. It is through this chain of ethical duty that lawyers and their work are affected with a public interest. Out of this duality of allegiance—for the interests of the client on the one hand, but within the bounds of ethical norms on the other—a genuine moral dilemma may arise.

This is especially so in the context of the large commercially driven corporation whose essential objectives are largely defined by the desire to maximize profitability. In such a business culture, the in-house professional may be trapped between a laudable desire to further the goals of the client-employer and restrictions on conduct imposed by the ethical norms prescribed by the Rules of Professional Conduct. Of course, the potential for such a dilemma is common to outside counsel as well. But, unlike their in-house counterparts, outside lawyers enjoy a measure of professional distance and economic independence that usually serves to lessen the pressure to bend or ignore professional norms. Here again, the distinguishing feature of the in-house attorney is a virtually complete dependence on the good will and confidence of a single employer to provide livelihood and career success.

The case for shielding the in-house attorney—among *all* corporate employees—from retaliation by the employer for either insisting on adhering to mandatory ethical norms of the profession or for refusing to violate them is thus clear. And because their professional work is by definition affected with a public interest, in-house attorneys are even more liable to conflicts between corporate goals and professional norms than their nonattorney colleagues. On this view, then, in-house counsel, forced to choose between the demands of the employer and the requirements of a professional code of ethics have, if anything, an *even more* powerful claim to judicial protection than their nonprofessional colleagues.

C

There is a substantial counterargument against permitting the pursuit of a retaliatory discharge *tort* claim by in-house counsel, one that also inheres in the essential nature of the attorney's professional role. Indeed, in the handful of reported cases dealing with the question, a majority of courts have refused to permit the maintenance of such suits on the ground that they pose *too great* a threat to the attorney-client relationship. This rationale is well illustrated in a trio of recent cases, each holding as a matter of law that retaliatory discharge suits by in-house counsel are not maintainable.

* * *

[The court here reviewed the cases of *Balla v. Gambro, Inc.*, 145 Ill.2d 492, 164 Ill.Dec. 892, 584 N.E.2d 104 (1991), *Herbster v. North American Co.*, 150 Ill.App.3d 21, 103 Ill.Dec. 322, 501 N.E.2d 343 (1986), and *Willy v. Coastal Corp.*, 647 F.Supp. 116 (S.D.Tex.1986), each of which rejected retaliatory discharge suits by fired in-house lawyers.]

Those courts that have declined to permit in-house counsel to pursue retaliatory discharge claims—in *Balla*, *Herbster*, and *Willy*—have rested their conclusion on two distinct grounds: First, because the fiducial qualities of their professional calling pervade the attorney-client relationship "lawyers are different." It is essential to the proper functioning of the lawyer's role that the client be assured that matters disclosed to counsel in confidence remain sacrosanct; to permit in-house attorneys to file suit against their clients can only harm that relationship. Second, to the extent that the retaliatory discharge tort rests on underpinnings designed to secure fundamental public policies, a tort remedy for in-house counsel is redundant—such attorneys are under an ethical obligation to sever their professional relationship with the erring client in any event—meaning, in the case of in-house counsel, resigning their employment.

D

There is no doubt that the Illinois courts in *Balla, supra,* 164 Ill.Dec. 892, 584 N.E.2d 104, and *Herbster, supra,* 103 Ill.Dec. 322, 501 N.E.2d 343, grappled conscientiously with the conflicting values presented by cases such as this one. If their reasoning and conclusions can be faulted, it is because one searches in vain for a principled link between the ethical duties of the in-house attorney and the courts' refusal to grant such an employee a tort remedy under conditions that directly implicate those professional obligations. As more than one critic of these opinions has pointed out, both cases appear to reflect not only an unspoken adherence to an anachronistic model of the attorney's place and role in contemporary society, but an inverted view of the consequences of the in-house attorney's essential professional role.

As one authoritative commentator on lawyers' ethics, criticizing the court's decision in *Balla, supra,* 164 Ill.Dec. 892, 584 N.E.2d 104, has written, "It is clear that there would have been a right of action had the employee not been a lawyer. It thus seems bizarre that a lawyer employee, who has affirmative duties concerning the administration of justice, should be denied redress for discharge resulting from trying to carry out those very duties. A good beginning point for analysis may well be the client's normal and broad right to discharge the lawyer, but that cannot be the ending point as well, for the lawyer-client relationship exists in a context of other law regulating both parties to that relationship, including the lawyer's duties to third persons, the courts, and the government." (1 Hazard & Hodes, The Law of Lawyering, *supra,* § 1.16.206 at p. 477, fns. omitted.)

Granted the priest-like license to receive the most intimate and damning disclosures of the client, granted the sanctity of the professional privilege, granted the uniquely influential position attorneys occupy in our society, it is precisely *because of* that role that attorneys should be accorded a retaliatory discharge remedy in those instances in which *mandatory ethical norms* embodied in the Rules of Professional Conduct *collide with illegitimate demands of the employer* and the attorney *insists on adhering to his or her clear professional duty.* It is, after all, the office of the retaliatory discharge tort to vindicate fundamental public policies by encouraging employees to act in ways that advance them. By providing the employee with a remedy in tort damages for resisting socially damaging organizational conduct, the courts mitigate the otherwise considerable economic and cultural pressures on the individual employee to silently conform.

Within their area of professional competence, in-house attorneys, more than other organizational employees, are imbued with ethical constraints on the direction their efforts may legitimately take. Among other strictures on their conduct, they may not be a party to the commission of a crime, destroy evidence or suborn perjury. They are forbidden to do these things by the very ethical codes that define their professional identity. It is a short step from this premise to the conclusion that in-house lawyers ought to have access to a judicial remedy in those instances in which their employment is terminated for adhering to the requirements of just such a mandatory professional duty, either by an *affirmative act* required by the ethical code or statute or by resisting a demand of the employer on the ground that it is unequivocally *barred* by the professional code.

* * *

In addition, the emphasis by the *Balla, Herbster* and *Willy* courts on the "remedy" of the in-house attorney's duty of "withdrawal" strikes us as illusory. Courts do not require nonlawyer employees to quietly surrender their jobs rather than "go along" with an employer's unlawful demands. Indeed, the retaliatory discharge tort claim is designed to encourage and support precisely the opposite reaction. Why, then, did the courts in these three cases content themselves with the bland announcement that the only "choice" of an attorney confronted with an employer's demand that he violate his professional oath by committing, say, a criminal act, is to voluntarily withdraw from employment, a course fraught with the possibility of economic catastrophe and professional banishment?

Whatever the reason, the withdrawal "remedy" fails to confront seriously the extraordinarily high cost that resignation entails. More importantly, it is virtually certain that, without the prospect of limited judicial access, in-house attorneys—especially those in mid-career who occupy senior positions—confronted with the dilemma of choosing between adhering to professional ethical norms and surrendering to the employer's unethical demands will almost always find silence the better part of valor. Declining to provide a limited remedy under defined circumstances will thus almost certainly foster a degradation of in-house counsel's professional stature.

E

In addition to retaliatory discharge claims founded on allegations that an in-house attorney was terminated for refusing to violate a mandatory ethical duty embodied in the Rules of Professional Conduct, judicial access ought logically extend to those limited circumstances in which in-house counsel's *nonattorney* colleagues would be permitted to pursue a retaliatory discharge claim *and* governing professional rules or statutes expressly remove the requirement of attorney confidentiality.

Thus, in determining whether an in-house attorney has a retaliatory discharge claim against his or her employer, a court must first ask whether the attorney was discharged for following a mandatory ethical obligation prescribed by professional rule or statute. If, for example, in-house counsel is asked to commit a crime, or to engage in an act of moral turpitude that would subject him to disbarment (see, e.g., Bus. & Prof.Code, §§ 6101, 6106 [providing, respectively, for disbarment on conviction of a felony or a misdemeanor involving moral turpitude, and for the "commission of any act involving moral turpitude, dishonesty or corruption"]), and is discharged for refusing to engage in such an act, counsel would have been discharged for adhering to a mandatory ethical obligation; under most circumstances, the attorney would have a retaliatory discharge cause of action against the employer.

If, on the other hand, the conduct in which the attorney has engaged is merely ethically *permissible*, but not *required* by statute or ethical code, then the inquiry facing the court is slightly more complex. Under these circumstances, a court must resolve *two* questions: First, whether the employer's conduct is of the kind that would give rise to a retaliatory discharge action by a nonattorney employee * * * second, the court must determine whether some statute or ethical rule, such as the statutory exceptions to the attorney-client privilege codified in the Evidence Code (see *id.*, §§ 956–958) specifically permits the attorney to depart from the usual requirement of confidentiality with respect to the client-employer and engage in the "nonfiduciary" conduct for which he was terminated.

We emphasize the limited scope of our conclusion that in-house counsel may state a cause of action in tort for retaliatory discharge. The lawyer's high duty of fidelity to the interests of the client work against a tort remedy that is coextensive with that available to the nonattorney employee. Although claims by in-house attorneys are cognate to those we approved in *Foley, supra*, 47 Cal.3d 654, 254 Cal.Rptr. 211, 765 P.2d 373, the underlying rationale differs somewhat, being grounded in the attorney's obligation to adhere to ethical norms specific to the profession. The cause of action is thus one designed to support in-house counsel in remaining faithful to those fundamental public policies reflected in the governing ethical code when carrying out professional assignments. Thus, in addition to the limitations on the scope of the retaliatory tort action mentioned above, the concerns expressed by the courts in *Balla, supra*, 164 Ill.Dec. 892, 584 N.E.2d 104, and *Herbster, supra*, 103 Ill.Dec. 322, 501 N.E.2d 343, for the integrity of the fiduciary aspects of the attorney-client relationship impose additional limitations.

First, those values that underlie the professional relationship—the fiduciary qualities of mutual trust and confidence—can be protected from the threat of damage by limiting judicial access to claims grounded in *explicit* and *unequivocal ethical norms* embodied in the Rules of Professional Responsibility and statutes, and claims which are maintainable by the nonattorney employee under our decision in *Gantt v. Sentry Insurance, supra*, 1 Cal.4th 1083, 4 Cal.Rptr.2d 874, 824 P.2d 680, under circumstances in which the Legislature has manifested a judgment that the principle of professional confidentiality *does not apply*. (See, e.g., Evid.Code, § 956.5 ["*There is no privilege* . . . if the lawyer reasonably believes that disclosure of any confidential communication . . . is necessary to prevent the client from committing a criminal act that the lawyer believes is likely to result in death or substantial bodily harm." [Italics added].]) [6]

Similarly, the in-house attorney who publicly exposes the client's secrets will usually find no sanctuary in the courts. Except in those rare instances when disclosure is explicitly permitted or mandated by an ethics code provision or statute, it is never the business of the lawyer to disclose publicly the secrets of the client. In any event, where the elements of a wrongful discharge in violation of fundamental public policy claim cannot, for reasons peculiar to the particular case, be fully established without breaching the attorney-client privilege, the suit must be dismissed in the interest of preserving the privilege. We underline the fact that such drastic action will seldom if ever be appropriate at the demurrer stage of litigation. Although General Dynamics argues that Rose's claims are barred from disclosure by the lawyer-client privilege, that is an issue that is incapable of resolution in a challenge to the facial sufficiency of the complaint. Indeed, in most wrongful termination suits brought by discharged in-house counsel, whether the attorney-client privilege precludes the plaintiff from recovery will not be resolvable at the demurrer stage. Rather, in the usual case, whether the privilege serves as a bar to the plaintiff's recovery will be litigated and determined in the context of motions for protective orders or to compel further discovery responses, as well as at the time of a motion for summary judgment.

Second, the contours of the statutory attorney-client privilege should continue to be strictly observed. We reject any suggestion that the scope of the privilege should be diluted in the context of in-house counsel and their corporate clients. Members of corporate legal departments are as fully subject to the demands of the privilege as their outside colleagues. It is likely, however, that many of the cases in which in-house counsel is faced with an ethical dilemma will lie outside the scope of the statutory privilege. Matters involving the commission of a crime or a fraud, or circumstances in which the attorney reasonably believes that disclosure is necessary to prevent the commission of a criminal act likely to result in death or substantial bodily harm, are statutory and well-recognized

---

6. As our discussion makes evident, in California, these ethical prescriptions are those embodied in the state's Rules of Professional Conduct and certain provisions of the Business and Professions Code (e.g., §§ 6068, 6090.5–6107). We expressly decline to adopt as a predicate for retaliatory discharge claims by in-house counsel either the Model Rules of Professional Conduct or the Model Code of Professional Responsibility, both of which have "no legal force of their own" (1 Hazard & Hodes, The Law of Lawyering, *supra*, § 206, at p. 1xx) and neither of which has been adopted by this court. Although the question is not before us in this case, we suggest that ethical issues arising in retaliatory discharge claims filed in California by out-of-state in-house attorneys against their employers and based on extrastate conduct will be resolved under governing choice-of-law rules.

exceptions to the attorney-client privilege. * * * Although their revelation in the course of a retaliatory discharge suit may do lasting damage to the expectations of the corporate client (or, more likely, a corporate executive) that disclosures to counsel would remain inviolate, a concern for protecting the fiduciary aspects of the relationship in the case of a client who confides in counsel for the purpose of planning a crime or practicing a fraud is misplaced; such disclosures do not violate the privilege.

Moreover, the trial courts can and should apply an array of ad hoc measures from their equitable arsenal designed to permit the attorney plaintiff to attempt to make the necessary proof while protecting from disclosure client confidences subject to the privilege. The use of sealing and protective orders, limited admissibility of evidence, orders restricting the use of testimony in successive proceedings, and, where appropriate, in camera proceedings, are but some of a number of measures that might usefully be explored by the trial courts as circumstances warrant. We are confident that by taking an aggressive managerial role, judges can minimize the dangers to the legitimate privilege interests the trial of such cases may present.

Finally, a handful of subsidiary rules will effectively raise the ante on the in-house attorney contemplating a tort action, thus deterring the incidence of strike suits or claims filed in bad faith. The contested ethical requirement must be clearly established by the ethics code or statutory provision; disagreements over policy are *not* actionable. The plaintiff, of course, bears the burden of establishing the *unequivocal* requirements of the ethical norm at issue and that the employer's conduct was motivated by impermissible considerations under a "but for" standard of causation. The ethical norm at issue must be one that is intended for the protection of the public at large; measures designed solely for the benefit of the attorney or the client will not suffice to support a retaliatory discharge claim. Moreover, an attorney who unsuccessfully pursues a retaliatory discharge suit, and in doing so discloses privileged client confidences, may be subject to State Bar disciplinary proceedings. Finally, of course, the defendant employer is always free to challenge plaintiff's claim by demonstrating the discharge was motivated by reasons other than a demand that counsel engage in conduct amounting to a breach of professional ethical norms.

VI

Applying the principles developed above to the complaint in this case, it is evident that as noted, plaintiff's first claim—for breach of an implied-in-fact just-cause agreement—adequately pleads the essential elements of the cause of action. It is less clear, however, that the allegations in support of relief under plaintiff's retaliatory discharge theory are sufficient. Plaintiff nowhere alleges that the conduct which allegedly led to his termination was required or supported by any requirement of our Rules of Professional Responsibility or a relevant statute.

* * *

CONCLUSION

The judgment of the Court of Appeal is affirmed and the cause is remanded to that court with directions to order further proceedings in accordance with the views expressed herein.

MULTIPLE CHOICE QUESTIONS

Answer these questions under the ABA Code
and the ABA Model Rules

1. A congressional investigating committee subpoenaed certain files from a governmental agency in connection with the committee's investigation of the agency's allegedly illegal expenditure of government funds. Lawyer Altmont (the agency's Chief Counsel) instructed lawyer Barker (the Deputy Chief Counsel) to gather up the files and prepare them for production. Barker, in turn, assigned the project to lawyer Crawford (a newly-hired junior lawyer). In giving Crawford the assignment, Barker said: "I wouldn't be surprised if all of these files have been shredded long ago, pursuant to our regular Document Storage and Retention Procedures Manual ('DSRPM')." Crawford discovered that the files still existed, even though the DSRPM called for their destruction six months earlier. Crawford dutifully shredded the files himself and then reported the fact to Barker. Barker responded by stating: "Good. I wonder if the computer backup for those files still exists?" Crawford interpreted this as an instruction to erase the computer backup material, which he promptly did. Barker then reported the full story to Altmont who informed the congressional investigating committee that both the files and the computer backup had been destroyed in accordance with the agency's regular procedures under the DSRPM. Which of the following is most nearly correct?

    A. Only Barker and Crawford are *subject to discipline.*

    B. Only Crawford is *subject to discipline.*

    C. Altmont, Barker, and Crawford are all *subject to discipline.*

    D. Neither Altmont, nor Barker, nor Crawford are *subject to discipline.*

2. Attorney Arlington is a young associate in the firm of Smith & Black. He is assisting senior partner Black in the discovery phase of a case in which the court has ordered Black's client to produce certain documents. Black asked Arlington to study the court order, to review several boxes of documents sent over by the client, and to decide which documents must be produced. Arlington did the work and presented his conclusions to Black. Black and Arlington disagree about one group of documents. Black maintains that the court order does not require them to be produced, but Arlington insists that a fair reading of the court

order does require them to be produced. The two attorneys agree that the question is a close one, but each is convinced that the other is incorrect. Which of the following is most nearly correct?

A. If Arlington gives in to Black's point of view, Arlington will be *subject to discipline,* since an attorney must not hold back what a court has ordered to be produced.

B. Since a subordinate attorney cannot be held accountable for following the directions of a supervising attorney, Arlington *must* accede to Black's point of view.

C. Since the point is a debatable one, Arlington *may* accede to Black's point of view.

D. Since an attorney is required to follow his own, independent judgment in handling a client's matter, Arlington *must* either insist that the documents be produced or else decline to work further on the case.

3. After 45 years of solo practice in the small town of Willow Creek, lawyer Lumire decided to sell his law practice and to retire. He advertised the practice for sale in the classified pages of the local bar journal, and in due course he found a buyer, an enthusiastic young attorney named Ames. The sale contract between Lumire and Ames provides that Ames will pay Lumire $65,000 for the small wood building that houses Lumire's office; $8,000 for the furniture, law books, office machines, and related items of personal property; and $10,000 for the good will of the practice. It further provides that Ames will pay Lumire $500 per month as a retirement benefit during Lumire's lifetime or until Lumire returns to law practice in Willow Creek. Is the sale contract *proper?*

A. Yes, even though it provides for the $500 monthly retirement benefit.

B. Yes, provided that the $500 monthly retirement benefit is reasonable in light of the good will value of the practice.

C. No, because the good will of a law practice cannot be bought and sold.

D. No, because Lumire and Ames have not previously been associated in law practice, either as partners or otherwise.

Chapter Fourteen

JUDICIAL CONDUCT

What This Chapter Covers

Reading Assignment

Wydick & Perschbacher, Chapter 14.

ABA Model Code of Judicial Conduct (1990).

ABA Model Rules:

Rules 1.12, 3.5, 8.3(b), and 8.4(f).

CRPC, Rule 5–300.

Supplemental Reading

ABA Model Code:

EC 7–34 through 7–36, 9–3, 9–4;

DR 1–103(B), 7–106(C)(6), 7–110(B), 9–101(A) and (C).

Hazard & Hodes:

Discussion of ABA Model Rules 1.12, 3.5, 8.3(b), and 8.4(f).

Wolfram:

Section 8.10.3 (former judge as private lawyer);

Sections 11.3.1 through 11.3.3 (lawyer-judge relationship);

Section 12.1.3 (courtroom decorum);

Section 12.2.1 (news reporting in courtroom);

Section 12.10.1 (duty to report misconduct).

———

Discussion Problems

1. Rosalind is a former law school classmate of yours. The two of you have practiced law in the same town, and over the years you have remained good friends. She has decided to run for a Superior Court judgeship, and you believe that she would make an excellent judge. A large part of your law practice involves cases in the Superior Court.

    a. May you work for and contribute money to Rosalind's campaign?

    b. If she is elected:

        1. May you represent clients in her court?

        2. May you continue to play tennis with her on Saturday mornings, as you have done for years?

        3. May you continue to exchange birthday gifts with her, as you have done for years?

2. Judge P. Farley Dibble is a full-time judge of the County Court. The County Court is the state court of original jurisdiction for all felonies and for all civil matters involving more than $2,500.

    a. Judge Dibble's former law partner is on trial in the United States District Court for federal tax fraud. He asks Judge Dibble to testify on his behalf as a character witness. How should Judge Dibble respond?

    b. Judge Dibble's good friend, Ralph, asks him to put in a telephone call to the loan officer at the First City Bank to put in a good word for Ralph, who is seeking a large loan for a real estate venture. How should Judge Dibble respond?

    c. Judge Dibble recently finished the trial of a complex water pollution case; he is now preparing his findings of fact and conclusions of law. A post-graduate student at the local university has offered to provide him with the results of some just-completed water pollution experiments. This material could be important to a wise and informed decision in the case. May Judge Dibble accept this offer of aid?

    d. The water pollution case raises several tricky legal issues that have been bungled in the parties' post-trial briefs. May Judge Dibble solicit the help of Professor Happing (who teaches environmental and water law at the local law school) in resolving these tricky issues?

3. Judge Linda Corbin was recently appointed to serve as a full-time judge of the State Court of Intermediate Appeals.

a. Before taking the bench, she was representing the defendants in a series of complicated civil cases pending in the United States District Court. She would like to see these cases through to a conclusion. Her clients have agreed to the association of a co-counsel who will take over the day-to-day work in the cases. Under what, if any, circumstances may Judge Corbin continue to serve as counsel in these cases?

b. Because of her expertise in labor law matters, she has been asked to serve as arbitrator in a dispute between the local school district and United Teachers of America, Local #583. May she serve?

c. During her years in law practice, Judge Corbin was a vigorous proponent of equal treatment for women in employment and job advancement. The President of the United States has asked her to serve on a specially-appointed Commission on Working Women, to advise him on important legal and political issues that affect women in the work force. May she serve?

4. Rubin Trinidad is a United States District Judge. His hobby is fly-fishing for trout, steelhead, and salmon.

a. He belongs to a non-profit conservation group called Nature's Advocates. The group takes public positions against water pollution, damming of wild rivers, and the like. He has been elected to the Board of Directors. May he serve?

b. May he engage in fund-raising activities for Nature's Advocates?

c. May he accept the invitation of the local university to engage in a public debate with an official from the U.S. Department of the Interior about a proposal to dam the Taranoga River, one of the last remaining white water rivers in the state?

d. If he does give the speech, may he accept the $100 honorarium that the university offers to all speakers who appear at events of this sort?

e. One of Judge Trinidad's life-long friends is Anthony, a local dentist who has no connection with any matter that might come before Judge Trinidad's court. Anthony's hobby is making fine split-bamboo fly fishing rods. As a birthday present, Anthony gives Judge Trinidad a beautiful handmade rod worth at least $300. May Judge Trinidad accept this gift?

f. May Judge Trinidad agree to be named in Anthony's will as the executor of Anthony's estate?

5. In which of the following situations must the judge disqualify him or herself?

a. Judge Martin attended the funeral of Ingram, a private investigator who had occasionally appeared as a witness before

Judge Martin. The judge had no other connection with Ingram. May he preside at the trial of Ingram's accused murderer?

b. Judge Olson publicly stated her intent to sentence all Clean Air Act violators to 30 months' imprisonment as a way of encouraging people to comply with the Act. The Act itself does not make a prison sentence mandatory. Must she disqualify herself in Clean Air Act cases that come before her?

c. State Supreme Court Justice Nguyen notes that the Supreme Court calendar for the coming term includes a tort case concerning a landlord's liability for a dangerous condition created by a tenant. The state law on this subject is unsettled. Justice Nguyen is himself the landlord-defendant in a similar suit now pending in one of the state's trial courts. Must Justice Nguyen disqualify himself in the Supreme Court proceedings?

d. One of the city's prominent lawyers, Mario Ortiz, was appointed as a *pro tempore* Administrative Law Officer (hearing examiner) for the State Farm Labor Relations Board. He was assigned to hear a dispute between Ardmore Farms, Inc. and a group of Ardmore's Mexican-American employees. In numerous prior cases, Ortiz had represented Mexican-American clients. Must he disqualify himself from hearing this dispute?

e. In the middle of a complex antitrust trial, the defendants asked United States District Judge Williams to disqualify herself for bias. They claimed that she had become an advocate for the plaintiffs by shielding plaintiffs' witnesses from effective cross-examination and by subjecting defendants' witnesses to withering cross-examination from the bench. The defendants further pointed out that she had ruled against them on 86% of the oral and written objections and motions that had been presented during the trial. Must Judge Williams disqualify herself?

f. United States District Judge Jennings is the sole trustee of a trust fund established to provide scholarships for needy students at the law school from which he graduated. The trust fund assets include a small number of AA tax-free municipal bonds issued by the City of Glencove. Under what, if any, circumstances may Judge Jennings hear a case in which the outcome may substantially affect the market price of the Glencove bonds?

JUDICIAL STANDARDS AND DISCIPLINE

The ABA Model Code of Judicial Conduct ("CJC") was adopted by the ABA House of Delegates in 1990. It is intended to be used as a model for the various states to follow in promulgating their own codes of conduct for judges. California and about half of the other states have adopted judicial codes based on the 1990 CJC. (The judicial codes of the remaining states are based on an earlier ABA model.) California's Code of Judicial Ethics (1996) differs from the 1990 CJC on a number of topics, but in this book we do not consider those differences.

All 50 states and the District of Columbia have adopted procedures for disciplining judges. Federal judges in Article III courts hold office "during good behavior" and can be removed from office only by impeachment for "treason, bribery, or other high crimes or misdemeanors." Impeachment is a long, tedious procedure and is seldom used. In 1980, Congress established a procedure that allows a panel of federal judges to discipline a fellow judge by censure and other sanctions short of removal from office. [*See* 28 U.S.C.A. § 372(c)(1)–(18) (1994).]

Discipline of California judges is the responsibility of the California Commission on Judicial Performance. [*See* Cal. Const. Art. 6, § 18 (West Supp.1996).] Before 1994, judges and lawyers formed a majority of the Commission, but in 1994 California voters passed a ballot proposition that changed the Commission membership to three judges (appointed by the Supreme Court), two attorneys (appointed by the Governor), and six lay persons (two appointed by the Governor, two by the Speaker of the Assembly, and two by the Senate Rules Committee). [*Id.*] The Commission may censure or remove a judge for willful misconduct in office, persistent failure or inability to perform the judge's duties, habitual intemperance in the use of alcohol or other drugs, or conduct that prejudices justice. [*Id.*] The Commission must remove a judge who is convicted of a felony or crime involving moral turpitude. [*Id.*] The Commission's disciplinary orders can be reviewed by petition to the California Supreme Court. [*Id.*]

McCULLOUGH v. COMMISSION ON JUDICIAL PERFORMANCE

Supreme Court of California, 1989.
49 Cal.3d 186, 260 Cal.Rptr. 557, 776 P.2d 259.

The Commission on Judicial Performance (hereafter the Commission) unanimously recommends that we remove Bernard P. McCullough from his office as judge of the Justice Court of the San Benito Judicial District, San Benito County. Judge McCullough asks us to reject the Commission's recommendation, alleging that it is not supported by the evidence. * * * After reviewing the record and the judge's objections, we adopt the Commission's recommendation.

BACKGROUND

Judge McCullough was born and raised in Hollister, California. After practicing law in San Francisco for almost 10 years, he returned to Hollister in 1967 to serve as District Attorney of San Benito County. In 1977, he was appointed to the Justice Court, and has since been elected and re-elected.

In April 1987, we publicly censured Judge McCullough for failing to decide a case for almost four years and for continuing to execute salary affidavits even though cases remained pending in his court for more than 90 days. * * * [w]e noted that he had ignored three private admonishments from the Commission to act promptly on the cases before him. * * *

In the instant matter, the Commission served Judge McCullough with a notice of formal proceedings. * * * Count 1 alleges that Judge McCullough abridged a defendant's right to trial by an impartial jury when he directed the jurors to find the defendant guilty. Count 2 alleges that he used his judicial office to advance the private interests of a personal friend by continuing the friend's case for over two years, and then dismissing it without explanation * * *. The third and fourth counts allege that the judge violated defendants' rights to representation when he ordered their trials to proceed in the absence of their attorneys. Count 5 involved the judge's failure to advise convicted misdemeanants of their rights on appeal * * *. The sixth count alleges that he failed to perform his judicial duties by not disposing of a matter pending before him for over six years.

* * *

[After a three day hearing before special masters, the Commission unanimously] recommended removal of Judge McCullough. * * * The judge then petitioned this court for review of the recommendation. * * *

Standard of Review

When disciplining a member of the judiciary, we undertake an independent evaluation of the record in order to determine whether clear and convincing evidence supports the Commission's recommendation. * * * In so doing, we give special weight both to the factual findings of the special masters, because of the masters' ability to evaluate the credibility of the witnesses at the hearing, and to the conclusions of the Commission, because of its expertise in matters of judicial conduct. * * *

We may censure or remove a judge for engaging in "wilful misconduct in office, persistent failure or inability to perform the judge's duties, habitual intemperance in the use of intoxicants or drugs, or conduct prejudicial to the administration of justice that brings the judicial office into disrepute." (Cal. Const., art. VI, § 18, subd. (c).) Wilful misconduct, the most serious charge, occurs when a judge commits acts (1) which he knows, or should know, are beyond his authority (2) for reasons other than the faithful discharge of his duties. * * * Though a judge must act in bad faith * * * in order to commit wilful misconduct, he need not necessarily seek to harm a particular litigant or attorney; disregard for the legal system in general will suffice. Unlike wilful misconduct, the charge of prejudicial conduct does not require the presence of bad faith. * * * It occurs when a judge, though acting in good faith, engages in conduct which adversely affects public opinion of the judiciary. Though "less grave" than wilful misconduct, prejudicial conduct may nevertheless, by itself, justify removal. Persistent failure, also an independent ground for removal, focuses on a judge's legal and administrative competence and omissions.

COUNT 1—THE SUMAYA MATTER

Count 1 alleges that Judge McCullough abridged Richard Sumaya's right to trial by an impartial jury by directing the jurors sitting on his case to find him guilty. Sumaya plead not guilty to a charge of riding a bicycle while under the influence of alcohol. The matter proceeded to trial. During the prosecution's closing argument to the jury, Judge McCullough interrupted the prosecutor, told him to "sit down," and then said to the jurors: "Ladies and gentlemen, I want you to go in that room and find the defendant guilty." Five minutes later, when the jurors returned with a guilty verdict, the judge commented that, "For a while there, ladies and gentlemen, I thought you were not going to follow my instructions." After conviction, the district attorney's office contacted Sumaya's counsel, advising him to appeal; following Sumaya's appeal, the appellate department of the superior court eventually reversed the conviction.

In response to this charge, Judge McCullough claims that he directed the jury to bring in a guilty verdict because Sumaya had admitted all elements of the offense on the witness stand. The record supports a finding, however, that Sumaya never actually testified at trial. He also asserts that, at the time of Sumaya's trial, he believed that federal law allowed a judge to direct a guilty verdict when the defendant's guilt is, in the view of the judge, undisputed. He now acknowledges that neither federal nor state law authorizes such an instruction, regardless of the judge's opinion of the defendant's guilt. Moreover, he clearly *should* have known that attempting to direct a jury to return a guilty verdict in a criminal action was beyond his judicial authority. * * *

We conclude that Judge McCullough's instruction to the jury directing a guilty verdict constituted wilful misconduct.

COUNT 2—THE CERRATO MATTER

Count 2 alleges that Judge McCullough used his judicial office to advance the private interests of Frank Cerrato, a personal friend of his, by continuing Cerrato's criminal case for over two years and then dismissing it without explanation * * *. The criminal action against Cerrato arose out of a domestic dispute between Cerrato and his wife. The police went to the Cerrato home in response to a call; when Mrs. Cerrato refused to file a criminal complaint against her husband, the district attorney's office charged him with obstructing a police officer in the performance of his duties.

Frank Cerrato and his twin brother Harold are lifelong friends of Judge McCullough; Harold was a member of the board of supervisors when the board first appointed the judge to the bench. The day before Frank's arraignment, the Cerratos went to the judge's home, where Frank told the judge the story of his arrest and asked the judge to excuse him from appearing on the next day. (The Cerratos owned an apricot orchard and Frank's arrest occurred in the midst of the harvest season.) Frank testified at the hearing before the special masters that Judge McCullough told him that the arresting officer had apparently "over-reacted" and that he "should go home and pick his apricots." Frank did not appear in court on either the next day or any later date, and testified that he "presumed" the district attorney had dismissed the case when the court returned the bail money to his brother two years later.

The judge admits that he committed the acts that form the basis of the Commission's charge—that he had an improper ex parte conversation with Frank, never arraigned him on the obstructing charge, continued the case approximately 20 times over a 2–year period, later took the case off calendar, and eventually dismissed the case, without ever explaining his actions or advising the district attorney's office. In addition, he failed to disqualify and recuse himself from the case even though he stated that he planned to do so.

In his defense, the judge alleges that he continued the case 20 times because he was waiting for some action by the district attorney's office, and that he dismissed the case because the office never took any action. However, the responsibility for the arraignment rested with Judge McCullough, as the presiding judge, not with the district attorney's office.

Using the power of the bench to benefit a friend is a casebook example of wilful misconduct. Judge McCullough certainly should have known that failing to arraign Cerrato, continuing the case several times, and then dismissing it was improper. * * * Moreover, in view of his extrajudicial discussion with the Cerrato brothers about Frank's arrest and his long-term friendship with them, he should have promptly disqualified himself from the case. (Cal.Code Jud.Conduct, canon 3C(1) ["Judges should disqualify themselves in a proceeding in which * * * his impartiality might reasonably be questioned, including but not limited to instances where: (a) he has a personal bias or prejudice concerning a party * * *"].) We conclude that the judge's handling of the Cerrato case constituted wilful misconduct.

Count 3—The O'Brien Matter

Count 3 alleges that the judge violated Amelia O'Brien's right to representation when he ordered her trial to proceed despite the absence of herself and her attorney. O'Brien was charged with driving while under the influence of alcohol. On the day before her scheduled trial in San Benito County, a court in another county had ordered O'Brien's attorney to appear before it on the following day. Due to the trial conflict, O'Brien's attorney had his secretary telephone Judge McCullough's chambers to request a continuance of the O'Brien trial. A court clerk advised the secretary to contact the district attorney's office. The district attorney had no objection to the continuance but informed the attorney that the court normally required 48 hours written notice of requests for continuances. Since he did not have sufficient time to prepare a written motion for a continuance, O'Brien's attorney arranged for a local attorney to make a special appearance at the trial to make the request. The local attorney, however, did not appear personally at the court on the following day, but instead telephoned the court with the request for a continuance.

Judge McCullough denied the request and ordered the trial to proceed—despite the absence of the defendant, her counsel of record, or the local attorney. Moreover, the prosecutor on the case informed the judge that he did not object to a continuance, and suggested that the judge impose sanctions on O'Brien's attorney for failing to comply with the court's 48–hour rule instead of ordering the trial to proceed. Later that day, O'Brien's counsel learned that the trial had proceeded without him or his client and made a motion for a new trial, which the judge granted.

Judge McCullough correctly asserts that the power to grant a continuance, along with the power to impose sanctions on parties who do not comply with the requirements for requesting a continuance, are discretionary under section 1050 of the Penal Code. Although section 1050 does make the granting of continuances and the imposition of sanctions discretionary, a judge *must* hold a hearing to determine whether the noncomplying request was made in good faith. Judge McCullough failed to hold such a hearing. * * *

The special masters found that the allegations of count 3 constituted wilful misconduct; the Commission disagreed and concluded that count 3 constituted only prejudicial conduct. We agree with the special masters. Conducting judicial proceedings in the absence of the defendant and her counsel seriously interferes with the defendant's Sixth Amendment right to representation. Though Judge McCullough may have intended to punish only O'Brien's attorney and not O'Brien, he acted intentionally and in bad faith. We thus conclude that the judge's action in the O'Brien case constituted wilful misconduct.

* * *

[The court's discussion of counts 4 and 5 is omitted.]

COUNT 6—THE BRASHEAR MATTER

Count 6 alleges that the judge failed to perform his judicial duties by not disposing of a matter pending before him for over six years. Kathy Brashear was the codefendant and cross-complainant in the case of Oakley v. Cheadle. On February 2, 1982, Judge McCullough granted her motions for judgment against plaintiffs and cross-defendants. A week later, Brashear's attorney sent the court a proposed judgment and request for costs and attorney's fees. Despite numerous telephone calls, written requests and trips to the court by Brashear's attorney over the next three years, Judge McCullough neither signed the judgment nor ruled on the request for costs and fees. The Commission eventually brought charges against the judge for his delay in this and other cases, and we publicly censured him in April 1987, finding that he had committed persistent failure and prejudicial conduct.

We are especially concerned with the judge's failure to act on the Brashear matter even after public censure. Instead of signing the judgment after his censure, the judge cavalierly told his clerk that he wanted nothing more to do with the case. Not until March 1988, after the Commission had instituted the present proceedings and more than six years after he actually granted the motions, did he sign the judgment.

We conclude that Judge McCullough's failure to sign the judgment form constituted persistent failure [to perform judicial duties.]

* * *

MITIGATING CIRCUMSTANCES

The Commission found that Judge McCullough is a hardworking judge who has critics but also friends in the community. Several parties testified to the judge's good character, and the San Benito County Bar Association filed an amicus curiae brief on his behalf. In addition, we take notice that the voters of San Benito County have twice elected him to judicial office.

DISPOSITION

We conclude that Judge McCullough has committed four acts of wilful misconduct and one act of persistent failure. He deprived criminal defendants of their constitutional rights, used his office to benefit a personal friend, and failed to perform the most basic of judicial duties. * * *

The purpose of these proceedings is not to punish errant judges but to protect the judicial system and those subject to the awesome power that judges wield. We conclude that that purpose is best served by adopting the recommendation of the Commission that Judge McCullough be removed from office.

We order that Judge Bernard P. McCullough, justice court judge of the San Benito Judicial District, San Benito County, be removed from office. He shall, however, if otherwise qualified, be permitted to resume the practice of law on the condition that he pass the Professional Responsibility Examination. He had a long career in private and public practice before coming onto the bench, and several parties have testified to his good character. Moreover, as an attorney, he will not have access to the power that he abused as a judge.

PERPICH v. CLEVELAND CLIFFS IRON CO.

United States District Court, Eastern District of Michigan, 1996.
927 F.Supp. 226.

Plaintiff seeks to disqualify this Court based upon a November 15, 1995 disclosure to counsel of the Court's former participation in his family's limited partnership which owned stock in General Electric

Company ("GE") and Westinghouse Corporation, two of the defendants in this case.[1] The November 15, 1995 letter to counsel stated:

> I have recently discovered that a family investment entity in which I was a limited partner has owned stock in General Electric Company and Westinghouse Corporation, which are parties to the above-referenced pending action. Prior to this discovery, I had no knowledge that the family limited partnership owned this stock. Several weeks ago, I divested myself of the limited partnership interest, and therefore, no longer have any interest in those stocks. I note from a review of the docket sheet that, thus far, I have rendered no substantive opinions or orders in this case.
>
> I have reviewed the pertinent statutes and law concerning disqualification and believe there is no requirement that I recuse myself in this case as I now have no financial interest and have rendered no substantive opinions. However, out of caution and prudence, I believe it is appropriate to bring this matter to your attention for whatever action, if any, you may deem necessary.

* * *

Disqualification of federal judges is governed by 28 U.S.C. § 455, which provides, in pertinent part:

> (a) Any justice, judge, or magistrate of the United States shall disqualify himself in any proceeding in which his impartiality might reasonably be questioned.
>
> (b) He shall also disqualify himself in the following circumstances:

*   *   *   *   *   *

> (4) He knows that he, individually or as a fiduciary, ... has a financial interest ... in a party to the proceeding, or any other interest that could be substantially affected by the outcome of the proceeding.
>
> (5) He or his spouse, or a person within the third degree of relationship to either of them, or the spouse of such person:

*   *   *   *   *   *

> (iii) Is known by the judge to have an interest that could be substantially affected by the outcome of the proceeding[.]

*   *   *   *   *   *

---

1. The limited partnership owned approximately 200 shares of Westinghouse and 400 shares of GE stock, although 200 shares of GE were sold in January 1994, before this case was assigned to this Court. The Court neither had nor has any role whatsoever in managing, or even making decisions about, the assets of the limited partnership.

(d) For the purposes of this section the following words or phrases shall have the meaning indicated:

* * * * * *

(2) the degree of relationship is calculated according to the civil law system;

* * * * * *

(4) "financial interest" means ownership of a legal or equitable interest, however small, or a relationship as a director, adviser, or other active participant in the affairs of a party . . . .

* * * * * *

(e) No justice, judge or magistrate shall accept from the parties to the proceeding a waiver of any ground for disqualification enumerated in subsection (b). Where the ground for disqualification arises only under subsection (a), waiver may be accepted provided it is preceded by a full disclosure on the record of the basis for disqualification.

(f) Notwithstanding the preceding provisions of this section, if any . . . judge . . . to whom a matter has been assigned would be disqualified, after substantial judicial time has been devoted to the matter, because of the appearance or discovery, after the matter was assigned to him or her, that he or she . . . has a financial interest in a party (other than an interest that could be substantially affected by the outcome), disqualification is not required if the . . . judge . . . divests himself or herself of the interest that provides the grounds for disqualification.

28 U.S.C. § 455 * * *

* * *

Plaintiff's principal disqualification argument is predicated on subsections (b)(4) (financial interest of the judge) and (b)(5) (known interest of family members) of Section 455. Secondarily, Plaintiff relies upon the "catch-all" general standard in subsection (a) of the statute which provides for disqualification in a proceeding in which a judge's "impartiality might reasonably be questioned."

Financial Interest in a Party

Plaintiff maintains that disqualification is mandated under § 455(b)(4) because the Court disclosed in November 1995 that it had just discovered that a family limited partnership (in which it was a limited partner) had owned some stock in General Electric Company and Westinghouse Corporation, two of the defendants in this case. Although Plaintiff acknowledges that the Court advised counsel for the parties that it had divested itself of the limited partnership interest "several weeks" earlier, Plaintiff nonetheless argues for disqualification because the Court did have a "financial interest" through the family limited partnership in Defendants GE and Westinghouse when the case was assigned to it in February 1995. Plaintiff asserts that he has "grave concerns" about the Court's impartiality since he does not know from the facts disclosed by the judge in November 1995 "the exact date he divested himself of any interest in the limited partnership, the number of shares [of the defendants' stock] the limited partnership owned and continues to own, the number of investors in the limited partnership, and the nature of the relationship the remaining partners share with Judge Rosen." * * *

As indicated * * *, the Court no longer has any interest in the family limited partnership or the GE or Westinghouse stocks. Indeed, even the family limited partnership no longer has an interest in the stock of either company. * * * [T]he Westinghouse stock was sold in June 1995, and the GE stock was sold in February 1996. * * *

An examination of the docket of this case indicates the following regarding this 20–month old case. Plaintiff filed his Complaint against five shipowner-employers and six nonemployer manufacturers of ship engines or component parts on August 29, 1994. The case was originally assigned to U.S. District Judge Bernard Friedman. The case remained with Judge Friedman for five months, until February 2, 1995, when Judge Friedman recused himself. The case was then reassigned to this Court. From February through November 1995, the parties engaged in discovery. * * * The docket, however, reveals that discovery disputes were minimal, and in fact, the Court entered only four orders in the case as of November 1995, none of which were substantive.

* * *

[T]he Court finds that the circumstances concerning its discovery and subsequent divestment of its interest in the family limited partnership are substantially similar to the facts presented in Union Carbide Corp. v. U.S. Cutting Service, Inc., 782 F.2d 710 (7th Cir.1986). That case involved a class action lawsuit filed on behalf of buyers of oxygen, nitrogen and argon. Two years after the complaint was filed, the federal district judge assigned to the case married a man whose self-managed retirement account happened to contain approximately $100,000 worth of IBM and Kodak stock. The judge had no reason to think that her marriage would have any effect on the propriety of her continuing to preside over the case since neither IBM nor Kodak were named plaintiffs, nor would it have seemed likely to persons without a technical background who would not know that liquid nitrogen is used by both companies in their technical processes that either company would be a member of the plaintiff class since, at the time of the judge's marriage, there was no list of class members.

In May 1984 and 1985, the judge filed her required financial disclosure statements, disclosing her husband's stock interests. In July

1985, Union Carbide moved for the recusal of the judge based on § 455(b)(4), pointing out that IBM and Kodak had in fact bought industrial gases from the defendants during the period covered in the complaint. The judge immediately ceased ruling on any motions in the case while the parties briefed the disqualification issue. All other motions in the case were referred to a magistrate or another judge for resolution. After the issue was briefed, the judge determined that she could properly preside over the case if her husband sold the IBM and Kodak stock. After he did so, she resumed control over the action.

Union Carbide appealed the district judge's refusal to recuse herself arguing that the sale of the stock did not cure the mandatory disqualification called for under section 455(b). The Seventh Circuit rejected Union Carbide's argument. The appellate court explained:

> When Judge Getzendanner discovered in July 1985 that she had a financial interest in a "party", she immediately suspended her involvement in the case. Although the case was not formally reassigned to another judge, any matters requiring a judicial ruling were referred to other judges; it was as if she had recused herself. Then however her husband sold the stock and she resumed control of the case. It was as if she had been reassigned to it. And when reassigned she no longer had a financial interest in it. Since the statute forbids only the knowing possession of a financial interest, since Judge Getzendanner relinquished control of the case as soon as she found out about the financial interest, and since she did not resume control until the financial interest was eliminated, at no time was she in literal violation of the statute.

> We must of course consider the purpose as well as the bare words of the statute. But the purpose as we have said is just to make sure that judges do not sit in cases in which they have a financial interest, however small. Judge Getzendanner has no financial interest in this case. If she were to rule in favor of the plaintiffs it could not put a nickel in her pocket, because neither she nor her husband owned securities of any member of the plaintiff class. Before she discovered she had a financial interest, she could have had no incentive to favor the plaintiffs; when she knew she had such an interest, she made no rulings in the case; now, when she has no interest, she cannot enrich herself by favoring the plaintiffs. The statutory purpose would not be served by forcing her to recuse herself.

782 F.2d at 714.

Just as was the case with Judge Getzendanner, this Court no longer has any financial interest in the case. It has had no financial interest in the stock of either company since, at the latest, October 31, 1995 when it severed its affiliation with the family limited partnership. Further, during the early part of the pendency of this case after its transfer to this Court's docket, the Court was unaware of the limited partnership's ownership of this stock, and once it learned of this interest (as well as of its interest in many other stocks), it moved to divest itself of its limited partnership interest. Moreover, even during the period before the Court divested itself of its partnership interest, the Court only entered a Scheduling Order. Other motions filed in that time frame were referred to a magistrate judge for resolution.

Notwithstanding that this Court, personally, did not enter any substantive orders during the nearly two-year pendency of this action, the parties and their counsel, as well as other judicial officers of the Eastern District have expended a substantial amount of time on this case, and the matter is ready for disposition, either by way of a summary judgment decision or trial.

Subsection (f) of § 455 provides:

> (f) Notwithstanding the preceding [disqualification] provisions of this section, if any justice, judge, magistrate or bankruptcy judge to whom a matter has been assigned would be disqualified, after substantial judicial time has been devoted to the matter, because of the appearance or discovery, after the matter was assigned to him or her, that he or she ... has a financial interest in a party (other than an interest that could be substantially affected by the outcome), disqualification is not required if the justice, judge, magistrate, bankruptcy judge, or his spouse, as the case may be, divests himself or herself of the interest that provides the grounds for the disqualification.

28 U.S.C. § 455.

Plaintiff argues that no "substantial judicial time" has been spent because the Court has not entered any substantive orders in the case. Plaintiff's narrow literal interpretation of subsection (f) is contrary to the spirit of this provision. As the Advisory Committee on Codes of Conduct of the Judicial Conference explained * * *, the statute, like the ABA Code of Judicial Conduct, "is couched in the present tense, providing that a judge should not sit when he or she 'has' an interest." As the district court noted in In re Industrial Gas Antitrust Litigation, No. 80 C 3479 (N.D.Ill. Sept. 24, 1985) * * *, the Advisory Committee considered the appearance of impropriety remote where the disqualifying interest comes to light "only after significant expenditures of time and energy by the judge, by counsel, and by the litigants." * * * While the Advisory Committee is not empowered to render opinions on the law and may only interpret the ABA Code of Judicial Conduct, Congress intended § 455 to conform generally to the Code. * * * Therefore, although not controlling, the Advisory Committee's opinion is entitled to some weight.

Recently, the Federal Circuit found that the divestiture of a judge's financial interest two months after the complaint was filed "fit squarely" within § 455(f) in Baldwin Hardware Corp. v. Franksu Enterprise Corp., 78 F.3d 550 (Fed.Cir.1996).

* * *

Based on the foregoing, the Court determines that there is no basis for mandatory disqualification under § 455(b)(4).

INTEREST OF FAMILY MEMBERS

Plaintiff also argues for disqualification based on § 455(b)(5) which calls for a judge's disqualification if a person "within the third degree of relationship" of either the judge or his spouse "is known by the judge to have an interest that could be substantially affected by the outcome of the proceeding." * * * [T]he following persons are within the third degree of relationship: children; grandchildren; great-grandchildren; parents; grandparents; great-grandparents; uncles; aunts; brothers; sisters; nephews; and nieces. * * *

The family limited partnership members consisted of the Court's father and two brothers. As indicated above, the partnership sold its shares of Westinghouse stock in June 1995, and the remainder (200 shares) of its GE stock in February 1996. Thus, the question is whether the partnership's interest in Defendant General Electric is one that may be "substantially affected by the outcome" of this case.

Whether an interest is one which could be "substantially affected" by the outcome of a proceeding depends on the interaction of two variables: the remoteness of the interest and its extent or degree. * * *

In NEC Corp. v. Intel Corp., 654 F.Supp. 1256 (N.D.Cal.1987), (subsequently vacated as moot, 835 F.2d 1546 (9th Cir.1988)), a copyright infringement action, the court was faced with a recusal motion based upon the "other interest" provision of § 455(b)(4) which contains the same "substantially affected by the outcome of the proceeding" language as in subsection (b)(5).[4] In NEC the district judge had an interest in a 24–member investment club. * * * The investment club held 60 shares of Intel Corporation. Upon discovery of the fund's ownership of Intel stock, the judge resigned from the investment club, and he relinquished his interest in the Intel stock, which was valued at $80.

The court determined that the judge was not required to disqualify himself from the case "because Judge Ingram's interest, considering its size and remoteness [i.e., a ¹⁄₂₄th share of 60 shares of Intel stock], was too slight" to be substantially affected by the outcome of the copyright infringement proceeding and "because Judge Ingram has divested himself of his interest in Intel." 654 F.Supp. at 1257. * * *

---

4. In addition to providing for disqualification of a judge who knows that he or she has a direct financial interest in a party or in the subject matter of the proceeding, § 455(b)(4) also provides for disqualification of a judge having "any other interest that could be substantially affected by the outcome of the proceeding."

Applying the foregoing authorities to the facts of this case, the Court finds that although his father and two brothers did have a shared limited partnership interest in 200 shares of GE stock until February 1996, given that they no longer have any interest in the stock, there is no basis whatsoever for an argument that the outcome of this single-plaintiff personal injury action could substantially affect their interest. Therefore, the Court finds no basis for disqualification under § 455(b)(5).

DISQUALIFICATION UNDER SECTION 455(A)

Plaintiff also alternatively seeks disqualification under the general "catch all" provision in Section 455(a). * * *

As the plain language of subsection (a) makes clear, disqualification is called for only when the judge's impartiality "might reasonably be questioned." The Sixth Circuit standard in disqualification motions under § 455(a) is that a district judge is required to recuse himself "only if a reasonable person with knowledge of all the facts would conclude that the judge's impartiality might reasonably be questioned." Wheeler v. Southland Corp., 875 F.2d 1246, 1251 (6th Cir.1989); Roberts v. Bailar, 625 F.2d 125, 129 (6th Cir.1980) (impartiality issue is to be determined from the view point of a reasonable person knowing all of the relevant facts). * * *

Although it is undisputed that the purpose of the disqualification statute is to avoid the appearance of impartiality (sic) * * * the legislative history of the 1974 amendments to Section 455 reveals that Congress intended the statute to be narrowly construed to prevent "judge shopping". For example, the Senate Judiciary Committee warned judges of applying section 455 too cavalierly:

> [I]n assessing the reasonableness of a challenge to his impartiality, each judge must be alert to avoid the possibility that those who would question his impartiality are in fact seeking to avoid the consequences of his expected adverse decision. Disqualification must have a reasonable basis. Nothing in this proposed legislation should be read to warrant the transformation of a litigant's fear that a judge may decide a question against him into a "reasonable fear" that the judge will not be impartial. Litigants ought not to have to face a judge where there is a reasonable question of impartiality, but they are not entitled to judges of their own choice.

* * *

* * *

In this case, * * * the Court did not discover until well into the pendency of this case that his family's limited partnership had a short-lived and relatively insubstantial stock ownership interest in two of the 11 defendants in this action. Upon discovery, the Court immediately moved to terminate its membership in the partnership. As further indicated, while the Court did have an unknown stock ownership interest from February through October 1995, during that period of time, it made no rulings whatsoever in the case, and entered no orders other than a scheduling order and two orders of reference, referring two discovery motions to the magistrate judge for resolution.

Given the foregoing, the Court finds that a reasonable person with knowledge of all of these facts would not reasonably question the Court's impartiality. Therefore, the Court will deny Plaintiffs' Motion for Disqualification.

MULTIPLE CHOICE QUESTIONS

Answer the following questions using the ABA Code of Judicial Conduct (1990).

1. Judge Agatha DuBois, age 67, is a full-time judge on the State Superior Court. She has a brother who is 13 years her senior. Her brother asked her to prepare a will for him. He said he wanted to leave her $1,000 in his will and to divide the rest of his estate equally among his grandchildren. Judge DuBois explained that she could not prepare the will for him and she suggested he have it done by Schmitts, one of the good estate planning lawyers in town. Which of the following statements are correct?

I. If the will names Judge DuBois as executrix, she *may* serve, assuming that it will not interfere with judicial duties.

II. If the will names First City Bank as executor and names Judge DuBois as attorney for the estate, she *may* serve, assuming that the estate will not be probated in her court or one under its appellate jurisdiction.

III. If the will leaves Judge DuBois $1,000, she *may* accept the money.

IV. It would have been *proper* for Judge DuBois to prepare the will for her brother, even though she would receive $1,000 under the will.

V. If Schmitts sends Judge DuBois a nice crate of Florida grapefruit, as a small token of thanks for the referral, she *may* eat the grapefruit.

    A. None of the above.

    B. Only IV.

    C. Only IV and V.

    D. Only I and III.

2. Judge Fenton Hardy has been assigned to hear a suit brought by the Smithfield Citizens Reacting Against Monopoly (SCRAM) against Atlantic Power and Light (APAL). Assuming that there is no reason whatsoever to doubt Judge Hardy's complete impartiality in the case, which of the following would require him to disqualify himself?

I. The husband of his wife's sister is the trial counsel for APAL.

II. He has personal knowledge that one of the key allegations in SCRAM's complaint is absolutely false.

III. His son, Joey (a minor living at home), owns two shares of Essex Mutual Fund (a gift from his grandmother), and Essex Mutual Fund owns .003% of the outstanding common stock of APAL.

IV. His nephew's wife will testify as a material witness for SCRAM.

V. His wife's cousin is on the Board of Directors of APAL.

VI. Five years ago, when Judge Hardy was still practicing law, one of his law partners defended APAL in a case arising out of the untimely death of a pet cat that was run over by an APAL repair truck.

    A. Only I, II, and IV.

    B. Only II, III, and V.

    C. Only I, IV, and V.

    D. Only II, IV, V, and VI.

3. Before her recent election to the State Supreme Court, Justice McDonald was very active in political, charitable, and religious activities. Now she must cut back that part of her life. In which of the following activities *may* she engage as a judge?

I. The other Supreme Court Justices have asked her, as junior Justice, to take up a collection from the court's personnel to pay for retirement parties, holiday parties, flowers for sick employees, and the like.

II. The pastor of her church has asked her to solicit funds in the church's annual door-to-door plea for money to buy food for impoverished people in the community.

III. The Fundamental Freedoms Party has asked her to solicit funds in the party's annual door-to-door plea for political donations.

IV. The Fundamental Freedoms Party has asked her to serve again next year as its Regional Chairperson.

V. The pastor of her church has asked her to serve again next year on the Board of Wardens, the governing body of the church.

    A. All of the above.

    B. None of the above.

    C. I, III, and IV only.

    D. I and V only.

4. Judge Janke is a full-time Superior Court Judge. She has been assigned to preside in the cases described below. Assume that the parties are not willing to waive the technical disqualification provisions of the Code of Judicial Conduct; assume, further, that even in light of the facts stated below there is no reasonable ground to doubt Judge Janke's impartiality. In which of the cases *may* she preside?

I. *People v. Adams*, a murder case in which Judge Janke's family physician will testify as a witness on behalf of the prosecution.

II. *Bennett v. Amalgamated Chemical Corp.*, a class action in which Amalgamated is charged with sex discrimination in employment. Fifteen years ago, before she went on the bench, Judge Janke represented Amalgamated in a state inventory tax case.

III. *Cressler v. Union Van & Storage Co.*, a breach of warranty action in which Cressler claims that Union Van ruined her grand piano. Judge Janke's mother, age 96, lives in a nursing home and owns 100 of the three million outstanding shares of Union Van's common stock.

IV. *Dimish v. City of Portmont*, a tort action in which Dimish claims that noise from the Portmont Municipal Airport has reduced the value of his home. Judge Janke owns $2,000 worth of general obligation bonds that were issued by the City of Portmont to fund a variety of municipal public works projects.

    A. All of the above.

    B. None of the above.

    C. I only.

    D. I, III, and IV only.

5. Judge Linch has served on the State Intermediate Appeals Court for the past 14 years. The state law requires judges to stand for election every 5 years. The general election is two months from now, and Eddie Slick (a local lawyer) is running against Judge Linch. Which of the following activities would be *proper* in Judge Linch's campaign?

I. Judge Linch proposes to walk from door to door in some precincts, meeting the voters personally, and asking for small contributions to help pay for billboard advertisements.

II. Judge Linch proposes to dress in a clown suit and ride a donkey in the County Fair parade, while passing out green balloons that say: "Eddie Slick Makes Me Sick."

III. Judge Linch proposes to respond in a dignified, factual manner to Eddie Slick's charge that Judge Linch is lazy and stupid.

IV. Judge Linch proposes to debate Eddie Slick, face to face, on a local television program in which both candidates will inform voters of their general views on civil rights, First Amendment freedoms, and like issues.

    A. All of the above.

    B. III and IV only.

    C. I, III, and IV only.

    D. I only.

6. Justice Celeste Jefferson has lifetime tenure on the Supreme Court of State X. Her husband, Fred Jefferson, is a candidate for election to the State X Senate. Fred plans to hold a political gathering at their home to solicit funds for his campaign. Which of the following *may* Justice Jefferson do?

I. Make a brief, dignified speech on Fred's behalf, urging the guests at the gathering to contribute to Fred's campaign.

II. Send out invitations to the gathering on Supreme Court stationery.

III. Serve tea and little sandwiches at the gathering.

IV. Act as hostess at the gathering.

    A. All of the above.

    B. None of the above.

    C. III and IV only.

    D. IV only.

Answers to the multiple choice questions will be found in the Appendix at the end of the book

APPENDIX

You may not always agree with these answers to the multiple choice questions. We have attempted to explain why we picked the answers we did; if you disagree, please write to us to explain why your answer is better.

CHAPTER TWO

1. **A.** ABA Code DR 3–101(B) and ABA Model Rule 5.5(a) [and CRPC 1–300(B)] prohibit Alford from practicing in a state where he is not admitted to practice. He can avoid this proscription if he is admitted *pro hac vice* to defend Clara in the State B case. [*See* Hazard & Hodes §§ 5.5:201–5.5:202.] Answer B is not correct because requiring admission to practice does not discriminate against non-residents; neither residents nor non-residents can practice law without being admitted. Answers C and D are not correct because if Alford is admitted *pro hac vice* he may represent Clara in the case even though it involves a State B business and the interpretation of a State B statute.

2. **B.** If Linda tells the bar of State B that her cousin is fit to practice law, when in fact she believes him to be thoroughly dishonest, she would knowingly be making a false statement of material fact in violation of ABA Model Rule 8.1(a) and ABA Code DR 1–101(B). [CRPC 1–200(A) & (B) are similar but appear to apply only to applications for admission to the *California* State Bar. However, CRPC 1–100(D)(1) makes the California Rules applicable to California bar members while practicing in State B.] Answers C and D are not correct for the same reason. Answer A is not correct—Linda's lack of membership in the bar of State B is beside the point. State A could discipline her for lying to the bar of State B. [*See* ABA Model Rule 8.5 and CRPC 1–100(D)(1).]

3. **D.** All states require bar applicants to demonstrate good moral character. *See generally*, Rhode, *Moral Character as a Professional Credential*, 94 Yale L.J. 491 (1985). A recent conviction for federal tax fraud is strong (though perhaps not conclusive) evidence that Samuel lacks good moral character. [*See generally* Hazard & Hodes § 8.4:301.] As for item I, the *Piper* case, 470 U.S. at 274–288, and those that follow it suggest that State C could not refuse to admit Samuel simply because he plans to live across the state line. As for item II, membership in the Communist Party is not, by itself, sufficient ground to deny admission to the bar. [*See Schware v. Board of Bar Examiners*, 353 U.S. 232, 77 S.Ct. 752, 1 L.Ed.2d 796 (1957). In California, *cf.* Bus. & Prof.Code § 6106.1.] As for item III, lack of U.S. citizenship is not, by itself,

sufficient ground to deny admission to the bar. [*See In re Griffiths*, 413 U.S. 717, 93 S.Ct. 2851, 37 L.Ed.2d 910 (1973).]

4. C. According to ABA Code DR 1–102(A), a lawyer is subject to discipline for engaging in "illegal conduct involving moral turpitude," or engaging in "conduct involving dishonesty, fraud, deceit, or misrepresentation." [*See also* ABA Model Rule 8.4(b) and (c) and Cal.Bus. & Prof.Code § 6106 (cause for discipline).] Leon's conduct was dishonest and involved moral turpitude for two reasons: first, he intentionally cheated the phone company, and second, he lied to the judge. On the other hand, Leona's conduct (although a felony) does not strike us as involving either moral turpitude or dishonesty.

5. A. ABA Model Rule 8.1 and ABA Code DR 1–101(A) require candor of a bar applicant on an application questionnaire. [*See* CRPC 1–200(A) (applicable only to California bar members).] Answer B is not correct; a bar applicant can overcome a prior criminal conviction by demonstrating rehabilitation. Answer C is not correct; the prior conviction is relevant to Sabrina's present moral character, although she can be admitted to practice if she demonstrates rehabilitation. Answer D is not correct; no case has extended the constitutional right of privacy this far, although it has been argued that privacy values ought to be given more attention in bar admission matters. *See* Rhode, *supra*, at 574–84.

6. B. *In re Wolff*, 490 A.2d 1118 (D.C. App. 1985), involved similar facts and resulted in discipline of the lawyer. Sale of the pornographic photographs was said to involve moral turpitude because it made the lawyer a link in a chain of activity that degrades and exploits children. Answer A is not correct; State C can discipline Arner even though his conduct took place elsewhere. [*See* ABA Model Rule 8.5 and CRPC 1–100(D)(1).] Answer C is not correct; an act of moral turpitude need not be connected with the practice of law to result in professional discipline. [*See* ABA Code DR 1–102(A)(3)–(6); ABA Model Rule 8.4(b)–(d); Cal. Bus. & Prof.Code § 6106.] Answer D is not correct because it is too broad; not every criminal act is grounds for professional discipline. [*Id.*]

7. A. ABA Code DR 1–103 and ABA Model Rule 8.3 require a lawyer to report a disciplinary offense by another lawyer. But that duty does not apply where the first lawyer learns about the offense through a privileged communication. Lindell's communication with Cathcart was subject to the attorney-client privilege, and none of the exceptions to the privilege would apply in this situation. Thus, Lindell has no duty to reveal the information, and if he did reveal it, he himself would be subject to discipline. [*See* ABA Code DR 4–101(B); ABA Model Rule 1.6.] Answers B, C, and D are not correct because each of them involves some form of prohibited disclosure of the confidential information. [California has no Rule in this area. *Cf.* CRPC 1–200(C).]

CHAPTER THREE

1. C. ABA Code DR 2–110(C)(3) states that one ground for permissive withdrawal is the lawyer's "inability to work with co-counsel,"

coupled with a belief that withdrawal will serve the client's best interests. [*See also* ABA Model Rule 1.16.] Asking for the client's consent makes the propriety of the withdrawal all the clearer. [*See* ABA Code DR 2–110(C)(5); *see also* ABA Model Rule 1.16.] Answer A is not as good as C, because it does not take into account Snyder's duty to give advance notice and to take other steps to avoid prejudice to the client. [*See* ABA Code DR 2–110(A)(2); *see also* ABA Model Rule 1.16.] Answer B is incorrect because it seems to assume that the choice of counsel is up to Snyder, rather than the client. Answer D suffers the same defect; further, it might be regarded as an improper interference with the contractual relations between Slick and the client. [*Cf.* ABA Code EC 2–30.] The answer and analysis would be the same under CRPC 3–700.

2. B. Item I is correct; the question states that the court rules require court permission for withdrawal, and, where that is true, the lawyer is subject to discipline for failing to get permission. [ABA Code DR 2–110(A)(1); *cf.* ABA Model Rule 1.16.] Item II is incorrect. Under ABA Code DR 2–110(C)(1)(d) and (f), Arbuckle had ample grounds for permissive withdrawal—Clauzoff failed to co-operate in the defense, and he ignored his fee agreement with Arbuckle. [*See also* ABA Model Rule 1.16.] Item III is correct; ABA Code DR 2–110(A)(2) requires the return of "all papers and property to which the client is entitled," and the question states that attorney liens on litigation files are not recognized in State A. [*See also* ABA Model Rule 1.16.] Item IV is incorrect; Arbuckle earned the $1,200 when he put in his first 20 hours on the case. [*See* ABA Code DR 2–110(A)(3); *see also* ABA Model Rule 1.16.] The analysis and answer would be the same under CRPC 3–700.

3. A. ABA Code EC 2–26 states the general rule: "A lawyer is under no obligation to act as advisor or advocate for every person who may wish to become his client * * *." While that general rule is subject to limitations, none of them would seem to apply here. There is no lack of skilled counsel in the community, the cause and client are not so unpopular as to shut off access to counsel, and Worthington has sufficient resources to obtain other counsel with more experience in the matter at hand. [*Cf.* ABA Model Rules 6.1 and 6.2.] The answer and analysis would be the same under Cal.Bus. & Prof.Code § 6068(h) and California case law.

4. C. One of the limitations on an attorney's ordinary freedom to turn down cases is where the court asks the attorney to serve as appointed counsel. [ABA Code EC 2–29; ABA Model Rule 6.2] An attorney should not seek to be excused from taking a court appointed case, except for a compelling reason. As explained in ABA Code EC 2–26 through 2–29, items I, III, and IV do not present compelling reasons. But the risk of unreasonable financial harm does present a compelling reason, according to ABA Model Rule 6.2(b). The CRPC are silent on this subject, but see Cal.Bus. & Prof.Code § 6068(h). We believe the analysis and answer would be the same in California.

5. B. According to ABA Code DR 2–110(C)(1)(e), one of the grounds for permissive withdrawal is where the client "insists, in a matter not pending before a tribunal, that the lawyer engage in conduct that is contrary to the judgment and advice of the lawyer but not prohibited under the Disciplinary Rules." Similarly, ABA Model Rule 1.16(b)(3) permits a lawyer to withdraw when the client "insists upon pursuing an objective that the lawyer considers repugnant or imprudent." Here the officers of the union are asking Yeager to include a provision that is against her best judgment, a provision that she regards as imprudent. Therefore, she is entitled to withdraw, assuming that she takes the ordinary steps to protect her client's interest upon withdrawal. [*See* ABA Model Rule 1.16(d); ABA Code DR 2–110(A).] The analysis and answer would be the same under CRPC 3–700(C)(1)(e).

CHAPTER FOUR

1. A. ABA Model Rule 7.2(c) prohibits a lawyer from giving "anything of value" to a person for "recommending the lawyer's services." [*See also* ABA Code DR 2–101(I), which prohibits compensating media reporters for publicity in a news item.] The items of gossip Philos feeds to Norris are items of value to Norris, and Norris's favorable comments about Philos are in the nature of recommendations of his services. Answer B is wrong because there is no such disciplinary rule. Answer C is wrong; Philos is subject to discipline on the ground stated in answer A. Answer D is wrong; we know of no case that extends free speech protection to this kind of activity.

2. D. The relevant authorities are ABA Code DR 2–102 and ABA Model Rule 7.5. Item I is correct; the name of a dead partner may be retained by a successor firm. Item II is incorrect; the firm name makes Trimble appear to be a partner when he is in fact an associate. Item III is incorrect; Snod's name should have been removed when he ceased the regular practice of law to enter government service. Item IV is incorrect; the sign on the door makes Tremble and Gangler appear to be partners when in fact they are not. Under CRPC 1–400 and Standard 7, the answer would be B; Items I, II, and III would be correct, and Item IV would be incorrect.

3. C. Item I is correct. [*See* ABA Code DR 2–101(D) and ABA Model Rule 7.2(b).] Item II is correct. Anton's advertisement states that the "*most*" he will charge for "*any* type of legal work" is $100 per hour. If in fact he charges $125 for complicated legal work, his advertisement is false. [*See* ABA Model Rule 7.1; ABA Code DR 2–101(A).] Item III is not correct; Anton has no obligation to disclose that other lawyers charge less than he does. If Anton's advertisement stated or implied that his fees are "the lowest in town," or something to that effect, that would be a different matter—but the facts stated in the question do not suggest any such statement or implication. The answer would be the same under CRPC 1–400.

4. A. Assuming that items I, II, and IV are truthful and not misleading, they are proper under ABA Model Rules 7.1 and 7.2, and even under the "laundry list" in ABA Code DR 2–101(B). The same would be true under CRPC 1–400. Item III might be thought to violate ABA Model Rule 7.4 and ABA Code DR 2–105(A), which purport to restrict use of the term "specialist." [See also, CRPC 1–400(D)(6), which purports to restrict use of the term "certified specialist."] However, those rules must be read in light of *Peel v. Attorney Reg. & Disciplinary Com'n*, 496 U.S. 91, 110 S.Ct. 2281, 110 L.Ed.2d 83 (1990), which held that an attorney could not be disciplined in a situation similar to this one.

5. D. Answers A, B and C are incorrect under the principles expressed in the *Zauderer* and *Shapero* cases. Question 5 also raises a different ethics issue that you will study later in this book. You will learn that ordinarily a lawyer should not serve as trial counsel in a case where he or she is "likely to be a necessary witness." Salmon saw the accident and is therefore a potential witness, but he is probably not a "necessary" witness because he was only one of a crowd of people that saw the accident.

6. B. If Gresler personally hung around hospitals, passing out his professional cards to personal injury victims, he would violate ABA Code DR 2–103(A) and ABA Model Rule 7.3. [*Accord* CRPC 1–400(B) and (C) and Standards 3 and 4.] Likewise, he is subject to discipline for inducing other persons to do what he himself could not do. [See ABA Model Rule 8.4(a); ABA Code DR 2–103(C); CRPC 1–120.] Further, California and many other states prohibit lawyers from using "runners or cappers" to solicit legal business. [*See, e.g.,* Cal.Bus. & Prof.Code §§ 6150–54.] Answer A is not correct for the reasons stated above. Answers C and D are not correct; no disciplinary rule prohibits Gresler from holding the seminar or dispensing accurate legal advice to those who attend. [*See generally* ABA Code EC 2–2 through 2–5.]

7. A. ABA Model Rule 7.5(a) permits a law firm to use a tradename, so long as the name is not false or misleading and does not imply a connection with a government agency or public or charitable legal services organization. [*Accord* CRPC 1–400 and Standard 6.] ABA Code DR 2–102(B) purports to prohibit the use of a law firm tradename that does not incorporate the surnames of one or more lawyers, live or dead, who practice or once practiced with the firm or predecessor firms. Despite *Friedman v. Rogers*, 440 U.S. 1, 99 S.Ct. 887, 59 L.Ed.2d 100 (1979) (upholding a Texas ban on the use of tradenames by shops that sell eye glasses), we believe that ABA Code DR 2–102(B) could not survive constitutional challenge on the facts given here. The rule is a quaint vestige of the days when lawyers could not advertise. [*See* G. Hazard & W. Hodes, *The Law of Lawyering* §§ 7.5:101–7.5:203 (2d ed. 1990).] Answers B, C, and D are not correct for the same reason.

8. A. ABA Model Rule 7.1 prohibits misleading communications about legal services. [*See also* ABA Code DR 2–101(A).] The term

"affiliate" is broad and vague, and it has been applied to many kinds of relationships between law firms. ABA Formal Opinion 94–388 (1994) says that when attorneys use "affiliate" on a letterhead or similar advertising, they must take the additional step of explaining precisely what they mean by it. The additional explanation need not be given to everyone; it is sufficient to give it to those prospective clients who may care about it. Answer B is wrong, for the reason stated above. Answer C is wrong because there is no such rule. Answer D is wrong because the referral of work by one of these firms to the other does not violate any rule about solicitation of clients.

CHAPTER FIVE

1. D. Item III is correct. ABA Model Rule 1.5(d)(2) and ABA Code DR 2–106(C) make Lenox subject to discipline for using a contingent fee in a criminal case. The policy behind this rule is debatable. [*See* G. Hazard & W. Hodes 119.] Item I is also correct; Lenox should not have taken this case on contingent fee, but since he did, he should at least have put the contingent fee agreement in writing. [*See* ABA Model Rule 1.5(c), which requires contingent fee agreements to be in writing, and ABA Code EC 2–19, which strongly encourages it.] Items II and IV are both correct. ABA Model Rule 1.8(e) and ABA Code DR 5–103(B) permit Lenox to advance the litigation expenses. Denmon's promise to pay back the advance is mandatory under ABA Code DR 5–103(B) and is permissive under ABA Model Rule 1.8(e). If the problem arose in California, the answer would be A. California has no disciplinary rule that prohibits criminal defense lawyers from using contingent fees.

2. A. When two lawyers or law firms work on a case together, they frequently submit separate bills to the client, and nothing in either the ABA Model Rules or the ABA Code suggests that this is not a proper practice. Answer B is not correct. ABA Code DR 2–103(B) and ABA Model Rule 7.2(c) prohibit Alvarez from paying Leland for the referral. Answer C is not correct for the same reason that answer A is correct. The two lawyers could have worked out a suitable fee splitting arrangement here, but nothing requires them to do so. Answer D is not correct. The $1,000 referral fee makes the arrangement improper, even if it did not increase the total amount Holiday paid. If the problem arose in California and were governed by the CRPC, the $1,000 referral fee would be proper if two conditions were met. First, Holiday would have to be fully informed of the referral fee and consent to it in writing. Second, the total fee charged by the two lawyers could not be higher than it would have been absent the $1,000 referral fee. [*See* CRPC 2–200(A).]

3. B. Under ABA Code DR 5–103(B) and ABA Model Rule 1.8(e), Aragon is subject to discipline. The $7,500 was for medical expenses, not litigation expenses. Answer A is not correct. This is the kind of case that lawyers commonly take on a contingent fee basis. Answer C is not correct. As you will learn in a later chapter, it is proper to pay a reasonable fee to an expert witness. [*See* ABA Code DR 7–109(C)(3); *see also* Comment to ABA Model Rule 3.4.] Answer D is not correct. The

expert witness fee is an expense of litigation and can thus be advanced by Aragon on Carlson's behalf. [*See* ABA Code DR 5–103(B) and ABA Model Rule 1.8(e).] If the problem arose under the CRPC, it would be proper for Aragon to lend Carlson $7,500 to pay the medical bill, provided that: (a) Carlson had already hired Aragon as his lawyer, and (b) Carlson agreed in writing to repay Aragon. [*See* CRPC 4–210(A)(2).]

4. A. Item B is incorrect; ABA Code DR 2–106(B)(4) and ABA Model Rule 1.5(a) state that one factor a lawyer may consider in setting a fee is "the amount involved and the results obtained." Item C is incorrect; a portion of Draxco's check did belong to Arnstein, but Arnstein's portion had not yet been determined. In that situation, it was proper to put the entire amount in the client trust account. [*See* ABA Code DR 9–102(A)(2); ABA Model Rule 1.15(c).] Item D is incorrect; where there is a fee dispute, it is proper to keep the disputed funds in the client trust account until the dispute is settled. [*See* ABA Code DR 9–102(A)(2); ABA Model Rule 1.15(c).] The analysis and conclusions would be the same under the CRPC. [*See* CRPC 4–100(A) and 4–200(B)(5).]

5. C. Items A and D are incorrect; when Lee drew the $350 check on her client trust account, she was misappropriating Fujitomi's money. [*See* ABA Code DR 9–102; ABA Model Rule 1.15.] Item B is incorrect; nothing in the ABA Code or the Model Rules suggests that Lee had an ethical obligation to allow Watkins to go to jail. Item C is correct; in these circumstances, the fine can be viewed as an expense of litigation, and lawyers are permitted to advance litigation expenses. [*See* ABA Code DR 5–103(b); ABA Model Rule 1.8(e).] The answer would be the same under the CRPC. CRPC 4–210(A)(3) would permit Lee to advance the $350 as a litigation expense. Alternatively, under CRPC 4–210(A)(2), Lee could simply lend the $350 to Watkins, provided that Watkins promised in writing to repay her.

6. C. Canfield authorized Ayers to accept any reasonable settlement offer and said, "try to get the horse if you can." Note that Canfield sued for specific performance, not for return of the bonds— Canfield obviously has a higher opinion of Thunderbolt than Ayers does. At the outset, Ayers could properly have counseled Canfield to seek the bonds rather than the horse. [*See* ABA Code EC 7–7 and 7–8; ABA Model Rule 1.2(a) and the Comment thereto.] But the time for counseling has passed; Ayers' duty at this point is to carry out his client's instructions. Thus, answers A and B are not correct. When Ayers gets the horse from Dennis, he must keep it in a safe place until Canfield returns. [ABA Model Rule 1.15(a); ABA Code DR 9–102(B)(2).] The bonded stable is a better choice than the pasture on Ayers' farm, mentioned in answer D; who knows what evil might befall Thunderbolt out in Ayers' pasture? The bonded stable will cost nearly $1,000, but in the circumstances it is proper for Ayers to incur this expense and to seek reimbursement from Canfield. [*See Restatement (Second) of Trusts* § 176 (1959); A. Scott, *Trusts* § 176 (3d ed. 1967); R. Brown, *Law of*

Personal Property § 11.10 (3d ed. 1975).] The analysis and conclusions would be the same under CRPC 4–100(B)(2).

CHAPTER SIX

1. **D.** ABA Code DR 6–101(A)(3) provides that a lawyer must not "neglect a legal matter entrusted to him." ABA Model Rule 1.3 provides that a lawyer must "act with reasonable diligence and promptness in representing a client." [*Cf.* CRPC 3–110(A) (duty of competence).] Further, ABA Model Rule 1.4 and CRPC 3–500 require a lawyer to keep the client "reasonably informed about the status of a matter," and ABA Model Rule 8.4(c) forbids lying and other dishonest conduct. [*See also* ABA Code EC 9–2.] Answer A is not correct. Even if Acevedo would have been able to do the work on time, he is subject to discipline for lying to Catlin about his progress on the matter. Answer B is not correct. Acevedo is subject to discipline even though Catlin was able to find another lawyer who could get the complaint filed in time. Answer C is not correct. Since Catlin was not injured by the delay, Acevedo is not liable for malpractice.

2. **C.** Item I is correct. The question states that any reasonably competent general practitioner would have discovered the more favorable law under the Lanham Act. Lloyd failed to discover it, and he is thus liable for the injury Cress suffered due to his negligence. Item II is correct. As the partner in charge of this case, Ames himself was probably negligent for taking the case to trial on state law theories only. Even if that were not true, partner Ames is liable for Lloyd's negligence under ordinary principles of *respondeat superior*. Item III is correct. As a partner in the firm, Baker is liable for the negligent acts of Lloyd and Ames. Item IV is not correct for the reasons explained above.

3. **C.** The question states that Landsman volunteered to represent CAH, not Cheng. If Landsman had purported to advise both CAH and Cheng in the transaction [*see* ABA Model Rule 2.2], then he would have owed a duty of care to Cheng, but nothing in the question suggests that he purported to advise Cheng. When a lawyer advises one party to an arms-length transaction, the lawyer is not liable for negligence that injures the other party. [*See* Wolfram § 5.6.4.] Answer A is not correct for the same reason. Answer B is not correct. The mere fact that Landsman was not working for a fee does not relieve him from malpractice liability. Answer D is not correct because the injury to Cheng would have been foreseen by a reasonably prudent lawyer.

4. **A.** When a lawyer represents one party to litigation, the lawyer is not liable for negligence that causes injury to the adversary party. [*See* Wolfram § 5.6.4.] Further, nothing in the question suggests that Applegate was negligent in the first place. A lawyer is liable to the adversary for intentional misconduct, for example, abuse of process. If Delta had sued Applegate for abuse of process, it would have had to prove that Applegate intentionally pursued a claim that he knew was baseless. The question states that Applegate believed that Delta had in

fact unlawfully discriminated against Cortez, even though Applegate was pessimistic about Cortez's chances of winning at trial. Answers B and D are not correct for the same reason. Answer C is not correct. If Applegate had owed a duty of care to Delta, and if Applegate had acted negligently, the actual cause element would have been easy for Delta to satisfy.

    5. D. Item I is correct. [*See* ABA Code DR 6–101(A); ABA Model Rule 1.1.] It would be proper for Abrams to charge Carmondy a nominal fee for finding a suitable specialist; to find a suitable expert takes time and requires careful judgment. As a practical matter, however, many lawyers in Abrams' position would elect not to charge a regular client for this service. Item II is correct. ABA Code DR 6–101(A)(1) and CRPC 3–100(B) specifically contemplate this approach, and the Comment to ABA Model Rule 1.1 is in accord. Item III is not correct because it fails to mention the need for Carmondy's consent to the arrangement. [*See* ABA Code DR 2–107(A)(1); ABA Model Rule 1.5(e); *but see* CRPC 3–100(B) (fails to require client consent).] Item IV is correct. ABA Code EC 6–3 and CRPC 3–110(B) allow Abrams to accept the employment in these circumstances, and the Comment to ABA Model Rule 1.1 is in accord.

    6. B. Item I is incorrect and Item III is correct for the following reasons. ABA Code DR 6–102(A) and ABA Model Rule 1.8(h) concern lawyers' efforts to exonerate themselves from liability for malpractice. The arbitration agreement in the contract between Aoki and Cramer does not violate either of those provisions. The arbitration agreement does not exonerate Aoki from anything; it simply provides a method of resolving disputes. In years gone by, courts regarded arbitration agreements as contrary to public policy because they "ousted courts of their jurisdiction." In modern times, courts have discovered that they do not suffer for lack of business. Further, federal and state legislation makes arbitration agreements enforceable, and arbitration has now become a "favored" method of dispute resolution. The Comment to ABA Model Rule 1.5 encourages lawyers to use bar-sponsored arbitration to resolve fee disputes. Neither the ABA Code nor the ABA Model Rules mention arbitration as a method of resolving malpractice claims, but its use has become commonplace in the medical profession, and there would seem to be no reason to resist it in the legal profession. If Aoki were a California lawyer, she would wish to consult Cal.Bar.Op. 1977–47, which states that there is nothing inherently wrong with an agreement to arbitrate legal malpractice claims, so long as the client is *fully informed of the consequences of the agreement.* [*See also Lawrence v. Walzer & Gabrielson,* 207 Cal.App.3d 1501, 256 Cal.Rptr. 6 (1989) (retainer agreement that called for binding arbitration of all disputes regarding "fees, costs, or any other aspect of our attorney-client relationship" did not require client to arbitrate a malpractice claim).] Item II is not correct. Lawyers are entitled to insist that clients observe their fee agreements. CRPC 3–700(C)(1)(f), ABA Code DR 2–110(C)(1)(f) and ABA Model Rule 1.16(b)(4) permit a lawyer to withdraw if a client deliberately disregards

the fee agreement. While it is true that a lawyer cannot leave a client in the lurch (shortly before trial, for example), and while a lawyer must take reasonable steps to protect the client's interests upon withdrawal, the question does not suggest that Aoki has acted improperly in refusing to do further work until she is paid. Item IV is correct. The ABA Code offers no specific guidance on this point, but ABA Model Rule 1.8(h) and CRPC 3–400(B) state that a lawyer who seeks to settle a malpractice claim with a client must advise the client in writing that independent representation is appropriate in connection with the settlement.

7. A. Item I is not correct. It is not uncommon for a lawyer to have a non-lawyer employee handle the day-to-day details of the client trust account, and neither the ABA Code nor the ABA Model Rules nor the CRPC forbid it. Items II and III are correct. ABA Model Rule 5.3 requires lawyers to train and adequately supervise their non-lawyer assistants. [*See also* Discussion following CRPC 3–110 (duty to supervise).] *In re Scanlan*, 144 Ariz. 334, 697 P.2d 1084 (1985), imposes discipline on a lawyer for conduct similar to that described in this question. Likewise, if Pearce was negligent in her supervision of Nelson, then Pearce is liable for malpractice under ordinary principles of *respondeat superior*. Item IV is not correct. Pearce's subjective, good faith belief is beside the point. The standard is an objective one: if a reasonably prudent lawyer would not have allowed Nelson to handle the client trust account, considering the facts stated in the question, then Pearce has breached her duty of care.

8. C. Item IV is correct. Liggett can be disciplined for ratifying Prentice's misconduct and for failing to take steps to mitigate its consequences. [ABA Model Rule 5.3(c); *see also* ABA Code DR 1–102(A)(2).] Item I is not correct. Searching through files for documents that have to be produced is the kind of task that is often delegated to a non-lawyer assistant; the delegation is proper so long as the lawyer adequately supervises the non-lawyer's work and takes ultimate responsibility for it. [*See* ABA Code EC 3–6; Comment to ABA Model Rule 5.5; Discussion following CRPC 3–110.] Item III is not correct. A lawyer is subject to discipline for harassing the adversary in discovery proceedings. [*See* ABA Model Rule 3.4(a), (c), and (d); ABA Code DR 7–102(A)(1) and (3), and DR 7–106(C)(7).] Fed.R.Civ.P. 34 states that "a party who produces documents for inspection shall produce them as they are kept in the usual course of business or shall organize and label them to correspond with the categories in the request." If Liggett himself had jumbled the documents, he could be sanctioned under Fed.R.Civ.P. 37 as well as disciplined by the bar. Here it was Prentice who jumbled the documents, but Liggett apparently ratified her conduct, or at least failed to take steps to mitigate its consequences. [ABA Model Rule 5.3(c).] Item II is not correct for the same reasons; it was not enough for Liggett to tell Prentice not to do such things in the future. He should have taken steps to mitigate the consequences of her misconduct [*Id.*]. For example, he might instruct her to put the documents back in the proper

order; if that is impossible, perhaps he would have to flag the harmful documents so that the adversary could find them.

CHAPTER SEVEN

1. C. The attorney-client privilege covers the information in item I. The tax accountant was simply acting as a conduit to help communicate information from the client to the attorney, and the tax accountant's role was to help further the attorney-client relationship. The information is also covered by the attorney's ethical duty to preserve confidential information. [*See* ABA Code DR 4–101(A); ABA Model Rule 1.6; Proposed CRPC 3–100.] The items of information in items II, III, and IV are likewise covered by the ethical duty, but they are not covered by the attorney-client privilege because the attorney did not obtain the information through confidential communications with the client. In item II, the information came from public land records. In item III, it came from a third party taxi driver. In item IV, it came from a public newspaper.

2. B. Item I is not correct. The attorney-client privilege does not apply when the client seeks the attorney's aid to commit a future crime, but under the modern view the future crime exception does not apply unless the client knew, or should have known, that the conduct was criminal. If the privilege applies, then item II is not correct and item IV is correct. Item III is correct; surely Alder may volunteer his advice in this context, even though Christenson will probably ignore it. The result in California would be the same.

3. C. ABA Code EC 4–3 and DR 4–101(D) recognize that lawyers often need to use employees and outside contractors to help them serve their clients. It is proper to do so, so long as the lawyer uses care in selecting such persons and properly instructs them about the need for confidentiality. [*See also*, ABA Model Rule 5.3 and the Comment thereto.] Answer A is not correct; the ethics rules do not require Lorenz to waste her time and her client's money in this fashion. Answer B is not correct. Lorenz may wish to make the copies on his own facilities, but the ethics rules do not require that. Answer D is not correct. Lorenz need not be there to supervise personally, so long as she selects a trustworthy copying firm and gives proper instructions about confidentiality. The result in California would be the same. [*Cf.* Los Angeles Bar Ops. 374 (1978) and 423 (1983).]

4. D. Answer D is correct under ABA Model Rule 1.6(b)(2) and ABA Code DR 4–101(C)(4). [*Accord* Proposed CRPC 3–100(C)(3)(b).] Answer A is not correct. The crime of extortion includes the obtaining of money by inducing fear in the victim. One common way of inducing that fear is by a threat to reveal the victim's secret. [*See, e.g.,* Calif. Penal Code §§ 518–19.] If Aquino's letter is not extortionate, it is at least coercive. Answer B is not correct. ABA Code EC 2–23 urges lawyers to try to settle fee disputes amicably and states that a lawyer should not sue to collect a fee unless necessary to prevent fraud or gross

imposition by the client. But neither the ABA Code nor the ABA Model Rules forbid suits to collect fees. [In California a lawyer must submit a fee dispute to arbitration if the client wants to arbitrate, but if the client waives arbitration, the lawyer may sue to collect the fee. (*See* Cal.Bus. & Prof. Code §§ 6200–6206.)] Answer C is not correct. When ABA Code EC 2–23 speaks of attempting to resolve fee disputes amicably, it does not mean by extortion or coercion.

5. A. ABA Code DR 4–101(B), ABA Model Rule 1.6(a), and Proposed CRPC 3–100 make a lawyer subject to discipline for revealing a client's confidential information. The future crime exception does not apply here. Colbert has revealed past crimes, not an intent to commit future crimes. She has now moved out of the house and is living in a distant town, and the facts stated in the question do not suggest that she intends to abuse the children further. Answer B is incorrect; Lamb has no discretion here. Answer C is incorrect. The state statute is directed to physicians and psychotherapists, not to attorneys. Indianapolis Bar Ass'n Op. 1–1986 (1986) involves a similar statute and holds that an attorney has no duty to report past instances of child abuse. Answer D is incorrect because the crimes are past crimes, not future crimes.

6. C. ABA Model Rule 1.6(a), ABA Code DR 4–101(B), and Proposed CRPC 3–100 require Arnott to keep Curtis's information in confidence, unless Curtis changes her mind and consents to have it revealed. [*See* Michigan State Bar Op. CI–1141 (1986).] Answer A is not correct; Arnott has no discretion here. Answer B is not correct. The holder of the attorney-client privilege (and the beneficiary of the ethical duty) is Curtis; whether or not Coleman's evasion of the law is a continuing crime, Curtis is still entitled to the protection of confidentiality. Answer D is not correct. Arnott would be breaching the duty of confidentiality even if he asked the prosecutor not to reveal the source of the information. The prosecutor might not comply with the request. Even if the prosecutor does, Coleman or one of the other friends of Curtis's ex-husband may be able to figure out where the information came from, thus putting Curtis and her children in danger.

7. A. Clark and Craddock were joint clients of Ling. As joint clients, both of them were holders of the attorney-client privilege. But in litigation between two former joint clients, neither of them is entitled to claim the attorney-client privilege. [*See* Cal. Evid. Code § 962; C. McCormick, *Evidence* § 91 at 219–20 (3d ed. 1984).] Therefore, the court was correct in ordering Ling to disclose what Clark said. Having been properly ordered by the court to disclose the information, Ling has neither an ethical right nor an ethical duty to withhold the information. [*See* ABA Code DR 4–101(C)(2); Comment to ABA Model Rule 1.6 ("The lawyer must comply with the final orders of a court * * * requiring the lawyer to give information about the client"); *Accord* Proposed CRPC 3–100(C)(2).] Further, it was proper for Ling to withdraw as counsel for Clark and Craddock because of the conflict between their interests. [ABA Model Rule 1.16(a)(1); ABA Code DR 2–110(B)(2); *Accord* CRPC 3–310(A).] Answer B is not correct; as noted above, Ling must disclose

what Clark said. Answer C is not correct. Ling's withdrawal was proper, and she must disclose what Clark said. Answer D is not correct; again, having been ordered to answer by the court, Ling must do so.

CHAPTER EIGHT

1. B. The relevant provisions are ABA Model Rule 3.3(a)(3) and ABA Code DR 7–106(B)(1). In item I, the United States Supreme Court case is adverse only by analogy between the State X statute and the federal Lanham Act. Further, the United States Supreme Court's interpretation of federal law is not controlling on a State X judge who is applying State X law. For the same reasons, the United States Court of Appeals case in item II need not be disclosed. The State Y case in item III need not be disclosed because State Y law is not controlling in a case governed by State X law. The State X case in item IV need not be disclosed because it is adverse only by analogy between trespass to real property and infringement of a trademark. There may be sound tactical reasons for counsel for Noxatox to call all of these cases to the court's attention, but the rules do not compel it. Note that the CRPC contains no provision concerning a lawyer's duty to disclose adverse legal authority. However, CRPC 5–200(B) and Cal. Bus. & Prof. Code § 6068(d) prohibit a lawyer from seeking to "mislead the judge or any judicial officer by an artifice or false statement of fact or law." Should "artifice" be read to include the failure to disclose a controlling adverse legal authority?

2. C. The ABA Code contains no specific guidance on this problem, but ABA Model Rule 3.3(d) requires a lawyer in an *ex parte* proceeding to disclose all of the relevant facts known to the lawyer, even the adverse facts. The Comment to Model Rule 3.3 explains why. There is no CRPC parallel to ABA Model Rule 3.3(d), but a California lawyer can be disciplined for failing to disclose important information to a judge in an *ex parte* matter. [*See DiSabatino v. State Bar,* 27 Cal.3d 159, 162 Cal.Rptr. 458, 606 P.2d 765 (1980) (lawyer got a night bail commissioner to reduce his client's bail without telling the commissioner that two judges had refused the bail reduction the same day); *Snyder v. State Bar*, 18 Cal.3d 286, 133 Cal.Rptr. 864, 555 P.2d 1104 (1976) (lawyer did not tell judge about earlier adverse order entered by a different judge).]

3. A. Carla's and Carl's disclosure to Anderson is confidential information, protected by ABA Model Rule 1.6 and ABA Code DR 4–101. [*Accord* Proposed CRPC 3–100.] ABA Code DR 7–102(B)(1) does not require Anderson to reveal their disclosure to the court because of the exception at the end of that provision. [*Accord* Proposed CRPC 3–100(E).] ABA Model Rule 3.3(a)(4) does not require disclosure for at least one and perhaps two reasons. First, since the adoption proceeding has come to a conclusion, the duty to disclose no longer applies. [ABA Model Rule 3.3(b).] Second, it is not clear from the facts stated in the question that Anderson "offered false evidence" in the adoption proceeding. She did offer the marriage certificate, but that document was not

false, and Anderson had no reason at the time to believe that Carla and Carl were not validly married. Answers C and D are incorrect for the same reasons. Answer B is incorrect as well. "Continuing fraud" is a foggy concept at best, but even assuming that Carl and Carla are committing a continuing fraud by keeping their adopted child and living together as husband and wife, there is no reason to assume that Anderson's advice would "assist" them in continuing the fraud.

4. D. ABA Model Rule 3.4(b) and ABA Code DR 7–102(A)(6) prohibit a lawyer from counseling or assisting a client (or any other witness) to testify falsely. [*See also* CRPC 3–210; 18 U.S.C. § 1622 (1982) (subornation of perjury); *Tedesco v. Mishkin*, 629 F.Supp. 1474 (S.D.N.Y. 1986).] Answer B is not correct. Lawyers should, and commonly do, talk with clients and other witnesses about the testimony they will give. But, as one judge put it long ago, the lawyer's task is "to extract the facts from the witness, not to put them into him." [*In re Eldridge*, 82 N.Y. 161 (1880).] Answer A is not correct. Canon 7 of the ABA Code says a lawyer should represent a client "zealously," but it does not end there. It says "zealously within the bounds of the law." The assertion in Answer C is accurate, but it is misapplied here. If the lawyer's object is to bend the witness's testimony, then ABA Code DR 7–102(A)(6) and ABA Model Rule 3.4(b) apply, even if the bending takes the form of a lecture on the law. [*See* Wolfram, § 12.4.3, at 648.]

5. B. ABA Formal Opinion 87–353 (1987), *supra*, and its predecessor, ABA Formal Opinion 287 (1953), use a version of this hypothetical to illustrate the hair-fine balance between zealously representing a client and actively misleading a court. [*See generally* G. Hazard & W. Hodes, §§ 3.3:202–3.3:205.] Bear in mind that this hypothetical involves the criminal process; the prosecutor carries the burden of proof, and the client is entitled to remain silent and to have the effective assistance of counsel. In this hypothetical, the adversary process has failed to produce the truth, and the client will get a windfall gain. If the lawyer responds as in item I or II, the lawyer has not actively misled the court. True, the lawyer has failed to correct the court's mistaken belief, but that is deceit only if there is a duty to speak out, and there is no duty here. In item III, the lawyer asserts that his client's "record is clean." That is the literal truth: the record is clean, though the client is not. Nonetheless, it seems to us that in item III the lawyer has stepped over the line and has actively misled the court in violation of ABA Code DR 7–102(A)(5) and ABA Model Rule 3.3(a)(1). [*Accord* CRPC 5–200(B).] In item IV, the lawyer has corrected the court's mistake, but he has breached the duty of confidentiality and is subject to discipline under ABA Model Rule 1.6 and ABA Code DR 4–101. [*See* Hazard & Hodes, *supra* § 3.3:205.]

6. A. Your duty here is to serve your client's best interests, and the way to do that is simply to call the mistake to Lauder's attention so it can be corrected. If your client signs the contract, knowing of the mistake, the contract is voidable; ultimately, your client may lose the benefit of the bargain, or end up in costly litigation, or both. [*See*

Restatement (Second) of Contracts § 153 (1981).] Answers B and C are incorrect. It is true that you should not give up one of your client's valuable legal rights without first consulting the client and obtaining his consent. [*See* Comment to ABA Model Rule 1.2; ABA Code EC 7–8.] But you are not giving up any legal right here; your knowledge of the mistake is imputed to your client, and your client thus has no legal right to hold the other party to the mistaken version of the contract. Answer D is incorrect for a reason that you will in a later Chapter. A lawyer must not communicate directly with a party on the opposite side of a matter if the lawyer knows that the party is represented by counsel. [ABA Model Rule 4.2; ABA Code DR 7–104(A)(1); CRPC 2–100.]

CHAPTER NINE

1. D. It is proper, indeed routine, for a lawyer to talk with a witness about his testimony before the witness testifies. It is also proper for a lawyer to use documents or other items to try to refresh a witness's memory of a once-known but now forgotten fact. In this process, the lawyer must bear in mind that the proper object is to "extract the facts from the witness, not to put them into him; to learn what the witness does know, not to teach him what he ought to know." [*In re Eldridge*, 82 N.Y. 161, 171 (1880).] Items II and II are incorrect, because the question does not indicate that Westerman exceeded these bounds in meeting with the investigator. Item III is correct; ABA Code DR 7–106(C)(6) prohibits a lawyer from degrading a court by undignified or discourteous conduct. [*See also* ABA Model Rule 3.5(c).] Item IV is correct; ABA Code DR 7–106(C)(7) and ABA Model Rule 3.4(c) prohibit a lawyer from intentionally violating an established rule of evidence law, and production of the notes was clearly required under Federal Rule of Evidence 612. Item V is correct; the judge ordered Westerman to bring the notes "the next morning," and Westerman intentionally failed to do so. [ABA Code DR 7–106(A); *cf.* ABA Model Rule 3.5(c).] The analysis and answer would be the same under Cal.Bus. & Prof.Code § 6103 and Cal.Evid. Code § 771.

2. D. ABA Code DR 7–104(A) and ABA Model Rule 4.2 both prohibit a lawyer from communicating with a "party" who is represented by a lawyer, without first getting the consent of that lawyer. The Comment to ABA Model Rule 4.2 explains that when the represented party is a legal entity (such as the church corporation in this question), a lawyer must get the consent of the entity's lawyer before talking directly with three classes of persons: (1) persons with managerial responsibility; (2) persons whose acts may be attributed to the entity for purposes of civil or criminal liability; and (3) persons whose statements "may constitute an admission on the part of" the entity. [*Cf. Upjohn Co. v. United States*, 449 U.S. 383, 101 S.Ct. 677, 66 L.Ed.2d 584 (1981) (defining scope of attorney-client privilege as to communications between corporate employees and attorneys for the corporation).] Even if the bookkeeper does not fall within class (1) or class (2), we believe that she falls within class (3). Under the broad, modern view of vicarious

admissions, her statements could probably be admitted against the church corporation over hearsay objection. [*See, e.g.,* Federal Rule of Evidence 801(d)(2)(D).] Thus, Lexington should have gotten the consent of counsel for the church corporation before talking with her. For a similar interpretation of ABA Code DR 7–104(A), see New York City Bar Op. 80–46 (1981). The answer and analysis would be the same under CRPC 2–100.

3. A. Altmont has violated ABA Code DR 7–105(A) by using a threat of criminal prosecution to gain an advantage in a civil matter, the fee dispute. [*Cf. Bluestein v. State Bar of California,* 13 Cal.3d 162, 118 Cal.Rptr. 175, 529 P.2d 599 (1974).] The ABA Model Rules do not contain a direct counterpart to ABA Code DR 7–105(A), but Altmont's threat would violate ABA Model Rule 1.8(b) (threat to use the client's confidential information to harm the client). Answers B and C are incorrect for the same reason that answer A is correct. Answer D is incorrect, first because it misses the point of the question, and second because it misinterprets ABA Code DR 2–104(A). That rule concerns the taking of legal business that arises from unsolicited advice, not the giving of unsolicited advice. The answer and analysis would be the same under CRPC 5–100.

4. A. If Daniels sent the carbon copy to Parker, he would violate ABA Code DR 7–104(A)(1) and ABA Model Rule 4.2, even if he is positive that Paxton did not convey the settlement offer to Parker. If Paxton has failed to convey the offer to Parker, then Paxton has violated his duty to keep Parker informed and to let Parker make the important decisions in the case. [*See* ABA Code EC 7–7; ABA Model Rule 1.2(a); CRPC 3–500 and 3–510. *See also* Cal.Bus. & Prof.Code § 6103.5.] But the proper remedy for that violation is for Daniels to bring Paxton's conduct to the attention of the judge to whom the case is assigned, not to deal directly with Parker. [*See* ABA Informal Op. 1348 (1975) (carbon copy of settlement offer sent to represented adversary in civil case); *see also* ABA Informal Op. 1373 (1976) (copy of offer to plea bargain sent to represented criminal defendant).] Answers B, C, and D are incorrect for the same reasons. The answer and analysis would be the same under CRPC 2–100.

5. D. Limpett's direct contact with Victoria violates ABA Code DR 7–104(A)(2) and ABA Model Rule 4.3. A lawyer may talk with a potential adversary who is not represented by counsel, but in doing so the lawyer must not purport to give the person legal advice (other than to retain counsel if that is appropriate). [*See* ABA Code DR 7–104(A)(2) and Comment to ABA Model Rule 4.3.] Note that Limpett's advice to Victoria is also misleading in part. If Crebs were held liable to Victoria, the so-called "collateral source" rule would probably allow her to collect her medical expenses from him, even though those expenses were covered by her own health insurance. Answers A, B, and C are incorrect for the reasons explained above. The CRPC have no counterpart to ABA Model Rule 4.3, but we believe the answer and analysis would be the same in California. [*See* Los Angeles Ethics Op. 334 (1973).]

CHAPTER TEN

1. C. Even though the decision is old, and in your view unsound, it is the controlling law in this jurisdiction. Under ABA Code DR 7–101(A) and 7–102(A), you are entitled—indeed, obliged—to use it if you think it may help Carter's defense. [*Cf.* ABA Model Rules 1.1 and 3.3.] Answer A is incorrect for two reasons. First, if you do find a way to use it effectively in Carter's defense, then you could only harm Carter by telling the court that you think the decision is unsound. Second, even if it were appropriate to disclose your qualms to the court, you should do it on the record, in open court, not *ex parte*. [*See* ABA Code DR 7–110(B); ABA Model Rule 3.5(b).] Answer B is incorrect for the same reason that answer C is correct. Answer D is incorrect because it is inconsistent with ABA Code EC 7–12. The decision about what use, if any, to make of an old, questionable precedent is one uniquely within the lawyer's area of special skill. Where the client is fully competent, the lawyer should certainly talk the problem over with the client and give the client's viewpoint full consideration. [*See* ABA Model Rule 1.2(a).] But on this kind of issue the ultimate responsibility should rest with the lawyer. Carter's handicap makes it even clearer that the ultimate responsibility should rest with you, as lawyer, not with him, as client. [*See* ABA Code EC 7–12; ABA Model Rule 1.14.] The CRPC do not speak directly to this point, but we believe the answer and analysis would be the same under CRPC 3–110. [*See also* CRPC 5–200.]

2. A. According to ABA Code EC 7–13 and EC 7–14, a public prosecutor should use discretion in bringing criminal charges. [*See also* ABA Model Rule 3.8.] The two Ethical Considerations do not give much guidance in staking the boundaries of that discretion, but ABA Standards for the Prosecution Function 3–3.9(b) (2nd Ed., Tentative Draft Approved February 12, 1979) offers clear guidance. It provides a partial list of the factors that a prosecutor may consider in exercising her discretion, and each of the items in the question is on the list. We believe the answer and analysis would be the same in California. [*See* CRPC 5–110.]

3. A. Sanford should disclose the information to Rossi's counsel because Beaumont's conclusion suggests that the fire was not caused by a criminal act. [*See* ABA Code DR 7–103(B); ABA Model Rule 3.8(d).] Answers C and D are accordingly incorrect. Answer B is incorrect. Beaumont's conclusion may or may not create a reasonable doubt about Rossi's guilt. Even if it does create a reasonable doubt in Sanford's mind, that would not oblige him to recommend dismissal, so long as there is other evidence to support probable cause. [*See* ABA Model Rule 3.8(a); ABA Code DR 7–103(A) and EC 7–13.] The CRPC have no counterpart to ABA Model Rule 3.8(d). The drafters of the CRPC explained that the relationship between prosecutors and criminal defendants is subject to continuing refinement in the case law and is not an appropriate topic for a disciplinary rule.

4. D. Items I and IV are proper. Loach is simply pointing out evidence in the record that tends to discredit the testimony of the Commission's witnesses, and he is inviting the court to draw its own conclusions about their credibility. Item II is not proper. Here Loach is trying to pander to the judge's sympathies. The judge's personal interest in duck hunting and the judge's memories of his father are irrelevant to the case. [*See* ABA Code DR 7–106(C)(1) and EC 7–36; ABA Model Rule 3.4(e).] Item III is not proper. Here Loach is trying to use his own personal knowledge and opinions as substitutes for evidence in the record. [*See* ABA Code DR 7–106(C)(3) and (4); ABA Model Rule 3.4(e).] The answer and analysis would be the same under CRPC 5–200(E).

5. A. ABA Code DR 7–104 states that, in the course of representing a client, a lawyer must not "give advice to a person who is not represented by a lawyer, other than the advice to secure counsel, if the interests of such person are or have a reasonable possibility of being in conflict with the interests of his client." [*Cf.* ABA Model Rules 1.7 and 4.3.] Further, ABA Code DR 7–109(B) states that a "lawyer shall not advise or cause a person to secrete himself or to leave the jurisdiction of a tribunal for the purposes of making him unavailable as a witness therein." [*Cf.* ABA Model Rule 3.4(a) and (f).] In this situation, the *only* proper advice that Dennert can give Katzenmeier is to consult his own lawyer for impartial counsel. The answer and analysis would be the same under CRPC 5–310(A).

6. C. In *Young v. United States ex rel. Vuitton et Fils S.A.*, 481 U.S. 787, 107 S.Ct. 2124, 95 L.Ed.2d 740 (1987), the Court considered the propriety of appointing a private attorney as special prosecutor in criminal contempt proceedings. In the exercise of its supervisory power over the federal judiciary, the Court held that "counsel for a party that is the beneficiary of a court order may not be appointed to undertake contempt prosecutions for alleged violations of that order." As counsel for the interested party, the private attorney owes that party a duty of loyal, zealous representation; that duty can too easily conflict with a prosecutor's duty to seek justice, not necessarily conviction. [*See* ABA Code DR 5–105(A); ABA Model Rule 1.7(a) and (b).] The appointment of private attorneys as special prosecutors is not itself improper, but it becomes improper when the special prosecutor also represents the party for whose benefit the court order was entered. Although the *Young* decision was based on the Court's supervisory power over the federal judiciary (not on the United States Constitution), the decision would doubtless be persuasive authority in state proceedings as well. [In fact, Justice Blackmun's concurring opinion argues that the decision should have been based on the due process clause, not on the supervisory power.] Accordingly, item IV is correct and item II is incorrect. Further, Lester's comments about wife beating and child molesting (unsupported by any evidence in the record) constitute gross prosecutorial misconduct. [*See* ABA Model Rule 3.4(e); ABA Code DR 7–106(C); *see also Stumbo v. Seabold*, 704 F.2d 910 (6th Cir. 1983) (in a murder case,

defendant was deprived of a fair trial by special prosecutor's improper questioning of witnesses and remarks not supported by evidence; the special prosecutor also represented the murder victim's family).] Thus, item I is correct, and item III is incorrect. The answer and analysis would be the same in California. [*See generally* CRPC 5–200.]

CHAPTER ELEVEN

1. Lenschell's client is Tina, not Timothy, no matter who may be paying fine or the legal fee. Therefore, Lenschell must not allow Timothy to orchestrate the case. [*See* ABA Code DR 5–107(B); ABA Model Rule 1.7(b); *Wood v. Georgia*, 450 U.S. 261, 101 S.Ct. 1097, 67 L.Ed.2d 220 (1981) (pornography shop employee defended by lawyer who was paid by shop owner)] The California rule is consistent, CRPC 3–310(E) (amendment pending). Whether to plead guilty or not guilty is for Tina to decide. [ABA Code EC 7–7; ABA Model Rule 1.2(a). *See also Employers Insurance of Wausau, supra.*] Thus, answers A and D are incorrect. Answer B is preferable to answer C. Lenschell has gotten this far with the case, and time is short since the case is about to be called on the criminal calendar. Assuming that Tina wants Lenschell to advise her about the plea, he should do so. The question does not provide enough facts to decide whether it would or would not be appropriate for Lenschell to continue representing Tina at subsequent stages of the case. Note that ABA Code DR 5–107(A)(1); ABA Model Rule 1.8(f) and CRPC 3–310(E) (amendment pending) all prohibit Lenschell from accepting the fee from Timothy without Tina's informed consent.

2. C. Once it becomes apparent that Markler will not cooperate, Lattimer's best course of action is to take the matter up with Markler's corporate superior, the Executive Vice President. [*See* ABA Model Rule 1.13; ABA Code EC 5–18; CRPC 3–600(B).] Answer C is preferable to answer D because C creates less risk of disrupting the corporate operations and revealing confidential information to outsiders. [*See* ABA Model Rule 1.13(b); CRPC 3–600(B).] Answer B is incorrect because B would breach Lattimer's duty of confidentiality. [*See* Cal.Bus. & Prof. Code § 6068(e).] Further, a competent lawyer would not need an advisory opinion from the Justice Department to know that phone calls between competitors about future prices raise antitrust problems. [*See, e.g., United States v. Container Corp. of America*, 393 U.S. 333, 89 S.Ct. 510, 21 L.Ed.2d 526 (1969).] Answer A is incorrect because Lattimer's client is the corporation, not Markler, and she has a duty to warn her client of Markler's activity. [*See* ABA Model Rule 1.13(b); ABA Code EC 5–18; CRPC 3–600(A) and (D).]

3. D. The financial interest held by Prentice is imputed to all lawyers in the firm. [*See* ABA Model Rule 1.10(a); ABA Code DR 5–105(D).] California has no imputed disqualification rule. California court decisions have either assumed an imputed rule applicable here or looked to the ABA rules for one. Since that interest is in conflict with the Alliance's interests, Tillis cannot accept the case without first

disclosing the conflict to the Alliance and obtaining the Alliance's consent. [*See* ABA Model Rule 1.7(b); ABA Code DR 5–101(A); CRPC 3–310(B) (amendment pending).] Item II is not correct. Vista del Oro is not now, and has never been, a client of the firm. Thus Vista del Oro's sentiments about the conflict are irrelevant. Neither item III nor item IV is a necessary condition of allowing Tillis to represent Alliance. If the Alliance consents after full disclosure of the conflict, that is sufficient; Prentice need not rid himself of his interest in Vista del Oro. Note that an alternative way to resolve the conflict of interest might be for Prentice to resign as a director and to sell his seven home sites, but that is not among the four answers offered in this question. Further, even if Prentice were to get rid of his interest in Vista del Oro, many firms would still disclose the situation to the Alliance, simply as a matter of good client relations. The answer would be the same under the CRPC.

4. B. The ABA Code and the ABA Model Rules produce the same answer, but the method of analysis is somewhat different. The relevant ABA Code provision is DR 5–101(B). Ordinarily a lawyer should not serve as trial counsel if he can foresee at the outset that he ought to be a witness, and the same is true if someone else in his firm ought to be a witness. But here the exceptions stated in DR 5–101(B)(1) and (2) seem applicable. The plaintiff may concede the authenticity of the letter, or its authenticity may be a mere formality as to which there is little or no chance of serious debate. If either exception applies, then both Smithers and Hillner could serve as defendant's trial counsel. Under the ABA Model Rules, the starting point of the analysis is Rule 1.7. Rule 1.7 would not bar Smithers from serving as defendant's trial counsel, provided that the defendant understands and accepts the fact that Smither's effectiveness may be somewhat reduced by his dual role as trial counsel and witness. ABA Model Rule 3.7 would not bar Smithers from serving as defendant's trial counsel, provided that the authenticity of the FTC letter is uncontested. [Hazard & Hodes § 3.7:202.] Finally, if Smithers could serve as defense trial counsel, then Hillner could also serve. Under the CRPC the answer is the same. According to CRPC 5–210 Smithers may not serve as counsel before a jury which will hear testimony from him, unless one of three exceptions applies. Exception (A)—the testimony relates to an uncontested matter—may apply, freeing Smithers to represent defendant. If not, Smithers can still obtain the informed, written consent of defendant, and act as counsel and witness. [CRPC 5–210(C).] The discussion following 5–210 states it does not apply if Hillner serves as counsel and Smithers is only a witness. [*See generally*, Wydick, *Trial Counsel as Witness: The Code and The Model Rules*, 15 U.C. Davis L. Rev. 651 (1982).]

5. B. Under ABA Model Rule 1.7(b) and ABA Code DR 5–101(A), client consent solves the problem. Further, under ABA Model Rule 1.7(b), client consent may be unnecessary if lawyer Ekimoto's financial interest is so small and indirect that it would not "materially" influence her representation of the plaintiff class. Answer C is incorrect for the same reason that answer B is correct. Answer A is incorrect because

neither the ABA Model Rules nor the ABA Code makes a general exception for the interest of a trust beneficiary. Answer D is incorrect because the availability of other counsel is irrelevant to this conflict of interest issue. In California, the reference is CRPC 3–310(A). Ekimoto's interest, if it counts as an "interest" under the Rule at all, requires the "affected clients' informed written consent." Under a pending amendment, CRPC 3–310(B) would require only written disclosure to the client, not the client's informed written consent. Thus the answer is the same.

6. D. Under ABA Code DR 5–103(A) and ABA Model Rule 1.8(j), a lawyer must not acquire an ownership interest in the subject of litigation that the lawyer is conducting for the client (subject to two exceptions that do not apply here). California law appears to be more lenient. CRPC 3–300 prohibits a member from knowingly acquiring an ownership or other pecuniary interest *adverse* to a client, but there is no general prohibition against acquiring a proprietary interest in the subject of litigation. Even if Lothrup's interest could be considered adverse to Belloni's interest, CRPC 3–300 would allow it if the transaction is fair and reasonable, disclosed in an understandable manner to the client in writing, and if the client consents in writing to the terms of the transaction after being advised in writing (and given a reasonable opportunity to act) that the client may seek the advice of a independent lawyer of the client's choice. At the other extreme, it is a misdemeanor for a lawyer to buy a claim with the intent to bring suit on it. Cal.Bus. & Prof.Code § 6129. The subject of this declaratory judgment action is Belloni's United States Patent, and Lothrup is acquiring a 10% interest in that patent. Answer A is incorrect for the same reason that answer D is correct. Answer B is incorrect because a lawyer may require the client to repay advanced litigation expenses, no matter what the outcome of the litigation. [*See* ABA Code DR 5–103(B); ABA Model Rule 1.8(e)(1); CRPC 4–210(A)(3); Hazard & Hodes § 1.8:1101.] Answer C is incorrect because a lawyer may advance litigation expenses in a civil case. [*Id.*]

7. A. The conflict of interest here is between Andrate (who wants to be paid for his work) and his indigent inmate clients (who want the medical treatment that the consent decree will give them). [*See* ABA Code DR 5–101(A); ABA Model Rule 1.7(b); *cf.* CRPC 3–310(A) (amendment pending).] All who have written about this issue agree on one basic point: the decision whether to accept or reject the settlement offer is for the client to make, not for the lawyer to make. [*See* ABA Model Rule 1.2; ABA Code EC 7–7. *See generally* Maute, *Allocation of Decisionmaking Authority Under the Model Rules of Professional Conduct*, 17 U.C.Davis L.Rev. 1049 (1984).] Answers B, C, and D are incorrect because in each instance the decision is made by the lawyer rather than the client. *Evans v. Jeff D.*, 475 U.S. 717, 106 S.Ct. 1531, 89 L.Ed.2d 747 (1986), concerns the settlement of a civil rights class action. A federal statute permits (but does not require) an award of attorney fees to the prevailing party in such an action. The defendant offered to

settle for a consent decree that would give the plaintiffs more injunctive relief than they probably would get by going to trial, provided that the plaintiffs would not seek an award of attorney fees. The issue before the Court was whether the trial judge was correct in approving the settlement containing the fee waiver. In a 6–3 decision, the Court said the trial judge was correct. Since Congress did not require fee awards, but only permitted them, the fee waiver was not antithetic to the purpose of the fee award statute. Further, to forbid fee waivers would impede settlements, because defendants naturally wish to clean up both the substantive issues and the fee issues at the same time. The dissenting opinion points out that to permit fee waivers will make attorneys far less willing to represent indigent plaintiffs in difficult civil rights cases. Is it ethically proper for a defendant to insist on a fee waiver as a condition of settlement? That issue remains a topic of hot debate. [*See* Ass'n Bar of City of New York Opinion 1987–4 (1987); Hazard & Hodes §§ 1.5:106–1.5:107.] In 1988, the California State Bar proposed CRPC 2–400:

> A member shall not make or present a settlement offer in any case involving a request by the opposing party for attorney's fees pursuant to private attorney general statutes which is conditioned on opposing counsel waiving all or substantially all fees. This rule does not preclude a member from making or presenting an offer of a lump sum to settle all claims including attorney's fees.

The California Supreme Court rejected the proposed rule, leaving the issue unresolved in California.

CHAPTER TWELVE

1. C. Under the ABA Model Rules, the applicable provision is Model Rule 1.8(i). The ABA Code does not speak specifically to this problem, but it has been ruled on by the ABA Committee on Ethics and Professional Responsibility. [ABA Formal Op. 340 (1975).] The opinion states that the mere fact of marriage creates no actual conflict of interest, but the closeness of the wife-husband relationship does create opportunities for inadvertent violations of the ethics rules. For instance, one spouse might inadvertently learn confidential information when taking a telephone message for the other spouse at their home. In light of this, both lawyers should call the situation to the attention of their respective clients. [*See* ABA Code EC 5–3 and 5–16.] If the two clients consent after full disclosure, then Cheryl and Dennis may participate on opposite sides of the case. [*See* Oregon State Bar Op. 502 (1984).] Under CRPC 3–320 the result should be the same. Cheryl and Dennis cannot represent different clients in the same matter unless each informs the client in writing of the relationship. Although client consent is not required, the rule suggests the marital relationship creates a possible conflict of interest, and the purpose of informing the client must be to give the client the option to seek other counsel. According to the Discussion, however, the rule only applies when the related lawyers have a direct involvement in the matter. This could excuse Dennis from

informing his client, although it would clearly be the better practice to do so.

2. B. Taking Norman's name off the pleading does not solve the conflict of interest. Norman remains the outside general counsel for North American, and North American may be liable on any judgment rendered against the joint venture in the suit brought by Eratec's French subsidiary. The proper course of action here would have been: (a) for Enid and Norman to decide whether they could effectively serve their respective clients in this situation; (b) if they concluded that they could, they should have made full disclosure of the problem to *both* sets of clients (not just to North American); (c) they should have obtained the consent of *both* sets of clients. [*See* ABA Code DR 5–105(A) through (D); ABA Model Rule 1.7.] The result would be the same under CRPC 3–310.

3. B. Even in a contingent fee case, it is the client, not the attorney, who decides whether to accept or reject a settlement offer. Here, attorney A's duty is to inform R, S, and T of U's offer, even though A may think it is ridiculously low. [*See* ABA Code EC 7–7; ABA Model Rules 1.2 and 1.4; Hazard & Hodes § 1.2:204, Illustrative Case.] Under California law, lawyers must communicate written settlement offers in civil cases and all offers in criminal cases. CRPC 3–510 and Cal. Bus. & Prof. Code § 6103.5; in any case clients must be kept "reasonably informed about significant developments." CRPC 3–500. Furthermore, a lawyer who represents several clients on the same side of a case has additional duties when the adversary makes an aggregate settlement offer. The lawyer must fully disclose the entire offer to each of the several clients, and the clients must reach their own decision about accepting it or rejecting it, and about how to share it if they do accept it. [*See* ABA Code DR 5–106; ABA Model Rule 1.8(g); CRPC 3–310(C) (amendment pending).]

4. D. Anna may represent both Wendy and Harry if she reasonably believes that she can serve both effectively, and if both of them consent to the joint representation after Anna explains to them the disadvantages of being represented by only one lawyer. [*See* ABA Code DR 5–105(C); ABA Model Rules 1.7 and 2.2; Hazard & Hodes § 1.7:306, Illustrative Case; CRPC 3–310; *see generally*, Moore, *Conflicts of Interest in the Simultaneous Representation of Multiple Clients*, 61 Texas L.Rev. 211, 245–58 (1982).] Answers A and C are incorrect for the same reason that answer D is correct. Answer B is incorrect because it does not meet the requirements of the rules cited above; further, obtaining a client's advance promise not to sue for legal malpractice is itself a disciplinary violation. [ABA Code DR 6–102; ABA Model Rule 1.8(h); CRPC 3–400(A).]

5. A. The relevant provisions are ABA Code DR 5–105(A) and (D) and ABA Model Rules 1.9 and 1.10. The service station dealers' antitrust case is "substantially related" to the proposed antitrust legislation. Further, DePew has received confidential information from Transpac

concerning the relationships between the integrated oil companies and their retail service station dealers. That information is clearly relevant to the dealers' antitrust case. Thus, DePew himself would be barred from taking the case, and the ordinary rule would also bar all of the other lawyers in DePew's firm. [*See* ABA Model Rule 1.10(a); ABA Code DR 5–105(D).] DePew's firm might try to invoke the so-called "ethical wall" or "Chinese Wall" theory (named in honor of the Great Wall of China), promising that DePew would be screened off from the service station dealers' case and would share no part of the fees earned in that case. [*Cf. Rosenfeld Construction Company, Inc. v. Superior Court, supra.*] Thus far, courts and ethics committees have been reluctant to extend the ethical wall theory to private law firms. The theory was created in response to the government's need for good lawyers, and it has generally been confined to conflicts involving former government lawyers who move into private law practice. [*See* Dist. Colum. Ethics Op. 174 (1986); Conn. Bar Op. 86–2 (1986); *compare Westinghouse Elect. Corp. v. Kerr-McGee Corp.*, 580 F.2d 1311 (7th Cir. 1978) (screening theory not accepted) *with Nemours Foundation v. Gilbane*, 632 F.Supp. 418 (D.C. Del. 1986) (screening theory accepted).] But the idea has gained acceptance in the ALI. [*See* Rest. (Third) Law Governing Lawyers § 204 (Tent.Draft No. 4, 1991).] The situation is less clear-cut in California, but A is still the best answer. CRPC 3–310should bar DePew from the case. There is no imputed disqualification rule in the CRPC, but California case law accepts the idea. [*See William H. Raley Co. v. Superior Court*, 149 Cal.App.3d 1042, 197 Cal.Rptr. 232 (1983).] California courts have been equally reluctant to accept screening or ethical wall procedures to limit imputed disqualifications. [*See Higdon v. Superior Court*, 227 Cal.App.3d 1667, 278 Cal.Rptr. 588 (1991) *cited in* the *Rosenfeld Construction* case, *supra.*]

6. B. The ABA Code provides no specific guidance on this problem, although DR 5–105 is some help. ABA Model Rule 6.3 does provide specific guidance, and it indicates that Leggett must not participate in the Board of Directors' decision. To participate and vote "yes" would be "incompatible" with his obligations to his firm's clients, a violation of Rule 6.3(a). To participate and vote "no" could "have a material adverse effect on the representation" of tenants who are the society's potential clients. [*Cf.* Hazard & Hodes § 6.3:202, Illustrative Case (a).] Thus answers C and D are not correct. Answer A is not correct. It is true that ABA Code DR 3–103 and ABA Model Rule 5.4(b) prohibit a lawyer from "forming a partnership" (or professional corporation) with a non-lawyer if any of the activities of the partnership (or professional corporation) consist of the practice of law. CRPC 1–310 contains the same prohibition. However, the boards of directors of legal aid societies typically include both lawyers and non-lawyers. Hazard and Hodes argue these regulations "sweep[ ] far too broadly." [Hazard & Hodes § 5.4:103, at 800.]

7. A. On a somewhat similar set of facts, a California court disqualified the entire county prosecutor's office. [*People v. Lepe*, 164 Cal.App.3d 685, 211 Cal.Rptr. 432 (1985). *But see People v. Hernandez*,

235 Cal.App.3d 674, 286 Cal.Rptr. 652 (1991) (limiting disqualification to lawyers who personally participated with former witness, now a defendant).] If Aldrich did a competent job as defense counsel in the two assault and battery cases, she undoubtedly talked with Costa in detail about his relationship with his brother-in-law, Vincent. The information she received as Costa's defense lawyer could become relevant in the murder prosecution—for example, to prove motive, intent, or premeditation. Thus, Aldrich herself would be barred from personally prosecuting Costa, and answer B is accordingly incorrect. Answer C is incorrect for the same reason; her "direct, immediate and personal supervision" would involve the same kind of conflict as if she personally prosecuted Costa. Answer D is incorrect because if she screens herself off from the case, she cannot exercise the "direct, immediate, and personal supervision" that the state statute mandates. We believe that ABA Model Rule 1.11(c)(1) does not apply to this problem, because the state statute allows the State Attorney General to take over cases in which the local prosecutor's office has a conflict of interest.

CHAPTER THIRTEEN

1. C. ABA Model Rules 5.1 and 5.2 apply here. The ABA Code provides no specific guidance on the respective duties of supervising and subordinate lawyers. A variety of federal and state statutes prohibit the destruction of subpoenaed documents. [See generally Wolfram § 12.3.5.] When Crawford shredded the files and later erased the computer backup, he doubtless violated one or more of these statutes; further, he is subject to professional discipline. [See ABA Model Rule 3.4(a); ABA Code DR 7–102(A)(3).] Even if Crawford thought that Barker had instructed him to destroy the material, Crawford is still subject to discipline—the ethical duty here is too clear to be subject to reasonable argument. [Compare ABA Model Rule 5.2(a) with 5.2(b).] Barker is also subject to discipline. When Barker learned that Crawford had shredded the files, Barker should have acted promptly to preserve the computer backup; instead, Barker made an ambiguous comment that an overzealous young lawyer might interpret as an instruction to erase the computer backup. [See ABA Model Rule 5.1(c)(2).] Altmont is subject to discipline for lying to the congressional committee about the destruction of the files and computer backup [ABA Model Rule 3.3(a)(1); ABA Code DR 7–102(A)(5)] and perhaps also for failing to make reasonable efforts to assure that Barker and Crawford would act ethically [ABA Model Rule 5.1(b)] or for ratifying their unethical conduct [ABA Model Rule 5.1(c)(1)].

2. C. Unlike ABA Model Rule 5.2, the ABA Code does not provide clear guidance on this question. But a common sense reading of ABA Code DR 5–107(B) suggests that a subordinate attorney should not be required to defy the professional judgment of a supervising attorney on a debatable question like this one. Here Black is the supervising attorney, and it is Black's client. Arlington is simply assisting Black, so Black should make the final judgments on close questions. Answer C is preferable to answer B because B is overbroad. Where the supervisor

and the subordinate are faced with a debatable question, the supervisor's judgment should prevail. But, if the question were not debatable, the subordinate would be subject to discipline, even though he was carrying out the directions of the supervisor. [ABA Model Rule 5.2(a) and (b); *see generally* Hazard & Hodes § 5.2:303, Illustrative case.]

3. A. The ABA Code does not speak to the issue, but ABA Model Rule 1.17 allows the sale of a law practice, subject to certain conditions. Rule 1.17 specifically permits the good will of a law practice to be sold, contrary to the prior law in most jurisdictions. The $500 monthly retirement benefit does not offend any provision of either the ABA Model Rules or the ABA Code. Answer B is wrong because there is no such "reasonableness" requirement. Answer C is wrong because it is contrary to the opening clause of ABA Model Rule 1.17. Answer D is wrong because there is no requirement that the buyer and seller of a practice have been previously associated in practice.

CHAPTER FOURTEEN

1. D. Item I is correct. The brother is a member of her family, and she may serve as executrix of his estate if it will not interfere with her judicial duties. [*See* CJC 4(E).] Item II is incorrect. CJC 4(G) prohibits a full-time judge from practicing law. Item III is correct. A judge may accept a bequest from a relative under CJC 5(D)(4)(e). Item IV is incorrect because CJC 4(G) prohibits a full-time judge from practicing law. As to the propriety of drafting a will in which the drafter is given a gift, *compare* ABA Code EC 5–5 *with* ABA Model Rule 1.8(c). Item V is incorrect for two reasons. First, the grapefruit does not fall within any of the exceptions to CJC 5(C)(4)'s general prohibition on accepting gifts. Second, lawyer Schmitts should not have sent a gift in thanks for the referral of legal business. [*See* ABA Code DR 2–103(B); ABA Model Rule 7.2(c).] The judge should not condone his conduct by accepting the gift. [*See* CJC 2(A).]

2. A. Item I requires disqualification under CJC 3(E)(1)(d)(2). Item II requires disqualification under CJC 3(E)(1)(a). Item III does not require disqualification. Son Joey comes within CJC 3(E)(1)(c), but ownership of these mutual fund shares does not create a "financial interest" as that term is defined in the Terminology section of the CJC. Item IV requires disqualification. The nephew's wife is a "relative" under CJC 3(E)(1)(d), and she will be a "material witness" under CJC 3(E)(1)(d)(iv). Item V does not require disqualification because the wife's cousin is not a "relative" within the meaning of CJC 3(E)(1)(d). Item VI does not require disqualification because SCRAM's lawsuit presumably does not involve the same "matter" as the dead cat incident. [*See* CJC 3(E)(1)(b).]

3. D. Item I is proper. Nothing in the Code of Judicial Conduct would prohibit her from taking up the collection from the court's personnel. Item II is improper. Under CJC 4(C)(3)(b)(1), a judge should not solicit funds for a religious organization. Item III is improper. CJC 5(A)(1)(e) prohibits a judge from soliciting funds for a political organization. Item IV is improper. CJC 5(A)(1)(a) states that a judge

should not act as a leader or hold an office in a political organization. Item V is proper. CJC 4(C)(3) allows a judge to serve as a trustee or director of a religious organization.

4. A. The question asks you to assume that the stated facts do not create a reasonable doubt about Judge Janke's impartiality. Item I does not require disqualification. Nothing in the Code of Judicial Conduct would require Judge Janke to disqualify herself simply because her family doctor will be a witness. [*Cf. United States ex rel. Perry v. Cuyler,* 584 F.2d 644 (3d Cir.1978).] Item II does not require disqualification. If Judge Janke had served as lawyer for Amalgamated in the "matter in controversy," then she would have to disqualify herself under CJC 3(E)(1)(b), but that is not the situation here. Item III does not require disqualification. Judge Janke's aged mother is a "relative" under CJC 3(E)(1)(d), but her interest in Union Van seems de minimis and is not likely to be "substantially affected by the proceedings." [*See* CJC 3(E)(1)(d)(iii).] Note that the more onerous provision in CJC 3(E)(1)(c) does not cover Judge Janke's mother, because she does not live in the judge's home. Item IV does not require disqualification. The Terminology section of the CJC defines "economic interest," as that term is used in CJC 3(E)(1)(c). The definition *excludes* the ownership of government securities unless the proceedings could substantially affect the value of the securities. That seems unlikely in this situation.

5. B. Judge Linch is a candidate for a judicial office, and his conduct is governed by CJC 5(A)(3) and 5(C). Item I is not proper. CJC 5(C)(2) prohibits a judicial candidate from personally soliciting campaign funds. Item II is not proper. CJC 5(A)(3)(a) requires a judicial candidate to "maintain the dignity appropriate to judicial office," and the clown suit, the donkey, and the balloons strike us as falling below that standard of dignity. Item III is proper. CJC 5(A)(3)(e) allows a judicial candidate to respond to a personal attack of this kind. Item IV is proper, provided that Judge Linch does not appear to commit himself to a particular position on an issue that is likely to come before his court. The former CJC (1972) prohibited judicial candidates from publicly announcing their views on "disputed legal or political issues." The present CJC deletes that prohibition; in its place, CJC 5(A)(3)(d)(ii) only prohibits a judicial candidate from making statements that "commit or appear to commit the candidate with respect to cases, controversies or issues that are likely to come before the court."

6. B. The applicable rule here is CJC 5(A)(1). Note that Justice Jefferson has lifetime tenure and is not a candidate for a judicial office. As we read CJC 5(A)(1), Justice Jefferson cannot even attend the political gathering, albeit in her own home. Thus, Items I, III, and IV are not proper. Item I is not proper for two additional reasons. CJC 5(A)(1)(b) prohibits a judge from publicly endorsing a candidate for public office, and CJC 5(A)(1)(e) prohibits a judge from soliciting campaign funds for a political candidate. Item II is not specifically covered by CJC 5(A)(1), but the use of the Supreme Court stationery would violate CJC 2(B), which prohibits a judge from lending the prestige of her office "to advance the private interests of * * * others."

*

Index

References are to Pages

†